Eccentric Spaces, Hidden Histories

Asian Religions & Cultures

Edited by

Carl Bielefeldt

Bernard Faure

Great Clarity: Daoism and Alchemy in Early Medieval China
Fabrizio Pregadio
2006

Chinese Poetry and Prophecy: The Written Oracle in East Asia
Michel Strickmann
Edited by Bernard Faure
2005

Chinese Magical Medicine
Michel Strickmann
Edited by Bernard Faure
2002

Living Images: Japanese Buddhist Icons in Context
Edited by Robert H. Sharf and Elizabeth Horton Sharf
2001

David T. Bialock

Eccentric Spaces, Hidden Histories

Narrative, Ritual, and Royal Authority
from *The Chronicles of Japan*
to *The Tale of the Heike*

Stanford University Press
Stanford, California 2007

Stanford University Press
Stanford, California

Printed in the United States of America on acid-free, archival-quality paper

Library of Congress Cataloging-in-Publication Data

Bialock, David T.
Eccentric spaces, hidden histories : narrative, ritual, and royal authority from The Chronicles of Japan to The Tale of the Heike / David T. Bialock.
  p. cm.—(Asian religions and cultures)
  Includes bibliographical references and index.
  ISBN-13: 978-0-8047-5158-2 (cloth : alk. paper)
  1. Japanese literature—To 1600—History and criticism.   2. Heike monogatari.
  3. History in literature.   4. Religion and literature—Japan.   I. Title.
II. Series: Asian religions & cultures.
PL726.115.B53 2007
895.6'09358—dc22

                                                                    2006005088

Typeset by Newgen in 10/14.5 Sabon

CONTENTS

PART THREE

ACKNOWLEDGMENTS

This book represents research going back a number of years. I would like to begin by expressing my thanks to Haruo Shirane, my former advisor at Columbia University, who has remained throughout the years a source of wise counsel and unfailing in his encouragement and support. In the course of several stays in Japan, my research benefited from the help of a number of scholars. I want to thank Hyōdō Hiromi for his support and generosity over the years. The inspiration that I received from his path-breaking work on *Heike monogatari* helped set me on the course of this study. My thanks to Saeki Shin'ichi for patiently answering countless questions and for all that I have learned from his *Heike* scholarship. My thanks to Komine Kazuaki for his hospitality and welcoming me into his study group. His wide-ranging research on medieval literature has been another source of inspiration. My thanks as well to Takagi Makoto for sharing his research over the years and for perceptive comments on my work. To the members of the Gunki katari-mono kenkyūkai and Engyōbon chūshaku no kai, I would like to express my thanks for the opportunity to share in their discussions. Special thanks also to Herman Ooms, Abe Yasurō, Shidachi Masatomo, Shimizu Masumi, Sakura Yoshiyasu, Deguchi Hisanori, Ōhashi Naoyoshi, and Makino Atsushi.

As the manuscript went through successive revisions, I benefited from the comments of a number of readers. I would like to thank Paul Rouzer for detailed and extremely helpful comments. I would like to thank Joan Piggott for taking time to read through an earlier draft and make many useful suggestions. My thanks to Lewis Cook for encouraging words and providing helpful comments on a portion of an earlier draft. I would like to thank Stephen Bokenkamp for taking time to read through parts of the manuscript and for pointing out errors and suggesting a number of improvements. I would also like to thank several anonymous readers who commented on versions of the manuscript, pointing out errors and offering astute advice. My thanks to Gaye Rowley, whose generosity made it possible for me to make use of Waseda's research library. My thanks to Kimura Saeko for help in checking portions of the bibliography. My thanks also to Alex Brown for assistance in obtaining copies of several articles. At the University of Southern California, I have been supported by wonderful colleagues in my department throughout the research and writing of this book. My heartfelt thanks to them all. Peter Nosco provided much needed support and guidance, Bettine Birge encouragement and wise advice, and Dominic Cheung friendship and counsel. And to Bill Noel, thanks for wise and humorous words at a great distance.

Lastly, I want to mention my family. I thank my daughter, Emily, who grew up during the years that I worked on this book, and Tomoko, who helped out in many ways. And I thank my parents, Sadie and Theodore Bialock, who have been an inspiration, and to whom this book is dedicated.

In the course of researching and writing this book, I have benefited from a number of grants. An Andrew Mellon Postdoctoral Fellowship in the Humanities provided a year of research at Stanford University that greatly helped out during an early phase of my research. A Junior Faculty Research Grant from the University of Southern California provided valuable writing time. A Japan Foundation Fellowship allowed me to complete final revisions to the manuscript.

ABBREVIATIONS

CHJ   *The Cambridge History of Japan.* Cambridge: Cambridge
      University Press, 1988–1999. 6 vols.

GK   *Gunki to katarimono*

HR   *History of Religions*

JJRS *Japanese Journal of Religious Studies*

KK   *Kokugo to kokubungaku*

KST   *Shintei zōho kokushi taikei.* Yoshikawa kōbunkan, 1929–
      1967. 66 vols.

MN   *Monumenta Nipponica*

NKBT *Nihon koten bungaku taikei.* Iwanami shoten, 1957–1968.
      102 vols.

NKBZ *Nihon koten bungaku zenshū.* Shōgakukan, 1970–1975.
      51 vols.

OMS   *Onmyōdō sōsho.* Meicho shuppan, 1991–1993. 4 vols.

SKT   *Shinshaku kanbun taikei.* Meiji shoin, 1960– . 114 vols.

SNKBT *Shin nihon koten bungaku taikei.* Iwanami shoten, 1989–
      2001. 100 vols.

ST   *Shintō taikei.* Shintō Taikei Hensankai, 1978–1992. 120 vols.

ZKT   *Zenshaku kanbun taikei.* Shūeisha, 1973–1980. 33 vols.

ZST   *Zōho shiryō taisei.* Kyoto: Rinsen shoten, 1965. 45 vols.

A NOTE TO THE READER

In Part Three of this study, I cite extensively from several variant *Heike* texts. Because this is not a textual study of *Heike*, I have not entered into debates, still inconclusive, on the formation, evolution, and dating of the variant texts. Interested readers are referred to my article in *Dictionary of Literary Biography, Volume 203: Medieval Japanese Writers*, ed. Steven Carter, which provides a summary of recent debates, and the earlier study by Kenneth Dean Butler, "The Textual Evolution of the *Heike monogatari*" (listed in the Bibliography), which, apart from its claims for the antiquity of the *Shibubon* variant, provides much valuable information on several of the variant texts. Readers will also find much useful information in Michael Watson's study, also listed in the Bibliography. Here I list the main variants discussed or cited in this study:

> *Engyōbon heike monogatari*. In six scrolls and twelve fascicles. The *Daitōkyū kinen bunkozō* manuscript, copied in 1419–1420, contains a second colophon indicating that it is a recopying of an earlier manuscript dated 1309–1310. Widely regarded as transmitting the oldest form of any extant *Heike* text.

> *Kakuichibon heike monogatari*. In twelve scrolls, plus a thirteenth scroll titled "Kanjō no maki." Extant in six variant manuscripts. The *Ryūkoku daigaku* manuscript contains two colophons: one at the end of the twelfth scroll with the date Ōan 3/11/29 (1370) and a second, at the end of the "Kanjō no maki," dating its dictation by the reciter Kakuichi to Ōan 4/3/15 (1371). This is the most widely read *Heike* variant, twice translated into English.

Nagatobon heike monogatari. In twenty scrolls. The extant manuscripts of this variant are all relatively late. Possibly assumed its present form in the late fourteenth to early fifteenth centuries.

Genpei seisuiki. At forty-eight scrolls, the longest version of *Heike*. All of the extant manuscripts and woodblock printed editions of this variant are late. Probably evolved over the course of the thirteenth and fourteenth centuries.

Finally, a word on reading the titles of the variants. Engyōbon instead of Enkyōbon is now the preferred usage. Apart from a few bibliographic entries, I have adopted this usage throughout. I have also followed the usage of most literature scholars and adopted the reading *Genpei jōsuiki* instead of *Genpei seisuiki* in the main text and notes. In conformance to standard bibliographic practice, however, *Genpei seisuiki* is retained in citations of the work.

Eccentric Spaces, Hidden Histories

INTRODUCTION

The present study is the result of a long engagement with the *Heike* textual corpus and the medieval world in which it took shape, roughly the thirteenth through the fourteenth centuries. Of its eight chapters, somewhat less than half, or most of the final three chapters, deal at length and in detail with *Heike* material and its medieval world. But it is also *Heike* and the problems that came to light in reading through several of its variants that have shaped the organization and concerns of the other five chapters, which include the three chapters of Part One on yin-yang and Daoist ideas in the Nara and early Heian periods and the two chapters of Part Two on various aspects of ritual, space, and narrative from *Kojiki* (712) to the late Heian historical narrative *Ōkagami*. If the time frame and selection of topics strike the reader as unorthodox, that is because they are aimed at reversing several canonical views of *Heike* that first took shape in the course of the twentieth century. Although Japanese scholarship on *Heike* since the late 1970s has moved well beyond these earlier canonical readings, the presentation of *Heike* as a major work of classical Japanese literature continues to be influenced by these earlier readings. This is especially the case in English, where there continues to be an absence of book-length studies on *Heike* comparable to those that we now have for other major works and genres of the classical period. The present study therefore aims not only to open up the discussion of *Heike* and its medieval world in Part Three but to locate it within a broader trajectory that reaches back through the Heian to Nara periods.

Heike *and the Canon*

When we speak of *The Tale of the Heike* (*Heike monogatari*) as a classic of Japanese literature, we are generally referring to the text that was dictated by the master reciter Kakuichi in the year 1371, which describes the rise and fall of the Heike warrior clan over the course of the twelfth century, culminating in their exile from the capital and eventually in their total defeat at the hands of their rival, the Genji warrior Minamoto no Yoritomo. Like many medieval and Heian period texts, however, *Heike* exists in a large number of variants. These variants often amount to radically different versions of the narrative presented in the more familiar Kakuichi *Heike*, the version available in several English translations. The Kakuichi *Heike*, for example, is consistently capital-centric in its presentation of events. When a messenger arrives at Kiyomori's Fukuhara residence to report on Yoritomo's uprising in the eastern provinces in scroll five, he disposes of those momentous events in the equivalent of a brief paragraph or two. In the Engyōbon *Heike* and several other variants of the so-called "read lineage,"[1] on the other hand, the battle unfolds in a lengthy narrative that brings the local topography and terrain into view with a wealth of concrete detail. *Genpei tōjōroku* (*The Battle Account of the Genpei*), a variant composed in a form of Chinese (*kanbun*), represents the events of this same Genpei War almost entirely from the viewpoint of local warrior groups, such as the Chiba, paying far less attention to the action that unfolds in the capital. Another variant, the Nagatobon *Heike*, contains many episodes that depict sites and topography associated with the activity of outcast reciters who wandered the regions of western Japan that bordered the shores of the Inner Sea. The *Heike* variants, in brief, are embedded in a variety of spatial practices, some projecting distinct regional histories that lay outside the more capital-centric viewpoint of the Kakuichi *Heike* and others relating local topographies connected to sacred sites and the activity of wandering storytellers. Even the Kakuichi *Heike*, as will be shown later in this study, harbors its own eccentric spaces inside its fiction of a dominant capital-centric space.

In the course of the twentieth century, the efforts of literature scholars and historians engaged in constructing a classical canon and narrative of Japan's national emergence all but effaced these local geographies and spaces in the interests of national unity and one national space. Equally important, *Heike*'s affiliations to a Sino-Japanese tradition embodied in a variety of textual practices and a symbolic language for speaking about and representing the authority of the emperor were obscured or downplayed. In one of two canonical narratives that anchored the modern reception of *Heike*, the mid-Heian flowering of vernacular literature in prose and poetry along with the Fujiwara practice of controlling the succession through regental rule, which is generally regarded as having broken with an earlier model of governance based on Chinese conceptions of sovereignty, came to represent the reaffirmation of an authentic indigenous culture freed from a distorting veneer of Chinese learning and culture. In a second narrative, the narrative of popular emergence, these same ideas were projected onto the warrior class, who were portrayed as throwing off the constraints of an effete, sinified court culture, a historical movement that was held to have given rise to the earliest "warrior chronicle" *Shōmonki* (*The Record of Masakado*) that later evolved into the genre of the vernacular warrior tale typified in *The Tale of the Heike*.[2]

Heike *and the Sino-Japanese Tradition*

One aim of the present study is to reposition *Heike* in relation to this Sino-Japanese tradition that extends back from the medieval to the Heian and Nara periods, not through a process of commentary and source tracing, but by producing a counternarrative to a classical canon that has tended to privilege certain peak moments of national emergence, typically represented by a vernacular *Man'yōshū* and *Kojiki* from the Nara period (710–794) and a flowering of court literature in imperial waka collections and *The Tale of Genji* (ca. 1000). The counternarrative that I construct in the first two parts of this study privileges instead a number of works that either belong to or took shape within this Sino-Japanese tradition. Thus, in Part One of this study, I read *Nihon shoki* (*The Chronicles of Japan*, 720) and the Nara period poetry of *Man'yōshū* (*Collection of Ten Thousand Leaves*) and *Kaifūsō* (*Fond Recollections of Poetry*, 751) through the prism of yin-yang and Daoist practices and symbolic language. Chapter 4 places *Kojiki* (*The Record of Ancient Matters*, 712) into a dialogical relation with *Nihon shoki*, and Chapter 5 highlights the relatively neglected late Heian vernacular "historical tale" *Ōkagami* (*The Great Mirror*), which is typically treated as an expression of court literature. The analysis that I propose presents it as a polyvocal history that encroaches into the sphere of official history in Chinese, but in a narrative that already anticipates the heterodox and nomadic speech of the medieval *Heike*. In privileging this counternarrative, I am not proposing a new canonical series but providing an eccentric reading of the earlier canon that recovers some of the discursive terrain of the medieval *Heike* that has been concealed by earlier canonical readings of the classical tradition.

By repositioning *Heike* inside the terrain of this Sino-Japanese tradition, I also aim to highlight a complicated yet neglected strand in the symbolic representation of royal authority that was centered on yin-yang and Daoist notions and practices. In its representation of royal authority, the *Heike* narratives project several competing, even contradictory, images of the ruler. The retired sovereign Go-Shirakawa (r. 1155–1158), for example, appears in his capacity as a Buddhist adept, wielding theurgic powers that placate demonic spirits in Antoku's birth scene and as a reincarnated sovereign endowed with Buddhist wisdom in his encounter with Kenreimon'in in "The Initiate's Scroll" ("Kanjō no maki"). A relatively minor presence in the Kakuichi *Heike*, he often takes center stage in the Engyōbon, where pride in his sacred powers as a Dharma sovereign (*hōō*) is castigated as a cause of demonic infestation.[3] Another image of royal authority in *Heike* is Takakura, who is portrayed as a Chinese-style sage ruler: "The Emperor finally passed away. The twelve years of his reign were a time of supremely humane governance, during which he revived the abandoned teachings of benevolence and righteousness explicated in the *Book of Poetry* and the *Book of Documents* and reestablished the lapsed tradition of correct government and bringing comfort to the people."[4] The reign of the sage ruler was typically portrayed as a time of equable seasons, moderate rains, and abundant harvests, all signs that his governance was in harmony with the yin and the yang. The idealization of the sage ruler is usually traced back to the period of the *Tale of Genji* when the reign of the Engi era sovereign Daigo (r. 897–930) began to be idealized as a golden age, with the emperor governing free from the meddling of the Fujiwara regents. Although it is true that Engi came to represent a golden age of imperial rule (a tradition transmitted in *Heike* recitation), historically by the late ninth and early tenth centuries, much of the symbolic apparatus that had once supported the Chinese-style sovereign of ritsuryō period rule had ceased to function in its original form. It was during Daigo's reign, for example, that the production official history in Chinese was discontinued. By this time as well, the Yin-Yang Bureau had altered many of its original functions. Instead of the symbolic activities of geomancy, calendrical calculations, and the prognostication of signs, which had formerly served to enhance the authority of the emperor (*tennō*), private yin-yang masters, who had taken over many of the Yin-Yang Bureau's functions, were now increasingly involved in ritual activity centered around pollution taboos and the expulsion of malign spirits. The idealization of the Engi era sovereign as a sage ruler is therefore best understood as echoing an even earlier period of the court when the figure of the Daoist-type sage was represented in a variety of texts and symbolic practices, including the poetry of *Man'yōshū*, Temmu's chronicle in *Nihon shoki*, the Chinese poetry of *Kaifūsō*, and ritual play at Yoshino. As an idealization, however, the Engi myth represents no more than an etiolated image of this earlier Daoist-type sage, whose ritual authority was premised on the ability to command and drive out threatening powers.

By the early thirteenth century, when *Heike* began to assume textual form, there were fresh efforts to revive Chinese-style historiography, this time in a more Confucian mode. At the same time, Buddhist priests were also engaged in the production of new forms of vernacular Buddhist historiography, exemplified in Jien's *Gukanshō*. These and other historiographical practices are combined to varying degrees in the *Heike* variants, creating a contradictory play between different representations of royal authority. It is here that another major theme of this study comes into consideration: the complex interplay between various symbolic practices of royal authority and the representation of space. Chinese-style historiography, the activities of the Yin-Yang Bureau, and the composition of poetry in Chinese were all practices that enforced a specific relation to space that supported the authority of the court. This is illustrated most vividly in the geomantic centering of the capital according to the principles of yin-yang correlative cosmology, commemorated in the Kakuichi *Heike*'s fifth scroll, but it is also evident in the graphic form and sequencing of certain *Man'yōshū* poems, which deploy similar correlative principles, as well as in the middle-kingdom ideology that organized space around a center–periphery opposition that was embodied in a refined culture identified with the capital and a periphery equated with the barbarous hinterlands. The devaluation of the graphic dimension of texts composed in Chinese in favor of a phonocentrism that privileged the vernacular reading of texts, a process that began with the national literature scholars and continued throughout much of the twentieth century,[5] was part of the same broad relegation of the Sino-Japanese tradition to marginal status that shaped several canonical views of *Heike*. Its effect has been to render many aspects of Nara period texts invisible, including ideas pertaining to yin-yang correlative cosmology and the Daoist pursuit of immortality, two subjects examined at length in Chapters 2 and 3.

Heike *and Competing Spatialities*

Far more than a rhetorical style for speaking about the emperor, the ideal of the sage ruler was a refraction of a specific ideology or practice of royal authority, embodied in a form of historiography (official histories), styles of poetry (in *Man'yōshū* and *Kaifūsō*), and ritual and symbolic activity (housed in the Yin-Yang Bureau). Over the course of the Nara and early Heian periods, these and other practices enforced a center–periphery view of space, but this was only one facet of a complex spatiality that interacted with a succession of ideologies of royal authority. By the mid-Heian period, under an increasingly dominant Buddhist episteme,[6] the ideology of the sage ruler was being displaced by a different spatial practice underpinned and supported by a variety of Buddhist doctrines, including ideas pertaining to defilement in Pure Land and later by nondual doctrines such as original enlightenment doctrine in the early medieval period. It is in the interplay between this earlier symbolic practice of royal authority and the shift to a more dominant Buddhist ideology from the mid-Heian period on that changes in the character of ritual space and the space of the body can be more readily grasped. As already noted, by the mid-Heian period, yin-yang masters, formerly under the authority of the tennō, were performing rituals whose ultimate effect was to inhibit the tennō's religio-political authority, even if they enhanced his symbolic sacrality as a ruler. One ritual performed by the yin-yang masters from as early as the mid-Heian period was the Seven Shallows Purification (*nanase no harae*). Performed along waterways inside the capital and at specified points throughout the provinces, the Seven Shallows Purification involved transferring defilement from the tennō to an effigy that was then cast into a stream of flowing water, symbolizing the expulsion of defilement from the central space. This was only one of many similar rituals performed at the borders of the capital district and at other specified sites, which continued to enforce a centered space. In the sphere of representation, however, the middle-kingdom ideology, with its view of a refined center and barbarous periphery, was gradually overlaid by a parallel set of ideas that equated the center with purity and the peripheries with defiled spaces inhabited by demonic beings.

By the early medieval period, this spatiality was further complicated by the representation of Japan as a "small country of the borderland," in which Japan was transformed from a center into a physical and metaphorical embodiment of liminality, which valorized the border as a site of dangerous yet numinous powers. This coincided with the full assimilation of defilement to the domain of Buddhist doctrine and practice and the apogee of Buddhist authority, which attempted to enforce its hegemony even over the body and person of the tennō. Much of Part Three of this study is taken up with an analysis of this complex spatiality and its play of contradictory symbolic codes, which achieves maximal play in the *Heike* textual corpus. Thus, in addition to the ideal of the sage ruler, who governs over a harmonious centered realm, there is the child emperor Antoku, a defiled emperor whose death by drowning at Dan no ura can be understood as a literal enactment of the Seven Shallows Purification in which the emperor's body is cast into the water. Other figures, like the retired sovereign Go-Shirakawa and Taira no Kiyomori, take on characteristics of a royal authority capable of trafficking in the defiled periphery.

Heike *and Narrative Assemblages*

Another area of concern in this study is the elements that combine into various narrative forms, broadly encompassing everything from sacred utterance, or what I refer to as nomadic speech, orthodox oral narrative (myth or *furukoto*), official history (*seishi*) and vernacular "fiction" (*monogatari*), and the medieval practice of commentary (*chūshaku*). I am especially interested in how these interacted with various kinds of ritual and ceremonial activity—that is, their performative aspects—and the role played by writing and forms of oral transmission in mediating them. Much of this material is taken up at length in the two chapters of Part Two and again in Chapter 8 of Part Three, which is devoted entirely to the apocryphal history of Kiyomori in *Heike*. Here, too, my initial point of departure was problems encountered in making sense of the complex narrative assemblages transmitted in the numerous *Heike* variants and the ways in which they interact with a Sino-Japanese tradition now intricately combined with Buddhist doctrinal debate, sermonizing, and storytelling. Earlier canonical views of *Heike*, which focused on the recited variant dictated from memory by Kakuichi, tended to emphasize either *Heike*'s affiliation to vernacular court fiction or the so-called warrior chronicle, which was held to have evolved into a vernacular form from the early gunki composed in Chinese. Other theories emphasized those aspects of *Heike* that may have originated in shamanic utterance, mediating the spirits of those who had died violent deaths. My own approach has been to locate the entire issue of vernacular narrative, including nomadic utterance, in the broad framework of the same Sino-Japanese tradition that helped to organize the various symbolic representations of royal authority.

Another aspect of the eccentric canon constructed in Part Two of this study, therefore, is to provide a diachronic view of the ways in which the construction of a physical and metaphorical center played out in a clash between official and unofficial forms of discourse, the former exemplified in Chinese-style historiography, and the latter in various forms of marginalized orthodox speech (as in Imibe Hironari's *Kogo shūi*), the early warrior chronicle *Shōmonki* (*The Record of Masakado*), and vernacular narratives like *Ōkagami*, with the last two read as appropriations of and encroachments into the territory of the metaphorical center embodied in the court.[7] Here, however, I must emphasize that I am not reverting to a dichotomy between Chinese writing (foreign) and vernacular speech (indigenous). *Kojiki* and the *Hitachi fudoki*, for example, are read in Chapter 4 as participating in the same construction of a ritual center of authority as *Nihon shoki*. Rather, I am highlighting the dialogical tension between the two. By reversing a more canonical reading that has tended to essentialize the vernacular, I show how the vernacular, in the process of defining itself against a more dominant discourse in Chinese, took on some of the latter's attributes. This allows the so-called indigenous mode of oracular speech or shamanic utterance, a type of nomadic speech, to commingle in strange ways with the gossip, rumor, and small talk that are thrust outside the main ambit of orthodox or official history. It also allows vernacular "fiction" to be read as participating both *within* but also at the edges of official discourse. In *Ōkagami*, a vernacular history that dates from the late Heian period, this gives rise to a narrative assemblage that I have characterized as ambulatory history, foreshadowing those *Heike* variants that were in the custody of wandering reciters known as biwa priests. In its medieval form, ambulatory history, which encompasses the ensemble of *Heike* variants but also large parts of *Taiheiki* and the medieval tradition of "prophecy records" (*miraiki*), has a twofold character. On the one hand, it transmits potentially dangerous heterodox speech made up of rumor, gossip, oracles, and the utterances of threatening or demonic spirits that centers of authority often seek to control. On the other hand, it belongs to a broader nomadization of late Heian and early medieval culture that parallels the emergence of rule by retired sovereigns, the social and religious phenomenon of the heteromorphic (*irui igyō*), and the reinvestment of borders as sites of power. Each of these topics is taken up at length in the three chapters of Part Three.

Some Theoretical and Methodological Issues

As a literature specialist with cross-disciplinary interests, I have drawn on a number of approaches from the fields of literary and cultural studies, which sharply distinguishes my work from the approach of many historians who have covered some of the same material and time periods. Thus, I have generally avoided the boundaries that have traditionally separated the disciplines of literature, history, and religious studies into isolated and autonomous domains. Like the new historicists and cultural geographers, rather than focusing on the text's neutral documentary value or on the text as autonomous literary structure, I have tried to emphasize the embeddedness of texts in the material conditions of their production (including their graphic form) and the ways in which they intersect with a variety of doctrinal, ritual, and symbolic practices.[8] In focusing on *representation* and *performance* rather than a narrative of "fact" and "events," I am interested in the ways power and authority are mediated through a variety of symbolic practices that cut across the false barrier that has been erected between "documents," which are held to transmit "facts" and reliable "evidence," and "literature," which is treated as an epiphenomenon. This latter practice has tended to enforce a sharp separation between literature (*bungaku*) on the one hand and history (*rekishi*) on the other, which has removed texts from their embeddedness in an ensemble of cultural practices, including ritual and ceremonial, and transformed them into abstractions in a discourse *about* rather than *of* the periods in question. By returning texts like *Nihon shoki* and *Man'yōshū* to their performative function (i.e., their embeddedness in an ensemble of cultural practices), we can better grasp their role in either enforcing or contesting specific ideologies of royal authority, irrespective of their historicity and factual accuracy.

In my discussions of space, I have also drawn on the ideas of the French thinker Henri Lefebvre, whose work represents one of the most thorough attempts to theorize the production of space in its social, political, and historical dimensions. Lefebvre's conceptual terminology for describing space is extremely fluid and not always used with consistency, but he provides three concepts—spatial practice (*la pratique spatiale*), representations of space (*les représentations de l'espace*), and representational spaces (*les espaces de représentation*)—which I have found useful in analyzing the complex spatiality of late Heian and early medieval Japan in Part Three of this study. A spatial practice can be characterized as a mode of activity whereby a particular view or "representation of space" is enforced. Thus, Lefebvre writes of how a "spatial practice of society secretes that society's space; it propounds and presupposes it, in a dialectical interaction; it produces it slowly and surely as it masters and appropriates it." Among the examples listed by Lefebvre are the network of roads that facilitated pilgrimages in medieval Europe, but it can also be understood as extending to forms of ritual practice. A representation of space, on the other hand, is "conceptualized space," or space that has been organized around various codes, as in the layout of an urban center in terms of Renaissance linear perspective and arrangements of architecture, where the monument or building is "embedded in a spatial context," which finds its analogy in the layout and architectural coding of ancient sites like Heijō and Heiankyō. Whereas representations of space tend to refer to the "dominant space in any society," representational space is Lefebvre's term for imaginary space, the lived space of people, which gets expressed in symbolic works, such as painting and other works of art and writing, but may often elude representation, remaining confined to the life of memories, dreams, and other images belonging to the submerged and hidden side of a culture.[9] Above all, it is Lefebvre's dialectical method, which allows for reversals and sedimentation of previous spatialities, that makes it especially productive as a mode of inquiry. Thus, an earlier practice of space that enforced the authority of the Daoist-sage type ruler lingers on as a representational space in the medieval idealization of the Engi era sovereigns, forming part of the medieval imaginary about royal authority. At the same time, as I show in Chapter 6, China held an ambiguous place in the medieval imaginary, alternately threatening site of the other and the figure for an emergent, decentered space of commercial and cultural exchange. Analyzed in this fashion, the space of a culture is seldom reducible to simple binary oppositions but is made up of competing and contradictory spaces that can coexist and even cooperate within a larger system.

My approach to texts and the problem of space differs therefore in significant ways from the recent study of the historian Bruce Batten.[10] Batten's work is a detailed and illuminating discussion of the role played by boundary concepts in constructing Japan's identity as a geopolitical and cultural space. His work is especially informative on the shifting and fluctuating sense of political and cultural boundaries in Japan, illuminating, on the one hand, the oscillation between strong and weak centers over the long stretch of time extending from the Nara through the early modern periods and the distinctions, on the other hand, between boundaries as sharply delimiting the inside and outside of cultural and political space and the vague zonal frontiers where cultural and political space is blurred. In presenting his argument, however, Batten takes the approach that "it is important to distinguish between worldviews, on the one hand, and geopolitical realities, on the other." [11] The present study approaches the problem of space from a different perspective, treating as primary the constructive role played by ritual, doctrine, and the imaginative discourse of texts that Batten subsumes under his worldviews. I premise my argument on the assumption that worldviews or ideology cannot easily be separated from geopolitical or other "realities." In brief, worldviews, or what I prefer to call "imaginaries," are constituted in and through specific textual, ritual, and spatial practices that not only shape perceptions of cultural, political, and geographical space but bring it into tangible presence. Hence, the ritual capture of sacred speech embodied in the performative gesture of a text like *Kojiki* and later in enshrinement rituals such as the Kitano Tenjin cult (both discussed in Chapter 4), yin-yang practices aimed at driving out defilement, and the annual repetition of rites to expel plague deities at specified points along the boundaries of the Kinai region are all concrete instances of practices that both create and enforce a particular experience of space. Likewise, the medieval representation of Japan as a "small, defiled country of the border" is not merely a rhetorical flourish or literary embellishment but an aspect of complex symbolic practices that brought into being certain ways of thinking about and relating to space that helped, in this case, to enforce the authority of powerful temples.

Finally, in my discussions of space, the nomadic, and the related social phenomenon of the heteromorphic—a medieval sign of ambiguous sacrality often associated with a bizarre appearance and animal traits that are exemplified in dengaku ("field music"), the pack phenomenon of the marauding akutō ("evil bands"), and the eerie behavior of the demonlike creatures tengu—I have also drawn on the coauthored work of Gilles Deleuze and Felix Guattari. In their theory of nomadology, in particular, I have found a useful vantage point for locating many of the social, political, and cultural phenomena pertaining to premodern ambulant populations that have been studied by Amino Yoshihiko and others.[12] Although geography prevented a classic nomadic culture from developing in Japan, the nomadic, in the extended sense of wandering, itinerancy, and vagabondage, is inseparable from the formation of centers and states. It is not surprising, then, that vagabondage and fear of the nomadic first emerged as a problem in the Nara period, a time of intense state formation. At once exterior to the state, or outside its cultural ambit, the nomadic, as Deleuze has shown, is invariably in conflict or at war with the state, at times even bringing about its deterritorialization. This allows a somewhat different reading of itinerancy and the related phenomenon of the heteromorphic (*igyō*), which have typically been viewed from inside the binary logic of the state, or what Amino has characterized in cultural terms as an opposition between sedentary agricultural and itinerant nonagricultural populations.[13] The bizarre effect produced by the heteromorphic, for example, which the center experiences as a confusion of its own categories, can also be viewed as belonging to the anomic or heterogeneous traits of the nomadic cultural assemblage, which stands outside the center's logic of inside–outside, high–low, and other binary oppositions characteristic of its hierarchical striated space. In this sense, medieval "sacrality," including aspects of original enlightenment doctrine, may be viewed as an effort to come to terms with the nomadization of the medieval state structure. These and other problems connected to the heteromorphic, space, and nomadic assemblages are examined in Chapters 4, 7, and in the discussion of Kiyomori's kaburo in Chapter 8.

Chapter Summaries

The eight chapters of this study are arranged into three parts. With the exception of Chapter 1, which deals with the modern academic discourse on yin-yang and Daoism, the first two parts move through the material largely in a diachronic fashion, whereas the three chapters of Part Three take more of a synchronic approach. The three interweaving themes are ritual, narrative, and space.

The three chapters of Part One reexamine the role of yin-yang and Daoist practices in shaping the symbolic representation of royal authority in both texts and rituals of the Nara and early Heian periods. Rather than influences or expressions of literary borrowing, I treat these practices as part of a hybrid cultural assemblage infused with yin-yang and Daoist elements. Chapter 1 begins the series with an analysis of how the construction of a modern academic discourse on China, exemplified in the work of Tsuda Sōkichi, paradoxically turned yin-yang and Daoism into objects of serious academic study while effectively removing them as significant factors in discussions of ancient Japanese religious practices, specifically as these bore on the tennō's authority in the ancient period. Chapter 2 looks at how yin-yang contributed to the symbolic language of royal authority by relating it to narrative structure in *Nihon shoki*, calendrical procedures, prognostication, geomancy, and the cosmogonic theories that informed the mythological portions of the chronicles. In Chapter 3, the discussion shifts to ritual and symbolic activity of a more Daoist cast, including the cultivation of immortality and the use of elixirs and their bearing on the ritual authority claimed by Temmu and other emperors. The second half of Chapter 3 takes up the problem of the Yin-Yang Bureau's transformation from an office initially engaged in enhancing the authority of the tennō into a ritual apparatus, now largely managed by private yin-yang masters, for managing pollution and expelling demonic infestations. Rather than the traditional view that understands this change as an indigenization of yin-yang, I relate it to contradictions in the ritual efficacy claimed by the tennō.

The two chapters of Part Two examine two groups of historical narrative: *Kojiki, Nihon shoki*, and the *Hitachi fudoki* in Chapter 4 and the vernacular historical tale *Ōkagami* in Chapter 5. In the first half of Chapter 4, I examine the two chronicles and fudoki as symbolic and ritual expressions of the tennō's claim to control space by monopolizing the authority to act as a mediator of sacred speech. The second half of the chapter examines how the construction of a religio-political center brought about a new awareness of the nomadic, understood as both itinerancy and volatile sacred speech, which now becomes the object of new efforts by the center to capture it ritually. In Chapter 5, I turn from space and ritual to the problem of written vernacular narrative as it emerges out of and then defines itself against the dominant discourse in Chinese, with sections devoted to *Kojiki* and *Kogo shūi*, but primarily focusing on the late Heian text *Ōkagami*, which is read as both a transmogrification and an early nomadization of court history that characterized the emergence of rule by retired sovereigns.

The three chapters of Part Three take up various aspects of late Heian and early medieval space, focusing on the interplay between centered, peripheral, and heterotopic space, the latter being my term for cryptic space or the space of the Other in the early medieval period, which can apply to a sacred enclosure, border, or even the body in its heteromorphic aspect. Chapter 6 looks at the ambiguous place of both the warrior and China in the medieval imaginary, which is examined through the close reading of a number of episodes from the *Heike* variants, including several centered on Kiyomori and Shigemori that relate to the Taira's commerce with China. Chapter 7 examines how changes in the conceptualization of defilement over the course of the late Heian and early medieval periods transformed the character of ritual space, ultimately undermining an earlier practice of royal authority. This is analyzed in relation to dengaku, or "field music," a semiritualized entertainment, shifts in the codes pertaining to dress and the use of space, and the weirdness associated with the heteromorphic. In these sections, I draw on a variety of episodes from the *Heike* narrative tradition to illustrate how several contradictory images of the tennō coexisted in the medieval imaginary about royal authority. The chapter also looks at how the Buddhist doctrines of Pure Land and "hongaku" (original enlightenment) helped to articulate the shift from centered to peripheral to heterotopic space. Through the comparison of several *Heike* variants of the Kikai-ga-shima sequence, these sections explore some of the paradoxes and contradictions underlying the medieval imaginary of sacred space, focusing in particular on the ambiguous character of heterotopic space as typified by borders and liminal sites. Chapter 8 concludes the study with an extended analysis of *Heike* as an apocryphal history of Kiyomori, focusing on three episodes, the kaburo or "pageboy cuts," who served Kiyomori as spies, legends of Kiyomori's heterodox royal parentage in the "Gion Lady" episode, and the identification of Kiyomori as the reincarnation of the demon-subjugating general, Jie Taishi.

Part One

Part One

HIDDEN TEXTS

The Modern Construction of Yin-Yang and Daoist Studies

Keichū and the Reading of Ancient Texts

Over the centuries, the poetry of *Man'yōshū*, Japan's oldest and most extensive collection of ancient poems, has passed through many phases of appreciation, reevaluation, and critical commentary. One keynote in the reception of this poetry is its supposed simplicity and naturalness, qualities that were sometimes associated with origins in a preliterate antiquity. An early and classic statement of this view is found in the work of the Edo period scholar Keichū (1640–1701), whose writings on *Man'yōshū* would later inspire nativist scholars like Motoori Norinaga (1730–1801) and continue to influence the poetry's reception well into the twentieth century:

> This realm is a divine country. Therefore, both the history books and court ritual always place the gods first and people afterwards. In ancient times, the emperor governed the realm solely through the way of the gods. Moreover, in addition to the simplicity of the times, there was no writing back then, and so things were transmitted orally just as they were. Unlike the Confucian classics, Buddhist sutras, and other writings, Shintō has left no interpretations. There are *Kujiki*, *Kojiki*, and *Nihongi*, but these only *record* matters since the age of the gods. The court rituals and various shrine rites alone transmit the ancient customs of the age of the gods.

> Although it grows faint generation after generation, poetry has still not
> faded; although it is in decline, the eight-fold fence of poetry lingers on,
> and this indeed is a sign of its divine origin.[1]

Poetry is here accorded the same numinous powers that invest the shinto
rites and court rituals that uphold the authority of the emperor. In both ritual and poetry, simplicity and spontaneous oral transmission are contrasted
with the mediated nature of written knowledge represented by Confucian
and Buddhist teachings. Even the oldest chronicles merely *record* divine matters; only ritual and poetry transmit their full plenitude.

Keichū's primitivism is deceptive, however. As Peter Nosco has observed,
it was arrived at through remarkably sophisticated philological methods. In
his effort to recover the sense of *Man'yōshū* poems, composed in an often ar-
cane, difficult to decipher system of Chinese graphs known as *man'yōgana*,
Keichū drew on a wide range of texts, including classical Chinese sources,
which allowed him to produce insightful interpretations of the poetry's frequently obscure vocabulary. It was a method, in brief, that remained alert
to the graphic implications of the man'yōgana. But Keichū's archaism, en-
capsulated in his well-known advice "to try to forget the spirit of your own
age and become part of the spirit of ancient man," could also become the
basis for rejecting the obvious graphic sense in favor of vernacular readings
that were deemed authentic expressions of the ancient spirit.[2] This tendency
would become especially pronounced in the nativist tradition that followed
Keichū, giving rise to a hermeneutic that accorded little status to the graphic
dimension of *Man'yōshū* poetry, eliminating in the process the kinds of interpretive possibilities that arise when Chinese and Buddhist writings are
brought to bear on the meaning of the written graphs.[3]

In an essay published in 1986, Mark Morris raised some interesting questions in this regard when he attempted to *read* several *Man'yōshū* poems
as Chinese poems, according the man'yōgana primary significance rather
than a merely instrumental function.[4] Morris's observations on the semantic
weight of Chinese in the poetry were one aspect of a wide-ranging essay that
questioned many of the literary assumptions that underlay established approaches to reading ancient Japanese poetry. The present chapter will also
attend to the implications of the Chinese graphs, but I am less concerned with
the literary possibilities of interpretation than with what happens when we
take two apparently straightforward "lyrical" poems from *Man'yōshū* and
relocate them in a discourse of yin-yang and Daoist ideas that constituted

an important element in the ideology that undergird ancient royal authority. Following this initial exercise in reinterpretation, I turn to the question of why such readings remained in a sense unavailable, or at best marginal, within a broader twentieth-century discourse about China and its relation to Japanese antiquity. Here we will see how ideas already adumbrated as early as Keichū were subsequently amplified and given a new direction in Meiji and early twentieth-century discussions about national emergence.

Yin-Yang and Daoist Motifs in Two Man'yōshū Poems

Among the half-dozen or so *Man'yōshū* poems attributed to Princess Uno, otherwise known as Empress Jitō (r. 690–697), one of the most famous is the following poem from early in the first scroll:

> 春過ぎて夏來るらし白栲の衣乾したり天の香具山

> Spring has passed / and summer seems to have come / white hempen robes / have been hung out to dry / near heavenly Mount Kaguyama

> (Haru sugite / natsu kitarurashi / shirotae no / koromo hoshitari / ama no kaguyama) (*MYS*, 1, 28)[5]

Even readers unfamiliar with the poetry of *Man'yōshū* may feel acquainted with this poem. It is found in a slightly modified form, for example, in *Hyaku-nin isshu*, the one-hundred-poem anthology, attributed to Fujiwara no Teika (1162–1241), that subsequently became the basis for the still popular New Year's card-game *karuta*.[6] The poem was also singled out early in the twentieth century by Masaoka Shiki (1867–1902), Saitō Mokichi (1882–1953), and other poets of the Araragi lineage of modern tanka poetry for the clarity, freshness, and realism of its nature description, qualities indicative of a new modern sensibility but also owing something to the pristine values and vitality admired by Keichū and later by the nativists. Cultural and literary factors have therefore combined to make this poem into a familiar icon of traditional Japan: a touchstone for the *Man'yōshū* style in particular, often celebrated for its pure and frank emotionalism, and for Japanese sensibility in general, typically perceived as exquisitely attuned to the natural world and the flow of the seasons.[7]

More recently, Ōhama Itsuhiko and Eguchi Kiyoshi have questioned the naturalistic and lyrical emphasis of this earlier approach to the poem.[8] In a study published in 1978, Ōhama, attentive to the poem's graphic shape in its original *man'yōgana*, went beyond the lyrical reading to discover a complex symbolism that was based on yin-yang correlative cosmology. Ōhama's approach took inspiration from the newly discovered wall paintings inside the late seventh-century Takamatsuzuka tumulus, which depict the four zoomorphs of Chinese astrology, specifically, the green dragon, white tiger, vermilion bird, and dark warrior on the east, west, south, and north walls of the tumulus, respectively.[9] It was the implications of this astral-geomantic symbolism in the interior of the tumulus, suggesting knowledge of yin-yang correlative cosmology, that led Ōhama and other scholars to reexamine the symbolic principles underlying the language and sequencing of poems in Japan's oldest poetry collection.[10]

In his analysis, Ōhama showed how the graphs could be read as mapping out a seasonal or temporal progression that runs from the spring and summer of the first and second lines to autumn and winter in lines three and five. This becomes clear when the poem is returned to its man'yōgana form:

春過而　夏來良之　白妙能　衣乾有　天之香來山

Although autumn and winter are not explicitly mentioned in the poem, they are indicated by the color and directional symbolism inscribed in the graphs. The color "white," embedded in the third ku's pillow word "shirotae no" 白妙能, corresponds in yin-yang five agents theory to the season autumn and the direction west; winter, on the other hand, is derived from the directional symbolism of Kaguyama, which Ōhama understood as lying north of the Kiyomihara Palace, where Empress Jitō is thought to have composed her poem.[11] To support this identification of Kaguyama with the direction north, Ōhama drew on the evidence of another *Man'yōshū* poem, also attributed to Jitō, in which she speaks of the departed spirit of the deceased Prince Ōama (posthumously named Temmu):

北山にたなびく雲の青雲の星離り行き月を離りて

On the northern mountain / trails a cloud / a whitish cloud / that parts company from the stars / parts company from the moon

(Kitayama ni / tanabiku kumo no / aogumo no / hoshi sakariyuki / tsuki wo sakarite) (*MYS*, 2, 161)[12]

The poem's first line, glossed in the vernacular as "On the northern mountain" (*kitayama ni*), when read according to the sense and order of the three Chinese graphs 向南山, yields the literal meaning of "facing-south-mountain." Ōhama understood this to mean Kaguyama as it would have appeared to Jitō had she looked due north toward the southward-facing Kaguyama from her Kiyomihara Palace. Returning to the first poem, Ōhama further discerned a deliberate balancing of heaven and earth in its structure, with the epithet or makura kotoba "heavenly" (*ama no*) balancing the earth associations of Kaguyama.[13] Reinforced by this geomantic balancing of the earthly and heavenly realms, the symbolism of the poem's spatiotemporal progression (spring–east, summer–south, autumn–west, winter–north) becomes a conscious expression of Empress Jitō's harmonious relationship to space and time.

In another study, Eguchi has extended and refined this exegetical approach. Although departing from some of Ōhama's interpretations, he has otherwise enriched the poetry's yin-yang cosmological determinations by bringing it into relation with a variety of Chinese texts and other poems in the collection. For example, when the graph glossed as "hoshitari" (drying) in *MYS*, 1, 28 is given its sinicized reading "ken," it suggests the compound *kenkon* 乾坤, which names the first two hexagrams in the *Yijing* (*Book of Changes*), with first graph "ken" yielding the correspondences heaven-yang and the directional meaning of west-north, and the second graph "kon" the correspondences earth–yin.[14] In place of Ōhama's locative designations of east, south, and west for the first three lines, respectively, Eguchi's analysis discloses a sequence of east, south, west, and west-north for the poem's first four lines. With the four directions distributed over the first four lines, the concluding fifth line, "heavenly Mount Kaguyama," is available for a new locative designation. This is disclosed by the graph "kō" 香 (*xiang*) in Kaguyama, which according to the arrangement of the five agents in *Master Lü's Spring and Autumn* (*Lüshi chunqiu*) corresponds to the "central space" (Jp. *chūō*) or "earth potency."[15] Eguchi also reads the phrase "facing-south-mountain" to imply more than a reference to Kaguyama's northerly location. More than simple wordplay, the graphic combination names Kaguyama viewed under its aspect as earthly counterpart to the polestar realm, whose ruler sits upon his throne facing south, a directional symbolism, Eguchi notes, that also influenced the architecture of Yakushiji Temple (built by Temmu for Jitō), the main gate of which faced south, as well as the positioning of Ise Shrine.[16] The epithet "heavenly" that ornaments Kaguyama would then further enhance the polestar associations of the Temmu/Jitō court. In addition to the directional and seasonal symbolism that Ōhama pointed out, Kaguyama also functions as the central space that mediates between the heavenly and earthly realms. The positive yang associations of the preceding fourth line's "ken," evoking the solar and celestial powers of the sun-myth, further highlight Kaguyama's symbolic status as a central space.[17]

The second poem also discloses a further range of meaning, suggesting a more complex view of Temmu's death. Traditionally, it has been read lyrically, an expression of Jitō's grief over the death of Prince Ōama.[18] Problems again arise out of trying to force modern conventions of interpretation upon the poem's imagery. In both the classical Chinese and Japanese traditions, the color connotations represented by the graph 青 (Jp. *aoshi*, Ch. *qing*) were quite different from the modern usage of "green" or "blue," and included a variable range of indeterminate shades from white to gray to green.[19] In *Man'yōshū* and *Kojiki*, for example, "aogumo no" could function as a pillow word for nouns connected to the color white, indicating that in classical Japanese green-blue and white evoked related color impressions. In the rhetorical patterning of classical Chinese verse, green-blue (*qing*) in the first verse of a couplet could be answered by white in the second verse, and in the correlative principles that organized some poems, the yang verse (corresponding to the directions east or south) with its red or green-blue might be answered by white or black in the following yin verse (corresponding to the directions west or north). In the present poem, just as the phrase "facing-south-mountain" in *MYS*, 2, 161, contains a hidden allusion to the direction north (reading it from the viewpoint of the speaker who looks north toward the south-facing mountain), the trailing cloud in the oddly doubled expression "kumo no aogumo" secretly alludes to a white cloud (identified with the north). Its deeper meaning, suggests Eguchi, is to evoke the white cloud on which a Daoist sage ascends to the realm of the immortals, as in the following passage from Zhuangzi: "When a sage wearies of this world after a lapse of a thousand years, he ascends among the immortals. Mounting upon a white cloud, he goes to the land of the celestial prince [*shangdi*]."[20] In addition to symbolizing the sorrowful parting of death, the white cloud also hints at Temmu's Daoist quest for immortality.

The studies of Ōhama and Eguchi belong to a growing body of work that has begun to reshape our understanding of Japanese antiquity, especially in relation to the impact of continental culture and thought on ancient Japanese ideas of rulership. Although the Confucian and Buddhist contributions to Japanese culture have been extensively explored for the ancient period, far less attention has been paid to the role of yin-yang five agents thought and Daoism during this same period.[21] The case is similar in English, where Daoism (including yin-yang thought and practice) has occupied a relatively small niche in the scholarship on the ancient period.[22] The 1993 volume on the ancient period in *The Cambridge History of Japan*, for example, which may be taken as a fair indication of the state of the field in the decade or so preceding its publication, includes extensive discussions of Buddhism, Shinto, and substantial if less detailed remarks on Confucianism but only a few cursory references to Daoism and yin-yang.[23]

Part of the problem is definitional. What is regularly referred to as an expression of Confucian, Buddhist, and Shinto belief is sometimes a Daoist or yin-yang practice that has shifted into a new cultic context. In his analysis of the combinatory methods practiced by shrine-temple multiplexes in the Heian period, for example, the scholar of religions Allan Grapard has shown how a variety of yin-yang and Daoist practices could operate in combination with both esoteric and exoteric Buddhist practices and shrine rites as well.[24] On the other hand, as Kuroda Toshio and other scholars have remarked, in the Nara period when texts like *Nihon shoki* were composed, the graphs 神道 (shintō) were used in China at this time as another term for Daoism.[25] We must also consider the permutations of the word "dōkyō," the standard Sino-Japanese term that gives us the word *Daoism* in English. In their essay "What Is Daoism," Sakai Tadao and Fukui Fumimasa have traced the term's earliest occurrence to Mozi (468–376 B.C.E.), where it refers to "the teaching of the Confucianists" and is broadly defined as "the teaching of the way of the sages and former kings" or "teaching that explains the way of the sages." By the time of the northern Wei in the fifth century, well after the introduction of Buddhism, the same term could also designate Buddhist teachings. Throughout this long period of time, the Chinese term dōkyō might thus refer to any one of what were commonly referred to as the three teachings: Confucianism, Buddhism, and Daoism. It was only after the emergence of organized Daoism that dōkyō acquired the more restrictive sense of Daoism, where it was used in opposition to Buddhism.[26] All of these factors obviously have an important bearing on how one construes the Daoist and yin-yang element in the mix of ancient Japanese religious practices and beliefs.[27] But there remains the problem of Daoism's and yin-yang's relative invisibility in modern scholarly readings of Japanese antiquity, especially among literature scholars. The remainder of this chapter will look more closely at the modern reception of

Daoist and yin-yang studies in Japan. By a kind of paradox, the marginalization Daoism and yin-yang occurred even as the Japanese study of China was
expanding and achieving a more systematic and "scientific" character.

Daoism and Japanese Sinology: The Case of Tsuda Sōkichi

The modern study of Daoism and yin-yang was influenced by a number of
sometimes contradictory factors. Under the initial influence of rationalism
and enlightenment philosophy, Meiji intellectuals came to view yin-yang
and Daoism as irrational and a hindrance to modernization. Viewed in relation to Buddhist and Confucian thought, which were held in relatively high
regard at this time, Daoism was regarded as heretical, vulgar, and rife with
superstitions and oddities. Political factors also contributed to yin-yang's
neglect when the office of yin-yang was abolished under the Tsuchimikado
Yin-Yang Abolition Act as part of the Meiji policy of transforming Japan
into a Shinto state. These developments in turn belonged to a much broader
intellectual endeavor, first articulated by the Tokugawa period nativists, to
distinguish the "pure" elements in Japanese culture by separating them out
from foreign influences. Just as the body of so-called Shinto beliefs was ar-
tificially "separated," or as Grapard prefers, dissociated, from Buddhism,
Chinese Buddhism was in turn purified of its extraneous and corrupting yin-
yang elements. In the field of folklore studies as well, developed by Yanagita
Kunio and others, yin-yang and Daoist beliefs were often ignored or treated
as the underlying expression of indigenous beliefs that had managed to survive intact, uninfluenced by continental trends.[28]

Yet if the Meiji tendency to devalue Daoism and yin-yang was one factor
in their lackluster modern reception, the subsequent de-emphasis of Daoism
and yin-yang in standard histories and cultural surveys of Japan cannot be
attributed solely to their scholarly neglect. In the 1920s, for example, Japanese scholars were involved in the publication of important primary sources
related to Daoism, including the massive *Daoist Canon* (*Daozang*, 1923–
1926), which helped stimulate research on Daoism both inside Japan and
abroad. One scholar even traveled from Japan to Paris in the late 1920s to
make copies of the Dunhuang manuscripts, discovered earlier in the century
by Aurel Stein.[29] Among scholars of the time, there was clearly an interest
in Daoist studies. But there were other factors at work in this intense level
of scholarly involvement with things Chinese in the early Shōwa period.

Much of the scholarship was stimulated by a fresh demand for knowledge about China arising from Japan's colonial activities in Manchuria, with both the Research Department for the Southern Manchuria Railroad (Mantetsu Chōsa-bu) and the Center for Oriental Research (Tōyō Kenkyū-jo) serving as magnets for much of this research in the 1930s. One of the main prewar venues for the publication of scholarship on Daoism was the journal *Shina bukkyō shigaku* (*Historical Studies in Chinese Buddhism*), which was published by the Society for the Study of Chinese Buddhism (Shina Bukkyōshi Gakkai) that was established in 1936. After the war, in 1950, Daoist scholars from the same Shina Bukkyōshi Gakkai regrouped and formed the Japanese Society for the Study of Daoism (Nihon Dōkyō Gakkai), which began publication of the journal *Tōyō shūkyō* (*The Journal of Eastern Religions*) in 1951. Today, the journal remains one of the main venues for publishing new research on Daoism in Japan.[30]

The activity of collecting and publishing primary sources, producing historical criticism of texts, and founding institutes or societies to sponsor the publication of research results in scholarly journals effectively transformed Daoism into an object of scientific study. The postwar reorganization of Daoist studies under the aegis of The Japanese Society for the Study of Daoism, which transformed the study of Daoism from a subfield of Buddhist studies into an independent field, was a further development of this process. The broader landscape of this scholarly activity, however, which encompassed the entire field of sinology, extended all the way back to the Meiji period when the modern academic disciplines of Japanese literary, historical, and religious studies first began to take shape. In discussing the emergence of historiographical practices in France and Italy, Michel de Certeau has defined such moments in the amplification of scholarly production as follows: "A work is 'scientific' when it produces a *redistribution* of space and when it consists, first of all, in *ascribing* a place for itself through the 'establishment of sources'—that is to say, through an institutionalizing action and through transformational techniques."[31] Certeau was here concerned with what happens when an already established archive, a collection of materials and ordered classifications, is reorganized into a new field. Although the time frame and conditions of production were different—late Renaissance in Europe and the Meiji Enlightenment in Japan—the establishment of sinology in Meiji Japan represented a comparable development. It was in the course of this redistribution of the cultural space that "tōyō," or "Japan's

Orient" to borrow Stefan Tanaka's apt phrase, emerged as both a discursive construct and a geopolitical and cultural sphere. The place of Daoist and yin-yang ideas and practices in the scholarly construction of Japanese antiquity is inseparable, I would suggest, from this concept of Japan's orient. One of the central figures in this activity was the historian Tsuda Sōkichi (1873–1961), whose scholarship played a pivotal role in helping to define the place of Daoism and yin-yang in historical and literary studies throughout much of the first half of the last century and whose influence extended to Western scholarship on Japan.[32] It is not surprising, then, that Tsuda was at the center of a lively exchange between two scholars of Daoism that was paradigmatic of the shift in the critical reception of Japanese Daoist and yin-yang studies that became especially pronounced from the late 1970s on. In the fall of 1982, the scholar of religions Fukui Fumimasa published a review that was sharply critical of the sinologist Fukunaga Mitsuji's study *Daoism and Japanese Culture* (*Dōkyō to nihon bunka*, 1982), which led to a lengthy exchange between the two in the pages of *Tōhō shūkyō*. While such exchanges are not uncommon, this one generated more than passing interest.[33] At issue was not simply a question of scholarly variance over the degree to which Daoist ideas and practice may or may not have influenced Japanese culture but a broader set of questions related to how the modern academic discourse about Japan's antiquity and its objects and categories of analysis have both enabled and constrained debate.

Written in a style accessible to the general reader, Fukunaga's study is a wide-ranging discussion on the formative influence of Daoist thought and practice in premodern Japanese culture, with a particular emphasis on how Daoism influenced conceptions of royal authority in antiquity. The polemical thrust of Fukunaga's book is evident in its opening pages, where he provides an explanation of why the study of Daoist influences in premodern Japanese culture languished throughout much of the twentieth century. He lists two principal causes: first, the nativism of Motoori Norinaga and others, which, in privileging the ancient period as the age of the gods (*kami*), interpreted Shinto as the authentic expression of Japanese divinity; and second, a tendency within early Japanese Buddhism to denigrate Daoism as an inferior form of what Fukunaga glosses as "shamanism" (*kidō*), a Daoist term (Ch. *guidao*) meaning the "way of demons." The combined influence of these two tendencies, according to Fukunaga, contributed to the neglect of Daoism in Japanese historical and religious studies in favor of Buddhism.

Two modern representatives cited by Fukunaga are the philosopher Watsuji Tetsurō (1889–1960) and the historian Tsuda Sōkichi.[34]

In his review, Fukui took issue with Fukunaga's claim that Daoist influences in Japanese culture had been neglected or ignored by Japanese scholars. As Fukui notes, Tsuda, in his well-known essay "Tennō kō" (published in 1920), had already traced the textual sources of the word *tennō* to a variety of Daoist contexts in ancient Chinese literary and historical texts. "The title 'tennō'," writes Tsuda in the conclusion to this early essay, "was adopted for usage in Japan because it contained a religious meaning; and there should be no doubt, as shown by the foregoing investigation, that the usage derived directly from Daoism."[35] Many of these Daoist associations examined by Tsuda—the polestar, Grand Monad, Purple Tenuity Palace, and others—are given detailed reconsideration in Fukunaga's study. What the citation does not convey, however, although it informs Fukui's criticism of Fukunaga's argument, is that for Tsuda these Daoist borrowings remained largely textual in nature, with no substantive influence on the Japanese tennō's political and religious character. This comes through in Fukui's reasons for rejecting Fukunaga's larger argument. Specifically, he questions Fukunaga's contention that Daoism was ever a "fundamental influence" underlying the adoption of the term "tennō" or the formation of the "emperor system" in the ancient period. On the contrary, suggests Fukui, we are not really talking about influence at all but literary borrowing and no more. Fukunaga was not really denying Tsuda's theory as he claimed but rather supplementing it with new evidence of his own.[36]

Fukunaga responded with a lengthy critique of Tsuda's views on Chinese culture as expressed in a number of studies, including the essay "Shina shisō to nihon" ("Chinese Thought and Japan," 1938) together with its Preface (added in 1959), Tsuda's volume *Nihon no shintō* (*Japanese Shinto*, 1954), and the early study "Tennō kō." After drawing attention to Tsuda's recommendation (in the 1959 Preface) that the study of Chinese literature be removed from the school curriculum, Fukunaga cites Tsuda's observations on cultural particularity: "Japan and China possess distinct histories, distinct cultures, and distinct civilizations. Being distinct worlds, a single orient did not come into being, a single oriental culture and civilization does not exist . . . The Japanese people developed their own particular lifestyle as Japanese and created their own particular culture. Although Chinese thought was esteemed as knowledge (*chishiki*) by learned people in the past, this was something far removed from the actual lives of Japanese people . . ."[37] As Fukunaga rightly suggests, this passage was in part a criticism of Okakura Tenshin's earlier views about the unity of the orient. The Japanese construction of the orient (*tōyō*) as a historical concept has been explored in Stefan Tanaka's study *Japan's Orient: Rendering Pasts into History*, which examines the emergence of modern historical studies in Japan. As Tanaka points out, the adoption of Western historical positivism in Meiji Japan, while initially perceived as an advance on earlier historical methods, carried its own problems. Because progress and modernity were marked as Western, the problem for Japanese historians became one of constructing a progressive history for Japan without reducing it to an incomplete and always inferior phase of the West.[38] One response to this dilemma was the construction of an academic discourse around the concept of "tōyō," a discursive as well as a geopolitical and cultural space in which Japan came to stand for the highest aspirations of the orient. Although Tsuda was a strong critic of the idea that the orient "was immanent in Japan," his own narrative of Japan's past, with its emphasis on cultural particularity, continued to operate within a discursive framework that was preoccupied with origins and deeply colored with nationalistic overtones.[39]

The notion, then, of cultural particularity, which Fukunaga singles out in his reply to Fukui, was fundamental to how Tsuda grasped cultural and religious influences. In Tsuda's scholarly idiolect, "knowledge" derived from writing is marked as that which is extraneous to those deeper cultural currents that fashion a national ethos. Here, of course, Tsuda is aligning himself with an intellectual tradition that goes back to Keichū and the later nativists, although we must also allow for influences derived from European debates about national origins that began to enter Japan as early as Meiji. This point is elaborated in the opening pages of *Nihon no shintō*, where Tsuda separates out the constituent elements in a vital religious tradition. The word *shinto*, he tells us, has a number of meanings that need to be carefully distinguished. First, it designates those religious beliefs (including magic) belonging to popular customs that were anciently transmitted to Japan. This, observes Tsuda, is the sense of the word *shinto* in its earliest occurrence in the literature, in *Nihon shoki*'s chronicles of Yōmei (r. 585–587) and Kōgyoku (r. 642–645), where it was used in contradistinction to Buddhism that had entered Japan from abroad and spread among the people. On the other hand, there were also foreign ideas that entered Japan, including Confucianism and Daoism. Confucianism, according to Tsuda, wasn't a religion but instruction in ethics and politics. In Japan, the Confucian rites were not studied in a practical fashion but only at a second remove through books. Likewise with Daoism: "There is no doubt that knowledge and classics connected to Daoism were transmitted to Japan, but Daoism as a religion did not enter Japan. Only Buddhism was possessed of energy as a religion in opposition to the indigenous popular religion, so it became necessary to use the name shintō to distinguish these popular beliefs from Buddhism."[40] And regarding the yin-yang explanation of the separation and division of earth and heaven, Tsuda observes: "Although found in stories about kami, the various expressions of yin-yang theory that appear in *Nihon shoki* are intellectually without religious meaning. In brief, Chinese ideas were adopted in various ways in writing, but in the minds of scholars who drew on such writings, they were for most part without meaning in a religious sense."[41]

To sum up, a religion (*shūkyō*) in Tsuda's discourse is a body of beliefs that has been vitalized through direct contact with the people. Although both Shinto and to a lesser extent Buddhism were infused with popular energies in Japan, Daoism, Confucianism, and yin-yang each remained largely a decorative phenomenon in Tsuda's account, a kind of graphic or textual trace empty of real content.[42] It is this view that Fukunaga rejects. In according primacy to the role of Daoism in ancient Japanese culture, he writes as a critic of Tsuda's low estimate of Chinese thought in Japan's cultural formation, not as Fukui's "epigone" of Tsuda. Notwithstanding Tsuda's contributions to Japanese sinology, his scholarship on China cannot be easily prized away from its ideological origins in the discussions about national emergence that characterized the debate about Japan's orient in the Meiji, Taishō, and early Shōwa periods.

One further criticism leveled by Fukui against Fukunaga's study related to its supposed methodological failings—terminological vagueness and the absence of citations, references, and bibliography. Indeed, for Fukui, this was perhaps the major shortcoming of Fukunaga's study. As the description of a style of scholarship once widely practiced but now fallen into increasing disfavor, the criticism certainly has validity. But even these methodological conventions, whose absence in a work aimed at a general readership is still not unusual, have their historical genealogy. In brief, the creation of a new narrative of national emergence and Tsuda's participation in that larger effort to produce an "objective" body of knowledge about China were parallel processes.[43] Echoing what was then a still prevalent view of the orient derived from nineteenth-century European historiography, Tsuda could confidently write: "Both China and India have long histories, but in reality one can say that only the time has been long while their histories are short. Hence, unlike the West they have no medieval or modern periods. Their contemporary histories did not develop in a fundamental sense; they are merely an extension of their antiquity."[44] Here, of course, we are back in the realm of Hegel's stagnant orient: timeless, without history, and unmoved by the power of the dialectic.[45] For Fukunaga, this remark is evidence of Tsuda's low regard for Chinese culture in general. For Fukui, on the other hand, such statements are an inducement to reflect on Tsuda's methodological sophistication. He notes, for example, that Tsuda could be equally scathing of Japan's own "backwardness and inferior status," as in the following remark that concludes one of Tsuda's essays on sinology: "In brief, compared to the research into Chinese thought by Western scholars, Japan is like a child."[46] For Fukui, such lapses by Tsuda into negative characterizations of Chinese culture (especially at the end of his career) must be placed in the broader context of a long career devoted to the "thorough and objective" (Fukui) investigation of Chinese thought "from a purely scholarly viewpoint" (Tsuda). Thus, although Tsuda could acknowledge the value of intuitive sympathy for one's subject matter, he was adamant in rejecting "a cranky obsession with or worship of China. The investigation of Chinese thought is always a scholarly investigation and must be critical. The old-fashioned Confucian begins right off by worshiping Chinese learning, treating it as something perfect; such an attitude must be fundamentally changed."[47] By exhorting scholars to exchange the Confucian attitude of reverence toward the past for the detached regard of the objective historian, Tsuda was arguing well beyond the nativist critique of China. He was giving a distinctively nationalist twist to a critique that had first emerged among late Qing intellectuals looking for a rationalist past in China's Confucian legacy.[48]

Conclusion

The scholarly exchange between Fukunaga and Fukui sheds considerable light on the discursive conditions that produced a body of knowledge that continues even now to influence assumptions about Japanese antiquity. If Fukui's argument that, prior to Fukunaga's study, there already existed a significant body of research on Japanese Daoism, including the seminal work of Tsuda, is well supported, equally pertinent are the specific institutional practices that have given rise to this knowledge and confined it within the disciplinary boundaries of literature, history, and religious studies. Let us go back for a moment to the discussion of the *Man'yōshū* poems that opened this chapter. As early as Keichū, there was already the beginning of a devaluation of the graphic or material dimension of poems in favor of their phonic values that would later be extended to other kinds of texts, notably to *Kojiki* by Motoori Norinaga, and lead to the benign neglect of others, such as the Chinese poetry composed by Japanese authors in the *Kaifūsō* (751). On one level, Tsuda (and many of his contemporaries) inherited this preference for the phonic as opposed to the graphic dimension of texts, but it was both reinforced and complicated by a number of Western-derived assumptions pertaining to the study of literature and history. In literature, the oral was implicitly identified with the authentic source of national expression or national characteristics. Writing and bookish knowledge, equivalent to Chinese learning in Tsuda, were inauthentic and bracketed as inessential to the deeper springs of national, or in this case, Japanese identity. At the same time, the new methodologies of literary and historical studies brought about a reclassification and reorganization of textual production and a separation of textual production in its entirety from its former embeddedness in various kinds of ritual practice. Texts, in other words, were no longer performative. In abstract terms, the newly created category of "literature" was subdivided into genres, and texts of a "historical" character were transformed into "sources" and "documents." *Man'yōshū* poems, which even in Keichū's time were still being identified with the realm of ritual and court rites, were reduced to generic expressions of the lyric, epic, or folk poem. A text like *Nihon shoki*, on the other hand, which clearly once had a performative function, was turned into a document that had to be cautiously scrutinized for its yield of underlying facts, which were then assembled into a narrative of events, a history.[49] To cite de Certeau once more on this process of producing documents and "changing their locus and status":

> This gesture consists in "isolating" a body—as in physics—and "denaturing" things in order to turn them into parts which will fill the lacunae inside an a priori totality. It forms the "collection" of documents. In the words of

Jean Baudrillard, it places things in a "marginal system." [50] It exiles them from practice in order to confer upon them the status of "abstract" objects of knowledge. Far from accepting "data," this gesture forms them. [51]

This process of placing things in a "marginal system" produced different effects depending on what was being set aside. Although removed from practice, texts like *Nihon shoki* gained a fresh cachet in their new incarnation as historical documents. On the other hand, texts as various as *Man'yōshū* poems and narratives like *Kojiki*, at least in historians' eyes, suffered a marked loss of status compared to those that were now invested with documentary value and that were held to be more reliable than literature for establishing narratives of fact about past realities. In the case of both Daoist and yin-yang thought and practice, things were somewhat more complicated. While these have been studied in their own right for some time now, their study has often been pursued by abstracting them from texts already divorced from their material conditions of production and the ritual contexts that supported them. Any attempt, in brief, to recover the symbolic and ritual implications of a yin-yang Daoist discourse in the ancient period must inevitably contend against the dispersal effect resulting from well-established disciplinary boundaries that have continued to enforce a hierarchy of values implicit in the institutionalized practices of modern literary and historical studies. Under such conditions, despite a wealth of specialized studies going back to the first years of Shōwa and even earlier, the role of Daoist and yin-yang ideas in the ideology of ancient royal authority has remained largely invisible and ignored. The two chapters that follow therefore are not an attempt to rewrite ancient Japanese history nor are they written with the aim of establishing a new narrative of fact. Rather, they are a speculative exercise in interpretation aimed at seeing what happens when the textual traces of Daoist and yin-yang thought are taken as signifiers of possible meaning, embedded in an underlying ritual practice of ancient royal authority.

THE YIN AND THE YANG OF POWER

Introduction

The Meiji effort to separate Daoism and yin-yang from the so-called pure forms of Buddhism, Confucianism, and Shinto and their subsequent marginalization, first within the field of Japanese sinology and later as a subfield within religious studies, has had several consequences. In English language scholarship, it has tended to remove yin-yang and Daoism from the purview of most literary-based approaches to the study of texts, especially for the Nara and Heian periods.[1] It occluded the contribution of Daoist and yin-yang thought to the weave of symbolic practices that legitimated ancient royal authority; and it fostered misunderstanding of the role played by Korean and Chinese culture in Japanese antiquity more generally. More recently, a number of scholars in the fields of historical and archeological studies have begun to remedy the latter by illuminating the complex ways in which ancient Japan interacted with the East Asian cultural sphere. The historian Joan Piggott, for example, has provided one of the most detailed discussions to date about the evolution of Japanese kingship from Himiko through the reign of Emperor Shōmu, with an especially rich analysis of the Chinese influences (including Confucian, Buddhist, and some Daoist ideas) that provided constructive elements in defining ancient Japanese principles of kingship.[2]

My own approach in this and the following chapter is different in kind from the work of Piggott and other historians. In focusing on the role of yin-yang and Daoism, which reverses the more usual emphasis on Buddhist and Confucian ideas in shaping the conduct of royal authority, I am neither proposing a new theory or narrative of ancient Japanese history nor am I engaged in a historical study per se. Rather, my aim is to highlight a much neglected strand in the *symbolic discourse of texts*, primarily from the Nara period. As a literature specialist with a strong interest in ritual, ceremonial, and symbolic activity, I am less concerned with the historian's focus on provable realities than with how power gets expressed in narrative, ritual, and symbolic thinking about space. My chief concern therefore is not with texts as documents and sources as such but with what texts tell us as expressions of power rather than as reflections of some underlying "reality" and narrative of events. That said, it is necessary to establish at the outset parameters for treating these yin-yang and Daoist ideas and practices. What this involves can best be clarified by looking at two contrasting approaches to articulating the phenomena of a yin-yang and Daoist matrix in Japan.

As already noted, the failure to accord Daoist and yin-yang ideas a scale of treatment at least on a par with that accorded to Buddhism, Confucianism, and Shinto in the ancient period has been partly a function of how these terms have been defined. We need to begin therefore by clarifying the use of the term yin-yang practices (*on'yōdō*) as it is applied to a taxonomy of ancient Japanese ritual and symbolic practices.[3] One well-established Japanese view is that whereas yin-yang (encompassing thought related to the five agents as well) provided constructive elements for all three of China's major philosophical and religious traditions—namely, Confucianism, Daoism, and Buddhism—it never constituted itself as an independent set of ritual practices as it did in Japan.[4] In Japan, it is argued, yin-yang was not only given formal and official status in the Yin-Yang Bureau, but its evolution into a distinctive way or practice (*michi*) known as *on'yōdō* in the course of the Heian period has generally been regarded as an important stage in its indigenization. We can characterize this as the teleological view because it stages the evolution of on'yōdō as the emergence of a distinctively Japanese set of ritual practices by projecting it onto an implicit narrative of national origins.

Murayama Shūichi has distilled this view of on'yōdō's development into four separate phases. An initial phase predating the Yamato state and the systematization of yin-yang practices in the ritsuryō codes was characterized by a gradual diffusion of prognostication techniques, including tortoise-shell casting, from the Korean Peninsula to Tsushima, Iki, and then eastward through Kyūshū. This was followed by a second phase that extended through the end of the Nara period, when a number of texts relating to yin-yang practices are supposed to have been transmitted by official embassies from the continent directly to the Yamato court. It was during this period that a succession of sovereigns are assumed to have begun the process of incorporating yin-yang procedures into court praxis and ideology, culminating in the official establishment of the Yin-Yang Bureau not long after the Jinshin Rebellion (672). The third phase, extending from the early Heian period up to about the tenth century, involved what Murayama and other scholars generally refer to as the gradual indigenization of yin-yang practices, a period which also saw the emergence of the first yin-yang "house specialists." It was during Murayama's fourth phase, which begins from about the mid-Heian period, that the two houses of the Kamo and Abe established preeminence at court in the field of yin-yang practice. It was also during this phase that yin-yang masters began to play an increasingly important role in numerous rituals pertaining to the management of pollution and purification, widely regarded as another indication of yin-yang's indigenization.[5]

In the teleological narrative just summarized, yin-yang refers in effect to two rather different sets of practices: one that was gradually disseminated to Japan by populations of immigrants arriving from the continent and a second based on a textual tradition that was transmitted directly to the court. Although Murayama generally employs the term "onmyōdō" (his preferred reading) to refer to both phenomena, thereby refusing the hierarchization that is otherwise implicit in his staged narrative, other scholars have adopted the term yin-yang thought (*in'yō shisō*) to distinguish between the intellectual system of correlative cosmology based on the yin-yang five agents cycles (*in'yō gogyō*), which had an elaborate textual tradition, and the term *on'yōdō* to refer to magical techniques (*jujutsu*) used in geomancy, purification, and other ritual practices. Shimode Sekiyo has gone so far as to characterize the intellectual system as a "surface" phenomenon and the ritual practices as fundamental in Japanese culture. Whereas the former was official, public, and thus readily available for analysis, the latter constituted the invisible but enduring substrate of ancient Japanese ritual practices.[6] In Shimode's effort to distinguish between surface and depth phenomena, there is an echo of the same tendency to essentialize the indigenous by privileging it over the foreign in Japanese culture that we found in the scholarship of Tsuda Sōkichi.

More recently, a much different view of Japanese yin-yang and Daoist practices has been developed by a number of historians, literature specialists, and experts in Chinese Daoist studies, including Shinkawa Tokio, Masuo Shin'ichirō, Noguchi Tetsurō, Tōno Haruyuki, and Ōyama Seiichi, to name only a few of what constitutes a large and loosely connected group. In contrast to the teleological narrative, which emphasizes the opposition between the foreign and indigenous, often couched in terms of elite versus popular tendencies, with the former typically aligned with the official transmission of written knowledge, the analyses of these scholars, conversant with what has sometimes been described as the "ideographic cultural sphere" (*kanji bunka ken*), evoke something much closer to cultural hybridity. By supplementing their research on texts with evidence derived from inscriptions on wooden tablets (*mokkan*) and other artifacts recovered from archeological sites, they present a far more complex picture of Nara and pre-Nara period culture, especially as regards its relationship to continental culture. Even when the tension between popular and elite tendencies is stressed, as is the case for Masuo Shin'ichirō, the popular tends to be treated as a dissonant rather than a merely indigenous voice, which participates in the same hybrid culture that is shared by the elites. Some of these issues will be taken up later in this and the following chapter. Here, I largely restrict my comments to the work of Shinkawa, whose theory on the fate of Daoism in the pre-Nara to early Heian periods provides a distillation of this more recent scholarly approach, as well as a suggestive contrast to the teleological model.[7]

As explained by Shinkawa, the establishment of the Yin-Yang Bureau (*Onmyōryō*) and the Medical Bureau (*Tenyakuryō*) early in the eighth century marked the transition from a prior period of cultural synthesis, in which Daoist, yin-yang, and Buddhist ideas were mingled together in a shared culture of the elites, to one in which the court under Temmu and his immediate successors attempted to achieve a new level of centralization and control. It was during this period that a sharpened awareness of yin-yang and Daoism in contradistinction to Buddhism crystallized. This shift is reflected not only in subtle changes in the language pertaining to Daoist-type techniques, first codified in the Taihō and later in the Yōrō legal codes but also in the early eighth-century phenomenon of returning "priests" (not synonymous with Buddhist priests) to secular status. During the Kiyomihara period, these priestlike figures, of which Hōzō in *Nihon shoki*'s Temmu chronicle is a representative figure, operated with relative freedom, performing Buddhist rites but also handling a variety of techniques based on yin-yang principles, including calendar manufacture, medical cures, prognostication, and Daoist-type spells or incantations. By the early decades of the eighth century, the use of these same techniques, including the preparation of medicines and elixirs, came to be increasingly viewed by the authorities as dangerous, and their unlicensed use was technically subject to severe punishments. In actual practice, however, because their techniques were valued, many of these same priests who were returned to lay status subsequently assumed important duties in the Yin-Yang Bureau and Medical Bureau. On one level, therefore, the establishment of the Yin-Yang Bureau and Medical Bureau was an attempt to monopolize such knowledge and practices by the court.[8]

The effort to monopolize and regulate the use of yin-yang and Daoist knowledge was one facet of a much broader legal codification of the ritsuryō state's authority. Knowledge and techniques that once belonged to a widely shared culture of the elites were now being rearticulated within a legal framework that *renamed* and thereby differentiated such knowledge and practices into (1) permissible activity, countenanced yet controlled by the state, and (2) prohibited activity that by the time of Prince Nagaya's "rebellion" (729) was being characterized as a form of heresy (*sadō*, literally sinister way) against the state.[9] What needs to be stressed, however, is that it wasn't the techniques or knowledge as such that were at issue but their distribution within a system of power. As the earlier cultural synthesis underwent a process of differentiation, for example, there was an overlap in the first half of the eighth century between Daoist-type magic (represented graphically as 持神咒) and another type associated with sutra chanting (represented by the graphs 経之咒). Although the activity was apparently the same, at the discursive level it was differentiated in a manner that gave priority to Buddhist chanting, which reflected the growing power of Buddhist rites and institutions.[10]

These observations place the debate over the status of Daoism and the related body of yin-yang knowledge and practices in a fresh, if somewhat paradoxical, light. Building on the results of previous scholarship, Shinkawa and others have presented a convincing picture of a culture that was deeply imbued with Daoist and yin-yang-derived practices dating from at least a century prior to Temmu's reign. Flourishing in the old temple enclaves of the prereform period, this Daoist, yin-yang, and Buddhist assemblage became the frequent catalyst of rebellions or attempts to seize power, the most successful arguably Temmu himself. It was Temmu, moreover, who seems to have first recognized the dangers associated with the techniques and knowledge that abetted his own accession to power. Hence, this paradox: The establishment of the Yin-Yang Bureau and Medical Bureau, which signified the court's monopolization of yin-yang and Daoist knowledge and practices, was also the beginning of a process that would invest these same practices with potentially heterodox meanings. But to emphasize the point made earlier, Daoist knowledge and yin-yang techniques were never simply ejected from official state ideology but *redistributed and made visible in officially named bureaus* and in a parallel process gradually folded into a body of ritual practice and doctrine where they were sanctioned as Buddhist rites.[11] Hence the ambiguous character of the yin-yang Daoist assemblage, especially in the period leading up to and following the ideological ferment that characterized the attempt by Temmu and his successors to establish a more centralized rule. Over the course of the Nara and early Heian periods, as Buddhist rites and institutions vied with the authority of the court, elements of this Daoist and yin-yang assemblage would periodically irrupt in dissonant counterpoint to the official ideology.

The remainder of this chapter looks at several aspects of this yin-yang Daoist cultural assemblage. It begins with an overview of what has sometimes been described as Han ideology, focusing on its blend of Confucian or juist (*ju*) thought with yin-yang–five agents, prognostication through omens, and the proto-Daoist practices of fangshi sorcery and immortality. My aim here is twofold. First, as already noted, one factor underlying the absence of yin-yang and Daoism in discussions of the ancient period is definitional. In rejecting the so-called irrationalism of Daoism and yin-yang, there has been a strong tendency to project a purified or rationalist Confucianism onto depictions of Japan's ancient period, which is then dismissed as superficial knowledge while the more "mystical" elements are reworked and presented as authentic indigenous tendencies. One aim of this first section is to refocus on the complexity of Han ideology, including its distinctive Confucianism. This is not to suggest that Han ideology was in any sense transmitted to Japan as a body of practice and thought. Rather, it was tributary to the broad cultural transmission—the hybrid continental culture discussed by Shinkawa and others—that reached Japan in successive waves, mediated in part by immigrants from the Korean kingdoms and China. A second aim in beginning with a discussion of Han ideology is heuristic and relates to the issue of sources and methodology. Going all the way back to Tsuda Sōkichi's studies, the search for Chinese precedents to illuminate the culture of Japan's ancient period, especially ideas pertaining to the emperor, has resembled at times a haphazard sifting of sources. In an earlier period, when written sources were the primary criteria for establishing historical veracity, the method had its justification. With the application of new theoretical models that aim to illuminate a discourse (namely, an ensemble of textual, ritual, and doctrinal practices) rather than establish direct lines of influence and that draw on the material evidence of artifacts as well as texts, the sovereign authority of written sources has been considerably eroded. This has certainly been the case for much recent scholarship on Daoist and yin-yang ideas in the Nara and pre-Nara periods, with its concept of cultural hybridity. In actual practice, however, this has meant that the search for sources, no longer constrained by the kind of temporal narratives favored by past scholarship, has expanded its range. In the case of the Nara and pre-Nara periods, this has been reinforced by the view that much of the written knowledge of the hybrid culture was mediated through digests and encyclopedic compilations rather than specific sources. A review of Han ideology has the advantage of providing a more focused discussion on a set of ideas and practices that, although subsequently mingled together with other practices in the hybrid culture, retain a certain cohesiveness of their own. Following this overview, I then turn to the main argument of the chapter on yin-yang-related practices. In these sections, I examine how yin-yang ideas relate to the organization of time, space, and the myths that helped to anchor the authority of the court, beginning with a look at yin-yang and weft-text knowledge in relation to Shōtoku Taishi's Seventeen Articles Constitution and descriptions of the ranking system. I further analyze the calendrical and yin-yang principles at work in *Nihon shoki*'s narrative strategies and look at a variety of yin-yang symbolism pertaining to palace architecture, the layout of the capital, and ritual activity aimed at enhancing the authority and prestige of the tennō. The chapter concludes with a discussion of the symbolic activity of the Yin-Yang Bureau and its relation to the cosmogonic theories that inform the mythological portions of the chronicles.

The Han Background

The importance of Han period thought as an influence on Japanese notions of sovereignty has been examined in a number of studies by Yasui Kōzan, Nakamura Shōhachi, and Endō Katsumi.[12] In addition to yin-yang five agents thought, characteristic elements of Han ideology discussed in their work include the interpretation of portents (*zaiyi*) and auspicious signs (*xiangrui*) and a tradition of prophecy based on omen-lore (*chenwei*). The omen-lore, which was collected and systematized in the weft-texts (*weishu*) during the Later Han, also included a variety of beliefs that would subsequently be absorbed into organized Daoism.[13] The connecting thread in Yasui's and Nakamura's view of Han ideology is the apocryphal lore of the weft-texts, which they identify as a characteristic of the so-called new-text (*jinwen*) Confucianism. According to one long-standing view, the new-text Confucianism of the Han period differed markedly in content from a supposedly earlier tradition of old-text (*guwen*) Confucianism. Recent debates, however, have cast doubt on the validity of the distinction, reading it as the creation of late Qing (1644–1912) controversies over the authenticity of certain Confucian classics, which subsequently merged into a broader ideological debate about the usefulness of Confucianism in confronting what was viewed as a technologically superior West. In this debate, old-text Confucianism was offered up as a more rational and authentic Confucianism.[14] Both Yasui and Nakamura have clearly drawn on aspects of this earlier scholarly tradition, yet from a perspective that aims to reverse a tradition of Japanese scholarship that has tended to dismiss a rationalizing Confucianism in the interests of affirming indigenous beliefs and practices. At issue, however, is neither rationalism nor its contrary but a style of thinking with its own logic. As Michael Nylan has shown, reliance on omenology, apocryphal lore, and yin-yang five agents cosmologizing was characteristic of many Confucian or juist scholars of Han times, irrespective of their adherence to old-text or new-text writings, which may have reflected little more than orthographic variations.[15] With these distinctions in mind, we can turn to our review of Han ideology.

I begin with a look at the emergence of several complementary cyclical arrangements of the five agents. Although the fragmentary nature of the extant textual record makes it difficult to provide an exact chronology, it is generally agreed that the synthesis of the yin and yang with the five agents into two distinct cycles of conquest (*sōkoku*) and generation (*sōsei*) was fully achieved by the middle of the Former Han (206 B.C.E.–8 C.E.). By this time, according to Yasui, the order of the five agents was most commonly represented in the three following arrangements:

1. Productive Sequence: water, fire, wood, metal, earth
2. Generative Cycle: wood, fire, earth, metal, water
3. Conquest Cycle: earth, wood, metal, fire, water

Although it has not been determined precisely when these three arrangements first appeared—Yasui surmises a time around the Spring and Autumn Annals or Warring States periods (403–221 B.C.E.)—it was the thinker Zou Yan (305–240 B.C.E.) who is generally credited with matching each of the five agents or potencies (*te*) to a specific dynasty according to the conquest order. The following correspondences are based on the chapter "Resonating with the Identical" in *Master Lü's Spring and Autumn,* a chapter widely thought to show the influence of Zou Yan's cosmological thinking:

Huangdi (Yellow Emperor)	earth
Xia	wood
Yin	metal
Zhou	fire
Qin	water

With Zou Yan's innovation, the five agents were transformed from what has sometimes been characterized as a protoscientific account of natural processes into a mysterious or esoteric knowledge that claimed to explain historical cycles of dynastic rise and fall.[16]

The conquest cycle prevailed in the period that extended roughly from the Warring States into the early Former Han. This was a time of violent revolutions and changes of power, and the first emperor of the Qin, the autocratic unifier Shi huangdi (r. 221–210 B.C.E.), clearly made use of the cycle to legitimate his own authority. With the collapse of the Qin in 207–206 B.C.E. after Shi huangdi's death in 210 B.C.E., China once again entered a period of warfare, which soon came to an end when Liu Bang defeated his rivals and was declared the first emperor of the Han, otherwise known as Han Gaozu. Interpreted according to the then prevailing conquest cycle, earth (Han) had defeated water (Qin), although it wasn't until the reign of Emperor Wu of the Han (141–87 B.C.E.) that the identification of the Han dynasty with the earth phase of the cycle was formally adopted.[17]

One of the works composed around this time that would later reach Japan and have a direct influence on *Nihon shoki*'s cosmogony was the *Huainan zi*. Put together by scholars in the service of the Prince of Huainan (180–122 B.C.E.), the *Huainan zi* successfully integrated yin-yang five agents thought with Daoist and Confucian ideas on the sage in a characteristic example of Han syncretism. As Isabelle Robinet writes: "The figure that ensures the metaphysical, theoretical, and ontological coherence of the various existing ideologies and assembles them from within is the Sage. He is, more precisely, a Sage who reconciles the high spiritual spheres in which the Sage of Zhuangzi evolved and the more mundane sphere of a political man. In this role, he is derived from the Sage of the *Book of Changes* and the Confucians, a cosmic civilizer and organizer. . . . The Sage of the *Huainan zi* is the incarnation of the Tao, of the Center-One." [18]

Another characteristic of Han ideology was the systematic integration of yin-yang five agents thought with the theory of portents. According to both Nakamura and Yasui, the Han integration of omenology with the yin-yang five agents cycles, although informed by the earlier concept of the unity or oneness of heaven and man found in Mengzi, Zhuangzi and other thinkers, marked a significant departure from previous uses of omens. Whereas the oneness of heaven and man put the primary emphasis on the notion of virtue, Han period thinkers amplified the principle of resonance between heavenly and human phenomena, already adumbrated in works like the *Shijing* (*Book of Songs*) and *Shujing* (*Book of Documents*), by establishing a complete macro-microcosmic correspondence between man and the universe. In *Master Lü's Spring and Autumn Annals*, for example, the natural portents or calamities are merely recorded as natural phenomena; there was as yet no connecting principle of natural resonance linking heaven and man. This was provided by introducing into the system of portents the yin-yang principle of *qi*, an innovation that appears to have owed much to the mystical thinker Dong Zhongshu (ca. 195–105 B.C.E.), an advisor to Emperor Wu and an important architect of the integration of portents with yin-yang cosmological thought.[19]

As explicated by Dong Zhongshu, when the virtue of the emperor and his governance benefited the people, heaven praised him by manifesting good omens such as beautiful cloud formations or auspicious animals like the phoenix. On the other hand, when his conduct harmed the people, he was rebuked and admonished by portents in the form of natural calamities such as earthquake or drought. Failure to modify his conduct resulted in the destruction of the country and the bestowal of the heavenly mandate upon a new dynasty. In summing up the political implications of Dong Zhongshu's system of thought, we can say that it worked to restrain the power of the Han emperors even as it became the basis of their legitimacy.[20]

Both Dong Zhongshu's systematic use of portents to admonish and praise and the *Huainan zi*'s virtuous sage ruler were made possible by a principle of resonance closely tied to an elaborate yin-yang correlative cosmology. The authors of the *Huainan zi* begin with the productive order of the five agents and then proceed to transpose them into their generative and conquest orders. This swing between conquest and generative cycles was closely tied to the alternating dominance of the two *qi* or pneuma of the yin and yang.[21] The political implications of this were considerable. By reinterpreting dynastic successions in accordance with the generative as opposed to the conquest cycle, new rulers could confer a legitimacy on their reigns that they might otherwise have lacked. According to one theory, this was the case for the usurping Emperor Wang Mang (r. 8–23 C.E.). Thus, at the end of the Former Han, the scholars Liu Xiang (79–6 B.C.E.) and his son Liu Xin (50 B.C.E.– 23 C.E.), who were proponents of the so-called old-text Confucianism, rearranged the order of the five potencies to reflect the generative as opposed to the conquest cycle. Han thereby changed from earth (in the conquest cycle) to fire (in the generative cycle), a fabrication, as Yasui suggests, that gave Wang Mang's usurpation of power the inevitability of a peaceful change of mandate. There were also other factors that may have assisted this change of potency. According to the principles of a solar calendar that was then in use and based on the triad of heaven-earth-man (*tian di ren*), the Han dynasty belonged to heaven and was thus identified with the color red, a view already current at the time of Dong Zhongshu. The identification of the Han dynasty with the potency of fire was then further reinforced by interpretations found in the weft-texts, about which more will be said later. By exploiting an already current idea that identified the Han dynasty with the potency of fire and anchoring it to the five potencies rearranged according to the generative cycle, Liu Xiang and Liu Xin were able to strengthen the identification of the Han dynasty with the potency of fire. From this point on, the generative cycle with its implicit logic of a peaceful succession from one dynasty to another prevailed throughout the remainder of the Han, further enhancing the legitimacy of its rule.[22]

As noted, one of the key aspects of Dong Zhongshu's thought was the integration of omens and portents into the yin-yang five agents cycles with the aim of legitimating and at the same time reigning in the authority of the Han emperors. The use of propitious omens as signs heralding virtuous rule, however, went back to a period well before the Han assumed power. In addition to propitious clouds (*ruiyun*) and propitious planets (*ruixing*), these could include a variety of natural phenomena connected to mountains, rivers, flowers, trees, and animals, the latter including the four supernatural creatures listed in the *Li ji* (*Record of Ceremony*): namely, the unicorn, phoenix, tortoise, and dragon.[23] In a well-known passage from the *Analects* (*Lunyu*), Confucius laments their absence as an indication of his own period's lack of a virtuous ruler: "The Master said, 'The Phoenix does not appear nor does the River offer up its Chart. I am done for.'"[24] Complementing the good omens were the category of portents or natural calamities, which the *Spring and Autumn Annals* differentiated into destructive natural events (*zai*) and deviations or natural prodigies (*yi*).[25] It was Dong Zhongshu who first made systematic use of natural calamities as a means of checking the authority of the emperors. Thus, in the "Xianliang duice," he states:

> When the empire is about to be destroyed by departing from the Way, heaven first sends destructive calamities (*zaihai*) as an admonition. If the emperor does not acknowledge this by reflecting on his actions, heaven sends prodigies (*guaiyi*) as a warning. If he still persists in his ignorance of these deviations, the empire is destroyed.[26]

Here, Dong Zhongshu observes the distinction made in the *Spring and Autumn Annals* between natural calamities and prodigies, with the latter performing the function of amplifying the warning to the erring emperor. By the end of the Former Han, the use of portents, specifically the natural prodigies, shifts from the function of merely restraining an emperor's authority, which was emphasized in Dong Zhongshu, to the function of prophecy, a shift that likewise occurs with the propitious omens.[27] It is in the so-called apocryphal or weft-texts, composed toward the end of the Former Han, that this prophetic function of signs, including both omens and portents, assumes a systematic written form.

As its name indicates, the weft-texts were understood as an esoteric thread of commentary or wei (literally woof-thread) on the prophetic signs (*chen*) that supplemented the warp (*jing*) of the orthodox interpretations found in the canonical texts (*jingshu*).[28] In an important study on their influence in Sixth Dynasty period Daoism, Anna Seidel argued that these prognostic texts themselves grew out of a much earlier tradition of "imperial treasure objects," including talismans (*fu*), charts (*tu*), registers (*lu*), and writs and tallies (*xie*), which were kept by dynastic houses as far back as the Zhou as a guarantee of the imperial mandate to rule. In the course of the Warring States period, a tradition of prognostication based on these objects developed that eventually gave rise to a body of written literature that was subsequently reduced to a systematic form in the weft-texts. Thus, the River Chart evolved from a stone "to a diagram, then to a text which interprets a diagram and finally to a whole series of texts constituting one of the sections of the chenwei literature." [29]

Although there is still uncertainty about when the prognostications first assumed written form in the weft-texts, by the time of Emperor Guangwu of the Han (r. 25–57 C.E.), they are under the control of the *fangshi* ("experts in techniques") and juist scholars, who use them to buttress the legitimacy of the Han emperors. Thus, whereas Wang Mang's use of *fu ming* (a heavenly mandate revealed through tallies) relied on the older tradition of auspicious objects to legitimate his seizure of power from the Han, Emperor Guangwu, who defeated him and restored the Han dynasty to power, made extensive use of the signs recorded in the weft-texts, initiating a practice that would be continued until the Han lost power. But as Nakamura also observes, no sooner had the prognostications been reduced to a systematic form in the weft-texts in the first half of the Former Han than writings criticizing them began to appear, an indication that their widespread circulation was perceived as a threat to the ruling power. [30] This trend has been aptly summarized by Seidel: "Probably all the various contenders for the throne in the period after Wang Mang used prognostications in what might be termed an ideological battle." [31] By the third century, the widespread use of omen-lore led to government prohibitions on their circulation. Apart from a few exceptions, almost all of the Han period weft-texts were lost or destroyed following the Han's collapse. [32] Much of their content, however, was eventually absorbed and elaborated upon in the revealed scriptures of organized Daoism, which took shape in the course of the second through fifth centuries.

Our review of Han ideology has so far focused on the yin-yang five agents, omens and portents, and the prognostications recorded in the weft-texts. Yet there were intellectual currents at this time that showed a distinctively proto-Daoist coloring. Of particular importance in this regard were the ideas and

practices of the aforementioned *fangshi*, who devoted themselves to astrology, divination, geomancy, and techniques for achieving longevity or "immortality." In her study of Daoism, Isabelle Robinet, after noting the strong
link between the theories of the *fangshi* and the Confucianism of the weft-
texts, states: "The affinity between the subjects studied by the *fangshi* and
those of interest to the Taoists was so great and lasted for so long that the
distinction between these thinkers and the Taoists is not easy to make—
to the point that many treatises on geomancy and divination that derive
from *fangshi* practices have been incorporated in the *Daozang*, the Taoist
canon."[33] To round out this review of the Han Chinese background, it will
be necessary to look at several of the Daoist strands in this thought.

Among the proto-Daoist elements in the syncretistic Han ideology were
practices and beliefs for becoming immortals (*shenxian*). Shi huangdi of the
Qin and Emperor Wu of the Han, for example, were both famous in legend
for their patronage of *fangshi* who guided them in alchemical and dietary
rites aimed at the achievement of immortality.[34] Although not much is known
about the specific content of these rites during the Qin and Han periods—
the accretion of legends around Emperor Wu must be attributed in part to
Daoism's later efforts to create its own history—in the revealed Daoist scriptures, written down in the course of the second through fifth centuries, the
induction of "pneumas" (*qi*) into the body and their proper regulation became one of the basic practices for achieving longevity. In the *Xiang'er* commentary, a Daoist scripture that also functioned as a guide to the enlightened
ruler and "whose concept of kingship," in Stephen R. Bokenkamp's words,
was "fully consonant with Han ideas of the thearch," considerable attention was paid to the proper management of *qi*.[35] In Daoist scriptures such
as the *Purple Texts*, on the other hand, metaphorical language based on the
analogy of alchemy and meditation became the basis for the symbolic representation of "the gradual perfection of the body through the ingestion of
solar and lunar essences."[36] These later Daoist elaborations on the notion
of a downward infusion of vitalizing cosmic "pneumas," whether of solar,
lunar, or planetary rays or "essences" (*jing*), are already prefigured in the
omen-lore transmitted in the weft-texts. Thus, central to Han notions of
thearchical rule was the idea that each founder of a dynasty was born from
the union between a semidivine being and a woman impregnated by the
infusion of a divine essence or *jing*. In the weft-texts, these legends of each
founding emperor's miraculous birth were arranged by potency according

to the five agents generative cycle. One legend tells how the founder of the Han dynasty, Liu Bang, was born of a woman impregnated by a red dragon, signaling the Han dynasty's identification with the potency of fire. In another legend, these same principles are worked out in the form of a prophecy delivered by a *fangshi*. According to an account in the *Han shu*, during the reign of the Han Emperor Ai (r. 7–1 B.C.E.), a period marked by peasant revolts, brigandage, and a host of natural calamities, the emperor was presented with a prophetic text that had been received from a *fangshi* of Qi, who had in turn received it from an immortal (*zhenren*), literally "true man," named Master Red Essence (Chijing zi). The text declared the following prophecy: "The historical cycle of the Han house is halfway exhausted; it will once again receive the mandate." In her discussion, Seidel has characterized this text as the earliest example of a revealed scripture in the Han dynasty. Yasui suggests that the Red Essence Prophecy was probably composed after the fact and intended to foreshadow the subsequent revival of the Han following the usurpation of Wang Mang.[37] Whatever the historical origins of this particular prophecy, it discloses the connection between the omen-lore of the weft-texts, the *fangshi*, and the principle of a downward infusion of vitalizing essence.

Weft-Texts, Chronologies, and Yin-Yang Numerology

> Winter, Tenth Month: A priest from Paekche named Kwalleuk
> arrived and presented the court with books on calendar-making,
> astrology, geomancy, and also books on the art of invisibility and
> magic.
>
> —NIHON SHOKI, *Suiko 10*

The textual evidence for the presence of an apocryphal strand of Chinese thought in ancient Japanese conceptualizations of rulership is the catalogue of books edited by Fujiwara Masayo titled *Nihonkoku genzaisho mokuroku* (*A Catalogue of Books Extant in Japan*, 889–898), which contains a special category listing more than eighty-five volumes of weft-texts. In addition to weft-text commentaries on such classics as the *Yijing*, *Book of Poetry*, *Book of Rites*, *Book of Music*, and *Spring and Autumn Annals*, it also lists volumes that deal specifically with the prognostication of portents and prodigies, including one volume of a work attributed to Dong Zhongshu on the interpretation of portents and prodigies in the *Spring and Autumn Annals*

(*Shunjū saii tōchūjō sen*). Although it is not known precisely when the texts listed in the catalogue were brought to Japan—Endō Katsumi proposes the Nara period for some of them—Yasui has surmised that weft-texts were already an influence and circulating in Japan by the end of the sixth century.[38] But the significance of chronology here exceeds the historian's concern with dating because the fact of chronology is itself one of the effects wrought by the introduction of yin-yang principles as a basis for legitimating ancient rule. This is evident not only in the way events are clustered together and structured in Japan's first official history, *Nihon shoki*, but above all in the calendrical principles that organized these events into a chronology and then linked the mythic time of the early cosmogonic portions of *Nihon shoki*'s narrative to what Emile Benveniste, in speaking of the emergence of chronicle time in general, has characterized as an "axial moment." In Japan's case, the axial moment was Jimmu's date of enthronement, which reconfigured time into an expression of the tennō's authority and thereby inaugurated a "new course of events."[39]

Except for a brief mention of two experts in divination and calendar-making during the fifteenth year of Kimmei's reign (554), *Nihon shoki*'s entry in the tenth year of Suiko's reign (602) regarding the Paekche priest Kwalleuk's presentation of books on calendar-making, astrology (*tenmon*), geomancy (*chiri*), and the art of becoming invisible (*tonkō*) and magic *(hōjuchi)* is generally regarded as the earliest textual evidence that clearly links the activities of the court to a knowledge of calendrical principles and yin-yang five agents theory.[40] One year later, the court instituted cap-ranks (*kan'i*); and in the twelfth year of Suiko's reign (604), the aforementioned "cap-ranks were for the first time granted to the various ministers" and the Seventeen Articles were promulgated.[41] Five reigns later, during the ninth year of Tenchi's reign (664), we find a similar clustering of notices pertaining to institutional reform and knowledge connected to activities that would shortly be assigned to the Yin-Yang Bureau established soon after Temmu's reign.[42] Thus, during the ninth year of Tenchi's reign, not only were the cap-ranks revised and augmented into twenty-six grades, but in the following year, a clepsydra, or water clock (*rōkoku*), "was placed in the new pavilion, and for the first time the hours were struck, and bells and drum sounded."[43] The way in which the symbolic activity of time reckoning either accompanies or affirms major acts of institutional reform—here the introduction of the cap-ranks and promulgation of the Seventeen Articles by Suiko and Tenchi's subsequent revision of the cap-ranks—points to the underlying yin-yang principles that regulated *Nihon shoki*'s temporal structure.[44]

The earliest exegesis of *Nihon shoki*'s calendrical principles as applied to its chronology, specifically the dating of Suiko's promulgation of the Seventeen Articles in 604 and Jimmu's enthronement in 660 B.C.E., was undertaken by the Heian period scholar Miyoshi Kiyoyuki (847–918). In his *Kakumei kanmon* (901?), Miyoshi drew on his knowledge of prophecy lore found in the weft-texts to argue for a change of era name to ward off anticipated disasters associated with a kanototori year, thought to be a time of revolutionary change and renewal of the heavenly mandate. Miyoshi's exegesis was based on passages found in weft commentaries on the *Book of Changes, Spring and Autumn Annals*, and *Book of Poetry*, which declared *kinoene* and *kanototori* years, the former corresponding with Suiko's promulgation and the latter with Jimmu's enthronement, as years portending a change in the heavenly mandate (*kakumei*). Subsequent studies have shown that the dating of Tenchi's revision of the cap-ranks in 664 was also based on a year of revolutionary change.[45]

In addition to regulating chronology in *Nihon shoki*, yin-yang knowledge and omen-lore derived from the weft-texts also appear to have informed the symbolic code of Suiko's cap-ranks and the Seventeen Articles. The Seventeen Articles attributed to Shōtoku Taishi, for example, reveal an extensive use of yin-yang symbolism and numerological theory in their construction and content that exceed a merely formal or ornamental function. In an early essay whose observations were further developed by Takigawa Masajirō, Okada Masayuki argued that the constitution's arrangement into seventeen articles was based on the sum of eight and nine, the two highest numbers in yin-yang numerology symbolizing the yin and yang, respectively, which derives from number symbolism in weft commentaries on the *Spring and Autumn Annals* and other works. Okada and Takigawa further argued that the moral qualities assigned to the six pairs of twelve cap-ranks, in the order of toku (virtue), jin (benevolence), rei (courtesy), shin (sincerity), gi (justice), and chi (wisdom), were arranged to accord with yin-yang five agents principles rather than the Confucian order of virtue, benevolence, justice, courtesy, wisdom, and sincerity; and that the distribution of the five colors likewise harmonized with yin-yang principles in an arrangement intended to ward off calamities and assure good fortune.[46] More recently, Takeda Sachiko has questioned the view that Suiko's Seventeen Articles were based on yin-yang five agents symbolism. Arguing that the circular logic of yin-yang five agents principles, with its balancing and harmonizing with periodic changes of reign, would have rendered its color symbolism unsuitable for establishing stable distinctions of rank, she has proposed that Confucian principles pertaining to the ceremonial order, where the emphasis was on rank and hierarchy, were more likely to have influenced the symbolism of Suiko's code. In making her argument, Takeda notes that because each dynasty in China ruled under a dominant agent with its associated color, the remaining colors were not available for marking distinctions of rank and class. Instead, these were rendered visible by the type of clothing, pattern of cloth, and accessories, which then functioned in tandem with the circular yin-yang logic that underlay the dominant color symbolism of the dynasty. While Takeda's analysis complicates any attempt to read the symbolic ramifications of ritsuryō period dress codes, it does so by assuming that the copresence of two different symbolic orders, one premised on circular logic and the other on binary and hierarchical principles, was a possibility in China but an improbability in ancient Japan. It also fails to allow for the ways in which such symbolic knowledge was adapted to local conditions of power. In conclusion, whether we accept Okada's and Takigawa's view that the dating of the constitution's promulgation to a revolutionary year was a deliberate strategy of its putative framer, Shōtoku Taishi, or Yasui's more likely hypothesis that such dating reflects knowledge closer to the period of *Nihon shoki*'s editing, it is reasonable to assume that yin-yang cosmological principles, derived in part from knowledge transmitted in the weft-texts, played a role in shaping its conception of ancient royal authority, although this doesn't rule out Takeda's arguments that more Confucian-like principles were also a factor.[47]

Polestars, Grand Monad, and the Purple Tenuity Palace

Perhaps the most intriguing evidence for yin-yang symbolism in the Seventeen Articles lies in the choice of twelve ranks, which has been thought to be based on the analogy of the twelve guardian stars that surround Grand Monad (*taiyi*), one of the two brightest stars in the polestar constellation.[48] The sources of the polestar symbolism, the Grand Monad, and the Purple Tenuity Palace in the weft-texts and other Chinese sources and their bearing on the choice of the term tennō as a title for the Japanese sovereign were discussed in an early essay by Tsuda Sōkichi.[49] Yet Tsuda, despite the richness of his exegesis, viewed this symbolic nexus as little more than a veneer of bookish learning. More recently, the significance of the polestar as a cosmological symbol for validating the authority of ancient Japanese sovereigns has been argued by Joan Piggott in her study of Japanese kingship. In characterizing Suiko's reign that followed Yūryaku's, she writes:

> Yūryaku's martial paramountcy was replaced by the idealized, universal reign of a Chinese-style sacral monarch—a polestar—who presided over a ranking system and a courtly ethic into which all chiefly elites of the realm were to be incorporated. A compelling cosmological revalidation established the "heavenly court" (*tenchō*) as a center of unprecedented virtue, contributing substantially to the waxing of the galactic center at the turn of seventh century.[50]

As Piggott notes, one possible source for the polestar basis of Suiko's reign is this well-known passage from the *Analects*: "The Master said, 'The rule of virtue can be compared to the Pole Star which commands the homage of the multitude of stars without leaving its place.'"[51] In light of the numerological symbolism in Shōtoku's constitution, it is likely that yin-yang knowledge underlay the polestar symbolism as well. It will be helpful at this point to sketch in the broader yin-yang and astrological basis for the polestar theory of ancient Japanese rulership.

In ancient Chinese astrology, the polestar and the constellations that revolved around it were viewed as the center point of the sky and the object of a complex astral mythology. A passage in the *Shi ji*'s (*Records of the Historian*) Officers of Heaven (*tianguan*), for example, characterizes the region about the polestar as the Palace, which was understood to have emerged from the polestar and its surrounding constellations.[52] Inside the Palace dwelled the Grand Monad, or Taiyi, one of several names for the polestar in its divine character, who was flanked in turn by stars personified as the Grand Heir (*taizi*) and Empress and the twelve guardians who surrounded them, all of whom were protected by the Wall of Purple Tenuity, a series of fifteen stars extending northeast of the polestar. Other astrological texts assigned different names to the stars and asterisms of the polestar region, including Heaven's Illustrious Great Theocrat (*Tianhuang dadi*) for the polestar and Theocrat (*Di*) for the brightest of the polar stars Kochab, also known as Grand Monad.[53] The mythological character of the polestar constellation is conveyed in the following description, cited by Edward H. Schafer, from the Han philosopher Wang Chong:

> The location in the sky of a Sky Divinity is just like the residence of a king. The royal one resides within a double barrier, and so the divinity of the sky is suitably placed within a hidden and secret place. As the royal person resides within the buildings of a palace, so the sky too has its Grand Palace of Purple Tenuity.

As Schafer goes on to note, "the 'Purple Palace' as it was sometimes called for short, was the residence of Heaven's Illustrious Great Theocrat, who reveals himself as Yilduz [Polaris], which is itself, like him, the secret embryo and quintessence of the god Grand Monad, revealed as Kochab."[54]

In the cosmogonic myths elaborated in works such as the *Huainan zi* and *Book of Changes*, Grand Monad of the astral myth was reworked by philosophers into the principle of the Grand Culmination (*Taiji*), which designates the primordial chaos or primitive material before its differentiation out of original oneness into first the yin and yang and then into the myriad forms that arise out of their interaction. According to the *Huainan zi*, the process of differentiation began when the buoyant or refined pneumas (*qi*) filled with light and rose upward to become the yang or heaven, while the heavy and dark pneumas of the yin sank to become earth. The yang in turn gave rise to the essence of fire, which became the sun, and the yin to the essence of water that became the moon. The interaction of the sun (*yang*) and moon (*yin*) in the heavens gave rise in turn to the five planets and stars, while fire (*yang*) and water (*yin*) combined on land to generate the five primordial elements of wood, fire, earth, metal, and water, whose continuous circulation was expressed as the five agents.[55] The philosophical reworking of the polestar myth, which combined a dynamic struggle between the dualistic yin and yang forces giving rise to the divisions of the seasons (time) and the four directions (space), with a principle of infinite circularity expressed in the five agents, ultimately transformed the ruler into the central expression of a harmonious balance of cosmological forces.

The extent to which Japan's ancient rulers made a deliberate use of polestar symbolism and the underlying cosmogonic myth grounded in yin-yang five agents theory is reflected not only in the principles that organized the Seventeen Articles but in a variety of textual, spatial, and architectural practices. As Kōnoshi Takamitsu has recently shown in a number of studies, the yin-yang cosmogony incorporated into the creation myth at the beginning of *Nihon shoki* (based on the *Huainan zi*) was not merely a superficial embellishment but fundamental to *Nihon shoki*'s ideology for legitimating the authority of the ruler.[56] Yoshino Hiroko, in addition to detailing the yin-yang symbolism that informed many of the court rituals, including the Gosechi dances and the Great Thanksgiving Service (*daijōsai*), has also speculated on the astral-geomantic principles that she believes to have informed the layout of the Ise shrine complex as early as the reign of Temmu. According to Yoshino, during Temmu's reign, the deity Amaterasu was being amalgamated with the polestar emanation of the Grand Monad in an architectural layout that identified the inner shrine (*naigū*) with Grand Monad and the outer shrine (*gaigū*) with the seven polestars of the Big Dipper.[57]

The polestar myth also influenced the geomantic positioning of capitals and the disposition of buildings inside them. Its symbolism regulated not only the northern siting of the Fujiwara Capital (Fujiwarakyō) and thereafter the increasingly northern locations of successive capitals, culminating in the establishment of Heiankyō, but also determined the placement of the Palace (*dairi*), which was generally located at the northern extremity of the capital.[58] As noted in the discussion of the astral symbolism of the polestar region, the constellation of fifteen stars stretching northeast of the polestar (roughly overlapping with Draco) was visualized in astrological lore as a protective wall known as the Wall of Purple Tenuity (*ziwei yuan*). By Han times, one of its stars was being visualized as the dwelling of the Heavenly Thearch (Tiandi) and called the Purple Tenuity Palace (*ziwei gong*), also sometimes abbreviated to *ziwei* or *zigong*. In the *Huainan zi*, composed in the Former Han, we find the graphs 紫宮 being used as a designation for the residence of the Heavenly Thearch;[59] and by the Later Han, the same polestar divinity, now designated by the graphs that would later be used for the Japanese *tennō* 天皇 (or "Heavenly Sovereign," to borrow Piggott's suggestive translation), is being conceptualized as dwelling in the Purple Tenuity Palace located in the realm of the immortals. According to Fukunaga, the main ceremonial hall (*shishinden*) of the dairi, whose first graph meaning "purple" is identical to the *zi* of "ziwei" (Purple Tenuity), was the counterpart to the Purple Tenuity Palace of the polestar deity.[60] Further allusions to the polestar symbolism and the underlying philosophical myth are contained in the name of The Great Hall of State (*daigokuden*), which was written with the same graphs used to designate the primordial chaos of the yin-yang cosmogonic myth discussed earlier. During the Heian period, the Daigokuden, which is mentioned as early as *Nihon shoki*, was located in the northern part of the Greater Palace (*daidairi*), where it functioned as the main throne room and ceremonial center of the court until its destruction by fire during the Angen era in the year 1177.[61]

Calamities, Omens, and Era Names

The cosmologizing of royal authority through the systematic application of yin-yang five agents principles and omen-lore transmitted in the weft-texts was clearly intended, on one level, to magnify and enhance the prestige of the Yamato court. However, since this knowledge was part of a shared culture that was slowly establishing discursive dominance among the elites, it was also available as a potential weapon in ideological and symbolic warfare among competing political factions. This is evident in the practice of interpreting natural calamities as criticism of royal lack of virtue, made possible by the yin-yang principle of micro-macrocosmic resonance. Shortly after the *Nihon shoki* notice regarding the transmission of yin-yang and calendrical knowledge to the court during the tenth year of Suiko's reign, the narrative is characterized by a sudden increase in entries recording all sorts of natural calamities and prodigies. Apart from the mention of floods and famine during the twenty-eighth year of Kimmei's reign (567), there is very little mention of calamities throughout the reigns of Bidatsu, Yōmei, and Sujun. In an analysis of this, Tamura Enchō has suggested that the meticulous recording of natural calamities and prodigies in Suiko's chronicle reflects the political power struggle that was then taking place between Suiko and the Soga clan, with the natural calamities and portents of flood, famine, eclipse, and so on functioning as signs of criticism against bad government. Since the calamities and prodigies recorded reflect criticism against both contenders in the power struggle, Tamura concludes that yin-yang knowledge of apocryphal signs was being manipulated simultaneously by both sides at this time. In other words, it was not yet a monopoly of the court or any one group.[62]

Whereas Suiko's chronicle provides the earliest evidence for a deliberate use of omen-lore in ideological battle, the portion of *Nihon shoki* extending from the reign of Kōtoku (645–654) through Jitō discloses a systematic use of both yin-yang five agents cycles and calendrical and geomantic principles to confer a cosmological sanction upon the succession of rulers. As was noted earlier in the chapter, by the time of the Former Han, there were in existence several competing cycles of change, the most important of which were (1) a generative cycle in the order of wood generates fire, fire generates earth, and so on through metal, water, and back to wood and (2) an active or conquest cycle in which the relationship was reversed, yielding the sequence of wood conquers earth, metal conquers wood, fire conquers metal, water conquers fire, and earth conquers water. Applied to the historical interpretation of events, these two cycles resulted in much different narratives. Whereas the former legitimated peaceful changes of mandate in which the abdicating sovereign willingly yielded to a successor's virtue, the conquest cycle provided a cosmological justification for sudden revolutions of power brought about by the active intervention of human agents. The potential for manipulating this symbolic code in political power struggles was considerable, and in ancient China, Daoist rebels were frequently linked to political movements resulting in the overthrow of rulers and revolutions in the state.[63] As we shall see later, this was one likely motive for the creation of an official Yin-Yang Bureau.

In her discussion of the underlying yin-yang principles that organize *Nihon shoki*'s narrative of successions from Kōtoku through Jitō, Yoshino has suggested that the editors constructed the narrative in emulation of Han notions of dynastic succession based on various arrangements of the five potencies.[64] According to this reading, the *Nihon shoki* scheme was arranged to accord with the generative cycle, but instead of beginning with the cycle's first agent, wood, it starts with water (Kōtoku Tennō), the last agent in the cycle, and then continues in order with wood (Tenchi), fire (Temmu), and earth (Jitō). The decision to begin with water, according to Yoshino, was probably motivated by (1) the apparent prestige accorded water in Chinese arrangements of the cycles and five potencies and (2) the Yamato rulers' identification with the polestar deity, whose northerly direction also corresponded with the element of water.[65] In explicating the yin-yang symbolism of the chronicle, Yoshino focuses primarily on the calendrical and geomantic coding of major events during each ruler's reign, including transfers of the capital, enthronements, investitures, inspections of the land, and the like. Thus, whereas Kōtoku's transfer of the capital to Naniwa corresponds by time, direction, and place to the element of water, Tenchi's transfer of the capital to Ōmi corresponds to the agent wood.[66] In addition to calendrical and geomantic principles, the chroniclers also made systematic use of good omens (*shōzui*) in the narrative. In the fifth year of Tenchi's reign, the chronicle records: "This winter the rats of the capital migrated towards Ōmi." Here the rats function as a propitious sign predicting the transfer of the capital to Ōmi in the following year, with the branch symbolism of the rat (identified with the direction north) further suggesting the northern pole-star associations of Tenchi's court.[67] Another example of omen-lore occurs in the narrative of Temmu's battle against Prince Ōtomo. At one point in the narrative, one of Prince Ōtomo's allies, Tanabe no Wosumi, decides to give his warriors the watchword "metal" to prevent them from being mistaken for enemy troops. Since metal conquers wood (the agent of Tenchi's reign) in the conquest cycle, it would have made little sense for an ally of the Tenchi faction of Prince Ōtomo to have deliberately chosen such an inauspicious watchword. It is more likely, as Yoshino suggests, that the editors of *Nihon shoki* inserted the anecdote as an auspicious sign presaging Temmu's conquest by fire (the ruling agent of his reign) of Prince Ōtomo's allies' agent metal. Set within the broader framework of the generative cycle implying a peaceable succession of rulers—Tenchi's wood yielding to Temmu's fire—this use of the conquest cycle inside Temmu's chronicle suitably conveys the ambitions of his warlike reign.[68]

The systematic use of favorable omens in this portion of *Nihon shoki* is also connected to what may very well be the most important political use of yin-yang symbolic knowledge: the creation and assigning of era names (*nengō*) to individual reigns, which occurs for the first time during Kōtoku's reign. For accruing legitimacy to the court and affirming its power, no single act held more symbolic weight than the court's decision to institute the practice of assigning era names to individual reigns. By this one act, the court reorganized the time of events into an image and expression of its own power and centrality in the cosmic processes. Although doubt has been cast on the authenticity of Taika and Hakuchi as historically legitimate era names, *Nihon shoki*'s detailed account of the events leading up to the change of era name from Taika to Hakuchi reveals, as Murayama has argued, both the symbolic significance attached to the establishing of era names and the central role played in this practice by yin-yang procedures.[69]

Briefly summarized, the *Nihon shoki* account consists of a lengthy and extremely detailed narration of the events surrounding the report of the favorable omen of a white pheasant that was captured and presented by the governor of the province of Anato to the court in the year preceding the era change from Taika to Hakuchi (650), the latter meaning White Pheasant.[70]

The account consists largely of the citation of numerous precedents, from both Chinese and Japanese sources, to support the favorable interpretation of white-colored animals and birds, "which appear when the ruler is sage and humane." The underlying yin-yang principles of interpretation that informed the symbolism of the era change to Hakuchi are as follows. As the most westerly location in Honshū, Anato would have been identified with the direction west. In the five agents system of correspondences, the direction west was identified with the agent of metal, the color white, and in the twelve branches or signs of the zodiac with the sign of the bird (*tori*). Since Kōtoku's own reign corresponded to the agent water, with metal assisting water in the generative cycle, the omen of the white pheasant was in all points the most favorable indication of Kōtoku's reign.[71] Whether the era names of Taika and Hakuchi are viewed as evidence of an actual precedent set by Kōtoku or as the work of chroniclers belonging to a later reign around the time of *Nihon shoki*'s editing, the practice of assigning era names inaugurated a new phase in the consolidation of the court's expanding political power. History was henceforth the temporal record of the activities, decisions, and ceremonials of the court, with each succeeding change in era name inaugurating a new cycle that reaffirmed the court's authority.

The Yin-Yang Bureau and Cosmogonic Myths

Among the reigns in *Nihon shoki*, Temmu's chronicle stands out conspicuously for its Daoist coloring and weft-text influences.[72] Since the end of Temmu's reign falls close to the period of *Nihon shoki*'s final redaction in 720, it is possible that his own chroniclers were responsible for the sequencing of reigns that culminates in his reign's potency of fire. In choosing red in direct opposition to Tenchi's white, Temmu, who as Prince Ōama seized the throne from Tenchi's son Prince Ōtomo, is thought to have been consciously modeling his reign after the founder of the Han dynasty, Gaozu, who also identified himself with the potency of fire (*katoku*).[73] It is intriguing, then, that the chronicle of Temmu, a ruler famed for his "skill in astronomy (*tenmon*)," also provides the earliest evidence for the existence of a Yin-Yang Bureau, recording that "for the first time a platform was erected for prognosticating by the stars."[74] The connection between this platform (*senseidai* 占星臺) and the Yin-Yang Bureau mentioned a few entries earlier in the same chronicle, and again between the Yin-Yang Bureau of Temmu's time and the one that was later housed in the Nakatsukasashō (Central Affairs Ministry) remains a matter of conjecture. But viewed in the broader context of *Nihon shoki*'s calendrical strategies, together with the use of omens and the cosmogonic myths that inaugurate its narrative, the Yin-Yang Bureau becomes a narrative sign of converging meanings.

One function of the tower was probably related to the observation of the heavens. As spelled out in the Yōrō Code of the Nara period, the responsibilities of the head of the Yin-Yang Bureau related to the four areas of heavenly portents, calendrical calculations, cloud forms, and aerial phenomena. One of the chief duties of the head officer was to report secretly to the tennō the occurrence of any unusual omens that might portend danger to the state. Among the subordinate officials under his control, the most important were six yin-yang masters charged with prognostication (*senzei* or *uranau*) and geomancy (*sōchi*), a calendar maker,[75] and a doctor of astrology (*tenmon no hakuji*) responsible for observing heavenly portents and reporting any unusual signs. The importance of time reckoning to the court is indicated by the provision for a timekeeper (*rōkoku no hakuji*) responsible for regulating the flow of time by the clepsydra, with the hours indicated by a drumbeat and the minutes by the ringing of a bell.[76] The operations of the Yin-Yang Bureau—investigation of portents, prognostication, and timekeeping—thus routinized at the ritual level the same symbolic practices that are incorporated into *Nihon shoki*'s narrative structure.

The astrological lore that fell within the purview of the Yin-Yang Bureau, and which appears to have been connected to the construction of Temmu's observation platform, also informed the sky myths and poetic language that helped to sanction the tennō's authority. The literary ramifications of this astrological lore will be looked at in more detail in the following chapter's examination of *Kaifūsō*, but here it is useful to take a closer look at Chinese cosmogonic thinking as its relates to the myths that anchored the tennō's authority.

No aspect of the study of ancient Japanese culture is more conducive to labyrinthine guesswork than the mythological skein that makes up much of *Kojiki* and the first two books of *Nihon shoki*. Some of the difficulty here lies in the nature of mythographic thought in general, which is not only compressed like all forms of poetic thinking but often consists of the multiple layering and cunning reworking of previous myths. No system of myth, in other words, is pure. In postwar Japan, anthropological, structuralist, and folklore perspectives have complicated our view of Japanese mythology by drawing attention to its diverse geographical origins and parallels with other systems of myth.[77] Notwithstanding this trend, for much of the twentieth century, discussion typically centered on separating out the indigenous from the foreign or Chinese elements in the myths, often to the detriment of the latter. Here, too, the work of Tsuda Sōkichi has been critical, especially in the way he conceptualized the place of "ten," or the heavenly realm in the system of Japanese myth.[78]

As described by Tsuda, Takama no hara was based on an ancient Japanese myth dating from before the mid-sixth century and was understood as forming the dwelling place of the sun deity, Amaterasu. At this time, there existed no other heavenly deity (*tenjin*) apart from the Japanese sun deity, who was the central figure of the age of the gods. "The sun deity dwells in Takama no hara and rules over it and Ashihara no naka tsu kuni (Central Land of the Reed Plains)." For Tsuda, Takama no hara "did not exist apart from the sun deity." So closely was Takama no hara identified with the sun deity in Tsuda's thinking that he understood its coming into being as occurring simultaneously with the sun deity's ascent up to Takama no hara, whereas following the descent of the deities to earth, Takama no hara became an empty void.[79]

Tsuda, of course, was well aware of the contradictions in Japanese mythological accounts. But he was also familiar, as noted in the previous chapter, with the connections between the term tennō and Chinese conceptions of the Heavenly Thearch embodied in terms like tennō taitei, kōten taitei, tai-itsu or Grand Monad, and other linguistic borrowings. To secure primacy of place to his notion of the Japanese sun deity, therefore, he had to empty the Chinese components in this sky mythology of their meaning. His treatment of the deity Takamimusubi is a case in point. In the *Nihon shoki* myths, which are thought by some scholars to be earlier than those found in *Kojiki*, Takamimusubi's name is written with the graphs 高皇産霊. In an analysis of the graphs, Hirohata Sukeo discerns two principles: a vitalizing or productive power represented by the graphs 産霊 and glossed in the vernacular as "musubi"; and a second principle represented by the combination of the two graphs 皇霊, which derives from the Heavenly Thearch or sky deity in ancient Chinese corresponding to Tianhuang dadi, or in its abbreviated form, Dadi, an aspect of Grand Monad. Takamimusubi also appears as one of the three original deities in *Kojiki*'s account of the cosmogonic opening and retains throughout the narrative, particularly in the critical descent portions when the assembly of deities issues its commands, a stature equal to, if not superior to, that of the later born Amaterasu, a role consistent with Takamimusubi's commanding presence in *Nihon shoki* as well. In brief, as the ancestral heavenly deity (*kōso tenjin*), Takamimusubi appears to have been constructed by analogy to the Chinese Heavenly Thearch.[80]

Tsuda himself recognized the Chinese origins of Takamimusubi's divine character, and Takamimusubi becomes the carrier of Chinese meaning in his reading of Japanese myth. But Takamimusubi along with his two companions, Ame no minaka nushi and Kamimusubi, were also latecomers "who did not have a fundamental connection to the narrative of divine history."[81] This is conveyed in an interpretation that amounts to a form of mythographic rewriting. Thus, once the deities have made their descent and Takama no hara has become an empty void, "the sun deity was no longer the sun deity as ancestral deity to the ruler, but merely the sun deity as sun, and its dwelling Takama no hara now merely the sky (*ten*)."[82] In a similar vein, Tsuda characterizes *Kojiki*'s Takama no hara at the moment of its opening, before Amaterasu's birth, "as simply the sky; that is, this sky is simply the sky of the Chinese graphs (*kanji*), the sky of Chinese thought (*shina shisō no ten*)."[83]

Tsuda's success in extracting a pure myth of the Japanese sun deity from the chronicles' tangled skein was a compound of many ironies. There is a modern disenchantment about Tsuda's Chinese sky, emptied as it is of its variegated mythological world following the descent of the deities to earth. Tsuda's re-creation of his country's myths, I would suggest, was fundamentally antimythological.[84] Another irony, perhaps unintended, lay in Tsuda's decision to characterize the abandoned Takama no hara as an empty void (*kūkyo*). Tsuda's knowledge of Chinese thought was extensive, but it has been suggested that he lacked a detailed knowledge of the cosmogonic vocabulary of the myths, which might account for his failure, rather than unwillingness, to connect the cosmogonies at the opening of the narratives in any fundamental way to the ancient emperor ideology.[85]

Ancient Chinese cosmogonists held three views of the sky. Two of these, the *gaitian* and *huntian* theories, remained current in the post-Han period and would have been known to scholars in ancient Japan as well. Of the third or "unrestricted night" (*xuanye*) theory, to borrow Schafer's tentative translation, little detailed knowledge survived in the post-Han period. All three are discussed in the massive northern Song compendium *Taiping yulan*

(983). According to the Daoist text *Baopu zi* (*Master Who Embraces Simplicity*, 317), cited in *Taiping yulan*, the sky of the xuanye cosmogony was an empty and vast void "without substance."[86] Was Tsuda familiar with this theory? If he was, then it was a subtle form of irony to make a forgotten Chinese cosmogony the basis of his description of the abandoned Takama no hara. In the more familiar gaitian theory, translated by Schafer as the "Canopy Sky," the sky is always characterized as a lid- or umbrella-like covering that floats in a void.[87] In contrast to the xuanye theory, the sky is here endowed with a physical or material existence, a conception that underlies the myth of the Japanese Takama no hara or Plain of Heaven. Yet neither the term nor references to the gaitian theory occur in any of Tsuda's accounts of Japanese myth; nor does Tsuda mention or allude to the huntian, or "Enveloping Sky," theory.[88] According to its description in the *Jin shu*, an official history of the Jin dynasty compiled in 648, the sky is like an egg with the yolk inside, which permits water to rise into the heavens and pour back thence into the seas. The huntian theory of the sky together with the related "cosmic sphere" or *hundun* cosmogony, possibly through the influence of the *Huainan zi*, shapes several portions of the Japanese cosmogonic myths.[89] Its most explicit expression is the opening portion of *Nihon shoki*'s cosmogony. It is also at work, as Hirohata observes, in *Kojiki*'s initial description of the formation of the land "resembling floating oil and drifting like jellyfish" and in the equivalent passage in *Nihon shoki* where the "land floats about like a fish sporting on the waves."[90] Possibly echoing Motoori's commentary on the *Nihon shoki* variant, Tsuda views this portion of the cosmogony, with its characterization of a formless earth, as a purely native myth, arguing that such a concept occurs nowhere in either the *Huainan zi* or *San wu li ji*. Yet these same accounts of heaven and earth arising out of a primitive material or primal chaos also call to mind the yin-yang cosmogonic theory of multiplicity arising out of an original oneness, namely, the Grand Monad yin-yang theory. It was this theory, most likely borrowed from the *Huainan zi*, that constructs the authority of the ancient Japanese tennō after the Chinese model of the Heavenly Thearch or tennō taitei, who was otherwise an aspect of the great oneness or originary chaos, Taiyi.[91] Even if we accept the argument for an indigenous, or possibly non-Chinese, origin for both *Kojiki*'s and *Nihon shoki*'s versions of the earth's formation, it need not mean that Chinese cosmogonic theories are of nugatory import here.[92] Just as the graphic representation of Takamimusubi's divine name allows what may well have been an "indigenous" deity to persist in a new linguistic frame of reference, the larger structure of the Chinese cosmogonic and mythographic model may be said to rearticulate without necessarily eliminating another structure of myth.

To return to the problem of Temmu's Yin-Yang Bureau and the construction of the observation platform, it was the same huntian view of the sky, I suggest, that provided the philosophical basis for the Yin-Yang Bureau's astrological activity—namely, the observance of planetary deviations, cloud forms, and other aerial phenomena and the reporting of them in secret to the emperor.[93] The Yin-Yang Bureau and observation platform mentioned in *Nihon shoki* were, in other words, not simply textual embellishments of dubious historical veracity—empty imitations of Chinese thought—but consistent with the symbolic representation of ancient royal authority elsewhere in *Nihon shoki*, in certain *Man'yōshū* poems, and in other texts and ritual practices to be discussed later in this study. Regarding the actual model for Temmu's senseidai or "observation platform," Hirohata has proposed the Tang Imperial Observatory (*sitian tai*) as a possibility, further speculating that an office connected to astrology was probably already in existence by Tenchi's time, with its organization completed in the reign of Temmu.[94] We need not, however, insist too closely on a direct borrowing of the Tang model, which was probably too late to have influenced the court of Temmu's day.[95] A more likely influence is suggested by another entry in *Nihon shoki* just prior to the mention of the platform, which speaks of a gathering of scholars from the Bureau of Learning, the Yin-Yang Bureau, and the Bureau of Outer Medicine and of visitors that included a prince from Paekche and workers from Silla. Cultural exchange between Yamato and the Korean kingdoms likely provided the impetus for the construction of the platform, a supposition strengthened by the fact that a similar structure, some nine meters in height, had already been erected by the Sillan king a few years earlier.[96]

The activities of the Yin-Yang Bureau crop up repeatedly in official Japanese court histories. Some idea of the scope of the yin-yang officers' learning is indicated by an entry in *Shoku nihongi* for the year 757, which charges the officers of the Yin-Yang Bureau to master the *Wuxing dayi* (*General Significances of the Five Agents*).[97] Throughout the Nara period, the prognostication of propitious omens was closely tied to the periodic change of era names, and it was the yin-yang masters' knowledge of the weft-texts and omen-lore that often determined such a change. According to an edict promulgated by Shōmu Tennō, the change of era name from Yōrō to Jinki (Sacred Tortoise) occurred when prognosticators drew on their knowledge of weft-text diagrams and interpreted the presentation of a white tortoise as a sign of Shōmu's virtuous rule, leading to a change of era name in the following year.[98] In addition to calendrical and astronomical functions, two other duties of the Yin-Yang Bureau that are detailed in the law codes and recorded in the official histories are geomancy and pacification rituals. A good example is the proclamation that was issued on the occasion of the court's move to Heijō. It opens with a declaration by Genmei Tennō that contains an unmistakable reference to the Heavenly Thearch's Purple Tenuity Palace: "Having reverently received the [mandate] from the profundity above, I stand before the realm as emperor. On account of my modest virtue, I occupy the dignity of the Purple Palace (*shikyū*)." The next passage illustrates the importance of yin-yang practices in securing the authority of the court: "From ancient times until the present, the measurement of the days and the inspection of the planets have established the foundation of the Palace. Prognosticating society for omens and observing signs in the earth have made secure the capital of the emperor (*teiō*). . . ." The chronicler then affirms the results of the geomantic siting of the new capital: "At the present time the earth of Heizei [Heijō] is in harmony with the Four Zoomorphs and the Chart, and the three mountains protect it. It is in accord with the tortoise shell and bamboo stalks, and suitable for the construction of a capital."[99] Far from empty rhetoric, the language of the proclamation is a clear acknowledgment of the central role played by yin-yang practitioners in securing for the court a harmonious relationship to space, time, and the cosmological principles revealed through the understanding of earthly and heavenly signs.[100]

Finally, there is the underlying astral symbolism of the four zoomorphs that determine the geomantic layout of the new capital. Designated here by the graphs 四离 (*shikin*, literally "four birds" or "four animals"), they were more commonly known as the "four deities" (*shijin*) or "four spirits" (*shirei*). In the geomantic rite based on the yin-yang five agents system, each of the four deities corresponded to a specific direction and geographical feature. Thus, according to the commentary of the yin-yang specialist Abe no Seimei, proper performance of the geomantic rite required a flowing stream to the east (green dragon), a marsh to the south (vermilion bird), a large road to the west (white tiger), and a high mountain to the north ("murky warrior").[101] In correlative cosmology, such an alignment was intended to protect the capital from the agents of fire (drought) and water (flood) and to channel productively wood (agriculture) and metal (warfare).[102] In the ancient Chinese astrological system, the four spirits referred to four constellations located one each in the four astral quarters or "palaces" (*guan*) that surrounded the central palace where the Heavenly Thearch resided. In the Officers of Heaven section of the *Shi ji*, the four astral quarters of the Eastern, Western, Southern, and Northern palaces are matched respectively to the green dragon (*cang long*), the vermilion bird (*zhu niao*), the Pool of Heaven (*xian chi*, but more typically the "white tiger," or *bai hu*), and the murky warrior (*xuan wu*).[103] Genmei's new capital, where she occupied the "dignity of the Purple Tenuity Palace," was a mirror image of its heavenly counterpart. The chapter that follows extends this discussion of the yin-yang Daoist basis of the tennō's authority by taking up the Daoist threads in this discourse, especially as they bear on ideas pertaining to immortality.

RECOVERING THE DAOIST TEXT

Introduction

The symbolic strategies that have thus far been examined—chronology, prognostication, cosmogony, and geomancy—were all related to knowledge and techniques housed in the Yin-Yang Bureau. Another current in Han ideology was a body of thought and practice centered on "immortality" and the pursuit of longevity. In the organized Daoism that took shape between the second and fifth centuries in China, ideas on immortality were systematically incorporated into both ritual and meditative practices centered on the management of the body's *qi* to bring it back into alignment with the "original breath," or Dao, the animating principle of the universe and the basis of the resonance that linked the microcosm of the body to the macrocosm of the universe. Just as the "ingesting" of pure *qi* served as one method for achieving immortality, the failure to balance or harmonize the breath was believed to result in demonic infestation, illness, and death.[1] This preoccupation with life-enhancing practices was further reflected in another characteristic of organized Daoism: the observance of "taboos and prohibitions" (*jinji*) aimed at warding off calamities and demonic infestation that result from improperly mourned spirits, dangers associated with burials or "woundings of the earth" (*fan tu*), and risks attending "transitional or disruptive events" such as travel, marriage, sacrifice, and the like.[2]

This Daoist emphasis on bodily well-being and protection against demonic infestation has obvious affinities to the magical functions of mid-Heian *on'yōdō*, which, in addition to guidance regarding directional taboos (*kata-tagae*), divination practices, and calendrical calculations for determining auspicious and inauspicious occasions, included a variety of rites aimed at expelling and protecting against demonic spirits. The resemblances suggest that Japanese on'yōdō was itself an adaptation of Daoism. Fukunaga Mitsuji, for example, has viewed mid-Heian on'yōdō with its emphasis on the health and well-being of the body as simply another name for the Daoist beliefs upon which it was based.[3] Shimode Sekiyo has likewise characterized Daoist magic (*dōjutsu*) as having been "dissolved or absorbed into Japanese yin-yang practices."[4] Yet where Fukunaga has treated the magical, life-enhancing aspects of on'yōdō as part of a broader Daoist discourse encompassing the conceptual framework of yin-yang five agents correlative cosmology that underlay the authority of the tennō, Shimode regards the Daoist substrate in on'yōdō as an occult or hidden influence that remained largely outside the prevailing ideologies of official Confucianism and Buddhism. To the extent that it was recognized at all by official ideology, it was done so under the name of "Shintō," meaning Daoism that was subsequently indigenized after having been introduced to Japan by immigrants from the continent.[5]

Although it is true that Daoism in Japan never constituted an official school or branch of study, the weft-texts not only contained much that was subsequently absorbed into organized Daoist religion but also constituted an element of the hybrid cultural assemblage. By focusing on the absence of organized Daoism in the pre-Nara and Nara periods, which belongs to the historically distinct development of official Tang Daoism, the culture of this earlier period with its mingling of yin-yang, proto-Daoist, and Buddhist practices is easily misunderstood.[6] The more fundamental issue lies less in the absence or presence of Daoist conceptions of royal authority in the ancient period—their influence now seems beyond dispute—but rather in the modification of these conceptions as they interacted with other ritual practices, notably, those centered on purity, defilement, and placation, which in turn were closely tied to ideological and institutional pressures that accompanied the increasing power of Buddhist authority and rites.[7]

In this chapter, I focus on two aspects of the Japanese yin-yang Daoist matrix: Daoist ritual and symbolic practices as they relate to an earlier conception of royal authority, including ideas centered on immortality; and the subsequent displacement of symbolic activity that was housed in the Yin-Yang Bureau and aimed primarily at enhancing the tennō's authority by new rituals that proliferate around pollution taboos and the expulsion of demonic infestations. Although characterized as an indigenization of yin-yang practices, it was related to an important shift in the ritual and political status of the tennō. Signs of this shift are already apparent in Temmu's reign, but it becomes more pronounced from the late ninth century and will thereafter reverberate well into the medieval period. Throughout this chapter, I pay special attention to the problems that arise when trying to recover the sense of symbolic and ritual practices that have been obscured by subsequent interpretive traditions. This involves not only interpreting *Nihon shoki* in accordance with the "letter," as opposed to the "spirit" (*tama*), of its text, recovering, in other words, the sense implied by the graphs, but also triangulating among what appear to be sharply differentiated ritual practices—the Daoist practice of ingesting "pneumas," the expulsion (*harai*) of defilements, and the pacification (*shizume*) of raging deities—to arrive at an understanding of ancient royal authority that has remained partially occluded.

The discussion begins with a brief look at the Daoist implications of several familiar Japanese terms, including "tennō," titles for deities, the royal regalia, and the like. The four sections that follow are organized around what might be characterized as four graphical nexi: an entry on a Daoist-like temple in Saimei's reign, Temmu's posthumous name, a reference to a "soul-summoning" rite in Temmu's chronicle, widely interpreted as the earliest instance of a "chinkon" (spirit-pacification) rite, and a mysterious reference to grottolike retreats on the occasion of Temmu's presentation of gifts to ritual entertainers. In each of these semantic nexi, there is a gap between the traditional vernacular reading of the text and the Daoist associations evident in the graphic representation. Using these gaps as a hermeneutical hook to move through this succession of Daoist topoi, the analysis attempts to recover the outlines of a symbolic landscape and ritual practice centered on the quest for immortality by making connections to a range of Chinese sources as well as interpretations of ritual in the Japanese law commentaries. These threads come together in the section on the Chinese poetry of *Kaifūsō*.

Often discussed for its literary qualities, it has received less attention as a symbolic expression of ancient royal authority. In this section, I look at how the poetry of *Kaifūsō* mythologizes the court as an immortal realm, reassessing as well the significance of such familiar topoi as the Tanabata festival and ritual play at Yoshino. The remaining sections of the chapter turn to the set of problems related to the emergence of yin-yang practices centered on defilement or pollution taboos. Through the analysis of such ritual practices as the Great Purification Rite (*ōharae*), magical expulsion rituals, the chinkon ceremony, and practices pertaining to pollution taboos, I show how an uneasy balance between overlapping ritual systems—one centered around a Daoist yin-yang articulation of pollution practices and the other around pacification rites and the management of defilement—became one of the preconditions for the emergence of Heian period on'yōdō. The chapter concludes with a look at the political landscape of competing power interests that characterized this transition.

Some Daoist Terms

A number of Daoist terms are found in terminology and ritual practices that have come to be identified more closely with Shinto. These include the term *tennō*, two of the three sacred regalia (*shinki*), the mirror and the sword, and ritual language found in the so-called Shinto prayers known as *norito*. In the vernacular readings of the graphs 天皇 ("sumera mikoto"), "sumera" has been understood as expressing the sacred and pure character of the sovereign, and "mikoto" the authority of his utterances as sumera. As the highest representative of the "heavenly deity" (*tenshin*), it was the sumera mikoto who acted as the mediator of sacred speech (*mikotomochi*).[8] In Chinese astrological lore, on the other hand, the term *tennō*, or *tennō taitei* (Heavenly Great Thearch) in its longer form, designated the polestar in its divine character. In Daoist lore, the term *tennō* was also associated with deities like Dong wang fu (King Father of the East), who was believed to reside in one of the several immortal realms. Tsuda Sōkichi, who was the first to bring to light many of these Daoist associations, traced much of the vocabulary to the *Zhenzhong ji*, a Tang period novel with many Daoist themes. Although Tsuda's views have been questioned, especially regarding likely textual sources and his dating of the term *tennō*'s first usage, they remain influential. In a critique of Tsuda's theory, Shimode argued that if the term *tennō* had in fact been chosen on the basis of being the highest deity of Daoism, the term ought to have been "genshi ten'ō," "taitei," or "tentei," the highest ranking deity in the *Zhenzhong ji*, not tennō. Instead, Shimode argued that the choice of the term *tennō* drew on the astrological thinking of *Shi ji*'s "Officers of Heaven" section. Yet as Tōno Haruyuki has observed, at the time the term *tennō* was adopted, Daoism, immortality thought, weft-text knowledge, and the astrology of official history were all inextricably intertwined. The term *tennō* is therefore best understood as deriving from Daoism broadly understood as encompassing both weft-text and astrological knowledge.[9]

By the Later Han, the thearch, or tennō taitei, was conceptualized as living in the Purple Tenuity Palace located in the realm of the immortals, where he was served by a hierarchy of officers of which the highest was the *zhenren* (*shinjin, mahito*), or "true person," a title indicating one who had achieved knowledge or mastery of "immortality" (*xian*). One of the principal symbols of the Heavenly Great Thearch's sacred authority was another familiar icon of Shintō mythology, the mirror and sword, or *shenqi* in Chinese. Although its earliest occurrence in Daoist literature dates only from the sixth century, the mirror and sword as symbols of royal authority already appear as early as the second century in the prophecy lore transmitted in the weft-texts.[10] When such evidence is set beside the myth of Amaterasu's heavenly origin, which recalls another Daoist belief—namely, that of the Heavenly Thearch or celestial master who advises the perfect ruler—it becomes reasonably certain that Daoist ideas had more than a formal influence on ancient Japanese ideas of rulership. Although it is difficult to ascertain when these ideas first reached Japan, it appears likely that at least by Tenchi's reign, and certainly by the time of the Temmu and Jitō courts, they were already figuring consciously in conceptions of royal authority.[11]

Temmu's reign in particular is deeply colored by Daoist motifs and a fascination with immortality.[12] It is reflected, for example, in the revision to the so-called eight hereditary titles (*yakusa no kabane*), recorded in *Nihon shoki*.[13] Among the eight grades, the highest grade was "mahito" 真人, the "true person" or "perfected" of the heavenly realm of the immortals, which functions as a pair with tennō or the polestar deity. The fifth grade in Temmu's eight hereditary titles was *dōshi* (literally "master of the way"), which designated an expert in Daoist learning.[14] One possible source for the pair "mahito" and "tennō" is the *Zhengao* (*Declarations of the Perfected*), a Daoist text collected and edited by Tao Hongjing (456–536), where the "true person" is characterized as one who serves the Heavenly Thearch.[15] Other Daoist terms that can be mentioned include the graphs 尊 and 命. Used to represent the names of divinities in *Nihon shoki* and *Kojiki*, they have traditionally been given the vernacular reading of "mikoto." The Daoist origin of these terms was remarked on as early as Tsuda and then more extensively in a study by Naba Toshisada, who traced the usage to the term *tianzun* (heavenly worthy), one of several titles for the highest deity of Daoism.[16]

Daoist Temples, Dragon Riders, and Hot-Spring Landscapes

I now turn to several of the more intriguing Daoist textual loci, beginning with the entry in Saimei's chronicle regarding what appears to be a Daoist belvedere (*daoguan*). In an entry recorded in the second year of Saimei's reign, immediately following the empress's removal to the new Palace of Asuka, the chronicler states: "Tamura Peak was crowned with a circular enclosure. Tamura 田身 is the name of a mountain; it is also written Tamu 大務. Moreover, next to two Tsuki trees on top of the peak, a tower (*takadono* 観) was erected. It was given the name of Futa-tsuki Palace. It was also called the Heavenly Palace (*ama tsu miya* 天宮)."[17] Earlier in the same chronicle, there occurs one of the most curious passages in *Nihon shoki*: "There was someone mounted on a dragon in the middle of the sky. In appearance, he resembled a Tang gentleman. He had on a broad hat of blue oiled silk. He rode swiftly from Kazuragi Peak and disappeared on Mount Ikoma. At the Hour of the Horse [around noon], he passed over Pine Peak of Suminoe and departed swiftly toward the west."[18] These two entries have been the subject of debate among Japanese scholars from as early as the Taishō period when Kuroita Katsumi (1874–1946) published an article in which he suggested that the graphs 起観 (to erect a tower) referred to the construction of a Daoist belvedere (*daoguan*) on the site of Saimei's Futa-tsuki Palace and that the dragon-mounted figure was a Daoist sage. Kuroita's theory soon gained a number of adherents, but in the postwar period, it was seriously questioned by a number of scholars, including Naba Toshisada, Kubo Noritada, and Shimode Sekiyo. Since then, the well-entrenched view that official Daoism left no traces in Japan has meant that Kuroita's claim for the existence of a Daoist belvedere in Japan was largely treated with a taboolike caution. More recently, renewed interest in the Daoist and yin-yang sources of ancient royal authority has scholars once more cautiously circling about the tower for its possible meaning.[19] The debate is of particular interest not only for the light it sheds on the existence of a hybrid cultural assemblage but also for the way it crystallizes several of the issues in the modern scholarly discourse on Daoism that are central to this study.

Critics of the theory have relied primarily on three textual cruxes: the existence of a traditional vernacular gloss on the graph 観; the lack of so-called corroborative textual evidence to support the Daoist reading; and an interpretation of the dragon-mounted figure in the late Heian Buddhist historical work *Fusō ryakki*, compiled by the Buddhist priest Kōen (d. 1169). Regarding the first point, Naba objected to Kuroita's Daoist reading on the grounds that the graph had several other possible meanings, including *rōkan*, or "lofty tower," a reading seemingly supported by the traditional vernacular gloss "takadono" that is found in the oldest manuscripts of *Nihon shoki*.[20] This point was developed by Shimode, who observed that *Nihon shoki* yielded no other examples of the graph "kan," used either in the implied sense of "takadono" or with the gloss "takadono" attached to it. Shimode further argued that the graph could not refer to the whole of the Futa-tsuki Palace because there were no other instances in *Nihon shoki* of its being used to express the idea of a "palace" (*miyadono, kyūden*). He also rejected the idea that the dragon-mounted figure referred to a Daoist master, citing (1) an oral tradition in the *Fusō ryakki* that made it the "spirit of the minister Soga no Toyoura [Emishi]" and (2) a gloss from *Teiō hennen ki* (*Annals of the Emperors*) stating that "many people died on account of his spirit."[21] Finally, Kubo objected that the Daoist reading lacked corroborative support. There was no mention, for example, of a "dōshi," which might have been expected in the context of a Daoist belvedere.

The critics present what appears to be a persuasive argument but by wrenching the obvious sense of the graph from its own context and locating its meaning in a subsequent interpretive tradition. It is a classic instance of the anachronistic historicizing of *Nihon shoki* that refuses to accord substantive meaning to the text's literal or graphic sense. As Shimode himself notes, and as Takashima Masato observes in his rebuttal of the theory's critics, the traditional gloss of "takadono" was itself already an interpretation, probably dating from no earlier than the Heian period. It is at least as likely that the chroniclers chose to use this particular graph precisely because the structure was different from the typical palace.[22]

Regarding the figure on a dragon, the interpretation offered by critics of the Daoist reading draws on what appears to have been a later, or possibly alternative, legend that accreted around Soga no Emishi as a result of his bitter death in the violence of the Taika reforms. The reference to the many deaths caused by his spirit in *Annals of the Emperors* is a classic instance of destructive wrath visited by a "vengeful spirit" (*onryō*), a motif that crops up with increasing frequency in the official histories from the ninth century on. The placation of vengeful spirits is an important ritual practice in ancient Japan, but there has been a tendency in modern scholarship to treat placation as an explanatory key to ancient Japanese religious experience in general, sometimes in contexts where it is not warranted. Although Soga no Emishi does have an association with Kazuragi, where he is said to have built an "ancestral temple" in the first year of Kōgyoku's reign,[23] in the case of the exegetical tradition invoked here, we are clearly dealing with a Buddhist-Shinto reworking, certainly post-Nara but probably dating from the Heian period, which has conveniently served the modern preference for a Buddhist-Shinto reading of the Kodai period that was discussed in Chapter 1.[24]

A reader open to the range of Daoist associations will be forcibly struck by the close proximity of the first entry that records the sighting of an immortal aloft upon a dragon and the second that details the construction of the mysterious *guan*, or Daoist belvedere. As will be discussed later, Mount Kazuragi was closely connected at this time to Daoist activities and would subsequently be associated with forbidden magic. Rather than placation, it is the link between dragons and immortals who command special powers, recorded in Daoist works like the *Zhuangzi, Baopu zi*, and *Shenxian zhuan* (*Biographies of Immortals*) that best illuminates this scene. In the *Zhuangzi*, the immortal who lives on Mount Guye "sucks the wind, drinks the dew, climbs up on the clouds and mist, rides a flying dragon, and wanders beyond the four seas." And in the "Golden Cinnabar" section of *Baopu zi*, it is related of Laozi's teacher Yuanjun that, "Skillfully harmonizing the yin and the yang, he commanded the demons and gods and the wind and rain. And as he coursed aloft upon nine dragons and twelve white tigers, the immortals throughout the realm all obeyed him."[25] In addition to these associations, the Daoist belvedere is provided with its own suggestive gloss, "ama tsu miya" 天宮 ("heavenly palace"), which recalls the Daoist name for the Heavenly Thearch's Palace. The epithet "ama no," which "embellishes" many verses in *Man'yōshū*, itself belongs to this same nexus of Daoist associations. In the *Man'yōshū* poem on Mount Kaguya that begins with the phrase "amoritsuku / ama no kaguyama" ("Heavenly descended / heavenly Mount Kaguya"), Mount Kaguya is represented by the graphic combination 芳來 that merges it with the Daoist immortal realm of Hōrai (Ch. *Penglai* 蓬莱).[26]

But what about the physical structure of Saimei's "tower"? What was its purpose and what kind of activities were pursued there? The following description of a Tang period belvedere or "watch-place" by Schafer is suggestive: "These well-appointed retreats were most frequently placed in remote mountain areas, not only because of the peace and quiet afforded to facilitate meditations and discipline of the residents, but because of the obvious benefits of the proximity of supernatural beings, both those who held court deep within the caverns of the mountains themselves, and those above, for whose spirit-places the high hills provided convenient courtyards and vestibules."[27] In addition to meditative practices, it can be assumed that purifications and vitality-enhancing exercises were also among the ritual activities pursued at such belvederes. For this, we must turn to another episode in Saimei's chronicle centered on the rebellion of Prince Arima.

Arima's narrative has several interrelated motifs running through it, one connected to his madness and fascination with hot springs and landscape viewing and a second to his supposed plot to overthrow Saimei, which revolves around an act of prognostication in a mysterious tower. *Nihon shoki* first takes up the Arima thread in the following passage: "Prince Arima was clever by nature, feigned madness, and so on. He went to the hot springs of Muro under the pretence of curing his illness, and upon his return he praised the landscape of the province, saying: 'Hardly had I gazed upon the land, then my illness disappeared of itself.'"[28] Favorably impressed by Arima's praise, Saimei decides to visit the hot springs herself, a motif that is repeated throughout her chronicle. When the chronicle next takes up Arima's story, he is addressed by Soga no Omi Akae in a speech that enumerates "the three faults" of Saimei's rule, which include wasteful levies of the people's wealth and lavish construction projects. The criticism is welcomed by Arima as an overture to take up arms: "Prince Arima went to the house of Akae, climbed up a tower (*rō* or *takadono* 楼), and plotted with him. An arm-rest broke by itself. Realizing that it was an unlucky omen, they both swore an oath and left off their plotting." Although Arima and his co-conspirator, Akae, appear to have forsworn their rebellion, in the sequel he and his co-conspirators "are arrested and sent to the hot springs of Ki." When questioned by the imperial prince about the reason for his rebellion, Arima mysteriously replies, "Heaven and Akae would know. I understand nothing of this." In the end,

Arima is strangled and the other conspirators are either executed or banished to the provinces.[29]

The fascination with towers, hot springs, and landscapes is explained in part by contemporary developments on the continent in the first half of the seventh century, when there was a boom in recreational visits to the hot springs east of Chang-an by the Tang Emperor Taizong (r. 627–649), an activity that would be resumed after a brief lull by Gaozong in 676. The journeys to this region that was the site of many daoguan were motivated by the cleansing and curative powers of viewing the scenery, which in turn was closely connected to the emperor's religio-political authority. By curing himself, he also cleansed and healed the people, building up a reservoir of goodwill among his subjects. With their lodges set amid forested mountains overhung with mist and clouds, the hot-spring landscapes were the equivalent of Daoist immortal realms, endowed with vitalizing powers that conferred longevity. Like Zhuangzi's immortal, one went there to "suck the wind" and "drink the dew." One famous Daoist watchtower, Louguan 楼観, near Chang-an, served as a site from which to contemplate stars and gaze at clouds for the purpose of prognostication.[30] Both the contemplation of hot-spring landscapes, which nourished the vitalizing *qi*, and the viewing of heavenly phenomena and cloud gazing (*wangqi* 望気) from watchtowers, can therefore be regarded as related activities.[31]

It is here as well that the exchange between Soga no Omi Akae and Prince Arima discloses its profounder meaning. The three faults listed by Akae all refer to Saimei's large-scale construction projects, which appear to have been aimed at transforming the landscape surrounding Tōnomine, the site of her tower, into a replica of a Daoist immortal realm. The criticisms attributed to Akae, on the other hand, imply that these undertakings wrought such environmental damage and so overtaxed the people that they had the contrary effect of undermining the health and well-being of the people. Although Saimei's landscaping project is criticized as exhibiting a want of virtue, the motif is echoed later in Temmu's plans to establish what amounts to an auxiliary capital in Shinano, a mountainous region east of the main capital in Yamato that was also known for the hot springs of Tsukama.[32] Although Temmu did not live to complete this project, which may have been undertaken in emulation of the Tang Emperor Gaozong, preparations for it were continued by his son Prince Ōtsu, who, like Arima, was subsequently accused of rebellion and executed by order of the court. As Shinkawa observes, Saimei's project and Arima's tower, landscape viewing, and feigned madness, the latter a likely reference to the mysterious behavior of the Daoist adept, were all related expressions of the same yin-yang Daoist cultural assemblage.[33]

Although *Nihon shoki* has often been read as the origin point of a long-enduring Japanese tradition of imperial authority, the chroniclers and editors who fashioned its discourse were participants in a broader East Asian dialogue. By the time of the Tang period, Chinese emperors such as Tang Gaozu (r. 618–628) were adopting Daoism as an official religion. In the year 647, during the reign of Emperor Taizong, the title of the Chinese emperor changed from *huangdi* to *tianhuang*, or tennō in Japanese. Its adoption by Japanese sovereigns at this time, possibly for the first time by Temmu, thus took place amid a surge of interest in Daoism that rapidly spread to other parts of the East Asian cultural sphere, including the Kingdom of Koguryŏ. As Ch'a Chu-hwan relates in a study of Korean Buddhism, Taizong actually dispatched Daoist masters to Koguryŏ, where the Korean king of the day had a Buddhist temple remade into a Daoist hall and elevated its Daoist masters to a position above that of the Confucian scholars.[34] The destruction of Koguryŏ and Paekche shortly afterward sent many Korean refugees to Japan, bringing with them a knowledge of Daoism. Like Temmu's observation tower and the Yin-Yang Bureau discussed in Chapter 2, Saimei's much debated belvedere is another point of convergence for a skein of motifs that have both symbolic as well as historical resonance.

Temmu's Posthumous Name

Another intriguing indication of a Daoist matrix is Temmu's posthumous name, or "okurina," 天淳中原瀛眞人天皇 (ama no nunahara oki no mahito no sumera mikoto), which is recorded twice in *Nihon shoki*, once each at the beginning of the two parts of his chronicle.[35] This complicated series of graphs with their Japanese glosses discloses several overlapping layers of meaning. The two graphs 眞人 (mahito) identify Temmu as the "true person" or "perfected" of Daoism, while the preceding graph 瀛 (*oki*), suggestive of a broad expanse of sea, is an abbreviated form for Yingzhou, one of the Three Sacred Mountains lying in the Eastern Sea, the other two being Penglai and Fangzhang. There on mountains that appeared as a cloud on the distant horizon of the sea, immortals were believed to gather, the immortality elixir was at hand, and the palaces were all made of gold and silver. Temmu, in brief, is being commemorated as both Heavenly Thearch and a master of the secrets of immortality, who now dwells on the sacred mountain of Yingzhou. The first four graphs evoke several further levels of meaning. According to Ueda Masaaki's analysis, they contain a reference to a pond that was excavated when Temmu constructed his Asuka Kiyomihara Palace. The graphs 淳中原 (nunahara) would thus mean something like "plain in the midst of the pond," the site of the Asuka Kiyomihara Palace.[36] In addition to this literal reference to Temmu's Kiyomihara Palace, the phrase may contain a more expansive meaning as well. If the first graph is included, the combination reads "plain in the midst of the heavenly pond." As I discussed earlier, the earthly emperor's residence was typically identified with the Heavenly Thearch's Purple Tenuity Palace of astral mythology. In Daoist lore, the thearch of Heaven was conceived of as an immortal and the heavenly topography easily merged with the Daoist vision of the immortal realms. As will be shown later in the discussion of poetic imagery in *Kaifūsō*, there was an overlap in the Japanese imaginary between the immortal realm of Hōrai, located in the sea, and the heavenly realm of the thearch, which was metaphorically identified with the tennō and his palace. In this sense, the Kiyomihara Palace can also be viewed as an immortal realm. One further level of meaning hints at the symbolic and ritual basis of Temmu's authority. In a note on Temmu's posthumous name, the editors of *Shoku nihongi* interpret the graphs 淳中原 as containing another sense pertaining to the production of a red stone or jewel, reading the phonemes *nunahara* as nu 瓊 + na (old variant of the particle *no*) + hara 原, which yields the meaning "plain which produces the red stone."[37] The literature of the weft-texts and the lore of immortals are filled with accounts of the vitalizing powers associated with the consumption of various mineral- and herbal-based compounds. In addition to its encomiastic function, then, Temmu's posthumous title encodes an allusion to a quest for the immortality elixir (*sen'yaku*), which was often compounded of ingredients that included a red stone or jewel.[38] Regarding this point, I now turn to several more entries in Temmu's chronicle.

Elixirs, Pharmacopoeias, and Spirit-Summoning Rites

In an entry for the Tenth Month, fourteenth year of Temmu's reign, the chronicler states: "The Paekche priest Pop-chang [Hōzō] and the lay priest Masuda no Atae, Konshū, were dispatched to Mino in order make an infusion of hakuchi 白朮." A few entries later in the following month, we are told: "On the twenty-fourth day, the priest Hōzō and Konshū presented the infusion of hakuchi. On this day, the spirit-summoning ritual (*shōkon* or *mitama-furi*) was performed for the tennō."[39] What was the purpose of the infusion and was there any connection between its presentation and the "spirit-summoning" ritual recorded on the same day? Both passages occur amid a series of entries detailing references to Temmu's declining health and various rites performed to cure it. According to the standard gloss on the herb, hakuchi (also read "okera") was a perennial of the chrysanthemum family (*Atractylis Ovata*) from which a medicinal infusion was made to treat stomach ailments. A well-established view of the "mitama-furi" rite or *chinkonsai*, moreover, holds that it was performed to prevent the tennō's spirit (*reikon*) from wandering from his body by calling it back and restoring his health to a flourishing state.[40] In remarks on this passage, Gary Ebersole comments on the function of the mitama-furi rite within the broader context of the tennō's cosmic authority: "the intention behind its annual performance was to recall and capture the imperial *tama* as found in the mythic paradigm of Amaterasu and her retreat into the rock-grotto. This ritual would ensure not only the health of the sovereign but the well-being and fertility of the entire country. To be sure, the mitama-furi rituals could be pressed into service in times of crisis and exceptional need when the sovereign fell ill, but in the annual ritual calendar the performance of this ritual functioned as a demonstration of the cosmic power of the sacred sovereign."[41] The mitama-furi was thus an important rite in the tennō's ritual repertoire. Yet as Ebersole also implies, its performance in the present context seems exceptional. Is it possible, then, that the combination of the infusion and the "spirit-summoning" rite was more than curative? The answer, I suggest, is yes. But before we see why, it will first be necessary to look at two factors that bore directly on the tennō's religio-political authority in the period of ritsuryō rule, the relationship between the tennō and care for the ill, and the underlying discourse pertaining to pharmacological knowledge and practices.

An entry in the eighth year of Temmu's chronicle records: "This month, the Emperor bestowed his bounty, succoring the poor and wretched and thereby providing assistance for the hungry and cold." A similar expression of largesse is recorded for the third year of Jitō's reign, shortly after the promulgation of the Kiyomihara Code: "The Empress bestowed rice upon the widows, widowers, orphans, the grievously ill, and the poor unable to provide for their own subsistence, and exempted them from the tax and labor corvée." [42] Both passages echo language recorded in the law codes pertaining to the care of the aged, impoverished, and ill. In a discussion of these passages, Maruyama Yumiko draws a contrast between the ritsuryō period tennō, who performed acts of charitable giving (*shingō*) to manifest virtue, with the post-ritsuryō tennō from the tenth century on, whose almsgiving was limited to earning merit aimed at his own salvation. Rather than displaying his authority and virtue through charitable acts that extended throughout the land as previously, the tennō now restricted his almsgiving to the narrow confines of the capital, where his relationship to illness, death, and the care of his own body was increasingly circumscribed by defilement taboos. [43]

If the collection and distribution of medicaments were one sign of the tennō's preeminent authority in the seventh and eighth centuries, reflective of the Confucian ideal of the virtuous sage ruler, there were Daoist medical practices that bore equally on the tennō's claim to command special powers. The foundational text for the systematic treatment of pharmacological knowledge in China was a seven-scroll work titled *Shennong bencao jing jizhu* (*Collected Commentaries on the Pharmacopoeia of Shennong*), usually abbreviated to *Bencao jizhu* (*Honzōshūchū*), composed around the year 500 by the Daoist adept Tao Hongjing. Tao Hongjing based his work on a four-scroll work titled *Shennong's Basic Pharmacopoeia* (*Shennong benjing*), a Han period medical book attributed to the legendary Emperor Shennong, and the *Record of Famous Physicians* (*Mingyi bielu*), which reedited medical lore by celebrated physicians, combining this material with three new scrolls of his own plus a preface and notes. Although Tao Hongjing's original work is no longer extant, having been absorbed by the much larger twenty-scroll herbal *The New and Revised Basic Pharmacopoeia* (*Xinxiu benjing*, 695), its basic structure and outline have been preserved by subsequent works. [44] In addition to *Honzōshūchū*'s specialized treatment of medical cures, there was an overlapping body of lore related to the ingestion of immortality elixirs transmitted in a number of Daoist texts. One of these, the *Zhengao*, was collected and edited by Tao Hongjing, but the extant literature survives in numerous Daoist compendia, including the *Baopu zi* and collections like *Biographies of Exemplary Immortals* (*Liexian zhuan*) and *Biographies of Immortals* (*Shenxian zhuan*). In Daoist practices aimed at the achievement of immortality, both herbal- and mineral-based elixirs were ingested, with the maximum effect believed to be obtained by ingesting elixirs in their raw form. It was above all the dangerous mineral-based elixirs, especially the red-colored cinnabar elixir (*tanyao*; Jp. *tan'yaku*), that were regarded as the most efficacious for achieving the state of an immortal.[45]

In seventh- and eighth-century Japan, both of these traditions coexisted, although there appears to have been a shift from the ingestion of immortality elixirs, cultivated by the elites in the Nara period and before, to an herbal-based pharmacopoeia for primarily curative purposes from the tenth century on. Related to this use of medicinals and elixirs were ceremonial and ritual activities like the numerous medicine hunts (*kusurigari*) recorded in *Nihon shoki* and *Man'yōshū*, which involved the seasonal gathering of herbs and deer horns. The gathering of special herbs such as irises (*ayame*) and mugwort (*yomogi*) early in the Fifth Month, widely practiced throughout the Nara period, and the medicine hunts associated with the earlier *tango* or Iris festival, coincided seasonally with a period in which the yang power increased in vigor, conferring upon the herbs that were gathered the power to prolong life and ward off malign or noxious spirits.[46]

In discussing these practices, Wada Atsumu surmised that texts like Tao Hongjing's *Honzōshūchū*, an important source of medical knowledge from about the time of Temmu, were valued chiefly for the information they provided on the ingestion of immortality elixirs, especially the dangerous cinnabar elixirs. Although the fascination with elixirs would linger into the Heian period, most notably in Emperor Nimmyō's (r. 833–850) consumption of a dangerous mineral-based elixir in the face of strong reservations from officers of the Medical Bureau,[47] the practice was gradually displaced by the later Tang pharmacopoeia, exemplified in Tanba no Yasuyori's *Ishinhō* (984), which emphasized the curative use of herbals while evincing caution regarding the dangerous mineral-based potions.[48] A somewhat different picture has been presented by Masuo Shin'ichirō. Drawing upon recent scholarship on ancient Chinese medical practices, Masuo suggests that Tao Hongjing's *Honzōshūchū*, whose classificatory scheme and Preface departed from earlier Daoist compendia by according priority to the curative use of herbs as opposed to immortality elixirs, would have been regarded primarily as an official guide for medical treatments in the early ritsuryō period. The well-attested Nara period fascination with immortality elixirs, on the other hand, exemplified in the poetic circles of Ōtomo no Tabito and others, would have drawn on texts like the Daoist *Baopu zi*.[49]

While Masuo's two lines of influence, one focused on cures and the other inspired by a Daoist literary tradition pertaining to the cultivation of

immortality, probably coexisted in some fashion throughout much of the
Nara period—alongside Confucian principles and Buddhist rites aimed at
healing and caring for the ill—the distinction, I suggest, would have been
far more blurred at this time than it is in the eyes of modern scholarship. As
elements in the hybrid cultural assemblage that has been discussed elsewhere,
all of these practices were entangled with ceremonial and ritual that bore directly on the authority of the tennō. The cultivation of immortality practices,
for example, was aimed not only at prolonging life in the physical body but
also at the acquisition of special powers. To quote once more the passage
cited earlier in the "Golden Cinnabar" section of *Baopu zi*, "Skillfully harmonizing the yin and the yang, he commanded the demons and gods and the
wind and rain." And elsewhere from the section on "Elixirs," the *Baopu zi*
tells how their ingestion gives one the power to command demonic and divine
spirits, to pass through fire without burning, enter water without getting wet,
and tread on swords without being cut.[50] Underlying the entire practice was
the harmonizing and transforming of *qi* in accordance with the principles of
yin-yang five agents correlative cosmology. As practices and knowledge that
both conferred power and upon which power depended, it is not surprising
that they were subsequently regulated and placed under the authority of the
Medical Bureau, including *jugon*, a Daoist-derived technique aimed at binding *qi*. Like other techniques and knowledge housed in the Yin-Yang Bureau,
all of these were critical to the tennō's exercise of power. With this in mind,
we can now return to Temmu's chinkon rite.

Although *Nihon shoki*'s entry on Temmu's rite is regarded as the earliest extant mention of the *chinkon* (spirit pacification), the graphs glossed
as "mitama-furi" in the text are actually 招魂 (*shōkon*), also read *tama-
yobai* ("soul summoning"). The conventional chinkon reading of the passage together with its vernacular gloss "mitama-furi" probably dates from
a commentarial tradition transmitted by the Urabe lineage. Thus, according
to a secret kun-reading given in the twenty-first scroll of *Shaku nihongi*, the
graphs were intended to be read "mitama-furi," a ritual elsewhere represented in *Shaku nihongi* by the graphs 鎮魂祭 (*chinkonsai*). This reading of
the graphs, now well established, was also argued for by Ban Nobutomo in
his classic study *Chinkon den*, where he noted that the phrase "should be
recorded as 為天皇鎮魂之, but one can surmise that it was written 招魂 in
conformance with the usual Chinese practice."[51]

Leaving aside for the present the distinction between chinkon and shōkon,
we can now turn to some descriptions of the chinkon rite in the law codes

and their commentaries, which have been the basis for most attempts to construct its ancient ritual function. These include the Taihō Code of 701 (extant only fragmentarily in the later Yōrō Code), the *Ryō no shūge* (selected in 833), and the *Ryō no gige* (selected prior to 868). According to the Taihō Code, the chinkonsai was held in midwinter in the Eleventh Month, on a *tora no hi* (day of the tiger), and followed by the daijōsai on a *u no hi* (day of the rabbit), a period that coincided with the winter solstice. In Chinese yin-yang five agents thought, both of these days were identified with the agent wood (the beginning of the cycle), which corresponded to the direction east and the season spring. Both the month and days were a time when the positive yang pneumas were believed to mount upward and all things were held to be in a state of movement. It was thus an ideal time for initiating activities such as royal accessions.[52]

Turning to some actual definitions of the chinkon rite, we find the following explanation in the *Ryō no gige* under the heading chinkon: "The graph 鎮 means to pacify. A person's yang spirit (*yōki*) is called soul (*tama* 魂). The tama moves about, meaning one summons back the tama that wanders about in a state of separation and pacifies it inside the body [literally "bowels"]. Therefore it is named "chinkon" (to pacify the soul)."[53] Another definition from the *Ryō no shūge* contains some additional details: "A person's yang spirit is called 'kon' 魂; it moves about. A person's yin spirit is called 'haku' 魄; it is white. Therefore one calls back the white soul 魄 wandering about in a state of separation and causes it to be pacified inside the bowels. Therefore it is called chinkon."[54]

The exact source for the ideas contained in these descriptions remains uncertain, but the language recalls ancient Chinese ideas about the fate of the soul after death. According to the *Li ji*, the yang *qi* of the "cloudsoul" (*hun*) rises up into the sky (*tian*) after death, whereas the yin or dark elements associated with the body or "whitesoul" (*po*) return to the earth.[55] Another passage in the *Li ji*, on the rites of mourning, speaks of summoning back the cloudsoul and returning it to the body (*po*).[56] It was under the influence of such commentaries, according to Watanabe Katsuyoshi, that modern scholars developed the idea of a "soul that wanders about in separation from its body" and interpreted chinkon as a rite primarily aimed at preventing such separation by placating the "tama" and thereby obviating the illness and death that were held to result from such separation.[57]

The yin-yang five agents principles and the related concept of "qi," which informed the ritual setting (temporal and geomantic) of the chinkonsai and the descriptive language of the law doctors, were fundamental, of course, to Chinese philosophical thought. In Daoism, the induction of *qi* into the body and its proper regulation became one of the basic practices for achieving longevity, a central concern of later Daoist literature, as in the *Xiang'er* commentary on the *Daode jing*, which also functioned as a guide to the enlightened ruler.[58] Thus, in Bokenkamp's paraphrase of one *Xiang'er* passage, "the pneumas of morning and evening should be caused to descend into the human body, where they should be mixed with the body's own pneumas so that they are evenly distributed throughout."[59] On the other hand, this time citing directly from the *Xiang'er*, "When the heart produces ill-omened and evil conduct, the Dao departs, leaving the sack [belly] empty. Once it is empty, deviance enters, killing the person."[60] As these citations make clear, the principle of balancing and harmonizing *qi* was of paramount importance; "deviance" (*xie*), on the other hand, arose from a failure to achieve a proper balance or mixing of pneumas resulting in illness and death.

Although it is unlikely that the Daoist *Xiang'er Commentary* had a direct influence on either the practice or conception of ancient Japanese royal authority, its concept of kingship drew upon the same Han ideas of the thearch elaborated in the weft-texts that influenced the symbolic language of royal authority in the Nara period and before. The emphasis in the *Xiang'er* passage on the belly, for example, recalls what Watanabe characterizes as the peculiar language of the law commentaries, where the aim of the rite was to draw the erring "tama" back into the "bowels." A related notion found in the *Chuxue ji*, a Tang period encyclopedia compiled at the order of Emperor Xuanzong (r. 712–756), states that on the winter solstice the yang *qi* is restored to the belly and hot things placed in it are easily digested.[61] If this Daoist medical advice offers a parallel to the ideas of the law doctors in their attempts to describe the chinkon rite, recipes for the production of immortality elixirs provide a suggestive context for understanding the relationship between the medicinal herb and Temmu's spirit-summoning rite. An entry from scroll seventy-seven on "elixirs" in *Yunji qiqian* (*Seven Lots from the Satchel of the Clouds*), an encyclopedia of older Daoist texts and extracts compiled under the Northern Song, describes a life-extending elixir called *lingwan* that allows one to "pacify the cloud souls, coagulate the white souls, and fly off into the seventy-four directions," and in another passage, "to sport about on the Five Mountain Peaks."[62] Not least interesting here is the combination of graphs 鎮魂 (*chinkon*, "pacify the cloud souls"), the same two graphs that are used for the Japanese chinkon or "mitama-furi" rite. Another entry from the *Inner Transmission of the Purple Sun Master* (*Ziyang zhenren neichuan*, 399), collected in scroll 106 of the *Yunji qiqian*, relates that the consumption of *zhu* 朮 over a period of five years—the same medicinal herb ingested by Temmu—produces a glow in the body, gives one a vision that can see right through to the five viscera, and enables one to become an immortal.[63]

By now, it should be evident that Temmu's ingestion of the herb hakuchi cannot be fully accounted for by a straightforward medical reading. The calendrical and yin-yang principles that informed its consumption and the accompanying shōkon rite belonged to the same sphere of symbolic activity that would soon be housed in the Yin-Yang Bureau and Medical Bureau, as the following notice from Jitō's chronicle makes clear: "The Yin-yang Doctors, the priest (hōshi) Hōzō and Dōki, received twenty ryō of silver."[64] The date of this third reference to Hōzō, just prior to the establishment of the official Yin-Yang Bureau, indicates that he was one of an important group of technical experts who mediated the cultural assemblage transmitted from the continent. Although it is impossible to determine the precise scope and nature of Hōzō's knowledge, some of its probable sources can be inferred from his Paekche origins.

Although the ingestion of the herb *zhu* (*hakuchi*) and its efficacy as both a medicinal and immortality elixir are well documented in Daoist lore and herbals, the practice seems to have especially flourished in the period of the Southern dynasties (420–589) when Tao Hongjing composed his herbal and Daoist works.[65] It can be assumed that Hōzō, a Paekche immigrant, would have been knowledgeable about this tradition—its influence having reached the Korean kingdom—as well as conversant with practices from Tao Hongjing's region that were outside the written transmission.[66] In addition to the Southern dynasties' tradition, it is also likely that Hōzō had absorbed more recent influences. One possibility, suggested by Shinkawa, is the early Tang work *Qianjin yaofang* (*Essential Prescriptions Worth a Hundred Weight in Gold*), composed by the Daoist master and physician Sun Simiao (d. 682) sometime between 650 and 658. Predating the Tang medical reforms, this text transmitted a tradition very close to the earlier Southern dynasties' tradition and contained detailed discussions on the preparation of *zhu* and its capacity to harmonize in accord with yin-yang five agents principles.[67]

This cosmological theory of resonance, much of which is recorded in the *Gogyō taigi* that reached Japan no later than the end of the seventh century, invests Temmu's ingestion of the elixir and the shōkon rite with its religio-political significance. Held in the Eleventh Month on a tora no hi (day of the tiger), the rite's timing corresponded to the agent wood and the direction east. In Daoist medical lore pertaining to the five viscera, the cloudsoul (*kon*) resided in the liver (*kan*), which was identified with the element wood and controlled the eyes, hair, nails, and muscles. The liver was also known as the Office of the General, the faculty responsible for wise counsel; and its element wood was identified with "virtue" (*jin*) that pacifies the myriad things, making it analogous to the ruler.[68] According to another text cited in *Gogyō taigi*, *The Lineage of Thearchs* (*Dixi pu* 帝系譜), "Heaven and earth first arose, then generated the Heavenly Thearch (*tennō*) who rules through the virtue wood," a formulation that derives from the symbolism of the hexagram *zhen* 震, identified variously with lightning, the dragon, and the dark springs. The *Yijing* states that the thearch and myriad things arise from zhen, with zhen identified with the direction east.[69] Although these correspondences add weight to the medical aim of this hybrid rite, they do so by locating Temmu at the center of a radiating cosmological order, which gains additional significance because the rite took place at a critical juncture when tennō was being newly adopted as a title of authority.[70]

Temmu's Grotto Hall

If rituals like the foregoing suggest a Daoist basis for Temmu's authority, its traces may also be discernible in architectural features of the Great Hall of State. The southward-facing Sun Gate 陽明門 (Yōmeimon), more literally the Yang Gate, recalls sites connected in Daoist thought to revitalizing solar influences and rites for achieving immortality. Two other gates, the Nikkamon 日華門 (Sun Gate) and Gekkamon (Moon Gate), likewise call to mind technical terms for Daoist rituals that involved inducting the vitalizing effluence of the solar and lunar rays, which are elaborated in texts like the *Zhengao* of Tao Hongjing. In the *shihōhai* ritual that was incorporated into court ritual during the early Heian period, the tennō would make obeisance to the four quarters and then face north toward his "birth-star" (*honmyōsei*), as magical prayers containing Daoist formulae were chanted for his well-being. Accounts of this rite recorded in Daoist scriptures indicate that there was a direct connection between ritual obeisance to the four quarters and the absorption of vitalizing breaths, or "pneumas."[71]

Returning to Temmu's chronicle, there are two more passages suggestive of Daoist-inspired rites and symbolic practices. In an entry for the first year of Shuchō, the chronicle states: "Today, the Emperor took up a position in front of the *grotto hall* (*mimurodono* 御窟殿) and made presents of varying worth to the performers. He also presented the singers with presents of clothing." And then in the Seventh Month of the same year: "Seventy persons who performed purifications were selected to retire from the world. A feast of vegetable food was provided in front of the *grotto hall in the Palace* (*miya no uchi no mimuro no machi* 宮中御窟院)."[72] Like the entry on Saimei's belvedere, these passages present us with an architectural anomaly. In both cases, the editors of *Nihon shoki* have been content to note that the part of the palace or building referred to here remains unknown. The use of the graph 院, in the second entry, appears to indicate that the grotto hall was partitioned off from the rest of the palace, suggesting a sequestered site suitable for activity of a ritual nature. Along with hidden mountain recesses and valleys, grottoes and caverns were central to Daoist imaginings about the immortal realms. In the type of analogical and macro-microcosmic thought cultivated by Daoist mythographers, the body itself was often conceptualized as a cavern. In one model expounded in the *Scripture of the Inner Light of the Yellow Court of Highest Clarity* (*Huangting neijing yujing*), for example, the Palace (*gong-dian*) of the Heavenly Thearch was envisioned as existing inside the cavern of the body, where various deities were believed to dwell.[73] I take the idiosyncratic graphic combination in these two passages (whose sense is lost in the vernacular gloss "mimuro") as one more sign of Temmu's absorption with Daoist rites and symbolism. As a final commentary on Temmu's grotto hall, this reflection from the *Baopu zi* is suggestive. "When ingesting pneumas one should always do it at a time of vitalizing pneumas and never when the pneumas are moribund. This is the reason for the saying, 'The sage ingests the six pneumas.'"[74]

Daoist and Yin-Yang Motifs in the Poetry of Kaifūsō

In this section, I turn from ritual to literary activity to take a more extended look at some of the ways in which Daoist and yin-yang ideas intersect with one of the central symbolic activities of the court, poetry. Of the two extant

Nara poetry collections, the slender *Kaifūsō* (751) has for obvious reasons received less attention than the voluminous and more varied *Man'yōshū*, one of the masterpieces of classical Japanese literature. Whereas many poems from *Man'yōshū* have been justly celebrated for the perfection of their style, *Kaifūsō*'s Chinese poetry has often been judged to be no more than a partially successful attempt to emulate Chinese poetic practice, especially in the Six Dynasties style. In the remarks that follow, I leave aside questions of *Kaifūsō*'s literary merit, a topic which has been treated by scholars elsewhere, and focus instead on the symbolic implications of its poetic lexicon.[75]

Among the topics treated in *Kaifūsō*, a large number deal with the seasons and important festive occasions, such as New Year's Day, the Tanabata festival, and excursions to Yoshino. The following pair of couplets, composed by Fujiwara no Fuhito (659–720) at the emperor's behest, opens a poem on the topic "New Year's Day":

正朝觀萬國	On New Year's morning, he gazes out upon the entire land,
元日臨兆民	On New Year's day, he looks out upon the populace;
齊政敷玄造	Ordering the heavenly bodies, he extends the hidden process,
撫機御紫宸	In control of the polestar, he arrives in the Purple Hall.

(KFS, 29)[76]

Here, the emperor appears in the full splendor of a polestar monarch, whose virtuous government mirrors the orderly movements of the heavens. The graph *zheng* 政 in line three, more literally translated as "government," can also refer in astrological lore to the seven heavenly bodies that revolve around the polestar. The second of the two graphs 撫機, translated as "in control of the polestar," was a variant of the graph 璣 (*ki*), the name for the third of the seven stars that make up the polestar constellation. The phrase may also allude to the Jade Armil (*senki*), also written 琁璣, an astronomical instrument used for observing the heavens. The idea expressed in the couplets is thus perfectly consonant with the activity and symbolic functions of the Yin-Yang Bureau. The expression "Purple Hall" also reinforces these associations. At first glance, it might be taken as a literal reference to the Shishinden, the main ceremonial hall of the palace. Yet this reading is problematic because it wasn't until Kōin 9 (818) that the Daianden was renamed Shishinden and the term came into current usage, well after Fuhito's time. A more likely possibility, and one that would accord with the polestar symbolism, is that shishin here refers to the Purple Tenuity Palace of the Heavenly Thearch (*tentei*).[77] This is supported by the language of other poems, including the following by Mushimaro, on the topic "In Attendance at a Banquet":

聖豫開芳序	His Sagely Joy inaugurates the flourishing season's change,
皇恩施品生	The Sovereign grace bestows his bounty on all;
流霞酒處泛	Flowing haze drifts about the banquet seats,
薰吹曲中輕	The fragrant breeze dallies amidst the music;
紫殿連珠絡	The *Purple Palace* is bedecked with inlaid pearls,
丹墀蕡草榮	Within its *vermilioned* walls the *ming* flowers blaze;
即此乘槎客	And like *that wanderer who rode upon the raft*,
俱欣天上情	I delight with everyone in this *heavenly scene*. (*KFS*, 81)[78]

In addition to the "Purple Palace" with its "vermilioned walls," the poem contains an allusion to an old legend, recorded in several versions, about a man who rode a raft up the course of the Yellow River until he reached the Heavenly River in the sky. In one version, it was the explorer Zhang Jian, who had been sent in the second century B.C.E. to seek the source of the Yellow River; and in another version, recorded in *Bowu zhi* (*The Treatise on the Investigation of Things*), it was an ordinary man who boarded the raft in its yearly passage along the river. References to this legend occur in several other *Kaifūsō* poems. In both poems, then, the emperor's palace is equated with the Palace of the Heavenly Thearch.[79]

Astral associations reappear in many other poems and combine with a second cluster of associations centered on Daoist immortals. The following couplets open a poem on the topic "Spring Day" and were composed by Mino no Kiyomaro at the behest of Emperor Mommu in the second year of Keiun (705):

玉燭凝紫宮	The jade candle freezes the *Purple Palace* in its glow,
淑氣潤芳春	The balmy air moistens with fragrant spring flowers;
曲浦戲嬌鴛	In a crook on the bay frolic the charming mandarin ducks,
瑤池躍潛鱗	In *Jade Pond* leap out the hiding fish. (*KFS*, 24)[80]

Kiyomaro uses the seasonal topic as an opportunity to celebrate Mommu's benevolent rule, expressed through the tranquil harmony of the season and the image of the leaping fish, always a propitious sign. The first of the two italicized expressions further exalts the emperor by suggesting an analogy between Mommu's rule and that of the Heavenly Thearch, who inhabits the Purple Tenuity Palace. Jade Pond (*yōchi*), on the other hand, was the name for a lake located on Mount Kunlun, which in Daoist lore was associated with Xi wang mu, the Queen Mother of the West, and another of the many legendary places inhabited by immortals. Daoist sacred loci and purple color symbolism weave their threads through many other poems. In one final example, *Kaifūsō* 67, the poet, Prince Nagaya (d. 729), sets up a parallel between the realm of the immortals and the palace of the emperor, this time invoking another haunt of immortals on Mount Kunlun, the "dim orchard" (*genbo*) which is balanced against the "purple garden" of the emperor's palace.[81]

Another frequent topic in *Kaifūsō* is the Tanabata or Star festival, which occurs on the seventh day of the Seventh Month and centers around the once yearly meeting between the Weaver Maid and the Ox Driver. Poems on the Tanabata legend later became one of the standard topics in the court-sponsored poetry collections. Unlike the later *Kokinshū* poems, however, which tend to center more narrowly around the erotic theme of the separated lovers, the Chinese poems of *Kaifūsō* typically evoke a grander skyscape that combines astral lore with Daoist motifs about immortals.[82] The following Tanabata poem is attributed to Fujiwara no Fusasaki (681–737), translated this time by Helen McCullough:

帝里初涼至	At the imperial seat, first-coolness comes;
神衿翫早秋	His majesty takes pleasure in early autumn.
瓊筵振雅藻	In the luxurious banquet room, elegant verse is composed;
金閣啓良遊	In the gold pavilion, refined amusements are provided.
鳳駕飛雲路	A phoenix palanquin flies the cloud path;
龍車越漢流	A dragon carriage crosses the Han flow.
欲知神仙會	If you want to know about the immortal's meeting,
靑鳥入瓊樓	Watch the bluebird entering the sumptuous tower. (*KFS*, 85)[83]

Making their appearance here as immortals, the Weaver Maid is matched with the "phoenix palanquin" and the Ox Herder with the "dragon carriage," two vehicles typically associated with emperors. The mythological background is too complex to take up in detail here, other than to note the connection between the blue bird and Emperor Wu. As discussed in Chapter 2, Emperor Wu was reputed to have been in constant quest of the immortality elixir, and allusions to him are a recurrent motif in *Kaifūsō*. According to one legend, while preparing for the Star festival one night, Emperor Wu was visited by a blue bird with a message from the Queen Mother of the West telling him of her plan to visit him. Originally a type of primitive earth goddess, the Queen Mother later figured in much Daoist lore about the immortals.[84]

That the linkage between the quest for immortality and the Tanabata festival was something more than mere poetic fashion is indicated in *Nihon shoki*'s account of Urashima in Yūryaku's chronicle:

> Autumn, Seventh Month. A man of Tsutsukawa, in the district of Yoza in the province of Tamba, the child Urashima of Mizunoe, got into a boat and went fishing. He caught a large tortoise, which upon the instant turned into a woman. Thereupon, the child Urashima fell in love and made her his wife. Following after her, he set out to sea and came to Mount Penglai, where he met with the immortals.[85]

Urashima's journey to the immortal realm of Mount Penglai, it will be noted, is recorded as having occurred in the Seventh Month of autumn, making it coincide with the Tanabata festival. Its calendrical and astrological significance can be inferred from several passages in the "Governors of Heaven" section of the *Shi ji*. First, in a formulation of the polestar or Heavenly Thearch's centrality in the cosmological harmony, echoed in the first of the *Kaifūsō* poems cited earlier, the *Shi ji* states: "He moves at the center, rules over the four directions, divides the yin and the yang, establishes the four seasons, moderates the activity of the five agents, and brings about the division of the seasons and the sky." And later, in the section describing the astrological attributes of the Heavenly River: "When the stars are numerous in the Heavenly River, floods are frequent; and when the stars are few, there is drought."[86] The polestar symbolism and the fact that Tanabata celebrations coincided calendrically with harvest festivals suggest that it was an important rite in the ritual calendar of the court from as early as Temmu's reign.[87] In several studies on the long sequence of Tanabata poems attributed to Hitomaro in the tenth scroll of *Man'yōshū*, Watase Masatada has shown how the arrangement of the poems into groups of four reflects temporal and spatial principles in accordance with yin-yang five agents theory. Specifically, their arrangement was symbolically structured to ward off drought during the period of the Temmu/Jitō court that ruled under the agent of fire, with the poems performed as a form of song-theater at a banquet that concluded the rites.[88] Although typically regarded as no more than a literary motif in classical waka, the Tanabata festival's basis in astrological lore and yin-yang five agents thinking would have invested it with equal importance as a symbolic rite that supported the tennō's authority.

Finally, there are a large number of *Kaifūsō* poems that were composed on the occasion of royal sojourns at Yoshino. Closely connected to the political and ritual authority of the Temmu/Jitō courts—Jitō is said to have made some thirty-two progresses to Yoshino—Yoshino and its surroundings are frequently mentioned in the chronicles and appear repeatedly as a site of poetic praise.[89] The following poem was composed by Takamuko Morotari on the topic "Accompanying His Majesty to Yoshino":

在昔釣魚士	Long ago there was a man who caught fish,
方今留鳳公	Now there is a lord who halts his phoenix carriage;
彈琴與仙戲	Plucking on our zithers, we frolic with immortals,
投江將神通	Reaching the river, we converse with the goddess;
柘歌泛寒渚	The mulberry song floats above the cold shore,
霞景飄秋風	The misty landscape wavers in the autumn wind;
誰謂姑射嶺	Who can speak of Guye's Peak?
駐蹕望仙宮	He halts his retinue at Wangxian Palace. (KFS, 102)[90]

Like the recasting of myth in the chronicles, where local deities may be said to persist within the lexical confines of the new graphic signs, the language of this poem raises intriguing questions about the relationship between Chinese as a metaphoric circuit for the new royal authority claimed by Temmu and his successors and their continuing dependence on competing, if not older, sources of myth and legitimation. By Temmu's time, Yoshino had taken on the character of an especially sacred site, and it stayed so throughout the Nara period when Kaifūsō was compiled. As late as the early Heian period, sacred Kuzu dancers and singers from Yoshino were still performing at court. Yet even prior to Temmu's time, there appears to have been a strong association between musico-shamanistic activity and Yoshino. The most famous example is an anecdote recorded in Kojiki about Yūryaku, who twice meets "maidens" beside the banks of the Yoshino River, and on the second occasion performs on the zither (koto) and sings about his longing for the "eternal land" (tokoyo) while the maiden performs a dance.[91]

In the present poem, Yoshino is recast as a site of ritualized play (asobi) that unfolds in a Daoist landscape of legend and myth. Guye Peak and Wangxian Palace were both Daoist loci connected to the quest for immortality, the former occurring in the "Free and Easy Wandering" (Xiaoyao you) section of Zhuangzi, and the latter, literally the Palace of Longing for Immortality, a structure said to have been built by Emperor Wu.[92] Yet behind the Daoist associations (and possibly echoing Yūryaku's legend as well) is a story about the legendary mulberry branch, which formed the basis of several Man'yōshū poems and has been pieced together from extant fragments. According to Man'yōshū kogi, there was once a man named Umashine who set traps in the Yoshino River and made his living catching fish. When a mulberry branch floated down the river and got caught in his trap one day, he took the branch home, where it turned into a beautiful woman. After marrying her, they lived together knowing neither age nor death, until one day the mulberry woman flew off into the eternal land.[93] Whatever the precise valence of the mulberry legend in this poem—another possible source for the poem's "river goddesses" are the "river nymphs" who appear in the *Wen xuan*'s "Shu Capital Rhapsody"[94]—Yoshino in this and other *Kaifūsō* poems is celebrated as a Daoist immortal realm.

A final example is this anonymous poem on the topic "Entertainment at Yoshino":

夏身夏色古	At Natsumi the colors of summer have faded,
秋津秋氣新	At Akitsu the breath of autumn blows fresh;
昔者聞汾后	Long ago, there was the Fen River goddess,
今之見吉賓	But now I look upon excellent guests;
靈仙駕鶴去	The sacred immortal rode off upon a crane,
星客乘査遶	And the star guest rode upon the raft and returned;
諸性担流水	Wise natures draw from the flowing streams,
素心開靜仁	Pure minds open their quiet virtue to the hills. (*KFS*, 32)[95]

In addition to the familiar topos of the legendary raft rider, the author has invoked one of the most celebrated immortals, Wang Qiao, the heir apparent of King Ling of Zhou, who, according to the *Biographies of Exemplary Immortals*, was fond of playing the sheng (mouth organ), cultivated immortality on lofty mountains, and was said to have finally mounted to the heavens on a white crane.[96] But the most interesting point is connected to the poem's topic, represented by the graph 遊. Although I have settled on the translation "entertainment," "asobi" suggests an activity far more complex, combining elements of ritual with song, dance, and music, and in its original Chinese sense suggesting the Daoist notion of "wandering" and "roaming." In remarks on its usage in *Kaifūsō*, Matsuda Tomohiro suggests that the activity evoked by the term "asobi" in these poems is congruent with its Daoist association with roaming (*xiaoyao*), artlessness or "wuwei" (sometimes translated as "inaction"), and communing with the natural scenery of mountains and rivers. Of the nine poems that have the topic "asobi" or "yūran" in *Kaifūsō*, seven are set at Yoshino, indicating that the detached villa at Yoshino, with its scenery of rivers and mountains, was viewed as a sacred site set apart from the main capital.[97]

Forbidden Magic and Mount Kazuraki

Even as the landscape of Yoshino took on the allure of a Daoist immortal realm, its isolated terrain and that of nearby mountains like Kazuraki were becoming associated with the cultivation of mysterious powers, in some cases provoking rumors of rebellion. The following notice, recorded in *Shoku nihongi*, is from the third year of Mommu's reign:

> E no Kimi Ozuno has been exiled to the island of Izu. At first, Ozuno lived on Mount Kazuraki and was celebrated for his skill in magic. He was the teacher of Karakuni no Muraji Hirotari, upper grade lower fifth rank. Afterwards, he ruined his talent and was accused of beguilements. For this reason, he was exiled to a distant place. People say the following of him: "Ozuno commanded demons and deities and had them draw water and gather kindling. If they didn't obey his command, he forthwith bound them with a spell." [98]

Linked in *Nihon shoki* to a dragon-mounted immortal, Kazuraki has now become the site of an apparent dispute involving proscribed activities. The "magic" cultivated by Ozuno probably involved the exorcistic technique *jugon*. A few years after this incident, in the year 732, the same Karakuni who is mentioned in the notice was appointed head of the Medical Bureau, which handled jugon and related techniques.[99] By manipulating *qi* through binding and loosening, jugon enabled the exorcist to expel and defend against the encroachment of dangerous spirits.[100] An idea of the technique can be gathered from this description in the mid-Heian law book *Seiji yōryaku* (*Essentials of Government*): "The exorcist (*jigonsha*) holds a sword and chants spells (*jumon*). He employs the method of binding *qi*. As a result, he does not suffer attack or injury from fierce beasts, tigers, foxes, poisonous insects, ghosts, brigands, and the five military weapons. Furthermore, by means of binding spells he hardens the body and becomes impervious to woundings from scalding water, fire, and swords." Another technique called "gego" allowed the exorcist to scatter and put to flight harmful spirits.[101] The likely source for such ideas was the *Baopu zi* and other Daoist texts, which elaborate the principles in detail. Thus, "The Highest Wisdom" section from scroll five of the *Baopu zi* explains how all things arise from *qi* and how "those who manage *qi* well, nourish it within and expel the bad qi out of themselves." It then goes on to illustrate the powers obtained through properly ingesting *qi*, including the capacity to enter plague-stricken lands, sleep beside the ill without getting sick, and expel calamities: "When evil spirits and mountain sprites attack people in their houses . . . the person able to manage qi binds them with [his] qi and on the instant they vanish. This is because qi enables one to bind demons and gods."[102]

The slander against Ozuno and his exile during the reign of Mommu points to an important shift in the status of figures like the priest Hōzō, who handled Temmu's *shōkon* rite. During the reigns of Mommu (697–707) and Genmei (707–715), shortly after the establishment of the Yin-Yang and Medical Bureaus, many of these ambiguous priestlike figures were "returned to lay status" and assigned duties in the Yin-Yang and Medical Bureaus, as the court sought to secure a monopoly over their techniques.[103] The accusation of "beguilements" (*yōwaku*) echoes the language of the Yōrō Code that explicitly proscribed such activity in the Regulations for Priests and Nuns (Sōniryō): "Priests and nuns who contemplate heavenly phenomena and deceptively interpret calamities and auspicious signs, speak words against the state [emperor], and beguile (*yōwaku*) the peasantry . . . are to be punished." As the article implies, the prognostication of heavenly phenomena is now the province of the Yin-Yang Bureau. At the same time, Daoist-type magical techniques, which were being assigned to the Medical Bureau, are also undergoing a process of redefinition as they are folded into Buddhist rites: "Priests and nuns who prognosticate and interpret good and bad omens, and cure illness through techniques of the lesser way (*shōdō*) and mediumship, all of these are to be returned to secular status. The curing of illness through Buddhist rites by means of spells (*shuji*) is the only practice not prohibited."[104] "Shuji" (the vernacular rendering for the graphs 持咒) was a form of jugon. In the earlier Taihō Code, whose language is cited in the *Collected Commentaries on the Administrative Code* (*Ryō no shūge*), these exorcistic techniques that involved the use of spells are explicitly equated with the Daoist techniques of Karakuni: "According to old records, spells (*shuji*) refer to sutra spells. Magical techniques (*dōjutsu*) and amulets for binding refer to the method of the Daoist master (*dōshi no hō*). These are what Karakuni no Muraji now performs." Both the Taihō and Yōrō Codes recognize the use of Daoist-type magical techniques, but whereas the former accords the sutra spells and Daoist techniques an equal status, the Yōrō language of the Sōniryō implies that Daoist techniques not sanctioned as Buddhist rites nor assigned to the Medical Bureau belong to the "lesser way," which by the Tenpyō era (729–749) is taking on the connotation of heretical practices (*jadō*).[105]

The ambiguous status of such magical techniques is disclosed in the following tale collected in *Nihon ryōiki* (mid-Heian), where Ozuno's powers are on full display:

> E no ubasoku was Kamo no E no Kimi, from whom the present day Taka-kamo no Ason is descended. He was from the village of Chihara in the district of Upper Kazuragi, in Yamato Province. He was clever by nature and was top in scholarship. He believed strongly in the three treasures of Buddhism and thus devoted himself to austerities. It was his constant wish to hang from a five-colored cloud, soar beyond the heavens, and join with the guests in the Palace of the Immortals; to roam in the Palace of Myriad Years, recline in flowering gardens, and drink freely of the nourishing mists. For these reasons, when he reached the end of his fortieth year, he took to dwelling in mountain grottoes, where he covered himself in robes of vines, ate of pine needles, and bathed in pure spring waters, cleansing himself of the world's grime. Devoting himself to the Peacock spell, he gained mastery of strange powers. He commanded the demons and spirits and did whatever he wished. Summoning sundry demons and spirits, he gathered them before him and said: "Suspend a bridge between the peaks of Kane no Take and Kazuraki no Take, in Yamato Province." All of the deities were vexed at this. During the reign of Emperor Mommu who ruled at Fujiwara Palace, the deity Hitokotonushi of Kazuraki Peak took possession of a medium and slandered him in these words: "E no Ubasoku is leading a plot to overthrow the emperor." [106]

In the sequel, the emperor orders E no Ubasoku's arrest, who manages to elude capture until he is lured into rescuing his mother. Exiled to the island of Izu, he continues to flaunt his powers, traveling at will through the sky to distant mountain peaks. At one point, after a false pardon, he is granted permission to return to the capital but chooses instead to fly off as an immortal to China, where he is subsequently met by a traveling Buddhist priest from Japan. Observing that the deity Hitokotonushi has never since been released from E no Ubasoku's magical spell, the story ends with praise for the awesome power of Buddhist rites.

Although E no Ubasoku's powers as a Daoist immortal are celebrated in the tale, they are identified with Buddhist rites. While there is an obvious intent to proselytize Buddhist doctrine, the tale also discloses the danger associated with Daoist magical powers, hinted at in Ubasoku's plot and subsequent contest with the empress, but above all in his capacity to command and bind demons and deities at will. Powers formerly vested in institutions under the emperor's control are here presented as an awesome sign of Buddhist authority.[107] In the remainder of this chapter, I examine how rites aimed at controlling and defending against demonic and divine powers, initially vested in the authority of the tennō, were gradually shifted onto the ground of pollution taboos that proliferated at court along with yin-yang practices or on'yōdō.

Expulsions, Magical Swords, and the Great Purification Rite

Among the rituals that came to be performed by yin-yang masters over the course of the Heian period, many were centered on the expulsion (*harai*) of defilements and harmful spirits and the pacification (*shizume*) of threatening powers. The most important expulsion ritual was the *ōharae*, which was performed on the last day of the Sixth Month and Twelfth Month. An entry in *Shoku nihongi* for the second year of Taihō (702) during Mommu's reign is generally regarded as the earliest recorded mention of the rite: "On the thirtieth day, the Great Purification Ceremony was suspended. However, the Yamato Kawachi no Fubito-be performed the expulsion (*harae*) as usual." [108] Although an order to perform the *ōharae* is recorded on three separate occasions in *Nihon shoki*'s chronicle of Temmu, this is the first instance that conforms to the calendrical timing prescribed by the Yōrō Code.[109] The article in the Yōrō Code describes two parts to the *ōharae*, one handled by both the Nakatomi shrine ritualists and the Yamato and Kawachi Fubito-be and a second handled exclusively by the Nakatomi and Urabe. In the first part, performed for the tennō, the Nakatomi ritualist would offer up the *ōharae nusa* (an object made of hemp and other plant fibers), and the Yamato and Kawachi no Fubito-be would present the exorcist's sword and intone an incantation. In the second part, the nobility were to gather at the site of the exorcism, where the Nakatomi would read out the prayer and the Urabe perform the expulsion. In the Taihō example cited earlier, for reasons that remain unclear, the part handled by the Nakatomi has been suspended, while the sword offering and its accompanying chant have been allowed to continue as prescribed.[110] It is the portion of the rite performed by the Fubito-be that I focus on here.

Although there is no indication that yin-yang masters were involved in the rite on this occasion, the ritual itself and the magical incantation that accompanied its performance were steeped in yin-yang and Daoist symbolism. The *Shoku nihongi* account does not record the magical formula chanted by the Fubito-be, but the text as well as details regarding its ritual performance have been preserved in the *Engi shiki*, where it is prefaced by the following words: "An Incantation Performed when the sword is presented by the Fumi no Imikibe of Yamato [Kawachi no Fumibe follows after]":

> Supreme Thearch of the Heavens
> Three Ministers of the Polestar
> Moon, sun, and stars
> Deities of the eight directions
> Deities who rule the life-force and keep judgments
> King Father of the East on the Left
> Queen Mother of the West on the Right
> Five Thearchs of the Five Directions
> Four breaths of the four seasons
> I make an offering of a silver effigy
> And pray that you remove calamities
> I make an offering of a gold sword
> And pray that you extend the ruler's reign
> I speak the incantation:
> To the East as far as the Land of the Mulberry
> To the West as far as the Land of the Sunset
> To the South as far as the Land of the Blazing Light
> To the North as far the Land of the Weak Waters
> May the thousand capitals and hundred palaces
> Be ruled in peace for ten thousands years
> Ten thousand years.[111]

As a linguistic artifact, the text is a nearly perfect projection of Daoist cosmological ideas. Starting with the opening invocation to the Supreme Thearch of the Heavens (Haotian shangdi), who was worshiped as a polestar deity, it proceeds by naming the various divisions of space and their presiding deities, continues with the divisions of the four times or seasons, regulated by the four breaths or pneumas, and ends with an evocation of Daoist immortal realms. In its projection of space, it is good example of what Robinet has characterized as the "centering and outward radiation" characteristic of the Daoist worldview.[112] The problem that needs to be addressed centers on the relationship between what is unmistakably a Daoist ritual invocation, traditionally intoned in Chinese, and one of the preeminent shrine rituals, the ōharae, which has generally been regarded as a rite aimed at the expulsion and purification of defilements.[113] Do we have a deliberate blending of two ritual systems here? Does the relatively late date of the Engi shiki (Procedures of the Engi Era) point to a Heian period innovation?[114] Or is the Fubito-be portion a legacy from an earlier period of ritual practice? And finally, what connection is there between the text of the Daoist incantation and the ritual for which it was intoned?

Discussions of the incantation have noted its resemblance to the prayer intoned at the Chinese-style *kōshi* (Ch. *jiaosi*) rite performed during the reigns of Kammu and Montoku. Like the ōharae incantation, this prayer was also addressed to the Supreme Thearch of the Heavens, but unlike the ōharae ceremony, the ritual itself was always held outside the capital, in the village of Katano in Kawachi province, on a specially designed platform constructed on a hilltop site from which magical prayers could be easily directed toward the sky. In the words of Shimode Sekiyo, the entire rite formally bore a strong resemblance to the rituals (*zhaijiao*) and ceremonial protocols (*keyi*) of organized Daoist religion, which were intended to drive off calamities and extend life. Despite such resemblances, Shimode concludes that the Daoist incantation was merely added on to the Shinto Great Purification Ceremony to add weight to its ritual function of driving out defilements and bringing about worldly benefits.[115]

Yet in addition to the symbolism of the incantation, Daoist and yin-yang principles are also at work in the ritual actions performed by the Fubito-be. Together with the "gold sword," the incantation makes reference to a "silver effigy." While effigies or human-shaped figures were widely used in later yin-yang rites as objects to which defilements were transferred and expelled (a function that has been attributed to their use here as well),[116] effigies recovered from archeological sites going back to the Nara period and before hint at additional usages. The same jugon officers of the Medical Bureau who employed techniques for manipulating *qi* also made effigies that served a curative function.[117] Here, both the effigy and the sword have a basis in Daoist techniques, the silver effigy to drive out calamities and the sword offered up as a magical object that embodies the tennō's power over demonic and other threatening spirits. The Engi era protocols for the Bureau of Carpentry provide detailed instructions on the manufacture of such ritual objects. For the ōharae, the protocols specified the use of two gold swords, two gold- and silver-foiled human effigies, and six swords dyed black with cuttlefish ink. The graphs 禄人 (*rokunin*) used in the text of the incantation, where the first graph has the more literal sense of "felicitous" or "propitious," indicate a human effigy painted gold and silver. The carefully prescribed color symbolism, as Murayama Shūichi suggests, discloses yin-yang principles at work, with the positive gold sword driving out the calamities or "defilements" symbolized by the effigies. To quote Murayama, "the harae ritual did not simply end with the expulsion of defilement, but was a Daoist yin-yang rite aimed at soliciting favorable omens."[118]

But why was it the Fubito-be who offered up the sword? An earlier school of scholarship tended to read the Fubito-be's presentation of the sword as an act symbolizing submission to the court.[119] Yet a reading attentive to the Daoist and yin-yang principles at work in the sword symbolism suggests a religio-political meaning more congruent with the military conquests of the Temmu/Jitō court.[120] According to *Nihon shoki* and *Shoku nihongi*, both the Yamato and Kawachi Fubito-be traced their ancestry back to two scribal lineages whose founders, Aichiki and Wang In, entered Japan from Paekche during the reign of Ōjin.[121] The *Kogo shūi* further indicates that these two lineages were closely connected to Temmu's court. According to its author, Imibe no Hironari, when Temmu reorganized the ranking system into eight grades—reflecting, it will be recalled, a strong Daoist influence—the "court took the fourth rank of Imiki and made it the surname of the Hada and Aya along with the Fumi from Paekche." In a note appended to this passage, Hironari adds: "And I believe that the custom of having the Fumi of Yamato and Kawachi present a sword at the purification ritual originated here."[122]

Both the Yamato and Kawachi Fubito-be appear on the occasion of Temmu's mourning ritual (*mogariya*), where they performed a martial dance called the tatafushi no mai, in which the performers wielded a shield and a sword.[123] Its performance during the period of the Temmu/Jitō court, along with the use of the felicitous phrase "manzai" ("ten thousand years") in the harae incantation, was probably in emulation of the Tang courts of Emperor Taizong and Empress Wu (r. 690–705), who had incorporated new music and martial dances like the *Pozhen yue* ("Music for Breaking the Armies") into their court ceremonial in celebration of recent military conquests.[124] The yin-yang principles enacted in these dances, of which an early example is the shield dance (*ganqi* 干戚) recorded in the *Li ji*, performed the dual function of ritually driving out evil spirits and affirming the harmonious balancing of the four breaths that regulated the seasons, heaven and earth, and the four directions—a motif echoed in the language of the ōharae incantation.[125] Rather than an act of submission, therefore, the Fubito-be's participation in martial dances and their presentation of the sword are best viewed as ritual reenactments of Temmu's military conquests that combined the expulsion of harmful spirits with the yin-yang principle of harmonizing time (the four seasons) and space (the four directions) under Temmu's and Jitō's rule.[126] The same principles were also operative in the symbolism of the sword ku-sanagi, which, as one of the three regalia, had a basis in Daoist lore pertaining to magically resonant swords. Thus, right after a notice recording the conferral of cap-ranks on skilled craftsmen, yin-yang masters, medical doctors, and scholars, *Nihon shoki* states: "When the illness of the tennō was prognosticated, it was attributed to the curse of the sword kusanagi." Here, Temmu's ailing body and the sword are symbolically linked, with changes in the one mirrored in the other in accordance with the yin-yang principle of harmonizing *qi*.[127]

To summarize, as religio-political authority was increasingly vested in the tennō from the end of the seventh into the early eighth centuries, a realm reflecting the "centering and outward radiation" characteristic of the Daoist worldview took shape in the Yamato region. As the mediator between heaven and earth and the ruler of the center, the tennō occupied a position that combined elements of the polestar monarch who inhabited the Purple Tenuity Palace and the Daoist sage, master of the secrets of immortality who kept the malign powers at bay. By the time the capital was transferred to Heiankyō at the beginning of the ninth century, there are already subtle changes in this picture. During Kammu's reign, the newly renamed Purple Hall (*shishinden*) of the Palace, formerly the Daianden, has taken on the symbolic attributes of an immortal realm in harmonious yin-yang balance with the demonic realm, but the entranceway to the latter is located northeast of the palace atop Hieizan's Shimegatake, the site of the Demon Gate (*kimon*), suggesting that Buddhist rites, managed by a coequal if not rival center of authority, are now claiming control over the demonic powers.[128] This supposition is strengthened by another change at the end of Junna's reign (823–833), as the practice of basing era names on good omens falls into abeyance.

Temmu's Paradoxes

> Defilement is a Japanese affair; in Tang, they do not observe defilement taboos.
>
> —FUJIWARA NO SANESUKE, *Shōyūki*[129]

Beginning with his flight to Yoshino as Prince Ōama, Temmu's actions are ambiguous in their intent.[130] "The reason I yield the throne and abandon the world is because I wish to heal my illness and preserve my life, living long for a hundred years."[131] Cast as a gesture of renunciation, Temmu's choice to cultivate longevity at Yoshino can also be read as the beginning of his training in various Daoist and yin-yang techniques, including the arts of astrology and invisibility for which he was later celebrated and which arguably helped him achieve victory in the Jinshin Rebellion.[132] It was perhaps at Yoshino as well that the future Temmu, under the guidance of Paekche ritualists, acquired a belief in the power to command the demons and gods. Yet if Temmu's reign was characterized by a fascination with the language, symbols, and practice of immortality, it is also the case that Temmu evinced an equally strong preoccupation with purity that was strangely intertwined with the military achievements of his reign. Right after his victory, he promptly instituted a purity cult. In an edict issued in the eighth year of his reign, he orders the aged and sick to be removed from the temples, where their confinement to narrow rooms as a result of incapacity causes "pure places to become defiled." Instead, they are to be nourished and given medicine in places set apart.[133] Other measures included initiating large-scale sutra copying and recitation in temples and in the palace, the creation of a special category of renunciants called "purifiers" (*jōgyōsha*), and the addition of new grades to the ranking system called "bright rank" (*myōi*) and "pure rank" (*jōi*).[134] Meanwhile, centenarian priests of Paekche—living immortals—are granted special house allotments, and Temmu himself is served by Hōzō and other priests who administer elixirs and perform rites intended to prolong his life.[135]

The bizarre logic that characterizes these actions—removal of the aged and ill from the temples as sources of defilement and the special status accorded centenarians as living immortals—hints at an aporia in the ritual basis of Temmu's and his successors' religio-political authority. As noted earlier in this chapter, one sign of the tennō's authority was the capacity to collect and distribute medicaments and engage in Confucian acts of charitable giving. The provision in Temmu's edict that the aged and ill be cared for and provided with medicines is an expression of this authority. Related to this prerogative was the tennō's ability to visit the sick and dying, unhampered by the threat of defilements in the case of severe illness and death.[136] Temmu's concern, expressed in the same edict, regarding the defilement of pure temple spaces is at variance with this prerogative. How do we explain such inconsistencies? Maruyama's observation that Buddhist rites and Confucian principles of sageship were already operating in tandem at this time is part of the answer,[137] but we must also keep in mind the ways in which Buddhist, Confucian, and Daoist ideas were mingled together at this time. Thus, Temmu's preoccupation with purity is one more facet of his Daoist-like quest for immortality (notwithstanding the seemingly Buddhist tonality to much of this ritual activity), yet the aspiration is already in contradiction with the increasingly sharp accentuation between life and death, purity and defilement, health and illness, which followed upon the violent imposition of a new ceremonial order.[138]

It is here that problems more typically associated with mid-Heian on'yōdō and pollution practices first make their appearance. In brief, as the binary logic of state formation took effect, defilement took on new meaning. To return to the problem of the Fubito-be, it will be recalled that Temmu bestowed upon them the rank of Imiki, a word that implies a connection to pollution taboos.[139] According to a register of court appointments stored in the Shōsōin, which is thought to date from the early Nara period, a member of this lineage by the name of Fumi no Imiki Hiromaro held an appointment as officer in the Yin-Yang Bureau.[140] This minor detail is significant in light of the widely held view that mid-Heian yin-yang practices were characterized above all by a new awareness of pollution taboos. The Fubito-be's connection to yin-yang points to something quite different. First, it suggests that officers of the Yin-Yang Bureau from Temmu's time or shortly thereafter were already involved in the performance of expulsion rituals, a supposition borne out by the example of the tsuina ritual that is discussed later. Second, it suggests that the ōharae, or at least that portion handled by the Fubito-be, was constructed out of a rearticulation of "defilement" in terms of yin-yang correlative principles. If this is the case, then mid-Heian on'yōdō differs from the earlier activities of the Yin-Yang Bureau not by virtue of its indigenization— that is, its involvement with pollution taboos[141]—but because its agents, the on'yōji, were now operating in an environment where defilement, already a factor in Temmu's time, was being invested with new meanings arising from institutional shifts and a redistribution of power. As a result, the tennō could no longer claim control over the demonic or threatening powers.

A Cosmology Defiled

Although the idea of a Chinese-style sage governing over a refined center would continue to be invoked throughout the Heian period and beyond,[142] in practice the character of the tennō's political and sacred authority changed significantly in the course of the ninth and tenth centuries, influenced in part by two concurrent developments in the political and religious spheres: the growing power of the Fujiwara regents, including the system of shrines under their authority, and the expanding power of Buddhist temples.[143] It was during this period that a rapid increase in the observance of pollution taboos (*monoimi*) at the court began to put burdensome constraints upon the activity and movements of the tennō.[144] The number, frequency, and scope of purification rites aimed at expelling malign spirits also increased dramatically. As yin-yang masters became increasingly involved with the penumbral region of managing defilements, advising on pollution and directional taboos, expelling and warding off attacks from plague deities (*ekijin, ekiki*), and handling spirit possessions (*mononoke*) and the like—a process also reflected in the shift from good omens to calamities (*saii*) as the basis for changing era names—they became complicit in a process that was subtly undermining the rationale that had initially guided their activity: to interpret signs on behalf of the tennō who governed in resonant accord with cosmological principles.[145] These developments may now be more easily grasped by locating them within the context of contemporaneous shrine rites (*saishi*) that were being managed under the Jingikan (Shrine Bureau) during the same period.

As has often been noted, magical expulsion rituals were originally the province of the Shrine Bureau. Among these, the border and road rituals are of special interest. Held at specified points and times along borders and roads, these rituals performed the twofold function of (1) warding off malign influences that encroached from outside in the form of plague deities and pestilence and (2) expelling dangerous pollution that had accumulated inside the borders of the interior space. It was the border rituals that gradually became the special province of yin-yang masters. Okada Shōji gives the year 914 as the earliest recorded instance of an on'yōji being summoned to perform an extraordinary (*rinji*) Four Corners and Four Borders rite (*shikaku shikyō no matsuri*) to drive out plague deities during a season of exceptional pestilence.[146]

Of these border-type rituals, the Great Demon Expulsion (*taida* or *daina*, but later called *tsuina*), or the Da nuo in Chinese, has a special bearing on the role played in managing such rites by the Shrine Bureau and yin-yang masters. In the Great Demon Expulsion, the exorcist, or "hōsōji" (Ch. *fangxiang shi*), armed with a halberd and shield for driving out the demons, would dress up in red robes and wrap himself in a bearskin with four golden eyes. Held regularly outside the palace gates, it was performed shortly after the winter solstice to expel pestilential vapors or evil spirits that were prone to break out in periods of seasonal transition when the yin and yang pneumas reversed course.[147] The earliest mention of this rite is an entry in *Shoku ni-hongi* for the third year of Keiun (706), Twelfth Month.[148] What makes it especially interesting is that it was managed from the start by the Yin-Yang Bureau at a time when the Shrine Bureau still performed magical expulsions. According to the words of the ritual prayer that was intoned by the yin-yang master who performed the rite, one of its aims was to drive out "defiled plague demons."[149]

Why were these rituals gradually transferred over from the Jingikan to yin-yang masters, despite the Engi era provisions that assigned many of them to the former? Part of the explanation lies in the nature of border and road rituals. Because these involved the use of animal skins, their already close tie to polluting activity and ritually impure sites would have been accentuated. As awareness of pollution deepened in court society, the Jingikan's sphere of activities tended to be restricted to nonpolluting forms of ritual, whereas the dangerous expulsion rituals, which had been at the core of the Jingikan's responsibilities, gradually became the preserve of yin-yang masters. The Jingikan, in brief, was redefined as the locus and custodian of purity (*seijō*), thereby enforcing an increasingly sharp opposition between purity and pollution.[150] The taking over of such rituals by yin-yang masters would therefore appear to be part of a broader rearticulation of the complex codes defining pollution and purity from about the ninth century on, which was related to the growing influence of Buddhist views regarding defilement and other unseen powers. The latter is evident in the sutra chanting of Buddhist priests that begins to work in tandem with on'yōdō in the management of plague spirits over the course of the ninth century.[151]

At the center of this system of pollution practices was the tennō. This is clearly reflected in the provisions pertaining to pollution management set forth in the Engi shiki, which disclose a concentric geographical structure radiating outward from a core of bodily purity in the tennō to the boundaries of the palace, the capital city, and thence to the borders of the Go-kinai and the outer provinces beyond.[152] Watching over the tennō day and night, yin-yang masters would regularly perform the treading ritual *henpai* to drive out malign spirits and threatening pollution whenever he moved from room to room in the palace or went on a journey outside the palace grounds.[153] The enmeshment of the tennō in a web of pollution-based practices can also be seen in the way it encroaches upon and affects the performance of rituals that once exemplified the tennō's command over dangerous powers. One of these was the chinkonsai.

The performance of the chinkonsai exemplified the tennō's singular capacity to demonstrate ritual control over the raging powers that would otherwise threaten the realm with destruction. To quote Watanabe Katsuyoshi: "For the tennō who stood at the apex and unified the provinces, the most important religious ceremony that he had to perform would have been placating (*shizumeyawasu*) the ancestral deities that were at the heart of the unification of each of the various clan groups in the provinces. The tennō alone was able to perform it, and it was the proof of his kingship." [154] In another passage, Watanabe describes the ritual shaking of the tennō's robe (*onzo shindō*), an important element in the chinkon rite: "Through the action of shaking the sacred robe the world order in its totality is opened. By this means, the evil spirits (*akuryō*), harmful demons (*akki*), and all of the defilement are simultaneously expelled and purified, and the tama (spirits) of the fearsome enraged deities are placated." [155] The chinkon rite thus accomplished three ritual acts—harai (expulsion), kiyome (purification), and shizume (pacification)—all of which were simultaneously present in the ritual of "tamashizume." [156] Watanabe's hypothesis that all three actions were accomplished simultaneously may seem problematic, but the seasonal and spatial basis of the chinkonsai, grounded in yin-yang correlative principles, parallels the logic of the ōharae rite analyzed earlier.[157]

But when we turn to notices of the chinkonsai's performance in the ninth and tenth centuries, defilement crops up as a frequent cause for its suspension or postponement.[158] Elements of the chinkonsai were also reappearing at this time in altered ritual contexts. In the Eighty Islands Rite (Yasoshima matsuri) held at Naniwa, for which the earliest recorded mention is 850, the ritual action of shaking the robe takes on the attributes of a "misogibarai" or purification, with the robe functioning as a symbolic substitute (*katashiro*) for the emperor's own body.[159] At the opposite extreme are changes in the character of the expulsion ritual of the ōharae. As harae-type rituals came to be performed for other members of the aristocracy, the tennō's personal harae developed into the ritual known as mi-aga, or the ōharae performed for the tennō by the Jingikan on the last day of every month, and also during the Jingonjiki[160] in the Sixth Month and Twelfth Month as well as before the niiname-sai in the Eleventh Month. By the time of Go-Suzaku's reign (r. 1036–1045), the mi-aga or purification ceremony was being performed for the tennō every day.[161]

In discussing the phenomenon, Itō Kiyoshi, Kuroda Toshio, and others have characterized it as a deliberate "mystification" of the tennō. By surrounding the person of the tennō with an ever more elaborate network of taboos and rites aimed at expelling potentially harmful defilements, the purity of the tennō, it is argued, was accentuated. Invested with magical authority, he was now expected "to preserve peace in the realm (*kokudo annon*), drive out disease and vengeful spirits, preserve vitality (*seimei*), and bring about worldly benefits and the purification of defilement." [162] Itō's characterization of the tennō's functions, which draws directly on language in the codes, bears a strong resemblance to the Daoist ideal of the sage emperor. Thus, in commenting on the homologous ritual functions of Daoist priest and sovereign in ancient China, Robinet notes that the latter were "ultimately 'cult agents' charged with maintaining order both in the human domain and in nature, warding off natural scourges, rebellions, floods, and evil spirits." [163] The problem lies with the word *defilement*. There are subtle yet important differences between the sacrilizing function of "kegare" (pollution, defilement) from about the tenth century on, which, as Itō observes, appears to have functioned symbolically in polar opposition to purity, and the correlative cosmology of the yin-yang five agents system with its principle of circulating *qi* (pneumas) that underlay the authority of the sage. Where the binary logic of the former inhibited and easily became the basis for control, the modulations of the latter were less subject to manipulation by one vested authority. The former, I suggest, ultimately made the tennō entirely dependent on the ritualists who defended and protected his purity, immobilizing him in an intricate web of restrictive taboos. The latter at least allowed the possibility of a self-correcting ritual practice, although here too there were risks to the tennō's authority. In the final section, I focus on some of these dangers as well as the tensions and overlaps between the two systems.

Bewitchments: Yin-Yang Reversed

If indigenous pollution beliefs were able to overwhelm or subvert the functions of the Yin-Yang Bureau, it was made possible in part by the very symbolic language its officers had charge of. As we saw in Chapter 2, in Han times, the prognostication of good and bad omens, specifically the systematic use of favorable omens and natural calamities and prodigies, was a two-edged sword that could be used to affirm as well as restrain the power of the ruler, the latter by interpreting bad omens as political criticism portending loss of virtue. It is not surprising, then, that Temmu and the sovereigns who succeeded him were sensitive to the potential threat posed to their authority by manipulations of the yin-yang symbolic code. It was not only the capacity of yin-yang and Daoist-based practices to symbolically enhance the ruler's authority but their potential to undermine it as well that partly explains the attempt to monopolize such knowledge by placing it under the strict control of the Yin-Yang Bureau. As Tamura Enchō has observed, the transmission of yin-yang knowledge during the earliest phase of the ritsuryō state was strictly prohibited and the written discourse carefully guarded.[164]

The vigilance of the court is borne out by the apparent rivalry during the Nara period between court yin-yang practices and those managed by Buddhist priests and the strong measures taken by the court to safeguard the secrecy of the textual tradition.[165] The Regulations for Priests and Nuns, cited earlier, prohibited either from making any use of Daoist magical charms (*jugon*) for driving out malign spirits and curing illnesses, reserving this privilege for the officers of the Medical Bureau. This contrasts with the Tang system that allowed for the dual use of both Daoist and Buddhist-type cures, leading Endō Katsumi to conclude that at the Nara court the two methods were in sharp opposition.[166] In a further indication of how easily yin-yang practices could be used for the purpose of making political criticisms, the Sōniryō also established severe punishments for those who engaged in the observation of heavenly portents for the purpose of interpreting good and bad omens to beguile peasants.[167] Ultimately, this led to a situation in which yin-yang related texts, including books on astrological lore, divination charts, and calendrical matters, as well as weft-texts and knowledge related to the prognostication of directions, were all prohibited for private use outside the court.[168]

But to read such prohibitions only in terms of an opposition between the Nara court and the growing power of Buddhist rites or of the elite's attempt to suppress popular resistance risks simplifying what in effect was a more ambiguous situation. For example, shortly after the Prince Nagaya incident in 729 during the reign of Shōmu, an edict was issued in which severe punishments were announced for whoever made use of heretical learning, from all members of the court bureaucracy down to and including the general population. In addition to prohibiting the cultivation of magic or "illusory arts" (*genjutsu*) and cursing with effigies and spells (*enmi juso*), the edict also forbade dwelling in the mountains and forests, teaching false Buddhist doctrine, concocting seals and talismans, and compounding medicines to make poisons.[169] If the edict discloses an awareness of what constitutes false as opposed to orthodox Buddhist teaching, it also suggests that elements of an earlier cultural assemblage that mingled together Daoist, yin-yang, and Buddhist practices are now taking on a heretical coloring. Hence, the weird rumors associated with the political demise of Prince Nagaya (684–729), who is thought to have committed suicide after an order was issued for his arrest on the charge of heresy (*sadō*). According to the popular rumor of the day, Prince Nagaya, who imposed a harsh ceremonial order on the court, was believed to have made use of a curse to kill the crown prince born to Kōmyōshi, the consort of Shōmu. As Shinkawa has suggested, however, the accusation of heresy was owing in part to the vague fears that had begun to invest certain Daoist-like practices at this time, which included the use of elixirs and incantations that the well-intentioned Prince Nagaya employed in rites *aimed at healing* the ailing crown prince.[170]

There was thus an inherent instability in the yin-yang Daoist discourse from the start, which was further accentuated during the period of legal codification as practices of a Daoist cast became invested with an aura of taboo. In addition to this, we must factor in the effects of pollution taboos that continued to operate at both the edges as well as inside the ambit of official ideology. On the one hand, symbolic language and practices related to ingesting elixirs and inducting qi—the entire emphasis on immortality— suggest that the ideology may have initially helped to circumvent the constraints of such pollution practices by relocating them within a logic of balancing and harmonizing qi. The imbrication, on the other hand, of yin-yang with pollution practices from the ninth century on indicates that the overarching edifice of the earlier cosmological discourse that was managed by the Yin-Yang Bureau and at the center of which stood the sage ruler was all too susceptible of being shifted onto the more hazardous terrain of these same pollution practices.

As the symbolic functions of the Yin-Yang Bureau shifted over to yin-yang masters and pollution practices that fell increasingly within the purview of Buddhist doctrinal concerns—a domain, in other words, of Buddhist authority—the court's control over the apparatus and symbolic language that legitimated its authority gradually slipped from its control. This accounts for the periodic attempts to suppress magical yin-yang practices over the period extending from the reigns of Kammu through Uda. During the reign of Kammu, for example, the head yin-yang master of the Yin-Yang Bureau, Yamanoue Ason Funenushi, in an incident that echoes the accusation against Prince Nagaya, was suspected of performing magical curses against Kammu and joining in a plot to rebel.[171] During the reign of Saga (r. 809–823), magical yin-yang practices were held vigorously in check, even as the gates and main hall of the palace were renamed in emulation of the Tang imperial palace that equated the *shishinden* with the Purple Tenuity Palace of the polestar ruler. Following the coup of Fujiwara no Yoshifusa (804–871) after the death of Saga, however, there was a resurgence in yin-yang practices during the reign of Nimmyō (r. 833–850) as the northern branch of the Fujiwara gained increasing control over the throne. A similar suppression of magical yin-yang practices accompanied by a reintroduction of Confucian principles occurs during the reign of Uda (r. 887–897).[172] Whether we characterize this tendency as a form of "rational" Confucianism or as an attempt to reassert autonomy on the part of the tennō, it is clear that up until the emergence of rule by retired sovereigns, or for about the first half of the Heian period, there was an ambiguous pull between a Daoist-type sage emperor who engaged actively in the political field and one that was becoming increasingly isolated, immobile, and at risk of defilement. It was now the yin-yang masters along with esoteric Buddhist priests who held the threatening powers at bay.

Part Two

Part Two

ROYALIZING THE REALM AND THE RITUALIZATION OF VIOLENCE

Introduction

Part One of this study examined texts from the Nara and early Heian periods with the aim of recovering some of the yin-yang and Daoist ideas that contributed to the symbolic representation of royal authority. The strategy of examining a discourse of the center from a position that has been marginal to the conventional view of the period has yielded a more open-ended understanding of its texts and their relation to a variety of ritual practices. Texts like *Nihon shoki* and *Man'yōshū* that have tended to be regarded as origin points in a narrative of national emergence, especially in the field of literature studies, can now be seen as participating within a broader East Asian culture, part of the ideographic cultural sphere.

The two chapters of Part Two extend this analysis to a series of historical narratives: *Kojiki* and *Nihon shoki* in Chapter 4 and the vernacular historical tale *Ōkagami* in Chapter 5. Of the two historical narratives examined in this chapter, it was *Nihon shoki* that established itself as the official history of the court. The role of *Kojiki*, on the other hand, has remained something of an enigma in view of its relegation to marginal status throughout much of the premodern period. Taking this as my starting point, I compare how

Nihon shoki and *Kojiki* manipulate legendary material, with a special focus on the Yamato Takeru narrative and Jimmu's subjugation chronicle as symbolic and ritual expressions of the tennō's claim to control territory by acting as a mediator of sacred speech. In these pages, I question the widely held view that this claim was founded on a peaceful submission to the center. Instead, I suggest that the tennō's claim to mediate sacred speech was inextricably linked to the violence that arose from the consolidation of a religio-political center. I further argue that *Kojiki*, in providing a ritual response to such violence, represented a historical project that was both complementary to and yet ultimately at odds with *Nihon shoki*'s ideology of the sage ruler. The second half of the chapter carries the discussion forward into the eighth, ninth, and first half of the tenth centuries. Here I examine how the construction of a geographical and metaphorical center created a set of discursive conditions that invested movement or wandering within the royalized center, including various manifestations of nomadic speech, with new meaning in the overlapping domains of secular and sacred authority. One of my aims here is to resituate the phenomenon of wandering, which has tended to function as a metaphorical site for projecting modern preoccupations with national essence, within its historical moment, a period often characterized as one of recurrent plagues and social instability. It was during this period that an earlier system of myth and ritual centered around raging deities and the capture of their speech began to be rearticulated within a Buddhist doctrinal framework. In the final sections, the phenomenon of nomadic speech is examined in relation to a number of incidents, including the suppression of shamanlike groups in Mino province, the instituting of the Jōgan era goryōe in response to outbreaks of spirit possession, and elite perceptions of popular unrest connected to the shidara no kami incident in the mid-tenth century, which climaxed in the enshrinement of Sugawara no Michizane's spirit at the Kitano shrine. Each of these incidents was closely connected to the construction of a religio-political center.

Complementarity in Historical Narrative

It is a curious accident of literary history that the earliest extant manuscript of *Kojiki* (712), the *Shinpukujibon* (1372), was copied only one year after Kakuichi dictated his now celebrated version of *The Tale of the Heike* in 1371. There is no question of any connection between these two events. But apart from the coincident of dating, the fact that both texts are famously tied to oral recitation (*Kojiki* dictated by the reciter Hiyeda no Are) does suggest some intriguing parallels. The cultural historian Hayashiya Tatsusaburō, for example, once proposed that the biwa hōshi might be late representatives of an ancient tradition of oral reciters stretching back from *Heike* through the Yotsugi narrator of *Ōkagami* to *Kojiki*'s Hiyeda no Are and the ancient "kataribe" of preliterate times.[1] Hayashiya's theory never gained wide acceptance among *Heike* scholars, but by positing the existence of a continuous oral tradition running through a succession of seemingly unrelated historical narratives, Hayashiya touched on a question of fundamental importance: the relationship between texts invested with or that claim authoritative status and those that flourish at their margins. Whereas *Nihon shoki*, for example, inaugurated the series of Six National Histories (*rikkokushi*) and continued to be the object of intensive interpretive activity throughout the Heian and medieval periods, *Kojiki* appears to have exercised its influence less overtly, as a supplementary text in the tradition of commentary on *Nihon shoki*. Only after Motoori elevated it to superior status through the "recovery" of its vernacular reading did *Kojiki* begin its ascent to the canon.[2]

Reflecting on some of these same issues, the historian Gomi Fumihiko has discerned a generic resemblance of sorts between *Heike* and *Kojiki*. Noting the tendency of historical narrative to double its more official version with a less official account, Gomi has suggested that narrative pairings such as *Nihon shoki* and *Kojiki*, the early medieval *Gukanshō* and *Heike*, and the Kamakura period warrior history *Azumakagami* (*Mirror of the East*) and *Soga monogatari* (*The Tale of the Soga*) functioned in each case as pairs of mutually complementary narratives encompassing single multilayered histories.[3] Thus, the story of the Soga brothers' revenge killing of their father's slayer, Suketsune, a retainer of Yoritomo (1147–1199), can also be read as narrative shorthand for the ritual slaying of the king whose death brings about the reinvigoration of diminished royal mystique. Although the role of victim is displaced onto Suketsune, the true royal figure in *Soga monogatari* is Yoritomo, who as outsider and exile from the capital is welcomed as the king in Tōgoku. The slaying of Suketsune and the hunting episodes centered on the ritualized killing of deer in *Soga monogatari* all belong to this larger myth about the birth of royal power.[4] In this fashion, the official "chronicle" (*nendaiki*) of *Azumakagami*, whose principal subject is the legitimate succession of royal power, is shadowed by the darker narrative, with its hints of a ritual slaying, that is recounted in *Soga monogatari*. The placation of the slain Soga brothers can therefore be said to conceal a deeper meaning about the violent origins of royal power. One has only to think about the exile and slaying of the once flourishing Heike clan, and balance this against the overt religio-political program argued for by the Buddhist prelate Jien, to see a similar pattern at work. What about *Kojiki* and *Nihon shoki*, the oldest extant pair of historical narratives, whose appearance was separated by only eight years? Does *Kojiki* represent a mythic or ritual counterpart to *Nihon shoki*'s official historical account, establishing a pattern of complementarity that would later reemerge in Gomi's medieval pairings? What might a comparison of the two reveal about the way royal authority was conceptualized in the ancient period? To shed light on these questions, I first turn to *Kojiki*'s Preface and then to several legendary cycles in *Kojiki* and *Nihon shoki*.

Two Versions of the Yamato Takeru Legend

In the Preface to *Kojiki*, Temmu's declared purpose is set forth in the following words:

> I have heard that the *teiki* and *honji* in possession of the various houses
> have deviated from the truth and accrued many falsehoods. If these errors
> are not remedied at the present time, before many years have passed, their
> meaning will be lost. This is the fabric of the state, the great foundation
> of the sovereign's influence. Therefore, recording the *teiki* and examining
> the *senji*, eliminating the falsehoods and establishing the truth, I intend to
> transmit them to later generations.[5]

The precise meaning of *teiki* in this passage has been debated, but its general sense is that of genealogical records pertaining to the imperial line. Since this is qualified as those in possession of the various houses, it suggests the competing claims of at least several *uji*, translated variously as clan, family, or "titled lineages."[6] This is borne out in the second reference a short while later to what is apparently the same record, only this time named *Sumera mikoto no hi tsugi* ("The Imperial Sun Lineage"), where it refers to the lineage of the reigning house. Whatever the precise nuance of the terms, the passage indicates Temmu's concern to adjust both the genealogical records (*teiki*) and foundation narratives (*honji*) (or "basic dicta," in Philippi's translation) of the various *uji* to make them conform to the new power structure.[7] This means that those genealogies and narratives that enter the record—some must have been suppressed altogether—will have been reshaped to reflect the imperial line's claims to legitimacy.

The narrative of Yamato Takeru, which literally means "Mighty One of Yamato," is a case in point. Widely differing versions exist both inside and outside the chronicles, and a comparison of these differences discloses the extent to which foundation narratives were manipulated in the interests of legitimating power. In the *Kojiki* and *Nihon shoki* versions, Yamato Takeru is dispatched by his father, the legendary Emperor Keikō (r. A.D. 71–130), to subdue numerous raging deities (*araburugami*) and rebellious peoples. In a variant found in *Hitachi fudoki*, the same Yamato Takeru is depicted as a tennō (sumera no mikoto) making a royal progress.[8] A portion of the *Kojiki* version of Yamato Takeru, on the other hand, appears to derive from an Izumo myth that was later appropriated by the center.[9] Since *Nihon shoki*'s treatment of the Izumo myth has an important bearing on the broader implications of the Yamato Takeru narrative, I begin with this chronologically earlier Izumo narrative.

As has frequently been noted, the earlier reigns in *Nihon shoki* have far fewer entries relative to the number of years covered than do the reigns in the second half of the work, especially from Suiko on. This has led some historians to view the density of the chronological entries as a sign of the narrative's increasing factual veracity and reliability as a source document. Although the Chinese methods of recordkeeping exemplified in Japanese historiographical practice did produce remarkably accurate accounts of court matters, there is an aspect to chronology that gets lost when attention is focused exclusively on its factual reliability—namely, its symbolic function of investing a narrative with authority. What gets placed under the sign of a dated entry, in brief, is already an indication of its importance to the recorder.[10] Hence, even those early portions of *Nihon shoki*, often treated as padding to eke out a lack of historical documentation, merit the closest scrutiny for what the chroniclers chose to include and arrange into a chronological sequence.

Why, for example, did the chroniclers of *Nihon shoki* choose to link together two dated entries regarding (1) a problem of royal succession and (2) an Izumo legend about a fratricide, recorded successively in the forty-eighth year and sixtieth year of Sūjin's reign? The first entry begins: "The emperor commanded Toyoki no Mikoto and Ikume no Mikoto, saying: 'Both of you, my sons, are alike in my affections. I don't know which of you to make my successor. Each of you go now and dream, and I will form an augury from your dreams.'" After interpreting the two dreams, Sūjin decides to make the elder son ruler of the East Country, where he becomes "the first ancestor of the Kimi of Kamitsuke and of the Kimi of Shimotsuke." The younger brother, on the other hand, is declared successor to the throne because "he looked down over all four quarters" instead of only to the East as did the elder brother.[11] The next entry begins: "Sūjin commanded his ministers, saying: 'Take hina teru no mikoto [another source says "Take hina tori," and another "Ame hina tori"] brought down the divine treasures (*kamu dakara*) from the heavens and stored them in the shrine of the Great Kami of Izumo. I wish to look upon them.' Thereupon, he dispatched Take moro sumi [one writing says, "Also called Oho moro sumi"], the ancestor of the Yata-be no Miyatsuko, to Izumo so that he could present him with the treasures." As it happens, Izumo Furune (the ancestor of the Izumo no Omi), who "had charge of the divine treasures," was away at this time in Tsukushi, so it was his younger brother Ihi iri ne who received the emperor's command and proceeded to turn over the divine treasures, thereby rendering them up to the court. When the elder brother Izumo Furune found out, he got angry and some years later succeeded in slaying the younger brother by tricking him with a wooden sword. Informed of the younger brother's murder, the court dispatched Kibi tsu hiko and Take nuna kawa, who executed Izumo Furune.[12]

Commenting on the Izumo legend, Fukushima Akiho has suggested that it reflects a ceremony in which a newly appointed kuni no miyatsuko ("country chieftain") felicitates the reign of the ruling sovereign by swearing an oath of submission and offering up the divine treasures to the court.[13] But in addition to this straightforward religio-political meaning, there is another motive in the chronicler's decision to link the Izumo legend to the preceding entry on the succession. Both entries, for example, revolve around a rivalry between two brothers: in the first over the succession and in the second over control of the divine treasures. Whereas the first ends peaceably, the latter irrupts into a fratricidal killing. The contrast, I suggest, serves to reinforce the prestige and authority of the court. This same emphasis on harmonious relations within the royal family informs *Nihon shoki*'s version of the Yamato Takeru narrative, although it is contradicted in the *Kojiki* version.

In both the *Kojiki* and *Nihon shoki* versions, Yamato Takeru is sent out on various missions of conquest. Although both versions represent the interests of the center, rewriting regional myths to give them a Yamato slant, in their sharply differing presentations of Yamato Takeru, they expose contradictions that underlay the effort to impose centralized rule. *Kojiki*, for example, develops the theme of Wo-usu-no-mikoto's (the younger brother's name prior to receiving the eulogistic title Yamato Takeru) murderous violence, his expulsion under the guise of a subjugating general, and his gradual transformation into the figure of a reluctant exile. The narrative begins by hinting at dissension inside the royal family when the elder brother tricks his father by marrying the maidens whom he was dispatched to present to his father. When the elder brother (Opo-usu-no-mikoto) fails to attend the morning and evening meals, his father dispatches the younger brother to "teach and admonish him." The future Yamato Takeru gives the following account of his success:

> "Early in the morning when he went into the privy, I waited and captured him, grasped him and crushed him, then pulled off his limbs, and wrapping them in a straw mat, threw them away." Hereupon the emperor fearing the *mighty and fierce temper* (*takeku araki kokoro*) of his son said: "In the West there are two Kumaso Takeru (two mighty ones of Kumaso); they are unsubmissive and lacking in manners. For this reason, kill them." [14]

Repeatedly dispatched to subdue raging deities and unsubmissive populations, Yamato Takeru accomplishes these tasks through a combination of trickery and brute force. In one episode, he comes upon the Kumaso Takeru as they are in the midst of a banquet to celebrate the building of a new pit-dwelling. Adopting the guise of a young girl, he sits down inside the pit-dwelling among the women, where he proceeds to slay first the elder and then the younger Kumaso Takeru with a sword that he has kept concealed beneath his clothes. He uses similar tactics of deception in slaying Izumo Takeru:

> Thereupon he entered the country of Izumo, and having come with the intention of slaying Izumo Takeru, he then swore an oath of friendship with him. Thereupon he secretly made a false sword out of Itipi wood, and wore it at his side. They bathed in the Hi River. Here, Yamato Takeru no mikoto got out of the river first and took the sword that Izumo Takeru had lain aside, put it on, and said: "Let us exchange swords." Whereupon, Izumo Takeru got out of the river and put on Yamato Takeru's false sword. Here, Yamato Takeru invited him, saying: "Let's cross swords." Then, as each one was drawing his sword, Izumo Takeru was unable to draw his. Here, Yamato Takeru no mikoto drew his sword and struck Izumo Takeru dead. [15]

Here, the motif of substituting a false wooden sword that had originally been transmitted locally in the Izumo region has been incorporated directly into the subjugation narrative of the Yamato court. [16] Equally interesting is how *Nihon shoki*'s account of a peaceful transfer of power from Izumo to the center (symbolized by the rendering up of the divine treasures) is here depicted as a violent conquest, with Yamato Takeru sharing, as it were, aspects of Izumo Furune's own identity. The *Kojiki* narrative, in other words, is double-voiced. Another tactic employed by Yamato Takeru is to pacify the raging deities through the ritual capture of their sacred speech, a peaceful means of conquest that stands in sharp contrast to his use of trickery and brute violence. This change of tactic is mirrored in Yamato Takeru's gradual weakening and death that follow his apparent violation of a taboo, the slaying of a white boar. At the end of the narrative, tamed of his once "mighty and fierce temper," Yamato Takeru is ritually mourned and deified in the form of a white bird.

The Yamato Takeru of *Nihon shoki* is a much different figure. The fratricidal and internecine strife foregrounded in *Kojiki*'s narrative—the same motif that is present in the original Izumo myth—is elided in favor of a narrative that stresses Opo-usu-no-mikoto's peaceful integration into the center.[17] *Nihon shoki* also frames Yamato Takeru's narrative in terms of the calendrical time originating with the newly established court, and within the narrative portrays him as the faithful executor of Keikō's command, already in possession of the eulogistic title Yamato Takeru.[18] Unlike the impulsively violent and fratricidal Wo-usu-no-Mikoto of *Kojiki*, the figure in *Nihon shoki* embodies all the virtues of the ideal warrior:

> Now we mark that you are mighty of stature and your countenance is of perfect beauty, you have strength sufficient to raise tripods, your fierceness is like thunder and lightening, wherever you turn your face, there is none to stand before you; whenever you attack you surely conquer. This we know, that whereas in outward form you are our child, in reality you are a god.[19]

As commentaries have long pointed out, this portrait of Yamato Takeru is a composite image of celebrated warrior figures described in the *Shi ji*, *Hou han shu* (*History of the Later Han*), and other works of Chinese historiography.[20] In the passage immediately preceding it, on the other hand, the barbarous traits and violence constituting the evil side of Yamato Takeru in *Kojiki* is displaced in *Nihon shoki* onto those whom he is sent out to subjugate, the Emishi, or Eastern Barbarians. Here follows a portion of the passage:

> Among these Eastern Barbarians, the Emishi are the most powerful. Their men and women are promiscuous, and they make no distinction between father and son. In the winter they dwell in holes; and in the summer, in

nests. They wear furs, drink blood, and brothers mistrust one another. They climb mountains in the manner of flying birds, and run through the grass like wild beasts. They are forgetful of favors done, and if they meet with an enemy (or wrong) they take vengeance. For this reason, they keep arrows in their top-knots, and hide swords in their clothing.[21]

Not found in the *Kojiki* version, the description is a classic instance of the middle-kingdom ideology adopted by the Yamato state. Borrowing its language from traditional Chinese views of the unassimilated populations located at the fringe of its empire, it projects an alien otherness upon the easterners who had refused to submit to the Yamato hegemony, providing the court with a justification for their subjugation.[22] Rhetoric of this type, especially the emphasis on bestiality and duplicity, will persist as part of a broader discourse of otherness that is projected by the "civilizing" (*fūka*) center upon populations who either opposed its interests or lay outside its effective control.

To return to our initial question, viewed strictly as historical narratives, *Kojiki* and *Nihon shoki* can well be characterized as exhibiting complementary narrative strategies. By combining in a single figure the roles of transgressor, conqueror, and victim together with the contradictory qualities of fierceness and gentleness, the *Kojiki* variant of the Yamato Takeru narrative registers the violence underlying the Yamato attempt to impose hegemony. This self-generating repetitive structure in which exile and violence are inevitably produced out of the establishment of a political order supplements, to anticipate Murasaki Shikibu's later formulation in *The Tale of Genji*, "the one-sided" view of *Nihon shoki*,[23] which suppresses the negative contrary underlying the Yamato court's rise to power by projecting the same violence that is integrated *into* the *Kojiki* narrative *outward* upon the subject population. By setting up a binary opposition between inner and outer, or between the refined cultural space of its own political order and the barbarian populations to the east and west, *Nihon shoki* elides the problematic violence of the court's origins, vividly conveyed in *Kojiki* and poignantly in these words spoken by Yamato Takeru:

> *Is it because the emperor wants me to die?* Why did he dispatch me to the West to attack the evil people of the West? Now that I have returned, and not even much time has elapsed, without giving me troops, will he once again dispatch me to subdue the evil people of the twelve regions of the East? When I reflect on this, *he must want me to die soon.*" Saying this, he lamented and cried.[24]

Here, the narrative hints at what the expulsion appeared to conceal—namely, the identity between the murdered elder brother and Yamato Takeru himself. In ritual or mythic terms, both figures can be read as displacements for a single figure, the doomed scapegoat of collective violence, who at the end of the narrative is deified in the form of a white bird.

But here, too, in this ambiguous presentation of Yamato Takeru, the model of complementarity becomes more problematic. As our attention shifts from narrative symmetries to ritual concerns, the two texts look less like complementary narrative strategies, with *Kojiki* supplementing *Nihon shoki*'s centered viewpoint, and more like contradictory legitimations of the tennō's religio-political authority. Thus, without discounting the place of explicit violence in *Nihon shoki*, its editors clearly had a different ideological purpose in mind in stressing the mandate to rule in accordance with Chinese conceptions of kingship. The very form of the history, modeled after official Chinese dynastic accounts, together with its yin-yang and Daoist cosmological worldview, locates the events of the Yamato court's rise to power within a much different narrative trajectory than does *Kojiki*'s treatment of these same events. *Kojiki*'s starker interest in the problematic violence that accompanied the imposition of centralized rule suggests an underlying ritual intent at odds with *Nihon shoki*'s larger claims, a difference that may explain *Kojiki*'s subsequent relegation to cryptically commenting on the official account of events.

Ritualized Violence and Subjugation Narratives

In several studies on Japanese kingship that speak directly to the issue of violence, the anthropologist Yamaguchi Masao has attempted to locate the Yamato Takeru narrative within a broader mythological framework that is held to have undergird Japanese notions of kingship from ancient times.[25] Central to Yamaguchi's reading is the thesis that any system of kingship will inevitably project in the form of myth those negative powers and forces that, although integral to kingship, would threaten the system were they explicitly acknowledged in the actual conduct of the ruler: "Herein lies the dilemma of kingship: to be integral it has to represent negative elements as well as positive ones. But as a lay authority, the king can express only that which is morally acceptable. The mythical dimension is introduced to solve this type of dilemma."[26] In mythological terms, this means that as power is consolidated in the ordered realm of the center, the unruly and destructive forces

(*aratama*) are banished to the periphery. At the same time, the periodic renewal of the center's authority also demands the regular reintroduction of
the "alien" power of the periphery. Drawing on Orikuchi Shinobu's theory
of the outsider, or the mysterious visitor from afar (*marebito*), and Lévi-
Strauss's structural anthropology, notably his well-known typology of the
trickster figure, Yamaguchi identifies Yamato Takeru as one of many ambiguous figures who performed the dual role of first introducing chaos and
then re-creating order "by establishing a kingdom." The ambiguous nature
of Yamato Takeru and of similar figures such as Susanoo no mikoto, embodying "the contradictory phases of a single process," reflects, according
to Yamaguchi, "the essential character of Japanese kingship."[27]

Yamaguchi's structuralist approach allows him to make connections
among a variety of ritual and cultural practices, including the management
of defilement, the placation of violent spirits, and the symbolic role of marginal reciters. Of particular interest is his insight into the occult link between
the violent and chaotic energies of the periphery and the authority of the
ruler who inhabits the center. As Yamaguchi notes, "The *Kojiki* chronicle
tells us of the internal wars carried on between the fifth and seventh centuries, almost in a ritual way, every time a king died."[28] The ritualized violence
connected to royal succession implied by this statement is then analogized by
Yamaguchi to the cultic function of itinerant reciters. Simultaneously identified with Orikuchi's "rare visitor" from afar and bearers of the "defilement"
that arises out of the order imposed by the center, such itinerant reciters are
identical, in Yamaguchi's view, to the king in his occult character as transgressor, taking on, in their role as victim and scapegoat, the threatening
powers that must be kept hidden in the king's public or official role.

Yamaguchi's reading certainly provides a compelling analysis of Japanese
kingship. Yet in treating a variety of disparate writings and ritual practices,
often widely separated in time, as a single cultural text inscribing an unchanging myth of Japanese kingship, the historical determinations of several
contradictory practices of royal power are effaced. There is a stark contrast,
for example, between *Nihon shoki*'s sage ruler, who occupied the center of
a royalized realm that was supported in part by yin-yang and Daoist principles, and the mid-Heian tennō, who, as the object of a purity cult, was
hedged round with pollution taboos. In brief, by displacing the central issue of royal authority's complicity with violence to the realm of myth, the
analysis obscures changes in the way violence was both ritually managed

and manipulated as conceptions of royal power changed over time. The argument's central premise regarding the fundamental ambiguity of Japanese royal authority need not be rejected, however, but historicized. We can begin this process by taking a closer look at *Kojiki*'s construction of the tennō's sacred authority.

In an important reassessment, Kōnoshi Takamitsu views *Kojiki* as fundamental to the ideology that legitimated the authority of the tennō.[29] Central to Kōnoshi's discussion is the problematic term "kotomuke," which has traditionally been interpreted to mean "to cause to submit through the power of words," or perhaps more literally, "to direct (*muke*) words (*koto*) toward" and thereby cause to submit.[30] According to Kōnoshi, "kotomuke," which is not found in *Nihon shoki*, meant something nearly the opposite—namely, "to cause the listener direct words over here." It would have therefore signified an act whereby "kami" (deities)—usually "raging deities" in *Kojiki*—were made to swear an oath of submission to the central authority embodied in the person of the tennō. Having sprung logically out of the center's attempt to impose order, the raging deities lay outside the system of Confucian rites (*rei*) that were integral to the project of royalizing (*ōka*) the realm. In exchange for their oath, they were brought under the center's civilizing influence and incorporated into a sacred order at the apex of which stood the tennō, who mediated and thereby monopolized all sacred speech. Among the eighteen instances of the lexeme "ara" (rough, wild, raging) that occur in *Kojiki*, nine are linked to araburugami. The majority, moreover, are concentrated in those portions of *Kojiki* most critical to the construction of a royal sphere: the "kuniyuzuri"(the central myth in which Ōkuninushi yields the land to the royal sun lineage), Jimmu's subjugation chronicle, and Keikō's chronicle, or the narrative of Yamato Takeru. The prominence of the expression "[araburugami] wo kotomuke yawashite" in the latter, where it occurs four times, makes the Yamato Takeru narrative critical to the formation of a royal sphere.[31]

Yet if the tennō stood at the apex of the ritual system, a status exemplified in his performance of the ancient chinkon rite, what connection did he have to the violence that accompanied imposition of centralized rule? Yamaguchi sought to answer this question by displacing the problem of real violence to the symbolic realm of myth and ritual. Another theory, proposed by Nishizawa Katsumi, would ground the tennō's authority in violence itself. Thus, *Kojiki*, in addition to the explicit violence of the Yamato Takeru narrative, repeatedly foregrounds, in the second and third scrolls that follow Jimmu's subjugation chronicle, the motifs of rebellion, regicide, and fratricide that arise out of disputes over the succession, narrating them serially and with a complete lack of the critical consciousness—that is, the use of interlinear glosses and the inclusion of variants—that is found in *Nihon shoki*. Royal power, in brief, has its origin in violence, and the repetition of violence reign after reign reveals an awareness that violence supported the royal order, with the survivor of internecine strife thereby increasing his own sacrality.[32] In contrast to Yamaguchi, therefore, who grants violence only metaphorical rights in the ritual apparatus, and Kōnoshi who emphasizes the tennō's authority that is grounded in the capacity to redirect the sacred speech (*kotomuke*) of pacified raging deities to the center, Nishizawa views the tennō's authority as arising out of his monopoly over violence itself. In an effort to shed additional light on this problem, I now turn to the problem of violence in Jimmu's subjugation chronicle.

Jimmu, Banquets, and the Tsuchigumo

Like the Yamato Takeru narrative, Jimmu's subjugation narrative maps out the construction of a royal sphere centered on the region of Yamato. But whereas Keikō's realm radiates eastward and westward from an already established center, Jimmu's chronicle traces out an earlier conquest that originates in Himuka in the far west and culminates in Yamato in the east.[33] Through the motif of repeated banquets and ritual transfers of speech by local "earthly deities" who willingly give up their names, the narrative represents the subjugation as by and large a peaceful submission to Jimmu. At Uda in Yamato, however, the narrative takes a sudden turn toward violence when the elder of two brothers refuses submission. Betrayed by the younger brother (Oto-ukashi), the elder brother (Ye-ukashi) is killed inside the very trap that he had prepared for his enemies: "They then pulled him out and *cut up and scattered [his body]*. Therefore, this place is called the *bloody fields of Uda*. Then the *banquet fare* (*ōmiae*) that had been offered by Oto-ukashi was bestowed upon the troops."[34]

After this ritual slaughter, the narrative continues with an account of Jimmu's defeat of the tsuchigumo. The tsuchigumo were probably local groups, possibly chieftains, who refused to submit to the center's authority. In *Nihon shoki*, their name is always represented by graphs meaning "earth spiders."

Although this usage may contain a reference to the cultic behavior of the tsuchigumo, its use in *Nihon shoki* belongs to that same rhetoric of otherness that is applied elsewhere to people outside the court's orbit of authority.[35] Their defeat at the hands of Jimmu's forces is described in the following passage from *Kojiki*:

> When he journeyed from that place [Uda] and arrived at the pit dwelling of Osaka, there were eighty fierce (*yaso takeru*) tsuchigumo waiting inside the pit dwelling making a clamor. Thereupon the child of the heavenly deity gave an order to make a *banquet* (*ae*) for the eighty fierce men. He then assigned eighty servers to the eighty fierce men, and had each one wear a sword. He then instructed the servers saying: "As they are listening to your song, strike them all at once." Then, to signal their intention to slay the tsuchigumo, they sang: "In the pit-dwelling of Osaka / there are / many people / although there are / many people / the gallant / boys of Kume / holding mallet-headed swords / stone-mallets / will strike them unceasingly / the gallant / boys of Kume / holding mallet-headed swords / stone-mallets / will now strike them." After they sang this, they drew their swords and struck them dead all at once.[36]

In commenting on this passage, the *Kojiki* scholar Saigō Nobutsuna has suggested that the Kume song that ends this account was a warrior song performed as a form of mock combat, normally in the setting of a banquet, suggesting that the episode represented an already formalized ritual occasion.[37] But what lies back of this ritual occasion? One well-established view, implicit in Saigō's reading, is that the offerings of song and dance presented at court banquets symbolized the act of political submission. The court's authority is thereby grounded in a relatively benign ritual transfer of power to the center.[38] But was this in fact the case? One striking feature in the episode is the doublings and mirror effects produced by the repeated use of the numeral eighty (a sacred number in Japanese), an effect also discernible in the pairing of the two brothers in the previous episode. The literary theorist René Girard has explained such effects as follows:

> The most delicately choreographed patterns, positions exchanged while partners remain face to face, mirroring effects—all of this can be read as the purified and schematized trace of past confrontations . . . In order to reproduce a model of the mimetic crisis in a spirit of social harmony, the enactment must be progressively emptied of all real violence so that only the "pure" form is allowed to survive.[39]

The mimetic crisis, as defined by Girard, refers to a process of escalating *imitative* violence within a community that leads to a complete breakdown of order, ultimately threatening the total destruction of the community. It is resolved when the violence that has taken possession of the community converges onto a single member, whose subsequent deification and the rituals that commemorate his death preempt further violence by reenacting it in symbolic form.[40] Although Girard's theory has been widely criticized as reductive,[41] by disturbing the sometimes overly facile aesthetic reading of much ritual behavior, it has raised important questions about the coincidence of ritual and violence found in a certain type of mythological or legendary narrative. In the present examples, the widely held view that ritualized offerings to the court, typically performed in the setting of a banquet, reflected the *peaceful submission* of the conquered looks less persuasive when set against the contradictions that emerge inside single narratives (as in these two examples from *Kojiki*'s version of Jimmu's subjugation narrative) or even more starkly when parallel accounts in *Nihon shoki* and *Kojiki* are compared (as in the Yamato Takeru narrative).

To return to *Kojiki*'s ritual intent, is it possible to reconcile *Kojiki*'s structural violence, understood as internal to the maintenance of the tennō's authority, with a tennō whose monopoly over sacred speech legitimated him in his role as civilizer? The answer, I suggest, lies in recognizing that *Kojiki* remains fundamentally ambivalent in its own representation of violence and on several accounts. First, the narrative of Yamato Takeru, who is deified at the end and thereby transformed from a dangerous to a beneficent power, is at once a repetition of the violence that accompanied the effort to impose centralized rule and an instance of the same ritual transfer of power to the center that Yamato Takeru effects through soliciting the raging deities to offer up their speech. In the most literal sense, *Kojiki* may be said to perform what it narrates, especially if we take into account Hiyeda no Are's revocalization of the text. But beyond this structural ambivalence, *Kojiki* is ambivalent in its claims:

> Prostrate, I consider how Her Imperial Majesty, gaining the One, illumines the Universe; being in communion with the Three, nurtures the populace.
> Ruling in the Purple Pavilion, her virtue extends to the limit of the horses' hoof-prints; dwelling in the Concealed Palace, her influence illumines the furthest extent of the prows of the boats.[42]

In this passage from the Preface, we are closer to the ideology of the sage ruler, to *Nihon shoki*'s magniloquent recasting of the Yamato Takeru legend, than the stark ritual violence of *Kojiki*'s world. This contradiction, I suggest, accounts for *Kojiki*'s relative neglect soon after its production. Just as the *chinkonsai*, the preeminent rite for placating the raging deities, was undermined by the unmanageable effects of defilement, the *Kojiki* appears to reflect a historical moment in which the ruler aspired to, without ever actually achieving, a ritual monopoly over the effects of violence that arose from the effort to impose centralized rule.

Ambulation and the Construction of a Central Space

So far, the focus has been on the narrative and ritual aspects of *Kojiki* and *Nihon shoki*. The establishment of a religio-political center also involved very specific ways of thinking about and relating to space. Among the variants of the Yamato Takeru legend, the version found in *Hitachi fudoki* is especially illuminating on this point. Although questions about the dating of the text mean that any inferences drawn from it about the ancient period must necessarily be tentative,[43] by placing it within the broader framework of exile narratives, which remained remarkably constant throughout the premodern period, we can gain insight into the relationship between space, ritual, and royal authority.

In *Hitachi fudoki*, Yamato Takeru is first introduced in the following passage: "One account says: 'When the emperor Yamato Takeru was *on a tour* of the land of the emishi in Azuma *making an inspection* of the Niibari District, he dispatched the district ruler Hinarasu no mikoto and ordered him to dig a new well. The well-water was transparently pure and worthy of praise. Thereupon he *stopped his palanquin* to praise the water, and while he was asperging his hands the sleeve of his robe dipped into the spring and got wet. Because he dipped his sleeve (*sode wo hitasu*), he named the country [Hitachi].'"[44] Unlike *Nihon shoki* and *Kojiki*, where Yamato Takeru is merely an agent of Keikō's authority, here he appears in the full dignity of an emperor (*tennō* or *sumera no mikoto*) on a tour of inspection. What are we to make of this change of perspective? According to Isomae Jun'ichi, the *fudoki*, although compiled by local officials for authorities in the center, are best viewed not as "conflicting with the *Kojiki* and *Nihon shoki* accounts" but as "supplementing them from a different perspective." In contrast to the latter, which "traced the process of expansion and consolidation of Yamato rule through a chronological account centered on the imperial lineage, the *fudoki* looked at this same issue spatially, surveying the geographical extent of the imperial line's involvement in the development of the land through tours and expeditions of pacification. While having different narrative purposes, these works complemented each other."[45] By locating the *fudoki* within the discourse of the center, Isomae is arguing, in effect, that Yamato Takeru acts on behalf of the center. The Hitachi Yamato Takeru may conduct himself like a local sovereign, but his acts of naming and surveying the land ultimately serve the political interests of the center. Mitani Kuniaki likewise argued that *Hitachi fudoki*'s legends about the origins of placenames paralleled the emergence and control of political power centered around the Yamato court.[46] A contrary view is presented by Kamio Tokiko. Drawing on Shida Jun'ichi's theory that the Yamato Takeru portion of *Hitachi fudoki* transmits a fragment of the original text that survived subsequent abridgements, Kamio reads the narrative as a countermyth to the official version in the chronicles that inscribes a heterodox sphere of royal authority in the Hitachi district of the Tōgoku region. In contrast to *Kojiki*'s Yamato Takeru, who names the land in the course of his *wanderings* after his expulsion from the center, the Hitachi Yamato Takeru inscribes the land while making a *royal progress* through it.[47]

Even if we assume that the Hitachi district possessed its own independent tennō ideology, or myth of royal authority—an argument supported, I believe, by the evidence of regional myths like that of Izumo Furune just examined—it is also the case that as the Yamato court consolidated power, achieving a position of relative dominance, counterclaimants were eventually compelled to speak in its language. In this sense, Isomae is probably right to view the *fudoki*, which are primarily about the toponymic reordering of the land,[48] as representing an extension of the center's authority in spatial terms.

Although belonging to a later period, probably the thirteenth to fourteenth centuries, an episode from *Hōgen monogatari* (*The Tale of Hōgen*) about the banishment of the warrior Minamoto no Tametomo provides a useful commentary on this problem. Early in the tale, Tametomo is introduced in the following words:

> This Tametomo was from boyhood of an *extraordinarily fierce nature* (*motte no hoka no aramono nite*), disdaining his elder brothers and

behaving as if he were the only one in the world. As a result, the Hōgan [his father Tameyoshi] was unable to manage him. Believing that if he left him in the capital things would come to harm, *he dispatched him to Chinzei.*[49]

The raging aspect of Tametomo, echoing the "mighty and fierce temper" (*takeku araki kokoro*) of Yamato Takeru, together with the hint of fraternal strife and Tametomo's banishment to the periphery, provides a close parallel to *Kojiki*'s account of the legendary hero.[50] On the other hand, Tametomo's appropriation of the language of royal authority in the next passage also gives him a curious resemblance to the Yamato Takeru depicted in *Hitachi fudoki*. Here, the captured Tametomo is being readied for exile to Tsukushi:

"You fellows, listen to me. Although for other people exile is a grief, for me it's a joy. Pampered like a virtuous sovereign, I am placed on a litter with an escort of guards and at every post-station inn treated with food and other attentions. Truly, is it not an honor to be dispatched to my place of exile like this! What glory could surpass it?"[51]

By likening his treatment to that of a virtuous sovereign, Tametomo evokes the image of an emperor about to make a royal progress, thereby inverting the negative implications of his expulsion from the center. As the comparison of these episodes suggests, the shift in Yamato Takeru's status from that of banished exile to tennō is really inverted images of the same figure, with movement under its negative sign coded as wandering, and circuitous movement in the form of a royal progress coded as a sign of authority. By the time of the *fudoki*, the latter was being claimed as the exclusive privilege of the emergent *ritsuryō* state embodied in the tennō.

As space was reorganized around a metaphorical and geographical center tied to the religious and political authority of the court, unauthorized *movement* inside or across its borders came to be seen as a sign of threat and subject to various forms of regulation, interdiction, and even suppression. According to the law codes, the unauthorized departure of a noble from the home district of the five central provinces was strictly forbidden and could be construed as an act of rebellion against the state; exiles, on the other hand, as in the example of the rebel Tachibana no Hayanari (d. 842), were reduced to the nonstatus signified by the term *hinin* (nonperson), a word that would later be applied in the medieval period to placeless wanderers and outcasts who handled or were otherwise implicated in defilement.[52]

If exile and wandering represented the inverse of ritualized movement in the form of imperial tours, they also had their parallel in the domain of sacred utterance. The contrary to the ritual capture of sacred speech (*kotomuke*) by the center—equivalent to inscribing, naming, and reordering the land under the authority of the court—was nomadic speech, which appears simultaneously with the creation of a geographical and metaphorical center. It is foreshadowed mythologically in a passage at the beginning of book two in *Nihon shoki*'s narrative of the Age of the Gods. Here, the deity Takamimusubi has just declared his intention to make his recently born grandchild, Amatsu-hiko-hiko-ho-no-ninigi, ruler of the Central Land of the Reed Plains: "But in the land, the deities sparkled like numerous fireflies, and the evil deities *buzzed* like flies. There were also plants and trees *every one of which was able to speak*. Thereupon, Takamimusubi no mikoto assembled all eighty of the gods and spoke as follows: 'I wish to have the *evil demons (akki)* in the Central Land of the Reed Plains *expelled and subdued*.'" [53] Here, in the abrupt style of myth, Takamimusubi no sooner utters his intent than the entire land is shown irrupting into a susurration of threatening speech sounds, prefiguring the religio-political conquest of the land exemplified in the journeys of Jimmu and Yamato Takeru. Just as the authority of the tennō was augmented on the ritual level by the capture and redirecting of speech toward the center—an act that the recitation and inscription of *Kojiki* may have symbolically performed—the control of terrain thereby achieved could be assured only as long as the center retained its capacity to mediate sacred speech. By the middle of the ninth century, the very period that saw the increasing involvement of yin-yang masters in expulsion rituals and the management of pollution taboos, the tennō's capacity to mediate sacred speech was clearly on the wane, to the extent that effects of internecine violence dating from the founding of Heiankyō were being newly conflated with spontaneous outbreaks of social and religious unrest in the provinces. Nomadic speech, encompassing the utterances and songs of itinerant groups and wandering shamans, now took on an increasingly threatening character that provoked suppression as well as renewed efforts by the center to co-opt it at the ritual level. One way to envision this change is as a reimagining of *Nihon shoki*'s myth of primordial speech in terms of new symbolic and ritual practices that included the assimilation of local deities within a Buddhist doctrinal framework.

Reassessing the Nomadic

As a glance at the scholarly literature published on premodern Japan during the 1970s and 1980s shows, there was a marked increase at this time in studies that organize their material around the concept of wandering.[54] This fresh interest in the nomadic was partly owing to the work of the historian Amino Yoshihiko. Amino turned his attention to a variety of nonagricultural peoples—hunters, traders, craftspeople, and performing artists—in an effort to complicate an analysis of premodern Japan that had been largely based on an agricultural model of social and economic development. Yet well before this turn in historical studies, folklorists and literature scholars like Yanagita Kunio and Orikuchi Shinobu had already begun to evince an intense interest in the nomadic and marginal. In 1928, Orikuchi published an essay on the medieval vagrants known as *gorotsuki*, whose origins he traced to a population of drifters (*ukarebito*) in the ancient period, Orikuchi's preferred vernacular reading for the graphs 浮浪.[55] In Orikuchi's account, the ukarebito had once served at court where they had charge of mysterious arts of a sacred nature. After their ties to the court weakened and to escape taxation, they are supposed to have fled to the mountains and forests where they led a wandering life, gradually merging over the centuries with other marginal groups. Among these, Orikuchi numbered Gyōki's mendicant followers, low-class yin-yang ritualists (*onmyōji*), and a host of medieval itinerants that included outcast preachers (*shōmonji*), mountain ascetics (*shugenja*), shrine menials (*jinnin*), yamabushi, and many others.[56] Readers familiar with Amino's work will recognize many of his nonagricultural types among Orikuchi's vagrants. Yet if Amino's work represents an attempt to question established ideas about Japanese identity, through a conscious act of historical recovery, Orikuchi's broken lineage of wanderers, who drift in and out of history, becoming almost invisible in times of strong governmental authority, have that element of the uncanny that the cultural anthropologist Marilyn Ivy has called "phantasmatic," a projection of the modern nostalgia for lost origins.[57]

Are the claims made for this nomadic culture, then, no more than a sign of modernity's preoccupation with absence and cultural identity? We can be helped here by placing this issue in a broader cultural and philosophical framework. As several studies by the historian Carlo Ginzburg have shown, wandering was characteristic of a variety of heterodox religious activities that were relegated to marginal status throughout much of the European and Asian cultural spheres in the early modern period. Among the wealth of evidence amassed by Ginzburg is the phenomenon of soul loss among the *benandanti*, or "good-walkers," of sixteenth-century Italy, who, according to their own accounts, would journey at night from their bodies to engage in ritual battle at harvest time with witches and other demonic spirits. Ginzburg surmises that the proliferation of such cults at the margins of premodern European society, which were denounced as heretical by defenders of religious orthodoxy, probably derived from a common source in ancient shamanistic practices.[58] In the case of Japan, it might be argued, the shaman or medium had a recognized place in both organized religious institutions and in rituals at the court going back to a period well before the onset of modernity. Shamanistic activity, in other words, hardly qualifies as a marginal religious behavior in premodern Japan. But this is only partially correct. If mediumistic practices were granted a place within sanctioned religious rites and at court, it is also the case that shamanistic and other forms of nomadic speech that proliferated outside the reach of court and temples tended to be viewed with suspicion and fear by the authorities. Moreover, they were often linked to wandering and an itinerant lifestyle. This becomes especially pronounced in the eighth century, the same period in which an awareness of the heretical or sinister way crystallizes a hitherto unknown fear of anomic behaviors that flourish at the confines of the court's power. Thus, during one of the most aggressive periods of state formation in Japan, fears over the use of illicit magic, bewitching speech, and other forms of sorcery merge into anxiety over widespread vagabondage and itinerant religious activity, all of this unfolding against a background of recurrent plagues and natural calamities. The authorities of the fledgling state feared the nomadic in all of its manifestations.

It is here that questions raised earlier in the chapter in regard to Yamaguchi Masao's structuralist reading of the Yamato Takeru legend return to disclose a fundamental problem presented by the nomadic. Yamaguchi, it will be recalled, interpreted the Yamato Takeru narrative as a mythic displacement for the occult link between the violent and chaotic energies of the periphery and the authority of the ruler who inhabits the center. In commenting on structuralism's inadequacy when confronted with such chaotic energies or "transformations," the philosopher Gilles Deleuze writes: "When structuralism encounters becomings of this kind pervading a society, it sees them only as phenomena of degradation representing a deviation from the true order and pertaining to the adventures of diachrony." Invoking the work of Jean Duvigand on heresy and subversion, he then asks if there are not "'anomic' phenomena pervading societies that are not degradations of the mythic order but irreducible dynamisms drawing lines of flight and implying other forms of expression than those of myth, even if myth recapitulates them in its own terms in order to curb them?"[59] Deleuze's answer to this question is the nomadic, and it casts the entire issue of ambulation and itinerancy in premodern Japan, including center–periphery relations, in a different light.

As originally defined by Deleuze in the philosophical work *Difference and Repetition*, the nomadic designated ways of relating to space that were opposed to thinking derived from agrarian habits of dividing things up, distinguishing parts, assigning attributes, and the like. "Then there is a completely other distribution which must be called nomadic, a nomad *nomos*, without property, enclosure or measure . . . To fill a space, to be distributed within it, is very different from distributing the space." To distribute space is the procedure of all states, which structure space and divide it up in accordance with binary logic, turning it into what Deleuze in later writings defines as "striated space." In *Difference and Repetition*, the nomadic

> distribution is demonic rather than divine, since it is a peculiarity of demons to operate in the intervals between the gods' fields of action, as it is to leap over the barriers or enclosures, thereby confounding the boundaries between properties. Oedipus' chorus cries: 'Which demon has leapt further than the longest leap?' The leap here bears witness to the unsettling difficulties that nomadic distributions introduce into the sedentary structures of representation.[60]

In his subsequent "nomadology," Deleuze developed this demonic side of the nomadic into a radical critique of the state that takes back for the nomadic the negative signs that the state typically ascribes to it. What the state interprets as signs of plague, contagion, and deviations from the established order belong, when viewed from the side of the nomadic, to the nomad's heterogeneous condition of becoming. If the state gives to this movement the form of an exile—as in Yamato Takeru and other myths—the nomadic is a "line of flight," known by its animal or "anomic" features, its pack characteristics, and tendency to associate by alliances rather than the filiations that obtain in the hierarchical striated space of the state.[61] Medieval Japan, a period of contracting state authority, also had a name for this set of behaviors, the "heteromorphic" (*igyō*)—"evil bands" (*akutō*) and birdlike tengu being two of its characteristic expressions—but the nomadic as a social and religious phenomenon is already becoming visible in the Nara period, a time of aggressive state formation and legal codification.

Of particular interest in this regard are a series of government decrees against vagabondage and prohibited religious activity, including groups associated with the itinerant priest Gyōki (668–749). The following passage from an edict issued in 717 details widespread vagabondage in the provinces:

> Commoners in the hinterlands wander about in all directions, evade the labor corvée, and end up working for the royals and ministers. Some desire to become retainers; and others to become monks. The powerful do not keep to their own properties, but wantonly make use of these commoners, place demands on districts and provinces, and do just as they want. As a result, they wander about in the open and do not return to their home places. If there are such fellows, you can easily take them in hand, and after assessing their crimes, mete out punishment. Do this in accordance with the penal and administrative codes. Moreover, in accordance with the codes, let the monks and nuns take those sixteen years of age and under who do not provide labor or tribute and make them into their servants.[62]

The picture evoked here is that of a rural landscape permeated by instability. In describing its underlying social and economic causes, the historian Wayne Farris writes of "the repeated outbreak of epidemics" that continued throughout much of the late seventh to ninth centuries. "Plagues slowed population growth, which in turn meant a shortage of labor for farming. Pestilence also fostered population mobility which was not conducive to the settled rice agriculture preferred by court aristocrats."[63] If population mobility brought about in part by plagues undermined the court's agricultural system, the same "hyakusho" or commoners who helped to swell the ranks of Gyōki's followers included not only farmers but people engaged in a variety of nonagricultural pursuits, many of which were connected to an itinerant lifestyle.[64] The following passage is from an edict issued about a month earlier regarding the activity of Gyōki:

> These days, the insignificant monk Gyōki and his disciples roil about in the streets, recklessly interpret bad and good omens, form gangs, and burn and peel the skin from their fingers and elbows. Going from house to house, they teach false doctrine, extort alms, speak lies that they denominate sacred doctrine, and beguile the commoners. The distinction between clerics and lay persons is confused, and the classes abandon their trades. Advancing, they disobey the Buddha's teaching; retreating, they violate the laws.[65]

Some of these activities remain imperfectly understood, but it is clear that Gyōki and his "gangs" from the viewpoint of the authorities were engaging in forms of prohibited speech, including "yōwaku" (beguilements), which was listed as a forbidden activity in the Codes for Priests and Nuns. Another of the charges, to "recklessly interpret bad and good omens," was also prohibited. As Janet Goodwin has remarked, Gyōki may have been deliberately stirring up resentment by "suggesting that disasters such as floods or famines were indications of government wrongdoing."[66] Although Gyōki, as Goodwin also points out, was subsequently enlisted by the authorities to assist in the construction of Tōdaiji, and thus co-opted by the establishment, similar edicts indicate that Gyōki's activity was merely one instance of a widespread phenomenon. In 729, for example, shortly after the Prince Nagaya incident, an edict couched in much the same language was again issued by the court. After fulminating against the activity of brigands in the capital and provinces, it switches to the provinces of Aki and Suwa, where people recklessly interpret evil and propitious signs, assemble in large crowds, and use magic in worshiping the dead. It then directs its attention toward "the woods and fields" just east of the capital, where people are "assembling in large crowds" and "beguiling the crowd with predictions."[67] In sharp contrast to the language of the administrative codes, with their distinctions of hierarchy, secular and sacred, and prohibited and allowable activity, the object of concern in these edicts are nameless crowds and gangs, who assemble at the border or outside the confines of the new capital Heijō or, in the case of Gyōki, in the market that was itself a gathering spot for drifters and vagabonds.[68] To quote Deleuze once more: "Sorcerers have always held the anomalous position, at the edge of the fields or woods. They haunt the fringes. They are at the borderline of the village, or *between* villages. The important thing is their affinity with alliance, with the pact, which gives them a status opposed to that of filiation. The relation with the anomalous is one of alliance. The sorcerer has a relation of alliance with the demon as the power of the anomalous."[69] As "the power of the anomalous," the demon is also linked to contagion and plague. Although Deleuze reads contagion from a position outside the logic of the state—that is, as a sign of the nomad's heterogeneous state of becoming—the state always confounds heterogeneity with plague. This doubtlessly contributed to the increasingly ambiguous status of ritualists in the Heian period, among them the court yin-yang masters, some of whom were closely involved in plague rites that made use of animal skins.

Nomadic Speech: From Shamans to Wandering Deities

The kinds of bewitching and prophetic speech that become the object of government censure in the Nara period belong in a broader view to the phenomenon of nomadic speech, which has a strong relationship to ritual, narrative, and space. In this broad sense, nomadic speech comprises everything from shamanistic or oracular utterance to prophetic songs (*wazauta*), rumor, and stories tied to specific groups, or much of what has come to be known as setsuwa-type narrative. The earliest collection of the latter, *Nihon ryōiki*, contains dozens of tales about strange transformations that clearly belong to an anomic cultural assemblage. Both *Kojiki* and *Heike monogatari* may be characterized as narratives that *assemble* nomadic utterance on a large scale, the former by anchoring it to the center and the latter by taking on the very form of a nomadic history (*yūgyō no rekishi*). The remainder of this chapter focuses on the relationship between nomadic speech and several large-scale efforts to capture or domestic it in new ritual behavior. I begin with a look at several incidents connected to shamanistic behavior in the Nara and early Heian periods.

Shamanism in Japan has been variously characterized as ambulatory or sedentary in form, a combination of the two, or as initially sedentary but taking on ambulatory characteristics after the breakdown of the ritsuryō state.[70] More recently, Nishimiya Hideki, drawing on a wide range of historical and literary sources, has concluded that "the shamans (*fugeki*) found among the people in ancient Japanese society have the singular characteristic of ambulation; there is no clear evidence for arguing the newness or antiquity of the sedentary type."[71] The description of asobibe in *Ryō no shūge* exemplifies the nomadic character of ancient mediums: "They often placate violent spirits, therefore they never employ themselves at anything; they evade the labor tax and *roam about* at will. Thus they are called *asobibe*." An additional gloss in the same commentary states: "Asobibe: those who pacify the evil and diseased spirits at the border that separates the living and the dead. They never employ themselves at anything, therefore they are called *asobibe*." In remarks on these passages, Gorai Shigeru has noted the affiliation between the asobibe and later ritualists such as *itako* ("shamanic medium"), *azusa miko* ("catalpa bow medium"), *kumano bikuni* ("Kumano nun"), and *aruki miko* ("walking shamanic medium"), all of whom led a wandering life.[72]

Eighth- and ninth-century references to the shamanlike figures represented by the graphs 巫覡 (*fugeki*) indicate that they engaged in a variety of practices, including spirit communication, magical cursings, prayers for good fortune, the cure of illness, and predictions.[73] Official attitudes during this same period ranged from ambivalence at best to outright hostility in some cases. A *Shoku nihongi* entry for the year 752, for example, records the capture in the capital of seventeen shamans (*fugeki*) and their expulsion to Izu, Oki, and Tosa, suggesting that they were viewed as a cause of social disorder in the capital.[74] Other sources indicate that the curing of illness, banned inside the capital, was given official sanction outside its borders.[75] On the other hand, the involvement of these shamanlike figures with magical prayers, curses, and oracular speech was clearly viewed by the government as a threat.[76] One frequently cited text is an entry in *The Veritable Record of Japan's Montoku Tennō* (*Nihon Montoku tennō jitsuroku*), which records the government's suppression in 827 of female shamans in Mino province:

> There were female shamans in the district of Mushiroda. Spirits roamed about secretly prying into people's minds. Their bands are rampant, and the people are plagued by them. For years, the officials have harbored a great fear of them, and they do not dare to enter the district. Takafusa entered with a unit of mounted warriors. He captured the whole lot; prompt and severe was their punishment. Not again will they plague people's minds with their prying.[77]

In a report that reflects the interests of the central authorities, it is difficult to judge the reliability of the description, but the language suggests that the shamans (represented by the graphs 妖巫) were involved in the manipulation of spirits.[78] The roaming may therefore refer as much to the spirits as to the shamans themselves inasmuch as the text is not clear on whether they were an ambulatory or sedentary cult. Although they are represented as a menace to the people, their suppression by an agent of the central authorities, as will be discussed later, may have had a political motivation.

In addition to the revulsion and terror evoked by local shaman cults at this time, aristocratic society in the capital was increasingly beset by vague fears connected to malign spirits. References to spirit possession in the national histories increase significantly at this time, with *Shoku nihon kōki* (869), compiled under the close supervision of Fujiwara no Yoshifusa (805–877), containing no less than thirteen references to malign spirits (*mononoke*).[79] New rituals aimed at placating them also proliferate. The following entry from *Nihon sandai jitsuroku* describes events surrounding the first officially sponsored spirit service (*go-ryōe*), which was held in the garden of the Greater Palace in the fifth year of Jōgan (863) to placate destructive plague deities and vengeful spirits:

> The spirits named are Sudō Tennō, Iyo Shinnō, Fujiwara no Yoshiko, the inspector, Tachibana no Hayanari, and Fun'ya no Miyatamaro. All of these were executed and have become vengeful spirits and demons. For some time now pestilence has raged and the number of dead is exceedingly high. Throughout the realm, it is believed that the disasters are the result of their spirits. They are spreading from the capital and home provinces to the outer provinces. Every summer and autumn placation rites are held without respite.[80]

Sudō Tennō was the posthumous name of Prince Sawara (d. 785), the younger brother of Kammu (r. 781–806).[81] Like Temmu and his nephew Prince Ōtomo during the Jinshin Rebellion, the two brothers became involved in an internecine struggle for power that eventually led to the founding of a new capital and political order in Heiankyō. Prince Sawara, who had originally been designated crown prince, died while en route to exile as a punishment for his alleged plot to gain power, in the course of which Kammu's close associate Fujiwara Tanetsugu was slain. Like *Nihon shoki*'s account of the Jinshin Rebellion, the official narrative of these events as transmitted in *Shoku nihongi* has been heavily abridged, possibly reflecting Kammu's care to give his reign greater legitimacy.[82]

While the Jōgan era go-ryōe was clearly intended to placate the vengeful spirits of those who had perished in the course of political violence, the events leading up to it also coincided with the rise of the northern Fujiwara, who from this time on would exercise increasing influence over the throne. As Neil McMullin has suggested, it is quite possible that there was a deliberate effort on the part of the Fujiwara at this time to gain control over the go-ryō cult and thereby channel popular fears arising from plague-causing spirits into a ritual system that supported their own political ambitions.[83] Notwithstanding such manipulation, it is unlikely that the widespread rumors linking Prince Sawara's violent spirit to natural disasters, which began shortly after his death, were entirely orchestrated from the start.[84] The account in *Sandai jitsuroku* portrays a situation close to collective hallucination, with the destructive spirits of Sudō and others slain in the political violence having become indistinguishable from outbreaks of natural calamities and social turmoil in the provinces. If the Fujiwara were successful in exploiting the situation, it was partly because such supernatural visitations further undermined the religio-political authority that had been claimed by tennō such as Temmu and his successors. As discussed in Chapter 2, in the yin-yang cosmological worldview that underwrote the center's authority, calamities coupled with popular unrest would have been viewed as signs portending the tennō's loss of virtue.[85] Not surprisingly, by Yōzei's reign (876–884), or only thirteen years after the Jōgan era go-ryōe of 863, the magical principle of naming eras in accordance with favorable omens yielded to the practice of assigning era names aimed at warding off disasters. Since it was during this same period that yin-yang taboos (including the first indications of the directional taboos known as *kata-tagae*) began to put extraordinary restraints upon the movements of the tennō, we can surmise that the perceived threat posed by demonic infestation at this time was closely connected to efforts aimed at protecting the tennō against defilement.[86] The go-ryōe of 863 was not an isolated event but the culmination of a lengthy program of border rituals performed throughout the country in the preceding months aimed at expelling harmful spirits and soliciting propitious signs.[87]

At the same time, the function of the go-ryōe extended well beyond the immediate purposes of placation and defending against demonic infestation. As the historian Kuroda Toshio has shown, it also served as a mechanism for rearticulating the sacred character of threatening plague deities and vengeful spirits by gradually transforming them from unstable, wandering manifestations of the sacred (*yūgyō no kami*) into pacified benefit-conferring deities, contained and enshrined within properly defined sites.[88] The process of constructing and redefining the attributes of such divinities was part of a continuing process of articulating and defending the boundaries of the core space that began to take shape during the Nara and pre-Nara periods.

The process was repeated in the establishment of the Kitano tenjin cult devoted to the worship of Sugawara no Michizane, who died in exile after a protracted struggle with the Fujiwara. Formally established in 947, the Kitano cult was preceded by the composition of *Dōken shōnin meido ki (The Record of the Holy Man Dōken's Journey to the Underworld)*, an elaborate mythographic text composed in 941 as one of several efforts to placate Sugawara's vengeful spirit.[89] In the following passage, Sugawara addresses the holy man Dōken:

"Thus I have afflicted the emperor and ministers, brought calamities upon the people, and been intent on destroying the land. I am the agent of all disease and disasters . . . However, Samantabhadra and Nagarjuna have made the secret doctrines flourish, and from the beginning my love for this teaching has been deep. As a result, a tenth of my rancor has ceased. Moreover, all the transformed Bodhisattvas, on the strength of their compassionate vows, have borrowed the name of enlightened deity and now dwell either in the midst of mountain forests or on the banks of rivers and seashores. Each of them, to the full extent of their wisdom, has continuously placated me. Therefore, I no longer bring about great harm. However, the one-hundred sixty-eight thousand *evil deities* who attend me bring calamities everywhere, and I am unable to control them." [90]

Like the spirits appeased in the Jōgan era go-ryōe, Sugawara now visits plague and disaster upon the land. At the same time, the process that will transform him from a threatening power into a beneficent deity is already underway thanks to the intercession of Bodhisattvas, who appear to be local deities that have been converted to Buddhism. Beyond Sugawara's control, however, are the myriad evil deities that continue to threaten the land with destruction.

Dōken shōnin meidoki was only one of many efforts to appease Sugawara's spirit that were made against a backdrop of political turmoil and widespread popular unrest in the provinces, the most dramatic being the shidara no kami incident.[91] In 945, or only four years after the suppression of Masakado and Sumitomo, an event known as the Rebellion of the Shōhei and Tengyō Eras, the capital was rife with rumors that numerous divinities were pouring into the capital from east and west.[92] On the twenty-fifth day of the Seventh Month, three sacred palanquins (*shin'yo*), said to be shidara [no] kami, arrived in Teshima district, and by the twenty-ninth of the same month, they had reached Yamashiro province. According to an entry in *Rihō ōki*, the three *shin'yo* had been brought up village by village all the way from Kyūshū and bore the names of Jizai Tenjin, held to be the spirit of the deceased Sugawara, Usa Haru Ōmiko, and Sumiyoshi Kami (Sumiyoshi god). The first was eventually enshrined at Iwashimizu Hachimangū before reaching the capital, its name having mysteriously changed to Usa Hachimangū Daibosatu Miyashiro.[93] With the formal establishment of Sugawara's cult at Kitano two years later, in 947, his angry spirit, now redefined as a beneficent deity, was finally brought into an economy of ritual placation and thereby made into a protector of the state.

The shidara incident exemplifies how closely the phenomenon of nomadic speech was tied to the articulation of a religio-political center. As both Kawane and Sakurai Yoshirō suggest, the movement of the sacred palanquins that embodied the energy of the wandering *kami* was on one level a popular or mass phenomenon of the time, related to dislocations arising from changing patterns of land tenure. At the same time, the sacred character of the event was reinforced by the threatening movement of the palanquins themselves, which Sakurai has connected to the activity of wandering shamanesses (*miko*) who were responsible for the "prophetic songs" (*wazauta*) that would announce the arrival of the shidara no kami's palanquin.[94] As in the case of the go-ryōe, nomadic speech and wandering movement that are initially perceived as a threat are subsequently captured by being enshrined in a specific locality. The connection with prophetic songs, moreover, gives to the shidara no kami event an explicitly political character. Prophetic songs appear as far back as *Nihon shoki*, where they frequently occur at the end of the chronicles of Kinmei, Kōgyoku, Saimei, and Tenchi, and also appear in connection with shaman-type figures in both *Nihon shoki* and several *Ryōiki* tales. In the Chinese tradition of prophecy, which was clearly at work in *Nihon shoki*, "children's songs" (*wazauta* 童謡) had a basis in yin-yang five agents theory and omen-lore and were believed to predict revolutions of state. By the Nara period, the illicit prophecies attributed to Gyōki and other unlicensed priests had begun to merge with this earlier shamanistic tradition.[95]

The connection of nomadic speech to both wandering spirits and oracular utterance of a political cast explains why it was such a potent source of threat to the authorities. According to *Shōmonki*, the rebellion of Masakado, which took place only four years prior to the shidara incident, was authorized by an oracle spoken by a female shaman claiming the authority of Sugawara's spirit:

> During the proceedings, a shamaness appeared and uttered the following statement: "I am a messenger of the Great Bodhisattva Hachiman. I hereby confer upon my son Masakado the title of emperor. The spirit of the Minister of the Right Sugawara no Ason, holder of the senior rank, has presented in writing the Certificate of Conferment of Rank wherein are written these words: 'The aforesaid great Bodhisattva Hachiman hereby calls together eighty thousand soldiers and confers upon Masakado the title of emperor.' With the Hymn of the Thirty-Two Signs, we must welcome the emperor without delay."[96]

It might seem strange that Masakado should seek legitimacy for his revolt in an oracle spoken in the name of Sugawara, but we must remember that at this time Sugawara's spirit had not yet been appeased. As Robert Borgen notes, the "incident is in keeping both with Michizane's mortal duties as a drafter of government documents and with his posthumous activities opposing the dominant political faction at court." It also shows, continues Borgen, "that by 940 an awareness of Michizane's ghost as an enemy of the court had spread all the way to the then-remote Kantō plain."[97] This latter point captures the peril posed to the court by the volatility of sacred rumor and the nomadic speech of wandering shamans. Interestingly, a variant account of the oracle, recorded in Kujō Kanezane's *Gyokuyō* (*Jeweled Leaves*), makes no mention of Michizane's vengeful spirit. In discussing this point, Higuchi Kunio surmises that those responsible for the extant version of *Shōmonki* may have grafted a Kinai version of the legend onto what had originally been a local account. If this is the case, then the 827 suppression of shaman guilds in the Tōgoku region, discussed earlier, may well have been a reaction to political resistance authorized by local shaman cults, foreshadowing the later regional Masakado legend cited in Kanezane's *Gyokuyō*.[98] Like the inverted images of Yamato Takeru discussed earlier, the same oracular speech that threatens the center becomes the source of Masakado's regional authority as a tennō.

Conclusion

The period extending from the ninth to tenth centuries marked an important change in the way the tennō was conceptualized as ruler. Whereas the ruler of the ancient period has been variously characterized as an *arahitogami* (a sacral ruler comparable to a Buddha or *kami*, but here understood as the *Kojiki*-type ruler who mediates sacred speech) and a Daoist- or Chinese-style sage, with the rise of Fujiwara *sekkan* rule in the course of the ninth and tenth centuries, the tennō not only loses political power but begins to take on an increasingly symbolic role as a locus of purity that must be continuously defended against defilements and demonic infestation. The suppression of wandering shaman cults in 827, the periodic outbreaks of so-called popular unrest accompanied by demonic infestation that led to the establishment of the go-ryōe in 863, the placation of Sugawara no Michizane, and the shidara event are not only significant historical and factual data but also symbolic of the tennō's diminishing religio-political status. In brief, the perceived threat to the center from nomadic speech that eluded its control was a sign that the tennō's capacity to mediate sacred authority had been seriously undermined. No longer able to mediate the transfer of sacred speech from the periphery to the center (and by extension, to manage the effects of violence that attended the imposition of centralized rule), the ritual economies implicit in texts like *Kojiki* and *Nihon shoki* had effectively collapsed. It is to the emergence of new forms of historical narrative in the course of the Heian period that I now turn.

PERIPHERIES OF POWER

Toward an Ambulatory History

Introduction

When the Buddhist prelate Jien composed *Gukanshō* in the early thirteenth century, a work regarded as the first attempt to write a Buddhist historiography in Japan, he consciously modeled his history upon the "succession tale" (*yotsugi ga monogatari*), which at the time meant vernacular narratives like *A Tale of Flowering Fortunes* and *Ōkagami*. But Jien also felt it necessary to defend his decision to write in the vernacular with an explanation of its advantages over the more dignified Chinese.[1] In the present chapter, I am primarily concerned with this alternative world of written vernacular narrative as it emerges out of and then defines itself against writing in Chinese. The majority of the chapter, roughly the final two-thirds, focuses on the late eleventh-century *Ōkagami*, in which historical narrative for the first time takes on an ambulatory form, registering an important shift as royal authority renews its ties with the dangerous powers of the periphery. But first I deal with two topics that are fundamental to understanding *Ōkagami*'s transformation of historical narrative. The first concerns the generic identity of vernacular narrative as it moved from the world of orality into the sphere of written discourse. To move from an oral to a written form in ancient Japan involved more than a passage across the literacy divide, but entry into a bilingual world where Chinese was the dominant written medium, a situation that finds a historical parallel in that of Roman literature. As the Russian theorist Bakhtin writes, "Roman literary consciousness was bilingual. . . . From start to finish, the creative literary consciousness of the Romans functioned against the background of the Greek language and Greek forms."[2] Chinese in Japan took on some of the same functions as Greek in Latin literature, not only affecting the structure of the language but providing a set of literary types that was both emulated and challenged throughout much of the premodern period.[3] After a brief review of the modern critique of phonocentricism, I look at several factors that had repercussions on the way vernacular narrative types came to be constituted as a distinct discourse alongside the more dominant discourse in Chinese, including (1) the practical consequences of representing Japanese sounds and meanings with Chinese graphs and (2) the relationship between authoritative versus nonauthoritative discourse, which grows out of the interaction between oral and written forms of narrative. The texts discussed include the Preface to *Kojiki*, several passages from Imibe no Hironari's *Kogo shūi* (*Gleanings of Old Words*, 807), and the well-known debate on fiction in the "Hotaru" ("Fireflies") scroll of Murasaki Shikibu's *Genji monogatari*. The second topic relates to the ceremonial and ritual setting of historical narrative and more generally to the symbolic function of the banquet as a site for affirming royal authority. This is exemplified in the lectures on *Nihongi*, which functioned as the principal means whereby official history was transmitted to successive generations at court up through the first half of the Heian period. In their final phase in the tenth century, the lectures underwent a transformation that already prefigures the ritual world of *Ōkagami*, reminding us of how closely historical narrative remained anchored to a ritual world.

Voice, Writing, and Authority

Chapter 1 began this study with a reconsideration of the tendency among Tokugawa nativists to privilege a phonocentric reading of ancient texts. Attempts to account for this early modern emphasis on the oral character of the Japanese language have given rise to an extensive scholarship. Murai Osamu, for example, views the privileged status of orality in the writings of Keichū and Motoori as arising, in part, from new methods of reading associated with the rise of "print culture" during the Tokugawa period, which allowed the "voice" alienated by print to come to consciousness as the inner essence of the "community."[4] For Naoki Sakai, on the other hand, a flourishing print culture was one symptom in a larger epistemic shift that reorganized the regimes of reading, writing, listening, and speaking: "It is a consequence of this phonocentric transformation that the co-presence of two heterogeneous inscriptional principles in Japanese writing began to be perceived as a marker of the 'peculiarity' of Japanese language and, by extension, Japanese culture in general." As Sakai goes on to observe, the installment of such phonocentrism allowed Motoori to "allocate these inscriptional ideologies according to geopolitical mapping, phonocentricism for Japan and ideography for China."[5] In the Meiji period, the nativist privileging of orality as an expression of the communal voice was given a more explicitly nationalistic inflection under the influence of European romantic theories about the origins of folk song and national folk epics, allowing texts like *Man'yōshū* and *Heike monogatari* to be recast as collective expressions of the national voice that validated Japan's status as a modern nation state.[6]

Although the critique of phonocentrism has performed a useful task in demystifying a type of cultural essentialism that becomes increasingly pronounced from the early modern period on, the phenomenon of orality must remain a factor in any account of the ancient period. An ancient term like *kotodama* (word-spirit), for example, although invoked as something uniquely Japanese, also points to the widely held belief that spoken language, uttered under certain conditions, has magical properties. The connection here is to ritual and performative acts.[7] In the case of *Man'yōshū* poems, the scriptive and performative functions might coexist in a single text, suggesting the existence of two sites (*ba*), one connected to the poem's ritual voicing (in the vernacular) and another to the act of inscription itself.[8] Then there are the interactions of orality and writing. In the case of medieval European literature, the relationship between Latin, an authoritative written language, and emergent vernacular literatures in English or French was often one of religious, political, and philosophical contestation. The medievalist Jesse Gellrich, for example, has shown how the proliferation of written vernacular histories that foregrounded the speaking voice in fourteenth-century Europe participated in a general destabilizing of the divine voice (*vox*), which until then had grounded authority in both the secular and sacred domains.[9] Neither of these two dimensions of orality, its use in ritual and performative acts and its

specific valence within a dominant writing practice (Latin or Chinese), is connected in any obvious way to later modern constructions about the meaning
of orality, although questions of authority and truth certainly come into play.
At the same time, the different cultural and linguistic systems represented by
Chinese writing in Japan, as opposed to Latin in Europe, necessarily had a
strong bearing on the way orality and its modifications into vernacular writing got constructed in relationship to the authoritative writing practice. In
the case of Japan, the adaptation of Chinese writing had consequences that
reached beyond the hierarchy of forms into perceptions about the phonetic
and morphological structure of the language that in turn became part of the
unique economy of vernacular expression. This can be seen by turning to the
remarks of the scribe Yasumaro in the Preface to *Kojiki*.

The collaboration between the reciter Hiyeda no Are and the scribe Yasumaro that resulted in the text of *Kojiki* has been the subject of considerable debate. The Preface to *Kojiki* states that Hiyeda no Are was endowed
with perfect auditory and visual recall, suggesting that he may have been
able to read the ancient writings as well as recite oral traditions from memory. Whether his recitation was based on rote memorization of previously
unrecorded traditions, traditions already recorded in Chinese writing, or
some combination thereof can only be conjectured. Improvisation, in view
of what is known about subsequent traditions like *Heike* recitation, seems
unlikely. Nishimiya Kazutami has argued that *Kojiki* is best understood as
the written transcription of Hiyeda no Are's revocalization of already extant
written texts.[10] Whatever conclusion one reaches about the precise nature
of Hiyeda no Are's contribution to the collaboration, the scribe Yasumaro
dwells at some length on the difficulties that he faced in devising a method
of writing that would accurately transcribe the performer's recitation. Here
is the first part of his observations:

> On the eighteenth day of the Ninth Month in the fourth year of Wadō, I,
> Yasumaro, was ordered to present and record the *Kuji* that Hiyeda no Are
> recited by imperial command. Reverently, in accordance with the imperial
> will, I took them up *in detail*. However, in ancient times, words and their
> meaning were both simple. Spreading [them] out into writing, building
> [them] into phrases is difficult with graphs. Expressed logographically, *the
> words do not reach to the meaning; strung out entirely in sounds, the pur-
> port of these matters becomes long.*[11]

At the most basic level, Yasumaro's statement is a straightforward observation on the imperfect fit between the graphs and the words that he wishes

to record. But it is worth noting that what gets emphasized in the process is the sense of *an excess of meaning and sound* that is not easily reducible to written form. Yasumaro takes up the revocalized *Kuji* "in detail," but either "the words do not reach to the meaning" (i.e., the graphs do not capture the full sense of the Japanese words) or "the purport of these matters becomes long," referring to the large number of graphs required to represent the polysyllabic Japanese words. Yasumaro's solution, which he describes afterward, was the combination of "ideographic and phonetic writing," with occasional glosses, that characterizes *Kojiki* as a text. In this way, he was able to convey "in detail" both the meaning and the sonorous dimension of Hiyeda no Are's performance.[12] Although Yasumaro's observations represent a unique instance, the experience he records must have been repeated countless times under similar conditions, creating perceptions about the vernacular that contributed to an awareness of its difference from Chinese writing, a point that will be returned to later.

If Yasumaro's observations are primarily about the practical difficulties of representing Japanese sounds and meanings with Chinese graphs, *Kogo shūi*, composed about a hundred years later, registers a gap between the oral and written that has begun to take on ideological overtones. In the opening passage of his work, Imibe no Hironari decries the loss of ancient oral traditions that has accompanied the advance of writing:

> As is often heard, in ancient times when letters did not yet exist, everyone, high and low, old and young, transmitted things orally, and the words and deeds of former days were not forgotten. Since the instituting of writing, people are no longer fond of talking about the past. Empty rhetoric flourishes and old men are mocked. The generations pass and succeed to the new; the ages pass by, and things undergo changes. When we reflect and ponder the ancient matters, it is no longer possible to understand their origins. Although *The National Histories* and House Records have transmitted the main matters, *there are details that have been left out.* Unless I myself speak of them, in all likelihood they will perish without being transmitted. Graciously, I have been favored with an imperial request and intend to express my pent up anger. Therefore, I have recorded the ancient traditions and present them to the court.[13]

At issue for Hironari is not the inadequacy of the writing system but the loss of oral traditions brought about by the use of writing, a development complicated, in Hironari's case, by his own *uji*'s increasingly marginal political status. For generations, the Imibe had charge of important religious cults and myths (later known as Shinto), but when Fujiwara no Kamatari, a member of the rival Nakatomi *uji*, achieved supremacy following the destruction of the Soga in 645, the Imibe were gradually excluded from their share in political and religious power, which was now centered in the ruling line established by Temmu. The Imibe's myths, in brief, were pushed to the margins of official discourse, which is indicated in Hironari's text by his pointed reference to *The National Histories*.[14] To better grasp what this meant for Hironari, we must take a closer look at how official discourse in Chinese began to reorganize the hierarchy of narrative types.

According to the literature scholar Fujii Sadakazu, the term *furukoto* (ancient words/matters), represented in the titles of works like *Kojiki* (*Record of Ancient Things*), *Kogo shūi*, and *Kuji* (*Ancient Matters*), designated oral narratives long fixed by tradition that had acquired an authoritative aura even before being put down in writing.[15] It was this fixity and perceived authority of *furukoto* that set them apart from other forms of narrative, not any fundamental distinction between the written as opposed to the oral form of the narratives.[16] Yet once writing had established itself as the principal medium for transmitting the orthodox narratives, the complex mechanisms of oral transmission began to break down, a process to which Hironari himself makes reference. Hironari's choice, then, was either to fix his traditions in writing and present them to the court or leave them to inevitable oblivion or an even unkindlier fate. What this latter might be is hinted at by Hironari at the end of his text, where, in a final appeal to the emperor, he refers to his own narratives in a striking phrase: "Even talk of the markets and streets (*gaikō no dan*) should be heeded at times; to cast aside the thoughts of a commoner is not an easy thing to do."[17] In the official discourse that overshadows Hironari's text from the start, "talk of the markets and streets" would have fallen within the range of meaning encompassed by the Chinese term *xiao shuo* (Jp. *shōsetsu*). In Han times, as Sheldon Lu discusses, *xiao shuo* was classified by the historian Ban Gu (32–92) as a subcategory of philosophical discourse, or "a form of philosophical and sophistic persuasion that complete[d] and challenge[d] the predominant discourse of the Confucian canons (*ching*)." Ban Gu further traced the origins of *xiao shuo* "to the ancient office of *pai-kuan* [*baiguan*], a minor historian-official whose responsibility was to channel the gossip of the back alleys and streets to the court." For the author of the seventh-century *Sui shu* (629–656), "*hsiao-shuo* [*xiao shuo*] were the talk of the streets." *Xiao shuo* thus encompassed a range of meanings, but all of them placed it in sharp opposition to the orthodoxy of official history (*shi*), and at its furthest remove, it was no more than trivial talk and gossip.[18]

To return to Hironari's closing appeal, it is possible of course that "gaikō no dan" was intended to convey a meaning less jarring than its literal sense. His use of the humilific pronoun *guchin* (foolish retainer) earlier in the same passage, for example, suggests that the phrase was, on one level, a formal gesture of deference toward the emperor. Fujii has further conjectured that the phrase may even have been intended ironically by Hironari as a way of asserting the legitimacy of his clan's ancient traditions (*furukoto*).[19] But is it likely that Hironari, who wrote of the eclipse of oral traditions under the shadow of official history, could have been unaware of the implied distinction between official and unofficial history in choosing such an expression? In short, if we hold to the plain sense of the text here, it seems reasonable to conclude that Hironari felt that his own uji's traditions were on the verge of becoming just what he states, "talk of the markets and streets," or everything that lay outside the official discourse of the day.

As a text, then, *Kogo shūi* suggests that the prestige of official history was already affecting the way orthodox oral traditions were being conceptualized. From here, it is but a short distance to the emergence of written vernacular narrative. In a now classic study, Mitani Eiichi argued that the term *monogatari* may initially have marked a distinction between the orthodox utterances (*furukoto*, *katarigoto*) of an uji's own deities and those narratives that belonged to deities outside the uji (*mono yosogami*). Once these orthodox narratives severed their ties to local cults and began to be disseminated broadly throughout society, they gradually became matter for entertainment, or written vernacular fiction (*monogatari*).[20] Mitani's theory, like Fujii's contrast between the fixed orthodox furukoto and other types of oral narrative, rests on distinctions internal to vernacular or oral narrative types; but by at least the time of Murasaki Shikibu, such distinctions were being articulated from inside a dominant practice of writing in Chinese, as the famous discussion about *monogatari* in the "Fireflies" chapter of *Genji monogatari* makes clear. In the most revealing passage, *monogatari* is defined in relation to the narrative tradition of *Nihongi*, a term that probably referred to the entire corpus of official history, and not simply *Nihon shoki*, the first in the series.[21] In responding to Genji's frivolous dismissal of *monogatari* as a species of idle lies, Tamakazura says: "Indeed, people accustomed to speaking falsehoods might reason in such a fashion. I myself think of [*monogatari*] as narrations of the truth pure and simple." Stung by the rebuff, Genji then undertakes to defend *monogatari*.

> "Most rudely, I have spoken ill of them. They have recorded matters in this world from the Age of the Gods. *Nihongi* and the rest are simply one-sided. In these [*monogatari*] there will be found edifying (*michimichishiku*) and detailed (*kuwashiki*) matters," said Genji with a smile.[22]

Whereas Genji had earlier characterized *monogatari* as fabrications and lies, here he ironically places them on a virtual equality with the narratives of *Nihongi*, which are characterized as only a "one-sided" expression of the truth.[23] The term *michimichishiku*, translated as "edifying," represents an ironic use of a term more usually associated with the canonical Chinese works, or *Sanshi wujing*, whose moral, ethical, and political concepts informed much of *Nihongi* and the ideology of the court.[24]

As the earliest attempt to articulate a defense of vernacular narrative, Murasaki's text has become the starting point for a good deal of theorizing on *monogatari* as a specific narrative type. But what did it mean to write *monogatari*? Did Murasaki set out to emulate history, challenge its authority, or parody its claims through something that approximates a kind of "fiction"?[25] Modern scholarship on *Genji* has tended to favor the view that Murasaki was writing a fictional (*kyokō*) as opposed to a factual (*jijitsu*) account of events. Yet an important strand in the medieval commentary on *Genji monogatari* viewed the work as a successor to the official histories. The *Myōjōshō* (ca. 1595) speaks of *Genji* as bridging in the gap left in the historical record for Daigo's reign that resulted from the discontinuance of official history after *Sandai jitsuroku*. The *Mingō nisso* (1598), a commentary compiled by Nakanoin Michikatsu (1556–1610), likewise draws comparisons between *Genji*, *Eiga monogatari*, and "succession tales" and the tradition of official history in Chinese represented by works like the *Shi ji* and the *Han shu*.[26] This tendency in medieval *Genji* scholarship can be dismissed as a strategy for enhancing the status of what by then was perceived as an inferior narrative type, but it also points back to the long-standing prestige of historical narrative in shaping perceptions of vernacular narrative.

But the relationship between the two was not merely one of *Nihongi* or official history lording it over vernacular narrative. Already in Murasaki, we find a writer who is poaching, as it were, on official history's own terrain, as in her ironic appropriation of the term *michimichishiku*. At the same time, the residual orality of written vernacular continued to be a factor in its perceived characteristics or narrative economy.[27] Thus, Genji's coupling of *monogatari* with the adjective "detailed" (*kuwashi*) recalls not only Hironari's reference to the "details" of an oral tradition that was left out of the official record but also that copiousness of sound and meaning that surfaced in Yasumaro's remarks on transcribing Hiyeda no Are's recitation. In articulating itself *against* official history, vernacular fiction became identified, I suggest, with a copiousness and multiplicity of view that were perceived to be absent in official discourse. The dialogical nature of monogatari, with its layering of "other voices," or heteroglossia,[28] along with its capacity to absorb other genres (as in the medieval *Heike*) derives in large measure from this marginal status and clash with authoritative discourse,[29] as does that intent to parody discerned by scholars like Takahashi Tōru and Norma Field. These same tendencies, as we will see later, break out with peculiar force in *Ōkagami*, where the gossip, rumor, and "talk of the streets" that were repressed from official history not only reassert themselves but, in merging with the nomadic sounds of sacred rumor, signal a reritualization of historical narrative.

Sendai kuji *and the Lectures on* Nihongi

In a notable departure from the practice of Chinese-style historiography, one of the main functions of *The National Histories* was to praise and magnify rather than censure the tennō. The idea is well expressed in the Kamakura period work *Godai teiō monogatari* (*Stories of Five Reigns and Their Emperors*): "The felicitous matters (*medetaki kotodomo*) of generations of emperors from the Age of the Gods can be seen in detail in *The National Histories*, the succession tales, and the house diaries." [30] This link between official history and the ceremonial function of celebrating the tennō's authority is nowhere more evident than in the "lectures on *Nihongi*" (*Nihongi-kō*), which were held seven times, or about once every generation, from 721 to 965. Attended by the cream of the nobility, the interpretive lectures constituted a type of "textual community" in which the oral recitation and explication of the inaugural history helped to reaffirm the bonds between the tennō and the court.[31] At the conclusion of the lectures, which extended over a period of years, a closing banquet was held during which participants would present congratulatory *waka*, singling out the various tennō who appear in the chronicle for their virtuous government, meritorious deeds, prosperity, and the like.[32] The termination of the lectures toward the end of the tenth century was probably not unrelated to the cessation of official court history earlier in the same century. Like the management of court records and documents that once went into the production of official history, the commentarial activity of the lectures on official history also gradually came under the management of private houses. At the same time, this development is also illuminated by being placed within the broader context of the court's increasing preoccupation with pollution taboos and the placation of violent spirits, which were both connected to changes in the tennō's sacred authority.

In a recent essay on *Sendai kuji hongi* (early tenth century) and the *Nihongi* lectures of the Shōhei era (965), Saitō Hideki has made a number of observations on the final lectures that have important implications for grasping the interrelationship between the production of history, ritual, and the ceremonial structure of the lectures and banquet at this particular historical juncture.[33] The *Sendai kuji* belonged to a group of texts (which included *Kogo shūi*) known collectively as *ujibumi* (uji writings). Dating from the eighth and ninth centuries, these writings transmitted ancient oral traditions of the various *uji* that had survived outside the official discourse of *Nihongi*. Unlike the earlier ujibumi, however, which transmitted traditions that predated *Nihon shoki* and *Kojiki*, the tenth-century *Sendai kuji*, argues Saitō, was the product of an effort to construct a new mythographical text, representing a postchronicle development that would eventually give rise to the medieval tradition of commentary on *Nihongi* exemplified in works like Urabe Kanekata's *Shaku nihongi*.[34] Comparing the earlier *Kogo shūi* with *Sendai kuji*, Saitō notes that the former constituted a protest on the part of the Imibe against the exclusion of their uji's traditions from official history at a time when the ritual structure of the Jingikan was being systematized under the ritsuryō codes. Hence, *Kogo shūi*'s critical view of written history and anti-Jingikan stance. The custodians of *Sendai kuji*, the Mononobe, on the other hand, represented a departure from both of these positions, and it is here that *Sendai kuji*'s connection to the official lectures is especially illuminating.

Until this point, the *Nihongi* lectures had been conducted exclusively by scholars of the Confucian branches of learning, who treated *Nihon shoki* and other official histories as orthodox texts; not a single member of the Jingikan had ever participated in the lectures. The participation of the non-

Confucian *Sendai kuji* custodians in the lectures was, as Saitō suggests, an epochal moment in the history of the lectures. Significantly, in contrast to the Imibe's rejection of official historiography, the custodians of *Sendai kuji* took pains to stress the orthodoxy of their own text's historiographical style, even claiming for it the status of Japan's oldest history by attributing its authorship to Ue no Miya no Miko (Shōtoku Taishi). In claiming a privileged status in the lectures for *Sendai kuji*, its custodians were laying claim to an orthodoxy that had formerly been the exclusive preserve of Confucian scholars in the service of the court. Saitō's most intriguing observations, however, concern the way in which *Sendai kuji* combines this claim to Confucian orthodoxy with its own mythographical aims, which center on an origin account of the *chinkonsai* in its third and seventh scrolls. As we saw earlier in this study, the *chinkonsai* (also known as *mitama-furi no matsuri*) had been one of the most important rituals conducted by the tennō in the ancient period. It was through the performance of this rite that the tennō demonstrated his sacred authority by placating the various raging deities.[35] By the tenth century, the ritual functions of placating, expelling, and managing violent spirits had become the prerogative of yin-yang masters and esoteric Buddhist priests. Reflecting this shift, *Sendai kuji*'s origin account of the chinkonsai devotes a great deal of attention to magical prayers for healing and revitalizing the dead.[36] Several conclusions can be drawn from this development. As Saitō suggests, in addition to representing an incursion into the Confucian preserve of orthodox historiography by the Jingikan, *Sendai kuji* was also an attempt to compete with yin-yang and esoteric Buddhist rites by means of its own magical placation practices.[37] At the same time, *Sendai kuji*'s chinkon myth was also connected to changes in the tennō's authority; for instead of accruing power to the tennō, the chinkonsai as explicated in *Sendai kuji* was now centered on ritual placation *aimed at protecting the tennō's person*, thereby mirroring a diminishment in his ritual and political authority.[38] This transformation of the *Nihongi* lectures in their twilight phase is an indication of how the historiographical discourse was slowly ebbing away from its former center of gravity in the court—in this case, to custodians with interests that diverged from an earlier practice of royal authority. With the new emphasis on placation and magical prayers aimed at healing and revitalization (which at this time also involved the management of pollutions), the reritualization of the *Nihongi* lectures by the custodians of *Sendai kuji* hints at the hidden side of their ceremonial function of celebrating the tennō's authority. Each of these elements—the appropriation of orthodox historiography for new ends, its ritualization within a lecture- and banquetlike setting, and the placation of spirits—will reappear in the eleventh-century historical narrative *Ōkagami.*

A Banquet at the Kawaranoin

The Kawaranoin residence of the Imperial Prince Minamoto Tōru (822–895), a son of Saga Tennō, exercised a deep hold on the imagination of the Heian aristocracy. Celebrated for its exquisite garden that was landscaped into an imitation of Shiogama Bay in distant Mutsu, the Kawaranoin appears as the site of uncanny happenings in a number of well-known episodes of Heian literature. According to one tradition of *Genji* commentary, it was the site of the ruinous residence to which Genji took Yūgao on the night that she died from fright induced by a spirit possession.[39] In the eighty-first episode of *The Tales of Ise*, the Kawaranoin appears under more flourishing conditions, but here, too, it is the setting for an unusual apparition. The occasion is a banquet during which the guests compose poems in praise of Tōru's residence:

> Long ago there was a Minister of the Left. In the neighborhood of Rokujō at the edge of the Kamogawa, he built an exquisite palace and took up residence there. Toward the end of the Tenth Month, when the chrysanthemum blossoms had peaked and were beginning to fade and the clusters of maple leaves had come into view, the Princes were sitting night after night, drinking wine and banqueting. As the dawn gradually broke, they composed poems in praise of the Minister's exquisite palace. An old beggar (*katai okina*) who happened to be there loitering about under the veranda, after waiting until everyone had finished his poem, recited: "Somehow I must have come to Shiogama; if only a fishing boat on the calm morning sea would hove in." He composed this poem because when he went to Michi no Kuni, there were many strange and exquisite places. Among the sixty provinces ruled by the sovereign, there is none that resembles the place called Shiogama. That's why the old man praised this place again with the phrase, "Somehow I must have come to Shiogama."[40]

The episode could stand as the very type of the celebratory banquet that affirms the authority of the center. Even its poetic geography, with the replicate of Shiogama Bay on the site of the Minister's grounds, seems to imply that the far-flung periphery of Michinoku now belongs to the center. Yet although the *Ise*, on one level, asks to be read as a text of the center, as Richard Okada has observed, the historical Ariwara no Narihira, who is the putative hero of the text, was confined throughout his life to positions well outside the ruling hierarchy of the time.[41] It is not surprising, then, that the okina figure, whose presence remains otherwise unexplained, should introduce a note of ambiguity and dissonance into the scene, which the commentaries, traditional and modern alike, seek to elucidate by attending to his identity, his precise location in the scene, and the implications of his poetic performance.[42]

According to one well-established reading, transmitted in medieval commentaries like *Waka chiken shū*, the okina figure is Narihira in disguise. Modern commentators like Yura Takuo, on the other hand, prefer to read him in more general terms as a stock figure of humor. In glossing his name, "katai okina," the commentaries propose readings that range from foolish or worthless old man to beggar (*kojiki*) and hence someone of extremely low social status.[43] Notions of hierarchy thus come into play in the various attempts to position him with respect to the aristocratic banqueters. In the *Ise* text, he is "itajiki no shita ni," indicating that he is somewhere "under the floorboards," but the commentaries have taken this in different senses. Some suggest that he is on the ground, presumably below the veranda (one possible reading of *itajiki*). Another commentary that follows a different textual line, which gives "daishiki" in place of "itajiki," suggests that he is on the ground beneath a viewing platform of some sort. Finally, there are other commentators who place him *inside* among the guests, but at the lower end (*shita*) of the seating arrangement, on the exposed floorboards (*itajiki*) as opposed to the matted area reserved for the nobles.[44] In all of these cases, the okina is perceived as an outsider, whose lack and imperfection (the literal sense of "katai") disturb the decorum and hierarchy of the banquet. It is here, too, that the evaluation of his poem comes into play. If, as some commentators argue, the aim was to compose a poem "in praise of the Minister's exquisite palace," then the okina's literalism misses the point, and the poem is a failure in keeping with his lowly social status. Other commentaries, on the other hand, read this same literalism or directness as an indication of the poem's charm, implying that the okina equaled if not surpassed the poetic skill of the nobles seated above.[45]

The discussion has so far stayed within the bounds of the *Ise* text and its commentarial tradition. But if we attend to the archetypal aspect of the old man, who makes his appearance just as dawn breaks, he also recalls,

as Tokuda Kazuo suggests, the deity who passes between worlds at moments of ritual play.[46] To draw out the implications of this observation, the
okina can be viewed as an aspect of the local deity whose sacred site is now
represented as physically incorporated into the center, here the Minister of
the Left's garden. If the okina as lowly beggar (the disguised Narihira of
the commentarial tradition) produces a poem that is superior to that of any
of the nobles sitting in formal array above, thereby inverting the hierarchical
order of the banquet (the political subtext of the episode), then the okina
as deity, by winning at *waka*, discloses the source of the banqueters' ritual
language—namely, the placenames (*meisho*) whose invocation affirmed the
center's possession of once autonomous sacred sites.[47] As the text hovers
between these two levels of meaning, not only is the center's claim to control
such ritual speech implicitly questioned but the very notion of a fixed center,
which shifts between Shiogama and the Heian site of the minister's palace,
is in doubt. From here, it is but a short distance to the wandering narrators of *Ōkagami*, a narrative, as we shall now see, in which official history
is transmogrified into something approximating its inverted double.

Ōkagami, *Ambulatory History, and the Urin'in*

"Recently, while attending an enlightenment lecture at the Urin'in Temple,
I met by chance two strange-looking old men (*okina*) aged far beyond ordinary people and an old woman, who appeared to have sat down in the same
place."[48] In this fashion, the unnamed recorder of *Ōkagami* begins the earliest example of a group of historical narratives that are collectively known as
the "mirror works" (*kagamimono*). Like the *okina* figure of the *Ise* episode,
there is something inexplicable in the chance presence of these aged figures
on the temple grounds, which is echoed in their sudden vanishing at the end
of the narrative. But whereas *Ise*'s okina is still attached to a particular site,
the narrators of *Ōkagami* are wanderers. In the subsequent mirror works,
this emphasis on wandering becomes even more pronounced. *Imakagami*
(*A Mirror for the Present*, ca. 1180), for example, is given as the oral narrative of an aged woman, over a century and a half old, heard by a capital
dweller while on a pilgrimage to Yamato temples.[49] Likewise, *Mizukagami*
(*The Water Mirror*, late twelfth century) is staged as the oral telling of an
ascetic who relates stories of ancient time that he in turn heard from an immortal.[50] In this fashion, *Ōkagami* registers the moment when wandering
reciters gain figural custody of historical narrative, which becomes literal

with the itinerant biwa reciters of the medieval *Heike*. Once the written production of court scholars, history has now become the utterance of wandering reciters at the margins of power.

Yet despite the appearance of a radical departure from the form of official history, the aged narrator of *Ōkagami* continues to view himself as one of its custodians. In the famous section known as the Second Preface, which comes right after a lengthy rehearsal of the genealogy and succession of sovereigns, Yotsugi delivers the following exhortation to his circle of listeners: "But instead of trivialities I am going to speak of serious business (*mameyakanaru koto*) now. Everyone listen well. Even as you must think of the exposition of the preacher today as intended for your enlightenment, so you must listen to my explications as if you were hearing the *Chronicles of Japan*."[51] The "trivialities" refer to the preceding mock-humorous exchange about mirrors between Yotsugi and his interlocutor Shigeki that constitutes the main topic of the Second Preface. Here, however, Yotsugi encourages his listeners to treat his recitation as an act that is comparable to the exegetical lectures on the official history, only now the site of the performance has shifted from the court to a location outside the capital on the occasion of an enlightenment sermon.

The Urin'in where the narrative of *Ōkagami* unfolds was both an important burial site for the Heian aristocracy and a gathering place for literati. Located at the periphery of the capital, it was like many temples a site where activities of a sacred and profane nature met and mingled and opposites mysteriously disclosed their identities. This accounts for one of the reasons *Ōkagami*'s narration of Michinaga's flowering fortunes is staged at Urin'in on the occasion of its enlightenment sermon (*bodaikō*). According to a tale found in *Konjaku monogatari shū* (15: 22), the bodaikō of Urin'in was instituted by a one-time thief who was delivered from punishment after a physiognomist predicted that his was the face of one "who would achieve rebirth."[52] The origins of the bodaikō, established by an "evil man" who subsequently proves to be a Buddhist saint, parallels the life story of Michinaga himself, who, despite hints of evil acts that darken his "flowering fortunes," is several times likened to an incarnation of the Buddha.[53] Viewed in this light, the setting of *Ōkagami* provides a sacred analogy for the acts of political violence that characterized Michinaga's and his family's rise to power.

But there is another aspect to the bodaikō, connected to Urin'in as a site of mortuary rites for the Heian aristocracy, which must also be factored into our understanding of *Ōkagami*'s historical narrative. Held in the Fifth Month of the second year of Manju (1025), the enlightenment sermon also overlapped with the forty-ninth-day mass that commemorated the death of Seishi, one of Emperor Sanjō's consorts and the mother of Prince Atsuakira (subsequently known by his title of Koichijōin). Although Atsuakira had been designated crown prince, he was coerced into resigning by Michinaga so the latter might further his own political aims. Prayers for Seishi's salvation were thus a form of placation intended to mollify the spirits of those alienated in the course of Michinaga's quest for power. This is darkly hinted at toward the end of part one of Michinaga's biography, as Yotsugi pauses in his celebratory account of the Fujiwara to make the following observation: "This year heavenly perturbations have been frequent and society seems rife with strange rumors. With Kishi pregnant like this, it is terrifying to hear that Kanshi, the retired sovereign Koichijōin's consort, appears to have been continuously afflicted throughout the year with her old ailment."[54] Although the cause of these "heavenly perturbations" is left unexplained in the passage, entries in the courtier journal *Shōyūki* record a series of natural calamities, including earthquake, pestilence, and drought, all concentrated in the Third Month of 1025, the very same month in which Seishi died in the course of a smallpox epidemic.[55] The deaths of both Kanshi and Michinaga's daughter Kishi in the Seventh Month and Eighth Month, respectively, Kanshi from illness and Kishi after having given birth to the future Emperor Go-Reizei, give Yotsugi's words the character of an ominous prophecy. Kanshi herself, moreover, was believed to have been afflicted by the vengeful spirits of Akimitsu and his daughter Enshi, both victims again of Michinaga's political machinations.[56] It is against this ominous backdrop of natural calamities and strange rumors that the bodaikō takes on additional importance as a ritual setting for the talk of *Ōkagami*'s mysterious speakers. The stories and hints about vengeful spirits, possessions, and prodigies (*kaii*) that circulate through the narrative of *Ōkagami* are the signs of a nomadic speech that has now *taken possession* of the court's history and is altering its very form.[57]

Polyvocality and Storytelling in the Round

Another characteristic of *Ōkagami* is its polyvocal form. The entire narrative is staged as a conversational exchange between Yotsugi and his interlocutor Shigeki, with occasional interruptions by an attendant in the audience and passages of straight narration from the anonymous recorder of the event. At the same time, the individual narrations are typically framed as the utterance of unnamed people (*yo no hito*), which adds yet another layer of voicing to an already richly polyvocal text.[58] Among the three principal interlocutors, Yotsugi largely assumes responsibility for praising Michinaga by focusing on the public view of events; Shigeki fills in the private details; and the "young attendant" (*aosamurai*) provides the occasional back view or glimpses into the political machinations of the Fujiwara.[59] Stated more schematically, as custodian of the official chronicle, consisting of the *genealogical records* of the tennō and of the glorious history of the Fujiwara regental house, Yotsugi performs the role of transmitter of felicitous words, whereas the young attendant and Shigeki supplement this positive function of felicitation with critical viewpoints, becoming at times the voice of those dispossessed in the course of Michinaga's and his family's rise to power.[60]

In treating the resignation of Prince Atsuakira from the position of crown prince (*tōgū*), for example, *Ōkagami* provides the audience with two separate accounts. After Yostugi's version, in which Atsuakira is represented as resigning by his own choice, the unnamed attendant breaks into the narration with these remarks:

> "That is very reasonable. However, regarding the affair of the Crown Prince, there is a much different account. I have personally heard about it in detail." To which Yotsugi replied: "That may well be so. I should very much like to hear what you have been told. It is a hobby of mine to listen to such talk."[61]

In the account of mingled rumor and gossip that follows, the resignation of Atsuakira is clearly attributed to pressure directly applied by Michinaga. This method of providing alternative viewpoints is typical of *Ōkagami*'s narration and distinguishes it from *Eiga monogatari*, which provides only a single version that represents Prince Atsuakira as resigning by his own choice.[62] As historical narrative, then, *Ōkagami*'s murmur of voices recovers that detailed and copious utterance that had been lost in the more monological narration of the official histories.

The narrative form in which several interlocutors take turns exchanging tales has been aptly characterized as "storytelling in the round" (*meguri monogatari*). An early example is the famous "rainy night" conversation on the ranking of women lovers in *The Tale of Genji*. In the medieval period, such narration frequently took the form of "tales of repentance" in which the individual speakers, as the result of a chance encounter, confess past sins that turn out to disclose mysterious karmic ties that lead to their Buddhist conversion or enlightenment.[63] In *Ōkagami*, this confessional tone often colors the alternative accounts of Shigeki and the young attendant, contrasting sharply with the more positive, felicitous tone of Yotsugi's narrative. In addition to the Prince Atsuakira narratives, the best example of this double structure is found in the section of "old tales" that make up the sixth and final section of *Ōkagami*, where Yotsugi's focus on the glory of Michinaga is set against the darker confessional tone of Shigeki's narratives. Thus, Shigeki prefaces his account of the sinful pursuit of hawking with the statement: "At this temple I wish to make my confession today."[64] In this way, the narrative of *Ōkagami* alternates between placation and felicitation, which is mirrored again in the movement from repentance to enlightenment. The vanishing of *Ōkagami*'s narrators at the end of their recitation also aligns their narration with the prophecy record (*miraiki*) that would flourish in the medieval period and of which notable examples are found in *Taiheiki*.[65] In these narratives, an exchange of tales among a chance gathering of speakers, often on the occasion of an all-night vigil at a temple, typically ends with the mysterious disappearance of the participants, signifying the sacred nature of their prophetic speech.

To summarize the argument so far, as historical narrative took on an ambulatory character in *Ōkagami*, the ritual logic inscribed and enacted in earlier texts such as *Kojiki* was reversed. At the same time, the shift in the site of historical narrative from court to temple hints at the claim of Buddhist temples—a claim asserted with even greater force in the medieval period—to act as sole effective mediators of threatening speech, whose nomadic character, conveyed in the reciters' bewitching words (*yōgen*) and strange rumors, is reflected figuratively in the circular form of *Ōkagami*'s narrative structure. Yet the invasion of historical narrative by nomadic speech represents only one facet of *Ōkagami*'s discourse. As we will see later, parodic elements in *Ōkagami* also disclose a heterodox character that is connected to the emergence of rule by retired sovereigns. But first, we must pause for a closer look at the problem of *Ōkagami*'s narrative form.

Ōkagami *and the Problem of Genre*

In the history of Heian vernacular narrative, no text occupies quite so anomalous or scandalous a position as *Ōkagami*. When it was rumored that Fujiwara no Kaneie's daughter Suishi, a consort of the crown prince (later

Emperor Sanjō), was having "an affair with the Consultant Minamoto Yori-sada," her ambitious half-brother Michinaga paid her a visit to verify the truth of the rumor:

> Suspicious of this unusual visit, Suishi drew her curtain-stand closer, but Michinaga pushed it aside. Her naturally gorgeous looks had been enhanced by cosmetics, and she looked even more beautiful than usual. "When I went to the Crown Prince, he told me about some things that he had heard, and I have come to see for myself. It would be a pity if he should give heed to baseless rumors." He then opened her robes and pinched her breast, and didn't he get a stream of milk in his face![66]

The crudeness of Michinaga's action sharply differentiates *Ōkagami*'s depiction of court life from that of its immediate predecessor, *A Tale of Flowering Fortunes*. As Komine Kazuaki remarks, in such passages, *Ōkagami* "subverts the entire tradition of court literature."[67] Or take the example of Fujiwara no Michitaka, who, according to *Eiga monogatari*, "was a man of elegant appearance, delicate sensibilities, and faultless decorum."[68] Not only is there no hint of this refinement in *Ōkagami*, but its biography of Michitaka consists of a series of comical anecdotes illustrating his near perpetual state of drunkenness.[69] One way to make sense of such episodes is to subordinate them to *Ōkagami*'s larger design, which in Yotsugi's words "is to describe Lord Michinaga's surpassing success in the world."[70] This is the approach taken by Helen McCullough. In the first example, however crude the action, the reader is to understand that Michinaga is being indirectly praised for his "resourcefulness" or that "knack for getting things done," which allowed him to triumph over his rivals, whereas, in the second, it is Michitaka's want of such ability that leads to the political failures of his own line even as it abets his brother Michinaga's successes.[71] Yet such crudities, or what might better be characterized as *Ōkagami*'s ludic tendencies, yield a much different reading when placed in the broader context of the late Heian shift from regental (*sekkan*) politics to rule by retired sovereigns, which was accompanied by the emergence of a ritualized parodic discourse.[72]

With its ambiguous tricksterlike qualities, *Ōkagami* is a text that resists easy classification. Modern literary histories generally classify it as a "historical tale" (*rekishi monogatari*), a term first introduced around the time that Haga Yaichi and other Meiji scholars were redefining Japanese literary kinds in accordance with Western notions of genre.[73] The notion of fictionalized history suggested by the term is quite different, however, from *Ōkagami*'s relationship to historical narrative. The "mirror" of the title, for example, alludes on one level to the traditional Chinese figure that likens history to a mirror for the present. In classical Japanese, moreover, *Ōkagami* and related works such as *Eiga monogatari* were typically designated by the term "yotsugi no monogatari," or "tale of succession."[74] As a form of historical narrative, the yotsugi no monogatari related in regular chronological order important events and episodes centered upon the court, with the interests of the imperial house and the Fujiwara regental house providing the main focus of attention. *Eiga monogatari*, the first in the series, makes matters like imperial successions and resignations the core of its narrative, a form taken over directly from *The Six National Histories*.[75] As the vernacular successor to official history, the succession tale would appear to be claiming at least quasi-legitimacy as historical narrative.

The question of *Ōkagami*'s narrative status is further complicated by the intricate form of its narration, which is presented by an unnamed recorder as the conversation between two superannuated speakers, Ōyake no Yotsugi and Natsuyama Shigeki, that is interrupted in turn by remarks from a low-ranking attendant, by the recorder's own observations, and by comments from several other speakers, including the wife of one of the aged narrators.[76] For some readers of *Ōkagami*, this degree of narrative complexity has suggested the self-conscious viewpoint of a fictional mode of address.[77] In medieval European literature, self-conscious distancing of this type has been viewed as marking the moment when "vernacular narrative" freed itself from the requirements of truth telling that regulated writing in Latin.[78] Peter Haidu, for example, has characterized European vernacular fiction as "parodic from its very inception," giving itself up to the play of ironic distortions as it subverts the authoritative modes of official Latin.[79] It is tempting to see a parallel here to the relationship in Heian Japan between so-called vernacular fiction and official discourse in Chinese, discussed earlier. Yet the equality that Murasaki, speaking through Genji, claims for vernacular narrative is not easily dismissed as mere play or hyperbole because something like it came to fruition in *A Tale of Flowering Fortunes*. These observations must caution us against insisting on the merely fictional status of *Ōkagami*.

But what about *Ōkagami*'s ludic tendencies? To the extent that the ludic is understood as privileging textuality for its own sake, the concept fails to account for vernacular narrative's dangerous proximity to official discourse, which invariably casts it in the role of the latter's hidden other. The Preface to *Sandai jitsuroku* is instructive here: "Events of the street, which serve no purpose of instruction, and reckless talk will be left out."[80] As part of an enumeration of items deemed worthy of inclusion in the history, the statement pithily encapsulates the monological character of official history. Unverified rumor, gossip, and talk of the streets (the latter echoing Hironari's phrase in *Kogo shūi*) are with one stroke of the brush rejected and thrust to the margins, into a discursive limbo. It is precisely this polyvocal excess, with its layered voicing and rumors, that constitutes vernacular narrative. In brief, to characterize *Ōkagami*'s narrative as only self-conscious textual play or the product of artifice is to lose sight of its tendency to encroach upon official history, an identification that Yotsugi himself makes when he likens his recitation to a reading of *Nihon shoki*. On the other hand, the ludic, understood as ritual behavior, is certainly an important factor in *Ōkagami*'s narrative world, affirming history's ties with festive or ritual forms, such as the banquet. The "staging" of *Ōkagami* with its multiple oral narration is perhaps best viewed as arising from performative and ritual as opposed to purely textual/literary motivations. This extends to the extraordinary age of its principal narrators as well as its setting at a temple. Although the longevity of the narrators has typically been read as no more than a literary device, it affiliates Yotsugi and his partner with Daoist immortals and therefore in command of the demonic powers whose presence circulates through their narrative.[81]

Mirrors and Other Matters

The author of *Eiga monogatari*, the first vernacular successor to *The Six National Histories*, took over not only the latter's strict chronological form but infused her narrative with its traditional language of praise, thereby investing her principal subject, the deeds and character of Fujiwara no Michinaga and the regental house, with the luster of an imperial aura.[82] The same ritually charged language infuses *Ōkagami*, especially those portions dealing with Michinaga's life. In the section known as the Second Preface at the end of scroll one, Yotsugi and his companion Shigeki engage in a spirited exchange that returns repeatedly to the image of the mirror that gives the work its title. Yotsugi begins by stating his reason for beginning with a recitation of the "imperial annals" (*teiki*):

> As for the succession of emperors, although I need not have spoken of them, if one thinks about why the Lay Priest Michinaga's fortunes blossomed,

then one must first talk about the situation of the emperor and empress. When planting a tree, to the extent that one tends carefully to the nurturing of the roots, the branches flourish and the tree produces fruit. Therefore, having first recalled the succession of emperors, I now intend to enlighten you about the Ministers of State.[83]

To which Shigeki replies:

On the contrary, it was most splendid. Having suspended a mirror before the forms of even such sovereigns, how much greater will appear the ministers and the rest. I now feel like one who, having faced darkness for many years, is about to meet the darting rays of the luminous morning sun. Moreover, accustomed as I am to the mirror which is kept closed up in my wife's comb-box at home, which scarcely reflects and cannot be polished; seeing my face before this brightly polished mirror, I feel ashamed at my reflection. Yet how rare the sight and what a delightful experience! I feel as if twenty years had been added to my life today.[84]

Buoyed up by the festive mood, Shigeki then initiates an exchange of poems that takes up the mirror imagery developed in the preceding passage: "When I face / this clear mirror / things of past / present and future / can now be seen" (*Akirakeki / kagami ni aeba / suginishi mo / ima ya yukusue / koto mo miekeri*). To which Yotsugi replies: "Of the sovereigns / the traces one after another / with nothing hidden / are seen anew / in the old mirror" (*Suberagi no / ato mo tsugitsugi / kakure naku / arata ni miyuru / furukagami ka mo*).[85] Following this exchange, Yotsugi, echoing Shigeki's humorous reference to his wife's mirror, asks: "Do you feel as if you were looking at a modish flower-shaped mirror kept in a mother-of-pearl box? You're wrong. Though they are in fashion, they cloud too easily. *But this mirror in the ancient style, with its white metal*, though never polished, shines bright indeed!"[86] After this bit of self-praise, the humor of which is duly noted by the anonymous recorder, Yotsugi exhorts his audience to accord his words the dignity of an official reading of history: "But instead of trivialities I am going to speak of serious business now. Everyone listen well. Even as you must think of the exposition of the preacher today as intended for your enlightenment, so you must listen to my explications as if you were hearing the *Chronicles of Japan*."[87]

With its rapid shifts in tone, ranging from the celebratory to the mock humorous, this conversational exchange between the aged narrators is representative of *Ōkagami*'s style throughout. The peculiar mood, difficult to pin down with precision, is in keeping with the supernatural aura of the narrators, who are characterized at the outset as "utategenaru," meaning "odd" or "weird-seeming" but possibly hinting at the intensity and rapid tempo of their speech.[88] By praising Yotsugi's narration with one of the standard formulas of felicitation, "ito imijū medetashi ya" ("it was most splendid"), which recurs like a leitmotif throughout the work, Shigeki draws attention to the congratulatory function of Yotsugi's speech, which is given transitive force by his direct reference to a feeling of renewed vigor: "I feel as if twenty years had been added to my life today."

In an essay on the origins of Japanese historical narrative, the cultural historian Hayashiya Tatsusaburō viewed this link between historical narrative and the ritual performance of felicitous words as fundamental: "The historical traditions of the *uji* recorded in ancient Japanese history are all felicitous words incorporated into the national history in the course of their submission to the Yamato Court."[89] In making this argument, Hayashiya linked both the mirror and okina narrator of *Ōkagami* to ancient precedents in *Nihon shoki*. The "white metal" mirror of Yotsugi, for example, is traced back to Kuma-wani's offering of a white copper mirror in the chronicle of Chūai, which Hayashiya reads as an act of ritual submission to the newly established court in Yamato.[90] Yotsugi, as the traditional okina who performs felicitous prayers for peace and longevity, is placed in a direct line of descent from the ancient guild reciters (*kataribe*) who originally had custodianship of sacred words that were presented to the court. Although Hayashiya's theory refocused attention on the ritual character of *Ōkagami*'s narrators, it did so by overstating the orthodoxy of *Ōkagami* as historical narrative.[91]

The polysemous implications of the mirror resonate quite differently when placed in the broader context of Chinese historiography. As has frequently been noted, in contrast to *Eiga monogatari*, which inherits the strictly annalistic form of *The Six National Histories*, *Ōkagami* is loosely modeled after the tripartite form perfected by Sima Qian in *Shi ji*, with its combination of imperial annals, biographies, and a concluding section of essays on various topics.[92] In a passage that the title of *Ōkagami* appears to recall, Sima Qian employs the image of a mirror to illustrate the value of historical narrative: "One who lives in the present age and considers the ways of the past has a mirror wherein he may see that the two are not necessarily alike."[93] Another explanation of the mirror is provided in the following passage from the Tang period handbook *Zhenguan zhengyao*:

> Taizong once said to his minister: "Using bronze one fashions a mirror, and is thereby able to straighten his cap. Using the past, one makes a mirror, and thereby is enabled to understand the rise and fall of events. Using people, one makes a mirror and is thereby enabled to illuminate good and bad. Always keeping these three mirrors, I have thereby guarded myself against errors. Now Weizhong has passed away, and I have lost a mirror. Thus I have wept for a long time." He then continued: "In the past, Weizhong alone showed me my errors. Since he has passed away, though I error, there is no one to point them out to me." [94]

Among the three mirrors mentioned in this passage, the first suggests the regard for comportment and etiquette that were fundamental to the Confucian rites, the second the normative value of past events as guides to proper governance, and the third the importance to a ruler of heeding the "voice of the people" to learn whether or not his rule was in harmony with the heavenly mandate. Together they provide criteria or standards for accurately assessing the present, thereby opening up the possibility for transforming historical narrative from the predominantly legitimating function it had in *The Six National Histories* into an evaluative mode, capable of representing opposing viewpoints and introducing critical judgments. Although *Ōkagami* evinces little interest in the normative value of historical events, it is full of anecdotes and observations that draw attention to apparent violations of decorum, etiquette, canons of taste, and other behavior that falls within the compass of Confucian rites; and in its pervasive reliance on rumor and the opinions of unnamed speakers, we also hear the distant murmur of the people. These concerns have been collectively referred to as *Ōkagami*'s "critical spirit" (*hihansei*), a phrase that has long had currency as an interpretive key to the work. In a 1924 essay, for example, Fujimura Tsukuru argued that *Ōkagami*'s critical viewpoint was based on aesthetic (*biteki*) as opposed to ethical or moral norms.[95] Although an essay published in 1941 by Fujisawa Kesao was largely dismissive of the theory, treating *Ōkagami*'s critical spirit as little more than an attitude of enlightened criticism directed toward Michinaga's style of governance, Fujisawa's tepid view, as Kawakita Noboru has noted, was also a reaction to the difficulty of debating matters that touched on the tennō and imperial history in the wartime climate. As might be expected, the theory acquired new life in the postwar period, with some scholars even detecting popular censure directed against the tennō himself.[96]

Several examples will help illustrate. In part two of Michinaga's biography, after a series of anecdotes about poetry composition at the courts of Uda and Daigo, the attendant interrupts Shigeki, who at this point in the narrative has taken over from Yotsugi, to ask about the Sone no Yoshitada incident on the occasion of Retired Emperor En'yū's Rat Day excursion to Murasakino:

> "Yes, that was a very interesting incident. Since the emperor was going to appraise poems without regard to social status, it was natural to wish to be present on such an occasion, but even to hide somewhere and compose a superior poem would have been a breach of etiquette (*burei*). To take a seat right among the participants was most shocking."[97]

For this breach of etiquette, Yoshitada was ordered removed, and Shigeki ends his account with a disapproving remark on Yoshitada's lack of judgment. The disruption of hierarchy in Yoshitada's failure to observe the proprieties of time and place, his "breach of etiquette," is typical of *Ōkagami*'s eye for behavior that violates the Confucian proprieties.[98] The following remarks addressed by Shigeki to Yotsugi, on the other hand, recall *Zhenguan zhengyao*'s third mirror, the admonition to heed the voice of the people. Yotsugi has just concluded a long speech in praise of Michinaga's construction of the Muryōjuin Buddha Hall [Shigeki]: "Yet it seems that people speak only of how unbearable are Michinaga's frequent demands for laborers to work on his temple. Haven't you heard of this?"[99] Although Yotsugi responds with a vigorous defense of Michinaga, Shigeki's remarks are typical of those glimpses into the backside of history that we find elsewhere in *Ōkagami*. These examples and others like them suggest that *Ōkagami*'s mirror borrows a good deal of its reflective power from the exemplary function it had in Chinese historiography.

But how do we account for the presence of a critical spirit in a work ostensibly aimed at praising the Fujiwara? Despite Yotsugi's declared purpose of celebrating the glory of the Fujiwara regental house, most scholarship dates the composition of *Ōkagami* to the reign of Shirakawa (1086–1107), a period well after the events described in the narrative. According to one theory proposed by Hirata Toshiharu, the author was Nakanoin Masasada, a Minamoto retainer (*kinshin*) of the retired sovereign, who viewed Michinaga's and the Fujiwara's history in light of his own family's thwarted political ambitions, dealing out both praise and criticism of Michinaga. In a similar vein, Sakamoto Tarō argued that *Ōkagami*'s subtle criticisms of the Fujiwara were made with the intention of exalting the tennō's authority above that of the regental house. Referring to the same Masasada, he suggested that he may have taken up an anti-Fujiwara position in an attempt to wrest control of the government through the avenue of the *insei* (government by retired sovereigns).[100] The critical view of Fujiwara regental power, reflecting the alliance of a hitherto marginalized court faction and a retired sovereign intent on reasserting the authority of the tennō that had been restrained under Fujiwara rule, might well account for *Ōkagami*'s innovative adaptation of Chinese historiography as a vehicle intended to censure as well as to praise. Viewed in this light, *Ōkagami* might be characterized as exploiting Chinese historiographical models to legitimate political aims that clashed with prevailing notions of power.

There are several objections, however, that might be made to such a reading. First, many of the critical asides that bring to light darker motives or draw attention to violations of Confucian decorum in *Ōkagami* come by way of whispered rumors or laughter-provoking gossip, which is precisely what the gravitas, or in Yotsugi's words, "the serious business" of official history, rejects. Another objection relates to the problem of reconciling a critical spirit with the longstanding ceremonial function of praising the tennō. A more sweeping objection, already touched on at the beginning of this chapter, was voiced by Helen McCullough, who argued that the perception of a "critical spirit" in *Ōkagami* resulted from a failure to discern the principal aim of *Ōkagami*'s author, which was to explain the source of Michinaga's and his line's political successes while accounting for the failures of rivals, especially other Fujiwara factions.[101]

All of these objections have merit. But before we can answer them, we must first return to the exchange between Shigeki and Yotsugi in the Second Preface. There, it will be recalled, both Shigeki and Yotsugi playfully invoke a fashionable vanity mirror as a figure for historical narrative—an odd figure that seems out of key with Yotsugi's declared purpose of praising Michinaga's line. In the extensive commentary on this expression, several interpretations have been proposed. According to Matsumoto Haruhisa, by "modish" (*imayō*) mirror, Yotsugi intends a negative appraisal of the prior *Eiga monogatari*, whose numerous errors he will correct by returning to the superior standard of *Nihon shoki*, the "mirror in the ancient style."[102] Hosaka Hiroshi, on the other hand, suggests that the "modish flower-shaped mirror" refers to the fashionable Japanese imitation of a Chinese-style mirror that had ceased to be imported following the closure of the Tang embassies.[103] These conflicting interpretations alert us to the ambiguity of *Ōkagami*'s relationship to prior historical narrative, which it is either emulating according to Matsumoto's reading or rejecting as something falsely derivative according to Hosaka. Unmentioned by either, however, is the parodic force of introducing a stylish vanity mirror as a metaphor for illuminating imperial history. As we shall now see, this parodic tone, together with *Ōkagami*'s character as nomadic history, is fundamental to its narrative and performative logic and closely connected to its congratulatory function as well as to its so-called "critical spirit."

Parody in Ōkagami

Central to the parodic strain in *Ōkagami* is the word "tamashii" or "yamatodamashii," generally defined as a combination of wit, common sense, and "the ability to get things done."[104] It was Michinaga's possession of this quality that contributed to his success. One of the more extensive illustrations of tamashii in *Ōkagami* occurs in the biography of Tokihira, fully half of which is devoted to the exile of Tokihira's political rival Sugawara no Michizane. After its account of Michizane's exile and the destruction that his angry spirit subsequently wreaked on Tokihira's offspring, the narrator Yotsugi observes: "Afterwards, none of Tokihira's sons lived past the age of thirty or forty. The reason was nothing less than the anger of the Kitano deity." The remainder of the biography is devoted to the subject of Tokihira's own character: "People say that Tokihira's descendants died out because he sinned in committing terrible acts of evil. That may be so, but he had a splendid endowment of *yamatodamashii*." Three anecdotes about Tokihira then follow. In the first, Tokihira arrives at the palace in showy attire that violates Daigo's recently promulgated prohibitions against extravagance (*kasa*) and is promptly ordered to leave. At the conclusion of the story, Yotsugi drops a rumor implying that Tokihira had actually arranged the incident with Daigo to get people to curb such extravagance. In the second anecdote, a standoff between Michizane and Tokihira regarding a ministerial matter is resolved when a wily court recorder sets up Tokihira, who is subject to fits of uncontrollable laughter, by deliberately farting as he ostentatiously presents Tokihira with a document during arguments in the council chamber. As a result, the discomposed Tokihira loses interest in the proceedings, which enables Michizane to settle the matter to his own liking. The third and final anecdote relates how Tokihira once brandished his sword and stared down (*niramiyarite*) the angry spirit of Michizane, which was terrifying the palace with thunder and lightning.[105]

Is there a narrative logic to the biography? Helen McCullough argued that the lengthy account of Michizane's exile and actions as an angry spirit was intended to explain why Tokihira's line ultimately failed to flourish. The stories about yamatodamashii were included because they illustrated traits admired by *Ōkagami*'s author. It was Michinaga's possession of tamashii, for example, that inspired his clever strategy of pinching his half-sister's breast to find out if she was pregnant.[106] Both portions of the biography accord with McCullough's view that *Ōkagami* is (1) slanted in favor of Michinaga's success—here aided by the extinction of Tokihira's line—and (2) not especially concerned with criticisms of the Fujiwara inasmuch as the possession of "yamatodamashii" appears to be cast in a positive light.

But does this fully account for the ambiguous role of "tamashii" in the biography? Even if we allow that *Ōkagami*'s author admired the wit and energy displayed by both Tokihira and the wily recorder, the violations against the dress code and ceremonial punctilio are clearly perceived as direct affronts to the hierarchical order that supported the authority of the tennō. Like the Sone no Yoshitada incident discussed earlier, the first anecdote involves a clear breach of decorum that threatens hierarchy and might well have been intended as veiled criticism. Is Tokihira being praised for his effrontery in flaunting the dress code? Or is he being praised for his resourcefulness in devising a strategy to assure compliance with the tennō's prohibition of extravagance? The second anecdote is equally ambiguous because it is not entirely clear who is being singled out for what: Tokihira for his irrepressible laughter or the recorder for devising a clever, albeit indecorous, strategy to resolve a dispute. What we in fact have here are a cluster of motifs— violations of order, raucous laughter, and a level of latent violence implicit in "tamashii" (hinting as well at Michizane's unappeased spirit)—that exceed the logic of any discernible authorial intention.

The ambiguous set of traits encompassed by the term "[yamato]damashii" is made somewhat clearer in the third anecdote that concludes the biography of Tokihira:

> One time, when Michizane became the thunder god of Kitano, he put on
> a frightening display of thunder and lightning. When it looked like he was

about to strike the Seiryōden, the Hon'in Minister [Tokihira] unsheathed his sword and said: "Even while alive, were you not second in rank to me? Even if you *are* a deity now, in this world you must yield place to me. Can it be otherwise?" And as he uttered these words, Tokihira glared fiercely upward. At once, Michizane's spirit was pacified. That's what people say. And yet it wasn't because the Minister Tokihira was superior, but because royal authority (*ōi*) is limitless that Michizane was made to submit to right and wrong.[107]

The disruption of hierarchy signified by extravagant dress and laughter in the first two anecdotes is here implicitly aligned with royal authority's control over demonic powers. Although Yotsugi is careful to correct the judgment of the anonymous purveyors of the anecdote, a habit he exhibits elsewhere in *Ōkagami*, no less than five high-ranking Fujiwara—Tokihira, Kaneie, Tadahira, Morosuke, and Michinaga—face down or confront demonic spirits or prodigies (*kaii*) in the course of *Ōkagami*.[108] In the case of Michinaga, the language is especially telling. "A man destined for greatness displays from a very early age a fierce spirit (*tamashii takeku*), and also enjoys special divine protection."[109] This remark by Yotsugi prefaces an anecdote in which the emperor challenges Michinaga and his two brothers, Michitaka and Michikane, to visit remote locations on the palace grounds on an especially eerie night. Michinaga alone accomplishes the task with a sang-froid indicative of one endowed with superior powers. The phrase "tamashii takeku," however, indicates more than mere pluck or resourcefulness. It not only recalls the epithet of the ambiguously violent trickster figure Yamato Takeru but also anticipates traits subsequently associated with Taira no Kiyomori, including authority over demonic powers. In brief, the disruptive potential of the demonic, implicit in "tamashii" and "yamatotamashii" and its accompaniment of normally forbidden behaviors, which inverts established hierarchies, derives from royal power itself. This, in turn, bears directly on the ritual character of the okina figures who narrate *Ōkagami*.

Yotsugi no Okina was also the name of one of three principal roles in *Shiki sanba*—the other two being Inatsumi no Okina and Chichi no jō—a celebratory play performed throughout the eleventh and twelfth centuries at Buddhist temples to encourage peace and abundant harvests. Later, it was incorporated into the *nō* repertoire, where it came to be performed as the auspicious opening piece in the standard cycle of five plays.[110] In an influential essay, Orikuchi Shinobu read the Okina of the play as the embodiment of the *marebito* whose performance of the auspicious opening dance (*modogi*) secured the ritual placation of the spirits (*mono*) in the succeeding plays.[111] The felicitous or celebratory tone of Yotsugi's narrative, aimed at praising the Fujiwara, is thus connected to the placation of violent spirits as well. Before its co-optation by Buddhist temples or its transformation into elite art in *nō*, *Shiki sanba* also belonged to the unofficial arts of *dengaku* ("field-music"). Originally performed at harvest rituals for the conjuration of evil spirits, by the late Heian period, *dengaku* had begun to blend with the traditions of *sangaku*, a general term covering various types of comic mime, dance, acrobatics, and other performing arts.[112] In the course of the eleventh and twelfth centuries, the same time that *Ōkagami* was taking shape, the festive dengaku sites became identified with extravagant behavior, including vestimentary and fashionable excesses (*kasa, fūryū*), that would later evolve into the dengaku and *basara* crazes of the early medieval period.[113] It is this ritual tie to festive or carnival energies that partly accounts for the ambiguous coloring of *Ōkagami*'s discourse, investing Yotsugi's history with parodic overtones that shade off into the irony and many critical asides that provide that view into the back side of history touched on earlier. Michinaga and other figures of power in *Ōkagami* belong to a much different world from the refined court depicted in *Eiga monogatari*, reflecting instead the late Heian mutation in royal authority under retired sovereigns that reaffirmed its connection to dangerous demonic powers.

As Abe Yasurō, Gomi Fumihiko, and other scholars have argued, one of the defining characteristics of late Heian royal authority was the increasingly close association between retired sovereigns and a variety of marginal entertainers, including sarugaku performers.[114] Linked to the unruly demonic powers, one of the hallmarks of parodic sarugaku was the boisterous laughter (*oko no warai*) that came at the climax of the performance, signaling a ritual inversion of hierarchy and a revivifying of sacred authority. Although this transformation in the ritual character of royal power would not achieve its fullest development until the early medieval period, where it is reflected in the many riotous banquets and mock-battle scenes depicted in *Heike*, *Taiheiki*, and other works, it is already present in the carnival atmosphere that suffuses a number of *Ōkagami* episodes, including the Tokihira anecdotes.

The narratives centered on the mad (*kurui*) Kazan-in are another case in point. In a series of anecdotes gathered together in the biography of Koremasa, we are given examples of Kazan-in's extraordinary supernatural powers, acquired through the practice of esoteric Buddhist rites that enable him to control spirits; his antic disregard of decorum; and his genius in a variety of arts, including poetry, architecture, gardening, and painting. The following anecdote discloses his affiliation to the world of parodic sarugaku:

> And everybody must have noticed the appearance of Kazan-in the year that he watched the Kamo Return; and this, moreover, when on the previous day there had been such an incident. And yet on the following day, when he ought not to have been parading about the streets, there he was with a big crowd milling behind his carriage, led by that boisterous favorite of his, Tall Hat Raisei. But it was his rosary more than anything that struck me. It was strung with small oranges in place of the usual beads, and interspersed with larger ones for the main beads. It was so long that it hung outside the carriage with his trousers. Was there ever a spectacle (*mimono*) to equal it?[115]

The incident referred to was a violent clash between the attendants of Kazan-in and Fujiwara no Kintō. According to the account found in *Shōyūki*, an edict was issued by Michinaga ordering the arrest of the ringleader, but the latter managed to escape punishment after Kazan-in had been forewarned by Fujiwara no Yukinari. In *Ōkagami*, these two incidents have apparently been conflated. For, as Yotsugi goes on to relate, when the imperial police were dispatched to arrest the pages (*warabe*) responsible for the previous day's incident, Yukinari forewarned the retired sovereign, and "his attendants fled like spiders scattered by the wind." Careless of public censure and in complete defiance of the decorum that befitted his rank, Kazan-in disports himself with an extravagance of behavior that recalls the excesses of late Heian dengaku spectacles, which were the frequent object of censure in official notices. In commenting on the flight of Kazan-in's attendants, Abe draws a parallel between the Tsuzumi Hōgan episode in *Heike monogatari*, in which Go-Shirawaka's attendant Tomoyasu engages in mock ritual combat with the forces of Yoshinaka. There, too, the climax of the episode occurs with the flight of the retired sovereign's crowd of defenders, a motif that evokes the raucous laugher of the sarugaku spectacle. Performed under the authority of the retired sovereign, such ludic play was aimed at opposing the military power that threatened the tennō even while symbolizing the violence inherent in royal power itself.[116]

Although in the present episode there are as yet no warriors who openly oppose Kazan-in's authority, we find this motif in another anecdote about Kazan-in in the biography of Michitaka. As recounted by Yotsugi, Kazan-in makes a wager with Fujiwara no Takaie that the latter will not be able to get past the gate of his residence. On the appointed day, Takaie, dressed in ceremonial attire that brings to mind the nobles "who dash across Murasakino during the Kamo Return," arrives before Kazan-in's gates with fifty or sixty attendants. On his side, the retired sovereign has mustered seventy or eighty valiant monks, temple pages, and others who are armed with "big rocks and five- or six-foot staves."

> Both sides had limited their weapons to sticks and stones. After a brief pause, Takaie took his carriage north from Kadenokōji to a point near the gate, only to be forced back again. The former monarch's vigilant battalions roared with laugher. Was there ever such a sight? *Royal authority is an awesome thing*; it was hopeless for Takaie to try to get by.[117]

The allusion to Murasakino in this context is especially significant because it was one of the important sites of the *goryō*-type festival aimed at driving out demonic spirits during the late Heian period and would later be associated with raucous dengaku spectacles. The ritualized combat that climaxes in a moment of uproarious laughter signifies royal authority's control over the unruly demonic powers.

Absent from court ceremonial and official history for much of the Heian period, the ambiguous character of royal authority reemerges as one of the keynotes of *Ōkagami*'s historical narrative. In its ritual preoccupation with placation and the dangerous demonic powers, it recovers something of *Kojiki*'s connection to archaic violent energies. But whereas *Kojiki* and earlier rites aimed at installing the wandering deity in the fixed sites of temple-shrine complexes represented an effort to augment and secure the authority of the center by stabilizing its space, in *Ōkagami* it is the nomadic that has now taken possession of the court. Figural here, this invasion of the nomadic takes on increasing reality as retired sovereigns set up liminal courts and migrate physically to the periphery, a phenomenon that overlaps with the period during which *Ōkagami* took shape as a text.

Part Three

CHINA IN THE MEDIEVAL
IMAGINARY

It is no concern of mine if the red flags subjugate the
barbarians.

—FUJIWARA NO TEIKA, *Meigetsuki*

Introduction

In the ethnographic text, observes Michel de Certeau, writing has typically
served to establish a site of the foreign other outside the text that then serves
to authenticate the voice that speaks from within the space of the text. "An
image of the other and the place of the text are simultaneously produced."[1]
In classical Greek historiography, this took the form of an opposition between the other as barbarian, the nomadic Scythians, and the sedentary
citizens of Athens, the audience for Herodotus's *Histories*. By the time of
Montaigne's celebrated text on cannibals, ethnography was serving subtler
ends. Now it was the voice of the savage himself, speaking from "a beautiful
body 'without divisions,' unsplit by any trade, partition, hierarchy, or lie,"
which authenticated Montaigne's own discourse. In de Certeau's concise
formulation: "the savage body obeys a law, the law of faithful and verifiable
speech."[2] Although Japan lacked (at least until the modern period) a colo-
nialist motive for constituting an ethnography of others—in the Tokugawa
period, "verifiable speech" speaks as an indigenous voice—the middle-
kingdom ideology of China had long since enabled a hybrid space for barbarian others throughout the East Asian cultural sphere.[3] The Yamato court

took shape within and against the geographical imaginary produced by this ethnographic gaze from the continent, with *Nihon shoki* redirecting this gaze to its own "barbarian" others that thereby enforced the authority of its own text and by extension that of the court's own cultural space. It is the fluctuating fortunes of this cultural and geographical imaginary, sustained by an awareness of China, that will form the starting point for this chapter's discussion of the medieval Japanese spatial imaginary.

Geographical Imaginaries and the Centering of the Court

From the picture evoked at the end of Chapter 4, one might reasonably conclude that mid-Heian Japan was a closed, inward-looking culture, set on edge by the pervasive fear of plague and demonic possession. But the picture presented there was one largely seen through the prism of texts conditioned by the interests of a localized court at a particular historical moment. A number of poems on travel themes from *Man'yōshū* will allow us to gauge subtle shifts in the perception of the cultural terrain from a position that is outside the narrow confines of the Heian court but already registering the effects of a geographical centering. The first poem is by Prince Nagata (d. 737):

> Today I saw / in the far distance / where the clouds dwell / the Satsuma Channel / of the Hayato people (Hayahito no / satsuma no seto wo / kumoi nasu / tōku mo ware wa / kyō mitsuru kamo) (*MYS*, 3, 248)[4]

Inhabiting the westernmost region of Tsukushi, or present-day Kyūshū, the Hayato people of Satsuma were still perceived, in the early eighth century, as outside the political and cultural reach of the Yamato court. Whether an actual or imaginary experience, the poem records the traveler's feelings at finding himself at the boundary of the familiar, at the edge of strange lands. Yet the same site evokes a quite different response in a poem by Ōtomo no Tabito (665–773), who was then governor of Dazaifu. It is preceded by the prefatory remark, "Composed while longing for the detached palace of distant Yoshino":

> Even the huge rocks in the channel / of the Hayato people / fail to match / the fish coursing / through the falls of Yoshino (Hayahito no / seto no iwao mo / ayu hashiru / yoshino no taki ni / nao shikazukeri) (*MYS*, 6, 960)[5]

Here, the anticipated pleasure in seeing an unfamiliar site is countered by the memory of superior scenic pleasures associated with the emperor's palace at

Yoshino. If both poems suggest an openness to the unfamiliar and strange, the second poem is complicated by a certain ambivalence, hinting at a perception of cultural and political space that has already begun to organize itself around the geographical center of the court. The following poem is the seventh in a series of eight travel poems by Hitomaro:

> Over a long road from barbarian lands / at the far reach of the heavens / I have come, yearning / and now at the Straights of Akashi / the island of Yamato comes into view (amazakaru / hina no nagajiyu / koikureba / akashi no to yori / yamato shima miyu) (*MYS*, 3, 255)[6]

Emotionally, the poem registers the returning traveler's sudden pleasure at catching his first glimpse of Yamato as it rises into view. At the rhetorical level, there is an explicit contrast between Yamato and the "barbarian lands" from which Hitomaro has just returned. As an epithet of distant things, "amazakaru" 天離 ("at the far reach of the heavens") was frequently attached to the noun "hina," which might be represented logographically by 鄙 or 夷, the first graph indicating the unrefined hinterland and the second the "barbarians" who lived there.[7] This contrast between the refined center (Yamato) and the barbarian hinterland is made explicitly in another *Man'yōshū* poem:

> Living for five years in this hinterland / at the far reaches of the heavens / I have forgotten / the customs of the capital (amazakaru / hina ni itsu tose / sumaitsutsu / miyako no teburi / wasuraenikeri) (*MYS*, 5, 880)[8]

This was one of three poems composed by Ōtomo no Tabito on the occasion of a farewell banquet that was held for him at the symbolically significant site of the library at Dazaifu. Tabito's service as governor of Dazaifu, which began in 728, was his second trip to the region. Eight years earlier, he had been dispatched there as the general in charge of subjugating the same Hayato. The connotations of the epithet "amazakaru" in this and the preceding poem are worth exploring a bit further. An initial reading might easily suggest a meaning closer to "distant skies," but it is the hinterland that is distant with respect to the capital, a sense nicely captured in Levy's translation of the phrase. As Ōkubo Hiroyuki notes, the epithet properly refers to the sky (*ten*) that doesn't exist in the hinterland, specifically the sky of the capital where the sovereign resides. "Hina" therefore evokes the image of a land beyond the civilizing reach of the tennō, a land still awaiting the rule of his authority.[9] But the range of implication encompasses more than the physical sky above of the capital. In the Hitomaro poem, composed in logographs, the graph 天 also evokes the Chinese astral mythology that anchored the tennō's political authority.[10]

Another poem by Tabito complicates this view of the hinterland. At a banquet held shortly after he took up his new duties as governor of Dazaifu, Tabito engaged in the following poetic exchange with the Vice-governor Ishikawa no Taruhito:

> Do you not yearn / for Mount Sahoyama / to be living there / in a courtier's house / among the flourishing bamboo? (sasu take no / ōmiyahito no / ie to sumu / saho no yama woba / omou ya mo kimi) (*MYS*, 6, 955)[11]

Sahoyama was located northeast of the capital Heijō in Yamato. The allusion elicited the following reply from Tabito:

> Since my Sovereign, ruler of the eight quarters, governs in this land / whether I am here or in Yamato / it is all the same in my thoughts (yasumishishi / wago ōkimi no / wosu kuni wa / yamato mo koko mo / onaji to so omou) (*MYS*, 6, 956)[12]

Whereas the previous poems establish a sharp opposition between the barbarian hinterlands and the civilized court, the latter centered in the Yamato region, Dazaifu is here imagined as identical with Yamato, a single realm united under the authority of the sovereign. Ōkubo reads these shifts in perspective as indicative of a growing split between the public and private attitudes of Tabito. If the present poem shows a complete identification of the "private" Tabito with the public persona of the court official who serves the sovereign, the previous poems reveal a private Tabito in whom subjective perceptions, including attitudes toward illness and death, are being projected onto the barbarous hinterlands beyond the reach of the capital.[13] The private–public dichotomy is a familiar topic in discussions of classical poetry, but its psychological reading gains here by being placed in a geographical context. The vacillations between an outward-looking and inward-looking viewpoint in these poems can also be read as indications of a geographical imaginary that is beginning to reshape perceptions of not only subjective space but cultural and political space as well. The observations of the historian Bruce Batten are pertinent here.

In commenting on the sharpening sense of boundaries during the Nara period, Batten writes: "With the establishment of the Nara state, boundary concepts become somewhat clearer. Much like in Rome, a sharp distinction came to be drawn between 'inner lands' (*kenai*), that is areas under direct

Japanese control, and the "outer lands" (*kegai*), that is areas outside the zone of administration but still located within the greater Japanese 'world.'"[14] As Batten further notes, this sharpening sense of boundaries during the Nara period occurred at a time of vigorous state formation accompanied by outward expansion, with the result that the boundaries at the fringes of the "state" tended to have the character of "zonal frontiers," where cultural spheres merged into one another. These observations help to account for the range of impressions conveyed in the series at *Man'yōshū* poems cited earlier. In the two Satsuma poems, the speakers, to use Batten's terminology, are in a zonal frontier and convey a corresponding sense of wonder that unfamiliar surroundings evoke. In Tabito's two Dazaifu poems, on the other hand, Dazaifu is both inside and outside, part of the tennō's or sovereign's realm in one poem and its uncivilized hinterland in the other. The first of these would be indicative of the expansive and growing power of the Nara state to which Batten refers.

If the geographical notions of the *Man'yōshū* poems indicate an expanding, but still fluctuating, center of cultural and political authority, then one might expect to see competing powers emerging in the areas that lay outside or at the edge of the center's reach; especially by the mid-Heian period, or early tenth century, when, as Batten notes, political authority was becoming more "fragmented among multiple power-holders."[15] In the eighth year of Jōgan (866), for example, or about seventy years before the nearly simultaneous rebellions of Masakado and Sumitomo in eastern and western Japan, a district governor of the western province of Bizen, which was located on the Inland Sea, formed a conspiracy with local magnates and men from Silla, with the intention of seizing Tsushima, an island northeast of present-day Kyūshū. Tsushima's strategic importance lay in the fact that it was a critical stopover for trading ships traveling between the mainland and the ports of Tsukushi. A similar event occurred four years later, in 870, when a high government official of the Dazaifu formed ties with the king of Silla in another plan for rebellion against the state. The central authorities invariably characterized such events as rebellions. But if we follow the historian Amino Yoshihiko and reorient our geographical coordinates away from the court, they appear in a much different light. Rather than rebellions, they become evidence of an extensive trading and geopolitical sphere that encompasses Japan, Korea, China, and the maritime zones of the Japan Sea and the Inner Sea, superceding, in Amino's words, the narrow concept of "state" embodied in the ritsuryō system centered on the inner provinces.[16]

Could such activity have coalesced into a self-conscious attempt to establish a rival center to the court? In the case of Sumitomo's rebellion, historians suggest that vertical ties between court and local power holders and an insufficient military base would have prevented such an effort from succeeding.[17] But even if we grant that political and military conditions militated against a successful outcome, there would have been nothing to prevent such "rebels" from exploiting the same middle-kingdom ideology as the court. In remarks on Japanese foreign relations in the ancient period, Mori Kimiyuki observes that although the Yamato court viewed itself, in its official relations, as a tributary of Tang China, internally it conceived of itself as a "small imperium" (*shō teikoku*) and even tried to enforce such a view in its relations with the Korean kingdoms. This small imperium ideology was shared, as Mori notes, by all countries on China's periphery.[18] The much-debated duplicate court of Masakado that was imagined by the author of *Shōmonki* emerges, I suggest, in this gap between the center's "small imperium" ideology, which the *Man'yōshū* poems show in the process of formation, and the broader East Asian geographical imaginary in which it participated.

In a famous passage that occurs in Masakado's letter to Fujiwara no Tadahira, Masakado defends his decision to declare himself the new emperor:

> "Humbly considering my ancestry, I am a fifth generation descendant of the Kashiwara Tennō. Without doubt, even were I to control half of the country for a long time to come, it could not be said that I did so lacking fortune. *Every history book tells of men who in ancient times seized empires through military might.* Heaven has given me [excellence] in the military art; and when I think about it, who among my peers can compare with me?"[19]

And again, in a debate with his brother on the legitimacy of his claims, the following words are attributed to Masakado:

> In today's world, people look upon those who are victorious through arms as princes and kings. Even if this is not so in our country, *it is true of all other lands*; like the Great King of the Khitans who in the Enchō era, on the first day of the New Year, captured the country of Bohai, changed its name to Dongdan, and ruled over it as lord. What cannot be taken and ruled by force?[20]

The Khitans of this second passage were a nomadic people from Mongolia, who had been making incursions against the Chinese empire as early as the age of the Northern and Southern Courts (317–589). Strengthened by new allies, they finally succeeded in crushing the country of Bohai, an enfeoffed kingdom of the Tang empire, in the fourth year of Enchō (926), or only twelve years before Masakado's own rebellion in 939. Past scholarship has tended to dismiss Masakado's words as unrealistic or intentional irony by a chronicler sympathetic to the court. This view has been questioned by the historian Morita Tei. In an essay that reconsiders *Shōmonki*'s authorship, Morita has speculated that its author was someone who not only opposed the political hegemony of the Fujiwara regents but condoned in principle the historical theory of seizing the throne through force that is attributed to Masakado in the text. Sympathetic to Masakado's cause, Morita's author was critically detached enough to justify a seizure of political power by invoking precedents from books—namely, Chinese histories—as well as recent events in East Asia.[21] By allowing Masakado, via his putative author, to speak on his own terms rather than the court's, Morita makes possible a more radical reading of the text. In the geographical imaginary envisioned by *Shōmonki*, the axial link with the center is replaced by an affiliation with a much broader East Asian geopolitical sphere, or in Masakado's words, "all other lands (*mina hito no kuni*)." *Shōmonki*, in brief, represents what may well have been the first contestation of official history in Japan, appropriating the metaphorical center even as it speaks from a position outside the court's own geographical locus. In theoretical terms, the text of *Shōmonki* inscribes a moment of increasing tension in the dialectic between the metaphorical (textual) and material (geographical) implications of centrality, which is described by Henri Lefebvre in the following passage from his study *The Production of Space*:

> Any centrality, once established, is destined to suffer dispersal, to dissolve or explode from the effects of saturation, attrition, outside aggressions and so on. This means that the "real" can never become completely fixed, that it is constantly in a state of mobilization. It also means that a general figure (that of the center and of "decentering") is in play which leaves room for both repetition and difference, for both time and juxtaposition.[22]

The "real," in this particular case, was not only the court as geographical locus but the totality of discourses and practices which invested that centrality with authority.

Apart from historiographical deformations like *Shōmonki* and *Mutsuwaki*, the signs of this decentering also included the late Heian fascination with collecting oral tales (*setsuwa*) of local and foreign provenance, as in

Konjaku monogatari shū (*Collection of Tales of Now and Then*), the reassembling of assorted Chinese writings in texts like Fujiwara no Akihira's (989–1066) *Honchō monzui* (*A Japanese Literary Anthology*, ca. 1058), and the fresh interest evinced at this time in the marvelous, the strange, and the nomadic. Japanese writers were once again recording the contours of a geographical imaginary that first appeared in the travel poems of *Man'yōshū*, but with a difference. We can glimpse it in the fascination with festive sites at the edge of the capital, which is conveyed in works like *Shin sarugaku ki* of Fujiwara no Akihira, with its descriptions of itinerant performing artists, including one of the earliest notices of the biwa hōshi. We also catch its note in the recorded impressions of *dengaku* spectacles in aristocratic journals like Fujiwara no Munetada's *Chūyūki* and *Rakuyō dengakuki* of Ōe no Masafusa (1041–1111), which disclose a fascination with odd details of dress, gesture, and other unusual behavior. Masafusa, who appears in later anecdotal literature as a prodigy of Chinese learning, was arguably one of the earliest ethnographers of Japanese folk customs.[23] In his *Kugutsuki*, Masafusa provides a brief account of the customs and manners of the itinerant performers known as *kugutsu* (puppeteers). Whereas the men, he tells us, are skilled in archery, horsemanship, and hunting, the women make themselves up, sing seductive songs, and are fond of one-night liaisons. But it is in the description of their nomadic lifestyle that Masafusa strikes his most interesting note:

> The *kugutsu* have no fixed abode and keep no dwellings. In tents and animal skins, they move about in pursuit of water and grass. They are just like the barbarians of the north . . . They till neither furrowed fields, nor pluck mulberry twigs. Because they do not belong to government districts and none of them is indigenous to the land, they are just like vagabonds. Moreover, ignorant of rulers and nobles, they have no fear of provincial governors. With no labor corvée, their life is one of pleasure.[24]

Masafusa clothes his description of the *kugutsu* in language borrowed from Chinese accounts of the Xiongnu and other nomadic peoples.[25] At the same time, his mention of fields, mulberry twigs, and freedom from labor corvée are unmistakable references to the stable space of Heian agricultural life. Mulberry trees, for example, were typically planted about dwellings in settled agricultural communities and often crop up in late Heian documents detailing disputes over estate boundaries between temples and provincial governments.[26] In his use of such details, Masafusa seems to be aiming at an exoticization of the domestic or local. But contrary to his picture of a completely nomadic people, the documentary evidence of "field exemptions" and complaints filed by the kugutsu over the confiscation of personal property from the late Heian and early Kamakura periods indicate that the itinerant kugutsu actually performed services for the provincial government (*kokuga*). Because they sold combs among other items, Amino has surmised that they were among the special provisioners (*kugonin*) who received protection from the court.[27] The exoticizing of the nomadic kugutsu against the familiar backdrop of Heian agricultural life belongs to a new geographical imaginary where the play of difference works both within and against the dominant ideology of the center. In this new discourse, China names not only the geographical entity but a corpus of texts, citations, and interweaving references that recombine to produce new representations of local and domestic space.

From Centered to Peripheral Space

If political and cultural space in the Nara and Heian periods was less centered than an exclusive focus on the court would lead us to believe, it was nonetheless true that throughout much of this period the world of the court continued to organize itself around a center–periphery view that opposed the capital and home provinces as a center of refined culture and religio-political authority to the barbarous hinterlands of the outer provinces. Drawing again on the work of Henri Lefebvre, we can characterize this as a representation of space (*représentation de l'espace*): a dominant system of knowledge consisting of codes and conceptual frameworks that rationally organize space, visibly embodied in styles of architecture and reinforced by a variety of spatial practices.[28] Specifically, the geomantic centering of the capital with its grid of intersecting avenues, its palace and temple architecture, and the implementation of purificatory rites at designated sites within the capital and along the borders of the home provinces constituted a set of spatial practices that was underpinned first by yin-yang five agents correlative principles and later, over the course of the Heian period, by increasingly elaborate rules for managing defilement. Operating throughout much of the Heian period, these spatial practices produced and continued to reinforce the sense of a centered space.

By the late Heian and early medieval periods, a combination of factors was bringing about a gradual shift from this older capital-centric space to what I refer to as peripheral space. These included a marked increase in maritime trade, the gradual introduction of coin-based exchange, and the concomitant erosion of estate boundaries. The intersection between changing perceptions of space, economic trade, and textual production is already evident in the late Heian setsuwa collection *Konjaku monogatari shū*, where the tripartite classification into the three geographical zones of India, China, and Japan registers the gradual decentering of the capital-centered discourse that had initially been linked to temporal and geographical referents inaugurated by the Nara court.[29] Like *Konjaku*, the two medieval setsuwa collections *Shiju hyakuin nenshū* (thirteenth century) and *Sangoku denki* (*Chronicles of Three Countries*, late fourteenth to early fifteenth century) also organized their material by a geographical classification that encompassed India, China, and Japan. That this was more than a mere literary principle of classification is suggested by the Preface to *Sangoku denki*, which thematizes the link between the narrative style of "storytelling in the round" and the new space that was opening up as a result of increasing maritime trade. After praising the Ashikaga ruler Yoshimitsu, under whose rule the four seas are tranquil and foreign trade flourishes, the author introduces the reader to two characters named Bongobō and Kanjirō, the first a Buddhist priest from India and the second a layperson from the Ming empire, who happen at this time to be visiting Japan. Having decided to go into retreat at Kiyomizu Temple, they find themselves together with a Japanese recluse named Waami. To pass the time, the three take turns telling tales about their respective countries, one each for India, China, and Japan in a repeating series of three, giving their entertainment the form of stories in the round, a structure already anticipated in *Ōkagami*.[30] Like the latter's mingling of oracular speech, gossip, and street talk that results in an ambulatory history, *Sangoku denki*'s Preface, with its fortuitous encounter of three travelers who exchange tales, becomes a textual enactment of the new geographical imaginary, a world of cultural exchange enabled by expanding maritime trade.

One conspicuous sign of the shift to peripheral space was a quickening of activity in the forbidden sites of the old capital sphere—namely, its margins, waysides, barriers, market districts, ports, and so on. In Buddhist spheres, this gave rise to a new representation of space that envisioned Japan as a small country of the margin (*shōkoku no hendo*)—a modification of the same three-country worldview inscribed in the setsuwa collections—thereby transforming the islands of Japan from a center organized geographically around the capital sphere into a liminal realm.[31] With this gradual shift to peripheral space, the older capital-centric representation of space did not disappear but persisted as both a set of spatial practices and an important element in the medieval imaginary. In Lefebvre's terminology, the old capital-centric sphere continued to retain diminished force as a representation of space even as it was gradually being reduced to symbolic value as a "space of representation," or representational space.[32] In the sections that follow, the interplay between this older capital-centric space and the emergent, more open-ended space of the late twelfth through fourteenth centuries will provide the conceptual framework for exploring the ambiguous place of China and the warrior in the medieval imaginary. China is here understood as both an actual place and an imaginary space. Whereas in the mid-Heian period the warrior was confined to a position at the periphery of the aristocracy's imaginative universe (however visible in the daily life of the capital), by the early medieval period, through the person of Kiyomori, he had gained a literal foothold at the center of the power structure. As a result, the warrior in the medieval imaginary, much like China itself, is alternatively the threatening sign of the other and the figure for an emergent, decentered space of commercial and cultural exchange.

Barbarians at the Gate

In the epigraph from *Meigetsuki* (*Chronicle of the Bright Moon*) that opens this chapter, the poet Teika has made a small change to a line of verse from Bo Juyi, substituting the word "barbarian" 戎 for the latter's "brigand" 賊. As Ivo Smits points out, in poetic terms, the change is negligible.[33] But for the elite warriors who were coming into political ascendancy in the late Heian and early medieval periods, the slight alteration betokens their increasingly ambiguous status. This can be seen by setting Teika's choice of the term "barbarian," one of four names for the barbarians of the four quarters in Chinese, beside the terms "court enemy" (*chōteki*) and "general" (*shōgun*). As Saeki Shin'ichi has shown, the term *chōteki*, which is used extensively in *Heike monogatari* and other military chronicles, only came into common usage with the medieval period.[34] Not originally a Chinese compound but a Japanese formation, the word was not found much before the period of the Genpei War. Used in conjunction with the term *shōgun*, *chōteki* effectively removed the ascendant class of elite warriors from the negative associations that continued to cling to various populations traditionally referred to in officialese as "brigands" (*zoku*) and uncouth barbarians. In *Heike*, for example, the numerous occurrences of the word "chōteki" and the examples of warriors claiming the status of shōgun who have subdued the court's enemies from of old belie the fact that these "court enemies" would have entered the historical record as "brigands," "pirates" (*kaizoku*), or any of the various other pejorative terms available in the official language.[35] In structural terms, the linguistic shift was not inconsequential. By elevating their adversary's status, elite warriors who claimed to be defending the interests of the court were also affirming their own prestige.[36] In brief, the shōgun–chōteki dyad belonged to a warrior- rather than a court-centered conception of geopolitical space, where warriors claimed a position at the center of authority rather than one relegated to ambiguous status at its periphery. Barbarian, on the other hand, as will be shown later, becomes entangled with medieval ideas pertaining to defilement.

A climactic turning point in the Kakuichi *Heike* occurs in the seventh scroll. After opening with an account of the rise of the rebellious Minamoto warrior Kiso Yoshinaka in the far north, it swiftly proceeds to narrate his rout of the Heike warriors at the battle of Kurikara, continues with the Heike's unsuccessful attempt to enlist the military aid of Enryakuji Temple, and finally comes to a slow end with a long narrative of the Heike's flight from the capital as their enemies press in upon them from the north and east. At one point, the forward movement of the narrative is suspended by a long reflection on the fleetingness of the Heike's glory, made all the more poignant in the context of their now precipitous flight. An elaborate opening passage that likens the abandoned Rokuhara residence of the Taira to the palace of a Han emperor suddenly widens into this geographical metaphor of their flight from the capital, here given in Helen McCullough's translation: "Earlier, the Heike had fortified the steep pass of the Han Valley and the Two Yao, but the barrier had been smashed by the northern barbarians; now, they had relied on the deep waters of the Great River, the Jing, and the Wei, but the rivers had been seized by eastern savages. Never could they have imagined this sudden expulsion from the center of civilization, this tearful flight into the benighted hinterland."[37] Translation can only partially convey the full effect of this passage and the ornate description of the abandoned Taira residence that precedes it. Both passages draw heavily on language and phrasing from works like the *Wen xuan* and *Wakan rōei shū* (*A Collection of Japanese and Chinese Poems for Chanting*) to create a felt contrast of style with the surrounding vernacular narrative.[38] But its effect is more than rhetorical and stylistic. In the passage just quoted, for example, the elaborate spatial metaphor, invoking the ancient center–periphery opposition that first appears in *Nihon shoki*, equates the capital where the Confucian rites and duties are observed (*reigi no kyō*)[39] with the high culture of Han China; grandiloquently identifies the bridges of the Seta and Uji Rivers (which were strategic approaches to the capital) with the steep pass of the Han Valley and the Two Yao; and likens the invading forces of Yoshinaka and Yoritomo to the northern and eastern barbarians of the Chinese periphery. In brief, it imbues the Taira with an aura of grandeur that evokes an earlier age of the court's glory.

This equation of the Taira with the Han emperors is more than nostalgia for an earlier court that is now in peril. The following passage concludes the description of Kiyomori's "flowering fortunes" in the first scroll:

> The Dragon-Fly Islands of Japan are made up of barely sixty-six provinces, and the more than thirty provinces now controlled by the Heike already exceeded more than half. In addition to these, they possessed countless estates and rice-fields. Overflowing with silks and damasks, their halls resembled flowering gardens. Congested with horses and carriages, the areas outside their gates were like markets. Yangzhou gold, Jingzhou pearls, Wujun damasks, and Shujian brocades—not one of the seven precious things and myriad treasures was lacking. And as for the halls and pavilions where they danced and sang, and entertained with performances of the fish-dragon and arrow-toss, not even the Palace of the Emperor or the Retired Sovereign's Grotto of the Immortals surpassed them.[40]

What looks again like rhetorical heightening—this time enhanced from phrases borrowed out of the *Wen xuan, The Bo Juyi Collection*, and *Honchō monzui*—opens out into a range of reference that is no longer strictly regulated by the claims of a court-centered literary tradition. As commentators have long noted, the itemization of precious objects in this passage, all of them products of the territory ruled by the Southern Song, brings to mind the goods acquired by the Taira in their maritime trade.[41] The word *market* (*ichiba*) is more than a figure of speech; rather, the itemized wealth and lexical riches flow into the passage from a new space of trade in which the contemporary world of Song China occupied an increasingly important place in the expanding commercial activity of medieval Japan—an activity in which the Taira played an early and not inconsiderable role. In the text's geographical imaginary, the mapping of the Taira's Rokuhara residence lies at the intersection of two discursive fields: one that draws it back into the centric space of ritsuryō-style rule and another that joins it to the emergent, more open-ended cultural space of medieval Japan.

That the Taira, now invested with a royal aura, should be driven out of the capital by "barbarians" pressing in from the periphery is an irony of no small consequence, constituting one of the Kakuichi *Heike*'s characteristic inversions.[42] As warriors, the Taira were apt to evoke far different associations in the minds of the Heian aristocracy than nostalgia for the past glory of the court. As we learn in the "Night Attack," where Tadamori's unprecedented entry into the Courtiers' Hall provokes a vague threat of impending violence, the Taira, "despite being descendants of the Kashiwabara Sovereign, had for some years become unfamiliar with life in the capital and behaved like *jige*."[43] The term *jige* is a jab at Tadamori's rustic manners acquired from long residence in the provinces. Technically, it referred to those of the sixth rank and below who were not permitted entry into the palace (Seiryōden); more literally, it denoted those with roots in the soil of the provinces. The *jige*, therefore, as autochthonous residents of the provinces, were the contrary of the *tenjōbito* or "dwellers above the clouds" (*kumo no ue bito*), who as courtiers enjoyed the privilege of frequenting the emperor's palace.[44] Behind the metaphorical range of meanings implicit in the jige–tenjōbito opposition, then, was a larger web of associations that organized the capital aristocracy's view of the world and that had come to bear strongly on their perceptions of the warrior, contributing to the ambiguous threat of violence that pervades the opening episode of "The Night Attack in the Courtiers' Hall."[45]

Outside In, Inside Out

In the early medieval period, the perception of the warrior as the "barbarian within" was further complicated by the event known as the Mongol invasion in the latter third of the thirteenth century, which overlapped in subtle ways with a negative view of the Bakufu as a government of barbarians.[46] In the years leading up to the Mongol invasions of 1274 and 1281, a series of portents, including a red comet in 1265, induced the court to order the performance of ritual prayers and acts of virtuous government as a way of warding off disasters. Three years later, when the first reports reached Japan from Korea regarding the intentions of the Mongols,[47] the court again ordered prayers and acts of clemency toward the people. Finally, in 1293, as reports circulated of Kublai Khan's plans for Japan's subjugation, Fushimi Tennō drafted an edict that drew attention to the government's peril by linking the foreign menace and recurring natural calamities to Fushimi's own lack of virtue, including in its fourth article his vow to exercise virtuous government as a remedy. In addition to these points, article 3 of the edict singled out "a decline in the country's policy and court ceremonial." The latter, according to Murai Shōsuke, was intended as a criticism of the autocratic rule of the Hōjō clan, who had come to be viewed as the internal equivalent of an invading barbarian force. This view of Japan as under the heel of barbarian rule is the subject of one of the dream revelations in "The Matter of Unkei's Prophecy Record" ("Unkei miraiki no koto") in book 27 of *Taiheiki*:

> Because the emperor is despised and it is the end-age when there is no reverence for even the gods and Buddhas, how could any other government be possible? And so the way of treachery takes its place. There is no doubt that those who take turns casting aspersions on one another will all perish without distinction. They are like a gathering *of mountain brigands and sea-pirates* who argue over the profit and loss of their wicked deeds. Eleven generations have now passed, from the time when Lord Yoritomo put the world under military rule some years back until the current rule of Hōjō Takatoki, and although it is certainly a deviation from what is right *for the world to be governed by barbarians of low status*, in these days of the end-age signs of warning have been ineffectual. The minister slays the sovereign, and the son slays his father. Having reached the point where matters are settled by force, the bottom conquers the top. The nobility and ministerial families are unable to exercise power jointly with one sovereign ruler, and *so the dregs and lower orders* devour the lands and four seas of the realm. The entire realm has fallen to the warriors.[48]

Another revelation earlier in the same prophecy record attributes the famous collapse of the dengaku viewing stand in the capital to a similar breakdown in hierarchy: "The spectators were made up of low-class commoners (*jigenin*) in the capital and peddlers. When the nobles who rule over the country of Japan promiscuously mingled among them, the Bodhisattva Shō-Hachiman, the Kasuga Divinity, and the Sannō avatar were filled with anger, which in turn roused up the infernal deities who control the earth, causing the stand to collapse from the shaking."[49] In these passages, the view of the warrior as internal barbarian has begun to overlap with the increasingly negative attitudes toward defilement.

This blurring of the boundary between inside and outside, which *Taiheiki* portrays as a complete inversion of hierarchy, or as "bottom conquers top," coincided with an increasing emphasis on class distinctions. The *Myōgoki* (1275), a Kamakura period dictionary of vernacular words, contains the following entry on the word *ebisu*:

> Why are the warriors of the hinterlands (*hendo no mononofu*) called ebisu? The ebisu are found in the four quarters: the Eastern Barbarians, the Southern Barbarians, the Western Barbarians, and the Northern Barbarians. The word ebisu is based on the sound reversals of *yase* (thin), *hami* (chew), and *seri*. Hair (*ke*) grows on their faces and they are big-boned (*hone taka*). Furthermore, the sound reversals of *ese* (food), *hami* (chew), and *seri* are based on the sense of *gehin* (unrefined).[50]

Two rather different perspectives on the warrior are combined in this gloss: one reflective of the Chinese middle-kingdom ideology that locates the foreign other outside the center and a second that is premised on hierarchical distinctions of class and locates the foreign other inside, but among the lower social strata.[51] To arrive at the meaning of "ebisu," *Myōgoki*'s author employs the Chinese procedure of "hansetsu," which involved the reversing and splicing together of sounds from different words to arrive at the phonetic structure of the word being defined.[52] Apart from "seri," whose meaning is uncertain, the words chosen for their sounds all evoke negative characteristics, mainly centered on eating and physical traits, which are neatly summed up in the entry's concluding word "unrefined."

The same trend can be observed in the medieval usage of the term *ezo*, which, in addition to denoting the populations of the far east and north of the archipelago, also began to overlap with the sense of *hinin* (outcast), once again suggesting a blurring between the foreign other who resides outside and the defiled other within.[53] In a study on the origins of samurai honor, Keiko Ikegami has observed how the warriors' close ties to hunting culture along with their profession of violence put them on a footing that was perilously close to that of outcasts in medieval society. As she points out, "the rise of the honorable samurai warrior as a hereditary social category virtually coincided with the emergence of the *hinin*."[54] By a kind of inverse logic, then, as elite warriors achieved greater authority, status, and prestige in the medieval period, emulating the refined culture of the center, these internal others were redefined and increasingly pushed into the lowest strata of the social hierarchy.

Two further examples will help to illustrate the ambiguous status of the warrior in the medieval imaginary. The first is another exercise in medieval etymologizing, with the exegete this time the Buddhist priest Gen'e (1269–1350), a celebrated Confucian scholar who appears a number of times in *Taiheiki*, most famously as the discoursing priest in the riotous banquet early in the first scroll.[55] In his commentary on *Shōtoku Taishi kenpō* (Prince Shōtoku's Constitution), Gen'e draws on the authority of the Chinese glossary *Shuowen jiezi* (ca. 1000) to derive the following meanings for the four principal barbarians. Extracting the radicals for each graph, he associates the Southern Barbarians 南蛮 with "insects," the Western Barbarians 西羌 with "sheep," the Northern Barbarians 北狄 with "dogs," and the Eastern Barbarians 東夷 with the "bow." In this way, the warrior/barbarian is singled out for his martial calling and removed from the animal associations of the other three.[56] The second example is the following passage from the Engyōbon variant of the *Heike* episode "Su Wu" ("Sobu"), which blends together the Chinese topos of the barbarian Xiongnu, medieval attitudes toward defilement, and a Heian poetic sensibility:

> Long ago in China there was an Emperor called Han Wu di. He had summoned several tens of thousands of *sendara* to keep guard over the Palace, and when their term expired, a barbarian (*teki*) from the country of the Xiongnu said: "Though I am called a barbarian of the country of the Xiongnu, I have taken my nature from the furrows in the rice-fields of Ji.[57] Morning and evening I listened to the melancholy night-cry of the monkey and the calls of journeying geese; and at the eaves of a rough thatched-hut, full of sadness, I am accustomed to hear the grieving wind in the sere reeds. Now that I have this opportunity to meet with your wise and virtuous Excellency, you ask me, 'What can I give you as a memento for your journey home?' This is my wish. Your majesty has three thousand consorts. I would like to receive one and return to my fortress among the Xiongnu."[58]

Here, the negative associations of *sendara* (Sanskrit *caṇḍāla*), a word that technically denotes members of the lowest social caste in India whose principal occupations were slaughtering and hunting, blends with lyrical imagery from the court tradition to create a strangely dissonant effect. In the mid-Kamakura dictionary *Chiribukuro* (*The Dust Bag*), for example, the word *sendara* is grouped together with *etori, eta, hinin,* and other low-status types who handled meat or were otherwise connected to the slaughter of animals.[59] As a Xiongnu of the Chinese classical tradition, who has been transformed from a nomadic horseman into an agriculturalist, he is at the same time capable of evoking associations more proper to certain aristocratic views of late Heian rural life, here conveyed through the journeying geese, thatched hut, and grieving wind, images that all derive from the tradition of court poetry.[60] The military arrangement, moreover, as Saeki Shin'ichi has noted, recalls the late Heian and early Kamakura system of rotating guard duty whereby warriors from the provinces would be assigned to periodic duty in the capital.[61] Although less explicit than the *Taiheiki* passage cited earlier, the Engyōbon passage discloses the same problematic status of the warrior in the medieval imaginary. Called a sendara (literally a "slaughterer," but also hinting at the hunting culture of the Tōgoku warriors), the Xiongnu warrior at the same time possesses a refined sense of poetic nostalgia for lands that have now been partially assimilated to the cultural sphere of the center.

If the preceding passage locates the warrior in an ambiguous cultural space, there are other episodes in the Engyōbon *Heike* that transmit a detailed knowledge of terrain and topography that suggests the hunter's familiarity with the land. The following episode comes from the Engyōbon version of Yoshitsune's daring descent from Hiyodori Pass in his surprise attack against the Heike, which is narrated in "Rōba" ("The Old Horse") in the ninth scroll of the more familiar Kakuichi variant. Since this variant is unfamiliar, I translate it in its entirety:

> At that moment a man of about fifty in bound up persimmon-colored trousers and with two reddish dogs in front of him passed just outside Kurō Yoshitsune's military encampment. He dispatched Edo no Genzō to summon him. As the old man came before Yoshitsune, he made a bow. "Who are you and why are you traveling deep in the mountains at this hour of the night?" asked Yoshitsune. "I am from the village of Aikawa at the foot of this mountain, but for fourteen years now I have sheltered and hunted in these mountains. My name is Ononoe." "Well, then you must know your way round in these mountains. Is there a path that leads down to the stronghold where the Heike have withdrawn? Tell me the truth." The old man replied: "From childhood until old age, I have wandered and hunted in these forests to earn my livelihood. I have reconnoitered every tree and visited every valley, but there is no path that leads down to the Heike's stronghold." "But surely deer must pass through here?" The old man replied: "On calm spring days when the evening sun has shifted eastward and melted the

ice in the ponds, deer from deep in the mountains of Tamba cross over to the meadows of Harima. And when red maple leaves carpet the valleys and the branches become bare, Harima deer crossing over to Tamba make a path at dusk among the trees. At those times they pass through here." "So deer do pass through. Any path that a deer takes a horse should be able to follow. Just like a race-course. But tell me, why is this mountain called Hiyodori Pass?" The old man replied: "I have heard that in the days when Emperor Tenchi was living at Nagae no Nishi no Miya in the Province of Tsu, he dined on large numbers of small birds and would catch the bulbul bird (Hiyodori) on the mountain peak where Mukoyama Mangaji Temple stands. An attendant of the Emperor named Ōtomo no Kimiie used to pass down the slope dangling bulbul birds, and so it came to be called Hiyodori Pass. But closer to our own days, during the season of thick spring haze when it is dim in the mountain fastnesses, the Hiyodori, a resident of the southern mountains, journeys across to the northern mountains, builds its nest, and gives birth to its young. After the autumn mists clear and the branches become bare, the Hiyodori still in the north, fearing the deep mountain snows, journeys back to the south. At that time, too, it crosses these mountains. That is why it is called Hiyodori Pass. It must be about four or five thousand feet down to the Heike's stronghold. Although the drop might be only a hundred feet, no horse or man can make it down there from here. You had better stop." Having spoken, he vanished leaving them feeling even more forlorn.[62]

In addition to its detailed knowledge of the local terrain, the Engyōbon variant discloses that familiarity with the diurnal and seasonal habits of deer and birds that only a hunter is likely to have possessed, a viewpoint entirely lacking in the more capital-centric Kakuichi *Heike*, which records the encounter with the hunter but omits his story. Medieval texts like the Engyōbon *Heike*, then, could transmit a complex, even contradictory, sense of early medieval cultural space, shifting from the unstable capital-centric viewpoint in the Xiongnu story to the observations of a local hunter for whom Emperor Tenchi is remembered as a consumer of fresh game.

But how might late Heian and early medieval Japan have looked from the center's periphery? An interesting case is presented by Soto-ga-hama, an old name for what is today the east half, or gulf side, of the Tsugaru Peninsula in Aomori Prefecture.[63] At this time, Soto-ga-hama was under the control of the Ōshū Fujiwara, whose base of power was the flourishing city of Hiraizumi. In the course of the eleventh and twelfth centuries, Hiraizumi had become a center of both overland trade to other parts of Japan and maritime trade abroad, with ships sailing from China to Hakata in western Japan (present-day Kyūshū) and from there directly up the Pacific coast to Hiraizumi. In the famous Chūsonji petition attributed to the Hiraizumi chief, Fujiwara no Kiyohira (1056–1128), Kiyohira boasts that the people of Dewa and Mutsu bend to him as grass bowing before the wind (a phrase that is also used of Kiyomori) and that even the sea pirates (*kaiban*) of the Shukushin and Yūrō submit to him like irises before the sun. Kiyohira's "sea pirates" literally refer to the Tungusic peoples mentioned in Chinese historical records, but for Kiyohira, they are likely a reference to the sea-hunting Ainu of what was then known as Ezo-ga-shima (modern-day Hokkaidō). Two further observations can be made. First, as Ōishi Naomasa remarks in his discussion of this petition, Kiyohira's boast is lacking in any awareness of Sota-ga-hama as an important boundary separating north and south. Second, in portraying his power as a ruler, Kiyohira freely appropriates the middle-kingdom ideology, characterizing what may have been the Ainu people as barbarians at the periphery of his own political realm.[64]

If Hiraizumi and Soto-ga-hama constituted a center of political power for the Ōshū Fujiwara, by the late Heian period, Soto-ga-hama was figuring in the old center's geographical imaginary as the easternmost limit of Japan. Although later negatively associated with expulsion and defilement,[65] at this time Sota-ga-hama and Ezo evoked the lure of the exotic. In what is thought to be the earliest reference to Soto-ga-hama in the literature, the poet Saigyō writes in one of his many poems of travel: "That which lures me / into the depths of the far reaches of Mutsu / the memorial stone of Tsubo / and the breeze of Soto-no-hama (*Mutsunoku no / okuyukashiku zo / omōyuru / tsubo no ishibumi / soto no hama kaze*)." [66] According to the late twelfth-century poetic treatise *Shūchūshō*, the village of Tsubo [Tsumo] was at "the eastern limit of Japan" (*nihon no higashi no hate*) and *also* the site of a memorial stone incised with the words "Nihon chūō" (center of Japan), presenting the paradox of a "Japan" that was outside its inside.[67] The same sites could also evoke responses like this poem by Fujiwara no Chikataka (1099?–1164):

> In Tsugaro where the Ezo live, the fields are abloom with clover;
> by now they will be setting up wooden trees,
> brocaded with desire.
> (Ezo ga sumu / tsugaro no nobe no / hagi sakari / koya nishikigi no /
>   taterunaruran)[68]

According to the same *Shūchūshō*, it was the custom of the ebisu of Michinoku to woo his lover by placing a colorfully stained wooden block before her gate, thereby distinguishing him from the capital lover who conveyed his desire in writing.[69] The exoticism of Chikataka's late Heian poem is best appreciated by setting it against an earlier evocation of the far north, the following exchange from the tenth-century *Ise monogatari* between two lovers in Michinoku: "If only there was a path / where I could pass secretly / into the Shinobu Mountains / I should be able to see deep / into the depths of your heart (*shinobu yama / shinobite kayou / michi mo gana / hito no kokoro no / oku mo mirubeku*)." To which the woman replies: "I think that is truly splendid, but what would happen were you to see into the ill-tempered heart of a such a barbarian (*ebisu*)?"[70] Whereas earlier in the Heian period Michinoku and the ebisu were likely to be invoked for their barbarous lack of refinement,[71] in Chikataka's poem the unlettered Ezo/ebisu of the far north have come to evoke the exotic charm of distant places.

Strange Trafficking: Kiyomori and Fukuhara

History tends to remember Kiyomori as the arrogant warrior who was punished for having overreached his rank, but his strategy for achieving political power was based in part on geopolitical calculations that involved him in active commerce with the periphery: control over the Pacific sea lanes and a burgeoning trade with China that included gold mined in the distant "barbarian" provinces of Mutsu. By the latter half of the twelfth century, Chinese trading ships had extended their shipping lines from Hakata, on the western island of Kyūshū, deep into the Inland Sea. In spatial terms, as Takahashi Kimiaki has observed, Kiyomori's strategy represented an attempt to transform the interior geopolitical sphere of the ancient home provinces, centered on the capital, into a flourishing center of trade open to the outside.[72] In moving the court to Fukuhara, for example, which was located close to the entrance of the Inland Sea, Kiyomori had in mind its strategic importance for controlling and overseeing his trade with China. Nor was the Taira's trade network limited to maritime commerce between Japan and China, but it extended over large parts of interior Japan as well: from Ōshū, in the far north, with its gold reserves and horse pastures, down to the port of Hakata in Kyūshū, where ships set sail to China. In his study of this activity, Gomi Fumihiko has shown how the Taira's trade was assisted, in part, through their connections with retainers like Chikuzen Sadayoshi, who held a position as groom in the Imperial Stables, which was attached to the Office of the Retired Sovereign (*in no chō*). Sadayoshi, who makes several appearances in *Heike*, acted as an important intermediary in the transport of goods, including gold and horses, from the far northern provinces of Ōshū to the port in Hakata.[73] The goods traded between Japan and China at this time included luxuries such as cloth, exotic animals, books, sutras, paper, ink-stones, tea, and paintings imported from China; and from Japan, exports such as gold, silver, pearls, sulfur, lumber, as well as finished products that included screens, fans, swords, and rice.[74] Kiyomori himself, whose residence overflowed "with silks and damasks" and contained "Yangzhou gold, Jingzhou pearls, Wujun damasks, and Shujian brocades," even managed to obtain a printed version of the *Taiping yulan*, the encyclopedic collection of quotes and passages so esteemed by the Chinese emperors that its export was strictly prohibited.[75]

How did the old court aristocracy view such activity? In 1170, only eight years after having undertaken the costly repair and construction of Ōwada Harbor, Taira no Kiyomori invited Go-Shirakawa to his recently completed residence at Fukuhara where he introduced him to a Song merchant whose ship was anchored at the nearby harbor. Reacting to the news of Kiyomori's mercantile activity, the head of the Fujiwara regental house, Kujō Kanezane, characterized it as "unheard of in Japan since Engi, the actions of one possessed by a demon" (*tenma no shoi*).[76] A few years later, in 1172, Kanezane characterized as "shameful" some gifts sent from Song to the retired emperor (*hōō*) and the Taira chancellor lay priest (*Hei shōkoku nyūdō*), which were accompanied by a letter that addressed the recipients as the Japanese sovereign (*Nihon kokuō*) and chancellor (*daijō daijin*). Subsequent entries disclose that Kiyomori and Go-Shirakawa, notwithstanding Kanezane's strong disapproval, not only accepted the gifts—beautiful and precious objects sent by the governor (*hanshi*) of the Song state of Ming—but reciprocated with presents and a letter of their own. On this occasion, Kanezane also expressed extreme surprise at what he termed a "newly established ceremony," as well as anxiety over Go-Shirakawa's use of the title "Great Abdicated Sovereign" (*tajō tennō*) as his signature in the letter.[77] As Hashiguchi Kusaku notes in his discussion of these entries, for Kanezane, the cooperation between the retired sovereign and Kiyomori in such matters represented an extreme breach of precedent. Underlying Kanezane's concern over the compromised status of the retired sovereign was his anxiety at seeing him drawn into the activity of foreign commerce at the instigation of Kiyomori, who was now being formally addressed as the chancellor of Japan.[78]

Despite Kanezane's strong criticisms, when we turn to accounts of these events in the *Heike* corpus, Kiyomori's actions are typically celebrated as praiseworthy deeds. *Genpei jōsuiki*, for example, concludes its celebratory account of Kiyomori's construction of Sutra Island, which transformed Ōwada Harbor into a safe haven for trading ships, with effusive praise for Kiyomori's mercantile activity: "And so this island was given the name of Sutra Island. With ships now plying their trade without fear, the island was a source of wealth for the country and an example for ages to come. Its fame reached all the way to the Tang Emperor, who called Kiyomori the Taira Prince Wada of Japan and sent him divers precious gifts such as not even the Emperor received. It was a splendid honor indeed."[79] The same encomium in the Engyōbon variant is preceded by this poetic evocation of Kiyomori's port:

Gradually, boats began to dock and small houses and other buildings appeared. The inn lanterns glittered like the stars, sun, and moon; and the wide vista of the blue sea was dim. As the saying goes, although it may take more than ten years, the sight of the flourishing pine always brings blessings. Add up a few more months and years, and the port will rival even renowned Muro and Takasago. As is their custom in this world, even the pleasure-girls are not loath to come. Immersed in reflections in their small boats, they grow lonely as they gaze out toward the western provinces. By two's or three's they come alongside and chant, "The white waves in the wake of the ship rowing out to sea . . ." Or inside the cabin of the boat, they chant out these and other poems: "In the boat on the waves, it is the joyful meeting of my life . . . Tuning the harp softly, I gaze deeply at the moon, as the Chinese oars are lifted high and the boat enters the watery haze." Striking the drum and beating out a measure, they sing about the regret of parting. It is the way of love to play on the flute and pluck the strings. By now even the roof-tiles of houses back home have been forgotten. Provincial governors and those of lesser rank scrape the bottom of their coffers, and merchants and their servants squander their funds. Regrets come later, but so too does death, which cannot be avoided in this world. When the news of Kiyomori's passing reached the Emperor of China, he bestowed upon him the title Taira Prince Wada of Japan and is said to have sent rare treasures that not even the Emperor received.[80]

Accustomed as we are to the descriptions of port life in Chikamatsu and other writers, it is worth reflecting on how new such evocations were at this time.[81] Blending together the rhythms of the new style songs with a rich imbrication of quotations from *Wakan rōei shū*, the passage combines the language and imagery of commerce and merchant ships with the world of pleasure-girls and travelers to evoke a space of fluid movement and drift, at once alluring and melancholy in tone. It is as if the wealth accumulated by Kiyomori in his trade with China had poured its riches into the very style of the passage. Equally notable is the absence of any hint of the old court sphere that informs the criticisms of Kanezane. Instead, in the text's geographical imaginary, the centrality of the old capital has yielded, as the closing eulogy of Kiyomori vividly conveys, to a sphere of trade and cultural mingling that was closer to the Song than the Japanese court.

Just as Kiyomori's commercial ambitions could provoke feelings of revulsion among conservative court factions, we find a similar ambivalence in early medieval views of Yoritomo's military conquests. In 1188, or only a few years after his animadversions against Kiyomori's China trade, Kanezane was warning the latter's erstwhile rival, Minamoto Yoritomo, against a similar act of geopolitical hubris, this time Yoritomo's plan to subjugate the liminal island of Kikai-ga-shima (widely believed to be the abode of demons) and thereby extend the Bakufu's military rule to the furthest reaches of the archipelago.[82] In the Engyōbon *Heike*, Yoritomo's political ambitions, criticized by Kanezane, are presented in a much different light:

> One night, Tōkurō Morinaga had a dream. "Hyōe no suke was seated upon the fortress watch-tower of Ashigara. With his left foot pressing upon Soto-no-hama and his right foot upon Kikai-ga-shima, the sun and moon emerged from under his left and right arms spreading out a bright light. The Ihō Priest came forward holding a gold wine-jar. Moritsuna then placed a gold goblet on a silver serving tray and advanced to his side. I took up a ladle, poured off some wine, and offered it to Hyōe no Suke, who drank of it three times." At this point, Morinaga woke up from his dream. After he related his dream to Hyōe no Suke, Kageyoshi spoke as follows: "This is a most auspicious dream. As Barbarian Subduing General you will govern the realm. Tradition states that the sun is the reigning sovereign, and the moon the retired sovereign. For the sun and moon to spread out their light from your left and right arms means that the nation's rulers will now be wrapped in the strength of their general. Everyone from Soto-no-hama in the east to Kikai-ga-shima in the west will submit to you."[83]

Despite Kujō Kanezane's warning against the danger of attempting the conquest of the eerily liminal Kikai-ga-shima, Yoritomo, who is recorded to have made use of maps in plotting out his far-flung conquests, was not dissuaded and subdued the island anyway.[84] As these facts and anecdotes attest, the Japan of Kiyomori and Yoritomo, members of the warrior class, and the Japan of the old aristocracy, represented by figures like Kujō Kanezane, were premised on radically opposed ways of looking at cultural and political space.

The Pine of Akoya and Disappearing Placenames

From as far back as the Nara period, exile and banishment have been an important means of enforcing political authority and a perennial theme in both historical and literary narrative. To be effective, however, both the political act of exile and its ritual equivalent, expulsion, require a stable notion of the center. In a text like the Kakuichi *Heike*, which calls into question the very possibility of fixed and established boundaries, it is not surprising that moments of exile should become occasions for thematizing the problem of cultural and political space. A curious instance occurs in "The Pine of Akoya" ("Akoya no matsu"), one of several episodes devoted to the fate of the Shishi no tani conspirators, several of whom were exiled by Kiyomori after he discovered their plot against him. The following passage is spoken by the exiled Naritsune, after having been falsely told by his captor that the journey to visit his father, Narichika (another victim of exile), would take twelve or thirteen days:

> "Long ago, Japan was made up of thirty-three provinces, but recently it has been divided up into sixty-six. Bizen, Bitchū, and Bingo, too, were originally one province. Long ago, moreover, the two provinces of Dewa and Michi-noku famous in the East were made up of one province of sixty-six districts, but some time ago twelve districts were broken off to form the province of Dewa. When the Middle Captain Sanekata was exiled to Ōshū, thinking he would visit the famous site of that province, the place called The Pine of Akoya, he searched throughout the province, and when he was unable to find it and on his way back, he met an old man and asked: 'You appear to be old in years. Surely, you know about the famous site of this province, the place called The Pine of Akoya.' 'It's certainly not in this province. It must be in the province of Dewa,' he replied. 'So even you don't know. Now that the world has entered the end-age, people have lost the ability to name even the famous sites.'"[85]

Naritsune's words suggest how the weakening of the old cultural sphere centered on the capital affected members of the elite class.[86] As Christopher Tilley writes in a study on the phenomenology of landscapes: "The specificity of place is an essential element in understanding its significance. It follows that the meanings of space always involve a subjective dimension and cannot be understood apart from the symbolically constructed lifeworlds of social actors. Space has no substantial essence in itself, but only has a relational significance, created through relations between peoples and places."[87] Playing off a progressive division against a former unity, the passage represents the division and reaggregation of space as a loss, which in the sphere of spoken utterance becomes an inability to even name or call forth the famous sites. The latter, as discussed in a previous chapter, were emblematic of how space was possessed by the cultured elite, including once autonomous sacred sites. Hence the significance of the "old man," who, according to the version in *Genpei jōsuiki*, is no other than the divinity of Shiogama.[88] Here, however, he makes his appearance in the guise of a diminished divinity, typically an auspicious numen associated with the pine tree. In the concluding phrase of the passage, this negative multiplication of space is identified with the time of the end-age, a period of the Buddhist law in which it was believed that the increasing distance in time from the origin point of the Buddha's entry into nirvana made it virtually impossible for ordinary human beings to achieve enlightenment. To cite Tilley again, "The experience of space is always shot through with temporalities, as spaces are always created, reproduced and transformed in relation to previously constructed spaces provided and established from the past."[89] The decentered space of Naritsune's perception is accordingly accompanied by a reflection on loss that gestures toward the empty time of the Buddhist end-age.

A Kingdom Divided

If Naritsune's story connects changes in the perception of cultural and political space and the consequent disappearance of localities to a failure of spoken utterance, another episode relates this same phenomenon to Chinese writing. Kiyomori's punishment of the Shishi no tani conspirators was followed a short time later by another act of political hubris, the exile of the forty-three ministers of state and the sequestering of the Retired Sovereign

Go-Shirakawa in the Seinan detached palace. Among the exiled ministers was the Chancellor Fujiwara no Moronaga, famous for his musical talent and scholarship. The following anecdote from the Engyōbon purports to explain the cause of Kiyomori's wrath against the Fujiwara chancellor:

> The reason Lord Moronaga was hated so much by the Heike is as follows. The Chinese court [*taitō*, literally Great Tang] composed some sentences of difficult graphs and presented them to the Japanese court. No one at court was able to read them, but Moronaga could, and for the Heike their import was bad. In the first there were three graphs. One was the enclosure for country 口; he read this as "a kingless country" 王ナキ国. In the second sentence, inside the enclosure for country, the graph meaning "division" 分 was written three times 圝. He read this as "the country is disordered and full of commotion." The third one was written with the graph "shin" 身 in the word "shindai" 身躰 ("body") written twice side by side 躬. He read this as "matters will be taken in hand." The last one was this sentence: "kachū chūchū, kuchū shichinichi yūhi, kaichū shichinichi yūhi" [90] Having looked at this phrase as well, Lord Moronaga opened his mouth wide in laughter and managed to read out the entire phrase, but the people who heard him were unable to remember it exactly. Afterwards people said: "Rumors of the Heike's evil deeds have reached foreign lands (*ikoku*), and these words are meant to insult our country's ruler." [91]

Among the several intriguing aspects of this text is the shift from "taitō" (Great Tang) at the beginning to "ikoku" (foreign country) at the end. In an analysis of the various ways for referring to China or Chinese subject matter in the Engyōbon, Hirano Satsuki has discerned three broad categories of words: (1) vague designations like the pronouns *kano* (that) or the temporal marker *mukashi* (in the past); (2) dynastic names such as Tang (*tō*), Han (*kan*), and the like; and (3) a category of evaluative nouns such as *taitō* (Great Tang), *taikoku* (Great Country), *ikoku* (foreign country), *ichō* (foreign dynasty), *takoku* (other country), and the like.[92] It is this last category that is especially interesting. According to Hirano, nouns containing the graph for "great" (*dai*) mark China as a positive realm of precedent, which permits it to function as a standard for criticizing Japan. A second group, containing the graph for "foreign/different" (*i*) or "other" (*ta*), set up a pattern whereby China is contrasted negatively with Japan. It is the play of these conflicting designations within single episodes or stretches of text that discloses a shifting and ambivalent view of China. In attempting to account for the shift from "taitō" (Great Tang) to "ikoku" (foreign country) in the present anecdote, for example, Hirano argues that the intention of criticizing the Heike by first invoking China as a positive realm ends up undermining the Japanese tennō's own authority through the implication that Japan has become a "kingless realm." The anecdote thereby corrects itself through marking out China as the foreign other (*ikoku*) at the end.[93]

Drawing on Hirano's observations, we can extend this analysis into the relationship that the text establishes between scriptive and political space. As a learned member of the conservative court faction, Moronaga is presented as the only person capable of interpreting the Chinese graphs that have been sent to the Japanese court by the Tang emperor. In an ingenious trope, the constitutive elements of the graphs, by means of which the court had for centuries promulgated its authority in the form of edicts and official histories, become emblematic of the country's collapse into division. The written language thereby enacts a figural fall into division, producing a multiplicity of realms where there had once been unity. This is developed with almost dialectical precision in the anecdote. First, the graphic system that inscribed the court's authority at first refuses to yield any sense at all. Kiyomori's usurpation of authority has triggered a breakdown in the representational system, conveyed by the opacity of a language that now refuses to signify. Next, Moronaga's successful interpretations yield the ominous forecast of division and disorder in the realm. The climactic moment occurs in the long series of apparently nonsensical graphs, which when spoken out loud produce something like the equivalent of gibberish or noise.

The theme of this anecdote, a display of erudition in which a court official defends Japan's honor vis-à-vis its continental exemplar, China, is not unusual in medieval setsuwa literature, and we will have occasion to examine a further example later. In this particular variation, however, the contest between China and Japan takes on a deeper significance. Although Moronaga, as spokesperson for the court, interprets the Chinese graphs to Kiyomori's disfavor, the text represents something more problematic. In the geographical imaginary of the text, China is now a doubly ambiguous realm: figuratively at the level of language and literally as a productive source of power in the form of trade and wealth. The shift from Great Tang (*taitō*) at the beginning of the text to "foreign land" at the end, the former magnifying Japan and the latter harboring a sense of threat in its implied meaning of "other realm," marks out the two extremes of this doubly ambiguous space.

Ambiguous Realms: China, Japan, and Constructions of the Other

No major figure in *Heike*, with the possible exception of Kiso Yoshinaka, is more apt to elicit contradictory responses from readers than Shigemori, the eldest son of Kiyomori. Imperial apologists in the Tokugawa period, taking umbrage at episodes like "Kane watashi" ("A Transmission of Gold"), condemned him for his sinophilia. Early modern scholars like Haga Yaichi and Yamada Yoshio, on the other hand, impressed by Shigemori's loyalty to the emperor in episodes like "The Admonition" ("Kyōkunjō"), enrolled him among the defenders of the emperor system.[94] For scholars in the postwar period, Shigemori became something of a Hamletic figure, with a number of studies focusing on his self-contradictions.[95] Modern readers, less troubled by the ideological implications of Shigemori's words, are apt to be put off by his piety and sanctimoniousness. Yet few episodes in *Heike* are richer in the ways that they foreground the ambiguous workings of "the other" and the status of China in medieval Japan, especially when the Kakuichi variant is set beside the much different versions recorded in the Engyōbon. Two of these episodes, "A Transmission of Gold" and "A Debate over a Physician" ("Ishi mondō"), are the focus of this and the following section.

The well-known Kakuichi variant of "Kane watashi" ("A Transmission of Gold") begins with the following statement by Shigemori: "Although I may plant strong roots of merit in our land, I cannot expect my descendants to pray for me forever. I would like to plant roots of merit in another land so that prayers will always be said for my future salvation." The remainder of the episode relates how Shigemori commissions a Song merchant from Chinzei named Miao Dian to present two gifts of gold, one to the monks of the Mount Yuwang monastery and another to the Chinese emperor, to assure that prayers will be performed for his future salvation. The trusted Song merchant performs his commission and the episode concludes: "And thus it is said that prayers for the rebirth in Paradise of the Japanese Minister of State Taira no Ason Shigemori have been said continuously until this very day."[96]

The longer and less familiar Engyōbon version of this same episode reveals some striking differences:

> This minister Shigemori did not only heap treasure on the gods and Buddhas of our land, he was also devoted to the Buddhist law of foreign realms

(*ichō*). Around spring of the second year of Jishō, he summoned the governor of Chikuzen Sadayoshi and held counsel with him: "As long as I am alive, I want to raise up halls and pagodas worthy to be remembered in our land and perform meritorious works, but it appears that the Lay Priest's prosperity will not outlast his life-time. Therefore, melancholy for some time now at the thought that my family's glory will exhaust itself and that after this house perishes we will instantly become like the dust of the mountains and fields, I feel that if I leave behind even a single meritorious work in the Great Country, that there will be no extinction for me even in worlds to come. You will go to Tang and accomplish my plan." He then summoned a ship's captain by the name of Miao Dian of Hakata who was in the capital at the time, and gave him twenty-three hundred catty of gold, which had been sent up as tribute from the district of Kisen in Ōshū that was controlled by the minister. "Of this gold, I give a hundred catty to you; bring twenty-two hundred catty to Great Tang, and give two hundred to the monks of Mount Yuwang, where the bones of the Buddha's mortal remains are kept, and they will hand it over to the Zen monk Zhang Lao. Present the remaining two thousand catty to the Emperor and have him donate mass-fields to that same temple." After saying this, he wrote out a letter and gave it to Miao Dian. Miao Dian received the gold, hastened to Tang, and having informed the Emperor of the matter, presented him with the letter. The Emperor perused the letter . . .[97] The Emperor couldn't keep back his joy. "As a minister of Japan, he has expressed a deep regard for our country." Shigemori's name was entered in the temple register, and right up to the present day the words "enshrined spirit Taira no Shigemori, Governor of Musashi State in the Great Country of Japan" continue to be intoned every day. How splendid.[98]

In place of the Kakuichi *Heike*'s emphasis on the planting of good merit and prayers for Shigemori's salvation or rebirth in Paradise, the keynote in this version is struck by the words "prosperity" (*eiga*) and "glory" (*eiyō*), neither of which appears in the Kakuichi variant and which are closely tied to the fortunes of the Heike "family" and "house" (*ichimon, tōke*). In brief, Buddhist piety yields to a preoccupation with worldly fame, a desire to "raise up pagodas and towers worthy to be remembered." Even the one phrase that approximates the Kakuichi Shigemori's concern for his own salvation hints ambiguously at worldly aspirations: "I feel that if I leave behind even a single meritorious work in the Great Country, there will be no *extinction* for me even in worlds to come" (daikoku nite wo mo shu shiokitaraba, Shigemori takai no nochi made mo *taiten araji* to oboyuru nari). The italicized expression might arguably refer to a lapse in prayers spoken for Shigemori's salvation, a future lapse in Shigemori's state, or the lapse of his memory and fame.[99] The specific mention of mass-fields (*kūden*) later in the text and the Engyōbon's choice of a title for the episode, "Komatsu dono daikoku nite zen wo shūshitamau koto" ("Concerning the Komatsu Lord's Performance of a Meritorious Work in China"), would seem to encourage the first reading—namely, Shigemori's wish that prayers on his behalf be performed unremittingly in worlds to come. But in contrast to the explicit Kakuichi version, the motivation for these prayers remains problematic.

If worldly fame is a major motif in this version, its magnitude is in direct proportion to the splendor and might of the Chinese empire. Yet here, too, as in the case of the Moronaga episode, the text betrays an ambivalence when naming China. Whereas Shigemori's own words consistently magnify China, twice naming it Great Country (*taikoku*) and Great Tang (*taitō*), the narration prefers either neutral terms or the distancing expression "foreign realm" (*ichō*). The one exception to this is the use of "ichō" by Shigemori in the letter (abridged in my translation) that he sends to the Chinese emperor. For Hirano, this marks the same double-bind of simultaneously invoking China as an exalted realm of precedent and "othering" it to safeguard Japan's own prestige. Hence, when Shigemori switches from taikoku–taitō in his own speech to "foreign realm" in his formal letter to the Chinese emperor, there is a shift, Hirano suggests, from a private level of speech, in which Shigemori speaks on his own behalf from an attitude of humility toward an exalted China (*taikoku*, *taitō*), to a court- or Japan-centered discourse, in which Shigemori assumes the public role of "minister of Japan" (*Nihonkoku jinka*), who out of deference to the Japanese tennō is obligated to address China as the "foreign" other.[100]

But does the magnification of China necessarily entail an attitude of humility on the part of Shigemori? While the "othering" of China suggests a strategy on the part of the Engyōbon editors of organizing geographical space as well as the text's own discursive space into a Japan–China opposition, Shigemori's own words and the viewpoint that they imply may actually derive from source materials—diaries and other documents—that once belonged to the Taira family.[101] Despite the attempt to rework this material by framing devices, it persists as a dissonant voice within the body of the text. Although there are no extant documents to corroborate the various *Heike* accounts of Shigemori's behest of gold, the very specificity of the Engyōbon account regarding the Taira's network of trade, the identification of mediators like Sadayoshi, and the precise amounts of gold involved in the transaction enhance the historical claims of the text.[102] Viewed in this light, Shigemori's magnification of China arises less from an attitude of humility than from a desire for self-magnification: In magnifying China, Shigemori magnifies himself. To read the episode in this fashion is to relocate it in the same spatial imaginary as texts celebrating Kiyomori's port, recovering thereby the lineaments of a Taira history that lies hidden within the larger claims of the Engyōbon's discourse.[103]

The Engyōbon's ambivalent view of China flowed from several different sources. In the two episodes just analyzed, the focus was on the attempt to enforce a Japan–China opposition in the face of changing geopolitical conditions of trade that threatened the authority of the old court-centered capital hegemony. Another source of this ambivalence derived from the contradictory premises underlying the geographical location of Japan within the medieval Buddhist worldview. As I mentioned earlier, the belief that the world had entered the period of the final law (*mappō*) was reinforced in Japan by the view of Japan as a country at the margin of the Buddhist world. Distance in time from the Buddha's entry into nirvana, which rendered ordinary means of achieving enlightenment ineffectual, was paralleled by Japan's geographical distance from Buddhism's country of origin. Paradoxically, it was the apparent limitation of this geographical worldview that became the basis of the medieval conception of Japan as a special country of the kami or "deities" (*shinkoku*), which was achieved by systematically identifying Japan's native deities (*jingi*) as the manifestations or hypostases (*suijaku*) of the Buddha's original ground (*honji*). The ontological deficiency of Japan's marginal status was thereby reversed.[104]

Traces of these ideas are found in many medieval texts of the thirteenth and fourteenth centuries, including the *Heike* variants, notably in the religio-political doctrine articulated by Shigemori in his long speech extending over the "The Admonition" and "The Matter of the Signal Fires" ("Hōka no sata"), where he reprimands his father, Kiyomori, for inappropriate conduct toward the Retired Sovereign Go-Shirakawa: "Although it is said that our land is a mere hinterland, a region scattered like millet seeds, nevertheless, ever since the descendants of Tenshō Daijin [Amaterasu Ōkami] and those of Amanokoyane no mikoto have been rulers of this land and governed this realm, hasn't it been a breach of etiquette for one who has attained the office of Chancellor to don helmet and armor?"[105] Later in the same speech, after invoking the wrath of Amaterasu and Hachiman, he declares: "Japan is the country of the kami (*nippon wa kore shinkoku nari*). The kami do not suffer breaches of etiquette." And in the continuation of his speech in "The Matter of the Signal Fires," he invokes the third element of this ideology: "How wretched that because of a past karma I have been born in this latter age (*matsudai*) and experienced such unhappiness."[106]

Although the medieval notion of Japan as the country of the kami would appear to invert Japan's marginal status among the three Buddhist lands of Tenjiku (India), Shintan (China), and Honchō (Japan) by transforming it into a center of sacred authority, it actually achieved something more subtle and paradoxical. This can be made clear by looking at how the elements of this ideology functioned in combination. For this, we can turn to the following passage from *Genpei jōsuiki*:

> For the sake of us who live in the end-age and wish to pray for our rebirth, it would seem that we must without fail pray to the divinities (*shinmei*). It is more than two thousand years since the Buddha entered nirvana, and thousands of leagues separate Japan from India. The sacred doctrines have only recently been transmitted to Japan; yet because the true dharma and phenomenal dharma have lapsed, it is difficult for people to perform austerities, and signs are rare. Therefore, out of their abundant compassion the Buddhas and Bodhisattvas have taken pity on those who have been born into an evil age in a Buddha deprived border-land (*sakai*), where there is no hope of salvation, and having manifested their traces as deities (*shintō*), they subdue demons (*akuma*), protect the Buddhist teachings, display rewards and punishments, and inspire faith. . . . As a look at the conditions of our land shows, were it not for the assistance of the divinities, who would soothe the people and who would bring tranquillity to the land (*kokudo*)? As a small, remote country of the borderland (*shōkoku hendo no sakai*), this country's strength is feeble and in this defiled time of the end-age (*masse joaku no kono koro*), people's hearts are foolish.[107]

Here, Japan's marginal and defiled status has become the very basis of its own sacrality. Japan, in other words, is simultaneously defiled margin and sacred center. The supervenient principle here is the principle of "otherness" or "difference" because it is only out of such difference that Japan's sacrality can be secured. According to *Hachiman gudō kun* (kō-variant), for example, a late thirteenth-century text of Sannō shintō that has much in common with the Engyōbon's religious ideology, the decline of Korea was the direct consequence of its failure to keep itself separate from China—in other words, a failure to maintain its difference. Japan, on the other hand, the same text asserts, never belonged to another country because it was protected by its divinities. The sacrality of Japan was dependent on keeping its difference intact.[108]

In relation to our discussion of the medieval geographical imaginary, several important points emerge. First, in a phrase such as "shōkoku hendo no sakai" (a small, remote country of the borderland), the "shōkoku" (small country) discloses what remains merely implicit in the opposition between nouns that magnify China, as in "taikoku" (Great Country) and "taitō" (Great Tang), and those like "ikoku" (foreign country) and "ichō" (foreign realm) that diminish by infusing an aura of "otherness" into their referent. In other words, the foreign other that regularly inserts itself into these texts belongs as much to Japan as to China and is perhaps best understood as arising from a structural need for a principle of otherness, not from any fundamental opposition between Japan and China. To clarify this point, we can now turn to "Ishi mondō."

Medical Matters: "Ishi mondō," or a Debate over a Physician

Like "Kanewatashi" and the episodes about Kiyomori's construction of the port at Fukuhara, "Ishi mondō" opens out directly into the world of the Taira's flourishing China trade. The episode centers on Shigemori's reasons for rejecting Kiyomori's advice that he seek treatment for an illness from a celebrated Song physician now visiting Japan. Although there is no mention of this particular incident in extant historical records, it reflects a reluctance, among the higher echelons of the aristocracy, over the propriety of being treated by doctors conversant with the new Song medical arts that were entering Japan via the China trade. The center of this activity were ports in Kyūshū and other parts of Japan, and the diaries of the day record instances of aristocrats seeking out medical treatments from such doctors, sometimes with a sense of doing something illicit. Kujō Kanezane himself records "secret" (*mitsumitsu*) consultations with these doctors as well as his anxieties over the rumors that might follow.[109]

In both the Engyōbon and Kakuichi versions of this episode, Shigemori rejects medical treatment from a Song physician on three grounds: (1) the illness is caused by factors beyond his control, variously referred to as *tenmyō* (heavenly mandate) in the Engyōbon, *un/unmei* (fate or luck) in the Kakuichi variant, and *jōgō* (karmic determination) in both versions; (2) receiving a foreign visitor in the capital will bring shame on Japan; (3) cure by a Song physician will bring shame (*haji*) on Japanese medical art. Both versions therefore set up an opposition between Japan and China in which the latter functions as a site of threat. The different ways in which each variant structures these elements, however, allow the main portion of Shigemori's speech, his citation of the Han Gaozu precedent in the Kakuichi variant, to be read in contrary ways. The following passage from the Engyōbon version begins with Kiyomori's message urging Shigemori to seek medical treatment:

"At this very moment as if by divine aid (*myōga*), a famous physician from the Song Court has journeyed over to our country and plans to come up secretly to the capital. I have heard that he is presently at the port in the Province of Tsu, and have made haste to send for him. [1] *This physician is practiced in the medical art and continues without break the ancient example of Shennong. Having inherited the craft of healing, he follows at a distance in the steps of Jīvaka and Bianque. Thus, he is the head of a third generation house and having early on achieved perfect mastery of the medical art, he has always served the Emperor of the realm and spreads his fame at will over the four seas. Meet with him at once and have him devise a cure.*" The message was transmitted to Shigemori. Although the minister was lying in his sick-bed, he listened to the Lay Priest's messenger, and then out of deference perhaps, he hastily raised himself up, put on his court cap, straightened his robes, and facing Sadayoshi delivered this reply: "I have received medical treatment in past times. However, regarding my present illness, I have already thought the matter through and will not seek a cure. So there is no need to meet with him now. My reason is as follows: [2] *Long ago, when Han Gaozu attacked Qing Bu of Huainan, he was struck by a stray arrow. When he was on the verge of death, Empress Lü summoned a famous physician to see him. The physician said: 'I will cure you; however, it will cost you five-hundred weight in gold.' Gaozu replied: 'I have girded myself with a three-foot sword and taken the empire. This was a heavenly mandate; and life is in heaven's control. Over a period of eight years I fought over seventeen times with Xiangyu. Yet as long as the heavenly mandate endured, I was not wounded once. Now the heavenly mandate has fallen to earth, and I am wounded. Even if a renowned physician were to heal my wound, he could not save my life. What good could even Bianque do? It is not a question of being stinting of gold.' As he said this, he bestowed five-hundred weight in gold upon the physician, but his wound was not treated, and he finally passed away. With the example of those words in my ears, I am struck to the heart."* [110]

When we compare this version with the equivalent passages in the Kakuichi version, a number of important differences stand out. First, although both versions contain Kiyomori's praise of the Song physician (section 1), in the Engyōbon version it takes the form of a rhetorically embellished encomium, far more elaborate than the Kakuichi *Heike*'s brief mention of the "famous physician from the Song Court." The diminished presence of the Song doctor in the Kakuichi version is mirrored in Shigemori's initial reason for rejecting medical treatment:

> The Engi era sovereign [Daigo] was regarded as an extremely sage ruler.
> But when he permitted a physiognomist from a foreign country to enter the
> capital, this sage ruler committed what has been viewed as an indiscretion
> that has brought shame on our land (*honchō*) for years to come. How much
> greater, then, would the disgrace to this country be were I, an ordinary mor-
> tal, to introduce a physician from a foreign land into the capital. [111]

It is only after this warning against the impropriety of admitting a foreign doctor into the heart of the capital (literally the "royal city," *ōjō*) that Shigemori proceeds to cite the precedent of Han Gaozu (section 2). The central moment in Shigemori's speech, an effulgent moment in the Engyōbon, is overshadowed from the start by the threat of the foreign other.

The Han Gaozu precedent in turn discloses a subtle yet significant shift in emphasis. Instead of the Engyōbon's "tenmyō," the Gaozu of the Kakuichi version speaks of "un" [unmei]: "My *luck* has run out; and *my life* is now in heaven's hands." [112] Already from as early as *Shōmonki*, such Chinese concepts were being used to confer upon the deeds of warriors an ennobling aura that approximates the notions of fate, luck, and chance that one finds in many other traditions of warrior narrative. [113] Exempla about celebrated warriors from Chinese history were one way of magnifying the deeds of warriors in Japanese battle narrative, not unlike the classical Greek rhetorical technique of *auxesis* (Latin, *amplificatio*). By the medieval period, usages such as "un," "unmei," and "inochi" (the vernacular reading of the second graph in the compounds *tenmyō* and *unmei*) were becoming a site of dialogic tension as they were drawn into the orbit of Buddhist concepts such as karmic deter-mination (*jōgō, zengō*). [114] In the Engyōbon version, Shigemori counters the celebrated reputation of the Song physician with the even more illustrious fame of Gaozu. The use of tenmyō keeps Shigemori's speech firmly within the lofty realm of ancient Chinese precedent—Hirano's realm of positive precedent—burnishing Shigemori's refusal with the luster of a past glory. In the Kakuichi version, the shift to karma-determined fate is made clear in the sequel:

> If my illness is karma-determined (*jōgō*), will not medical treatment be ineffectual? And if it is not the result of karma (*higō*), it will heal itself without the application of a cure. When the medical art of the renowned Jīvaka failed, and Śākyamuni preached nirvanic extinction beside the Hiran-yavati River, it was in order to demonstrate that a karma-determined illness could not be cured. Were a karma-determined illness curable, why would Śākyamuni have entered nirvana? This was a clear indication that a karma-determined illness cannot be healed. He who was to be healed was the Buddha (*butsutai*); and the healer was Jīvaka. I, however, am not a Buddha, nor is the physician Jīvaka. Even were he to consult the Four Medical Books and prove master of a hundred cures, how could he heal this defiled body of mine (*udai no eshin*). Even if he had a detailed knowledge of the Five Medical Classics and experience curing many illnesses, how could he cure a karmic illness (*gōbyō*) from a former life? And were I to live as a result of his medical treatment, it would be as if there were no medical art in our land. If his medical art is to be without effect, there is no reason to meet him. Moreover, for a Minister of State of the Japanese court to meet with the visitor of a foreign court is both a shame for the country and an indication of political decline. Even if it means dying, how can I not be concerned about the honor of our country?[115]

The circular structure of Shigemori's entire speech, moving from (1) the shame of admitting a foreign visitor to the capital to (2) the ancient precedent of Han Gaozu, (3) the disquisition on karmic determination, and (4) back to the shame of meeting with a foreign physician, essentially negates the positive function of the Han precedent by turning it into an illustration of karmic causality, traces of which appear throughout the Kakuichi *Heike*. The circular, or ringlike, structure also discloses another pattern of associations that draws together the negative connotations of the foreign doctor (*ikoku no ishi*) and the state of Shigemori's own body. In explaining the karma-determined nature of illness, Shigemori refers to his own body as defiled. The Buddhist term employed by Shigemori, "eshin," technically means the dependent body that arises from mental constructions and that would therefore have no permanent ontological status. In medieval Japanese usage, however, the term *eshin* 依身 ("dependent body") was frequently represented in writing by the graphs *e* 穢 (defilement) and *shin* 身 (body), as it is in the passage from Shigemori's speech in the Kakuichi variant.[116] The bodily locus of defilement belongs to the same discourse that conceptualized Japan as a marginal and defiled land. The threat, in other words, posed by the foreign other, the introduction of a Song medical doctor into the sphere of the "royal city," and the defiled state of Shigemori's own body, arising from karmic determination, are in fact related symptoms, mirror effects, in a larger discourse connected to the ways "defilement" (*kegare*) was being reconceptualized from the late Heian period on. By way of summary, then, we can state that the Kakuichi variant of "Ishi mondō" brackets and, in a sense, erases the Chinese space of Shigemori's Han precedent—the world of trade, new medical arts, and also a new language of political power—by surrounding it with reflections on the foreign other and the karmic causality of illness. Although these appear unrelated, they are in fact connected through an underlying discourse on defilement.

The older Engyōbon version of "Ishi mondō" contains all of the elements or anecdotal material that has just been analyzed for the Kakuichi variant, but in contrast to the latter's integrated ringlike structure, the Engyōbon editors have merely linked them together as a series of discrete anecdotes. The Engyōbon version of the Han Gaozu precedent, cited earlier, is followed by two additional anecdotes on physicians and a final speech by Shigemori that closely resembles the Kakuichi disquisition on the karmic determination of illness. Although the two anecdotes are given as the direct speech of Shigemori, they derive from earlier anecdotes or setsuwa that have been reworked by the Engyōbon editors.[117] The technique of grouping together related anecdotes in the Engyōbon is a typical feature of the prompt books used by preachers of the Agui sect, whose influence is discernible here and elsewhere in much of the Engyōbon. The juxtaposition of individual setsuwa combined with the unfinished state of the Engyōbon text as a whole, which went through successive and partial phases of editing, has left us with a text that exposes its ideological sedimentations much more clearly than is the case for the Kakuichi *Heike*, which was reworked and "unified" by the reciters and their assistants.[118] The second anecdote (the first to follow the Han Gaozu precedent), a variant of which is also collected in the setsuwa collection *Jikkinshō* (*Miscellany of Ten Maxims*),[119] relates a story about a renowned Japanese physician who is invited to Tang to cure an empress's grave illness:

Recently in our own country, during the reign of Sanjō no In, the head of
the Medical Bureau was the physician Masatada. He cured illnesses difficult
to cure and made lives difficult to live livable, so people at the time won-
dered: "He must be the manifestation of Yakushi Nyorai, or Jivaka come to
life again." Though he lived in Japan, his renown spread to the Tang Court.
In those days, the empress of the *foreign land* had been suffering from a
malignant tumor for many years. At the time, the famous physicians of the
foreign land exhausted their medical arts and applied treatments, but they
were without effect, and so a letter arrived from the *foreign land* asking that
Masatada be sent over. Due to the rarity in our land of such an astonishing
request, the nobles met in frequent council. "To receive a request from the
Great Country is rare in our land and an honor for Masatada. However, he
must not go to Tang. If the cure is without effect, it will be a disgrace to our
country. And if it is efficacious, the practice of medicine in the Great Country will be lost for a long time to come. Moreover, why should it matter to
our court if the empress of another land dies?" When the Vice-Governor
and head officer of the Home Affairs Bureau Lord Tsunenobu expressed his
firm opinion,[120] everyone assented, and it was decided not to send Masatada. At this time, the Middle Counselor, Lord Masafusa, held the post of
Governor of Dazai and was living at Dazaifu. Because of this he was unable
to attend the council, so he was ordered by the Emperor to compose a reply
privately. In his letter poem, Masafusa said: "The two carp will not reach
the waves of the Phoenix Pond; how will Pianque enter the clouds of the
Crane Forest?" He wrote it down and sent it. It is said that this letter impressed the courts of both China and Japan.[121]

By alluding to an old story about a pair of carp that were the bearers of
a letter extracted from their insides, Masafusa's poem obliquely states that
Masatada will not go. Although hints from this anecdote have passed into
the Kakuichi version, nothing remains of the dialogical tension with the
preceding celebration of the Song physician.[122] The editor who inserted this
second anecdote not only intended to correct and comment on the aspirations of the first anecdote but disclosed, perhaps unwittingly, the medieval
ambivalence toward China. The repeated emphasis on China's foreignness
(*ikoku*) combined with the fame of the Japanese physician inverts the logic
of the previous anecdote. The reversal is then carried to an almost comic
pitch when the prospect of the Japanese doctor's success—now dependent
on the superiority of the country that confers recognition, thereby triggering
the shift from *ikoku* to *daikoku*[123]—suddenly threatens to obliterate the difference between China and Japan. Difference, fundamental to the medieval
discursive formation, must be maintained at any cost. It is only when the

learned Masafusa finally puts an end to the dilemma through a masterful display of innuendo that the Japanese court is rescued from the disgrace that menaces it in its trafficking with foreign realms.

The final anecdote delves back even further into the past and openly adverts to the taboo against a tennō's consulting foreign doctors:

> Moreover, long ago, after Emperor Hanzei had passed away, the fourth child of Emperor Nintoku, Emperor Ingyō—at this time he was still a prince—had long been suffering from a serious ailment. Nevertheless, due to the persistent urgings of the ministers, he acceded to the throne. When the physicians of our land had exhausted their art, they dispatched an envoy to the country of Silla, brought back one of that country's physicians, had him treat the Emperor's illness; and when after a short while he was cured, they praised him profusely and sent him back. This was a complete failure of judgment by the Japanese court, and an unparalleled act of mockery from a foreign country. Having heard of this precedent, despite the insistent demand from the foreign country to dispatch the chief of the Medical Bureau Masatada, Masafusa made a prompt judgment, and they ended by not sending him.[124]

The incident recalled here is recorded in both of Japan's earliest histories, *Nihon shoki* and *Kojiki*. Neither of these, however, hints at any cause for shame, and *Nihon shoki* actually portrays the incident in a positive light: "The physician arrived from Silla, and was forthwith made to treat the Emperor's disease. No long time after, he was healed of his disease. The Emperor was rejoiced, and having rewarded the physician liberally, sent him back to his own country."[125] The Engyōbon's and *Nihon shoki*'s sharply opposed views of the tennō's commerce with foreign doctors, the former's shadowed by the threat of defilement, points to the radically changed status of the late Heian and early medieval emperor. Whereas Temmu, Jitō, and early Nara period sovereigns magnanimously displayed their virtue by distributing medicaments and charity throughout the land, even visiting those who were mortally ill, the late Heian and early medieval emperors are constrained by the karmic affliction that besets their own bodies. This brings us back once more to one of the central concerns of this study: the impact upon royal authority arising from changes in the conceptualization of defilement over the course of the Heian period. To fully grasp this shift, we must now turn to the problem of heterotopic space, peripheral space in its ritual and sacred character, which is the topic of the following chapter.

REIMAGINING LATE HEIAN
AND EARLY MEDIEVAL SPACE

Introduction

Whereas the previous chapter explored several facets of the medieval imaginary of China, this chapter looks at medieval space in its ritual character.
Medieval here refers to the period that extends roughly from the late eleventh to the late fourteenth centuries, beginning with the emergence of rule by
retired sovereigns and ending with the appearance of *Taiheiki* after the defeat
of Go-Daigo that forms a major part of its subject matter. It was during
this period that defilement, under an increasingly dominant Buddhist religio-
political ideology, was transformed from something that could be eliminated
by expulsion into an interior phenomenon with both a somatic and subjective character, thereby effecting changes in the experience of space, especially
in its ritual character. I have characterized this shift as one from centered to
peripheral space. To give an example, the middle-kingdom ideology with its
notion of a refined center and barbarous periphery, which helped to organize
elite perceptions of cultural space from at least the early eighth century, was
overlaid during this later period by an image of Japan as a small country of
the margin that was simultaneously numinous—or in medieval terminology,
"a divine country"—and defiled, creating an intricate play between space

(encompassing the body) experienced as both center and a state of liminality invested with strange powers. In ritual as well as social behavior, this shift to peripheral space was often perceived by the capital elites as disorder in the social sphere, although it could also take on positive connotations. Underlying this perception of disorder was a breakdown in the symbolic codes that had been integral to the center's ritual management of space, embodied in such practices as placating the "raging deities," installing the nomadic or wandering deity in specific sites, and expelling demonic and harmful spirits, all of which have been discussed in previous chapters. One of its more visible signs was the outbreaks of vestimentary excess and other forms of extravagant behavior from the late Heian period on, often perceived as social unrest. As this activity overflowed the ritual sites, it took on an increasingly uncanny character that eventually became the early medieval sign of the heteromorphic (*igyō*), denoting an odd, weird, or strange appearance and behavior that hovered ambiguously between the sacred and profane. Historians have sometimes characterized these waves of riotous excess as indications of popular resistance to the government, but much of their effect on the religious and secular elites arose, I suggest, from this transformation in the ontological character of defilement.

In a well-known study, Amino Yoshihiko has characterized Go-Daigo's rule as that of a heteromorphic court. By affiliating himself with marginals, outcasts, and esoteric ritsu priests like Monkan (1278–1357), Go-Daigo, Amino argues, was attempting to invest his own royal authority with a new mystique that derived from his capacity to traffic in otherwise forbidden spheres—spheres implicated in defiling activity that had largely become the preserve of powerful Buddhist temples.[1] As I try to show in this chapter, however, Go-Daigo's court, at least in its liminality, represented the culmination of a ritual economy whose beginnings are already evident in *Ōkagami*, with its portrait of the extravagant and mad tennō Kazan-in and its renewed interest in royal authority's claim over demonic powers. During the reigns of Shirakawa and Toba, for example, the court of the retired sovereigns was already beginning to migrate physically to the periphery, or to the heterotopic sites of the capital. By the time of Go-Shirakawa, who was known for his cultivation of marginal performers, his deep devotion to Buddhist rites, and his trafficking in the profane military sphere, this transmogrification of the court was already well advanced.

We can observe this shift at many levels, both at the microlevel that defines the use of interior space at the court and in the permutation of codes pertaining to musical and other kinds of ritual or playful activity. In a study on the musical culture at the courts of Toba and Sutoku, for example, Tsuchiya Megumi has shown how the transformation of court ceremonial into a heterotopic site could extend even to formal court music like *bugaku*, which took on some of the same connotations for Sutoku as Go-Shirakawa's cultivation of *imayō*. In Sutoku's case, the unorthodox elements consisted in getting performers of widely disparate social status to compete in performing bugaku dances in normally prohibited or restricted areas of the palace. Among his preferred pieces were the Dragon King, in particular the section known as the Wild Prelude (*Kōjo*). On one occasion, he summoned courtiers to watch his high-ranking lover Fujiwara Tamemichi secretly perform the Dragon King dance in the courtyard (*niwa*), a site normally reserved for viewing performances of the Wild Prelude by low-class performers (*jige no maibito*). On other occasions, he would judge the skill of courtiers (*tenjōbito*) and low-ranking jige dancers performing together in the same site. In addition to judging the skills of others, Sutoku-in also cultivated the art of bugaku himself, devoting special attention to the "secret work" of the Dragon King dance.[2]

Over the course of the twelfth and thirteenth centuries, these violations of normative usages would frequently elicit strong criticisms in Buddhist and conservative court spheres, as was the case for Go-Toba. The author of the thirteenth-century *Jōkyūki* (*Chronicle of the Jōkyū Era*), for example, has this to say about Go-Toba's cultivation of shirabyōshi dancers:

> Excessively fond of entertainment, he assembled shirabyōshi from every quarter of the country and favorites from among his guardsmen, allowing them to *trample and defile* the Twelve Palace Offices and carpets of brocade where he summoned them. To see the royal authority and dignity thus lowered was truly loathsome. He feted them on the estates held by generations of nobility and court nobles, and having confiscated ten fields whose income had been designated for worship of the kami and lectures on the sutras, he combined them into five fields and bestowed them upon the shirabyōshi[3]

The use of the term "brocade" (*nishiki*) in conjunction with a defiling activity, as will be shown later, is typical of the behavior characterized as heteromorphic, which is closely tied to the violation of codes that define dress, music, and the use of space. In another study of the changing function of the interior space in imperial residences at this time, Akiyama Kiyoko, drawing on Teika's *Meigetsuki* and other sources, has described the collapse of hierarchical order that was characteristic of Go-Toba's detached villa at Minase.[4] An entry from *Meigetsuki* for the year 1206, for example, describes a scene at Go-Toba's detached Palace Babaden that shows Go-Toba performing on the biwa, an instrument preferred for its esoteric aura over the orthodox *kin* (modern *koto*) from the late Heian period on, while a gathering of low-class entertainers and retainers, headed by a jester figure named Yukifusa, engages in games of hide-and-seek and *sugoroku*. As Akiyama notes, the extravagant banqueting in Go-Toba's detached villa already anticipates the disorderly atmosphere of the *bureikō* of Go-Daigo's time that is described in *Taiheiki*.[5]

This chapter examines this shift to peripheral space from a number of perspectives. After reviewing the spatial logic underlying the ritual management of defilement in the Heian period and its rearticulation under the influence of Pure Land Buddhism, I then look at a variety of passages from documents, diaries, and literary texts that describe elite perceptions of dengaku and other spectacles connected to the ritual management of defilement and demonic infestation, focusing on symbolic codes pertaining to dress, music, and other forms of behavior. In this fashion, I build up a thick description of how changes in the conceptualization of defilement were transforming the character of ritual space, ultimately undermining an earlier practice of royal authority. In the middle sections, I draw on a variety of texts from *Heike* narrative that illustrate two contrasting images of the tennō that coexisted in the medieval imaginary about royal authority, representing inverted images of one another: the sage ruler, typified by Takakura and the Engi period sovereigns, who governed a harmonious, centered realm, and the defiled emperor, typified by the child emperor Antoku, whose reign is identified with a complete collapse of the sage ruler's realm. In these pages, we will also see how yin-yang masters who once sanctioned the authority of the sage ruler and later defended the tennō's purity have now taken on a duplicitous character indicative of the defilement of royal authority. Finally, in the concluding sections, I look at the critical place of medieval Buddhist doctrine, specifically "hongaku" (original enlightenment) doctrine. Through the comparison of several *Heike* variants of the Kikai-ga-shima sequence, these sections examine the ambiguous character of heterotopic space as typified by borders and liminal sites.

From Centered to Heterotopic Space

As we saw in Chapter 4, the period leading up to the establishment of the first spirit festival (*goryōe*) in 863 coincided with a rapid intensification in pollution consciousness at court and a transformation in the character of the Yin-Yang Bureau. By the tenth century, as anxiety about defilement spread among the aristocracy at large, a class of private yin-yang masters, distinct from those who had staffed the Yin-Yang Bureau, had become a constant presence in court society as they guided the aristocracy through the intricacies of an increasingly onerous system of prohibitions and directional taboos, a state of affairs amply documented in official records as well as in the vernacular literature of the period.[6]

In an analysis of regulations pertaining to pollution management set forth in the *Engi shiki*, Ōyama Kyōhei and other scholars have characterized the ritual system in terms of a twofold structure: (1) a vertical hierarchy with the tennō at the apex embodying purity and the "purifiers" (*kiyome*) at the bottom managing pollution, and (2) mirrored by a concentric geographical structure radiating outward from the tennō to the palace, the capital city, and thence to the borders of the five home provinces and the outer provinces.[7] A ritual prayer collected in the same *Engi shiki* (scroll sixteen, Onmyōryō), which accompanied the performance of the tsuina, gives an idea of the system's geographical scope: "Cause to be expelled all the defiled demons of disease wherever they lurk—in whatever place, in whatever village, a thousand ri away and more, at the boundaries on all sides, from Mutsu in the east, Chiga in the west, Tosa in the south and Sado in the north, from the countless places where the teeming disease demons dwell. Expel them."[8]

As the ritual system grew in complexity over the Heian period, it achieved greater geographical scope and coverage. In the Seven Shallows Purification, for example, a human effigy (*nademono*) was presented to the tennō at the palace, who would symbolically fill it with his breath and rub his body with it front and back. The effigy would then be brought to designated sites along the riverside, which in the capital venue were located at the confluence of the Kamo and Takano Rivers as well as at six points where the avenues of Ichijō, Tsuchimikado, Konoe, Nakamikado, Ōinomikado, and Nijō met the river. With the court retainers facing the river, the yin-yang master would place the effigy in the flowing stream to wash away the defilement that was believed to have attached itself to and invaded the tennō's body. After the purification, the effigy would be returned to the tennō, who would mime the act of consuming it.[9] Conducted primarily by yin-yang masters of the Yin-Yang Bureau, the ritual was widely performed from the mid-Heian period on at specified locations both inside and outside the capital, as well as at locations in the surrounding home provinces. Similar rituals, performed at designated points along the rivers throughout the five home provinces and along seashores at the far extremities of the archipelago, were intended to wash away the accumulated defilement from not only the Kinai watershed but throughout the length and breadth of Japan.[10]

The aim of this ritual system was to keep the tennō and the capital free from the dangerous effects of defilement, expelling defilements that had accumulated within and defending against their encroachment from without.[11] By necessity, the system demanded a finely articulated sense of space. For example, the *kō-otsu heitei* system set forth in the *Engi shiki* provided minutely detailed rules for determining the severity and degree of an initial defilement and then for calculating its potential risk as it was propagated outward from its point of origin.[12] As a rule, defilement was thought to accumulate inside enclosed spaces and dissipate in open spaces. Barriers, fences, gates, and the like that were erected to inhibit and prevent the spread or entry of defilement into a specific space could likewise increase the degree of intensity of the defilement once it had occurred.[13] It is not surprising that difficult cases were sometimes resolved by providing interpretations that were ambiguous or bent the rules. The following passage from *Honchō seiki* for the year 994 illustrates the fear that the threat of defilement could provoke in the capital populace: "Today there are weird rumors that plague deities are roaming about. It is said that in the capital men and women are unable to go out. As a result, everyone from the nobles to the commoners has shut gates and doors, and there is nobody on the roads." Another entry, this one from the journal *Hyōhanki* for the year 1153, provides an interesting case of how the risk from road defilement was managed. On this occasion, a palanquin for a shrine ritual was prevented from crossing the Uji Bridge, where corpses had recently been transported in a cart. After a consultation, the Uji elders, although lacking a precedent, decided that the taboo could be nullified in the case of a major road (*tairo*), and the palanquin was allowed to cross the bridge.[14] The accepted view is that major roads, provided one did not come into direct contact with defilement on them, neither spread defilement nor constituted defiled sites, a condition that also held for flowing water, which was believed to disperse defilement away from the site of purification.[15] Yet as Okada Shōji has noted in his discussion of these passages, although in this particular case the taboo was suspended out of convenience, roads and border regions, as the principal ingress points for demonic infestation, remained extremely perilous and were often the site of special roadside effigies and placations intended to ward off the danger of defilement. The inherent dangers of such sites, he suggests, were one reason their management was shifted away from the Jingikan to the Yin-Yang Bureau earlier in the Heian period.[16] On the other hand, there are examples in the Heian period of outriders and attendants who, due to their temporary defilement, were prohibited from entering the palace but still were allowed to make up an insufficiency in the tennō's entourage on the occasion of an imperial procession. This has been interpreted as clear evidence that roads could not become defiled spaces.[17] But it seems equally plausible to attribute this to the fact that roads were not and could not become pure spaces. Defilement, in brief, depended on a principle of difference and finely shaded degrees.

Whatever conclusions we reach about the degree to which particular spaces were prone or not prone to defilement, it is clear that for the apparatus aimed at managing defilement to function at all effectively, the integrity of boundaries demarcating inside and outside and something like a stable perception of space were essential. By the end of the Heian period, these conditions no longer fully obtained. Among the several possible causes, one was the expanding network of trade and commerce, which was not only altering the Heian aristocracy's perception of space but interacting in complex ways with the topography of the ritual sites. It is here that Kujō Kanezane's characterization of Kiyomori's and Go-Shirakawa's meeting with a Song merchant at Fukuhara as "a demonic act" (*tenma no shoi*)—discussed in the previous chapter—takes on a more complex signification. In addition to making an overt political criticism, Kanezane was also hinting at the dangers that a place such as Fukuhara, located on the Suma and Akashi coast, would inevitably evoke in the mind of a conservative court aristocrat. Only a short distance from Fukuhara was the Harima–Settsu border, one of ten sites designated in the Engi shiki for rituals aimed at warding off the invasion of plague deities in the home provinces. In terms of Engi shiki's geographical logic, anything west of this point was outside the center and defiled.[18] Fukuhara was only one of many such sites that now overlapped with the locales and spaces of a variety of commercial activities. Kanezane's expression of revulsion at

Kiyomori's move to Fukuhara, as well as at Yoritomo's plan to subjugate the remote demon-infested island of Kikai-ga-shima a few years later, owed some of its vehemence to the shudder induced by a taboo violation.

One indication that the center's ritual economy was breaking down are the mysterious rumors connected to the circulation of coins from the late Heian period on. An entry in *Hyakurenshō* for the third year of Jishō (1179), for example, mentions the spread of a "strange illness" (*kibyō*) called "coin sickness" (*zeni no yamai*).[19] Although this has usually been cited as evidence of official concern over the introduction of coins into Japan as a result of the increased China trade, it hints as well at an occult connection between the circulation of coins and pestilence (*ekibyō*), typically attributed to demonic infestation and defilement. During the same year, in fact, the court issued an edict forbidding the importation of Song coins, which had been undermining the system of regulated exchange based on rice, grains, and cloth. Because revenues derived from rights over land (*shiki*) were paid in kind, the introduction of coins and currency-based trade posed a major threat to the agriculture-based economy that supported the capital power structure. By the latter half of the thirteenth century, the competition over rights to land revenues had reached a point where, in Amino's words, "the *shiki*-system that underlay the capital power-structure began to collapse from the bottom up." There were also widespread fears at this time (thirteenth and fourteenth centuries) over the baleful and demonic powers of currency, which coincided with a sharp increase in moneylending and currency dealing by marginal groups such as provisioners to the court, sacred shrine menials (*jinnin*), temple dependents (*yoriudo*), and craftspeople (*shōkō*).[20]

The shift to a money-based economy has often been viewed as the beginning of a gradual change from a sacred to a secular order.[21] In late Heian and early medieval Japan, the initial effects of trade and currency-based exchange—namely, the breakdown of boundaries demarcating inner and outer and the erosion of the land-tenure system—seem to have been accompanied by an amplification of activity and signs in the sacred domain. How do we account for this? Commenting on Lefebvre's reading of a similar transition to a trade-based economy in medieval Europe, the cultural geographer Derek Gregory writes: "In most agrarian societies, Lefebvre argues, nontributary exchange and long-distance trade were present only in the interstices—in "heterotopias"—and were not part of the dominant spatial structure. The political city was thus threatened by the market, by merchants, and most of all by the insurgent power of the most mobile of all property forms: money." [22] Together with money, the key word here is "heterotopias." In Lefebvre's lexicon, the concept appears in a variety of formulations, but at its most general level, it can refer to any place, site, or fragment of space that persists at the margins of a more dominant spatial regime. The secularization of society resulting from capital accumulation in medieval Europe, for example, transformed the older magical cosmos and spaces of ancient times into what Lefebvre describes as "'heterotopical' places, places of sorcery and madness, places inhabited by demonic forces—places which were fascinating but tabooed." [23] Elsewhere, in a more general reflection on space that makes use of a theatrical metaphor, Lefebvre observes how "walls, enclosures and facades serve to define both a *scene* (where something takes place) and an *obscene* area to which everything that cannot or may not happen on the scene is relegated: whatever is inadmissible, be it malefic or forbidden, thus has its own hidden space on the near or far side of a frontier." [24] It was out of such heterotopias or marginal places—borders, roads, ports, seashores, barriers, and the like—that medieval Japan's burgeoning centers of commerce and trade would emerge. Yet unlike Lefebvre's twelfth-century Europe, these Japanese heterotopias belonged to a still dominant economy of ritual space, albeit one that was verging on collapse. It was this overlapping of commercial and ritual space in the roughly 300-year period extending from the twelfth through fourteenth centuries that invested sites like the Eastern Market (Higashi no ichi) in Heiankyō, Katase in Kamakura, Fukuhara, and Kikai-ga-shima with their aura of taboo and weird charm.[25]

Pure Land Buddhism and Defilement

Even as the changing topography of trade was altering the center's relations with the proscribed periphery, developments in the sphere of Buddhist doctrine and ideology had been effecting a radical shift in the symbolic and ontological meaning of defilement that would further complicate its ritual management. One paradox of these doctrinal developments was that they undermined the efficacy of the capital-centered apparatus for managing defilement, which had been premised on a spatial logic that sharply distinguished inner and outer, while at the same time investing the signs of defilement with an even greater aura of the sacred. The two doctrines in question are Pure Land Buddhism and original enlightenment. In this section, I deal mainly with effects of the former, reserving discussion of *hongaku* and the medieval imaginary of space for later in the chapter.

With its stark emphasis on escaping from the polluted conditions of this world (*enri edo*) to a Pure Land (*jōdo*) associated with light, Pure Land Buddhism played an instrumental role in solidifying the increasingly negative view of defilement from the mid-Heian period on.[26] In aristocratic spheres, texts like Genshin's *Ōjō yōshū* (*Essentials of Rebirth*), with its emphasis on the corruptible nature of the flesh, and meditative practices such as *fujōkan* (contemplating impurity), where the practitioner dwelled on various aspects of bodily decay as a spur to eliminating carnal attachments, helped transform the body into a site of defilement. Doctrine, in brief, was now extending its domain into the body as impurity (*fujō*), was interiorized, and defilement took on the meaning of sinful karmic obstruction (*zaishō*).[27] By the medieval period, the body itself is defiled. Thus, to return to Shigemori's rejection of medical treatment: "Even were he to consult the Four Medical Books and prove master of a hundred cures, how could he heal this defiled body of mine (*udai no eshin*)?" As was noted in our earlier discussion, the word *eshin* properly denotes the body as dependent existence, a product of the subjective activity of the mind, and hence a delusion of unenlightened thought. Not only is the nondual logic of "eshin" subverted in Shigemori's statement, but the notion of a thoroughly defiled body that resists even the curative techniques of Song medical art represents a radical inversion of the Daoist and yin-yang principles that had once affirmed the sacrality of the tennō.

The consequences of this conceptual shift were considerable. At the broadest social level, as Pure Land beliefs, with their emphasis on the defiled state of this world and of the bodies that dwelled there, spread beyond the aristocracy to broader swaths of the population, Buddhist temples were able to greatly expand their power base, becoming not only important agents in the management of pollution via the outcast groups under their control but, as Michele Marra has shown, the purveyors of doctrines offering salvation as well.[28] By multiplying conditions that induced a fear of defilement—for example, through the enactment of prohibitions against the taking of life (*sesshō kindan*)—the temples also created conditions favorable to the dissemination of such doctrines, which were often propagated by wandering *hijiri* types.[29] Activities that had hitherto been unmarked as sinful were now subject to punishment in various Buddhist hells. As a religious ideology, it was a self-generating structure that simultaneously produced consciousness of sin and the desire to escape its consequences.[30] It was a doctrine, finally, whose effects reached right into the body of the tennō. In the medieval period, we read of tennō who have fallen into Buddhist hells (Daigo, Kyōgoku), are driven into exile (Sutoku, Go-Toba), or in the case of Antoku, die in exile by drowning.[31] With Sutoku and Antoku, who both perished in exile, the analogy is clearly to the expulsion ritual, with Antoku's *jusui* amounting to a literal enactment of the Seven Shallows Ritual in which the tennō's own body is cast into the water.

The Yasurai Festival, Fūryū, and Popular Excess

The body's transformation into a site of defilement wrought perceptible changes in the sphere of ritual activity. Once defilement had merged into an effect of karmic determination (*jōgō*), it pervaded the body, and this in turn altered the way that defilement was articulated in space. Throughout much of the Heian period, illnesses, destructive plagues, and the assorted phenomena associated with spirits (*mononoke*) had been viewed essentially as malign influences *brought in from the outside*, which could be managed through the proper observance of taboos, exorcisms, or rites of expulsion performed at the borders of the imperial domain as prescribed in the law codes. With defilement now interwoven with the body through karmic determination, in a kind of ontological entangling, the effectiveness of the rituals for expelling malign spirits was undermined, as those who had formerly acted as agents of purification became defiled themselves.[32] One striking example is the changing character of the *tsuina*, the border ritual based on the Chinese Great Exorcism that had typically been performed around the first of the year from as early as the Nara period. As performed throughout most of the Heian period, the chief ritualist of the tsuina would lead a band of twenty attendants (*warawabe*) in driving out the plague-causing demons from the palace and capital. By the twelfth century, the exorcist had mysteriously shifted roles, switching from the agent who drove out the plague demons to the embodiment of the plague demon itself.[33]

The change of the exorcist from agent of purification to object of defilement had effects that reached far beyond the ritual space, ultimately altering the way ritualists and those connected to the management of defilement were perceived. Historically, such sites had always been critical points of exchange between the culture of the center (capital) and the peripheral sphere of popular culture. As the swirl of activity around these sites intensified in the late Heian period, it gradually merged into the broader movements of popular unrest that extended over a 300-year period from the great dengaku spectacles of the late eleventh century, notably the Eichō Era Great Field Music event (*Eichō dai dengaku*) of 1096, the Yasurai festival of 1154, to the basara craze of the late thirteenth and fourteenth centuries.[34] Characterized initially by the pursuit of excess (*kasa*) and extravagant fashions in dress and behavior (*fūryū*), these movements gradually took on an increasingly threatening and uncanny character for the elite classes who saw and experienced them, registered by the verbal shift from *kasa*, *fūryū*, and *iyō* (oddness) in the late Heian period to *igyō* and *basara* (literally the vajra or diamond-staff employed to drive out demons but later, through an association with the bizarre appearance of the demon-quelling deity, designating any extravagant and odd appearance) of the early medieval period.[35] It was out of this social ferment that the ambiguous category of borderline outcast entertainers emerged, many of whom would later act as mediators of royal authority (*ōbō*) and Buddhist authority (*buppō*), including the biwa hōshi who had charge of *Heike*. It will be useful therefore to take a closer look at the phenomenon.

The famous Yasurai festival of 1154, which took place on the eve of the Genpei War, is one the most frequently discussed examples of this popular excess.[36] The following account is from *Ryōjin hishō kudenshū*:

> Recently around the Third Month of the first year of Kyūju, men and women from nearby the capital assembled in crowds at Murasaki Shrine's purification ceremony engaging in gaudy entertainments (*fūryō no asobi*) with song and flute music, drums, and metal clappers, calling them sacred entertainments. They performed songs that resembled neither imayō nor the sounds and rhythms of wild dances and fast songs. The vocal style was not in the orthodox manner. They stuck gaudy flowers (*fūryū no hana*) atop their hats and dressed children up in hunting-robes to look like attendants. With drums attached to their chests, several dozen [of the attendants] mimicked wild dances in time to the rhythm. A figure whom they named evil sprite had his head smeared in red dye to give him the look of a demon and wore the mask Noble Virtue. He [and the attendants] raged about shouting and screaming in the manner of rough demons of the Twelfth Month. Those making offerings at the shrine and circling before the shrine deity were numerous. From the capital nobles and commoners came wrapped in silk finery and wearing tall hats, and even the highest echelons of the aristocracy

crowded inside the shrine to watch the spectacle. At night, under the illumination of pine torches, everyone carried on wildly.[37]

The Murasaki Shrine purification that provides the setting for this event belonged to the same class of pacification rituals known as *goryōe*, for which the prototype was the famous Jōgan era goryōe of 863 held in the garden of the Greater Palace.[38] The aim of the Jōgan era goryōe, it will be recalled, was to drive out demonic infestation believed to be the cause of pestilence and other natural calamities. Here, however, the shrine ceremony has become the occasion for a spectacle that mingles together ritual actions and a variety of song and dance entertainments, the bizarre character of which has attracted the regard of the author. Most notably, the figure who should be driving out the evil spirits now performs in the role of demon. In the Nara and Heian periods, the exorcist in the tsuina expulsion ritual would lead a band of twenty attendants into the courtyard of the palace where he would wield a shield and halberd to drive out plague demons, assisted by court officers who fired arrows. Afterward, the entire group would exit the West Gate of the palace and perform the ritual outside the palace to expel the demons from the entire capital. According to Kawane Yoshiyasu's well-known reading, the entire Yasurai spectacle was *staged* as a mock-tsuina exorcism. Organized by the Bifukumon-in faction in concert with disaffected court musicians, it was intended as a protest against the political machinations of Fujiwara no Yorinaga during the Hōgen disturbance. By exploiting popular unrest against the government, their intention, argued Kawane, was to cast the royal exorcist supposed to symbolize the virtue of the government as the embodiment of the malign spirits (*akki*) to be expelled.[39]

Kawane's theory provides a historically plausible reading of the Yasurai festival's political ramifications and popular character. The excesses of the 1154 Yasurai were in fact suppressed a few days later by imperial decree.[40] But we still need to account for the more general structural transmogrification of the ritual site. What sets the Yasurai festival apart from its ancient prototypes, such as the 863 Goryōe, are its heterodox elements of dress, gesture, and music. For example, the flowers stuck into the hats, the extravagant use of silk finery, the tall hats (*ichimegasa*), and other details are notable for the way in which they combine an article of elegant court dress or ornamentation with either uncouth gestures or objects of less refined associations.[41] The same mingling of registers applies to the music of the Yasurai festival. Throughout the Nara and much of the Heian period, the ethos of court music, strongly influenced by Confucian notions of propriety, had typically enforced a strict separation between refined music (*gagaku*) and the inferior sounds of rustic provenance.[42] Accounts of the 863 Goryōe, which incorporated performances of formal court music into its ritual, put a great deal of emphasis on the noble lineage of the participants. Here, however, the sounds of rustic musical instruments and "unorthodox" (*makoto shirazu*) vocal styles, "enveloped," in the words of one scholar, "in heteromorphic vocal sounds," create a dissonant effect as they combine with the more orthodox elements of the court tradition, specifically the mask of the bugaku dance Noble Virtue that is worn by the demon.[43]

The notation of odd details of dress, gesture, and behavior by the author of the *kudenshū* also characterizes other accounts of late Heian dengaku spectacles. Ōe no Masafusa, the author of *Rakuyō dengakuki* (*A Record of Field Music in the Capital*), mentions the wearing of "embroidered brocades" (*kinshū*) and ornaments of gold and silver by commoners, the flourishing of outsized fans attached to the end of sticks (*takaōgi*) by aristocrats, displays of nakedness, disheveled hair (*zanbaragami*), and toward the end of his account, he notes the odd reversals that characterized the riotous antics in this striking phrase: "At one moment, stark naked, they wrapped crimson robes around their haunches; at another, onto wildly flying hair, they put on a rice-planting hat (*tagasa*)."[44] For a dengaku event that took place in 1094, the author of the journal *Chūyūki* characterizes the behavior of his low-ranking attendants, which included going about naked and hatless, as "odd-looking and weird" (*itai kii*). Some of these attendants, who later engage in raucous fighting, turn out to be military guards and court musicians.[45]

Why did excessive behaviors and styles of dress become the object of fascination for the aristocrats who observed these events from the eleventh century on? And what was the source of the oddness that recurs throughout their accounts? Since the reaction of the aristocracy to the unfamiliar routines and behaviors of commoners typically ranged from bemused perplexity to revulsion, one might attribute their fascination to the social chasm that separated the observers from the popular crowds of the festive sites. Yet the class contempt that characterizes Sei Shōnagon's observations of the peasantry in *The Pillow Book* and the detached regard of *Eiga monogatari*'s narrator as she notes down the unusual dress and musical instruments of field music performers strike a decidedly different tone.[46] On the other hand, some of these notations may be attributable to a new taste for the exotic among the lettered class, as in the example of Ōe no Masafusa's *Yūjoki*, discussed earlier. But in the case of the Yasurai festival and dengaku spectacles, which were the frequent object of governmental prohibitions, we are dealing with a phenomenon of a different magnitude. By the thirteenth and fourteenth centuries, the rage for dengaku was being widely spoken of as an illness (*dengaku no yamai*) and a cause of plague and pestilence, and diarists of the day were referring to its excesses as *tenma no shoi*, or "acts of demonic possession." Dengaku itself, which often involved the singing of prophetic songs, came to be viewed as an ominous sign of the country's imminent destruction.[47] To account for this mixture of fascination, revulsion, and anxiety that was directed toward behaviors in the ritual sphere from the late Heian period on, we must therefore look for other causes.

The Semiotics of Dress

Among the codes that regulate conduct in a culture, those pertaining to dress are especially important as bearers of a meaning that transcends the intention of any one individual or class. True for modern societies where class structures tend to be less rigidly defined, it is far truer in cultures where social norms are strongly hierarchical. In the feudal society of medieval Europe, the slightest variation in dress conveyed a weight of symbolic meaning.[48] In medieval Japan as well, the vestimentary code was a symbolic site where political, ritual, and social meanings converged and conflicted. Of particular interest in this regard is the broad group of outcasts types (*hinin*) that included lepers (*raisha*), shrine menials (*inu jinnin*), riverside dwellers (*kawaramono*), yamabushi, and others. In both writing and iconography, these figures are frequently depicted as wearing persimmon (*kakiiro*), white, or red robes or attired in straw raincoats and hats (*minokasa*). In several studies, Amino and others have suggested that the particular styles and colors of dress associated with outcast types were signs of sacred authority in the medieval period. Depictions of *yamabushi*, for example, often overlapped with that of *tengu* (a kind of goblin or demon), suggesting a connection with supernatural powers, while the *minokasa* recalls the sacred otherness of Orikuchi's marebito figure.[49]

But what precisely is meant by the category of the sacred in the medieval context? The styles of dress associated with outcast types and other marginal groups in the medieval period were often characterized as *igyō* or "irui igyō" (literally "different in kind, different in shape"), both of which took on increasingly negative connotations. The *Ippen hijiri e* (late thirteenth century) identifies irui igyō as those who engage in slaughter, and a Muromachi period dictionary defines them as "various types of animals." For Amino, these characterizations are indicative of the declining social status of outcasts, who by the fifteenth century have shifted from a sacred category to an ostracized group that is the object of social discrimination.[50] In the following anecdote from the medieval setsuwa compilation *Shasekishū* (*Sand and Pebbles*), the Buddhist priest Eichō delivers a sermon attacking the lax behavior of Buddhist monks that sheds additional light on the problem of the sacred:

> Although they half-heartedly call themselves priests, take alms, and perform masses, they are a bizarre and weird-looking breed of priests (*fukashigi no irui igyō no hōshi*) that throng the provinces, defiling the name of Buddha's disciples (*hotoke deshi no na wo kegashi*) and observing none of the precepts. Some have wives; and others bear weapons, hunt and fish, and show not the least reluctance to engage in fighting and killing. . . . I see one sitting right here [subsequently identified as a yamabushi]. At first glance, I wonder if he is a layperson, yet he is wearing what looks like a priest's stole. He doesn't wear a hat, and is neither child, priest, nor servant; he is not even shit, but is something like diarrhea.[51]

For Eichō, who speaks in the capacity of the orthodox priest insisting on sharp distinctions between the sacred and profane spheres, the behavior and appearance of the "weird-looking breed of priests" (*irui igyō no hōshi*) and the yamabushi in the audience constitute a confusion of categories that arouses revulsion. Behind Eichō's criticisms lies an implicit system of categories and classifications pertaining to dress, hair style, age, and the like—in other words, a specific articulation of the sacred and profane that was now verging on collapse.[52] The heteromorphic, I suggest, was one of the names for this perceived confusion, and therein lay part of its ambiguous appeal throughout much of the early medieval period. In this sense, the sacred aura that invests medieval outcasts, which has been viewed as continuous with an ancient prototype, is more accurately described as marking a rupture with earlier articulations of the sacred. To better grasp this point, we must take a closer look at the codes pertaining to dress.

Among the many criticisms leveled at the Taira was their habit of indulging in ostentatious styles of dress. The following passage is from the first scroll of *Heike*:

> Even in these latter days of the Law, it could only be accounted bizarre (*fukashigi*) that descendants of Tadamori, a man whose very presence in the Courtiers' Hall had provoked resentment, should be granted permission to wear *forbidden colors* and informal attire, *deck themselves out in figured silks and embroidered brocades*, combine the offices of Minister of State and Major Captain—and, as brothers, hold major captaincies at the same time.[53]

And another passage records this observation on the dress of the Taira retainers: "Samurai with painted pictures and embroidered flowers on their robes came and went as though Kiyomori's mansion were the Emperor's Palace or a retired sovereign's residence."[54] Both passages indicate that the license to wear certain clothes depended on a strict hierarchy of ranks. As the dress codes increased in complexity over the Heian period, regulations came to encompass not only colors but specific patterns and materials as well. Among the "forbidden colors" (*kinjiki*) were the "figured silks and embroidered brocades" (*ryōra kinshū*), mentioned here and in the earlier dengaku account, and the elaborately dyed attire known as *surigoromo*. Both were normally restricted to the use of nobles on ceremonial occasions.[55] Like the distinction between refined court music and the disorderly sounds of the hinterlands, the rationale for classifications of dress was based in part on a combination of yin-yang principles and notions of Confucian propriety going back to the ancient period. Although primarily ceremonial in character and aimed at enforcing distinctions of rank, violations of the code and the wearing of certain colors might also be viewed as signs portending natural calamities and the loss of imperial virtue. In the course of the eighth and ninth centuries, for example, the court-issued edicts prohibiting the wearing of red-dyed clothes; and in one famous incident in the Jōgan era, during a court fashion for clothes dyed a deep-crimson color, the scholar Miyoshi Kiyoyuki, connecting the color to the high incidence of fires, advised the court to issue a prohibition.[56] In characterizing the Taira's license to wear forbidden attire as "bizarre" (*fukashigi*), the narrator is alluding to the ominous implications of such excess, shortly borne out in the disasters that follow. But there are other factors at work in the sinister tone of such condemnations.

By at least the late Heian period, the ceremonial codes pertaining to dress had begun to overlap with codes marking purity and defilement.[57] This is best illustrated in the peculiar vestimentary habits of the imperial police (*kebiishi*). Throughout much of the Heian period, the Kebiishi, in addition to exercising broad judicial and police powers, also managed a wide range of activities that were meant to obviate any potential source of defilement to the tennō. The latter included sweeping streets and grounds on ceremonial occasions, disposal of corpses, and the investigation into possible sources of pollution arising from untimely deaths, illness, menstruation, and the like.[58] It is something of a paradox, then, that the *hōmen*, low-ranking attendants at the very bottom of the *Kebiishi* hierarchy whose duties included escorting criminals to execution sites,[59] should openly don the elaborate formal attire normally restricted to nobles on special ceremonial occasions. This is illustrated in a picture from the thirty-third scroll of *Hōnen shōnin eden* (1207), which depicts the execution of Hōnen's disciple Anrakubō at the Rokujō riverbed.[60] In this scene, Anrakubō is surrounded by a group of imperial police officers, including two hōmen. All of the imperial police officials and attendants depicted in the scene, including the head officer, Fujiwara Hideyoshi, are impeccably dressed in showy attire, producing a strange contrast with the grim business in hand, the execution of Anrakubō. But it is especially in the two hōmen, the central figures in the scene, that the function of dress is most marked. Both wear long flowing beards, tall hats (*tate eboshi*), and hunting robes (*kariginu*) that have been dyed with elaborate motifs—a pattern produced by a technique of rubbing the cloth over a leaf pattern as it was pressed against a wooden board—creating a visual effect of extreme richness.[61] In addition to the hat, beards, and showy attire, one of the figures is holding an elaborately shaped halberd, further accentuating the effect of visual splendor.

The link between hōmen and gorgeous attire goes back much earlier, to at least the first half of the eleventh century. The following passage from Ōe no Masafusa's *Gōdanshō* (*Selection of Ōe's Conversations*) records an exchange between Fujiwara no Takaie and Fujiwara no Suminobu on the occasion of the Kamo festival: [Takaie:] "Is it because they are attendants of Imperial Police Officials that the hōmen wear figured silks and embroidered brocades?" [Suminobu:] "Because they are outcasts (*hinin*), they disregard the taboos."[62] This exchange raises a number of questions. Were the hōmen given a special license to wear forbidden colors? And if so, why? Or was it their status as pardoned criminals (the literal meaning of hōmen), and hence outcasts outside the system of class distinctions, which exempted them from the prohibitions regarding dress? In his study of the Kebiishi, Niunoya Tetsuichi notes that even for its highest officers, there were strict requirements regarding demeanor, comportment, wealth, and lineage, which were related to their close involvement with defilement.[63] In elucidating the showy attire of the hōmen in the scene depicting the execution of Anrakubō, Niunoya suggests that crime (*tsumi*) conceptualized in the medieval period as a form of pollution had transformed the execution site into a *kiyome no ba*, or a purifying site, implying that the gorgeous attire was in some sense prophylactic.[64] On the other hand, the increasingly close proximity to the tennō of a variety of outcast types—hōmen, shrine menials, Kiyomizu slope people, and the like—all engaged in purification and the disposal of defilement, also constituted, in the words of Itō Kiyoshi, "a structure that further accentuated the purity [of the tennō]."[65] In brief, the strict requirements regarding physical appearance and deportment for Kebiishi officials were a way of both warding off and at the same *accentuating* the defilement, with the aim of enhancing the symbolic status of the tennō as a site of bodily purity. The hōmen, who appear to have been granted a tacit license to wear prohibited attire, would therefore have marked the extreme limit of the symbolic structure, the point where the entire system was most vulnerable to unraveling. This seems to be borne out by several edicts, including one issued in 1114, which prohibited the hōmen from wearing the forbidden colors that had previously gone unpunished and coincided with a broader crackdown on extravagant dress among the capital roughs, including stone throwers (*tsubute*) and gamblers (*bakuto*). Despite these prohibitions, the hōmen's dress became even more extravagant and the practice more widespread.[66]

The sacrilization of the tennō's person, achieved by surrounding him with an elaborate system of taboos and rites of purification, was thus dependent on a finely yet precariously balanced semiotic code. Even so, by the twelfth century, violations of the code by outcast types were becoming widespread enough inside the capital to incur official censure. An entry in *Chūyūki* for the Second Month in the year 1114 reads: "These days, in the capital, people wearing *surigoromo* and sugoroku players (*hakugi*) fill the streets. By all means this must be forbidden."[67] Although prohibitions were issued, another entry recorded for the Fifth Month of same year indicates that the fashion had also penetrated the office of the retired sovereign (*in no chō*), leading to further prohibitions and the arrest of underlings (*shimobe*) in the retired sovereign's service.[68] But the trend outpaced the prohibitions, and by the late twelfth and thirteen centuries, the fashion of wearing forbidden attire had spread to include ox drivers, comic mimes (*sarugaku, dengaku bōshi*), capital roughs (*kyōwarawa*), gangs of ruffians (*akutō*), and stone throwers and stick throwers.[69] A reference to this extravagance can be heard in the captious remark of the poet Teika. Commenting on his contemporaries' wasteful habit of always exchanging clothes, this reliable barometer of conservative court values observes, "they are no different from the exorcists."[70] The exorcists (*jushi*, also pronounced *zushi*) originally played an important role in driving out evil spirits during the Buddhist ceremony *shushōe*, usually by spinning rapidly about before the altar as they carved out a ritual space with a sword or a bell. By the eleventh century, their acrobatic techniques were being imitated by the comic sarugaku performers.[71] The extravagance alluded to by Teika refers to the custom of bestowing gifts of clothes ("shōzoku tabawari") upon the jushi as a reward for their performance. The practice became so widespread in the late Heian period, as patrons outvied one another in the lavishness of their gifts, that it became the object of censure and frequent prohibitions.[72] A statement in Kujō Michie's journal, *Gyokuzui*, for the year 1212 sums up the official view of such wild behavior: "Commoners disregard distinctions of class, and high and low vie in their pursuit of extravagance (*fūryū*). This will be the ruin of the country. The laws must be enforced and a firm stop put to such excess."[73]

Heteromorphic Signs

By the early medieval period, not only had the ritualist exchanged roles with the demon whom he was supposed to expel, but the spread of extravagant behavior beyond the confines of the ritual site, decried by court conservatives and subject to frequent prohibitions, soon amplified a localized phenomenon into a perception of widespread demonic infestation threatening social collapse. With the officers of the imperial police now viewed as the literal embodiment of the demonic officers of Lord Emma, leading their victims to punishment in the Buddhist hells,[74] we are close to the hallucinatory world of medieval picture scrolls like *Tengu zōshi* and *Gaki zōshi*, where shadowy defiled hells overlap with the ordinary daylight scenes and ruinous demon-infested temples become the site of riotous banqueting. By the late thirteenth and early fourteenth centuries, this turn toward the demonic takes on an even more sinister tone. The aura of strangeness that enveloped dengaku and other spectacles of the late Heian period now metamorphoses into the uncanny and bizarre, captured in the untranslatable phrase "irui igyō." This corresponded to the observable shift from the excess, strangeness, and extravagant pursuit of elegance that had characterized the liminal spheres of late Heian and early medieval festive sites to the unrestrained rebelliousness of the basara phenomenon associated with the "evil gangs" (akutō) in the fourteenth century.[75]

Underlying this perceptual shift to the uncanny was a change in attitudes toward defilement, as gestures and behaviors that had earlier been singled out as odd or strange in connection to the dengaku spectacles, or that were traceable to specific gestures used in rituals of purification, began to evoke feelings of revulsion. One striking example is the unkempt hair (*sakagami*) of the principal performer in the court dance Batō no mai, which in the medieval period becomes a sign of ambiguous sacrality. A famous instance is the character Sakagami in Zeami's nō play *Semimaru*. In her introductory speech, Sakagami explains the reason for her mad wanderings:

> I am the third child of the Engi Emperor,
> And am called Sakagami.
> Although I was born a princess,
> As the result of some karmic seed
> I have become crazed
> And am now a mad wanderer of distant borders and hinterlands.
> My glossy hair shoots up toward the sky
> And however much I smooth it down
> It doesn't lie flat.
> Hey, you children over there. Why do you laugh? Why does my hair
>   stand up so? How marvelous! Truly, that it should stand up so is truly
>   marvelous!
> But more than my hair, it is your laughter that is out of place. Marvelous,
>   how marvelous![76]

As she tells us in her speech, Sakagami is a mad wanderer of the forbidden borders and margins of society (*hendo enkyō no kyōjin*). Even her name, which means something like "backward hair," contains a punning allusion to her liminal status, suggested by saka (slope) and sakai (border). Like the blindness and *minokasa* (straw raincoat and hat) of her brother Semimaru in the same play, Sakagami's hair that points wildly toward the sky is a heteromorphic sign, which came to be identified with defilement and outcast status in the medieval period. In this passage, shared between Sakagami and the chorus as she performs an agitated dance, she betrays the origins of her strange hair:

> CHORUS: The wind combing out the willow's hair
> SAKAGAMI: Cannot unknot it;
>   Nor will my hair be parted by my hands;
> CHORUS: Shaking my sleeves, I would tear it out
> SAKAGAMI: As in the dance called *Tearing out the Hair*,
>   How loathsome![77]

The dance to which Sakagami alludes originally belonged to the repertoire of court dances known as Bugaku, which in the course of the Heian period were incorporated into purificatory rituals (*harae*) aimed at driving out plague deities and other harmful spirits. The Bugaku repertoire also included the dances *Ryūō* (Dragon King) and *Kitoku* (Noble Virtue), all three of which appear in late Heian accounts of the dengaku spectacles and the Yasurai festival. Among the several extant descriptions of Batō, the early medieval musical treatise *Kyōkunshō* states that it was based on a Tang dance first performed by a woman whom jealousy had turned into a raging demon and that it involved gestures in which the dancer shook her hair wildly.[78] In his study of the Sakagami legend, Hattori Yukio has further traced aspects of Sakagami's ritual character to the figure of the possessed shamaness who dwelled beside the sacred pools and springs that were typically located near barriers (*seki*) at border regions, like the one in Zeami's play. By Zeami's time, however, the sacred signs of the exorcist and possessed medium had taken on grotesque connotations, the object of contempt and laughter, marking a reversal in their status that would eventually transform the heteromorphic sign of Sakagami's wild hair (*zanbaragami*, *hōhatsu*) into a physical sign of leprosy by the late medieval and Edo periods.[79]

In the fourteenth-century military chronicle *Taiheiki*, aptly likened by Matsuoka Shinpei to the verbal equivalent of a dengaku performance, the ambiguous workings of the heteromorphic are put on full display.[80] In book five, for example, we learn that one of the favorite pastimes of the Sagami lay monk and his fellow revelers was to entertain themselves at banquets with the performances of dengaku actors, "bedecking them out to extravagant lengths *with ornaments of gold, silver, precious gems and figured silks and brocades*," and going so far on one occasion as to strip themselves of their own clothes to reward the performers, an example of the ostentatious bestowing of clothes that was earlier deplored by Teika. On one such evening, a lady-in-waiting, curious to have a look at the banquet, peered through a gap in the sliding door: "Not a single one of those who appeared to be performers of the New and Original troops was a human being. Instead there were creatures that looked like kites with curved beaks and others that had the shape of mountain priests (*yamabushi*) sprouting wings on their bodies. They were all bizarre and oddly shaped changelings (*irui igyō no bakemono*) that had assumed human form." When the Sagami lay priest looked into the same room a short while later, "it seemed certain to him that there had been a gathering of demons (*tengu*); the floor mats had been defiled (*fumikegashitaru*) with the numerous tracks of birds and animals."[81] Like the ritualist turned demon in the Yasurai festival, here, too, everything has been turned inside out.

In an effort to pin down the heteromorphic effect of this dengaku performance as bodily spectacle, Matsuoka observes that dengaku actors evoke, by the speed and lightness of their movements, birds beating their wings in flight and the rapid cutting movements of the sharp angular beaks of the tobi bird.[82] To account for the eerie ill-omened feeling produced by the sensory effects of dengaku, especially in its overlap with tengu behaviors, he suggests that the dengaku performance opens up a glimpse into the hidden other of the ritual space, producing a momentary sense that the social world is on the verge of annihilation.[83] Drawing out the social and political implications of Matsuoka's performance theory, Hashimoto Hiroyuki has further argued that dengaku's link to the heteromorphic and prophecies of disaster pointed to nothing less than the total destruction of the state.[84]

To these observations must be added the anomic aspects of *Taiheiki*'s dengaku performance—namely, its link to deviant dress and animal and birdlike traits, which are identified in the episode with yamabushi. All of these traits answered to more than the binary logic of the state and were characteristic of two other groups that make frequent appearances in *Taiheiki* and the corpus of *Heike* texts, the guerrillalike "akutō" (literally "evil gangs") and the so-called warrior monks (*shūto*) and their leaders the "akusō" ("evil priests," but with "aku" also suggesting "fierce"). Just as dengaku performers would put on monkey masks, don costly capes of gold-threaded brocade, and leap about on the stage in tiger-skin footwear, provoking admiration in the audience but revulsion and condemnation from the authorities,[85] the akutō and akusō, who were fond of styling themselves as demon and tengu, aroused tremendous fear in the authorities.

As an ambiguous presence within the temples, the behavior of the akusō subverted the normal distinctions between the secular and sacred domains. Simultaneously priest and warrior, some engaged in lucrative trade, and over time, the most powerful among them transformed areas inside the temples into autonomous military enclaves and private holdings.[86] The mass assemblies (*sengi*) of the warrior monks, often dominated and provoked by the akusō, and their frequent descents to the capital throughout the late Heian period terrified the aristocratic populace.[87] The following entries from *Chūyūki* for the first year of Tennin (1108) describe the visual impression of these night gatherings on the aristocratic observer in the capital below:

> Tonight, they have made fires on the summit of Mount Nyoi on the Tendai Peaks. Several thousand soldier monks are roaming back and forth and the fires look indeed as if they will turn to a great conflagration.
>
> Tonight, the monks are descending to the capital; holding up torches, they descend along the mountain valleys, looking like a line of stars.[88]

The reference to continuous roaming movement to and fro (*ōtan*) from the temple is a frequent locution in descriptions of the akusō, and hints at their nomadic character that threatens the sedentary logic of the center, transgressive of all established boundaries. In assembly, the warrior monks concealed their appearance (leaving only their eyes exposed) by wrapping their heads in a monk's stole (*kesa*), whence the name *katō*, literally "wrapped heads."[89] The following passage from *Genpei jōsuiki* describes one such assembly, purportedly in the words of the akusō Gōun speaking to Go-Shirakawa:

> The assemblies of the Three Mountains are conducted in a strange manner. It is neither the sound of a voice chanting a poem, nor that of a voice expounding the sutras and their commentaries. It is also different from the manner of people holding mutual converse. It is as in the dancing of the "Dance of the Former King," when the nose is wrinkled up under the mask. In the assemblies of the three compounds, three thousand warrior monks meet in the courtyard of the Main Lecture Hall. They wrap their heads in a torn stole, and striking each a three foot staff called a Hall Entering Staff, they sweep the dew from the grass, take a small stone each, and sit down in a row upon them. Then, so that they won't be recognized by either their assistants or hall companions, pressing on their noses they alter their voices

and say, "Monks of the whole mountain stand round." In debating the intent of the protest, they express their accord by saying, "Yes, most reasonable"; and when the argument is without sense, they declare, "It is unreasonable."[90]

With its emphasis on concealment and transformation, which mark the assembly off from the normative activity of temple life, and on the auditory, where the voice is rendered into something eerily unlike the familiar sounds of human converse, the description highlights the absolute unknowability of the akusō.[91]

If the akusō represent an incursion of the nomadic into the precincts of the temples that was eventually co-opted and integrated into the power structure, the akutō belonged to a different order of threat. Dressing up basara-style in heterogeneous attire that mingled women's fashions with strange weaponry and glittering ornaments, the akutō, with their long forked beards reminiscent of the hōmen, spelled confusion and chaos for the capital elites.[92] As a social phenomenon outside the logic of the center, the akutō are best related to what Deleuze has characterized as the nomadic war machine: an anomic assemblage whose high-speed guerrilla tactics and "becoming-intense" and "becoming-animal," periodically wars against the state, threatening it with destruction until defeated or co-opted.[93]

Each of these groups overlapped with the sphere of dengaku, sarugaku, and other forms of heteromorphic entertainment.[94] At the same time, as several studies have made clear, yamabushi, hijiri, and later the akutō, all of whom were identified with tengu-like activity and animal traits, were also itinerants who pursued various crafts such as metallurgy, forestry, transport, and the like. The centers relied on these groups for building projects, but they also came into conflict with them, especially along disputed boundaries.[95] What *Taiheiki*'s dengaku spectacle presents us with, then, and Kiyomori's kaburo as will be shown in Chapter 8, is a *bordering* phenomenon of the nomadic, in which there is no inside–outside but only exteriority in a continuous state of becoming. Although this anomic assemblage, or the heteromorphic in medieval terminology, was decried as a threat, at another level it also signaled the deterritorialization of the medieval state, exemplified in Kiyomori's transgressive spatial tactics—his move to Fukuhara, for example—and in the wanderings of retired sovereigns for whom incessant pilgrimage to dangerous sites becomes a sign of sacred authority. The powerful temples, on the other hand, countered this nomadization by staging sacred spectacles that attempted to appropriate the heteromorphic's eerie threat for their own advantage.

Sage Ruler and Defiled Tennō: Daigo and Antoku

The 300-year period extending from the end of the eleventh century, when extravagance in the ritual sphere first began to attract the notice of aristocratic observers, to the appearance of *Taiheiki* at the end of the fourteenth century, which narrates the rise and fall of Go-Daigo's court, was characterized by the existence of several overlapping symbolic systems. In one of these, the centric space of the old capital domain, premised on boundaries separating inner and outer, although verging on collapse throughout much of this period, persisted in the routinized forms of ritual practice. As a symbolic system, it continued to affirm a ritually pure tennō whose sacrality was sustained by an elaborate network of taboos and rites of purification. In the sphere of representation, this took the form of the tennō as sage ruler in resonant accord with cosmological principles, a symbolic stature that echoed the earlier period of ritsuyrō-style rule.

In the Kakuichi *Heike*, language evoking the ritsuryō ideal of the sage ruler recurs throughout the narrative, including several episodes at the beginning of scroll six memorializing the death of Takakura, celebrated for his wise and beneficent rule. But it is the special transmission in Heike recitation (*heikyoku*) known as "Engi seidai" ("The Sacred Reign of Engi"), one of two "Lesser Secret Compositions" (*shōhiji*) managed by the guild reciters of *Heike*,[96] that best embodies this myth. After detailing Daigo's parentage and the stages of his accession to the rank of "son of heaven," it continues with the following description of his reign:

> From that moment on, he reverenced the deities, believed in the Buddhist law, showed compassion toward the people, brought blessings upon the populace, established the codes, performed the Buddhist rites, corrected what was wrong, and made proper government his priority. As a result, the entire realm was tranquil and throughout the four seas there was peace. His rule was not inferior to the ancient examples of the Three Emperors and surpassed the rule of the Five Emperors of long ago. Timely tenth day rains did no damage to the earth and fifth day winds barely rustled the branches of the trees. In the capital there were no calamities from the Fire God; and throughout the land griefs from drought were unheard of. Furthermore,

military disturbances and armed rebellions were not seen even in dreams. Bows and arrows were kept in storage, and halberds and shields were hidden away. The barbarians of the East, West, South, and North, including Silla, Paekche, Koguryŏ, and the Khitans, loosened their hunting collars and trembled. Offering up tribute, they expressed their reverence. Even the grass and trees bent, and flying birds showed obedience.[97]

Although the reigns of Uda and Daigo were already being idealized by the time of *The Tale of Genji* as an age when the sovereigns governed without interference from the Fujiwara regents, it was in the *Heike* narrative tradition that this was distilled into a mythlike representation of imperial rule. The Daigo portrayed here has the stature of a sage ruler, governing over a refined center and mirroring his virtue in the yin-yang balance of the natural cycles that keeps his realm free of calamities and at peace. The remaining two sections of "Engi seidai" reinforce this image. The first highlights the performative power of imperial speech in the story about a heron (*sagi*) rewarded by Daigo for obeying an imperial command (*senji*)—an anecdote also found at the end of "Chōteki zoroe" ("An Array of Court Enemies") in the fifth scroll of the Kakuichi *Heike*—and the final section illustrates Daigo's compassion toward his subjects:

In times of bitter cold on frosty moonlit winter nights, the emperor would speak of how cold the nation's people must feel, and sleep in his chamber without any bed-clothes. Excursions outside the Palace were not an easy matter for an emperor, who would be attended by members of the palace entourage and accompanied by hundreds of officers. Daigo, however, made excursions to the imperial garden, Kitano, Saga, and the Ōi River. These excursions were not for the sake of amusement or hunting trips. Rather, thinking that the complaints of the people and peasantry in the various provinces and seven circuits probably were not reaching his ears, he undertook these trips in order to learn for himself. Moreover, knowing that a grave demeanor would make it difficult for the people to speak their hearts, he put on an extremely cheerful countenance whenever he went abroad. In this fashion, none of the people harbored resentment or concealed their complaints. Although punishments had been established for crimes, years went by without any need to enforce them. Because the people did not break the laws, they forgot about locking the doors on their houses; and the barriers at the toll-gates were left unguarded. During the thirty years that the emperor governed the land, thick moss grew on the admonition drum and the bulrushes of the punishment whip rotted. There has been no such precedent throughout the twenty-seven reigns from Suiko to the present day. It was a splendid reign.[98]

Here, Daigo's concern to heed the voice of the people exemplifies the wise conduct of the Confucian-style sage. Other elements of this passage, such as Daigo's willingness to endure the bitter cold of winter nights out of sympathy for the commoners, are also found in *Heike*'s portrait of Takakura, who in "Kōyō" ("Autumn Leaves") is directly compared to the exemplary Daigo.

With its vision of a golden age, "Engi seidai" exemplifies the ideal of the sage ruler. But the piece was also performed in the context of various guild rituals that disclose other facets of the medieval imaginary of royal authority. Once every year, on the sixteenth day of the Second Month, it was performed during the ritual of "sekitōkai," as a form of congratulatory words aimed at assuring "peace and tranquility throughout the realm." [99] Sekitōkai itself was a widely practiced form of ritual prayer for the dead that involved piling up stones in the form of a pagoda. According to *Tōdōyōshū* (*Collected Essentials of the Guild*) and *Enpekiken ki*, it was performed several times a year along the banks of the Kamo River at the intersection of Shijō Avenue. Although the guild notices are relatively late, the incorporation of sekitōkai into the guild's ceremonial structure is thought to reflect older magical rites pertaining to the dead that blind reciters performed along riverbanks even before the period of *Heike*.[100] The combination of congratulatory words that celebrate the virtues of the sage ruler and ritual prayers for the dead along the banks of a flowing stream, a site closely tied to ritual purification, reflects a routinized stage in the guild's ceremonial structure that preserves traces of the late Heian and early medieval overlap between the Chinese-style sage ruler and the tennō whose ritual purity had to be maintained.

The theoretically pure sage ruler inhabiting a space that was organized around a logic of inside–outside and hierarchically structured difference, or Deleuze's "striated space," constituted only one side of royal authority in the early medieval imaginary. In the heteromorphic state, the boundary no longer strictly demarcated inside from outside, as it did within the logic of centered space, but was reinvested with ambiguous powers as the privileged site of transformations. Medieval Buddhism, as noted earlier, imaged this shift spatially in the idea of Japan as a defiled boundary country that was simultaneously numinous. Although medieval emperors, including retired sovereigns like Go-Shirakawa and the emperor Go-Daigo, claimed the authority to traffic in the defiled realms, under such radically changed conditions the notion of a theoretically pure tennō at the apex of a sociopolitical hierarchy became increasingly difficult to sustain. Hence, alongside the myth of the sage ruler in "Engi seidai," we find Daigo's antitype in the defiled tennō.

In the *Heike* narrative tradition, the symbolic opposition between the sage ruler, whose authority is based on yin-yang cosmological principles, and the defiled tennō who heads a collapsing ritual structure is refracted from a variety of perspectives. In scroll five, for example, the description of Kiyomori's transfer of the capital to Fukuhara in "Miyako utsuri" ("The Transfer of the Capital") is followed by a long recitation of previous transfers that culminated in the establishment of Heiankyō:

> Upon investigating the topography of the land, the presence of a green dragon on the left, a white tiger on the right, a vermilion bird in the front, and a tortoise behind show that the site is in harmony with the four divinities. It is perfect for establishing an imperial capital.[101]

In the yin-yang five agents system, the presence of the four geomantic signs or divinities corresponded to a flowing stream on the east (green dragon), a broad road on the west (white tiger), a marsh on the south (vermilion bird), and a lofty mountain on the north (tortoise). The record of the geomantic report thus delivered is introduced at this point to recall the capital's ancient conformity to cosmological principles, an emphasis further reflected in the nostalgic passage on the harmonious rule of former sage emperors that rounds out the episode.[102] The geomantic report on the founding of Heiankyō is followed by a passage on the Mound of the General (*shōgun ga tsuka*), the site of an armed iron-clad effigy that was said to have been constructed by Emperor Kammu atop Mount Hiei and that "always rumbles and mutters whenever any untoward event threatens the land."[103] The northeast peak on Mount Hiei where the Mound of the General stood was also the site of the Demon Gate, which in yin-yang thought was a point of egress and ingress for baleful, demonic forces. In Daoist terms, the Demon Gate's location in the northeast quarter was in harmonious balance with the immortal realm (*sen*) embodied in the palace of the emperor.[104] In the Engyōbon and *Genpei jōsuiki*, the geomantic implications of Kiyomori's transfer of the capital become the occasion for an elaborate debate between a yin-yang master in the service of Kiyomori and an anonymous critic. The version that follows is from *Genpei jōsuiki*:

> Somebody then spoke: "Regarding this [transfer], Fukuhara lies west of the Heian capital. This year, the Great General is in the west, and the direction is blocked. What should be done?" The yin-yang master Abe no Suehiro

was summoned and asked to deliver an interpretation. This was his interpretation. "The writing states: 'The Great General and the Royal Aspect
should be avoided as taboo in all cases, without regard to proximity or distance. However, in the matter of transferring the capital, precedents should
not be ignored. On the twenty-first day of the Tenth Month in the thirteenth
year of Enryaku in Emperor Kammu's reign, the capital was moved from
the capital of Nagaoka to the capital of Kadono [Kazuno]. That year, the
Great General corresponded to the northern quarter, the direction of the
Royal Aspect.' Pondering therefore on the auspicious precedent of the Enryaku era, which was nonetheless a transfer in the direction of the Great
General, why should there be any hesitation?" So spoke Suehiro.

When people heard this, they clicked their tongues in amazement. Someone then spoke: "The Enryaku transfer was a change of direction. Moreover, in this matter of abandoning the capital after a long period of time,
directional taboos should not be violated to this extent. If one interprets the
prognostication, however one looks at it, it is toward a blocked direction.
Suehiro's interpretation is a sham. Ponder well the meaning of the following
example. Long ago in China, they constructed a tower one-hundred feet in
height as a platform for observing the heavens, and stationed a doctor of
astrology upon it. This astrologer's duty was to observe heavenly anomalies and interpret their auspicious and inauspicious meaning. During the
two reigns of the Han emperors Yuandi and Chengdi, who were father and
son, the government was evil and heavenly anomalies frequent. The light of
the polestar dimmed and the five planets flickered red like fire. Flashing a
baleful light, they agitated the horn star and pierced the three terrace stars,
partially destroying the upper terrace and breaking the middle terrace. Such
anomalies infallibly portended disorder in the world and the destruction of
the country. Although the astrologer observed these signs, he feared the evil
ways of his ruler, and flattering the emperor's wishes on each occasion, he
merely stated, 'Propitious signs and auspicious omens bring joy; and heavenly prodigies portend long-lasting fortune.' As a result, the government
was not corrected, the country fell into disorder, and the emperor perished.
And now Suehiro, fearing the Lay Priest's evil governance, omits any mention of the directional taboos." Thus did he speak ill of Suehiro.[105]

Cast in the role of apologist, Suehiro's attempt to justify the transfer is based
on the authority of a dubious precedent that he uses to trump the interdiction
of a blocked direction (*kata-futagari*). One of eight divine generals who determined calendrical calculations, the Great General was ruled by the planet
Venus (*Taihaku*) and normally blocked travel in any direction that fell under
its influence, which was believed to remain harmful for a period of three

years.[106] His anonymous critic responds by arguing that the earlier transfer of the Enryaku era was preceded by a "change of direction" (*kata-tagae*) and thus in conformance to yin-yang protocols.[107] The anecdote about the cowardly Chinese astrologer that follows reinforces the deviant character of Kiyomori's transfer, foreshadowing the baleful portents and demonic infestation that break out at Kiyomori's Fukuhara Palace.[108]

Having broken with a nearly 400-year precedent, Kiyomori's transfer of the capital is portrayed as jeopardizing the entire symbolic edifice of ancient royal authority. Following the news of Yoritomo's rebellion in the east and the long list of former court enemies, the destruction of royal authority is commemorated in the account of the heron who obeyed a royal command, here cited in the Kakuichi version:

> Although in these days the royal rank is held in little esteem, in ancient days the recitation of an imperial edict caused withered plants and trees to suddenly flower and bear fruit, and flying birds to show obedience. The following incident occurred in the recent past. When the sovereign of the Engi era made a visit to the Shinzen'en Garden, there was a heron standing at the edge of the pond. Summoning a chamberlain of the sixth rank, the sovereign ordered him to go and bring back the bird. Although he had no idea how he would catch the bird, because it was a royal order, he walked towards it. The heron preened its feathers and prepared to fly off. When the chamberlain uttered the words "By imperial command," the heron flattened itself to the ground and didn't fly off. He then picked it up and brought it to the sovereign. "How splendid that you came in obedience to an imperial edict. You shall be raised immediately to the fifth rank." And saying this, he promoted the heron to the fifth rank. Then, writing out a plaque that read "From this day henceforth you shall be the king of the herons," the sovereign hung it on the heron's neck. He had absolutely no use for a heron, but wanted to learn the extent of royal authority.[109]

As noted, the heron episode belonged to the myth of the sage ruler that was transmitted by the guild reciters in their secret composition "Engi seidai." In the main narrative of the Kakuichi *Heike*, however, this same myth is inverted, first in the figure of Kiyomori, whose accession to power mimics many of the attributes of the sage ruler, and later in the figure of the heterodox tennō, Kiso Yoshinaka, whose rise to prominence follows immediately upon Kiyomori's death. If Yoshinaka's brief success amounts to a parody of royal authority, then "Tsuzumi Hōgan" ("The Tsuzumi Police Lieutenant"), where royal speech proves totally inefficacious, must be counted as its complete debasement. In the passage that follows, a Kebiishi officer by the name of Tomoyasu, having donned a helmet painted with images of the Four Heavenly Kings, performs a ritual dance to defend the Retired Sovereign Go-Shirakawa against the attack of Kiso no Yoshinaka:

> When Kiso attempted to advance to the West Gate of the Hōjūji mansion, Tsuzumi Hōgan Tomoyasu took charge of the battle. Tomoyasu was wearing a red brocade hitatare, but had deliberately refrained from donning armor. He wore only a helmet. The helmet was painted with a design of the Four Guardian Kings; it was with this that he defended himself. He climbed atop the west earthen wall of the Palace and planted himself there. In one hand, he held a spear, and in the other he held a vajra bell. Shaking the vajra bell, he would sometimes dance about. Some young nobles and courtiers mocked him saying: "How unseemly; Tomoyasu is possessed by a demon *(tengu)*." Raising up a mighty voice, Tomoyasu reviled them saying: "In the past when one recited an imperial edict, it was the custom for even withered grass and trees to flower and bear fruit. Evil demons and evil deities also submitted *(akki akujin mo shitagaikeri)*. Even if it is the end-age, how can you draw your bows against a virtuous sovereign *(jūzen teiō)*. The arrows you release will return to strike your own bodies; the swords you draw will cut you down." "Don't let him speak like this," said Kiso, and he raised the battle cry.[110]

Here, Tomoyasu invokes the same power of imperial speech that was commemorated in the heron episode, engaging in ritual combat on behalf of the retired sovereign, which is reflected in the ceremonial expression "he took charge of the battle" *(ikusa no gyōji uketamawatte)*.[111] Despite this show of power, Tomoyasu and his band of defenders scatter in flight. Thwarted in his attempt to defend against harmful spirits and defilements, the agent of purification, Tomoyasu, in an exact parallel to the inverted tsuina ritual, has now become the very embodiment of demonic infestation.[112] This is reflected not only in the ineffective power of imperial speech but in the composition of Go-Shirakawa's own forces, which include warrior priests and a motley crowd of outcasts:

> [Go-Shirakawa] did not give his orders to dependable warriors but had the Tendai Abbot and head priests of the temples summon fierce monks *(akusō)* of Miidera temple and Mount Hiei. As for the forces summoned by the nobles and courtiers, they consisted of stone-throwers *(mukaetsubute)*, stick-wielding commoners *(inji)*, worthless young drifters *(tsuji kanjabara)*, and beggar priests *(kotsujiki hōshi)*.[113]

Although the presence of Tomoyasu, an officer of the Kebiishi, clearly points to the late Heian and early medieval alliance between retired sovereigns and low-status marginals, including militarylike personnel as well as sarugaku performers and other entertainers, in the Kakuichi *Heike* the entire episode is cast as a comical debasement of diminished royal prestige.

If the Tomoyasu episode points to the defiled state of the tennō, it is the child tennō Antoku, whose lineage is overtly repudiated in both the Engyōbon and *Genpei jōsuiki*, who embodies royal defilement at its most extreme. In the Kakuichi *Heike*, this is hinted at in a more oblique fashion through the activity of the yin-yang masters, which often takes on the parodic tone that was one of the hallmarks of the heteromorphic as defiling behavior. Summoned to assist at critical turns of event—the birth of Antoku, outbreaks of natural calamities, and the loss of the sword—the yin-yang masters with their magical techniques and prognostications were in principle a visible guarantor that the court was functioning in harmony with the cosmological order. Yet in the Kakuichi *Heike*, where ritsuryō-style rule achieves a kind of mythologization, their divinations are quickly outpaced by the collapse of the order that they are being called upon to interpret, and on several occasions, their ritual actions are either marred by ominous lapses in execution or attended by raucous laughter. On the eve of Antoku's birth, there is a sudden increase in portents and heavenly signs, as in this passage from the beginning of scroll three: "A comet became visible in the east on the Seventh of the First Month. It was the kind called Chi You's Banner (*shiyūki*) or Red Spirit. Its brilliance increased on the Eighteenth." [114] Astrological phenomena of this sort belonged to the category of *tenmon*. Although no yin-yang master is summoned to interpret at this point, the dire import of the comet's appearance is conveyed in this definition from the Kamakura period dictionary *Myōgoki*: "Writings indicate that comets appear in the heavens when griefs arise among the people . . . As the griefs of the people worsen, natural disturbances appear, sorrows pile up, and calamities break out." [115] The next citation occurs in an episode from early in *Heike*'s third scroll that describes events relating to Kenreimon'in's confinement prior to giving birth to the future emperor Antoku:

> Furthermore, there was the matter of the thousand repetitions of the purification ritual, for which seven Yin-Yang Masters were summoned. One
> of the seven, an elderly gentleman called Tokiharu, who was Director of
> the Bureau of Housekeeping, came with only a few attendants. The people

assembled at the mansion were crowded together like bamboo shoots, like "rice and hemp, bamboo and reeds." "I have an official function to perform," Tokiharu said. "Open up!" He lost his right shoe while he was pushing his way through, and when he paused, someone knocked off his hat as well. The younger nobles and courtiers burst into laughter, irresistibly amused by the sight of an old man, clad in formal court robes, advancing at a measured pace with his top-hair exposed on such an occasion. We are told that Yin-Yang Masters adopt a special gait to ensure that they will never so much as take a false step—yet now there was this strange occurrence. People thought little of it at the time, but many later events called it to mind.[116]

The "special gait" refers to *henpai*, a treading step ritually performed by yin-yang masters throughout much of the Heian period to clear away evil spirits, and its success depended on a flawless execution. In the present case, however, the execution is compromised by Tokiharu's loss of his shoe and the even more egregious exposure of his topknot. These lapses in decorum are all the more ominous in that they take place on the occasion of an imperial birth, a liminal period at extreme risk of attack from malign spirits and polluting influences. The irruption of raucous laughter, more appropriate to a sarugaku or dengaku spectacle, adds the final touch to a scene of mayhem that becomes, as the narrator hints, premonitory of the collapse of order that is soon to follow. The result is a parody of the court chronicle that the narrative claims to be furnishing. The symbolic activity of the yin-yang masters is thereby inverted, becoming a sign emblematic of the destruction of ancient ritsuryō rule, although the fiction of its continuance is paradoxically sustained right through to the end of the Kakuichi *Heike*'s main narrative.

But it is in the Engyōbon and *Genpei jōsuiki* that we find the most explicit reflection on Antoku's defiled status.[117] In the following passage, which occurs right after the account of Antoku's death by drowning, the narrator of the Engyōbon, commenting on Antoku's questionable legitimacy, cites the opinion of several experts in precedents: "When someone remarked, 'The First Emperor of the Qin ruled the empire for thirty-eight years, although he was not the son of King Zhuangxiang but of Lü Buwei,' another person replied: 'In foreign lands, examples like this are numerous. The emperor known as Zhonghua came from the people; and Gaozu, although the child of Daigong, acceded to the throne. In our land, it is said that a child of ministerial rank has never before ascended to the throne. How could he be a legitimate heir of the imperial line?'" [118] *Genpei jōsuiki* goes even further in casting doubt on Antoku's legitimacy, reporting the rumor that Antoku was the incestuous offspring of Munemori and his younger sister Kenreimon-in: "And how wretched and pitiable the Minister Munemori looked just now. Regarding him I have heard something utterly loathsome (*imaimashiki koto*). It is said that while the Lay Priest was still living in society, he became intimate with his younger sister Kenreimon-in, and that the child born of the union was passed off as the offspring of the Retired Sovereign Takakura and appointed to the rank of sovereign." [119] Although the speaker goes on to cast doubt on the rumor, that such rumors were recorded at all is indicative of medieval views on the questionable purity of the imperial line. Antoku, in fact, was merely one instantiation of a complex structural shift that translated into a generalized perception of an imperial line increasingly vulnerable to defilement. Its consequences are conveyed in the following account of Antoku's reign from the Engyōbon that comes right after the narration of his death by drowning in the eleventh scroll:

> This sovereign's name was Antoku Tennō. On the day of his succession, there were sundry strange prodigies. A dog defiled the border of his bedding in the day-room, and a mountain dove took refuge behind the curtain of his night chamber. On the day of his accession a woman suddenly expired behind the high seat, and on the day of purification a menial stationed himself right outside the pavilion. During the three years that he occupied the throne, calamities of heaven and earth continued without cease. Various shrines and temples made frequent reports of strange prodigies. Spring and summer there were droughts and floods, and in autumn'and winter there were typhoons and destructive pests. The Fifth Month rains never ceased, icy winds rose up, the seedlings withered, and the grains did not sprout. Frost fell in the Ninth Month, and the autumns were unseasonably cold. The ten thousand grasses drooped, and the ears of rice did not mature. As a result, people throughout the land perished from hunger. People who were barely alive abandoned the localities where they had lived for generations and crossed over borders. Having lost their homes, they scattered over hill and field or followed the seashores. Vagrants collapsed in the cross-roads and grieving voices filled the villages. On every road and at every barrier there were robbers; and on every bay and every inlet, pirates. In the eastern and northern provinces, rebellion was rife. The times and seasons were marked by famine and pestilence, military revolts, and destructive fires. Not one of the three calamities and seven disasters was absent. In

ancient times, there was the drought of Jōgan and the typhoon of Eisō, but nothing has ever been reported to match the calamities of this reign.[120]

From the defilements that attended Antoku's birth and marred his accession ceremony—dogs and birds being among the most egregious forms of medieval defilement[121]—to the natural calamities that continued throughout his reign, the thrust of the entire passage is to identify Antoku as the cause of cosmological and social disorder, making him the very antithesis of the sage ruler who holds sway over the yin and yang. The geographical centeredness of the rule of Daigo and other sage rulers is here displaced by the image of a collapsing central space. Significantly, movement as a sign of disorder is represented as an uprooting of once stable populations who have "crossed over borders" (*sakai wo koe*) and "scattered over hill and field." Roads, barriers, and the watery domains of bays and seashores, the principal sites of the ancient purification ceremonies, are now infested with robbers and pirates and defiled by death resulting from starvation. The collapse into nondifferentiation that irrupts from the moment of Antoku's birth mirrors the defilement of the imperial line.

In the logic of centered space, the polar extremes of Daigo and Antoku represent inverted aspects of the same realm. In the heterotopic space of medieval Japan, on the other hand, such inversions become signs of sacred authority and a contested site of power. In Buddhist spheres, the defilement that imperiled the imperial line translated into a religio-political ideology that attempted to subordinate royal authority to Buddhist law. Royal authority's own response was the paradoxical move of migrating to the dangerous periphery, giving rise to what Amino has characterized as the heteromorphic court. To grasp the logic underlying such a move, we must now turn to the problem of "original enlightenment," which enabled two apparently contradictory regimes of space to function in a mutually reinforcing fashion. It was this mutually reinforcing structure that enabled defilement to be converted into signs of enlightenment and thus tokens of sacred authority.

Original Enlightenment and Space

If the propagation of Pure Land Buddhism by large temples affected the ritual management of defilement, there was another side to medieval Buddhism's ideological dominance that arose from the contradictory effects of original enlightenment doctrine. Briefly stated, hongaku doctrine permitted Buddhist ideologues to affirm the present world and its political order through a conception of the state that encompassed every existent being from the tennō down to the people, trees, and grass. Underlying this affirmation of present reality was the idea that all created beings were innately endowed with Buddha nature. As one of the basic supports of the exoteric–esoteric power structure's worldly authority in the late Heian and early medieval periods, hongaku has sometimes been criticized as constituting a substantialist heresy that distorted the nondual basis of correct Buddhist doctrine and resulted in discriminatory practices.[122]

One frequently cited formulation of original enlightenment doctrine from Annen's *Shinjō sōmoku jōbutsu ki* (ninth century) states, "Grass, trees, and the earthly realm all achieve Buddhahood" (*sōmoku kokudo shikkai jōbutsu*). A somewhat later formulation, attributed to Ryōgen but probably dating from the period of rule by retired sovereigns, restates this more expansively as, "Grass and trees are already endowed with the four aspects of birth, abiding, change, and perishing; namely, grass and trees have the form of conversion, practices, enlightenment, and extinction."[123] In commenting on these two statements, Sueki Fumihiko shows how the first citation, drawn from the work of the Chinese Tendai priest Zhanran (711–782), must be understood in relation to a larger argument on the absolute perspective of the void (*kū*), which relativizes the distinction between grass and trees (*sōmoku*) and human beings (*shujō*). More precisely, it is a human being's subjective existence resulting from past karmic effects (*shōhō*) that causes the dependent or environing world (*ehō*) to arise. From this perspective "grass and trees" as environment (*ehō*) are merely an effect of subjective existence (*shōhō*), a position of nonduality neatly summarized in the phrase "eshō funi" (environment and subject are nondual) and echoed in other Mahayanist formulations, such as "bonnō soku bodai" (defilements are identical to enlightenment) and "shōji soku nehan" (samsara is identical to nirvana). There was nothing to suggest, according to Sueki, that the expression "grass, trees, and the earthly realm all achieve Buddhahood" was to be taken as an affirmation of the phenomenal world. In the second formulation, on the other hand, which dates from the latter half of the Heian period, the absolute perspective of the void is diluted, and "grass and trees" are affirmed *in their difference* as concrete existences that manifest enlightenment.[124] It is this coexistence of difference and an enlightened state that has led scholars like Hakamaya Noriaki to critique hongaku as a doctrine that condoned discriminatory practices under the cloak of a false teaching of religious enlightenment. As Jaqueline Stone writes, summarizing Hakamaya's argument: "To say that 'rivers and mountains, grasses and trees, have all attained the Buddha Way' may sound egalitarian, but the claim that 'all things, just as they are, are Buddha' sacralizes the given social order and thus works to legitimate discrimination and other injustices."[125]

Between these two applications of hongaku doctrine there appears to be an unbridgeable gap. Whereas the former privileges a subject position where the occurrence of enlightenment is, in the literal sense, *utopian* by virtue of its absolute independence of place, the latter affirms a phenomenal realm of already enlightened space(s): enclosed spaces ontologically saturated with numinous powers. Although the shift from one position to the other is illogical and inconsistent, it was fundamental to the ideological dominance of the exoteric–esoteric system. This can be seen in another well-known formulation of Tendai hongaku doctrine, "this earth is identical with the Pure Land" (*shido soku jōdo*), which properly means that the moment a person sees with enlightened vision, this defiled world (*edo*) of the present is seen to be identical with the Pure Land. As Sato Hiroo has observed, despite the nondual position that affirms the identity of this world and the Pure Land, in actual practice Pure Lands were confined to delimited sites within the precincts of shrine-temple complexes.[126] The contradiction here is fundamental and unresolvable because it was at the basis of sacred authority in medieval Japan. Nor is it uniquely attributable, I suggest, to hongaku doctrine but arises out of the aporias of nondualistic thought at a specific historical juncture characterized by radical changes in material and economic conditions. This can be illustrated by comparing several *Heike* variants of the Kikai-ga-shima sequence.

Kikai-ga-shima and the Heterotopic Margin

The Kikai-ga-shima sequence describes the fates of Yasuyori, Naritsune, and Bishop Shunkan, all of whom were exiled to the island of Kikai-ga-shima by Kiyomori for their involvement in the Shishi no tani plot.[127] Although both Yasuyori and Naritsune are eventually pardoned by Kiyomori, Shunkan's name is not on the list, and he is left behind to die a wretched death, with the "whirlwind" and other ominous signs that soon follow suggesting that he has joined the ranks of the vengeful spirits and other malign forces that will soon bring about the destruction of the ancient power structure. The entire sequence consists of six separate episodes spread over scrolls two and three of the Kakuichi *Heike*, which incorporate narrative matter ranging from traveler stories about Kikai-ga-shima that circulated in the capital, local accounts originating in and about the Nine Provinces (present-day Kyūshū), to Buddhist miracle tales that were once managed by the Mount Kōya shrine-temple complex and later disseminated by wandering hijiri. Scholarly discussion has tended to focus on the placatory elements in the tales, especially the role played by wandering hijiri of Mount Kōya in propagating the Ariō account of Shunkan's death throughout Japan. But it is the complex geographical origins of the sequence together with much interesting Buddhist doctrinal debate in the read variants, notably the Engyōbon and *Genpei jōsuiki*, that make the sequence into an illuminating series of texts for grasping the interplay between Buddhist doctrine and the medieval imaginary of space.[128]

In the Kakuichi *Heike*, the island of Kikai-ga-shima is first introduced with the following description at the beginning of the episode "The Death of the Major Counselor" in the second scroll:

> In the meantime, Bishop Shunkan, the head of Hosshōji, the Lieutenant Yasuyori, and the Lesser Captain were all three exiled to Satsuma Bay at Kikai-ga-shima. To get to this island, one leaves the capital and endures a long voyage over the waves. Ordinarily, ships do not approach it. There are hardly any people on the island; and the few people that are there do not resemble the people of our land. They are black like oxen; hair often grows on their bodies; and their words are unintelligible. The men do not wear hats, and the women do not let their hair hang down. Because they have no clothes, they do not look like people. Because there is no food, they put great emphasis on killing. Because they do not till the fields, there are no grains. And since they do not harvest mulberry gardens, there isn't any silk. In the midst of the island, there is a lofty mountain, which forever belches fire. It is full of what we call sulfur. On this account, it is also known as Sulfur Island. Thunder is always rumbling up and down, and rain falls at its base. It does not look like a place where a human-being might live for even a single day.[129]

The picture presented here is of a world that completely inverts the norms of the center. In place of a settled agricultural society, the exiles find themselves among a population of hunting and gathering types, who go about unclothed and live off the slaughter of animals. The behaviors attributed to the island inhabitants, specifically hatlessness, nakedness, and a meat diet that necessitated killing, recall descriptions of the barbarous hinterlands found as early as *Nihon shoki*, but by the early medieval period (thirteenth to fourteenth century), these same behaviors have acquired an aura of the weird and heteromorphic. The mid-fourteenth century *Suwa Deity Picture Scroll* (*Suwa daimyōjin ekotoba*), for example, attributes identical traits to the inhabitants of Soto-ga-hama, Tsugaro (Tsugaru), and Ezo-ga-chishima.[130] In contrast to Kikai-ga-shima's far western location, Soto-ga-hama and Ezo-ga-chishima marked the far eastern limit of the center's cultural and political reach. In the medieval geographical imaginary of the capital residents, however, these regions were symbolically identical, a defiled realm engirdling the center that had lost whatever allure it had as a site of exotic imaginings in the Nara and again in the late Heian periods. Indeed, by the early Kamakura period, these regions had become the source of sinister omens. When a deformed nine-legged horse appeared in Awaji Province in the early Kamakura period, the Bakufu ordered its expulsion to Soto-ga-hama; and for the year 1247, an entry in *Azumakagami* recorded that the waters along the seashore of Ōshū turned an ominous red as the result of a strange human-shaped fish that had drifted ashore at Tsugaru, which was interpreted as a portent of impending rebellion.[131] Once viewed as a barbarous and incult region, outside the refined culture of the center, the periphery had now become the source and destination of defilements.

Later in the sequence, when Shunkan's young servant Ariō journeys to the island and gets his first glimpse of a bedraggled, seaweed entangled figure, whose "hair shoots up skyward," he is led to reflect: "I have seen many beggars (*kotsugai*) in the capital, but I have yet to see someone like this. The sutra states, 'The various Asuras dwell by the Great Ocean.' And the Buddha has explained that the Three Evil Realms and the Four Realms of the Asuras lie deep in the mountains and by the Great Ocean. Is it possible that I have come to the realm of famished spirits?"[132] Shunkan, whose own appearance has now taken on the heteromorphic characteristics of the islanders—his zanbaragami hairstyle recalls Sakagami of the nō play *Semimaru*—has become an inhabitant of one of the Buddhist hells or realms of reincarnation.[133] A short while later, however, in telling Ariō of his strategy for surviving on the island, Shunkan explains: "Because there is nothing for a human being to eat on this island, as long as I had the strength, I would climb up into the mountains and dig out what they call sulfur and sell it to traders (*akibito*) from the Nine Provinces in exchange for some food. But having grown weaker with each passing day, I am no longer capable of such exertion. On days when the weather is calm like today, I go out to the seashore and beg fish of the hook and net fisherman, with hands clasped and on bended knees. Or when the tide is low, I gather shells, seaweed, and moss from the rocky shore. In this fashion, I have extended my dewlike life." [134] As Takahashi Kimiaki has remarked of this passage, the viewpoint here is no longer that of the capital dweller but has slipped into the world of traders and the easy abundance of a fishing culture. The Nine Provinces and the cluster of islands to which Kikai-ga-shima (also called Iōjima) belonged were in fact part of a maritime sphere that included a thriving trade in sulfur with distant centers in Song China. Unlike the Kakuichi *Heike*, which represents the placename Kikai-ga-shima with graphs meaning something like Border Island of Demons 鬼界嶋, texts composed in literary Chinese, such as *Shin sarugakuki* (*New Account of Sarugaku*) and *Azumakagami*, show a preference for graphic combinations evocative of a wealthy maritime sphere. [135]

Like the layered transparencies of an atlas, the overlapping geographies have given us three different islands called Kikai-ga-shima: a defiled periphery, a Buddhist hell, and a maritime sphere inhabited by fishermen and frequented by sea traders who keep the exiles supplied "with shipments of food and clothing." But Kikai-ga-shima has still not exhausted its protean transformations. When Yasuyori and Naritsune wander its terrain looking for a site to establish a Kumano branch temple, the island suddenly takes on a look of "surpassing beauty" (*hoka yorimo nao suguretari*) that rivals the sacred scenery of Kumano, with trees that produce leaves like "embroidered red brocade" (*kōkinshū no yosoi shinajina ni*) and mountain slopes that shimmer like "green gossamer" (*heki raryō no iro*). [136] Sequentially, this episode is the first to follow the description of the naked inhabitants that initially defines Kikai-ga-shima for the listener. The inconsistency has been noted by scholars and attributed to the complex origins of the sequence, which combines at least two distinct story cycles of diverse provenance. [137] Yet juxtaposed with the earlier description, the textile metaphors, while not unusual in descriptions of sacred scenery, suggest a narrative logic that resembles the peculiar technique of late Heian dengaku entertainments, where the normally gorgeous court attire is put to such outlandish use—"at one moment, stark naked, they wrapped crimson robes around their haunches; at another, onto wildly flying hair, they put on a rice-planting hat"—that articles otherwise refined turn into their opposites, becoming odd, or in the medieval lexicon, heteromorphic.[138] At issue here is a stylistic economy in the Kakuichi *Heike* in which rapid juxtapositions and reversals have the effect of exposing what is normally concealed and of revealing the identity of apparent opposites. In this way, the incult and defiled island of Kikai-ga-shima reappears under its sacrilized aspect as Kumano; the rustic Taira of the opening become by *Heike*'s end the embodiment of courtly refinement, living in an exiled court that floats upon the waves; and the dragon, an agent of destruction throughout much of the narrative, becomes at the end the locus of enlightenment.[139] On another level, these same inversions can also be read as a transposition into narrative language, to borrow a musical metaphor, of a chordal harmony resonating from the sacred geography of Kumano itself. For this, we must turn to the ritual economy that underlay the *mōde* (sacred traverse) that is undertaken by Yasuyori and Naritsune on the island Kikai-ga-shima.

The Kumano mōde

In scroll ten of the Kakuichi *Heike*, when the fugitive Koremori reaches the Iwada River in the course of his Kumano pilgrimage, he pauses to reflect: "It is said that for whoever crosses the water of this stream even a single time, evil karma, defilements, and sins that have no beginning vanish away."[140] Koremori's statement refers to the mysterious source of Kumano's renown in the late Heian and medieval periods: its capacity to convert defilements into salvation and enlightenment. Paradoxically, it was Kumano's own defilement that made it into one of the preeminent sacred sites in the medieval period. Going all the way back to the ancient period, the Kii Peninsula, where both the Kumano and Kōyasan Temple complexes were located, was closely connected in mythological and religious lore to the realms of the dead. By the medieval period, Kōyasan had become a major depot, linked by a radiating network of pilgrimage routes, for housing funerary remains from all over Japan.[141] In addition to these necrotopic associations, Kumano's deities were known for the violent nature of their sacred character. *Shozan engi* (1192) describes Kumano's main deity, Ketsumiko, as so violent that it would sometimes run about the mountains putting obstacles in the way of worshipers. To ward off these dangers, the same text prescribed special ritual precautions and charms, such as smearing the face with the fragrance of sandalwood and bean-paste or wearing hats woven of sacred evergreen leaves.[142] It was this terrifying aspect of Kumano's sacred sites that invested the austerities performed in its precincts with a special cachet of authority. One of the more extreme examples was the esoteric Shingon practice Kongōdōji-hō. According to the rules set forth in the Shingon text *Byakuhōshō*, the adepts were to demonstrate proof of their superior powers, in the period of end-law, through confrontations with a host of demonic forces that swarmed in the earth of Kumano's sacred places threatening them with dangers to both body and spirit.[143] The Kongōdōji rite was a difficult esoteric training for adepts of mountain religion, but similar perils awaited the practitioner of the more familiar Kumano mōde.

Before setting out on the traverse (*mōde*) of Kumano's sacred circuit, the adept would enter a purification hut (*shōjiya*) for an initial period of fasting and austerities (*ketsusai shōjin*) preparatory for the journey, which in the medieval period took the form of entry into the Pure Land embodied physically in Kumano's Main Hall.[144] During the late Heian period of rule by retired sovereigns, the adept was assisted in this initial purification by a yin-yang master who would ritually transfer defilements to an effigy in a rite similar to the Seven Shallows Ritual discussed earlier in the chapter, a role that was subsequently taken over during the Kamakura period by the guide (*sendatsu*), usually a devotee of mountain religion (*shugendō*). The most important part of the traverse was the staged journey through Kumano's sacred sites, which was organized around the principle of transgressing boundaries and characterized by a dual structure of purifications. While on the journey, the adept performed ritual purifications in the morning before setting off and again in the evening at the conclusion of the day's journey, a practice called "the morning and evening method" (*gyōseki no shosa*).[145] The most intriguing aspect of the traverse was the irregular purifications (*kori*), which were performed during pauses in the journey at specified sites, a practice known as *hizugori*. Because of this dual structure, with midjourney purifications accumulating between the morning and evening rites, the physical act of journeying was transformed into nothing less than a defiling process for the adept, with maximal points of danger at the boundary sites. Based on an examination of Heian and Kamakura period diaries, Nanami Hiroaki has classified the boundaries into riversides, mountain passes, slopes, field paths, seashores, and provincial boundaries. At these moments of delay for purification (*hizukori*), conducted by the guide, the journey took on the character of a dramatic struggle against the danger of crossing defiled border sites.[146] In a sequence of such moments from *Shozan engi*, the traveler's journey is brought to a halt by a blood defilement on the path, a corpse floating in a river, a woman in childbirth, and a pile of horse and cow carcasses that are being consumed by a woman. With guidance from the assistant, or sometimes with the intervention of a deity, the traveler eventually negotiates the dangerous crossing. As Nanami remarks, "The danger of crossing boundaries assumes the form of defilement." At the same time, the intervention of the divinity makes the same defilement encountered physically on the journey into an interior expression of the traveler's sinful karmic obstruction (*zaishō*). The symbolic language of the traverse was variable, and other journeys took the form of struggles against a variety of demonic presences.[147] Like the multiple aspects of Kikai-ga-shima, the beautiful scenery of Kumano's mountains and valleys was simultaneously a geography of defiled places, charnel hells, and demonic realms, where the traveler's journey involved repeated encounters with the *obscene* spaces and times of the boundary crossings.

A Doctrinal Debate on Kikai-ga-shima

As the foregoing discussion of the Kumano mōde makes clear, the boundary was more than just a geographical marker separating inside from outside; it was a valorized site invested with numinous powers of its own. The center to periphery logic of space is turned inside out. Viewed in this light, Kikai-ga-shima, or Border Island of Demons, Kumano's sacred precincts, and Japan visualized as a small country of the border are facets of the same place in the medieval imaginary. That this was to remain a secret or hidden knowledge, however, is dramatized in the Engyōbon version of the Kikai-ga-shima sequence. In addition to providing the most detailed and concrete description of the exiles' traverse of the island's Kumano-style circuit, the Engyōbon contains a lengthy debate between two of the exiles, Shunkan and Yasuyori, in which the former demolishes the hidden doctrinal basis of Kumano's sacred space. It begins with the Lay Priest Yasuyori explaining the characteristics of the divinities (*kami*) worshiped on Kikai-ga-shima:

> "Well then, about three miles south of where the islanders dwell there is an isolated mountain called Barbarian Peak. The inhabitants of Kikai no Shima say: 'On Barbarian Peak, we worship the deity Lord Ebisu Saburō and have given him the name Iwadono. When sulphurous fires suddenly

gush out and it becomes completely unbearable for us on the island, we worship by making various offerings. Then the sulphurous fires stop, the typhoons blow calmly, and we island residents feel quite at ease serving him.'" When he heard this, the Lesser Captain Naritsune said: "If that's true, then they are calling that dwelling place of demons in the midst of sulphurous fires a *kami*." The Lay Priest Yasuyori replied: "That is certainly so. That which is called the Kingdom of Emma is also a dwelling place for demons in the midst of sulphurous fires. But even they are called the Ten Kings, the Ten Deities, and the Ten-form Deity, who dwell side by side. All the reason more that this island, one of the islands of the divine country of Japan, should be the dwelling place of Lord Ebisu Saburō.

"Now then, regarding my pilgrimage to sacred Kumano, although my vow may have been made with impure concentration, I have completed the eighteenth stage. In order to obtain rebirth in paradise in the next life, I intend to accomplish the remaining fifteen stages at Iwadono. Since great *kami* and small *kami* manifest themselves at the temples where they are solicited, the avatar will surely appear and accept my prayers. What do each of you think?" The Lesser Captain straightaway replied: "I will now lead the way and make the pilgrimage."

Following Yasuyori's initial defense of the demonic character of Kikai-ga-shima's principal deity and the medieval system of honji-suijaku (original ground/ trace-manifestation), whereby lower or "small," and frequently threatening, deities were conceptualized as the earthly manifestations of the more benign Buddha's original ground,[148] Shunkan responds with a skeptical attack on the existence of the kami, which is then rebutted as heretical by Yasuyori:

Shunkan thought it very odd and for a long while made no reply. After a long lapse of time, he said: "Japan is called the country of the kami, and when the minister Moriya recorded the names of the kami in the register, he said that there were thirteen thousand *kami*. I have not yet seen the *kami* called Iwadono of Kikai no Shima in that register of divine names. Moreover, Ebisu Saburō Dono takes possession of mediums, and by the looks of him seems to be quite worthless. On the whole, he is without reliable benefit. Even with the Kumano Avatar, eighteen pilgrimages have turned out to be useless, and you have met with this disaster. At the same time, it would be shameful to have it rumored back home: 'In his extremity, he who was a prelate of Hosshōji Temple worshiped Ebisu Saburō as he walked about sprinkling himself with holy water.' To have that spoken of me by family and strangers would be most loathsome."

"Next, even if one does not necessarily address the *kami* for enlightenment in the after-life, shouldn't chanting the nenbutsu be sufficient? It is said that 'He who believes in the *kami* as *kami* (*shinmei*) incurs the karma of heresy, and for a long period of time does not know separation from self. Simply meditate on Amida Nyorai's original ground, and even before the window of the ten evils and five violations, he will welcome you.' So it is explicated in the *Meditation Sutra*. Well, I have not yet grasped the Jōdo sect's teaching. But for the sake of dull and witless people, it turns the mind entirely toward a single object of thought. Thus it is an expedient means without real meaning."

[A] As for the great net of the Buddhist law, it is argued in both the esoteric doctrine and the exoteric doctrine that there is no distinction between lay person and saint, and that apart from one's own mind neither Buddhist law nor divinities exist. When one grasps that the *three worlds are the mind alone* (*sangai yui isshin*), neither the mundane world (*yokukai*) nor the corporeal world (*shikikai*) lie outside.[149] Both hells and other life forms arise from one's own heart. Both the human world and the heavenly world are in our minds. Enlightenment through hearing the dharma preached, through meditation on the twelve causes, and those called Bodhisattvas, none of these exists outside the mind. All creation, absolute and relative truth, the entire phenomenal universe exist in the law of self-being and one mind. In conditional truth, one names the erring mind *kami* and the enlightened mind Buddha. Error and enlightenment do not originate outside the mind. This is the marvelous truth that wrong and right are one. And so the teaching of Zen is called a special transmission outside the doctrine, whose wondrous truth stops speech. In one generation it surpassed the holy teaching of Śākyamuni, attaining the zenith of the eight and nine sects.

[B] "At this time at Hosshōji Temple is one called the honorable Ritsu Master Hongū, a Zen priest who traveled to Tang. Formerly, before he went to Tang, he was a scholar of Shingon Tendai, a practitioner of the four types of meditation, and a master of the water-consecration ritual; but when he switched to the Zen sect, he became the number one priest of non-action. He neither reverenced the gods, nor reverenced the Buddha; for him there was nothing to despise in becoming a beggar or an outcast. Laughing loudly, he would call the Shingon, Tendai, and Jōdo sects the melon-rind sects. He was always humming these words, said to be a phrase of the Zen master Huineng: 'The bodhi is not a tree, the mirror has no stand; from the beginning there is nothing; how can there be a speck of dust?' So he chanted, wearing neither a bell nor Buddhist robes. He made no offerings of flowers or incense to the Buddha. He neither chanted the *nenbutsu*, nor intoned the sutras.

"When someone asked, 'Why don't you do *zazen*?' he laughed loudly and said: 'What do you mean by *zazen*? Among the various doctrines, it is a rule practiced by novice ascetics. In the Tendai sect, there is thought-cessation *zazen*; in the Shingon doctrine, there is the *zazen* of meditating on the Sanskrit letter *A*, and in the Jōdo sect, there is the *zazen* of meditating on the sun, and there are others. It is not a practice proper to Zen. Though well buried in the mud, gold-dust is still gold; and wrapped in a brocade bag it is still gold. One does not grasp the zen doctrine all at once. Novices, though they practice *zazen* day and night, morning and evening, do not attain the highest level. According to Dharma's verse: 'Of those who grasp the Buddha through *zazen*, are there any who get more than a tranquil floor? However pure the white waves, their belief is in Master Zen Floor.' Daruma never practiced *zazen*: 'Gazing into the far off sky where the six flowers bloom from the six roots, I gaze upon myself.' This is what is meant by being a master of *zazen*."

"Speaking like this, he gorged himself on the five forbidden flavors, and on wine, meat, and vegetables, and at rest on his pillow of sloth and shamelessness, he slept all the time. Indeed, I too have grasped Zen master Huineng's phrases. 'The Bodhi is not a tree,' means there is nothing that is a Buddha; 'The bright mirror has no stand,' means there cannot be a Pure Land; the law that 'From the beginning there is not one thing,' means all Buddhist law is empty; and meditation on 'How can there be a speck of dust,' reveals that errors of sight and mind and the dust of karmic sin are like a dream-vision. All the more be assured of this: he who is called the Kumano Avatar, he who is called Ebisu Saburō Dono are the false illusions of benighted minds, entanglements as real as fur on a tortoise and horns on a rabbit."

And neither sympathizing with them nor accompanying them, Shunkan stayed behind alone. While he lingered behind alone in a rocky crevice beneath the shade of a pine tree meditating on the phenomena of the various laws, a wind suddenly blew up, the earth all at once quaked violently, and as the whole mountain shook, the rocky slopes crumbled into the sea. At that moment he recalled some old zen songs and began to chant: "The banks crumble and kill the fish; yet the banks do not experience pain; the wind rises and makes offerings of the flowers; does the wind achieve enlightenment?" And so he chanted as he sat.

The Lay Priest Yasuyori: "The import of Buddhist doctrine appears to be the Kegon sect's doctrine that the dharma world is the mind alone. Thus the wondrous logic of the unchanging truth and the talk of truth and error being empty alike. It is ever new and difficult to express in speech. Next, there is the doctrine of Zen, that the Buddha is ultimately inexpressible in speech.

Mahākāśyapa alone has understood its meaning. Because it negates cause and effect, it is not Buddhist doctrine. Because it is not Buddhist doctrine, it is a heretical teaching. For base commoners, it is completely inadequate for inducing belief. It neither reverences the Buddha, nor believes in the *kami*. Its followers do not practice good works, and because they talk thoughtlessly of evil karma, in one generation it has the reputation of a great heresy that completely destroys the Buddha's teaching. It must never be propagated openly. Causing all living beings to fall into hell, this is no other than a latter-day Devadatta. How sad! If there are no disciples of Śākya Sugata, who will receive the protection of the beneficent guardian deities! As for enlightenment, because people are by nature dull and ignorant, in Shingon doctrine they believe in achieving Buddhahood while still in bodily form through external means (*kaji no sokushin jōbutsu*), and in the Jōdo sect they believe in rebirth through external aid (*tariki*). Therefore, both the Paradise of the Ten Directions and the Eight Great Hells lie outside, and since we believe that both the Buddhas of the Three Worlds and the Avatars of the Three Places reside outside, let us be off, Lesser Captain," and together they went to worship Iwadono.[150]

In his lengthy speech, Shunkan draws on a variety of nondualistic doctrines, mainly Kegon (section A) and Zen (section B), but also containing significant references to the Pure Land emphasis on chanting the Buddha's name (*nenbutsu*), to assert that all kami, including those worshiped by Yasuyori and Naritsune, are nonexistent and hence a form of heretical belief. The proposed pilgrimage is therefore useless, premised as it is on the worship of nonexistent divinities.

The layering of Kegon and Zen doctrine in Shunkan's argument is thought to reflect several stages in the editing process of the Engyōbon. In the Zen portions of Shunkan's speech, for example, we find references to *The Platform Sutra of the Sixth Patriarch*, which records the teaching of the Chinese Zen master Huineng (638–713),[151] together with passages that link Shunkan's doctrine with the maligned teachings of Dainichi Nōnin (dates unknown). Nōnin, according to tradition, was the founder of the so-called Daruma shū (Bodhi Dharma sect), a name that later became a byword for incomprehensibility, as in the expression *daruma uta* ("nonsense poem") that was applied to the obscure style of Teika's early waka. Although little is known about the origins of the Daruma sect, tradition holds that Nōnin sent two of his disciples to China in 1189 to secure an official sanction from the Chinese Zen master Zhuoan Deguang (1144–1203), after which Nōnin began propagating the teaching under the name of the Daruma shū.[152] In

1194, Nōnin, together with Eisai (1141–1215), the founder of Rinzai Zen in Japan, was placed under a ban by Enryakuji Temple. Although Nōnin's Daruma sect eventually died out, with his disciples going over to Dōgen's sect, his brand of Zen was popular enough to elicit a strong written attack from Eisai in which he tried to distance himself from Nōnin's teachings.

As Akamatsu Toshihide showed some time ago, the doctrine espoused by Shunkan's Zen master Hongū bears a great similarity to Eisai's characterization of the Daruma shū in his *Kōzen gokoku ron* (*Treatise on the Propagation of Zen for the Protection of the Country*).[153] In the section titled "Resolving the Doctrinal Doubts of Lay People," Eisai cites the following passage as a statement of Daruma shū practices: "Practice neither rites nor perform austerities. From the beginning there are no carnal attachments and [the mind] is originally enlightened. Therefore, one need not observe the injunctions nor practice rites. Simply sleep as one likes. Why take trouble to practice the *nenbutsu*, to make offerings to the Buddha, or to abstain from meat or fast?"[154] The tenor of this passage corresponds almost point for point with the Zen doctrine of Shunkan's Hongū. Whether Hongū, as Akamatsu suggests, is a specific reference to Nōnin and the beliefs of the Daruma shū, or merely a straw man for attacking beliefs regarded as Zen, it is easy to see why Buddhist defenders of the power structure were eager to limit the circulation of such beliefs. The cavalier disregard for injunctions against meat eating, for example, coupled with the attack on the divinities, undermined the place of defilement within the sacred economy of the exoteric–esoteric system. In this regard, it is interesting to compare Shunkan's mocking tone, "He [Hongū] neither reverenced the gods, nor reverenced the Buddha; for him there was nothing to despise in becoming a beggar or an outcast (*hinin*)," with the fact that even as late as 1344, when Zen had already gained a strong following among warriors, Mount Hiei clerics could still scorn Zen and nenbutsu sects as weird and heteromorphic types (*irui igyō*) who "wander along waysides."[155] Yasuyori's strong rebuttal of Shunkan's Zen doctrine would therefore reflect an early phase of the Engyōbon's evolution, the first decades of the thirteenth century, when Enryakuji placed both Nōnin and Eisai under a ban for propagating Zen.

The Kegon elements (section A), on the other hand, represent a somewhat later accretion to the text, involving a fusion of Kegon and Zen doctrine that flourished at Kōyasan's Daidenpōin between 1250 and 1300, and thus a period when the Engyōbon manuscript passed from Tendai into Shingon spheres. This is the view of Makino Kazuo, who has suggested that the debate between Shunkan and Yasuyori registers a period of doctrinal strife at Kōyasan in the latter half of the thirteenth century between the supporters of Kegon-Zen (Shunkan) and Shingon Pure Land (Yasuyori). The Shingon Pure Land doctrine first assumed shape when Kakuban (1095–1143) incorporated *nenbutsu* into esoteric Shingon in an effort to reform the Kōyasan complex. As developed by Kakuban's followers, Shingon Pure Land emphasized reliance on the magical power (*kaji*) of Dainichi Nyorai to achieve Buddhahood in the body (*sokushin jōbutsu*) with little effort on one's own part.[156]

The crux of this debate, then, lies in Shunkan's nondualistic position that negates the distinction between inner and outer, denying the bodily and material existence of both divinities (*shinmei*) and hells (*jigoku*) and therefore the basis of Enryakuji's and Kōyasan's institutional authority. As Yamamoto Hiroko has noted in her analysis of this episode, whereas Shunkan adopts the Zen position that the gods and Buddhas (*shinbutsu*) are an interior or subjective phenomenon (a position that approximates *hongaku* in its earlier or "correct" formulation), Yasuyori asserts the exterior reality of the Bodhisattva and reliance for salvation on the outside aid of the divinities in their manifest form (*suijaku*).[157] Hence, in responding to Shunkan's attack, Yasuyori declares his mixture of Kegon and Zen beliefs to be a "heretical teaching" (*gedō*) that "negates cause and effect" and therefore "is not Buddhist doctrine." He concludes with the following affirmation of the divinities whose reality Shunkan has denied: "'because people are by nature dull and ignorant, in Shingon doctrine they believe in achieving Buddhahood while still in bodily form through external means, and in the Jōdo sect, they believe in rebirth through external aid.[158] Therefore, both the Paradise of the Ten Directions and the Eight Great Hells lie outside (*hoka ni ari*), and since we believe that both the Buddhas of the Three Worlds and the Avatars of the Three Places reside outside, let us be off, Lesser Captain,' and together they went to worship Iwadono." The logic of outside–inside, although denied in the utopian space of the border realm, still had to be affirmed by Yasuyori because it was indispensable for sustaining belief in external means (*tariki*) and the array of Buddhist hells and Pure Land paradises of Kumano's sacred space. Just as the sacred sites (*reijō*) where the kami had manifested themselves gave an external reality to the dwelling place of the kami, likewise the Main Hall at Kumano, by the Kamakura period, had taken on the character of an actual material embodiment of the Pure Land. As Allan Grapard has shown in several studies of Mount Hiko's sacred landscape, even the wordless journey through such landscapes, as the one undertaken by Yasuyori in the Engyōbon, might function as physical analogues to prayer or esoteric meditative practices.[159]

Although Shunkan's argument is conducted largely in the language of nondualistic Kegon-Zen doctrine, it also hints at the potentially subversive power of vocal nenbutsu. In characterizing Shunkan's attack against the divinities as a heretical doctrine, for example, Yasuyori's reply recalls similar denunciations made against the practice of exclusive nenbutsu practitioners (*ikkō senju*), who were also condemned for rejecting the divinities. Shunkan nowhere offers a specific defense of exclusive nenbutsu, but at one point, he skirts briefly past a doctrinal point that hints at another position from which his argument could have evolved instead of the Kegon-Zen angle that he subsequently takes. After rejecting Ebisu Saburō as a worthless divinity, he asks, "Wouldn't chanting the nenbutsu be sufficient? It is said that 'He who believes in the *kami* as *kami* incurs the retribution of heresy (*jadō no mukui*), and for a long period of time does not know separation from self.'" Here, Shunkan follows a mild endorsement of nenbutsu chanting with an allusion to the belief, widespread among certain sects of exclusive nenbutsu practitioners, that the worship of divinities incurred the punishment of falling into a long cycle of transmigration. In *Genpei jōsuiki*, this point is developed more fully, where it assumes the form of an attack against the kami under their "real" (*jissha*) as opposed to provisional (*gonja*) form. The kami as *jissha* appear in the form of "evil spirits" (*akuryō*) and "dead spirits" (*shiryō*) who lay curses upon people. Pursuing his attack, Shunkan then states, "According to a certain text, 'Whoever once glances at or bows to any of the various earthly deities (*shingi*) straightaway takes on the form of a snake for a period of five hundred years.'"[160] Shunkan's negative characterization of the *jissha* echoes a nearly identical view found in the *Shoshin hongai shū* of Zonkaku (1290–1373), which was widely shared by exclusive nenbutsu proponents in their attacks against the worship of kami.[161] In summarizing his argument in the *Genpei jōsuiki* version, Shunkan passes in review much of what constituted the doctrinal basis for the authority of powerful temple complexes like Kumano, only to reject it with a strong affirmation of the doctrine of original enlightenment:

> Those called divinities also include the provisional kami (*gonja no kami*) and hypostasizations (*suijaku*) that have temporarily descended as the manifest form of the Buddha Bodhisattva. Directly searching out the meaning of

the original ground [or more literally, directly exploring the landscape of the original ground (*honji no fūkō*)], one enters the path of renunciation. Next, relying on the nenbutsu in expectation of rebirth, intoning the Buddha's name whether moving, standing, sitting, reclining, and with the mind concentrated on Paradise at every thought and at every step, one awaits Amida Buddha's welcome at one's death. In practicing the way of enlightenment, there is no distinction between lay person and saint. The Buddha is not to be sought outside oneself. Wrong and right are by nature undifferentiated truth (*ichinyo*). Outside the ground of self there is no Pure Land. When one grasps that the three worlds are one mind, hell and heaven are not outside. Having once grasped that mind, Buddha, and all living beings are one, acquired enlightenment (*shikaku*) and original enlightenment occur without separation from the body. When one contemplates that one's body is already endowed from the start with the original Buddha of one's self-nature, the response of the enlightened Buddha who is without limits is like the answer of an echoing voice. The practice of contemplating the extinction of life and death is the short path that surpasses all speech. In the direct method of the Bodhidharma, the secret art of achieving Buddhahood is self-seeing, which opens the storage mind of the self. There are no divinities outside, but only mind. There are no hypostasizations outside; the main hall of the self is all." [162]

Shunkan's affirmation of original enlightenment doctrine in this passage, which oscillates between nonduality premised on the void and the so-called substantialist heresy of a somatically grounded sacrality, amounts to the same relativization of enclosed sacred space in its material or landscaped form that we saw in the Engyōbon. In the phrase, "Outside the ground of the self (*jido*) there is no Pure Land," the use of the graph for "ground" or "land" in *jido* 自土 enforces the utopian aspect of Shunkan's Pure Land. By rejecting the divinities and space of the temples, or the Buddha Lands (*butsudo* 仏土) in medieval terminology, Shunkan was also rejecting the elaborate ritual economy, exemplified in the Kumano mōde analyzed earlier, that converted defilement into an expression of sacred authority. Shunkan's nondual position, in brief, does not admit the ontological validity of defilement.

Yasuyori's counterargument in the *Genpei jōsuiki* version, on the other hand, pivots around the principle of defilement. He grounds his defense of the gods and Buddhas on the fact that the country of Japan, located at a vast distance in time and space from the Buddha's entry into nirvana, is where various compassionate Bodhisattvas have manifested their traces in the form of divinities: "In brief, this arises from the earnest expedient of bringing good to living beings and is named the benefit of divinities dimming their radiance and mingling with the dust of this world." And elsewhere, "Being a small country of the border regions, the country is feeble of strength; and because it is the end-age, a period of defilements and evils, people's minds are benighted."[163] The paradox is that it is ultimately the same hongaku doctrine that underlies both the sacred authority of the Buddha Lands defended by Yasuyori and Shunkan's already enlightened mind–body. If we substitute body for the earth of the Tendai hongaku formulation cited earlier, "this earth is identical with the Pure Land," we end up with more or less the same position advocated by Shunkan, which abolishes any special authority that Kumano might claim as the embodiment of the Pure Land.

Original Enlightenment Reconsidered

The ideological dominance of the exoteric–esoteric system appears to have rested precariously on a contradiction within its own discourse. This can be characterized as involving a continual slippage back and forth among nondualistic, monistic, and dualistic modes of thought. Thus, at one level of doctrinal activity, enlightenment meant grasping all phenomena as the illusory product of differential thinking. At another level, this was translated into the affirmation of a world where "Grass, trees, and the earthly realm all achieve Buddhahood." It was at this point that the notion of an innate or immanent "Buddha nature" that pervades all things gave rise to what Hakamaya and other modern critics have characterized as a form of substantialism, which amounts to a mystical monism in which matter and spirit are conceived as indistinguishable. A common-sensical view might reason that nondualistic enlightenment required the scaffolding of dualities and differential thinking to achieve its insight. But once enlightenment occurred, the scaffolding, like Wittgenstein's ladder, was supposed to fall away.[164] That this did not always occur is attributable not only to misunderstandings of the abstruse nature of nonduality but to medieval Buddhism's entanglement in worldly political ambitions. This is most evident in its manipulations of defilement, itself dependent on a strict dualism, which became the principal sign for both working out understandings of nondual insight and then displaying the results of such insight as signs of sacred authority dramatized as the conversion of defilements into enlightenment. To put it crudely, defilements, which grasped nondualistically were an illusory product of constructural thinking, retained at the base their material essence that fueled the sacred economy of medieval Buddhism's power structure.

Was original enlightenment doctrine therefore a cause of oppressive social practices during the late Heian and early medieval periods—an ideology complicit with notions of political absolutism? Or was medieval hongaku itself rather an effect or symptom of a more complex discursive formation? The material examined in this and the preceding chapters suggests that it was the reshaping of the medieval geographical imaginary brought about in part by new forms of trade and economic exchange that created conditions favorable to the flourishing of a variety of logics founded on the play between difference and identity. At the most obvious level, this allowed the temples to traffic in the worldly business of land acquisition, trade, military action, and the like, without abandoning their claims to sacred authority.[165] At the archeological level posited by Foucault, the coexistence of such mutually contradictory systems of thought suggests that the early medieval period constituted a discursive formation that kept the exoteric–esoteric system in power.[166] Contradiction and paradox were the language of not only doctrinal debate but of historical theorizing as well.[167] The existence of a discursive formation, which tolerates contradictions, would explain how powerful Buddhist institutions could simultaneously exploit a range of nondual and dualistic logics, manufacturing arguments that attacked as heretical the very same doctrines that supported their religio-political authority. Here, too, the medieval tradition of "secret transmission" (*kuden*) comes into play, which permitted a network of heterodox teachings to operate cryptically in the interstices of the system. In spatial terms, the paradox declared itself in the heightened awareness of the boundary, which functioned simultaneously as the marker of difference and as the site of its abolition. The closure suggested by a Foucaultian episteme, however, where everything serves the interests of power that gets expressed through the discursive formation, does not fully capture the power dynamics of early medieval Japan. In brief, there were a variety of positions available within the medieval religious imaginary for asserting as well as resisting authority by privileging either aspect of the logic of identity and difference. This is nowhere more evident than in the category of the heteromorphic, which straddled the demonic as well as the defiled realms. Underlying its uncanny power was the unstable ontology of defilement in the medieval religious imaginary, where the strict dualism that opposed defilement to purity clashed and secretly combined with a range of nondualistic Buddhist doctrines. On the one hand, heteromorphic groups, such as *inu jinnin* and other outcast populations, served as visible embodiments of the defiled realms under the authority of the powerful temples. On the other hand, there were groups, including the akutō and akusō discussed earlier, who exploited its uncanny signs as a tactic of terror. As the inverted and hidden side of the Buddhist power structure, the realm of the heteromorphic and demonic, like the secret transmissions at the discursive level, was both indispensable as well as a threat to its authority.[168]

THE APOCRYPHAL HISTORY
OF KIYOMORI

Introduction

The subject of this final chapter is Kiyomori as a heterodox figure of royal authority, whose partially submerged history straddled the worlds of both the elite centers of power and the marginal social strata of medieval Japan. To highlight this counterhistory, the discussion focuses around three episodes: the enigmatic kaburo or "pageboy cuts," who served Kiyomori as henchmen and spies; legends of Kiyomori's royal parentage in the Gion Lady episode; and the posthumous account of Kiyomori as the reincarnation of the Buddhist holy man Jie Taishi. The comparison of different versions of these episodes in the *Heike* variants reveals a far more complex view of Kiyomori's history than a reading confined to the more familiar Kakuichi *Heike* would otherwise suggest. By attending to these other versions of Kiyomori's history, we will recover some sense of how *Heike* would have resonated for medieval audiences that heard it performed, as well for those who helped to produce and mediate *Heike*, which included writers of Chinese-style historiography, commentators on the classics, Buddhist priests, and the nameless disseminators of a world of oral story, rumor, and song.

The discussion pays particular attention to the ways in which these episodes ramify into the contemporaneous worlds of popular rumor and storytelling, learned commentary, and exegesis, the latter including esoteric transmissions and debates over the implications of Buddhist doctrine, while keeping equally focused on their embeddedness in a concrete social and religious topography that reflects various facets of the medieval spatial imaginary. In the course of this chapter, many of the themes discussed in the previous chapters are revisited. The clash between official and unofficial historical narrative that formed a major theme in Part Two resurfaces in the apocryphal narrative world of the kaburo, which in turn marks a paradoxical inversion of the weft-text lore and yin-yang Daoist assemblage (discussed in Part One) that formed a major strand in the ideology underpinning sovereignty in the ancient period. The medieval attempt to reestablish an official mode of historical narrative in the Confucian style, as will be shown in the case of the kaburo episodes, was entangled from the start in the counterclaims of this apocryphal lore that resurfaced to flourish in both the literate and nonliterate spheres of medieval culture. At the same time, as we will see in the discussion of the Gion Lady, there are echoes of this same clash that characterizes medieval historical narrative in the sphere of secret Tendai transmissions. Just as heterotopic sites are invested with ambiguous powers in the medieval spatial imaginary, heterodox speech takes on peculiar roles in the hierarchy of discursive modes that organize the Tendai secret transmission. It is in these cryptic or hidden sites of medieval discourse and place that Kiyomori's heterodox authority flourishes. Although I am primarily concerned with the medieval imaginary of royal authority—Kiyomori as a figure of myth—there is also a sense in which the historical Kiyomori actually did establish a heterotopic court. By achieving symbolic authority over the demonic and defiled realms, Kiyomori's authority mirrored, like their shadowy double, the practice of such emperors as the Retired Sovereign Go-Shirakawa and the even later Go-Daigo.

The Kaburo

Although the kaburo make only one major appearance in the Kakuichi *Heike*,[1] their importance is indicated by their having an entire episode to themselves, which is placed prominently in the opening sequence of the narrative that celebrates Kiyomori's unprecedented rise to power:

> Now no matter how wise the governance of kings and sovereigns or the precautions taken by chancellor and regent, there are always trouble-makers

cast aside by society who, in places where they cannot be heard or seen, are ready to slander and criticize any point. However, when the Lay Priest Kiyomori was at the height of his power, there was not a single person who indulged in the slightest back-talk. This is the reason why. The Lay Priest Chancellor Kiyomori hit on the stratagem of hiring three hundred boys from fourteen to sixteen years of age, cut their hair in the roundish style worn by boys, dressed them in red *hitatare*, and let them roam at will throughout the entire city. If someone happened to bad-mouth the Heike, as soon as one of them got wind of it, he alerted the rest of the gang, and they would burst into the house, confiscate his belongings and effects, tie the culprit up, and bring him back to Rokuhara. As a result, not a single person dared to mention whatever he had observed with his eyes or knew in his heart. At the mere sound of the words "The Rokuhara boys!" people would swerve aside their horses and carriages to let them pass. "They went in and out of the Palace gates, but no one dared to ask their names. The great ones of the city appeared to avert their eyes."[2]

For the reader familiar with the McCullough version, where "kaburo" is translated as "page-boy cuts," the appearance of Kiyomori's spies may well evoke feelings at odds with their rough, even cruel, treatment of the capital populace. For a medieval audience, the kaburo hairstyle, dress, and overall appearance would likely have aroused sensations akin to the weirdness associated with the heteromorphic. As the *Heike* scholar Mizuhara Hajime has remarked, the duties performed by the kaburo resembled those of the hōmen, the low-ranking officers who worked as enforcers for the Kebiishi, while their hairstyle shared elements in common with outcast priests (*ransō*) and the carrion scavengers called "etori," who provided food for hawk breeders. Likewise, the historian Takahashi Masaaki, noting that successive generations of the Taira held appointments in the Kebiishi, suggests that the red color worn by the kaburo, which medieval picture scrolls identify with Kebiishi officers, discloses a probable link to outcast groups that lived in and around the Taira's Rokuhara compound.[3]

If the appearance of the kaburo was apt to provoke feelings of taboo avoidance, the same kaburo hairstyle, where the hair hung loose to a point just above the shoulders, also associates them with the figure of the warawabe (also pronounced waranbe) and rumor. Here, too, the innocuous connotations suggested by "child" must be avoided. Going hatless with unbound hair was a prohibited behavior for most classes of people in the medieval period, and its license (as in the case of children but also etori and other outcast types) was a sign of liminal status, evoking under certain conditions an aura of the sacred.[4] Warawabe in the medieval period, which would have included the young "capital roughs" known as *kyōwarawa/kyōwarabe*, were believed to be conduits of rumor, sometimes of a supernatural character. Just as they were permitted to violate the norms of dress, this same liminal status granted them the right of verbal abuse, including mockery and lampooning. Social and political criticism was in part mediated through the verbal license permitted to such figures.[5] In this connection, the kaburo's association with birds, suggested by Mizuhara's carrion scavengers, or etori, is worth pursuing a bit further.

Birdlike associations also surface in the language used to characterize the speech of rumor and mockery for which the warawabe figure served as a conduit. Two such expressions are *saezuri* (to twitter or make unintelligible sounds like a rustic) and *kyōsuzume* (capital sparrow), used of rumor mongers in the capital. In *Shōtoku Taishi denki* (*The Chronicle and Legends of Prince Shōtoku*, late Kamakura), we find the idea succinctly conveyed in this well-known medieval topos, ultimately derived from Chinese: "Heaven lacks a mouth, so it expresses these matters through human sounds (*hito no saezuri*)."[6] The fusion between bird and human being suggested by the phrase "hito no saezuri" is made explicit in variants of the kaburo tale. According to *Genpei jōsuiki*, each one of Kiyomori's 300 kaburo walked about holding a bird in his hand with bells and red tokens attached to its feathers.[7] The Nagatobon *Heike* doesn't include this detail but relates that the kaburo "were named Heike birds and had red tokens attached to their wings." Both of these variants also describe these birds as "sacred bird messengers of the kami," hinting, as will be discussed later, at the kaburo's prophetic function.[8]

To complete this preliminary sketch of Kiyomori's kaburo, there is one more detail about their behavior that must be mentioned. At the beginning of the Kakuichi variant of "Sutra Island," there is an enumeration of the "strange things" that occurred on the night of Kiyomori's death, including a fire and the untimely sounds of singing and laughter. In the Kakuichi variant, the singing is first thought to be the "act of goblins" (*tengu no shoi*) but is subsequently attributed to a group of banqueting samurai. The Engyōbon, on the other hand, informs us that "among the *kaburo* who served Kiyomori there mingled many tengu who shouted raucously to the sounds of field-music."[9] Although the Engyōbon doesn't tell us what went on at this banquet, as we have seen in the case of *Taiheiki*'s account of the dengaku performers, in the medieval imaginary there was a strong connection among dengaku, tengu, defilement, and animal/bird traits. This is important for several reasons. First, it enforces the historical link between the kaburo and the Kebiishi because the latter, as several studies have shown, had close ties with performers of dengaku and related entertainments.[10] At the same time, the presence of the birdlike tengu, who also appear in the *Taiheiki* episode, brings to the fore the kaburo's close ties with (1) an anomic cultural assemblage, characterized by animal (including bird) traits and speed, and (2) rumor of a prophetic sort. In *Taiheiki*, for example, tengu and tengu-like yamabushi ("mountain priests"), famous for their extraordinary speed, appear on a number of occasions as mediators of prophetic rumor predicting rebellion and other news.[11] The significance of these traits will be made clear later in the discussion of the apocryphal Engyōbon version of the kaburo. Here, however, I would simply note that the kaburo episode has typically been read as an illustration of Kiyomori's arrogance and high-handed ways, and therefore foreshadowing his subsequent fall. But this only partially accounts for the kaburo's role in an episode that revolves around the fearful effects of rumor and slander. Although the role assigned to them by Kiyomori in the Kakuichi variant is to spy on the populace and check the spread of rumor, the kaburo themselves are rumor's very embodiment.

Kiyomori's Ambiguous Royalty

So far, I have looked at what little can be gleaned about the historical background to the kaburo and touched on their place in the broader cultural imaginary of medieval Japan, including ties to rumor and an anomic cultural assemblage.[12] But what about the episode's placement in the Kakuichi *Heike*? In other words, is there a narrative logic that might account for the prominence accorded to the kaburo at this point early in Kiyomori's history, all the more salient for being their only appearance apart from a reference to their death in scroll twelve?

In the Kakuichi *Heike*, the kaburo episode famously concludes with the following phrase from Bo Juyi's "Song of Everlasting Sorrow," a literary favorite among the Heian aristocracy from at least the time of *The Tale of Genji*: "They went in and out of the Palace gates, but no one dared to ask their names. The high officials of the capital appeared to avert their eyes."

The allusion here is to the well-known story about the Tang Emperor Xuan-zong's infatuation for his consort Yang Guifei, which led him to neglect his governance of the empire, eventually provoking the rebellion of the trai-torous minister Lushan. If we follow the standard commentary, it would appear that the impudent behavior of the kaburo is being likened to that of Yang Guifei's relatives and family, who brazenly flaunt their access to the emperor's palace.[13] Lushan, of course, is one of the four Chinese rebels to the throne who are listed in *Heike*'s Preface: "If we investigate the examples of distant foreign lands, Zhao Gao of Qin, Wang Mang of Han, Zhu Yi of Liang, and Lushan of Tang, all of these deviated from the government of former kings and emperors, and pursued to the limit the pleasures of wealth; and because they disregarded the admonitions, were unaware of the immi-nent disorder in the empire, and ignored the people's distress, they did not endure long and all of them perished."[14] Interpreted according to the Pref-ace's karmic logic of cause and effect (*ingaron*)—namely, that evil actions beget evil consequences—the outrageous behavior of Kiyomori's kaburo is easily interpreted as premonitory of Kiyomori's and his family's subsequent destruction. This in fact is in one well-established reading.

But how did this allusion work for the medieval audiences who may have heard *Heike* recited? Although it clearly highlights the brazen conduct of Kiyomori's kaburo (without openly condemning it), it can also be under-stood as implicitly aligning Kiyomori with the Emperor Xuanzong—not with the rebel Lushan who brought his reign to an end.[15] As Kuroda Akira has shown, Chinese allusions of this type were "polysemic" because they were largely mediated through a commentarial tradition, where they took on different meanings, rather than based directly on the original sources.[16] Equally significant is the tone of the sequence that narrates Kiyomori's and his family's spectacular rise to power, which suggests Kiyomori's identifica-tion with an emperor-type figure.

If we except the famous Preface placed at the beginning of *Heike*, Kiyo-mori's narrative proper begins in the style of a standard imperial history, with a lengthy genealogy of his forebears. Once past "The Night Attack at the Courtiers' Hall," in which Kiyomori's father, Tadamori, is represented as a warrior who transgresses into the forbidden space of the palace, the language takes on the felicitous or celebratory tone appropriate to official history. Before long, Kiyomori himself is taking on the luster of a sovereign. In "The Sea Bass" ("Suzuki"), for example, which occurs right after the account of Kiyomori's swift and unprecedented rise to the position of chancellor, the narrator records: "The Statue says, 'The Chancellor acts as preceptor for the Emperor and as exemplar for the Four Seas. He keeps the state in order, inculcates moral principles, and holds sway over the yin and yang. The post is to remain vacant if there is no qualified person to fill it.' But Kiyomori held the whole country in the palm of his hand, and objections were futile." [17] The narrative here, learnedly weaving in references to ancient legal codes and historical documents pertaining to the ritsuryō state, is typical of *Heike*'s style in the chroniclelike portions of its narrative. The ninth-century *Commentaries on the Collected Administrative Codes*, which this passages draws upon, states: "He who holds sway over the yin and yang interprets the four seasons and conducts government affairs. This means that he opposes neither the yin and yang nor the seasons." As the *Heike* scholar Tomikura Tokujirō, in his gloss on the law code, explains: "Through virtuous governance seasonable winds and rains are obtained in harmony with heaven and earth, and heat and cold occur beneficially." [18] Shortly after this passage, this time in the "Kaburo" episode, we learn that Kiyomori, "stricken by illness," decided to take Buddhist vows and adopt the religious name of Jōkai: "Perhaps through divine response, the stubborn ailment disappeared overnight and he was spared. Other men obeyed his commands as grass bends before wind; people everywhere looked to him for aid as soil welcomes moistening rain." [19] The language here is based in part upon a well-known passage in the Confucian *Analects*: "The virtue of the gentleman is like the wind; the virtue of the small man is like the grass. Let the wind blow over the grass and it is sure to bend." [20] Here, the metaphor of a moistening rain, echoing the previous citation from the law codes, likewise evokes associations that link Kiyomori to the figure of the sage ruler who governs in harmony with the productive yin-yang powers. Finally, at the end of "Waga mi no eiga" ("Flowering Fortunes"), a title that itself evokes royal associations, the Taira's residence, in ornate language borrowed from the *Wen xuan* and other Chinese sources, is magnificently likened to the emperor's palace and the retired sovereign's Grotto of the Immortals.

In the Kakuichi *Heike*, then, Kiyomori is invested from early on with an aura of royal authority. Although it is a dubious sovereignty, which will give rise to numerous violations of precedent and failed rites—for example, the parodic henpai ritual performed by the yin-yang master Tokiharu on the occasion of Antoku's birth—it bears directly on the role of Kiyomori's kaburo, who are at one level agents of Kiyomori's royal authority, not merely harbingers of his destruction. Whereas sovereignty in the Kakuichi *Heike*—and not only Kiyomori's but sovereignty in general—is typically cast in ambiguous terms,[21] in the Engyōbon Kiyomori's history takes on an explicitly apocryphal character, which subsists like a dissonant voice at odds with the Engyōbon's larger aim of projecting a semiofficial history in a Confucian and Buddhist mode. To illustrate this, I now turn to the Engyōbon version of the kaburo.

Fish, Birds, and Heavenly Essences

The Engyōbon account of Kiyomori's kaburo is part of a longer section that narrates Kiyomori's unprecedented rise to power, including the stages of his promotions and several strange or miraculous occurrences of a prophetic character.[22] As in the equivalent stretch of the Kakuichi *Heike*, the language throughout is in the celebratory strain appropriate to an imperial chronicle.[23] The sequence of strange occurrences begins with the story about a fish that leaps into Kiyomori's boat on his way to Kumano (corresponding to the Kakuichi *Heike*'s "The Sea Bass"), continues with a dream in which Kiyomori ingests a vitality enhancing food, and ends with the account of the kaburo. I begin with "The Sea Bass" in the familiar Kakuichi version:

> It is said that the prosperity of the Heike was owing to the benefit of the Kumano avatar. The reason is as follows. Long ago, before Kiyomori had become governor of Aki province, he was making his way by boat to Kumano when a huge sea bass leapt into the boat. The ascetic said, "That fish is a benefit of the Kumano avatar. Make haste and eat it." Kiyomori replied, "Long ago, a white fish leapt into the boat of King Wu of Zhou. This is a propitious sign." Although it was a time for strict observance of the Ten Prohibitions and dietary abstinence, Kiyomori prepared the fish and fed it to his house servants and retainers. As a result, he has had nothing but continuous good fortune, making it all the way to Chancellor, while the promotions of his grandsons have been swifter than a dragon mounts to the clouds. That he should surpass nine generations of his ancestors was truly a matter for congratulations.[24]

In the Engyōbon as well, it is the ascetic who attributes the miraculous sign to the agency of the Kumano avatar and Kiyomori who points out the precedent in Chinese dynastic history. The source for Kiyomori's precedent remains unclear, but according to the *Shi ji*, when King Wu was crossing a river, a white fish leapt into his boat predicting a revolution in dynastic power. Later, the Han scholar Ma Rong (79–166) interpreted the fish as the symbol of the warrior and the color white as the official color of Yin, thereby foretelling King Wu's defeat of his rival, King Zhou of Yin.[25] The Han precedent suggests that Kiyomori's rise to power is being implicitly likened to a revolution in dynastic succession. In the Engyōbon, however, there is a subtle tension between Kiyomori and the ascetic. When the fish leaps into the boat, the astonished ascetic looks up its meaning in a "book of prognostications" (*kannagibumi*) and, after judging it to be "a favorable sign entirely without precedent," pronounces it to be "a benefit of the avatar." It is then that Kiyomori recalls the Chinese precedent of the white fish. Uncertain about the source of the sign's authority, he ends with this remark: "Whatever, since you have divined its meaning, the sign is half due to the Avatar. This is surely a most auspicious event." [26] Whereas the ascetic attributes the sign entirely to the authority of Kumano, Kiyomori allows the avatar only half the credit.

The next anecdote is an even stranger account, unique to the Engyōbon, of how Kiyomori came by his fierce warrior spirit:

> Again, when Kiyomori was thirty-seven years of age, around midnight on the thirteenth day of the Second Month, he had a dream in which a voice from heaven said to him, "Open your mouth, open your mouth." Wide awake and trembling with fear, he opened his mouth. Then, the voice said: "This is warrior's essence. Those who are warrior generals receive their essence from heaven." What appeared to be very cold fledgling birds were thrice placed in his mouth. Afterwards, he began to grow fierce and proud (*kokoro mo takeku ogorihajimekeri*).[27]

With this episode, Kiyomori's history takes on a distinctly apocryphal tone, echoing in a different key the motif of consumption that also appears in "The Sea Bass" episode. There, it will be recalled, Kiyomori and his companions consume the fish, even though the act violates the rule of dietary abstinence that Kiyomori is supposed to be observing.[28] Such transgressive acts were often a means of accruing power.[29] But whereas in the Kakuichi variant, the ascetic urges Kiyomori to "eat" the fish by employing the neutral verb "mairu," in the Engyōbon, he employs "yashinau," a marked verb that also brings to mind vitality enhancing practices. In the second episode, the consumption of meat (birds), or the ingesting of an "essence from heaven," takes up this same motif of transgression but locates it in a Chinese-style apocryphal tradition that subverts the logic of *Heike*'s Preface.

As has often been pointed out, the Preface or "Gion shōja" is in several respects a contradictory statement of the Buddhist principle of imperma-nence.[30] This is especially clear in the more overtly ideological Engyōbon, where the exemplum on the destruction of Chinese and Japanese rebels is followed by this statement: "Though human actions may deceive, the Way of Heaven is difficult to deceive; if this is true for rulers, then all the more should ministers and retainers exercise caution."[31] The Confucian concept of heaven was invoked in the medieval period as a transcendent principle that was above even the emperor.[32] In the Preface, this combines with the karmic logic of cause and effect to reinforce the message that emperors, war-riors, and ministers were all subordinate to and dependent on the power of Buddhist authority. Yet the excesses for which Kiyomori and other rebels are criticized in the Preface—"a proud heart and fierce deeds"—take on posi-tive connotations in the dream. Instead of the Confucian-style heaven whose logic informs the Preface, the heaven of the dream is closer to the world of the omen-lore, where one of the signs that typically invested a ruler was a divine "essence" (*jing*) originating from above that signaled possession of the heavenly mandate to rule. The Engyōbon variant of the kaburo episode falls squarely in this tradition.

The Engyōbon Kaburo and Kiyomori's Apocryphal History

In the Engyōbon, the kaburo account consists of two parts: the first resem-bling the Kakuichi variant and the second an exchange between an unnamed speaker and an individual referred to as "a certain Confucian scholar," who offers to explain the significance of Kiyomori's kaburo:

> Around that time, there was somebody who said: "I really can't understand these kaburo boys. For example, although it is said that Kiyomori employs them for the purpose of eavesdropping throughout the capital, he could make use of ordinary boys (*warawa*). Why does he always fit them out as kaburo? It's also strange that if even one goes missing, he intervenes and keeps their number at exactly three hundred. There must be some reason for this." A certain Confucian scholar said: "I have heard of such a precedent in a foreign land. During the reign of the Han Emperor, there was a minister named Wang Mang of outstanding talent and wisdom. Craving to become emperor of the country, he devised the following stratagem. He went out to the seashore and gathered together many thousands of tortoises, wrote the word 'Victory' on their shells, and released them into each bay. Next he

made copper horses and men, and placed them inside the hollow of bamboo stalks. He hid lots of these in a nearby bamboo forest. Meanwhile, he gathered together three hundred women who were seven months pregnant, boiled up some red cinnabar, mixed it with a potion called *man'yaku* and had them drink it. They gave birth at the full moon [or "at full term"], and the offspring were red in color and looked just like demons. Without informing anyone of these boys, he hid them deep in the mountains and brought them up there. As they gradually increased in size, he made a song and taught it to them: 'On the shell of a tortoise, there is written the word "Victory." In a bamboo forest, there are copper men and horses. These are signs that Wang Mang will possess the realm.'"

"When they were fourteen or fifteen years of age, he cut their hair so it fell about their shoulders and sent them into the capital, where, beating out a rhythm, all three hundred would sing the song in unison. Since it was an unusual sight, people marveled and reported it to the Emperor. He then summoned the boys into the southern courtyard. When beating out a rhythm as before, they faced the courtyard and sang the song, the Emperor marveled exceedingly. A council of the nobles was convened, and in order to determine the truth or falsehood of the song, the Emperor commanded the fishermen in all the bays to bring in the tortoises. Among them were many tortoises with the word 'Victory' written on their shells. Next, when he searched in the nearby bamboo forest, he discovered many copper horses and men there. Dumbfounded at this, the Emperor quickly resigned the throne and bestowed it upon Wang Mang. He is said to have ruled the realm for eighteen years. And so the Lay Priest as well, alluding to this, kept three hundred *kaburo* in his service. Perhaps he had his heart set on the throne as well. It was difficult to know." [33]

With differences in detail, this anecdote is also found in the other main variants of the read lineage of *Heike* texts.[34] Like the kaburo, however, whose historical origins remain an object of conjecture, there is no single known source for the anecdote; and many of its details, such as the references to writing on the tortoise shells and the copper horsemen in the bamboo, remain untraceable or in doubt. Even Yanase Kiyoshi's recent suggestion that the tortoise shell writing and copper horsemen reveal intriguing parallels with legends found in the Dunhuang collection of Daoist texts only confirms that we are dealing with a tradition of prophecy lore that lay outside the more mainstream medieval Confucian tradition.[35]

But leaving aside for now the question of sources, all the elements found in the more familiar Kakuichi kaburo—their red color, hairstyle, and connection with rumor—are present here but now firmly located in the cryptic lore of prognostication charts (*toshin*), prophetic signs (*shin'i*), and infusions of mysterious elixirs (*man'yaku*). Although the explanation is presented as the opinion of a Confucian scholar, which gives it an air of greater legitimacy, the medieval tradition of prophecy records (*miraiki*) to which the anecdote belongs transmitted mysterious knowledge portending revolutions of power that opposed orthodox Confucian teaching.[36] In orthodox history, for example, Wang Mang, who is one of the four Chinese rebels cited in the Preface, is usually presented in unambiguously negative terms, as in the following passage from *Genpei jōsuiki* regarding Kiso Yoshinaka's ambitions:

> Long ago, the retainer known as Wang Mang killed Emperor Ping of the Han, seized the throne, and held it for a period of eighteen years. Ruling selfishly over the four seas, he did not understand the griefs of the people, and as a result the populace suffered greatly. The ninth generation descendant of Gaozu, known by the name of Wenshu, destroyed Wang Mang and eventually ascended the throne. This was Emperor Guangwu of the Later Han. Although the lad Kiso did not succeed in seizing the throne, after the Heike fled the capital, his selfish behavior was no different from Wang Mang's.[37]

In the Engyōbon kaburo episode by contrast, Wang Mang is not only cast in a favorable light, but the clever manipulation of prophetic signs that makes Wang Mang the very type of the false claimant to the throne is praised as an indication of his and therefore Kiyomori's wisdom.[38]

In the Engyōbon, not only do the kaburo assume their prophetic role as conduits of rumor, but their miraculous birth invests their red color with mysterious powers. Red, for example, was the color of the fire essence associated with the Red Star Keiwakusei (also pronounced Keikokusho), or Yinghou in Chinese, who appeared in the guise of childlike figures who sang prophetic songs.[39] In the following passage from *Shōtoku Taishi denryaku* (*The Record and Legends of Prince Shōtoku*, late Heian), the link between Keiwaku's color symbolism and yin-yang five agents thought is made clear:

> Ninth year of Bidatsu (a kanoene year), summer, Sixth Month. There was a man who addressed the Emperor as follows: "Hachi no Muraji Yashima beats all others in the chanting of songs. One night, a man came and engaged him in a singing contest. The man's voice was unusual, and Yashima thought it was odd, so he followed him to find out who he was. The man

went as far as Sumiyoshi no Hama, and there he entered the sea just as dawn broke in the sky." Prince Shōtoku happened to be at the Emperor's side and said: "This is the star Keikoku." The Emperor was greatly surprised and asked, "What do you mean?" The Prince replied: "There are five stars in the sky, and they govern the five agents and produce the five colors. The star Seisei is blue and controls the East; its element is wood. Keikoku is red and controls the south; its element is fire. Keikoku descends from the sky and becomes a human being. He plays among children and is fond of composing songs. He sings of things that are yet to occur. This man was certainly a star." The Emperor was greatly pleased.[40]

The Fire Planet's baneful aspect is conveyed in this passage from *Shōtoku Taishi denki*, cited earlier:

> This star is the planet called the Fire Deity (Keijin Wakasei). Whenever the calamities of rebellion, starvation, and bad harvests are imminent in society, this planet takes on the form of a child, mingles among human kind, composes songs prophetic of future good and evil, and spreads them abroad. Heaven lacks a mouth, so it expresses these matters through human sounds.[41]

Because Keiwaku often portended disasters and the decline of imperial reigns, the kaburo's red color might be interpreted as a sign presaging Kiyomori's fall.[42] But Keiwaku, as the preceding citation indicates, composes songs prophetic of good as well as evil, leaving open the possibility of contrary interpretations. Why this is particularly so in the case of Kiyomori will be explained later, but there are several other points related to the red color symbolism that need to be touched on first.

In the Engyōbon, the kaburo's red color derives directly from the potion compounded of red cinnabar and the elixir man'yaku that is ingested by the women who give them birth. In the Nagatobon, this elixir is called "mansen'yaku" 万仙薬, leaving no doubt that it was an immortality elixir. As we saw in Chapter 3, red was the color of the most potent of the immortality elixirs, specifically the mineral-based elixirs made from cinnabar. In addition to red's association with elixirs, there is also the prophetic use of red symbolism in the omen-lore, where red in the conquest order of the five agents frequently signals a revolutionary change in the mandate.[43] I have already touched on the red color symbolism that threads through Temmu's chronicle, including the era-name Red Bird, widely held to derive from omen-lore transmitted in weft-texts. Two figures often mentioned in the omen-lore are the founder of the Zhou dynasty, Xi Bochang, otherwise known as King Wen (Jp. Bun'ō), and his son and successor King Wu (Jp. Buō), whose reigns were identified with red and repeatedly foretold by the auspicious omens of various red birds. According to one weft-text, when a red bird holding the vermilion book (*danshu*) in its beak arrived in Bochang's village and stopped before his door, Bochang bowed to the earth and accepted it. The prediction was that Bochang would destroy Yin and become emperor.[44]

In the Engyōbon, interestingly enough, Xi Bochang, or Seihakushō in Japanese, is mistakenly identified as the beneficiary of the white fish omen in its version of "Suzuki."[45] Although this may be no more than a slip on the part of the editor, it is of a piece with the apocryphal influences at work in the entire sequence, raising the possibility that the red tokens (*shiruji*) attached to each of the kaburo's birds were intended to function as a prophetic sign of some sort. One final point. The red color of the oni-like kaburo, who were born by the aid of an elixir, also hints at the magical property of red to drive out demonic or evil spirits.[46] Each of these connotations of red—its association with vitality enhancing elixirs, its auspicious symbolism in omen-lore, and its magical power to drive out demonic spirits—fits the overall logic of the kaburo anecdote and the trajectory of Kiyomori's counterhistory.

I now to turn to my principal reason for rejecting the view that Kiyomori's kaburo are intended to foreshadow his subsequent fall. The Engyōbon version, both by placement and tone—it is grouped with other auspicious episodes in a section titled "The Matter of Kiyomori's Prosperity"—is celebratory from beginning to end. There is no hint of disapproval in the Confucianist's exegesis.[47] This comes through most clearly in *Genpei jōsuiki*'s effort to account for Kiyomori's use of kaburo and birds. In seeking a precedent for this, the *Genpei jōsuiki* author likens Kiyomori's stratagem to the example of a wise Han minister named Hachiyō, whose governance was no different from that of the fabled Emperors Yao and Shun. Like Kiyomori, Hachiyō also gathers together many kaburo, provides them with birds known as Konkichō, and stations them in all the villages of each province. Unlike Kiyomori, however, Hachiyō's purpose is to make sure that the griefs of all the people throughout the land reach the emperor's ears. As a result, the country flourishes, the people are happy, and virtuous government extends throughout the empire. At the end of this exemplum, for which no known source has been found, the author makes a point of contrasting Hachiyō's

"good kaburo" with Kiyomori's "evil kaburo," disclosing his didactic purpose and judgment of Kiyomori's actions.[48] The *Genpei jōsuiki* author thus
assumes the role proper to an orthodox Confucianist, which is entirely lacking in the Engyōbon variant. Moreover, the "fictitious" exemplum, drawing
on the Confucian principle that the wise emperor should heed the voice of
the people and take appropriate counsel, completely inverts the role of the
Engyōbon's kaburo, who, in the style of apocryphal history, act as mysterious conduits of prophetic rumor. Taken as a group, then, the three miraculous tales in the narrative of Kiyomori's rise to power—the sea bass, the
ingestion of warrior essence, and the kaburo—suggest the lineaments of a
heterodox history that runs counter to the more orthodox history in which
it is embedded.

Apocryphal Histories and the Problem of Orality

How do we account for this apocryphal strand in a narrative that explicitly
warns about the consequences of rebellion? One factor is the ambiguous
nature of rumor in medieval culture. As the contrast between the kaburo
of heterodox lore and the kaburo of the more Confucian-minded *Genpei
jōsuiki* makes clear, rumor had both a dangerous as well as a beneficial side
to it. The beneficial side is reflected in orthodox historiography, where attending to rumor, or the "voice of the people," was viewed as indispensable
to the conduct of virtuous government. It is here that the biwa hōshi who
had custody of several *Heike* versions is important. As frequenters of the
markets and waysides where rumor proliferated, plying their itinerant trade
in the liminal district adjacent to the Taira's Rokuhara compound, the biwa
hōshi were from the start potential mediators of such speech, which is no
doubt one reason they became custodians of Kiyomori's history.[49] How was
this brought about? It is here that Shinzei's project for reviving an orthodox
form of Confucian-style history and its possible bearing on *Heike*'s formation raises some intriguing questions.

In the twelfth century, Fujiwara no Michinori (d. 1159), more commonly
known by his Buddhist name Shinzei, undertook in concert with Toba and
Go-Shirakawa a major program of reforms that was aimed at strengthen-
ing the authority of the court.[50] In addition to initiating palace repairs and
reordering the rites and music (*reigaku*), Shinzei took measures to revive the
practice of compiling official court histories, the fruit of which was *Honchō*

seiki, today regarded as a private history. He also evinced a strong interest in the musical and performing arts (*geinō*), including court music as well as the new style songs (*imayō*) performed by shirabyōshi dancers. Most important, Shinzei's interests and wide learning, aimed at articulating a new ideology of royal authority, were transmitted to his sons. His seventh son, Chōken (1126–1203), and Chōken's own son Shōkaku (1167–1235) were both major figures in Tendai religious spheres and founders of the Agui school of Buddhist preaching, which *Heike* scholars have long recognized as having played a major role in the formation and transmission of early *Heike* texts, notably the Engyōbon.[51] This nexus of historiographical and musical activity converges in the *Heike* tradition mediated by the biwa reciters.

In several essays that reexamine the link between blind reciters and historical narrative, the *Heike* scholar Shimizu Masumi has uncovered some intriguing facts about Shinzei's procedures.[52] The most important document in compiling an official history was the *geki nikki*, or Secretary's Diary (also known as the *shikanki*), which provided guidance to the emperor in the conduct of governance. Although the geki was no longer in existence by the twelfth century, the Nakahara family, who had historical ties to the office, were in possession of private family records, including kanbun journals, that Shinzei apparently deemed crucial to his project for reviving official history. In addition to their historical ties to the geki, the Nakahara family was also in charge of prognostication (*tenmon*) and the office responsible for overseeing activities in the market. In his *Honchō seiki*, Shinzei records not only the names of several Nakahara family members but notes their appointment to the office in charge of the Eastern Market. Located in the same region east of the river occupied by the Rokuhara compound, the Eastern Market was frequented throughout the medieval period by biwa hōshi.[53] The Nakahara's connection to the market would have kept them in close touch with popular rumor, or "the voice of the people," which was essential to their responsibility as compilers of records aimed at providing guidance to the ruler.[54]

Based on this evidence, Shimizu proposes that *Heike* may have represented one such effort to reestablish a tradition of Confucian-style historiography, mediated at an early stage by those closely affiliated to the Heike family and also by Shinzei's descendants, founders of the Agui sect that specialized in vocal and musical arts for the purpose of disseminating doctrine.[55] By acting as a mediator of the people's voice (*tami no koe*), the biwa hōshi would have helped to instruct the ruler on the wisdom or folly of his governance. To cite from several Chinese texts that may have provided the ideological basis for such an undertaking: "The blind present the music and the chronicler presents the history . . . and afterwards the ruler takes counsel." Or this quote from the old-text *Xiaojing*: "The ruler makes use of music, reflects on the customs of all peoples, and thereby understands flourishing and decline; through instrumental and vocal music one grasps these matters." With its reference to "flourishing and decline," the latter of these two passages sounds the very note of *Heike*'s famous Gion shōja Preface.[56]

Although it can be debated whether or not this project, as envisioned by Shimizu, was ever fully realized in the medieval *Heike*, the theory provides a useful interpretive framework for the Confucian strain in *Heike* texts and for the strong interest in knowledge pertaining to tenmon and yin-yang, especially in the Engyōbon, Nagatobon, and *Genpei jōsuiki*. At the same time, as a response to another school of *Heike* scholarship that has stressed the link between the biwa hōshi and placation in the formation of *Heike*, the theory casts fresh light on the problem of orality in *Heike*, especially as it bears on the role of the reciters who had charge of its performance.[57] The problem in the present case is that while this Confucian model suits the tenor of *Genpei jōsuiki*'s kaburo narrative, and possibly the Kakuichi version if one accepts the traditional didactic reading, it doesn't account for the apocryphal Engyōbon variant, unless one reads it as a criticism of Kiyomori along the lines of the traitorous Wang Mang.[58] In reassessing the text–orality issue in *Heike* formation, it proposes a performance model that accounts for orality while still according priority to the written text. A similar tendency is found in the work of Kuroda Akira, who views portions of *Heike*, including the kaburo episode, as the product of a complex interaction between the *Heike* manuscript tradition and medieval commentaries on works such as the *Shi ji*, *Wakan rōei shū*, and other Chinese works. The unstable identity of rebel figures like Wang Mang and others, according to Kuroda, is generated by the polysemy of the commentarial tradition rather than dictated by stable textual sources.[59] Motifs like the red color symbolism that runs through the kaburo tale are textual phenomena that owe nothing to reality. The following passage from a rōei commentary, for example, is cited to account for the red attire and other features in the kaburo tale:

> According to a story, when Guangwu di was a child, there was a warrior in the world named Wang Mang. Wishing to seize the throne, he revolved many different stratagems. He gathered together a thousand women who were pregnant and made them drink a red potion. The children were all

born red. This is the reason why a newly-born is called *akaji* [infant, but literally red child]. When these one thousand infants matured, at seven or eight years of age, he made red attire, clothed them in it, and taught them a song.[60]

The details are different from the Engyōbon variant, but the resemblance is close enough to permit the conjecture that the *Heike* variants and the tradition of rōei commentary may have been based on a common source.[61] But was the source necessarily textual? Or can it be assumed that the commentarial tradition was in full possession of the medieval oral tradition?[62] By prefacing the commentary with the phrase "according to a story" (monogatari ni iwaku), for example, the author of the commentary leaves open the possibility that some of this material originated outside the written transmission in a world of oral anecdote. A textual approach to *Heike*, in brief, is valuable to the extent that it shows how the world of Chinese learning continued to branch out into areas well beyond the immediate sphere of the court, reaching ever broader swaths of medieval society. But a focus on textuality and written transmission, even one as malleable as the commentarial tradition that continuously reworked its imaginative world, can easily lose sight of the role played by an oral culture that continued to mediate, interact with, and even appropriate the written tradition. Nor will it adequately account for the traces of material culture or indications of performativity in texts. It is entirely possible, for example, that the Engyōbon editors obtained a version of the kaburo tale from an unknown written or oral source, say, a story that once circulated in the environs of Kiyomori's Rokuhara compound, and inserted it into the text without ever fully realizing their intention of reworking it, as they did other tales, for the purpose of inculcating admonitory lessons. With this hypothesis in mind, I want to return once more to the kaburo tale, this time reframing its apocryphal elements as a nomadic tale, taking account of its orality and performativity.

Kiyomori's War Machine

Perhaps the biggest obstacle to gaining a view of the historical Kiyomori is that so much of his story has been presented to us through the ethos of the center. As the crude warrior, possibly deformed in appearance (his father Tadamori was said to have been "squint-eyed"), clever but also violent and cruel, a usurper who was punished for his sins, and the head of a defiled lineage that was rumored to be the product of an incestuous union, Kiyomori bears all the negative signs that form one pole of the duality that constitutes the state. On the other hand, these same traits hint at another Kiyomori, the same figure glimpsed in the apocryphal tales. As the prototypical warrior, Kiyomori *also* represents an incursion of the nomadic into the sedentary space of the old center, both through his alliance with anomic groups and through his connection to warring and trade.[63] It is here that the actuality of rumor in the kaburo tale and its relationship to space come to the fore.

Prophetic rumor in the Engyōbon kaburo is not only about narrative, opposing an apocryphal to a more orthodox Confucian history, but also about a clash over space. Although the center invariably tries to oppose or capture the nomadic, there is a continuous translation of the organized, or striated, space of the center into the smooth space of the nomos—the acentric marine space, for example, glimpsed in the evocation of Kiyomori's Ōwada Harbor discussed in Chapter 6—and vice versa.[64] Nomadic stories are about groups without strong affiliations to the center, but once they are captured and in the hands of the center (understood here as the Confucian- or Buddhist-minded historian), these same stories are converted into a binary style—made didactic, moral, doctrinal—and thereafter support the interests of the center. The animal and bird theme, for example, that runs through the apocryphal sequence—the consumption of the sea bass, the ingestion of "warrior essence" or birds, and the kaburo ties to birds and tengu—has a twofold character. On the one hand, it hints at a nomadic assemblage in its character as a pack, or bordering phenomenon, possibly connected to populations of itinerants in Kiyomori's service, or itinerants whose stories were drawn into the orbit of his history. Hence, the traces of a metallurgical theme in the Engyōbon variant of the kaburo episode, specifically the references to copper bamboo and the mixing of red cinnabar to produce the elixir, form a motif that also comes out in the Nagatobon, where the verb for smelting is actually used.[65] Such details, no longer fully recoverable, hint at Kiyomori's and the Taira's ties to itinerant craft groups.[66] On the other hand, the same animal theme also participates in the binary logic of the center—namely, the transgression against taboos that accrues power as well as the taboos associated with certain activities connected to animals and defilement.

These two tendencies are difficult to disentangle in the kaburo tale. In *Genpei jōsuiki*'s account of the kaburo who walk about holding birds with red tokens attached to their feathers, one can discern evidence of Kiyomori's strategic deployment of the signs of the anomic or heteromorphic to inspire fear in the capital populace. This comes through vividly in the Nagatobon variant, where the kaburo are described as "hastening toward their [prey] and destroying them demon-like in a flash." [67] It is possible, in other words, that Kiyomori exploited the taboolike fears associated with defilement and the demonic, very much in the style of the akutō and akusō, another anomic grouping, discussed in Chapter 7. As a tactician of the nomadic, however, Kiyomori made another use of the kaburo. Kiyomori's gang of kaburo constituted, I suggest, a capture of the rumor machine; a war tactic that deployed the kaburo to hold and occupy the space of the capital, disrupting but also transforming its striated space into the smooth space of the nomos. (Later, he would boldly "transfer" the capital to Fukuhara.) Even details of the operation and mode of employ for Kiyomori's rumor machine can be gleaned from the variants. The kaburo, for example, "filled the capital and roamed about" in the Kakuichi *Heike* or "were made to wander about" in *Genpei jōsuiki*, both of which convey their manner of holding space. *Genpei jōsuiki*, moreover, specifies how the kaburo were stationed along the gridwork of the capital's striated space (*jōri*)—namely, its streets, alleyways, gates, and doorways—and indicates with topographical precision the extent of the space held. [68] Even what the speaker in the Engyōbon refers to as Kiyomori's strange tactic of employing 300 kaburo and always keeping their ranks filled can be understood as an aspect of his war machine. As Deleuze shows, "number" was crucial to how the nomadic occupied space, arising out of its characteristic as a pack phenomenon or multiplicity. [69] But the most *telling* trait of Kiyomori's rumor machine is the red tokens attached to the birds of the kaburo, which seem to have been intended as prophetic signs of Kiyomori's rise to power. In this way, Kiyomori's rumor machine, deployed to hold the space of the capital, also appears to have manipulated rumor, with something like the prediction of Kiyomori's ascent to power strategically circulated at large in the capital and enhanced in its effectiveness by the weird appearance of the birdlike kaburo. Kiyomori's rumor machine was aimed not only at checking the spread of rumor that was potentially dangerous to himself but at actively propagating it as well.

To conclude, the apocryphal tradition that emerged in medieval Japan, perhaps best exemplified in works like the late Heian *Shōtoku Taishi denryaku* and fourteenth-century *Taiheiki* but also coloring many *Heike* variants, flourished at a historical moment *when the very notion of what constituted a center, let alone an orthodox or official history,* was in doubt. This not only accounts for its nomadic character but also for the tone of duplicity and sham that flows through much of the apocryphal textual tradition. If one strand of *Heike* narrative represents an effort to establish an orthodox Confucian-style historiography, it was entangled from the very outset in this apocryphal lore, giving rise to a counterhistory that straddled the divide between the world of oral culture and the manuscript tradition controlled by various elites. In addition to the kaburo episode just examined, this heterodox tradition colors the world of the Gion Consort legend.

The Gion Lady

"The Gion Consort" ("Gion nyōgo") is the third of three episodes relating marvelous tales of Kiyomori following his death in scroll six. According to the version in the Kakuichi *Heike*, the Retired Emperor Shirakawa was in the habit of visiting an imperial favorite "who lived in the Gion district at the foot of the Eastern Mountains." On one occasion, in the eerie darkness of a rainy Fifth Month night, Shirakawa, a few courtiers, and his retinue of guards were surprised by a "shining figure, which seemed to have a head covered with glittering, polished silver needles, and to be grasping a kind of mallet and a source of light in its raised left and right hands." With his attendants in a panic, Shirakawa summoned Tadamori, then still a low-ranking member of the North Guards. "I think you are the best man for this job. Either shoot the creature dead or kill it with your sword."[70] The quick-witted Tadamori, suspecting it to be a fox or a tanuki, decided to take it alive. After grappling the creature down, however, it turned out to be not a "transformed being" (*henge no mono*) but a "chapel serving-priest" (*midō no jōji bōshi*).[71] "To avoid being soaked in the downpour, he had fashioned himself a hat by tying up a bundle of wheat straws, which glittered like silver needles in the light from the flame." Impressed by Tadamori's prudence, Shirakawa rewarded him with his beloved consort, the Gion Lady, who was already pregnant with his child. Kiyomori thus turns out to be of illustrious lineage, and after invoking a precedent from the days of Emperor Tenchi, the narrator rounds off the story with this reflection: "With such a precedent from antiquity, it seems likely enough that Kiyomori was in truth Retired Emperor Shirakawa's son. It is not surprising that he should have determined on the formidable undertaking of transferring the capital."[72]

Like many oral-derived stories, the account of Kiyomori's birth reveals a good deal of typification in its structure and motifs. It has elements of both the demon-subjugating motif (*oni taiji*), in which a warrior is rewarded for subduing a dangerous prodigy, and the rich man story motif, in which there is a sudden change in fortune from poverty and low social status to a position of wealth and power.[73] But it is the slight variations on such standard motifs, details of topography and rank, that often provide the most telling clues to their meaning. This is the case for the many variants of the Gion Lady.[74] In both the Engyōbon and Nagatobon, for example, Tadamori's encounter with what at first appears to be a supernatural being takes place, not in the Gion district as in the Kakuichi *Heike*, but on the grounds of the palace. In both these variants, moreover, it is not the Gion Lady but a lady-in-waiting (*nyōbō*) that serves the Gion Lady at the palace (*chūgū*) who becomes the object of Shirakawa's affections and subsequently gives birth to Kiyomori.[75] In *Genpei jōsuiki*, on the other hand, several different accounts of Kiyomori's parentage are given. One (discussed later) makes him the offspring of the Gion Lady who lives in the Gion district; and the other implies that he is the offspring of the lady-in-waiting who serves the Gion Lady at the palace.[76] It is the Kakuichi *Heike* alone that gives a single version of the tale, making her both a resident of the Gion district and the mother of Shirakawa's child Kiyomori.

Who was the Gion Lady? The read lineage of *Heike* texts that portray her as a consort or lady-in-waiting who resided in the palace suggests that she may have been someone of aristocratic origins. That the Gion Lady may have existed is suggested by *Imakagami* (*The Mirror of Today*) and other historical documents, which speak of an imperial consort, sometimes identified by the name of Gion Nyōgo, who sponsored a mass at Kiyomori's grandfather Taira no Masamori's Rokuhara Mitsudō chapel in 1113 and who appears to have been instrumental in Masamori's rise in the world.[77] I will return to this point, but first I want to look at the more circumstantial account of the Gion Lady's encounter with Shirakawa in one of *Genpei jōsuiki*'s versions of the tale:

> Older people used to say that Kiyomori was not the child of Tadamori
> but of Retired Emperor Shirakawa. The reason is as follows. The Emperor
> used to worship at Kanjin-in and made frequent trips there. One day, in the
> road at the West Gate of Gion, there was a strange woman from a small
> house drawing water. Gathering up the hem of her hempen robe, she set the
> water jug down at the well-curb and looked up at the Emperor's progress.
> Charmed by her look, upon his return the Emperor summoned her to the
> Palace, where he kept her continuously by his side.[78]

Here, the precise descriptive details, as in the adjective *ayashiki* ("strange," "odd"), the "small house," and the coarse material of the woman's "hempen robe," build up a concrete picture of the Gion Lady's extremely low social status. The area adjoining the West Gate of Gion was in a fact a typical medieval "gate village," whose dwellings (*zaike*) were inhabited by low-status entertainers and people who served the needs of pilgrims to the shrines and temples in the vicinity.[79] The expression "chapel serving-priest" (*midō jōji bōshi*) used in the Kakuichi variant was a typical designation for someone of outcast status, whose duties would have included cleaning the shrine grounds and tending to the altar implements.

Famed for its "eerie charm," the Gion district was part of the proscribed area east of the Kamo River and technically outside the capital.[80] At the easternmost edge of this district stood the Kiyomizu Temple and the nearby Toribeno burial grounds. In 1112, just one year prior to the Gion Nyōgo mass mentioned earlier, Taira no Masamori is recorded to have made a request for proprietary rights over land held by the Rokudō Chin'ōji Temple in Toribeno cemetery. Documents suggest that Masamori's motive was not to acquire and open up agricultural land but rather to obtain space for the construction of the humble *zaike*-style dwellings used by people engaged in repairs, cleaning, and other activities associated with the temple's management of burials.[81] Because of the connection to defilement, these activities were primarily the responsibility of outcasts or hinin.

The story of the Gion Lady, then, is more than a fable about Kiyomori's royal parentage, and it hints at the origins of his family's heterodox authority in the proscribed sphere of defiling activity. The following anecdote from *Kojidan* (*Talks on Ancient Matters*, 1212–1215) about a hawk breeder in the employ of Kiyomori's son Tadanori will make this even clearer:

> The matter of Katō Nariie who violated the Retired Emperor Shirakawa's prohibition that forbade the taking of life.
>
> When the Retired Emperor Shirakawa issued a decree against taking life, he heard that Katō Taiyu Nariie, notwithstanding the strict prohibition, was still hawking. When an order was issued to the Imperial Police Bureau to summon Nariie, he promptly came up to the capital and went straight to the Palace, setting his hawk at his elbow-guard outside the Palace gate. Two underlings did the same. The Retired Sovereign spoke through his messenger: "It is now several years since I issued the order against killing living things. What do you think you are doing still hawking? Your actions are an offense to the Court! Be quick and explain yourself." Nariie replied: "It is

true. I presently have two or three hawks at my house. However, because I don't have any underlings, I wasn't able to bring them. I am a hereditary retainer of the Lord Punishments Minister [Tadamori], and every day the Gion Consort orders lots of fresh game for her repast; if I am remiss, I will be severely punished. As is the custom with the Genji and Heishi, punishment means having one's head cut off. In the profession of hunting, on some days game is hunted and on others it is not. I hunt because otherwise I would certainly lose my head, and I cherish my worthless life. On the other hand, if I incurred imperial censure, I might be put in prison or sent into exile but I wouldn't lose my life, so I eagerly hastened over here." When this was reported to the Palace, the Retired Emperor issued this order: "Banish the rascal!"[82]

The Buddhist injunction against killing had been given almost juridical weight through Shirakawa's promulgation of the law against killing bird, fish, or beast (*seshō kindan*) inside specified geographical boundaries. On one level, then, the sardonic tone hints at the psychological complicity that developed between warrior retainers and retired sovereigns as a direct consequence of the prohibition, which has been commented on by Gomi Fumihiko.[83] But as Higuchi Kunio has remarked, the viewpoint of the episode also betrays its origins among those who were opposed to such promulgations. The Taira retainer, for example, gets off with what amounts to a scolding, while the lady of the Gion district, now ensconced as consort in Shirakawa's palace, indulges a relish for meat-eating that makes light of her connection to prohibited activities.[84] The *Kojidan*'s date of composition, early thirteenth century, indicates that tales of the Gion Lady were already circulating broadly throughout society during the earliest stage of *Heike*'s formation. Some of these, including several found in the Engyōbon and Nagatobon, probably circulated in court circles. But the Kakuichi and *Genpei jōsuiki* variants that make Kiyomori the offspring of an emperor and a mother of probable outcast status most likely originated among those who lived and worked in and about the Taira's Rokuhara compound. Kiyomori's apocryphal history was also the story of the outcasts who once lived under his patronage and authority.

Heterodox Speech and Secret Traditions

Heike episodes about the Gion Lady, like the kaburo tales examined earlier, largely belong to the world of unofficial discourse, or *katari*. These oral-derived genres that flourished in the medieval period, which included forms of social chatter and gossip that modern scholarship designates as *setsuwa*, often project a world that inverts the social, political, and religious norms associated with works composed in Chinese-style histories, kanbun journals, and other forms of discourse that had a quasi-official sanction. In Chapter 5, I suggested that rumor and gossip gave rise to new forms of vernacular history as it invaded the sphere of historical narrative in works like *Ōkagami*. In *Heike*, these began to combine in unprecedented ways with official document style and other formal rhetorical modes, ultimately disrupting, inverting, and relativizing the hierarchy of styles that had prevailed up to about the eleventh century. This shift in discursive codes was mirrored as well in medieval space, which reinvested border regions and liminal sites with new levels of numinous power in political and religious spheres. I now turn to a version of the Gion Lady legend from the secret Tendai transmission *Keiranjūyōshū* that highlights this intersection between the heterotopic spheres of medieval social and religious space and unorthodox forms of oral discourse.

What happens when narrative of an oral type, characterized by forms of social chatter and gossip, is incorporated into the "margins" of orthodox Buddhist discourse? In the sphere of Buddhist discourse, such narrative code shifting operates under a number of constraints. Drawing on the authority of the *Lotus Sutra*, for example, the use of profane or poetic speech has a doctrinal justification as *hōben* ("expedient means"), for which the locus classicus in Japanese literature is the *monogatari-ron* in *The Tale of Genji*'s "Hotaru Chapter."[85] From about the mid-Heian period, another defense of profane words, mediated through Bo Juyi's well-known phrase *kyōgen kigo* ("mad words and fancy language"), is increasingly invoked as a justification for combining profane and sacred language. One of the codicils to the Engyōbon, for example, characterizes its narrative as a deliberate use of "the errors of wild words and fancy language."[86] There is an important distinction, however, between *hōben* and this new defense of profane language in that the latter exceeds the former's normative didactic usage, acquiring a radical and absolute sense, validated ontologically, as already enlightened speech.[87]

The assimilation of profane speech (as opposed to poetic language) into the secret oral traditions of Tendai learning (*Tendai kuden hōmon*) from the Kamakura period on marks one of the most radical changes in the organization of discursive styles within medieval Buddhist spheres.[88] Composed in the early fourteenth century, the *Keiranjūyōshū* transmitted in written form a secret transmission of oral provenance, encompassing Tendai, Shingon, and other doctrine, which began to take shape around the period of rule by retired sovereigns (late eleventh to twelfth centuries). In its oral phase, transmission occurred face to face from master to disciple. As new interpretations were added by subsequent masters, the tradition took on a multi-layered quality, with framing devices such as "shi iwaku" (the master says), "tsutaiiwaku" (it is handed down), and the like indicating hierarchical levels of authority within the transmission. At some point in the course of the thirteenth century, the oral transmission assumed a written form, eventually culminating in *Keiranjūyōshū*.[89] The following anecdote about Bishop Ikkai both exemplifies the procedure and illuminates another level of meaning in the Gion Lady's story:

> He inquired about the matter of Bishop Ikkai's secret offering. "What was the manner of Bishop Ikkai's secret offering?" He explained: "Regarding this Bishop's secret offering, it is as follows. Taking a dumpling, he sprinkled soybean flour on it, and made an offering of it while it was still warm. It was plainly a secret offering. This is what became known as Bishop Ikkai's Fat Child. The following story is told about him. 'This Bishop was Ninkai of Ono. On Mount Inari, he performed this rite for a period of a thousand days. The place is now called Bishop's Peak. Everyday throughout that period, the daughter of a priest who served at Gion sent him his daily ration of food. As a reward for this service, the woman became empress. She is the one who is known today as the Gion Consort. Ninkai became the personal priest of this consort, and as a result he immediately rose to the position of Bishop. This is why he is known as Bishop Ikkai.'"[90]

The ritual described here was an esoteric Buddhist practice that belonged to Dakiniten worship. Regarded as heterodox in most contexts, the worship of Dakiniten was thought to be efficacious in obtaining the worldly benefits of wealth and power. Drawing on recent debates related to categories of oral and oral-derived narrative (*monogatari, katari, setsuwa*), Tanaka Takako has characterized the use of *monogatari* in the secret transmission of Tendai learning as a form of heterodox discourse that proliferates at the margins of the orthodox transmission, arising in part out of a rivalry between oral and written forms of transmission.[91] The use of specific words for framing and setting off stretches of narrative within *Keiranjūyōshū* discloses a discursive strategy, according to Tanaka, that sets up a clear hierarchy of styles. The Ikkai anecdote, for example, begins as an exchange between master and disciple, with the disciple's question (*tazunete iwaku*) followed by the master's explanation that is introduced by the phrase "shimeshite iwaku" ("he explained"). The anecdote about Ninkai and the Gion Lady, on the other hand, is introduced by the phrase "the following story is told" ("chinami ni monogatari iwaku" 因物語云), setting it off from the main body of the oral transmission, or *kuden*.[92] In other sections of *Keiranjūyōshū*, an anecdote in the monogatari style may be further marked off from a following anecdote by being prefaced by the phrase "hōdan no tsugi ni" ("according to the following [Buddhist] talk"). The "hōdan" category of anecdote was acceptable material in orthodox Buddhist preaching styles (*seppō*) during the medieval period. The boxlike structure, in which an anecdote introduced by the phrase "chinami ni monogatari iwaku" is followed by another prefaced by "hōdan tsugi ni," establishes a subtle hierarchy of styles, with the former taking on some of the disruptive force of the profane *zōdan* ("miscellaneous talk") category of medieval discourse.[93] The strategy of distinguishing "monogatari," therefore, from the category of "hōdan" (sometimes introduced by its verb form *dan*) is an indication of the former's heterodox character. In another passage from *Keiranjūyōshū*, this time from an older manuscript version of the work, the priest who is speaking slips in an anecdote (*shi monogatari iwaku*) with the ostensible purpose of illustrating the esoteric doctrine of *santai en'yū*.[94] A certain priest, the story goes, skilled at drawing cartoons cleverly depicted a heteromorphic Fudō in a variety of scenes, including Fudō sleeping with a boy, exciting carnal passions after having assumed the form of a woman, and having diarrhea in the privy.[95] In brief, monogatari irrupt into the orthodox discourse of the secret transmission as forms of rumor, gossip, and parodic talk, establishing a circuitry of exchange between the orthodox world of the *kuden* and the profane world of the anecdotes (*monogatari*). But in contrast to the didactic *hōben*, let alone *kyōgen kigo*, to be efficacious, heterodox language had to maintain its otherness. Belying the complicity and interdependence of the two narrative types, the hierarchy is maintained at all times and is further emphasized in the contrast between the formal Chinese style of the orthodox transmission and the mixed Japanese kana style of the profane monogatari.

Heterodox speech therefore presents this paradox: To successfully profane sacred speech, it must remain radically other even as its anecdotal content suggests a conversion or inversion of profane into sacred. In this fashion, the procedures of the Tendai secret transmission provide a parallel to the Kakuichi *Heike*'s own narrative world, where the Heike's history unfolds as a continuous inversion of court history into its heterodox other, with the Taira transformed from the threatening outsider (Tadamori) of "The Night Attack" into a figure who rapidly takes on the attributes of a sage ruler (Kiyomori), later to be succeeded by the parodic anti-tennō, Kiso Yoshinaka. As in the case of *Keiranjūyōshū*'s Ikkai episode, such inversions belong to the Kakuichi *Heike*'s narrative world, but outside the specific discursive practices of Tendai secret transmission and *Heike* narrative, anecdotes like those about the Gion Lady in *Heike* and Bishop Ikkai in *Keiranjūyōshū* participate in a broader discourse about the heterodox source of medieval royal authority, which brings us back to the role of the Gion Lady in these episodes.

In the *Keiranjūyōshū* text, the liminal status of the Gion Lady combines with the heretical practice of the dakini rite to produce a powerful representation of profane to sacred conversion. Apart from a few limited usages, such as certain forms of the enthronement ritual, the dakini rite was prohibited as a dangerous and heterodox practice. In the first scroll of the Kakuichi *Heike*, for example, Tokudaiji Sanesada performs the rite to gain a desired promotion, which provokes a divine punishment in the form of a lightning strike.[96] In the case of Ninkai, however, who is singled out in a *Kojidan* anecdote for his meat-eating propensities,[97] its performance gains him an extraordinary promotion to the rank of bishop. The *Keiranjūyōshū* anecdote also allows for several different interpretations, one of which makes it possible to attribute Ninkai's success to the mediation of the Gion Lady herself, who as the daughter of the outcast priest (*shōji bōshi*)—the same figure who appears in the *Heike* anecdote—may have belonged to the class of miko who dwelled beneath the floorboards of certain shrines.[98] In the Kakuichi *Heike*, the Gion Lady's tale can be read on one level as the projection of the inhabitants in the districts adjacent to the Taira family's Rokuhara compound, but set beside the Ninkai episode from *Keiranjūyōshū*, it also becomes an episode in the history of a heterodox royal lineage—Shirakawa/Gion Lady/Kiyomori—that accrues its power from profane origins in proscribed spheres.

Kiyomori's Buddha Relics

Another thread in the complex skein of the Gion Lady's legend bears directly on the heterodox character of Kiyomori's royal authority. Apart from the episodic lore that was absorbed into the *Heike* manuscript tradition, one of the few pieces of documentary evidence regarding Kiyomori's blood tie to Shirakawa-in is a text known as *Busshari sōshō shidai* (*The Record of the Transmission of the Buddha Relic*, ca. 1235), which records that Kiyomori was the offspring of Shirakawa-in and a younger sister of the Gion Nyōgo. Since its discovery in the early part of the last century, *Busshari sōshō shidai* has been at the center of debates among historians and *Heike* scholars regarding the historicity of Kiyomori's royal parentage.[99] However, as recent scholarship on the function of relics in medieval Japan has shown, the historical factuality of such documents is of less importance than their symbolic function in a ritual economy of power.[100] *Busshari sōshō shidai* also participated in a mythological and ritual discourse centered on numinously charged talismans. By virtue of their liminality, Buddha relics, musical instruments (including the biwa), and other precious objects operated as powerful symbols of a heterodox royal authority in the period of rule by retired sovereigns.[101]

In an analysis of medieval documents that record transmissions of such talismans, Tanaka has reconstructed several lines of transmission, including one that shows the Buddha relics passing from the Retired Sovereign Shirakawa, to the Gion Lady, to the Retired Sovereign Toba, to Bifukumon'in, to Hachijōin, and so on.[102] Another document, the *Gebusshari bunpu hachiryū* transmitted in a text from Raikōji Temple, records a transmission of the relics from Taira no Kiyomori to the deity Kannon. The Buddha relics of Raikōji Temple were believed to be in the possession of the Dragon King, who resided in the Dragon Palace located in a recess of the nearby Nunobiki Falls, in the province of Settsu.[103] Extrapolating between these variants of the transmission, Tanaka has suggested that *Busshari sōshō shidai* records a stage in the transmission when the relics passed from the Gion Lady to Kiyomori, thereby pointing to a lineage of royal authority passing through Shirakawa to the Gion Lady and Kiyomori. In a further twist to this transmission, Buddhist mythographers grafted the Buddha relic legend onto ancient chronicle legends of the divine sea king, substituting the Buddha relic for the magical power-conferring water jewel of the sea-king's daughters. In this myth, the roles of the sea king, his two daughters, and the suitor are distributed among Shirakawa, the Gion Lady and her younger sister, and Kiyomori's father, Tadamori, resulting in a new myth of royal authority, whose origins lie in the radical otherness of the Gion Lady and the Buddha relics stored in the Dragon Palace.[104]

Although the Kakuichi *Heike* does not touch directly on this aspect of the Gion Lady legend, hinting instead at her outcast origins, another episode found in *Heiji monogatari* (*The Tale of Heiji*) records how Kiyomori came into possession of the talismanic Buddha relic.[105] According to *Heiji monogatari*, which records the Heike's defeat of Minamoto no Yoshitomo during the Heiji Rebellion, the Minamoto warrior Akugenda Yoshihira, who was beheaded by the Taira retainer Nanba no Saburō Tsunefusa, later returned in the form of a lightning bolt and struck Tsunefusa dead in an act revenge. In one version of the episode transmitted in the older lineage of *Heiji monogatari* texts, Tsunefusa is struck after returning from a visit to Nunobiki Falls, identified, as we saw earlier, with the Dragon King in possession of the Buddha relics transmitted to Kiyomori. In another version of the same episode, recorded in the Kotohirabon,[106] Tsunefusa is struck by the bolt in Tsu province after having made a pilgrimage to Minoo Falls, where he has the following experience:

> Meanwhile, after Nanba no Saburō Tsunefusa beheaded Akugenda, he felt continuously beset by evil spirits. When Tsunefusa asked, "How can I rid myself of these evil spirits?" somebody said: "They say that if a person goes to Minoo Falls in the province of Tsu and lets himself be struck by the waterfall, that the possessing spirits will vanish." Tsunefusa promptly made a visit to Minoo, and when he saw the waterfall, he said, "I wonder how deep it is?" The temple priests replied, "It is said to be one ri deep." He then experienced his usual attack of evil spirits and plunged into the basin of the falls. Not knowing where he was going, he made his way deep into the hollow, and came to a place where there was no water. The spot was like a beautifully ornamented Palace. As he stood before the entrance gate, from inside a voice said, "Who is it?" "I am the Heike retainer, Nanba no Saburō Tsunefusa." "So, you're a Nanba are you? Go back at once. When you learn how matters stand in the world of humans, then pay a visit." "Where am I? What shall I say when I get back?" "This is the Dragon Palace. As a sign that you have visited here, take this." He was then given a fragment of the Buddha relic from the crystal tower. He took it and placed it in the fold of his robe; then, thinking that he was exiting the gate, he found that he had floated back up to the basin of the waterfall. When he recounted what had happened to the priests, they felt their hair stand on end. Meanwhile, he went up to the capital and informed Kiyomori, who experienced a weird sensation and had the Buddha relic placed in the Kōkokuji Temple at the outskirts of Nishiyama. It was very strange indeed.[107]

In a detailed discussion of this episode, Kusaka Tsutomu has shown how the region of Tsu province where Minoo Falls was located constituted a virtual labyrinth of grottoes, caves, and waterfalls identified with various manifestations of the Dragon King. Together with Chikubushima, Enoshima, and Itsukushima, it was one of four medieval centers of dragon worship centered on the Buddhist deity Benzaiten. The well-established ritual ties between biwa reciters and serpent/dragon cults suggest that this particular version of the episode was possibly shaped by the biwa reciters.[108] Set within the broader context of medieval relic worship and transmission, it also provides another refraction of the heterodox royal lineage represented by Shirakawa/Gion Lady/Kiyomori, with Kōkokuji Temple at the western edge of the capital here assuming a function analogous to Shirakawa's Rengeōin treasure house. The latter, located *inside* Kiyomori's Rokuhara compound, was another of the many heterotopic sites that anchored medieval royal authority.[109]

A Sinner in Hell: The Death of Kiyomori

One of the climaxes in *Heike* is the description of Kiyomori's final illness and death in the sixth scroll. Contemporary accounts in *Gyokuyō*, *Meigetsuki*, and other records all mention the onset of a wasting fever. According to the most detailed of these accounts, Kiyomori's illness began as a head cold, and developed two days later into an extreme fever, which, in the medical language of the day, "caused his five viscera to turn black." Although attempts were made to cool Kiyomori's feverish body by means of cold presses and immersions in water, "smoke rose up from his vitals as the snow and water evaporated."[110] By the late thirteenth century, when *Heike* was being recited in the streets of the capital, Kiyomori's death agony had become the stuff of religious moralizing, a terrifying vision of an evildoer fallen into the consuming fires of the Avici Hell. The following passage is from the Kakuichi variant:

> From the day the illness took hold, the Lay Priest Chancellor could put nothing in his mouth, not even water. The fever in his body burnt like a fire . . . Thinking to bring him some relief, they directed water from a bamboo pipe, but it fizzled away without reaching him as though the pipes were fiery stones or iron. Whatever water did reach him burst into flames, so that black smoke filled the hall right up to the ceiling and flames swirled upwards. So must it have been long ago when Bishop Hōzō, wishing to find

out about his mother's rebirth, accepted the invitation of the compassionate Lord Emma, who had him escorted by the infernal guards to the Tapana Hot Hell. When he passed through the iron gate, and saw the flames rising up into the sky like shooting stars to what must have been a distance of hundreds and thousands of *yoyanas*, Hōzō finally understood. The principal wife of the Lay Priest Chancellor, the Nun of the Second Rank, had a terrifying dream. A carriage that was burning furiously was brought inside the gates. Standing in front and back were what looked like horse-faced and ox-faced creatures. At the front of the carriage an iron plaque had been affixed on which appeared the sole letter Mu. When the Nun of the Second Rank asked herself where the carriage had come from, someone said, "We have come from the tribunal of Emma to fetch Lord Kiyomori, the Heike Chancellor and Lay Priest." [111]

The letter "mu," as the speaker goes on to explain, signifies Hell Without Intermission (*muken jigoku*), otherwise known as Abi Jigoku or Avici Hell. Nethermost of the Eight Great Hells, the Avici Hell contained a lake of molten iron, a burning mountain, and was infested with demonic birds and evil serpents. It was also the destined place of punishment for those who had committed blasphemous acts against Buddhism, which, in Kiyomori's case, is specified as the burning of the Vairocana Buddha. A medieval audience hearing the recitation of this scene would have recalled the graphic depiction of sufferings in the painted hell-scrolls of the day. [112]

Horrific as the episode is, for medieval audiences who heard it performed, which must have included some thieves and blasphemers, there would have been entertainment and even solace in the three episodes that followed, consisting of "Sutra Island" ("Tsukishima"), "Jishinbō," and "The Gion Lady" examined earlier. [113] In these stories, the didactic intent of moralizing the consequences of evil acts (*akugyō*) is dissipated and even contradicted. Each of the stories celebrates a marvelous aspect of Kiyomori's character, illustrating the narrator's observation that Kiyomori "was not an ordinary person." [114] For example, "Sutra Island" begins with an enumeration of the "strange things" that occurred on the night of Kiyomori's death, including a fire and the untimely sounds of singing and laughter, and concludes with an admiring account of Kiyomori's pious act of inscribing sutra texts into the stones used for constructing the island barrier at his new Ōwada Harbor; and the third episode makes Kiyomori the offspring of the Emperor Shirakawa and the mysterious Gion Lady. But it is "Jishinbō," the second of the three episodes in the Kakuichi variant, that would have most effectively dispelled the lingering gloom of the death scene.[115] "Old men used to say that Kiyomori, despite the appearance of being an evil man (*akunin*), was actually the reincarnation of Archbishop Jie."[116] It is the implications of the apparent contradiction between these two images of Kiyomori that forms the substance of the discussion that follows.

A Journey to the Underworld

As the story goes on to relate, a former scholar monk of Mount Hiei by the name of Jishinbō Son'e had taken up residence at the mountain temple of Seichōji in Settsu province, where he was revered as a reciter of the *Lotus Sutra*. One night, in the second year of Shōan (1171), while performing sutra recitations, he was visited by a messenger from King Emma's palace with an invitation to participate in a partial reading of 100,000 Lotus Sutras by 100,000 sutra votaries. With some reluctance, Son'e accepted, and a few days later, after falling asleep, he journeyed in his dream to Emma's awesome palace. In an exchange with King Emma, he inquired about the prospects of his own future rebirth and was told: "Whether a person is reborn or not reborn depends on that person's belief or unbelief." (At these words, any thief in the audience may well have perked up his ears.) Emma then proceeded to have the casket containing the record of Son'e's good deeds fetched by an officer. After hearing a recital of its contents, Son'e "wept from grief" and begged Emma to instruct him in the way of enlightenment. Emma responded with the recital of some menacing verses about sinners shrieking in hell (dampening, no doubt, the thief's spirits again), which elicited a curious reaction from the priest: "Son'e was overjoyed. 'A person known as the Taira Great Chancellor of Japan has constructed buildings on more than five acres of land on the cape of Wada in Settsu Province. Like your own gathering of one-hundred thousand priests here today, he has assembled large numbers of sutra votaries, seated them to capacity in each cloister, and has had them diligently perform readings and chantings of the sutras.'" Rejoiced by the news, King Emma then stated: "The Lay Priest you speak of is no ordinary person. He is the manifestation (*keshin*) of Archbishop Jie, reborn in Japan in order to protect the Tendai doctrines. For this reason, there is a verse that I recite three times each day in praise of him. Take this verse and present it to him. 'I salute Archbishop Jie / Protector of Tendai doctrines / He manifests himself as a great general / His evil deeds likewise bring benefits to sentient beings.'" (With these words echoing in his ears, the thief may well be plotting out his next theft on a grand scale.) After Son'e returned with the verses and presented them to Kiyomori, the narrator remarks: "It is said that Kiyomori was unusually pleased. He entertained Son'e lavishly, bestowed various gifts upon him, and rewarded him with a promotion to the rank of Master of Discipline."[117]

If I have taken the liberty of tracking the reactions of a hypothetical thief, it is merely to highlight the mixed signals that a performance of this episode might have provoked in a medieval audience, whether at one of the sub-scription performances (*kanjin*) held at a temple or in the open spaces of the markets and streets, where the blind reciters often plied their trade.[118] Ever since Gotō Tanji established the connection between "Jishinbō" and *Meido sosei ki* (*A Record of the Underworld and Rebirth*), this episode has been the starting point for numerous theories about *Heike* and its relation to Buddhist proselytizing activity.[119] Composed in hentai-kanbun, *Meido sosei ki* purports to be Son'e's own record of four dream visits that he made to the underworld in Shōan 2 (1171), Shōan 3 (1172), Shōan 4 (1174), and the first year of Angen (1175). It was the first of these underworld visits by Son'e that was incorporated into *Heike*, which climaxes in King Emma's recognition of Kiyomori's patronage of Buddhism and his presentation of the verses that identify Kiyomori as the reincarnation of Archbishop Jie. One of the aims of *Meido sosei ki* was to encourage the activity of proselytizing and raising funds on behalf of Seichōji Temple in Settsu province. This aspect comes through most clearly in the Engyōbon variant of Jishinbō, which incorporates almost the entirety of *Meido soseiki*'s account of Son'e's first journey to the underworld.[120] The truncating of certain passages from the Kakuichi variant, on the other hand, partly explains its rather inconsistent portrayal of Jishinbō, who weeps and rejoices without a clearly defined motive. In the Engyōbon variant, for example, when Son'e replies that the reason for his visit is "to learn the place of his future rebirth," Emma states: "In the province of Settsu there are five earthly sites of rebirth, and Seichōji is one of them: it is a land of Buddhas and devotion to the sutras, the site of the Buddha and Future Buddha's manifestation. Whether a person is reborn or not reborn depends on that person's belief or unbelief."[121] This is then followed by Emma's order to retrieve the casket containing the record of Son'e's entire life's good works. Whereas the Kakuichi abridges the content of the record, the Engyōbon, following *Meido sosei ki*, provides a meticulous account of the merits already obtained by Son'e as well as future acts he has yet to perform. Having listened to this daunting recital, the priest "weeps from grief"—a reaction that remains unexplained in the Kakuichi *Heike*—and proceeds to make this request of Emma: "Holy Sovereign Emma, please take pity on me and teach me how to escape the cycle of life and death. Show me the direct way to enlightenment." Emma responds by writing down a lengthy list of injunctions, only several of which are included in the Kakuichi variant, and then addresses Son'e as follows: "For the sake of all people, I have copied out these sentences for proselytizing. Anyone who reads or hears them will certainly be converted. Take these sentences with you and from this time forth proselytize base and noble everywhere, solicit everyone from high to low, and you will accomplish your own vows and bring to fulfillment the vows of others. This is the way to guide along the path those already having a karmic tie and to indoctrinate sentient beings lacking karmic affinity." [122] At the conclusion of this exhortation, Emma presents Son'e with the sentences (officially acknowledging his right to proselytize), which elicits an expression of joy from Son'e, an emotional reaction that remains unexplained in the Kakuichi variant. Finally, Son'e recalls Kiyomori's sponsorship of sutra readings and lectures at Ōwada Harbor in Settsu province. There follows Emma's praise of Kiyomori, his recitation of the verses identifying Kiyomori as the reincarnation of Jie, and Son'e's return from the underworld and meeting with Kiyomori.

As this summary of the Engyōbon version of Jishinbō makes clear, the portion of the original *Meido sosei ki* that forms the basis of the tale (incorporated in the Engyōbon with only minor variations) was clearly intended to celebrate Kiyomori as a sponsor of Buddhist rites. Historical records, in fact, confirm that Kiyomori sponsored a "thousand priest mass" (*sensō kuyō*) on two separate occasions at Fukuhara, in 1169 and 1172, as well as a "sendan Amida kyō" at Ōwada Harbor, also in 1172. For the *Heike* scholar Atsumi Kaoru, the description of Emma's supernatural character as well as Son'e as a "sublime devotee of the *Lotus Sutra*" serves to enhance Kiyomori's own stature in the episode.[123] But there is more at work in the episode's praise of Kiyomori than a simple intent to celebrate his piety. It here that the *apparent* contradiction between the portrayal of Kiyomori as an illustrious protector of Buddhist doctrine and the graphic account of his evil deeds and punishment comes into play. To elucidate this, we must return to the central point of the Jishinbō episode, Kiyomori's identification with Archbishop Jie.

Demon-Subjugating Generals

Ryōgen (912–985), otherwise known by his posthumous name Jie, was a Tendai abbot renowned during his lifetime for his extraordinary eloquence and efforts to reorganize the religious life of Buddhist monks at Enryakuji Temple.[124] Like many charismatic religious figures, in his posthumous existence, Ryōgen took on attributes and characteristics that seem to contradict the historical personage. In one of the few extant texts thought to have been composed by Ryōgen, the *Nijūroku kajō seishiki* (Twenty-six Articles for Regulating Conduct, 970), he castigates the behavior of unruly monks:

> There are monks who unite in leagues and form gangs. They forget their obligations and take revenge. They conceal swords in their robes and go in and out of their cells as they please. They carry bows and arrows on their persons and wander back and forth over the temple grounds. In their intent to inflict harm, they are no different from butchers. In their propensity for violence, they are just like drunken elephants (Nineteenth Article).[125]

Ryōgen was here interested in regulating the behavior of monks who would later emerge as a semimilitarized priesthood in the late Heian and early medieval periods, the most notorious among them known as *akusō*.[126] Yet by the late Heian period, after the emergence of the religious cult centered on Ryōgen, Jie himself was being worshiped as the patron protector of the warrior priests. In 1204, for example, when battles broke out among the scholar monks and worker monks, the former performed subjugation prayers before the image of Jie Taishi. According to a legend recorded in the Buddhist historical work *Genkō shakusho* (1322), Ryōgen's own visage reflected in a mirror would drive away demonic spirits. The magical images of Jie, which were hoisted up onto poles or installed in various halls, depicted an eerie tengu-like demon.[127]

What was Jie's role, then, within Enryakuji's religious culture? In a petition of Kujō Michiie, Jie Taishi is invoked as one who rules over *majun*. The term *majun* was a contracted form for *tenma* (*deva-māra*) and *hajun* (*pāpīyas*), two terms, often used interchangeably for an order of demonic beings who inhabited the sixth and highest realm of the Deva Heaven (*dairokuten*). As Makino Kazuo observes, this suggests that Jie had taken on the role of the Demon King Mara (*maō*) himself. The phrase "He manifests himself as a great general" (*jigen saishō shōgunjin*) in the verses identifying Kiyomori with Jie in *Meido soseiki* and the Jishinbō episode would therefore point to

Jie's, and by association Kiyomori's, capacity to subdue demonic forces.[128]
A passage in *Gonsenhū*, a collection of prayers and petitions compiled by
the Agui sect of preachers, further identifies Jie as the *honji* (original ground)
of Sankō Ten'ō and *suijaku* (trace-manifestation) of Hachidai Ryūō, one
of the dragon kings and another facet of Jie's supernatural character. Within
the religious culture of medieval Enryakuji, Jie Taishi had come to embody
the ambiguous presence of demonic and supernatural powers, which both
supported the temple's authority but were also a latent threat to its internal
order in the often violent battles that broke out among the factions of monks.

The close identification of Hiei's sacred site with the demonic is captured
in the following passage from the Engyōbon, which occurs in the long narrative centered on the violent strife between the Hiei monks and the Retired
Sovereign Go-Shirakawa's North Guards that erupted after the killing of
several Enryakuji-affiliated shrine attendants:

> The reverence shown to the Northern Peaks by reign after reign of emperors
> has surpassed that of all other mountains. Because Buddhist law and royal
> law mutually protect one another, the one vehicle and the myriad vehicles
> flourish together. Thus the complaints of the Mountain Gate are not lim-
> ited to the griefs of the warrior monks and the wrath of the Sannō deity
> alone. Rather, it is matter of gravest concern to the state and a lament of
> the entire realm under heaven. "The ruler dwells in the divine country, is
> the heir of the divine age, and worships the divinities. If the court practices
> virtuous government and inclines to the Sannō divinity, why has there been
> no judgment?" So people spoke, bowing their heads in disapproval. Truly,
> Buddhist law and royal law are like the Five Mountains: it is not possible
> for one to be lacking. When there is law the country is tranquil. If Buddhist
> law is destroyed, how can royal law be preserved? If the Mountain Gate
> is destroyed, how can the perfect doctrine continue to exist? It is already
> over two-hundred years since the world entered the period of the final law,
> a time dominated by wars. Demonic powers (*ninma, tenma*) strengthen in
> power, and people cannot control their hearts. It is said that the sight of
> Mount Hiei's earthly form resembles that of a couchant lion. There is a say-
> ing that a person's heart resembles the place it dwells in, conforming to it
> like water in a vessel. Occupying dwellings on lofty heights, continuously
> ascending and descending precipitous slopes, the minds of the monks have
> become fierce and are dominated by arrogance. Thus long ago, Masakado
> was honored with an imperial decree and ascended Hiei with an imperial
> envoy. As he looked down upon the capital from a place called Lofty Peak,
> seeing it practically in the grasp of his hand, he suddenly grew rebellious in

his heart. This was the result of a brief ascent up the mountain. Imagine the effect of dwelling day and night on its summit![129]

After beginning with a classic statement of Hiei's ideology of *chingo kokka* ("pacification and defense of the nation") and the doctrine of the mutual dependence of Buddhist law and royal law, the passage turns into a curious reflection on the danger immanent in the site of Enryakuji Temple itself. The physical loftiness of Mount Hiei, typically emblematic of strength and spiritual preeminence, also becomes the source of arrogance, one of the Buddhist categories of sinful conduct. Arrogance, or kyōman, as another passage in the Engyōbon tells us, could easily become a connection (*en*) for attracting thought-deluding demons who threw obstacles in the way of believers: "Thus, the Retired sovereign's arrogant mind at once became the enabling connection (*en*) for the Demon King to come, and the *tengu* of all sixty-six provinces have intermingled with the mountain monks and brought to nothing all your splendid former austerities."[130] This passage comes at the end of a long disquisition by the Sumiyoshi Deity to the Retired Sovereign Go-Shirakawa on the various types and causes of demonic possession understood as deluded thinking. Its occasion is the anger of the Enryakuji monks provoked by Go-Shirakawa's plan to undergo the "Water Consecration Ritual" at Miidera Temple instead of the traditional site of Enryakuji Temple.[131] Earlier in the same disquisition, the Sumiyoshi deity enlightens Go-Shirakawa on the ambiguous character of demonic consciousness: "Know this above all: The demon king Mara resembles the form of all existing beings. And because the sixth form of consciousness (*dairoku no ishiki*) when reversed turns into Mara, the form of Mara also resembles all existing beings."[132] The insight articulated here derives from the secret tradition of original enlightenment doctrine, where the reversibility of the two states, the enlightened mind of sixth form consciousness and the state of deluded mind identified with Mara (*Maō*), amounts to their fundamental identity.[133] It also points us back to the underlying ambiguity of Mount Hiei's topography, at a once preeminent sacred site yet harboring in its physical form the capacity to provoke dangerous demonic obstructions.

It is ironic that the same Jie, who as the Demon King Mara governed the unruly demonic presences on Mount Hiei, should also have been credited, under his priest's name Ryōgen, with the authorship of several secret transmissions devoted to hongaku doctrine that may have been a factor in the outbreaks of violence among the monks at Mount Hiei. Among the four verses recited by King Emma in praise of Kiyomori, the enigmatic fourth and final verse, "akugō shujō dō riyaku" (his evil deeds likewise bring benefits to sentient beings), touches directly on this problem. Makino has described it as a characteristic expression of the hongaku doctrine, "good and evil are nondual" (*zen'aku funi*).[134] Tomikura Tokujirō, on the other hand, in what has become the standard reading, glossed the third and fourth verses as "Kiyomori has now appeared as a superb general (*jigen saishō shōgunjin*), and because he has taught that evil deeds are to be feared, he has brought benefits to sentient beings in the same way as the Archbishop brought benefits to sentient beings."[135] By avoiding the inherent ambiguity of the phrase, more literally translated as "his evil deeds likewise bring benefits to sentient beings," Tomikura brought the verse's meaning into line with the didactic purpose enunciated in *Heike*'s Preface—namely, that arrogance of mind and evil deeds will eventually be punished—a message that also underlay the proselytizing activity of Tendai priests. However, as Makino has argued, the two capping verses celebrating Jie, "I salute Archbishop Jie" (*kyōrai Jie daisōjō*) and "He manifests himself as a great general" (*jigen saishō shōgunjin*), were already circulating among the monks of Mount Hiei by the 1171 date given as the time of Son'e's first visit to the underworld in *Meido soseiki*.[136] The appearance of the Seichōji legend celebrating Kiyomori as the reincarnation of Jie at this time would therefore correspond to the period Kiyomori was at the apogee of his worldly success, cultivating extremely close ties with the powerful Hiei prelate Meiun and sponsoring *Lotus Sutra* readings at Fukuhara (1169, 1172) in Settsu province, not far from the site of Seichōji. The identification of Kiyomori with Jie Taishi at this time locates him squarely within the affirmative discourse of the supernatural demon-subjugating general.

It is likely therefore that "evil deeds" (*akugō*) in Emma's verse praising Kiyomori had a more ambiguous reference than a straightforward didactic message about the consequences of evil actions. We have already seen two such examples in the discussion of the kaburo tale: Kiyomori's consumption of the sea bass and his ingestion of warrior essence in the form of birds. In the first of these, Kiyomori not only breaks his fast but also violates the prohibition against taking life. Yet despite its evil nature, Kiyomori's act is praised as the cause of his good fortune. In an essay that attempts to establish the character of the historical Kiyomori's religious beliefs, Akamatsu Toshihide cites these and other examples of Kiyomori's behavior, including his willful destruction of temples, as evidence of Kiyomori's adherence to the nondual doctrine of "enlightenment in this very body" (*sokushin jōbutsu*), one of many manifestations of original enlightenment doctrine.[137] The radical implications of this doctrine are illustrated in the following passage from the Engyōbon variant of the Hiei monks' retaliatory burning of Kiyomizu-dera Temple:

> For some reason, the fire on the Pagoda went out, and as a result the entire Main Hall was left standing. Thereupon a Mūdōji monk, the Hōki Examiner named Jōen, a fierce scholar monk, stepped forward and deliberated: "*Sinful acts from the beginning have no reality. They arise from delusions and confusions of thought. Because the mind-nature is pure at its source, sentient beings are already Buddhas.* Set the Main Hall on fire and burn it down, fellows." The warrior monks shouted their assent, and lighting a flame, set fire to the four corners of the Hall. The smoke mounted all the way to the clouds, rivaling that of the Xiangyang Palace in a foreign land. In a moment it was consumed by flames. To call it shameful is inadequate.[138]

By his statement of the nondual principle that "sinful acts" (*zaigō*) have no real existence, the akusō Jōen shows how original enlightenment doctrine could influence the conduct of Hiei's armed monks.[139] Similar formulations are found in passages like the following from the hongaku text *Shinnyokan* (*Contemplation of Suchness*), one of the apocryphal texts attributed to Ryōgen: "Contemplating the meaning of the suchness of evil karma (*aku no gō*), sins quickly melt away like frost or dew touched by the rays of the sun. The *Fugenkyō* says, 'The entire sea of karmic obstruction *arises from delusions of thought* (*mōzō yori shōzu*). Those who desire release sit still and contemplate reality (*jissō*).' Reality is another name for suchness (*shinyo*). Like frost and dew, sins readily melt away in the sun's light." [140] The attempt to resolve doubts concerning the relationship between doctrine and action could lead to problematic solutions, as in the following example from the hongaku text *Kankō ruiju*: "Killing and thieving are evil acts, yet can a practitioner of insightful contemplation (*shikan no gyōja*) who is without fear do and act as he likes?" To which the teacher replies: "It would be nowise different than if one were to perform evils acts without attachment and spontaneously. It is like Kannon's manifesting herself as a fisherman and killing various fish and insects." The ambiguity of such replies, as Tamura Yoshirō remarks, could lead to dangerous consequences.[141]

Expounding Evil: Kiyomori and Devadatta

Despite its potentially radical influence on individual conduct, medieval hongaku doctrine was more than a matter of personal belief or of local abuses
inside temples. Rather, as I argued in the previous chapter, it arose in part
out of contradictions characteristic of a historical moment that privileged a
variety of logics founded on the play between difference and identity. This
is vividly illustrated in the Engyōbon's sequel to Jishinbō, which attempts to
clarify the meaning of Kiyomori's identification with Jie. After rounding off
its account of Jishinbō's trip to the underworld with the statement, "Thus
people understood that Kiyomori was the reincarnation of Archbishop Jie,"
the Engyōbon continues with a sermonlike passage that interprets the meaning of Kiyomori's identification with Archbishop Jie:

> [1a] However, supposing that Kiyomori were a provisional incarnation
> (*gonja*), a gon always appears in the world in order to bring forth the truth.
> "Performing evil deeds (*akugō*) and destroying the Buddhist law, by what
> logic can these conduce to truth?" So did each person express doubt and
> disbelief. Among the sutra commentaries, there is the following Buddhist
> verse that explains this logic: "The boar polishes the gold mountain; and
> the wind increases the kura-insect." [142] The phrase, 'The boar polishes
> the gold mountain,' means that when the boar digs up the gold mountain,
> he exposes the gold, causing the mountain to glow with a golden light.
> 'The wind increases the kura-insect,' refers to the existence in the world of
> the insect called "kura." Whenever the wind blows, they drift about and
> appear to be in danger. However, each time they are struck by the wind,
> their vitality increases greatly and their strength waxes mightily. The ben-
> efit brought about by a provisional incarnation is no different from these
> examples. For the sake of bringing good to people, even the commission of
> sins brings an increase in benefits.
>
> [1b] The way that good and evil together produce benefits varies in ac-
> cordance with the occasion. For example, when the Buddha Thus-Come-
> One, whose entire life was devoted to teaching, turned the five wheels of
> Buddhist law and brought benefits to all sentient beings, the ninety-five
> kinds of heresy sprang up vying for mastery, and the Thus-Come-One's
> teaching fell into disuse and was of no benefit. It was during this period
> that Devadatta was born. As head of the ninety-five kinds of heresy, he
> committed the three evils, the ten evils, and other sins, fighting against the
> Thus-Come-One. In retribution for that sinful act, the earth split open and
> [Devadatta], fully alive and in his present form, fell into the Hell Without
> Intermission. The rest of his fellow heretics, trembling with fear at the

sight of Devadatta's fall into hell, reformed their deluded minds and submitted to the Thus-Come-One. Ever since then, the Buddha's teaching has flourished.

[1c] The nature of the Thus-Come-One as Bodhisattva is not even understood. The teaching of a gonja cannot be fathomed by the average person. After Devadatta had fallen into the Hell Without Intermission, Śākya-muni sent for his disciples and interrogated Devadatta as follows: "Just how unbearable are the pains of the Hell Without Intermission?" Devadatta replied: "The pains of the Hell Without Intermission are just like the three varieties of pleasure." Upon hearing these words, one might think that Devadatta, with his evil mind still unreformed even in the midst of the fires of hell, was mocking the Thus-Come-One. However, when the Thus-Come-One was explicating the *Lotus Sutra* on Sacred Eagle Mountain, he said: "The One Buddha's enlightenment was achieved through the power of the one vehicle of the *Lotus Sutra*. I came into possession of the *Lotus Sutra* having learned it from my teacher Devadatta, as a reward for a thousand years of service." He then explicated this ancient karmic affinity. Thus, Devadatta is not merely Devadatta. He is Devadatta the provisional form. Nor are the pains of hell mere pains of hell. Having grasped that "pain and pleasure are nondual," Devadatta replied, with splendid insight, that the pains of hell "were like the three varieties of pleasure." Therefore, Kiyomori, too, is a gonja, and his evil deeds are no different from the evil deeds of Devadatta. *To destroy Buddhist law and mock royal law, to make manifest these evil deeds in his present body, and finally to contract a fever and after his death cause the destruction of his descendants—this was surely an example of promoting good and chastising evil.*

[2] Again, since evil and good are one law (*zen'aku wa ichigu no hō nareba*), Śākyamuni and Devadatta were born with the same nature and revealed the two flows of evil and good. In the same way, Kiyomori was also the offspring of the Retired Sovereign Shirakawa. Shirakawa-in was reborn as the holy man Kishinjikyō and revitalized Kōbō Daishi's Mount Kōya. The Retired Sovereign brought forth a forest of merits and planted the roots of virtuous deeds. Kiyomori accumulated acts of merit and evil deeds together and brought benefits to both society and individuals. This is no different from the benefits of Devadatta's and Śākyamuni's one nature. Because he was such a person, his reverence for the shrine deities and his worship of the Buddhist law surpassed all others. It seemed that his worship at Hiyoshi Shrine was unsurpassed by even the Regent's pilgrimages to the Kamo and Kasuga shrines. He continuously dispatched courtiers, mounted warriors, the highest ranking nobles and others to the shrine. At Hiyoshi Shrine, he selected even the sutra votaries for a thousand priest mass. These were awesome deeds.[143]

It is clear that the editor of the Engyōbon was troubled enough by the ambiguous implications of Kiyomori's identification with Archbishop Jie, expressed in the verse "akugō shujō dō riyaku" (his evil deeds likewise bring benefits to sentient beings), to append the equivalent of an exegetical sermon on its meaning. In attempting to clarify its meaning, however, and thereby bring the episode into line with the logic of cause and effect enunciated in the Preface, the exegesis, which reflects techniques commonly employed by preachers of the Agui sect, exposes further ambiguities.[144] It begins (section 1a) with several analogies of apparently harmful actions producing beneficial results. This sets the stage for the central analogy that likens Kiyomori to the evil disciple Devadatta, who, according to a legend that is not recorded in the *Lotus Sutra*, not only propagated heretical teachings but grew envious of Śākyamuni and attempted to kill him. The first part of this section (section 1b) illustrates how actions that are to all appearances evil may nonetheless bring about benefits, in this case the flourishing of Śākyamuni's teachings. At this point, the analogy is unambiguous in its meaning, casting Kiyomori as a bad example from which others learn valuable lessons.[145] In the following section (section 1c), however, the editor/preacher introduces the subtler principle of nonduality, already hinted at in the *gonjitsu* doctrine stated at the beginning of his sermon. Having complicated the relatively straightforward evil Devadatta–Kiyomori analogy, he then abruptly pulls his sermon back into the ambit of more easily understood dualities, with a classic statement of "kanzen chōaku" (promoting good and chastising evil), a Confucian didactic principle that is foreign to the doctrine of nonduality. The final section (section 2) is the most intriguing. As Saeki Shin'ichi has argued, it reflects an effort by the editor to interpret the entire Engyōbon sequence centered on Kiyomori's death, including the story that he was the offspring of Shirakawa, as an illustration of the doctrine that "good and evil are one" (*zen'aku ichigu*). Just as Devadatta and Śākyamuni represent the evil and good of a single nature that brings forth benefits, so also do Kiyomori (offspring) and Shirakawa (progenitor) perform evil actions and good actions that result in benefits.[146] The problem, of course, is that the preacher/narrator credits Kiyomori with both virtuous acts (*kudoku*) and evil deeds (*akugō*). While this affirms the logic of "good and evil are one," it undermines the didactic message articulated earlier in the exegesis. This is especially striking in the concluding lines (italicized), which eulogize Kiyomori for his patronage of Mount Hiei's Hiyoshi Shrine. Despite its effort at clarification, the Engyōbon's exegesis is unable to escape the aporia involved in attempting to reconcile a dualistic didactic message with the nondual doctrine that good and evil are one. It remains a self-contradictory text.

Fukuhara Revisited

The foregoing analysis suggests that Kiyomori, celebrated during his lifetime as a sponsor of *Lotus Sutra* readings and patron of Enryakuji Temple, was also celebrated as one imbued with special powers over the demonic realm. It is this, I suggest, rather than the didactic message that evil acts beget evil consequences, that underlies *Meido soseiki*'s identification of Kiyomori with the demon-subduing Jie Taishi, who took on the very characteristics of the demonic powers that he controlled. There remains the important question of *Meido soseiki*'s sacred topography. In his four successive visits to the underworld, Son'e returned each time with a copy of the *Lotus Sutra*, presenting one each to the emperor, Seichōji Temple, Onsenji Temple, and Shitennōji Temple. The *Meido soseiki* also states: "In the province of Settsu there are five earthly sites of rebirth, and Seichōji is one of them." The four additional sites were the temples of Onsenji, Chūzanji, Shitennōji, and Rengeji. In an analysis of *Meido soseiki* and related temple engi in Settsu province, Murakami Mitoshi has shown that Seichōji was located at the center of a radiating network of temples, each of which was simultaneously earthly Pure Land and gateway to the underworld. Geographically, these were organized along a northeast–southwest axis that began at Enryakuji Temple's Demon Gate, northeast of the capital, and extended southwest through the Palace (Dairi), Tada-in, Chūzanji Temple, Seichōji Temple, and Onsenji Temple, until reaching Akashi Ōto (The Great Gate of Akashi). Akashi Ōto, which was the name for the passage into the rough waters of the Akashi Straits, was a threshold site beyond which lay the entry into the demon world. With Seichōji occupying the exact geographical center and Rengeji and Shitennōji lying northwest and southeast respectively, the sacred sites had the form of a quadrant mapped in accordance with the five agents of the yin-yang cycle.[147]

With this topography in mind, we can turn to Kiyomori's contest with the malign powers that irrupt after his transfer of the palace to Fukuhara in scroll five:

After he moved the capital to Fukuhara, the Heike people had many bad dreams. Their minds were always on edge, and there were numerous ghosts.

One night, as the Lay Priest was lying down, the face of something larger than the space of a single bay stood and peered in at him. *The Lay Priest kept perfectly calm, and as he glared straight at it, it vanished in a twinkling.* The place known as the Hill Palace had only been recently made, and although there was nothing one could call a large tree, one night there was the sound of a tree crashing and then loud laughter equivalent to thirty human voices. Thinking that it must be the deed of a *tengu*, he stationed one hundred guards by night and fifty by day, whom he named the humming bulb watch. When he had them fire their humming bulbs in the direction where the *tengu* were, there was no sound; and when they fired in the direction where they were not, there was loud laughter. Again, one morning, the Lay Priest Chancellor Kiyomori left his curtained alcove and pushed open a side door. As he looked out into the inner courtyard, it was filled with the skulls of innumerable dead people, one on top of the other, which kept rolling together and rolling apart, now heaping up towards the middle and now spreading out toward the edges of the pile. In the midst of this frightful clatter, the Lay Priest Chancellor summoned his attendants. "Is anybody there, is anybody there?" But at the time nobody was on guard. At that point, the numerous skulls came together into a single dense heap larger than the entire inner courtyard, a veritable mountain more than a hundred and forty or fifty feet high. In that huge head, there appeared thousands of large eyes like those of living human beings, which glared straight at Kiyomori, without blinking. *Not in the least fazed, Kiyomori stood his ground and stared back, until the huge head, stared down by the force of his gaze, vanished without a trace, like frost or dew touched by the morning sun.*[148]

This episode invites several possible interpretations. At the simplest level, it reads like a variation on the common *Heike* motif of oni-taiji, or "demon-subjugation," the best known being Yorimasa's slaying of the "nue" ("thrush monster") in scroll four. A wider view that takes into account *Meido soseiki*'s sacred topography suggests that Kiyomori is performing here in his capacity as demon-subduing general on par with Enryakuji's Jie Taishi. Through this act, Kiyomori establishes Fukuhara as a heterotopic court. Finally, a third reading is suggested by the debate between Yasuyori and Shunkan on the demon-border of Kikai-ga-shima. It is likely that Yasuyori and Shunkan would have taken opposite sides in a debate concerning the reality of the beings who appear to Kiyomori at Fukuhara, the former affirming their existence and the latter dismissing them as an illusion of false thinking. In the medieval imaginary, the magical powers claimed by exoteric rites and the contemplative powers achieved through the insights explicated in the *Con-*

templation of Suchness and other secret transmissions were, on one level, nothing more than inverted aspects of one another. To quote a passage cited earlier from the *Contemplation of Suchness*: "Contemplating the meaning of the suchness of evil karma, sins quickly melt away like frost or dew touched by the rays of the sun." To speak of evil melting away "like frost or dew touched by the morning sun" is to evoke evil's unreality for the enlightened mind. The archetypal instance of such insight was Śākyamuni's subjugation of the demonic powers as he sat beneath the Bodhi tree, the eighth and final stage in the eight phases of his enlightenment. It rests with the reader to decide whether Kiyomori is the enlightened Śākyamuni or his evil disciple Devadatta.

EPILOGUE

To return to the aims laid out in the Introduction, this study has attempted three things: to cast light on a body of knowledge and ritual praxis related to Daoist and yin-yang ideas that has remained relatively hidden from view in English-language scholarship on Japan; to complicate our ways of speaking about the relationship between space and narrative in their cultural, ritual, and political manifestations; and to locate both sets of problems in a literary and historical trajectory that extends to the world of *Heike* and other medieval texts. If Kiyomori's attempt to establish a capital at Fukuhara asks us to rethink the center–periphery binary that has tended to characterize discussions of cultural and political space in Japan, his apocryphal history suggests that the most instructive exchanges in any dialogue about *Heike* and its affiliations may well lie with earlier periods such as Nara, which like medieval times was also characterized by a vigorous cultural exchange with the continent.

These problems are connected in turn to another theme implicitly addressed in this study, the problem of cultural memory, or the way the past is remembered, which I would like to reflect on in these concluding remarks. In the fifth year of Tenpyō Shōhō (753), the Tang priest Ganjin (688–763) crossed over to Japan, where he established the first ordination platform at Tōdaiji Temple and administered the precepts to Emperor Shōmu and other members of the court. Ganjin, who figures prominently in standard histories on Japan, is likely to be familiar to most students of ancient Japanese history. But as recounted in Ōmi no Mifune's *Tōdai wajō tōseiden* (779), his biography is strangely intertwined with the legacy of Daoism in Japan. According to Mifune, the Tang Emperor Xuanzong had repeatedly declined requests from Japanese envoys that Ganjin be allowed to journey to Japan, insisting that Ganjin be accompanied by a Daoist master, an indication of the important place of official Tang Daoism at this time. The envoy Fujiwara no Kiyokawa replied, "The Japanese sovereign has not previously worshiped the rites of the Daoist master." In the end, Kiyokawa left behind four of his fellow Japanese to study under a Daoist master and finally succeeded in getting Ganjin to Japan. Although conjectures have been made about the identities of these four students, their fate has remained a mystery. Composed in the late Nara period, Mifune's account of this rejection of official Tang Daoism shows that the Daoist legacy of an earlier time was already in the process of being effaced from the cultural and historical memory of Japan.[1]

The refashioning of the past by the present has been at the heart of debates about the meaning and role of culture for much of the past century and increasingly so in the past few decades. In the middle of the twentieth century, the poet T. S. Eliot drew attention to the power of new works of literature to alter and disturb the established canon. Dating back more than 700 years, *The Tale of the Heike* can hardly be characterized as new literature. What the present study has sought to achieve, however, is to question *Heike*'s haecceity as a canonical work—a procedure that goes somewhat counter to Eliot's notion of a canon whose primary function is to resist change—and thereby recover its affiliations to an earlier cultural landscape that predates the period of the court literature, whose luster has kept *Heike* in the shadows. But the effort to recover historical memory is always intertwined, as Mifune's biography of Ganjin shows, with the continuous process of refashioning the past. If the past is multiple, its alterity and fundamental strangeness, however deeply we may long for such an encounter, are seldom knowable on their own terms. The Argentine writer Jorge Luis Borges, going beyond Eliot's notion of an enduring canon, had his fictitious author Pierre Menard rewrite *Quixote* in the exact words used by Cervantes, ironically producing a superior version of the classic. "Historical truth, for him, is not what happened; it is what we judge to have happened."[2] In Borges's parable, which anticipated our already elapsed postmodernity, the past is no longer even available. That there are philosophical as well as moral dilemmas here cannot be denied. The present study makes no claim to have resolved them, but neither do I view the attempt as fraught only with peril. Carefully negotiated, what has come to be called the situatedness of any intellectual endeavor can become the basis for new dialogues, much like Shunkan's and Yasuyori's exchange on the island of Kikai-ga-shima, where a border becomes the setting for a debate about centrality.

To return to several examples from the preceding chapters, scholars concerned with the sociological and historical issue of discrimination in Japan may well view the traits attributed to the medieval heteromorphic as a stage in an evolution toward the early modern classification of outcasts (*hinin*) as a legally defined class. But is there continuity between the two or historical rupture? It may be that our concern to come to grips with long-neglected discriminatory practices has drawn our attention to a phenomenon that only looks like discrimination. A related effect concerns the fascination with trade and commerce as a site invested with an exotic allure, another theme addressed in this study. In the 1950s, the novelist Yoshikawa Eiji made a point of celebrating *Heike* for its outward-looking international perspective, comparing it favorably to the inward-looking literature and culture of the court. Yoshikawa's *Heike* was a sign for an economically renewed postwar Japan.[3] But medieval commerce, especially as it is portrayed in episodes like the Engyōbon's account of Kiyomori's port, thrived at the edges or even outside the ambit of a nation-centered imaginary, including the divine country worldview that Yoshikawa and others of his generation would later repudiate. Despite Yoshikawa's and his contemporaries' fascination with this aspect of *Heike*, medieval trade was not commensurate with modern state nationalism. At the present time, these issues of cultural memory and nationality have begun to resonate once again. It is not fortuitous that the conceptual framework of an ideographic cultural sphere has emerged against the background of mainland China's growing presence in Japan's national awareness, even as the prime minister's visits to the most potent symbol of Japanese nationalism, the Yasukuni Shrine, have become a contentious issue of debate between the two countries.

The writing and research of this study were largely conducted in two locations, Los Angeles and Tokyo, at opposite sides of what has come to be called the Pacific Rim. Much like Shunkan's and Yasuyori's island of Kikai-ga-shima, it is a border region and a provocation to think outside or around our notions of centrality. At times, the effect can be that of a liberating lightness. At an early stage of my research, the chance remark of a friend regarding the geomantic practice of feng shui made me curiously aware of how my research, despite its seemingly abstruse nature, connected with the quotidian in Los Angeles, where a traditional, even ancient, Chinese practice qualifies as familiar knowledge. Upon arriving in Tokyo at the opposite side of the Pacific Rim for the final phase of writing, after an absence of nearly twelve years, I was struck by another observation made in the bookstores. Ranged on the shelves alongside the volumes of a flourishing scholarly debate on Daoism and yin-yang was the leftover stock of an already dwindling 1990s boom in popular Daoism and related Chinese esoterica. If such experiences have the effect of unsettling the boundary between scholarship and its contingent present, they can also help restore perspective to the scholarly investigation of the past, which all too often presents its results as the recovery of facts undisturbed by any sense of our own historical moment. If the present study has tried to make this awareness of contingency and its eccentric spaces a part of its discussion of the past, it has done so in the belief that these are now an inescapable part of our relationship to the past.

Tokyo, Los Angeles

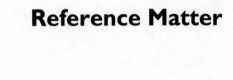

Reference Matter

Reference Matter

Introduction

1. Japanese scholars have traditionally divided the *Heike* texts into two broad categories: those that were intended for oral recitation, such as the Kakuichi-dictated text, and texts that were intended for private reading or oral declamation. The former are referred to as texts of the recited lineage (*kataribon-kei*) and the latter as texts of the read lineage (*yomihon-kei*).

2. For a detailed discussion of these points, see David T. Bialock, "Nation and Epic: *The Tale of the Heike* as Modern Classic," in *Inventing the Classics: Modernity, National Identity, and Japanese Literature*, eds. Haruo Shirane and Tomi Suzuki (Stanford, CA: Stanford University Press, 2000), 151–178; and my essay, "*The Tale of the Heike:* Its Modern Critics and the Medieval Past," *Issues of Canonicity and Canon Formation in Japanese Literary Studies, PAJLS (Proceedings for the Association of Japanese Literary Studies)*, 1 (Summer 2000), 141–152.

3. See David T. Bialock, "Outcasts, Emperorship, and Dragon Cults in *The Tale of the Heike*," in *Buddhist Priests, Kings and Marginals: Studies on Medieval Japanese Buddhism*, vol. 13 of *Cahiers d'Extrême-Asie* (2002–2003), 244–251; and Makino Atsushi, "Engyōbon *Heike monogatari* hōō go-kanjō no koto ronri: Dōsen risshi to idaten no monogatari to sono shaku wo tegakari ni," *GK*, 34 (March 1998), 55–65, esp. 62.

4. *Heike monogatari* jō, *NKBT*, vol. 32, 388.

5. For several critiques of phonocentrism, see Naoki Sakai, *Voices of the Past: The Status of Language in Eighteenth-Century Japanese Discourse* (Ithaca, NY: Cornell University Press, 1991); Tomiko Yoda, "Literary History Against the National Frame, or Gender and the Emergence of Heian Kana Writing," *Positions: East Asia Cultures Critique*, 8: 2 (Fall 2000), 465–497; and Thomas LaMarre, *Uncovering Heian Japan: An Archaeology of Sensation and Inscription* (Durham, NC: Duke University Press, 2000).

6. On the idea of a medieval Buddhist episteme, see Fabio Rambelli, "True Words, Silence, and the Adamantine Dance: On Japanese Mikkyō and the Formation of the Shingon Discourse," *JJRS*, 21: 4 (December 1994), 373–405.

7. For reasons of space, an extended discussion of the *National Histories*, and *Shōmonki, Mutsuwaki*, and other early *gunkimono* has been abridged, but the gist of the matter in relation to *Shōmonki* is examined in the opening section of Chapter 6.

8. As Claire Colebrook explains in her discussion of new historicist methodology, "texts are neither the reflection nor the effect of stable and static structures. Texts are, rather, forms of cultural labor which work upon heterogeneous materials from within received symbolic practices." Claire Colebrook, *New Literary Histories: New Historicism and Contemporary Criticism* (Manchester and New York: Manchester University Press, 1997), 218.

9. Henri Lefebvre, *The Production of Space*, trans. Donald Nicholson-Smith (Oxford and Cambridge, MA: Blackwell, 1991), 38–45.

10. Bruce L. Batten, *To the Ends of Japan: Premodern Frontiers, Boundaries, and Interactions* (Honolulu: University of Hawaii Press, 2003).

11. Ibid., 28 and 37.

12. Gilles Deleuze and Felix Guattari, *A Thousand Plateaus: Capitalism and Schizophrenia*, trans. Brian Massumi (Minneapolis and London: University of Minnesota Press, 1987). See esp. "Treatise on Nomadology: The War Machine," 351–423.

13. Amino Yoshihiko, *Nihon chūsei no hinōgyōmin to tennō* (Iwanami shoten, 1984).

Chapter 1

1. From Keichū's *Man'yō daishōki* (*A Stand-in's Chronicle of the Man'yōshū*), in *Keichū zenshū*, vol. 1, ed. Hisamatsu Sen'ichi (Iwanami shoten, 1973), 158. Cited and discussed in Murai Osamu, *Moji no yokuatsu: kokugaku ideorogī no seiritsu* (Seikyūsha, 1989), 22.

2. On these two tendencies in Keichū's work, see Peter Nosco, *Remembering Paradise: Nativism and Nostalgia in Eighteenth-Century Japan* (Cambridge and London: Council on East Asian Studies, Harvard University Press, 1990), 55–60. The quotation from *Man'yō daishōki: zassetsu* is cited on p. 59.

3. Keichū's own tracing of the textual sources for *Man'yōshū* poetry was of the highest quality. See Kojima Noriyuki, *Jōdai nihon bungaku to chūgoku bungaku* jō: *shuttenron wo chūshin to suru hikaku bungakuteki kōsatsu* (Hirakawa shobō, 1962), 133.

4. Mark Morris, "Waka and Form, Waka and History," *Harvard Journal of Asiatic Studies*, 46: 2 (December 1986), 577–578.

5. *Man'yōshū* 1, NKBT, vol. 4, 26–27.

6. On *Hyakunin isshu*, see Joshua S. Mostow, *Pictures of the Heart: The Hyakunin Isshu in Word and Image* (Honolulu: University of Hawaii Press, 1996). For the historical background to karuta, see p. 38.

7. For Saitō Mokichi's lyrical reading of the poem, see *Man'yōshū kenkyū* (jō) (Iwanami shoten, 1940), 136–138. The poem's reception is reviewed by Eguchi Kiyoshi, *Kodai tennō to onmyōryō no shisō: Jitō tennōka no kaidoku yori* (Kawade shobō shinsha, 1999), 11–12.

8. Ōhama Itsuhiko, *Man'yō genshikō* (Shūeisha, 1978), 163–192, esp. 174–182; and Eguchi, *Onmyōryō*, 11–36. Ōhama's theory is discussed in Eguchi, *Onmyōryō*, 13–18.

9. The Takamatsuzuka tumulus, located in Nara Prefecture, was first opened up by archeologists in 1972. For a detailed description of the tumulus, see J. Edward Kidder, "The Newly Discovered Takamatsuzuka Tomb," in *MN*, 27: 3 (Autumn 1972), 245–251; and Wayne Farris, *Sacred Texts and Buried Treasures* (Honolulu: University of Hawaii Press, 1998), 87–95, who looks at the archeological evidence in relation to possible Korean and Chinese influences.

10. For Ōhama's remarks on the Takamatsuzuka wall paintings, see *Man'yō genshikō*, 175, 179. Among literature scholars, mention also needs to be made of Watase Masatada, who has produced an extensive body of work relating the archeological finds of the Takamatsuzuka tumulus and other sites to the reinterpretation of Nara period literature, especially the poetry of *Man'yōshū* and Hitomaro. Many of these studies have recently been republished in vols. 4 and 6 of his collected works. See, for example, his chapter "Takamatsuzuka kofun no hekiga to hitomaro no sekai," in *Shima no miya no bungaku, Watase Masatada chosakushū*, vol. 4 (Ōfū, 2002), 51–72. Originally published under the same title in *Nihon bungaku kenkyū*, 12 (January 1973).

11. Ōhama, *Man'yō genshikō*, 174–175. The following chart, adapted from Ōhama, p. 174, provides the correspondences:

Five Agents	Wood	Fire	Earth	Metal	Water
Five Colors	Green	Red	Yellow	White	Black
Four Directions	East	South	Center	West	North
Four Seasons	Spring	Summer		Autumn	Winter
Four Zoomorphs	Green Dragon	Vermilion Bird		White Tiger	Dark Warrior

12. *Man'yōshū* 1, *NKBT*, vol. 4, 94–95.

13. Ōhama, *Man'yō genshikō*, 179.

14. For the hexagrams, see Suzuki Yoshijirō, *Ekikyō* jō, *ZKT*, vol. 9, 59–60, 100–105; and Richard Wilhelm, *The I Ching or Book of Changes*, trans. Cary F. Baynes, with a foreword by C. C. Jung (London and Melbourne: Routledge & Kegan Paul, 1951, 1965), 3–15 and 269–271.

15. Eguchi, *Onmyōryō*, 19–21. This change in directional symbolism also allows Eguchi to shift the viewpoint of the poem from Kiyomihara to the nearby Fujiwara Palace. For the full set of correspondences for the "Central Region" in the *Lüshi chunqiu*, see John Knoblock and Jeffrey Riegel, *The Annals of Lü*

Buwei: A Complete Translation and Study (Stanford, CA: Stanford University Press, 2000), Book 6/1.8, 156.

16. Eguchi, *Onmyōryō*, 14–15. On a ceremonial occasion, Temmu is recorded to have taken up a position at the South Gate of Asuka Temple. See *Nihon shoki ge* (Temmu 6/8/15), 428–429. On the yin-yang symbolism and astral-geomantic positioning of Ise Shrine, see Yoshino Hiroko, *In'yō gogyō shisō kara mita nihon no matsuri: Ise jingū saishi daijōsai wo chūshin toshite* (Kōbundō, 1978), 105–132.

17. Eguchi, *Onmyōryō*, 20.

18. The headnote to the poem in the Iwanami taikei edition, p. 94, glosses the poem's meaning as "in this fashion, the Prince has departed leaving me behind."

19. Fujimori Tomoo's painterly evocation of the first of these two poems is a good example of this modern naturalistic approach: "It is as if one can see the entire scene in the vividness of the green Mount Kaguya viewed to the east of the Fujiwara Palace and in the impressionistic whiteness of summer robes drenched in the early summer sun." In Saitō Mokichi, "Hitomaro mae no sakusha 3," in *Man'yōshū kenkyū* (jō), 128. Cited in Ōhama, 177. On Saitō Mokichi's admiration for *Man'yōshū*, see Amy Vladeck Heinrich, *Fragments of Rainbows: The Life and Poetry of Saito Mokichi, 1882–1953* (New York: Columbia University Press, 1983), 97–103.

20. Burton Watson, *The Complete Works of Chuang Tzu* (New York: Columbia University Press, 1968), 130; and Ichikawa Yasushi, Endō Tetsuo, *Sōshi ge, SKT*, vol. 8, 374. For the usage of the pillow word "aogumo no" as an epithet suggestive of white, see *MYS*, 13, 3329, in *Man'yōshū 3, NKBT*, vol. 6, 393; and *Kojiki*, in *Kojiki norito, NKBT*, vol. 1, 151. In the former, "aogumo no" is placed in a parallel relation with "shiragumo" ("white cloud") and "amagumo no" ("heavenly cloud"); and in the latter, "aogumo no" modifies Shirakata no tsu (Bay of Shirakata) in the phrase "aogumo no shirakata no tsu" 青雲之白肩津, where the placename Shirakata literally translates as "white sandbank." See *The Kojiki: Records of Ancient Matters*, trans. Basil Hall Chamberlain (Tokyo: Charles E. Tuttle, 1981), 159–160. All of these points are discussed in detail by Eguchi, *Onmyōryō*, 21–26. For a useful discussion of *qing yun* 青雲 and problems associated with its translation into English, see Edward H. Schafer, "Blue Green Clouds," *Journal of the American Oriental Society* 102: 1 (January–March 1982), 91–92.

21. Eguchi, *Onmyōryō*, 3. For a more extended discussion, see Araki Michio, "Onmyōdō," in *Nihon shisō 2, Iwanami kōza tōyō shisō, vol. 16* (Iwanami shoten, 1989), 315–344.

22. In French, there is the pioneering study on Heian period *on'yōdō* by Bernard Frank, which provides a detailed analysis of directional and other types of taboos. Originally published in 1958, it was recently reissued in a revised edition. See Bernard Frank, *Kata-imi et kata-tagae: Étude sur les interdits de direction à l'époque Heian* (Paris: Collège de France, Institut des Hautes Études Japonaises, 1998). In English, there is Felicia G. Bock's study and translation of Daoist materials, *Classical Learning and Taoist Practices in Early Japan*, with a translation of Books XVI and XX of the Engi-Shiki, Occasional Paper No. 17

(Tempe: Center for Asian Studies, Arizona State University, 1985); and more recently, *Daoism Handbook*, ed. Livia Kohn (Leiden and Boston: E. J. Brill, 2000), with essays and excellent bibliographies on all aspects of Daoism in East Asia, including Masuo Shin'ichirō's overview, "Daoism in Japan," 821–842.

23. *CHJ*, vol. 1, *Ancient Japan*, ed. Delmer M. Brown (Cambridge: Cambridge University Press, 1993). Two studies that can also be mentioned in this regard are Joseph M. Kitagawa, *On Understanding Japanese Religion* (Princeton, NJ: Princeton University Press, 1987); and Gary L. Ebersole, *Ritual Poetry and the Politics of Death in Early Japan* (Princeton, NJ: Princeton University Press, 1989). Extremely informative on Buddhism, Shinto, and indigenous Japanese religious practices, they contain only glancing references to Daoist and yin-yang ideas.

24. Allan G. Grapard, "Religious Practices," *CHJ*, vol. 2, *Heian Japan*, ed. Donald H. Shively and William H. McCullough (Cambridge: Cambridge University Press, 1999), 517–575, esp. 520–523, for a concise explanation of the combinatory theory; and 547–559, for a discussion of yin-yang and Daoist practices. In this chapter, Grapard provides the most thorough discussion to date in English of the important role of Daoist and yin-yang practices both at court and in the shrines and temples of the Heian period.

25. See Kuroda Toshio, "Shinto in the History of Japanese Religion," trans. James C. Dobbins and Suzanne Gay, *MN*, 7: 1 (Winter 1981), 1–21; esp. 5–7.

26. Sakai Tadao, Fukui Fumimasa, "Dōkyō to wa nanika: dōkyō, dōka, dōjutsu, dōshi," in *Dōkyō no sōgōteki kenkyū*, ed. Sakai Tadao (Kokusho kankōkai, 1977; 1981), 429–449, esp. 432–438. As the authors also note, 434–437, the related term *dōka*, which is often interpreted in English as "philosophical Daoism" in contrast to "religious Daoism" (*dōkyō*), was also used by at least the Later Han in the broad sense of Daoism, including meanings connected to immortality, religion, elixirs, and longevity. The shift from *dōka* to *dōkyō* in the fifth century, according to the authors, arose when the need was felt for a term to contrast with Buddhism.

27. For example, there is also the Daoism of the so-called spurious Buddhist sutras that were an important influence in the Kodai period. See Masuo Shin'ichirō, "Nihon kodai no dōkyō juyō to gigi kyōten," in *Dōkyō no rekishi to bunka*, ed. Yamada Toshiaki and Tanaka Fumio (Yūzankaku shuppan, 1998), 297–320.

28. Araki, "Onmyōdō," 316–318; Sakai Tadao, "Nihon ni okeru dōkyō kenkyū," in *Dōkyō no sōgōteki kenkyū*, 419–428, esp. 419–420; and Allan G. Grapard, "Japan's Ignored Cultural Revolution: The Separation of Shinto and Buddhist Divinities in Meiji (*shimbutsu bunri*) and a Case Study: Tōnomine," *HR*, 23: 3 (February 1984), 240–265, esp. 241.

29. Sakai, "Nihon ni okeru dōkyō kenkyū," 421.

30. On these points and for a list of scholarly studies on Daoism in the 1920s and 1930s, see Sakai, "Nihon ni okeru dōkyō kenkyū," 420–423.

31. Michel de Certeau, *The Writing of History*, trans. Tom Conley (New York: Columbia University Press, 1988), 75.

32. One example is the elegantly written historical surveys of George Sansom. Although Sansom accords a good deal of space to discussion of the Chinese contribution to Nara and Heian period culture, generally viewing it in a positive light, the pen that wrote the following statement seems to have been dipped in the inkwell of Tsuda Sōkichi: "Thus the native language had to struggle against a powerful enemy or rival, and its successes testify to the strength of a reaction against Chinese learning, or rather against the pretensions of Chinese scholarship—a reaction that was gathering strength during the ninth century, and reached a climax at its close." In his bibliography, Sansom mentions Tsuda, along with Hori Ichirō, as among the most useful works that he found. See George Sansom, *A History of Japan to 1334* (Stanford, CA: Stanford University Press, 1958), 132.

33. For Fukui's initial review, see Fukui Fumimasa, "Fukunaga Mitsuji cho *Dōkyō to nihon bunka*," *Tōhō shūkyō*, 60 (October 1982), 87–90. The debate continued with Fukunaga Mitsuji, "Kenkyū nōto: Tsuda Sōkichi hakushi to dōkyō: Fukui Fumimasa shi no shohyō *Dōkyō to Nihon bunka* ni kotaete," *Tōhō shūkyō*, 61 (May 1983), 65–79; and Fukui's response, Fukui Fumimasa, "Kenkyū no nōto: Fukunaga kyōju no hanron ni tsuite," *Tōhō shūkyō*, 62 (October 1983), 60–73. For additional assessments of Fukunaga's work on Daoism, see also Satō Akira, "Fukunaga Mitsuji-shi no 'dōkyō' to 'nihon bunka' ni kansuru ichiren no kenkyū wo megutte," *Chugoku tetsugaku ronshū*, 14 (October 1988), 19–34; and Sakai Tadao, "Shohyō: *Dōkyō jiten* tsuketari *Dōkyō no daijiten*," *Shikyū*, 29 (September 1994), 153–162.

34. Fukunaga Mitsuji, *Dōkyō to nihon bunka* (Jinbun shoin, 1982), 7–8.

35. All citations are from *Tsuda Sōkichi zenshū*, 33 vols. (Iwanami shoten, 1963–1966); henceforth, *Zenshū*. For his essay "Tennō kō," see *Nihon jōdaishi no kenkyū*, in *Zenshū*, vol. 3, 474–491; and for the citation, 490. It is cited in Fukui (October 1982), 88.

36. Fukui (October 1982), 88.

37. Tsuda, "Shina shisō to nihon" (maegaki), in *Rekishigaku to rekishi kyōiku*, 195, in *Zenshū*, vol. 20. Cited and discussed in Fukunaga (May 1983), 68–69.

38. Stefan Tanaka, *Japan's Orient: Rendering Pasts into History* (Berkeley: University of California Press, 1993), 45–47; and on Okakura's concept of the orient, see Tanaka, 13.

39. On Tanaka's somewhat different reading of Tsuda's views, see *Japan's Orient*, 278–281.

40. Tsuda, *Nihon no shintō*, 1–2, *Zenshū*, vol. 9; and Fukunaga (May 1983), 70.

41. Tsuda, *Nihon no shintō*, *Zenshū*, vol. 9, 26; and Fukunaga (May 1983), 71.

42. Although writing of the early phase of the Japanese adaptation of Chinese script, David Pollack's description of the process is equally suited to Tsuda's intentions: "when they began for the first time to use the Chinese script, the Japanese were already emptying these handy semiotic markers of their culture-

bound Chinese content, even though the script had been brought to them quite full." David Pollack, *The Fracture of Meaning: Japan's Synthesis of China from the Eighth Through the Eighteenth Centuries* (Princeton, NJ: Princeton University Press, 1986), 27.

43. On the emergence of literary studies as an academic discipline in Meiji Japan, which paralleled the creation of historical studies described by Tanaka, see Michael C. Brownstein's essay, "From *Kokugaku* to *Kokubungaku*: Canon-Formation in the Meiji Period," *Harvard Journal of Asiatic Studies*, 47 (December 1987), 35–60.

44. Tsuda, "Shina shisō to nihon," *Zenshū*, vol. 20, 332; Fukunaga (May 1983), 73.

45. On Hegel's view of China, echoed here by Tsuda, see Praesenjit Duara, *Rescuing History from the Nation: Questioning Narratives of Modern China* (Chicago: University of Chicago Press, 1995), 17–27.

46. Tsuda, "Shina shisō kenkyū no taido," in *Shisō, bungei, nihongo, Zenshū*, vol. 21, 367. Originally published in *Waseda gakuhō* (October 1934); cited in Fukui (October 1983), 65.

47. Tsuda, "Shina shisō kenkyū no taido," *Zenshū*, vol. 21, 353; and Fukui (October 1982), 65.

48. On the late Qing and early twentieth-century critique of Confucianism by Kang Youwei (1858–1927) and other Chinese intellectuals, see Hans Van Ess, "The Old Text/New Text Controversy: Has the 20th Century Got It Wrong?" *T'oung pao*, 80 (1994), 146–170.

49. To cite Hayden White on this point: "It is they [modern historians] who have made narrativity into a value, the presence of which in a discourse having to do with 'real' events signals at once its objectivity, its seriousness, and its realism." Hayden White, *The Content of the Form* (Baltimore and London: Johns Hopkins University Press, 1987), 24.

50. Jean Baudrillard, "La Collection," in *Système des objets* (Paris: Gallimard, 1968), 120–150.

51. De Certeau, *The Writing of History*, 72–73.

Chapter 2

1. Several notable exceptions include Michele Marra's discussion of Daoism in *Taketori monogatari* (*The Tale of the Bamboo Cutter*), in *The Aesthetics of Discontent: Politics and Reclusion in Medieval Japanese Literature* (Honolulu: University of Hawaii Press, 1991); and Arthur H. Thornhill's examination of yin-yang influences in medieval nō treatises, *Six Circles, One Dewdrop: The Religio-Aesthetic World of Komparu Zenchiku* (Princeton, NJ: Princeton University Press, 1993). Remarks on yin-yang and Daoism can also be found in Marian Ury, "The Oe Conversations," *MN*, 48: 3 (Autumn 1993), 359–380; and Susan B. Klein, "Allegories of Desire, Poetry and Eroticism in Ise Monogatari Zuino," *MN*, 52: 4 (Winter 1997), 441–465. Nonliterary approaches include Lee A. Butler on medieval on'yōdō, "The Way of Yin and Yang: A Tradition

Revived, Sold, Adopted," *MN*, 51: 2 (Summer 1996), 189–217; and the remarks on Japanese Daoist practices in Michel Strickmann, *Chinese Magical Medicine*, ed. Bernard Faure (Stanford, CA: Stanford University Press, 2002).

2. Joan R. Piggott, *The Emergence of Japanese Kingship* (Stanford, CA: Stanford University Press, 1997). In addition to Batten and Farris, both cited previously, other studies include Gina L. Barnes, *China, Korea and Japan: The Rise of Civilization in East Asia* (London and New York: Thames & Hudson, 1993); and Charles Holcombe, *The Genesis of East Asia, 221 B.C–A.D. 907* (Honolulu: Association for Asian Studies and University of Hawaii Press, 2001).

3. The vernacular reading and romanization of the graphs 陰陽道 are very inconsistent, with onmyōdō generally preferred to on'yōdō. Although both readings are attested from the medieval period on, the second, according to Yamashita Katsuaki, has greater authority. When used as a technical term in the main text or notes, I follow Yamashita and employ on'yōdō but have retained Onmyōryō for the Yin-Yang Bureau. When citing book titles or articles, I have tried to follow the author's preference when indicated but have otherwise romanized the term as onmyōdō. See Yamashita Katsuaki, *Heian jidai no shūkyō bunka to on'yōdō* (Iwata shoin, 1996), 8 (note 1).

4. For a representative statement of this view, see Endō Katsumi, *Kinsei onmyōdōshi no kenkyū* (Mirai kōbō, 1985), 29; and for an analysis of the Japanese modification of yin-yang thought, see Shimode Sekiyo, "Nihon ni okeru onmyōdō no shiteki isō," *OMS*, vol. 4, *Tokuron*, 1–6. The term on'yōdō, as used by Japanese scholars, is to be distinguished from the pre-Han "school of Yin and Yang" listed in the *Shi ji*, which referred to the *fangshi* ("experts in techniques") who traced their origins back to the mystic philosopher Zou Yan. See A. C. Graham, *Disputers of the Tao: Philosophical Argument in Ancient China* (La Salle, IL: Open Court Publishing, 1989), 328 and 377.

5. Murayama Shūichi, "Kodai nihon no onmyōdō," *OMS*, vol. 1, *Kodai*, 17–31. For an overview in English, see Felicia G. Bock, *Classical Learning and Taoist Practices in Early Japan*, 9–22.

6. Shimode Sekiyo, "Nihon ni okeru onmyōdō no shiteki isō," *OMS*, vol. 4, 5–10.

7. Shinkawa Tokio, "Nihon kodai ni okeru bukkyō to dōkyō," in *Kodai bunka no tenkai to dōkyō*, vol. 2 of *Senshū dōkyō to nihon*, ed. Noguchi Tetsurō and Nakamura Shōhachi (Yūzankaku, 1997), 51–83; Shinkawa, *Nihon kodai no girei to hyōgen: Ajia no naka no seiji bunka* (Yoshikawa kōbunkan, 1999); and Shinkawa, *Dōkyō wo meguru kōbō: Nihon no kun'nō, dōshi no hō wo agamezu*, Ajia bukkusu 13 (Taishūkan shoten, 1999), where he synthesizes his views on Japanese Daoism for a more general readership.

8. On the phenomenon of genzoku (returning priests to secular status), see Hashimoto Masayoshi, "Chokumei genzoku to hōki kanryō no keisei," *OMS*, vol. 1, *Kodai*, 83–119; and Shinkawa, "Nihon kodai ni okeru bukkyō to dōkyō," 78–79. For a brief account, see also Masuo Shin'ichirō, "Nihon kodai no shūkyō bunka to dōkyō," in *Ajia sho-chiiki to dōkyō*, vol. 6 of *Kōza dōkyō*,

ed. Noguchi Testurō, Yusa Noboru, Nozaki Mitsuhiko, and Masuo Shin'ichirō (Yūzankaku, 2001), 259–260.

9. Shinkawa, "Nihon kodai ni okeru bukkyō to dōkyō," 72–73; and also his chapter on Prince Nagaya in *Dōkyō wo meguru kōbō*, 166–233.

10. Shinkawa, "Nihon kodai ni okeru bukkyō to dōkyō," 62–68. The precise meaning of these phrases is debated, but both activities involved the use of spells for healing disease.

11. On the ejection of Daoist-type magic from the state, see Shimode Sekiyo, *Nihon kodai no jingi to dōkyō* (Yoshikawa kōbunkan, 1972), 208.

12. Yasui Kōzan, *Chūgoku shinpi shisō no nihon e no tenkai*, Taishō daigaku sensho 5 (Taishō daigaku shuppanbu, 1983); and for concise overviews, see Nakamura Shōhachi, *Nihon onmyōdōsho no kenkyū* (Kyūko shoin, 1985), 3–24; and Endō Katsumi, *Kinsei onmyōdōshi no kenkyū*, 3–39.

13. For an overview of the weft-texts in relation to portents and prophecy, see Nakamura Shōhachi, "Onmyōdō ni juyō sareta 'isho' ni tsuite," *OMS*, vol. 4, 259–277. One of the earliest studies of the weft-texts in Japan is that of the Edo period nativist Hirata Atsutane (1776–1843). See Yasui Kōzan, "Hirata Atsutane no ishogaku: Shunjū meireki jokō wo chūshin toshite," in *Dōkyō kenkyū ronshū: Dōkyō no shisō to bunka Yoshioka Hakushi kanreki kinen*, ed. Yoshioka Yoshitoyo Hakushi Kanreki Kinen Ronshū Kankōkai (Kokusho kankōkai, 1977), 735–751. Many of the weft-texts have been collected in the six volumes of *Jūshū isho shūsei*, ed. Yasui Kōzan and Nakamura Shōhachi (Meitoku shuppansha, 1973–1983). In English, see also Jack L. Dull, "A Historical Introduction to the Apocryphal (Ch'an-wei) Texts of the Han Dynasty" (PhD diss., University of Washington, 1966).

14. On these points, see Michael Nylan, "The *Chin wen/Ku wen* Controversy in Han," *T'oung pao* 80 (1994), 83–145; Nylan, "A Problematic Model: The Han 'Orthodox Synthesis,' Then and Now," in *Imagining Boundaries: Changing Confucian Doctrines, Texts, and Hermeneutics*, ed. Kai-wing Chow, On-cho Ng, and John B. Henderson (Albany: SUNY Press, 1999), 17–56; and Hans van Ess, "The Old Text/New Text Controversy," cited earlier.

15. Nylan, "The *Chin wen/Ku wen* Controversy in Han," 110–112.

16. Yasui, *Isho to chūgoku no shinpi shisō* (Hirakawa shuppansha, 1988), 144–153, esp. 151; and for a translation of the relevant chapter in *Lüshi chunqiu*, see Knoblock and Riegel, *The Annals of Lü Buwei*, Book 13/2.1, 282–283. In addition to the conquest and generative cycles, Yasui also discusses, pp. 147–148, the existence of four additional arrangements for the five phases from the fourth century *Tso Commentary* (*Zuo zhuan*), the Hong fan chapter of the *Book of Documents* (*Shujing*), the Later Han *Baihu tongyi* of Ban Gu, and the Wuxing zhi section in Ban Gu's *Han shu*. For the arrangement in the *Book of Documents*, see Katō Jōken, *Shokyō* jō, *SKT*, vol. 25, 151. On the *Tso Commentary*'s cycle, see also the remarks of Graham, *Disputers of the Tao*, 325–330.

17. The Han debate over what potency to adopt for its dynasty is discussed in Yasui, *Isho to chūgoku no shinpi shisō*, 154–155; and Dull, "Apocryphal Texts," 21–24.

18. Isabelle Robinet, *Taoism: Growth of a Religion*, trans. Phyllis Brooks (Stanford, CA: Stanford University Press), 47–48.

19. Nakamura Shōhachi, "Onmyōdō ni juyō sareta 'isho' ni tsuite," 265; Yasui, *Isho to chūgoku no shinpi shisō*, 28–34, esp. 33; and Yamashita, *Heian jidai no shūkyō bunka to on'yōdō*, 213–216. On Dong Zhongshu's thought, see also Dull, "Apocryphal Texts," 26–34; and Michael Loewe's chapter, "Imperial Sovereignty: Tung Chung-shu's Contribution and His Predecessors," in *Divination, Mythology and Monarchy in Han China* (Cambridge: Cambridge University Press, 1994), 121–141. For a complete study and reassessment of Dong Zhongshu's thought, see Sarah A. Queen, *From Chronicle to Canon: The Hermeneutics of the Spring and Autumn, According to Tung Chung-shu* (Cambridge and New York: Cambridge University Press, 1996). In her "Introduction" (p. 3), Queen suggests that Dong Zhongshu's role in systematizing yin-yang and five agents has been overstated. For a brief discussion of Dong Zhongshu's theory of portents and an excerpt from his *Chunqiu fanlu* [*Ch'un-ch'iu fan-lu*] (*Deep Significance of the Spring and Autumn Annals*), see *Sources of Chinese Tradition*, vol. 1, ed. William Theodore de Bary et al. (New York: Columbia University Press, 1960), 170–174.

20. Nakamura, "Onmyōdō ni juyō sareta 'isho' ni tsuite," 265–266; Yasui, *Isho to chūgoku no shinpi shisō*, 194–196; and Yamashita, *Heian jidai no shūkyō bunka to on'yōdō*, 213–216.

21. Murayama, *Nihon onmyōdōshi sōsetsu*, 8; for a complete description of *Huainan zi*'s cosmology, see Graham, *Disputers of the Tao*, 330–340; and for a translation and discussion of the key chapter dealing with resonance, see Charles Le Blanc, *Huai-Nan Tzu: Philosophical Synthesis in Early Han Thought, The Idea of Resonance (Kan-Ying), with a Translation and Analysis of Chapter Six* (Hong Kong: Hong Kong University Press, 1985), 110–163.

22. Yasui Kōzan, *Isho to chūgoku no shinpi shisō*, 156–157. On the manipulation of the cycles during Wang Mang's reign, see also Loewe, 57–58 and 91–93. The second theory related to the solar calendar (*santong li*), summarized by Yasui, was proposed by Kuno Shōichi in "Zenkan makkan katoku setsu tonaerareta riyū ni tsuite," jō-ge, *Tōyō gakuhō*, 25: 3 (1938), 418–455 and 567–599. The debate over the color and potency of the Han dynasty and the connection to calendrical reforms are also discussed in Dull, "Apocryphal Texts," 23–25. On the solar calendar, see Nōda Chūryō, *Koyomi: Gijutsu no ue kara jidai no rekishi wo miru* zōhoban, in Nihon rekishi shinsho (Shibundō, 1966, 1980), 62–66.

23. Takeuchi Teruo, *Raiki* jō, *SKT*, vol. 27, 353.

24. D. C. Lau, *Confucius: The Analects (Lun yü)* (London: Penguin Books, 1979), 97; and Yoshida Kenkō, *Rongo*, SKT, vol. 1, 197.

25. Yasui, *Isho to chūgoku no shinpi shisō*, 29–30.

26. Cited in Yasui, *Isho to chūgoku to shinpi shisō*, 33. See also the biography of Dong Zhongshu in the *Han shu*.

27. According to Yasui, Dong Zhongshu himself had a negative view of this prophetic use of portents, but it was advanced by his disciple. See Yasui, *Isho to*

chūgoku no shinpi shisō, 35–36; and Dull, "Apocryphal Texts," 33. Also discussed in Itano Chōhachi, *Jukyō seiritsushi no kenkyū* (Iwanami shoten, 1995), 157–164.

28. Dull, "Apocryphal Texts," 5–6.

29. Anna K. Seidel, "Imperial Treasures and Taoist Sacraments: Taoist Roots in the Apocrypha," in *Tantric and Taoist Studies in Honour of R. A. Stein*, vol. 2, *Melanges chinois et bouddhiques*, no. 21, ed. Michel Strickmann (Brussels: Institut Belge des Hautes Études Chínoises, 1983), 292–300 and 300 for the citation.

30. Nakamura Shōhachi, "Onmyōdō ni juyō sareta 'isho' ni tsuite," 267–272. Nakamura suggests that Wang Mang's use of the fu ming reflects the old-text Confucianism in a deliberate attempt to break from new-text practice, which by his time was firmly identified with the Han dynasty. Yasui, on the other hand, suggests that weft-text confirmations of Wang Mang's legitimacy may have been deliberately removed from the historical record at a later date. Yasui, *Isho to chūgoku no shinpi shisō*, 205–210 and 213–217.

31. Seidel, "Imperial Treasures and Taoist Sacraments," 305.

32. Nakamura, "Onmyōdō ni juyō sareta 'isho' ni tsuite," 274. Nakamura lists the year 267 as one such date, followed by subsequent prohibitions in 444, 457, and 466.

33. Robinet, *Taoism*, 43.

34. Fukunaga, *Dōkyō to nihon bunka*, 46–48; and Benjamin Schwartz, *The World of Thought in Ancient China* (Cambridge, MA: Belknap Press of Harvard University Press, 1985), 376–378.

35. Stephen R. Bokenkamp, *Early Daoist Scriptures* (Berkeley, Los Angeles, and London: University of California Press, 1997), 15–16 and 56.

36. Ibid., 290–292.

37. Yasui, *Isho to chūgoku no shinpi shisō*, 198–200; Yasui Kōzan, *Isho no seiritsu to sono tenkai* (Kokusho kankōkai, 1979), 291–294; and Seidel, 305.

38. On the content of the catalogue, see Yasui, *Chūgoku shinpi shisō no nihon e no tenkai*, 114–115; Fukunaga, *Dōkyō to nihon bunka*, 86–87; Yasui Kōzan and Nakamura Shōhachi, *Isho no kisoteki kenkyū*, 283–286; and the detailed remarks by Matsuda Tomohiro, in *Kodai nihon no dōkyō juyō to sennin* (Iwata shoin, 1999), 260–268. The major study of the catalogue, including a complete listing of its contents by category, is Yajima Genryō, *Nihonkoku genzaisho mokuroku: shūshō to kenkyū* (Kyūko shoin, 1984). For his discussion of the historical reception of the catalogue, see 237–264. For additional remarks on catalogues of Chinese books in Heian Japan, see also Ivo Smits, *The Pursuit of Loneliness: Chinese and Japanese Nature Poetry in Medieval Japan, ca. 1050–1150* (Stuttgart: Franz Steiner Verlag, 1995), 40–44.

39. Emile Benveniste, *Problèmes de linguistique générale* (Paris: Gallimard, 1974) 2: 67–78. Discussed in Paul Ricoeur, *Time and Narrative*, vol. 3 (Chicago: University of Chicago Press, 1985), 104–109.

40. W. G. Aston, *Nihongi: Chronicles of Japan from the Earliest Times to A.D. 697*, vol. 2 (Rutland, Tokyo: Charles E. Tuttle, 1972), 126; and *Nihon shoki ge*, NKBT, vol. 68, 108–109 and 178–179. For a listing and discussion

of all passages in *Nihon shoki* pertaining to the transmission of yin-yang thought to Japan, see Noda Kōsaburō, "Onmyōdō no seiritsu," *OMS*, vol. 1, 65–66. On the recent discovery of mokkan providing evidence of Kwalleuk's existence, see Masuo, "Nihon kodai no shūkyō bunka to dōkyō," 259.

41. Suiko 11/12/5, 12/4/3. *Nihon shoki* ge, 180–186; Aston, *Nihongi*, vol. 2, 127–133.

42. The first doctor of yin-yang was appointed in 689 (Jitō 3) as part of the restructuring of the Kiyomihara Code. Under the Taihō Code (701), the office became the Onmyōryō.

43. Tenchi 4/25. Aston, *Nihongi*, vol. 2, 296; and *Nihon shoki* ge, 376–77.

44. Eguchi, *Onmyōryō*, 70–76.

45. Discussed in Nakamura Shōhachi, "Onmyōdō ni juyō sareta 'isho' ni tsuite," 259; and Yasui, *Chūgoku shinpi shisō no nihon e no tenkai*, 23–42, esp. 38–42. A text of "Kakumei kanmon" can be found in *Kodai seiji shakai shisō*, vol. 8 of *Nihon shisō taikei*, ed. Yamagishi Tokuhei et al. (Iwanami shoten, 1979), 50–58.

46. On these points, see Okada Masayuki, "Kenpō jū shichi jō ni tsuite," in *Ōmi nara chō no kanbungaku* (Nara-ken Tanbaichi-chō: Yōtokusha, 1946), 37–51, esp. 46–50; and Takigawa Masajirō, "Kokka seihō no hajime, Jōgū taishi kenpō jū shichi kajō," in *Ritsuryō kyakushiki no kenkyū* (Kadokawa shoten, 1967), 15–78, esp. 31, 38, 54. A brief review of Okada's and Takigawa Masajirō's theories and their yin-yang principles can be found in Yoshino Hiroko, *Eki to nihon no saishi: shintō e no ichi shiten* (Kyoto: Jinbun shoin, 1984), 62–79, esp. 62–68. For another reading of the Seventeen Articles, see Piggott, *Japanese Kingship*, 85–92.

47. Takeda Sachiko, *Kodai kokka no keisei to ifukusei: hakama to kantōi* (Yoshikawa kōbunkan, 1984), 129–182, esp. 149–150; and Yasui, *Chūgoku shinpi shisō no nihon e no tenkai*, 152. It is my feeling that the arguments of Okada, Takigawa, and Takeda, valuable in their details, continue to be colored by the false opposition, discussed earlier, between a rationalizing Confucianism and a more mystical trend exemplified in the weft-texts. As I will argue in Chapter 3, however, we are dealing rather with a clash between competing symbolic orders (one premised on binary and the other on circular logic), which partly accounts for the peculiar workings of defilement in relation to yin-yang five agents principles.

48. Murayama, *Sōsetsu*, 29–30; and Takigawa, *Ritsuryō kyakushiki no kenkyū*, 94–108.

49. Tsuda, "Tennō kō," in *Zenshū*, 3, 477–482.

50. Piggott, *Japanese Kingship*, 67.

51. Lau, *The Analects*, 63; Yoshida, *Rongo*, *SKT*, vol. 1, 34. For Piggott's discussion, see *Japanese Kingship*, 83.

52. Yoshida Kenkō, *Shiki* 4 (Hassho), *SKT*, vol. 41, 145; and Édouard Chavannes, *Les Mémoires Historiques de Se-Ma Ts'ien*, Tome Troisième (Paris: A. Maisonneuve, 1967), 339–341. Discussed in Yoshino Hiroko, *In'yō gogyō shisō*, 35–37.

53. For a discussion of the astrological symbolism of Great Monad, see Edward H. Schafer, *Pacing the Void: T'ang Approaches to the Stars* (Berkeley: University of California Press, 1977), 42–53. I have adopted many of Schafer's translations for the astrological terms.

54. Ibid., 47.

55. Kusuyama Haruki, *Enanji jō,* "Tenmon," *SKT,* vol. 54, 130–132. Discussed in Yoshino, *In'yō gogyō,* 36–37.

56. See, for example, the essays on the mythological sections of *Nihon shoki* by Kōnoshi Takamitsu, Yonetani Masafumi, and Nishizawa Kazumitsu in *Ronshū: Nihon shoki jindai,* Izumi sensho 82, ed. Kōnoshi Takamitsu (Izumi shoin, 1993), 1–62. In addition to these studies, there is also the detailed analysis of the cosmogonic portions of the chronicles' myth cycles in Hirohata Sukeo, *Bansei ikkei ōchō shisō: Jimmu tennō no densetsu* (Kasama shoin, 1993), 1–62. This topic will be taken up in detail later.

57. Yoshino, *In'yō gogyō shisō,* 105–132; and Murayama, *Sōsetsu,* 35.

58. On the topographical coordinates of Fujiwarakyō and its parallel with Chang-an, see Tamura Yoshinaga, *Asukakyō Fujiwarakyō kōshō* (Kyoto: Sōgeisha, 1965), 32–36; and Murayama, *Sōsetsu,* 41–43.

59. Kusuyama, *Enanji jō,* "Tenmon," *SKT,* vol. 54, 144.

60. As the name for the main ceremonial hall, Shishinden was in use by the time of Kammu when it may have been adopted in emulation of the Tang practice. For a discussion of these points, see Fukunaga, *Dōkyō to nihon bunka,* 13–14 and 233; and Fukunaga's chapter, "Tennō to shikyū to mahito—chūgoku kodai no shintō," in his volume *Dōkyō shisōshi kenkyū* (Iwanami shoten, 1987), 383–411, esp. 390–397. Originally published under the same title in *shisō,* no. 637 (July 1977), 1–19.

61. For a description of the Daigokuden and an idea of its imposing nature, see William H. McCullough and Helen Craig McCullough, *A Tale of Flowering Fortunes,* vol. 2 (Stanford, CA: Stanford University Press, 1980), 836. Its symbolic importance is evident in the lengthy account of its history that closes out *Heike*'s first scroll, following its destruction by fire.

62. Tamura Enchō, "Onmyōryō seiritsu izen," *OMS,* vol. 1, *Kodai,* 35–60. On Suiko's chronicle, see esp. 37–44, which also contains a chart tracking the frequency and type of all natural calamities and portents for sovereigns from Keitai through Temmu.

63. On Daoist-inspired rebellions, see Robinet, *Taoism,* 53–77; and Araki, "Onmyōdō," in *Nihon shisō 2,* 322–323.

64. Yoshino, *In'yō gogyō shisō,* 82–104.

65. Ibid., 85.

66. Kōtoku, Taika 1/12/9. *Nihon shoki ge,* 279. In the branch symbolism for the date of Kōtoku's transfer of the capital from Yamato to Naniwa in Taika 1/12/9 (winter), both the day (*mizunoto*) and the season (winter) corresponded to the agent water. Directionally, Naniwa lay north-northwest of Yamato, corresponding to the twelfth branch *i* 亥 and again to the agent water. Naniwa itself

was also linked to water. See Yoshino, *In'yō gogyō shisō*, 86; and for an analysis of Tenchi's transfer to Omi, 89–90.

67. Tenchi 5/10. *Nihon shoki ge*, 364–365; Aston, *Nihongi*, vol. 2, 285; Yoshino, *In'yō gogyō shisō*, 90.

68. Temmu 1/7/5. *Nihon shoki ge*, 398–399; Aston, *Nihongi*, vol. 2, 313. As Yoshino also points out, *In'yō gogyō shisō*, 96, the narrative here is more likely to reflect the viewpoint of the victorious Temmu. On yin-yang symbolism and portents in *Nihon shoki*, see also Murayama Shūichi's chapter, "*Nihon shoki* ni okeru onmyōdōteki kiji to yōchō shisō no henten," in *Shugen onmyōdō to shaji shiryō* (Hōzōkan, 1997), 91–107.

69. Murayama, *OMS*, vol. 1, 20–21.

70. *Nihon shoki ge*, 312–316; Aston, *Nihongi*, vol. 2, 236–240.

71. Yoshino, *In'yō gogyō shisō*, 87.

72. Yahagi Takeshi, "Temmu-ki to sono shūhen: dōkyō isho ni kanren shite," in *Jōdai bungaku to kanbungaku*, Wakan hikaku bungaku sōsho, 2 (Kyūko shoin, 1986), 123–142; and Murayama, *Sōsetsu*, 36.

73. On Temmu's adoption of red in emulation of Han Gaozu, see Yahagi, "Temmu-ki to sono shūhen: dōkyō isho ni kanren shite," 133; Ihara Akira, "Temmu tennō no aru ichimen," in *Man'yōshū kenkyū*, vol. 9, ed. Gomi Tomohide and Kojima Noriyuki (Hanawa shobō, 1980), 177–203; and Murayama, *Sōsetsu*, 34. On possible Chinese sources for the uses of red color symbolism in Jimmu, Temmu, and other emperors, see also Hirohata, "Shūbuō koji to Jimmu densetsu," in his study *Bansei ikkei ōchō shisō: Jimmu tennō no densetsu*, 300–331. More recently, Shinkawa has suggested that the red symbolism in Temmu's reign may also have been connected to red's magical power to drive out evil spirits. See *Dōkyō wo meguru kōbō*, 56–57. Temmu's deft use of portents and favorable omens is discussed by Tamura in "Onmyōryō seiritsu izen," *OMS*, vol. 1, 49–55.

74. Temmu 4/1/5. *Nihon shoki ge*, 416; Aston, *Nihongi*, vol. 2, 326.

75. In the period of ritsuryō rule, the Onmyōryō produced a 166-scroll calendar for presentation to the tennō once every year. See Yamashita, *Heian jidai no shūkyō bunka to on'yōdō*, 221–226, esp. 221–222.

76. The duties of the Yin-Yang Bureau were originally set forth in the Taihō Administrative Code (701) and are transmitted in what is left of the Yōrō code (begun 718, promulgated 757) as reconstructed from the two commentaries *Ryō no gige* and *Ryō no shūge*. See *Ritsuryō*, ed. Inoue Mitsusada, Seki Akira, Tsuchida Naoshige, and Aoki Kazuo, *Nihon shisō taikei* (Iwanami shoten, 1976; reprinted 1994), 164–165. On the structure of the Onmyōryō, see also Noda Kōsaburō, *OMS*, vol. 1, 65–74; Murayama, *Sōsetsu*, 38–39; and Yasui, *Chūgoku shinpi shisō no nihon e no tenkai*, 115. For the Engi period protocols on the Onmyōryō, see *Engi shiki*, *KST*, vol. 26, 435–444; and for a complete translation into English of the relevant article, see Bock, *Classical Learning and Taoist Practices in Early Japan*, 13–14.

77. For an overview of recent scholarship on Japanese mythology, see Saitō Hideki, "Sōron / Nihon shinwa: sono kōzō to seisei," in *Nihon shinwa: sono*

kōzō to seisei, Nihon bungaku wo yomikaeru 1, ed. Saitō Hideki (Yūseidō, 1995), 2–16.

78. The discussion that follows is based on Tsuda's writings on ancient Japanese mythology in *Nihon koten no kenkyū* (jō, ge), *Zenshū*, vols. 1 and 2; and Hirohata's extensive analysis of Tsuda's theory in his chapter "Tsuda setsu no kentō," in *Jimmu tennō no densetsu*, 1–62.

79. Tsuda, *Nihon koten no kenkyū*, jō, *Zenshū*, vol. 1, 644–645; Hirohata, *Jimmu tennō no densetsu*, 42.

80. Hirohata, *Jimmu tennō no densetsu*, 2 and 8–9.

81. Tsuda, *Nihon koten no kenkyū*, jō, *Zenshū*, vol. 1, 331, 333–334; Hirohata, *Jimmu tennō no densetsu*, 7.

82. Tsuda, *Nihon koten no kenkyū*, jō, *Zenshū*, vol. 1, 645; Hirohata, *Jimmu tennō no densetsu*, 42–43.

83. Tsuda, *Nihon koten no kenkyū*, ge, *Zenshū*, vol. 2, 306; Hirohata, *Jimmu tennō no densetsu*, 43.

84. A stance that would have been in perfect accord with Tsuda's broader view of Japanese history as fundamentally progressive, evolving through a process of change and conflict, expressed most vividly in its national literature. On Tsuda's progressive view of Japanese literature, including *Heike*, see Bialock, "*The Tale of the Heike* as Modern Classic," in *Inventing the Classics*, 172–173.

85. The debate regarding the extent of Tsuda's knowledge of Chinese cosmogony is discussed in Hirohata, *Jimmu tennō no densetsu*, 46–47.

86. These theories and the relevant Chinese citations are discussed in Hirohata, "Nihon koten ni okeru shinsensetsu oyobi chūgoku tenmonsetsu no eikyō," in *Dōkyō kenkyū ronshū: Dōkyō no shisō to bunka Yoshioka Hakushi kanreki kinen*, ed. Yoshioka Yoshitoyo Hakushi Kanreki Kinen Ronshū Kankōkai (Kokusho kankōkai, 1977), 652–653. In English, there is an excellent account in Schafer's *Pacing the Void*, 21–41. On the "Unrestricted Night" theory, see 38.

87. Hirohata, "Nihon koten ni okeru shinsensetsu oyobi chūgoku tenmonsetsu no eikyō," 652. Its description from the *Ku pien i* (Gu bian yi) is rendered by Schafer: "Observing the shape of the sky from below, it is like the canopy of a carriage, and the stars are interlinked like strings of beads." *Pacing the Void*, 35.

88. Hirohata, *Jimmu tennō no densetsu*, 46–47 and 50–51. Enveloping Sky is Schafer's translation. See *Pacing the Void*, 35–36.

89. On the "cosmic sphere" cosmogony, see Schafer, *Pacing the Void*, 26–27, where he cites its description from the *San wu li ji*: "Before there was Heaven and Earth, the aspect of the cosmic sphere (*hun-t'un*) was like that of an egg. A boundless haze began to sprout—an all-encompassing mist budded and proliferated."

90. The huntian theory is discussed in Hirohata, "Nihon koten ni okeru shinsensetsu oyobi chūgoku tenmonsetsu no eikyō," 653; and Hirohata, *Jimmu tennō no densetsu*, 46–47. For its classic expression in *Nihon shoki*'s opening cosmogony, see *Nihon shoki* jō, 76–77; and Aston, *Nihongi*, vol. 1, 1–2.

91. Tsuda, *Nihon koten no kenkyū*, jō, 327; Hirohata, *Jimmu tennō no densetsu*, 50–51.

92. For example, in a comparative analysis of the *Nihon shoki* and *Kojiki* variants of the myths, Kōnoshi Takamitsu contrasts the yin-yang basis of the former with what he construes as the more monistic principle of *Kojiki*'s *musubi* logic. Nowhere is it implied, however, that the latter is an indigenous myth. What we do have are probably contemporaneous and competing systems of myth. See Kōnoshi, "Kiki shinwa ron kara no dakkyaku," in *Ronshū: Nihon shoki shindai*, 1–14; and for another study that examines Chinese conceptions of the sky in the myth portions of the chronicles, see Furui Gen, "Kojiki ni okeru shinwa no tōgō to rinen," in *Tennō no keifu to shinwa* (Hanawa shobō, 1967), 255–357, esp. 264–275.

93. On the connection between the huntian theory and the operations of the Yin-Yang Bureau, see Hirohata, "Nihon koten ni okeru shinsensetsu oyobi chūgoku tenmonsetsu no eikyō," 653–654.

94. Ibid., 654.

95. According to Dennis Twitchett, it was only in 758 that the Imperial Observatory, or Ssu-t'ien t'ai (Sitian tai), came into existence, when it replaced the earlier Han period Imperial Observatory, or T'ai-shih chu (Tai shi zhu), making it considerably later than the structure mentioned in Temmu's chronicle. Dennis Twitchett, *The Writing of Official History Under the T'ang* (Cambridge: Cambridge University Press, 1992), 12.

96. Temmu 4/1/1. *Nihon shoki* ge, 416–417; and Aston, *Nihongi*, vol. 2, 326. For Eguchi's remarks, see *Onmyōryō*, 73–74 and 82. The Sillan king was Zentoku (r. 632–646).

97. Tenpyō Hōji 1/11/9. *Shoku nihongi* 3, *SNKBT*, vol. 14, 137. The only extant manuscript of *Wuxing dayi* (Jp. *Gogyō taigi*) is in Japan. On its reception in the Nara through Edo periods, see Nakamura Shōhachi, *Gogyō taigi*, Chūgoku koten shinsho (Meitoku shuppansha, 1973), 25–48. See also Frank, *Kata-imi et Kata-tagae* 33–34. For a complete text with detailed commentary, see Nakamura Shōhachi, Kotō Tomoko, and Shimizu Hiroko, *Gogyō taigi* jō-ge, Shinpen kanbunsen, shisō rekishi shirīzu 7, 8 (Meiji shoin, 1998).

98. Yōrō 7/10/11. *Shoku nihongi* 2, *SNKBT*, vol. 13, 134–137; and Yasui, *Chūgoku shinpi shisō no nihon e no tenkai*, 113–115. On the use of auspicious omens in making era-name changes, see Murayama, *Sōsetsu*, 54–59.

99. *Shoku nihongi* 1, *SNKBT*, vol. 12, 131.

100. Murayama, *Sōsetsu*, 42.

101. From the *Hoki naiden*, cited in *Shoku nihongi* 1, *SNKBT*, vol. 12, 131 (footnote 14). See also Nakamura, *Gogyō taigi* ge, 237–242, which elaborates some of the underlying symbolic principles of the four spirits.

102. Communication from Stephen Bokenkamp.

103. Yoshida, *Shiki* 4 (hassho), *SKT*, vol. 41, 148–154. Discussed in Hirohata, "Nihon koten ni okeru shinsensetsu oyobi chūgoku tenmonsetsu no eikyō," 661. See also Chavannes, *Les Mémoires Historiques de Se-Ma Ts'ien*, Tome Troisième, 343–356.

Chapter 3

1. Robinet, *Taoism*, 105–113.

2. On these points, see Peter Nickerson, "The Great Petition for Sepulchral Plaints," in Bokenkamp, *Early Daoist Scriptures*, 230–260; and Strickmann, *Chinese Magical Medicine*, 50–57 and chap. 2 passim.

3. Fukunaga, *Dōkyō to nihon bunka*, 92–99.

4. Shimode Sekiyo, *Dōkyō: sono kōdō to shisō*, in Nihonjin no kōdō to shisō 10 (Hyōronsha, 1971), 242.

5. Shimode Sekiyo, *Nihon kodai no dōkyō onmyōdō to jingi* (Yoshikawa kōbunkan, 1997), 1–38, esp. 5–10 and 20–22.

6. On the important distinction between earlier Daoism and official Tang Daoism in the East Asian cultural sphere, see Shinkawa, *Dōkyō wo meguru kōbō*, 251–257.

7. I have found very little scholarship that addresses the issue of defilement and Daoism, but see the exchange on purity, "Jō no mondai: dōkyō to bukkyō," in Fukunaga Mitsuji, Ueda Masaaki, and Ueyama Shunpei, *Dōkyō to kodai no tennōsei: Nihon kodaishi shinkō* (Tokuma shoten, 1978; 1986), 161–175.

8. See Kobayashi Toshio, "Ō, daiō-gō to tennō-gō, sumera mikoto kō," in *Kodai tennōsei no kisoteki kenkyū* (Azekura shoten, 1994), 49–76, esp. 66–71. Kobayashi traces the meaning of sumera to "sube" (to govern, to control) and "sumu" (referring to the "purity" of the sovereign) and rejects, 53–54, any link between the Japanese conception of "ten" (heaven), which is remote and far away like the sea (also "ama"), and the Chinese concept of sovereignty represented by the graphs "tennō." For related views, see Umemura Takashi, "Tennō no koshō," in *Tōchiteki sho kinō to tennōkan, Kōza zenkindai no tennō*, vol. 4 (Aoki shoten, 1995), 9–42; and Saigō Nobutsuna, "Sumera mikoto kō," in *Shinwa to kokka: kodai ronshū*, in Heibonsha sensho 53 (Heibonsha, 1977), 119–144.

9. Shimode Sekiyo, *Shinsen shisō* (Yoshikawa kōbunkan, 1968), 79–107, esp. 86; Tōno Haruyuki, "Tennō-gō no seiritsu nendai ni tsuite," in *Shōsōin bunsho to mokkan no kenkyū* (Hanawa shobō, 1977), 408–409, 418, first published in *Shoku nihongi kenkyū*, vols. 144–145 (1969); and Fukunaga, *Dōkyō shisōshi kenkyū*, 123–155. For a brief overview of the debate, see Masuo, "Nihon kodai no shūkyō bunka to dōkyō," 262–265.

10. Fukunaga, *Dōkyō to nihon bunka*, 14–16; and also his detailed discussion "Dōkyō ni okeru kagami to tsurugi," in *Dōkyō shisōshi kenkyū*, 1–16.

11. Tsuda's dating of the term *tennō* (inscribed on the pedestal of the Hōryūji Buddha) to the year 607 of Suiko's reign is no longer widely accepted. Ōyama Seiichi now proposes a date closer to Tenchi's reign, while Tōno Haruyuki, Masuo Shin'ichirō and others favor a date closer to the Temmu/Jitō courts. See Ōyama Seiichi, *Nagaya ōke mokkan to kinsekibun* (Yoshikawa kōbunkan, 1998), 210; and Tōno Haruyuki, *Shōsōin bunsho to mokkan no kenkyū*, 400, 408.

12. According to Piggott, the reading at Temmu's Kiyomihara included "Taoist teachings on sagehood and immortality," with the *Zhuangzi, Laozi,*

and *Yijing* among the most popular books. Piggott, *The Emergence of Japanese Kingship*, 133.

13. Temmu 14/1/21. *Nihon shoki* ge, 467–468; Aston, *Nihongi*, vol. 2, 364–365.

14. Discussed in Fukunaga, *Dōkyō to nihon bunka*, 7; and Fukunaga, *Dōkyō to kodai no tennōsei: Nihon kodaishi, shinkō*, 25.

15. Takashima Masato, "Shichi hasseki ni okeru nihon no dōkyō," in *Rekishi ni okeru minshū to bunka: Sakai Tadao Sensei koki shukuga kinen ronshū*, ed. Sakai Tadao Sensei Koki Shukuga Kinen no Kai (Kokusho Kankōkai, 1982), 931–932.

16. See Tsuda, *Nihon koten no kenkyū* ge, *Zenshū*, 2, 323; and Naba Toshisada, "Dōkyō no nihonkoku e no ruden ni tsukite (1), *Tōhō shūkyō*, 1: 2 (September 1952), 15–22. Also discussed in Shimode, *Dōkyō: sono kōdō to shisō*, 57.

17. Saimei 2/9. *Nihon shoki* ge, 328–329; Aston, *Nihongi*, vol. 2, 250.

18. Saimei, summer, 1/5/1. *Nihon shoki* ge, 326–328; Aston, *Nihongi*, vol. 2, 248.

19. Kuroita Katsumi presented his original theory in "Waga jōdai ni okeru dōka shisō oyobi dōkyō ni tsuite," *Shirin*, 8: 1 (January 1923), 40–54, esp. 50–51. Essays in support of the theory included Oyanagi Shigeta, "Dōkyō shingon mikkyō to no kankei wo ronjite shugendō ni oyobu," *Tetsugaku zasshi*, 39: 450 (August 1924), 617–645, and 451 (September 1924), 733–746; and Tsumaki Chokuryō, "Nihon ni okeru dōkyō shisō," in *Ryūkoku gakuhō*, 306, 308. The theory was reprised and seriously questioned in the early fifties by Naba Toshisada in two articles, "Dōkyō no nihonkoku e no ruden ni tsukite (1)," *Tōhō shūkyō*, 1: 2 (September 1952), 1–22; and Naba, "Dōkyō no nihonkoku e no ruden ni tsukite (2)," *Tōhō shūkyō*, 1: 4–5 (January 1954), 58–122. For Naba's summary of Kuroita's original theory, see "Dōkyō no nihonkoku e no ruden ni tsukite (1)," 4–8. For Shimode's critique, see "Saimei ki no Futa-tsuki no miya ni tsuite: shoki no dōkyō kiji kō," in *Zoku nihon kodaishi ronshū*, jō, ed. Sakamoto Tarō Hakushi Koki Kinenkai (Yoshikawa Kōbunkan, 1972), 171–196; and Shimode, *Dōkyō: sono kōdō to shisō*, 56–57 and 76–77. Kubo's critique can be found in *Nitchū shūkyō bunka kōshōshi: kōshin shinkō no kenkyū*, jō (Hara shobō, 1980), 679. Takashima replies to the theory's skeptics in "Shichi hasseki ni okeru nihon no dōkyō," 932–936. It is also discussed in Yahagi Takeshi, "Temmu ki to sono shūhen: dōkyō isho ni kanren shite," 127.

20. Nawa, "Dōkyō no nihonkoku e no ruden ni tsuite" (1), 6–7.

21. Shimode, "Saimei ki no Futa-tsuki no miya ni tsuite," 178–184 and 189. Both glosses are cited in *Nihon shoki* ge, 326 (headnote 14).

22. Takashima, "Shichi hasseki ni okeru nihon no dōkyō," 932–933.

23. Kōgyoku 1. *Nihon shoki* ge, 244–245; and Aston, *Nihongi*, vol. 2, 178. For the political background, see Delmar M. Brown, *CHJ*, vol. 1, *Ancient Japan*, 160–161.

24. Takashima, "Shichi hasseki ni okeru nihon no dōkyō," 933–936. Ta-

kashima suggests that when *Nihon shoki* underwent its final stage of editing in the early eighth century, there was already an effort underway to suppress the Daoist elements in favor of Buddhism.

25. Watson, *The Complete Works of Chuang Tzu*, 33; and Akatsuka Kiyoshi, *Sōshi* jō, ZKT, vol. 16, 47–48. For the *Baopu zi* passage, see Nakamura's selected Chinese text in *Hōbokushi*, Chūgoku koten shinsho, 63. On the use of clouds, dragons, tigers, and other creatures as vehicles by immortals, see Fukunaga, *Dōkyō shisōshi kenkyū*, 107–116; and on Daoist toponyms in *Nihon shoki* and *Kojiki* and Kazuraki as an immortal realm, Matsuda, *Kodai nihon no dōkyō*, 193 and 197.

26. MYS, 3, 257, NKBT, vol. 4, 150–152. Observation of Hirohata in "Nihon koten ni okeru shinsensetsu oyobi chūgoku tenmonsetsu no eikyō," 651.

27. Schafer, *Pacing the Void*, 227.

28. Saimei 3/9. *Nihon shoki* ge, 330; Aston, *Nihongi*, vol. 2, 251.

29. Saimei 4/11/3, 5, and 9. *Nihon shoki* ge, 334–335; Aston, *Nihongi*, vol. 2, 255–256.

30. Louguan was associated with the legendary Daoist Yin Xi, who according to tradition received the *Daode jing* from Laozi. The first graph in Louguan is the same used for Arima's tower.

31. Shinkawa, *Dōkyō wo meguru kōbō*, 133.

32. Temmu 14/10/10. *Nihon shoki* ge, 472–473.

33. Shinkawa, *Dōkyō wo meguru kōbō*, 131–133; and on Prince Ōtsu's rebellion, 102–126.

34. Discussed in Ch'a Chu-hwan, *Chōsen no Dōkyō*, trans. Miura Kunio and Nozaki Mitsuhiko (Kyoto: Jinbun shoin, 1990), 291–294.

35. *Nihon shoki* ge, 382, 410; Aston, *Nihongi*, vol. 2, 300 and 320.

36. Ueda, *Dōkyō to kodai no tennōsei*, 69–70; and Ueda, "Wafū shigō to shindaishi," in *Akamatsu Toshihide kyōju taikan kinen kokushi ronshū* (Kyoto: Akamatsu Toshihide Kyōju Taikan Kinen Jigyōkai, 1972), 124.

37. *Shoku nihongi* 1, SNKBT, vol. 12, 240 (supplementary note 4). The editors of *Nihon shoki*, on the other hand, present two theories without reaching a definitive conclusion. According to one theory, the phoneme "nuna" means nu 瓊 + the particle "na" (no), referencing MYS, 13, 3247, where the phrase "nunakawa no soko naru tama" is interpreted to mean the river that produces "hisui" (jade). The same usage in Temmu's posthumous name can be read as an epithet of praise. The second theory reads "nuna" as "numa no naka no ta," or "the field in the midst of the pond," arguing that at the time of *Nihon shoki*'s editing, the phoneme *nuna* was always represented by either the graphic combination 淳中 or 淳名. "Nuna" would have therefore been understood to mean "nu" 沼 + "na" 中. See *Nihon shoki* ge, 108 (headnote 5); and *Man'yōshū* 3, NKBT, vol. 6, 349.

38. Discussed in Yahagi, "Temmu ki to sono shūhen: dōkyō isho ni kanren shite," 129; and Eguchi, *Onmyōryō*, 104–105.

39. Temmu 14/10/4, 14/11/24. *Nihon shoki* ge, 472–473; and Aston, *Nihongi*, vol. 2, 371–373.

40. Discussed in Watanabe Katsuyoshi, *Chinkonsai no kenkyū* (Meicho shuppan, 1994), 224 and 261 (endnote 4) for a list of representative studies expressing this viewpoint.

41. Gary L. Ebersole, *Ritual Poetry and the Politics of Death in Early Japan*, 160.

42. Temmu 8/2; and Jitō 4/1/17. *Nihon shoki* ge, 434 and 500; Aston, *Nihongi*, vol. 2, 341 and 396.

43. Maruyama Yumiko, "Kodai no tennō to byōsha," in *Kosumoroji to shintai*, vol. 8 of *Iwanami kōza: Tennō to ōken wo kangaeru*, ed. Amino Yoshihiko et al. (Iwanami shoten, 2002), 203–226. For the relevant articles in the law codes, see House Codes, Articles 5, 11, 19, and 32, in *Ritsuryō*, 226, 228, 230–231, and 235. These are discussed in Maruyama, "Kodai no tennō to byōsha," 207. On the Confucian-style duty of charitable giving in the *Li ji* and other texts, see Maruyama, 212–215.

44. Wada Atsumu, "Kusurigari to *Honzōshūchū*: Nihon kodai no minkan dōkyō no jittai," *Shirin*, 61: 3 (March 1978), 1–46, esp. 20–22; and Masuo Shin'ichirō, *Man'yō kajin to chūgoku shisō* (Yoshikawa kōbunkan, 1997), 227–236.

45. Wada, "Kusurigari to *Honzōshūchū*, 26–30.

46. Ibid., 7–16.

47. Kashō 3/3/25. *Shoku-nihon kōki*, in *Nihon kōki, Shoku-nihon kōki, Montoku tennō jitsuroku, KST*, vol. 3, 238–239.

48. On these points, see Wada, "Kusurigari to *Honzōshūchū*," 24, 34, 36, and 39–40; and Shimode, *Nihon kodai no jingi to dōkyō*, 223, on Nimmyō's and Junna's ingestion of mineral-based elixirs. The properties of these potent "golden liquid" elixirs (*jinye*) are detailed in scroll four of *Baopu zi*, in the section "Gold and Cinnabar" (*jindan*). *Hōbokushi, Ressenden, Sengaikyō*, vol. 8 of *Chūgoku koten bungaku taikei*, trans. Honda Wataru, Sawada Mizuho, and Kōma Miyoshi (Heibonsha, 1969), 25–28; and Nakamura, *Hōbokushi*, 116–120.

49. Masuo, *Man'yō kajin*, 232–235. In the same study, 89–118, 181–214, 215–227, Masuo provides a detailed look at the Daoist background to Man'yō-period poetic circles, including the ambivalent attitude toward the consumption of elixirs in the poetry of Ōtomo Tabito, *MYS*, 5, 847 and 848, and others.

50. Scroll eleven, "Elixirs," Inner Division of *Baopu zi*, in *Hōbokushi*, vol. 8 of *Chūgoku koten bungaku taikei*, 74–75.

51. Ban Nobutomo, *Ban Nobutomo zenshū*, vol. 2 (Kokusho kankōkai, 1907), 653–654; discussed in Watanabe, *Chinkonsai no kenkyū*, 201–202. For the relevant passages in *Shaku nihongi*, see *Shaku nihongi* (scroll twenty-one), vol. 5 of *ST*, koten chūshaku-hen, 560; and *Shaku nihongi* (scroll fifteen), 373–374, for the commentary on the meaning of Temmu's shōkon rite.

52. Watanabe, *Chinkonsai no kenkyū*, 224–225.

53. Original citation from *Ritsu/Ryō no gige, KST*, vol. 22, 29. Discussed in Watanabe, *Chinkonsai no kenkyū*, 225.

54. *Ryō no shūge: zenpen, KST*, vol. 23, 31. Cited and discussed in Watanabe, *Chinkonsai no kenkyū*, 225–226.

55. Translated by James Legge as, "The body and the animal soul go downwards; and the intelligent spirit on high." *Li Chi: Book of Rites, An Encyclopedia of Ancient Usages, Religious Creeds, and Social Institutions,* vol. 1, trans. James Legge (New York: University Books, 1967), 369; and Takeuchi, *Raiki* chū, *SKT,* vol. 28, 412.

56. Watanabe, *Chinkonsai no kenkyū,* 202–230. On the Chinese background, see also Joseph Needham, *Science and Civilization in China,* in *Chemistry and Chemical Technology,* Part 2, *Spagyrical Discovery and Invention: Magisteries of Gold and Immortality,* vol. 5 (Cambridge: Cambridge University Press, 1974), 85–93.

57. Watanabe, *Chinkonsai no kenkyū,* 226–228. Watanabe rejects this view of the chinkon rite, alleging misunderstanding by the law doctors regarding Chinese attitudes about soul and body. On his view of the chinkon as the preeminent rite for displaying the tennō's ritual authority, see the discussion that follows.

58. Bokenkamp, *Early Daoist Scriptures,* 15–16.

59. Ibid., 41.

60. Ibid., 78.

61. Watanabe, *Chinkonsai no kenkyū,* 230.

62. *Yunji qiqian,* vol. 4 (Beijing: Zhonghua shu ju, 2003), 1737 and 1741. Discussed in Watanabe, *Chinkonsai no kenkyū,* 168–169.

63. *Yunji qiqian,* vol. 5, 2297. Discussed in Yahagi, "Temmu ki to sono shūhen: dōkyō isho ni kanren shite," 135.

64. Jitō 6/2/11. *Nihon shoki* ge, 512–513; Aston, *Nihongi,* vol. 2, 405.

65. On the popularity of the herb *zhu* in Tao Hongjing's district, see Sunayama Minoru, *Zui Tō dōkyō shisōshi kenkyū* (Hirakawa shuppansha, 1990), 114. In addition to the *Yunji qiqian,* references to the vitalizing properties of *zhu* are found in the *Biographies of Immortals* and other texts, some according it the rank of an immortality elixir that extends life for several centuries and in one case for 600 years. See Wada, "Kusurigari to *Honzōshūchū,*" 27 and 32 (note 15); and Shinkawa, *Dōkyō wo meguru kōbō,* 71.

66. Observation of Shinkawa, *Dōkyō wo meguru kōbō,* 75–77.

67. Ibid., 85–86. *Qianjin yaofang* is listed in *Nihonkoku genzaisho mokuroku* and was frequently cited in *Ishinhō* and other Japanese medical texts. Maruyama Yumiko, *Nihon kodai no iryō seido,* Rekishigaku sōsho (Meichō kankōkai, 1998), 287–288.

68. The details of these micro-macrocosmic correspondences are laid out in *Gogyō taigi:* on the liver as the seat of the cloudsoul, vol. 1 (jō), 296; on the liver as the office of military prowess, vol. 2 (ge), 188; and on the liver as the faculty of sight, vol. 2 (ge), 219.

69. *The Lineage of Thearchs* was a two-scroll text that is no longer extant. The relevant passage is cited in *Gogyō taigi* ge, 124. For the *Yijing* passage on the hexagram zhen, see Suzuki, *Ekikyō* ge, vol. 10 of *ZKT,* 437–438.

70. Shinkawa, *Dōkyō wo meguru kōbō,* 89–90.

71. Fukunaga, *Dōkyō to nihon bunka,* 232–233; Murayama, *Sōsetsu,* 95–96; and Grapard, "Religious Practices," *CHJ,* vol. 2, *Heian Japan,* 552, who

gives 860 as the year when the tennō first performed the shihōhai. According to the *Zhengao*, the ingestion of solar and lunar essences prolongs life, cures illnesses, and gives one power over calamities brought by the hundred demons and thousand evils. See Ishii Masako, *Shinkō* [*Zhengao*], Chūgoku koten shinsho zokuhen (Meitoku shuppansha, 1991), 129–130.

72. Temmu, Shuchō 1/1/18, 1/7/28. *Nihon shoki* ge, 474–475 and 480–481; Aston, *Nihongi*, vol. 2, 375 and 379.

73. Miura Kunio, "Dōten fukuchi shōron," *Tōhō shūkyō*, no. 61 (May 1983), 1–23; 15. On the symbolism of the Daoist body, see also Kristopher Schipper, "The Taoist Body," *HR*, 17, 3–4 (February–May 1978), 355–385; and on the symbolic languages bearing on the tennō's body, Grapard, "Religious Practices," *CHJ*, vol. 2, *Heian Japan*, 528–531.

74. The passage, from *Baopu zi*, scroll eight, "Explaining Difficult Matters," continues: "The day and night have twelve hours. From midnight to noon, there are six hours of vitalizing pneumas; and from noon to midnight six hours of moribund pneumas. There is no benefit in ingesting pneumas during periods of moribund pneumas." The practice xingqi ("circulating the breath") was one of three techniques for achieving longevity, the other two being fangzhong and fuyao (ingestion of elixirs). Nakamura, *Hōbokushi*, 74–77; and discussed in Miura, "Dōten fukuchi shōron," 16. On Temmu's grotto hall, see also Yahagi, "Temmu ki to sono shūhen," 136–137.

75. On the literary background to *Kaifūsō*, see Helen Craig McCullough, *Brocade By Night: "Kokin wakashū" and the Court Style in Japanese Classical Poetry* (Stanford, CA: Stanford University Press, 1985), 86–97; Konishi Jin'ichi, *A History of Japanese Literature*, vol. 1, *The Archaic and Ancient Ages*, trans. Aileen Gatten and Nicholas Teele, ed. Earl Miner (Princeton, NJ: Princeton University Press, 1984), 315–323 and 377–392; and Donald Keene, *Seeds in the Heart: Japanese Literature from Earliest Times to the Late Sixteenth Century* (New York: Henry Holt, 1993), 74–78. In Japanese, the classic study by Kojima Noriyuki, editor of the Taikei text, covers many of the Daoist sources. See Kojima, *Jōdai nihon bungaku to chūgoku bungaku* jō, 133–164. For an overview of more recent studies, see Takahashi Yōichirō, "*Kaifūsō* to chūgoku bungaku," *Jōdai bungaku to kanbungaku*, Wakan hikaku bungaku sōsho 2, ed. Wakan hikaku bungakukai (Kyōko shoin, 1986), 191–207, and the same volume, 324–327, for a bibliography of mainly literary studies on the collection.

76. *Kaifūsō, bunka shūreishū, honchō monzui*, NKBT, vol. 69, ed. Kojima Noriyuki (Iwanami shoten, 1964), 99.

77. Hirohata, "Nihon koten ni okeru shinsensetsu oyobi chūgoku tenmonsetsu no eikyō," 646–649, esp. 646–647.

78. *Kaifūsō*, NKBT, vol. 69, 142.

79. On the background to these allusions, in addition to Kojima's headnotes, see Hirohata, "Nihon koten ni okeru shinsensetsu oyobi chūgoku tenmonsetsu no eikyō," 647–648.

80. *Kaifūsō*, NKBT, vol. 69, 94.

81. Ibid., 132; and for a further instance of this parallel, see also *KFS*, 40; *NKBT*, vol. 69, 108.

82. On the Tanabata motif in poetry from Hitomaro through *Kokinshū*, see Inaoka Kōji's chapter in *Hitomaro no hyōgen sekai: kotaika kara shintaika e* (Iwanami shoten, 1991), 217–260 and 248–260 for his discussion of *Kaifūsō*'s Tanabata poems; and in English, McCullough, *Brocade by Night*, 126–128.

83. McCullough, *Brocade by Night*, 89; *Kaifūsō*, *NKBT*, vol. 69, 145–146.

84. On the legendary background to the blue bird allusion, see Kominami Ichirō in his study of the Queen Mother/Star festival mythic complex, *Seiōbo to tanabata denshō* (Heibonsha, 1991), 85–95.

85. *Nihon shoki* jō, 497; Aston, *Nihongi*, vol. 1, 368.

86. Yoshida, *Shiki* 4 (hassho), *SKT*, vol. 41, 146 and 194; and Chavannes, *Les memoires*, vol. 3, 342. Discussed in Eguchi, *Onmyōryō*, 82–83.

87. Eguchi, *Onmyōryō*, 79–84. Eguchi here questions two conventional views regarding the Tanabata complex: (1) that the Tanabata legend was first transmitted to Japan by the Tang embassies, arguing instead for an earlier transmission together with the astrological knowledge associated with Temmu's Yin-Yang Bureau; and (2) that the Tanabata banquet was at first a private fashion during the reign of Temmu that only later became a public court ritual. He surmises that both were connected to Temmu's royal authority from the start.

88. Watase Masatada, "Hitomaro kashū tanabata kagun no kōzō," in *Man'yō*, no. 169 (April 1999), 30–42, esp. 41–42. For an English version of this article, see *Hitomaro kashū hi ryakutaika ron* ge, *Tanabata kagun ron*, in *Watase Masatada chosakushū*, vol. 4 (Ōfū, 2002), 346–376, originally published in *Acta Asiatica*, 77 (July 1999).

89. On Yoshino as a sacred Daoist site during the reigns of Temmu and Jitō, see Ueda Masaaki, *Dōkyō to kodai no tennōsei*, 71–74; and Wada Atsumu, "Jitō jotei no Yoshino miya gyōkō," in *Matsurigoto no tenkai*, ed. Kishi Toshio, *Nihon no kodai* 7 (Chūō kōronsha, 1996), 71–98.

90. *Kaifūsō*, *NKBT*, vol. 69, 163.

91. For the anecdote, see Philippi, *Kojiki*, 357; and *Kojiki norito*, *NKBT*, vol. 1, 313–314. The episode is discussed in Ueda, *Dōkyō to kodai no tennōsei*, 73.

92. On Mount Guye (Ku-she), see Watson, *The Complete Works of Chuang Tzu*, 33.

93. For background to the mulberry goddess legend, see Matsuda, *Kodai nihon no dōkyō juyō to sennin*, 169. My summary of the legend is based on the passage from *Man'yōshū kogi* cited in Matsuda. For the three *Man'yōshū* poems (*MYS*, 3, 385–387), see *Man'yōshū* 1, *NKBT*, vol. 4, 188–190. A translation can be found in Ian Hideo Levy, *The Ten Thousand Leaves: A Translation of the Man'yōshū, Japan's Premier Anthology of Classical Poetry*, vol. 1 (Princeton, NJ: Princeton University Press, 1981), 201–202.

94. See *Wen xuan, or, Selections of Refined Literature / Xiao Tong*, vol. 1, in *Rhapsodies on Metropolises and Capitals*, trans. David R. Knechtges (Princeton, NJ: Princeton University Press, 1982), 367.

95. *Kaifūsō, NKBT*, vol. 69, 101.

96. In the *Wen xuan*'s "Western Capital Rhapsody" (lines 303–308), Wangzi Qiao appears as one of the immortals sought after by Emperor Wu. See Knechtges, *Wen xuan*, 134–135.

97. See Matsuda, *Kodai nihon no dōkyō juyō to sennin*, 165–173, esp. 166–167. The concluding couplet of *KFS* 32 would seem to support this Daoist reading. Unfortunately, the text presents problems, so my translation follows the suggestion of Kojima, who cites the following passage from the *Analects*, vol. 6, 23, as a possible source for the couplet's formal parallelism: "The wise delight in water, the benevolent delight in mountains. The wise are active, the benevolent are still." Yoshida, *Rongo, SKT*, vol. 1, 139; and D. C. Lau, *Confucius: The Analects*, 84.

98. Mommu 3/5/25. *Shoku nihongi* 2, *SNKBT*, vol. 13, 16–17.

99. On Karakuni's background, see Shimode, *Nihon kodai no jingi to dōkyō*, 285; and Shinkawa, "Nihon kodai ni okeru bukkyō to dōkyō," 53.

100. Both of these techniques are listed in the duties assigned to the Jugon no shō (officer of jugon) in Article 14 in the Codes for Curing Illness. See *Ritsuryō*, 425–426.

101. *Seiji yōryaku*, scroll ninety-five, *KST*, vol. 28, 701. Also discussed in Shinkawa, "Nihon kodai ni okeru bukkyō to dōkyō," 54.

102. Nakamura, *Hōbokushi*, 71–72; Honda, *Hōbokushi, Chūgoku koten bungaku taikei*, vol. 8, 45–46; and Shinkawa, "Nihon kodai ni okeru bukkyō to dōkyō," 54.

103. See Hashimoto, "Chokumei genzoku to hōki kanryō no keisei," *OMS*, vol. 1, 83–119, cited previously.

104. *Ritsuryō*, "Sōniryō," Articles 1 and 2, 216.

105. *Ryō no shūge: zenpen, KST*, vol. 23, 215; and Shinkawa, "Nihon kodai ni okeru bukkyō to dōkyō," 52, 81–82, who discusses the Taihō language from the *Ryō no shūge* that comments on the Yōrō's "Sōniryō," Article 2. Based on the definition in *Ryō no shūge*, the lesser or inferior way (*shōdō*) involved the use of a type of amulet for driving out malign spirits (厭符之類). The *Koki* likewise characterizes it as a lesser technique involving the use of amulets for the purpose of driving out spirits. See *Ritsuryō*, 216 (headnote 2); and *Ryō no shūge: zenpen, KST*, vol. 23, 215. The discrepancies between the Taihō and Yōrō Codes have given rise to a long-standing debate that generally divides into two broad camps: (1) scholars like Kuroita Masao and Shimode Sekiyo who view both codes as strictly prohibiting Buddhist priests from using the techniques named 小道巫術 in the Yōrō Code's "Sōniryō" (Article 3) and 道術符禁謂道士法 in *Ryō no shūge*'s gloss on the passage; and (2) those scholars who regard the earlier language of the Taihō Code as permitting their use to Buddhist priests, a theory first presented by Miura Hiroyuki in 1919 and later taken up by Sakamoto Tarō in the 1960s. For proponents of the first theory, it was ritsuryō policy from the start to expel Daoist magical techniques from Buddhist spheres, which included returning violators to lay status. On the debate, see Shimode, *Nihon kodai no jingi to dōkyō*, 207–215; Masuo, *Man'yō kajin*, 106–108. For the earlier studies, see

Kuroita Masao, "Nara jidai no dōjutsu ni tsuite no shiron," originally published in 1936 in *Nara bukkyō to higashi ajia*, in *Ronshū nara bukkyō*, vol. 5, ed. Nakai Shinkō (Yūzankaku, 1995), 185–199; Miura Hiroyuki, "Sōniryō ni kansuru hōsei no kigen," in *Hōseishi no kenkyū* (Iwanami shoten, 1919); and Sakamoto Tarō, "Taihōryō to yōrōryō," in *Nihon shiseki ronshū* jō, ed. Iwahashi Koyata (Yoshikawa kōbunkan, 1969).

106. Nakada Norio, *Nihon ryōiki*, NKBZ, vol. 6, 116–119 and *Miraculous Stories from the Japanese Buddhist Tradition: The Nihon ryōiki of the Monk Kyōkai*, trans. Kyoko Motomochi Nakamura (Cambridge, MA: Harvard University Press, 1973, 140–142.

107. The Kazuraki Kamo had been responsible for interpreting portents (*tenmon*) and making calendars in the Taihō period, a connection suggested in the *Ryōiki* tale by the reference to Ubasoku's descendant, Takakamo no Ason. See Shinkawa, "Nihon kodai ni okeru bukkyō to dōkyō," 56.

108. Taihō 2/12/13. *Shoku nihongi*, vol. 1, 62–63.

109. Temmu 5/8/16; 10/7/30; Shuchō 1/7/3. *Nihon shoki* ge, 424, 448, and 478; Aston, *Nihongi*, vol. 2, 333, 352, and 378. Discussed in Yamamoto Kōji, *Kegare to ōharae*, Heibonsha sensho, 144 (Heibonsha, 1992), 166–168.

110. "Jingi ryō," Article 18, *Ritsuryō*, 215. Discussed by Okada Shōji, "Onmyōdō saishi no seiritsu to tenkai," OMS, vol. 1, 172; and *Shoku nihongi*, vol. 1, 349 (supplementary note 172). The suspension of a portion of the Taihō rite may have been due to the death of Empress Jitō, who had passed away on the twenty-second day of the same month.

111. The text of the incantation is collected in *Engi shiki*, scroll eight, section "Jingi." See *Kōtai shiki/Engi shiki/Kōnin shiki*, KST, vol. 26, 170. In making the present translation, I have used the text collected in *Kojiki norito*, NKBT, vol. 1, 427–428, consulting the version of Donald L. Philippi, *Norito: A Translation of the Ancient Japanese Ritual Prayers*, with a new Preface by Joseph M. Kitagawa (Princeton, NJ: Princeton University Press, 1990), 50.

112. Robinet, *Taoism*, 15.

113. Shimode, *Dōkyō: sono kōdō to shisō*, 206. More recently, Yamamoto has questioned the established view that the ōharae performed the expulsion of defilements (*kegare*). See *Kegare to ōharae*, 162–185.

114. Ordered in 905, selected in 927, and implemented over the course of the tenth century.

115. Shimode, *Dōkyō: sono kōdō to shisō*, 206–209.

116. On this point, see *Ritsuryō*, 539 (supplementary note 18c).

117. "Wooden slips" (*mokkan*) connected to the Medical Bureau, which have been unearthed on the site of the Fujiwara Palace, depict figures intended to cure eye diseases. See Yamashita, *Heian jidai no shūkyō bunka to on'yōdō*, 36–37.

118. *Engi shiki* jō (article on harae), vol. 11 of *ST*, koten-hen, 39; and *Engi shiki* ge, vol. 12 of *ST*, koten-hen, 404–405, which details the Bureau of Carpentry specifications for the swords and effigies. Discussed in Murayama, *Sōsetsu*, 71–72; Okada, "Onmyōdō saishi no seiritsu to tenkai," OMS, vol. 1, 173; Kuroita, "Waga jōdai ni okeru dōka shisō oyobi dōkyō ni tsuite," 44–45.

119. Hayashiya Tatsusaburō, *Chūsei geinōshi no kenkyū: kodai kara no keishō to sōzō* (Iwanami shoten, 1960), 169–170; and more recently, Yukawa Hisamitsu, "Kikajin no fukuzoku girei / sono keisei to igi: Yamato Kawachi Fumi Imiki-be no norito wo megutte," *Jōdai bungaku*, no. 52 (April 1984), 76–88.

120. Shinkawa, *Nihon kodai no girei to hyōgen*, 104–128; Yamashita, "On'yōdō to goshin-ken / hateki-ken," *Heian jidai no shūkyō bunka to on'yōdō*, 171–188; and on the Chinese background, Fukunaga, "Dōkyō ni okeru kagami to tsurugi," in *Dōkyō shisōshi kenkyū*, 1–69.

121. Ōjin, 15. *Nihon shoki* jō, 372–374; Aston, *Nihongi*, 261–263; and *Shoku nihongi* 5, SNKBT, vol. 16, 497–499. According to *Shoku nihongi*, Wang In was a descendant of the Han Emperor Gaozu. Discussed in Hayashiya, *Chūsei geinōshi no kenkyū*, 169.

122. John R. Bentley, *Historiographical Trends in Early Japan*, Japanese Studies, vol. 15 (Lewiston, NY: Edwin Mellen Press, 2002), 86; and *Kogo shūi: tsuketari chūshaku*, vol. 5 of ST, koten-hen, 40.

123. Jitō 2/11/4. *Nihon shoki* ge, 492–493; Aston, *Nihongi*, vol. 2, 388.

124. Shinkawa, *Nihon kodai no girei to hyōgen*, 109 and 112–113.

125. On the shield dance and music as an expression of yin-yang balancing and an aid to driving out evil spirits, see "Record of Music" (*Yue ji*), section 19 of the *Li ji*, in Takeuchi, *Raiki* chū, SKT, vol. 28, 566–567. For further remarks on the Chinese background, see Shinkawa, *Nihon kodai no girei to hyōgen*, 115; and Yamashita, *Heian jidai no shūkyō bunka to on'yōdō*, 180–183, for a discussion of the sword's yin-yang Daoist symbolism in relation to the language of the incantation and the expulsion aspect of the rite.

126. Hayashiya, on the other hand, derives the meaning of "tatafushi" etymologically from the verb "tatakau" (to fight), which in the dance took on the sense of the conquered "laying aside" (*fushi*) their "shields" (*tate*) in an act symbolic of submission to the Yamato court. *Chūsei geinōshi no kenkyū*, 164–167, esp. 167.

127. Temmu, Shuchō 1/6/10. *Nihon shoki* ge, 478–479; Aston, *Nihongi*, vol. 2, 388; discussed in Shinkawa, *Nihon kodai no girei to hyōgen*, 120–124. On magically resonant swords in Daoist texts like *Gujin daojian lu* (*Record of Swords Old and New*) and *Zhengao*, see Fukunaga, 9–12 and 42–48. Kishi Toshio has devoted several detailed studies to engraved swords that have been recovered from kofun (tumuli) and other archeological sites. In these studies, Kishi relates the astrological symbolism and other imagery incised on the swords to a range of Daoist writings, including the *Zhengao*, *Baopu zi*, and weft-texts. See, for example, Kishi's chapter "Kodai tōkenmei to Inariyama tekkenmei," in his study *Nihon kodai funbutsu no kenkyū* (Hirakawa shobō, 1988), 10–41.

128. On the Daoist geomantic balancing of the Shishinden and the Demon's Gate, see Fukunaga, *Dōkyō to nihon bunka*, 233–234.

129. Manju 4/8/25 (1027). *Shōyūki* 8, vol. 8 of *Dai nihon kokiroku*, ed. Shiryō hensanjo (Iwanami shoten, 1976), 22.

130. Shinkawa, *Dōkyō wo meguru kōbō*, 59–66.

131. Temmu 1/5. *Nihon shoki* ge, 385; Aston, *Nihongi*, vol. 2, 304.

132. Tonkō 遁甲, for example, which was manipulated by those questing for immortality, could also refer to calendrical and prognostication techniques employed in military strategy or a commander's avoidance 遁 of specific times 甲—those indicated by the zodiacal branches kinoe ne, kinoe inu, kinoe saru, kinoe uma, kinoe tatsu, and kinoe tora—when leading his forces into battle. In this sense, Temmu's guerrillalike tactic of flight and retreat to Yoshino was an aspect of his mastery of invisibility. On the military aspects of "tonkō," see Takigawa Masajirō, "Ritsuryō to onmyōdō," in *Tōhō shūkyō*, no. 35 (July 1970), 18.

133. Temmu 8/10/11. *Nihon shoki* ge, 438–439; Aston, *Nihongi*, vol. 2, 344.

134. Temmu 10/7/15, 12/7/5, 14/1/21, Shuchō 1/7/28. *Nihon shoki* ge, 448, 458, 468, and 480; Aston, *Nihongi*, vol. 2, 352, 360, 368, and 379.

135. Temmu 14/10/4, Shuchō 1/6/28. *Nihon shoki* ge, 472 and 478; Aston, *Nihongi*, vol. 2, 371 and 378. On these points, see also Shinkawa, *Dōkyō wo meguru kōbō*, 45–54.

136. Discussed in Maruyama, "Kodai no tennō to byōsha," 206.

137. Ibid., 214–215.

138. Exemplified in the austere maxim of performing one's office and rank with "bright, pure, honest sincerity of mind." Mommu 1/8/17. *Shoku nihongi* 1, *SNKBT*, vol. 12, 5. Discussed in Shinkawa, 52–53.

139. Temmu 13/10/1. *Nihon shoki* ge, 464–465. The headnote lists the meaning as unknown, noting only that it was a rank conferred upon naturalized immigrant families.

140. Discussed by Okada, "Onmyōdō saishi no seiritsu to tenkai," *OMS*, vol. 1, 173–174.

141. Working back from medieval pollution practices, Yokoi Kiyoshi has suggested that on'yōdō was overlaid onto older indigenous beliefs centered on taboos (*monoimi*) and defilement. For Yokoi, this fusion was aided by the fact that Chinese yin-yang and five agents theory had already evolved, even before its dissemination to Japan, from its naturalistic and philosophical form into an "occult" or "mystical" practice. Yokoi thereby eliminates the element of yin-yang five agents correlative cosmology as a factor in earlier yin-yang techniques. See Yokoi Kiyoshi, *Chūsei minshū no seikatsu bunka* (Tokyo daigaku shuppankai, 1975), 268–270.

142. On the Heian ideal of the sage king, see Marian Ury, "Chinese Learning and Intellectual Life," *CHJ*, vol. 2, *Heian Japan*, 355–359.

143. As Grapard notes, in the Heian period, the Fujiwara "consolidated its grip over the country in part through the formation and administration of shrine-temple multiplexes to which the imperial house made offerings." See Grapard, "Religious Practices," *CHJ*, vol. 2, *Heian Japan*, 528.

144. Murayama, *Sōsetsu*, 90–91.

145. Noda Kōsaburō, "Onmyōdō no ichisokumen: Heian chūki wo chūshin toshite," *OMS*, vol. 1, 132–138; Yamashita, *Heian jidai no shūkyō bunka to on'yōdō*, 223–227. As Yamashita notes, in the course of the tenth century, the

production of the calendar by the Yin-Yang Bureau ossifies, and by the eleventh century, it has become a monopoly of the Kamo yin-yang house. The new calendars, moreover, no longer noted planetary movements and heavenly phenomena but provided guidance pertaining to taboos (*kinki*). Most important, the function of secretly reporting anomalies to the emperor has devolved from the yin-yang doctor and head of the Onmyōryō to the chancellor (*daijin*) and chamberlain (*kurando*)—in other words, the direct link between the tennō and Yin-Yang Bureau is sundered. In his recent study of mid-Heian "onmyōdō," Shigeta Shini'ichi likewise shows how the official apparatus of the Yin-Yang Bureau and its officers was essentially swallowed up and absorbed by practitioners of on'yōdō. See Shigeta, *Onmyōji to kizoku shakai* (Yoshikawa kōbunkan, 2004), 227–260, esp. 230.

146. On border rituals, see Okada, "Onmyōdō saishi no seiritsu to tenkai," *OMS*, vol. 1, 167; and the same author's *Heian jidai no kokka to saishi* (Zoku gunsho ruijū kanseikai, 1994), 621–669, esp. 633–640. See also Masuo, "Tojō no chinsai to 'ekigami' saigi no tenkai," in *Kankyō to shinsei no kattō*, *Kankyō to shinsei no bunkashi* 3 (ge), ed. Masuo Shin'ichirō et al. (Bensei shuppan, 2003), 316–341, esp. 323–335; and Miyazaki Kenji, "Nara-matsu Heian shoki ni okeru ekigami saishi," in *Nihon kodai no shakai to shūkyō*, Ryūkoku daigaku bukkyō bunka kenkyū sōsho 6, ed. Hino Akira (Kyoto: Ryūkoku daigaku bukkyō bunka kenkyūjo, 1996), 151–168.

147. The best brief account of the tsuina with citation of relevant sources is in Yamanaka Yutaka, *Heianchō no nenchū gyōji*, Hanawa sensho 75 (Hirakawa shobō, 1973), 262–269. On its relation to on'yōdō, see Okada, "Onmyōdō saishi no seiritsu to tenkai," *OMS*, vol. 1, 165–167; Noda, "Onmyōdō no ichisokumen: Heian chūki wo chūshin toshite," *OMS*, vol. 1, 138–142; and the remarks of Masuo, "Tojō no chinsai to 'ekigami' saigi no tenkai," 323–327.

148. Keiun 3/12. *Shoku nihongi* 1, *SNKBT*, vol. 12, 109.

149. *Engi shiki*, scroll sixteen, "Onmyōryō," *KST*, vol. 26, 443; and *Kojiki norito*, *NKBT*, vol. 1, 456–458.

150. Okada, "Onmyōdō saishi no seiritsu to tenkai," *OMS*, vol. 1, 171 and 178–179.

151. This latter point is made by Yamashita, *Heian jidai no shūkyō bunka to on'yōdō*, 36.

152. Ōyama Kyōhei, *Nihon chūsei nōsonshi no kenkyū* (Iwanami shoten, 1978), 390–399; and Murai Shōsuke, *Ajia no naka no chūsei nihon* (Azekura shobō, 1988), 108–112.

153. Hayashiya, *Chūsei geinō shi no kenkyū*, 348.

154. Watanabe, *Chinkonsai*, 149–150.

155. Ibid., 206.

156. Ibid., 352.

157. Ibid., 159–197; esp. 165–167 and 172–184.

158. Ibid., 279–281. Some of the defilements listed by Watanabe include mourning for a deceased emperor (Jōgan 13/11/18, 871), postponement due to

illness within the imperial house (Tenryaku 3, 949), postponement due to death defilement (Jōgan 16/11/16, 874), defilement from the birth of a dog (Genkei 4/11/16, 880), death defilement (Genkei 7/12/24, 883), unspecified defilement (Engi 15/12/19, 915, and Tenryaku 5/11/23, 951), and three defilements from the death of a dog (Enchō 1/11/17, 923, Ōwa 2/11/12, 962, and Kōhō 2/11/10, 965). For a complete chart of all occurrences of the chinkonsai, including postponements and suspensions, supplemented with the relevant citations from *Sandai jitsuroku* and other histories, see Watanabe, 287–301.

159. See Tanaka Taku, "Futatabi yasoshima matsuri ni tsuite: Okada Seiji-shi setsu no hihan," *Shintōshi kenkyū*, 25: 3 (May 1977), 2–23; also discussed in Watanabe, *Chinkonsai*, 351.

160. The Jingonjiki was a Heian period ritual (*kamigoto*) held on the eve of the tsukinami no matsuri in the Sixth Month and Twelfth Month in the Shinkaden of the palace, where the tennō was supposed to worship Amaterasu ōmikami by making an offering of sacred food that he prepared from old grains at a sacred fire. After partaking of this meal, he reposed in the presence of the kami.

161. Discussed in Okada, "Onmyōdō saishi no seiritsu to tenkai," *OMS*, vol. 1, 177.

162. Itō Kiyoshi, *Nihon chūsei no ōken to ken'i* (Kyoto: Shibunkaku shuppan, 1993), 74 and 138–145.

163. Robinet, *Taoism*, 22.

164. Tamura Enchō, "Onmyōryō seiritsu izen," *OMS*, vol. 1, 36.

165. For example, Murayama, *Sōsetsu*, 63–65, discusses the example of the Buddhist priest Dōkyō as an indication of how Buddhist magic was beginning to oppress the Nara court's own monopoly of yin-yang practices. Dōkyō is thought to have made use of a Buddhist or Indian form of yin-yang prognostication (*sukuyōdō*) in his political machinations against the court. On Empress Shōtoku's collusion with Dōkyō to establish a pro-Buddhist policy, see also Kuroda, "Shinto in the History of Japanese Religion," 8; and on the Buddhist technique of prognostication sukuyōdō, see Grapard, "Religious Practices," *CHJ*, vol. 2, 548–549.

166. Endō Katsumi, *Kinsei onmyōdōshi no kenkyū*, 25–26.

167. Murayama, *Sōsetsu*, 26.

168. On prohibited texts in the Nara period, see the two studies by Saeki Arikiyo, "Hasseki no nihon ni okeru kinsho to hanran" and "Ritsuryō jidai no kinsho to kin heikisei," in *Nihon kodai no seiji to shakai* (Yoshikawa kōbunkan, 1970), 145–161 and 162–178.

169. Tenpyō 1/4/3. *Shoku nihongi* 2, *SNKBT*, vol. 13, 210–211. Discussed in Shinkawa, "Nihon kodai ni okeru bukkyō to dōkyō," 71–77; and Masuo, *Man'yō kajin*, 66–67.

170. Shinkawa, *Dōkyō wo meguru kōbō*, 166–233, esp. 199–209.

171. Enryaku 1/3/26. *Shoku nihongi* 5, *SNKBT*, vol. 16, 233–234. The accusation was "enmi," the fabrication of effigies with intent to harm. Discussed in

Yamashita, *Heian jidai no shūkyō bunka to on'yōdō*, 31–32. The fear of magical curses and plots from yin-yang masters lingered on in mid-Heian court society. It is discussed in Shigeta, *Onmyōji to kizoku shakai*, 212–226.

172. Regarding the swing between Daoist/yin-yang and Confucian periods of dominance, see Endō, *Kinsei onmyōdōshi no kenkyū*, 31; and Murayama, *Sōsetsu*, 81–98. As Murayama notes, the increasing frequency of yin-yang rituals at the court during this period also helped to enhance the prestige of the Fujiwara. Although Saga strongly resisted such trends, he was opposed by Fujiwara no Yoshifusa. See Yamashita, *Heian jidai no shūkyō bunka to on'yōdō*, 34–35.

Chapter 4

1. Hayashiya, *Chūsei geinōshi no kenkyū*, 321.

2. On the ways in which *Kojiki* was excerpted, adapted, and incorporated into the commentaries on *Nihon shoki*, see Kōnoshi Takamitsu, "Constructing Imperial Mythology: *Kojiki* and *Nihon shoki*," in *Inventing the Classics*, 56–62.

3. Gomi Fumihiko, *Azumakagami no hōhō: jijitsu to shinwa ni miru chūsei* (Yoshikawa kōbunkan, 1990), 43–48.

4. Ibid., 48–56. For several studies of the regicide motif in *Soga monogatari*, see Takagi Makoto, "Seisei hen'yō suru 'sekai' aruiwa manabon *Soga monogatari*: 'kami' no tanjō to 'tsumi' no hassei," in *Gikeiki, soga monogatari*, Nihon bungaku kenkyū taisei, ed. Murakami Manabu (Kokusho kankōkai, 1993), 357–371; and Takagi, "Hangyaku no gengo/seido no gengo: Manabon *Soga monogatari* no hyōgen to kōzō," *Nagoya daigaku kokugo kokubungaku*, 64 (July 1989), 1–17. Much of the anthropological background for this motif was introduced in a series of essays by Yamaguchi Masao, many collected in his book *Tennōsei no bunka jinruigaku* (Rippū shobō, 1989), 23–91. Yamaguchi's theory will be discussed later.

5. *Kojiki norito*, NKBT, vol. 1, 45–47.

6. On the term "uji," see Piggott, *The Emergence of Japanese Kingship*, 55; and Bentley, *Historiographical Trends in Early Japan*, 5.

7. Introduction to *Kojiki norito*, NKBT, vol. 1, 11; and Philippi's extensive remarks in *Kojiki*, 8–15.

8. For the *Fudoki* variant, see Akimoto Kichirō, *Fudoki*, NKBT, vol. 2, 51–53; also Akimoto Yoshinori, ed., *Hitachi Fudoki*, in *Hitachi no kuni fudoki zen yakuchū*, vol. 1 (Kōdansha, 1979), 56–57; and for a translation into English, Michiko Y. Aoki, in *Records of Wind and Earth: A Translation of Fudoki with Introduction and Commentaries*, Monograph and Occasional Paper Series, no. 53 (Ann Arbor, MI: Association for Asian Studies, 1997), 47–49.

9. Tsugita Masaki, *Kojiki* (chū), Kōdansha gakujutsu bunko 208 (Kōdansha, 1980), 145.

10. White, *The Content of the Form*, 1–25, esp. 9–11.

11. Sūjin, spring, 48/1/10. *Nihon shoki* jō, 250–251; Aston, *Nihongi*, vol. 1, 161.

12. Sūjin, autumn, 60/7/14. *Nihon shoki* jō, 250–251; Aston, *Nihongi*, vol. 1, 162.

13. Fukushima Akiho, *Kiki shinwa densetsu no kenkyū* (Rokkō shuppan, 1988), 307.

14. *Kojiki norito*, NKBT, vol. 1, 207.

15. Ibid., 211.

16. Tsugita Masaki, *Nihon shinwa no kōsei* (Meiji shoin, 1973), 56.

17. Aston, *Nihongi*, vol. 1, 202–203; *Nihon shoki* jō, 301.

18. These points are discussed by Yamashita Hiroaki in "Ikusa monogatari hyōgenshi I: *Kojiki* to *Nihon shoki*," *Nagoya daigaku bungakubu kenkyū ronshū*, 35 (March 1989), 203–204.

19. Aston, *Nihongi*, vol. 1, 204, slightly modified by the author; *Nihon shoki* jō, 302–303.

20. Chinese sources for both the description of Yamato Takeru and the Emishi include *Shi ji, Hou han shu, Wen xuan,* and *Han shu.* A complete commentary on the Chinese sources of *Nihon shoki* was first undertaken by Kawamura Hidene (1723–1792) in his monumental study, *Shoki shikkai,* vols. 1–4 (Kyoto: Rinsen shoten, 1969).

21. *Nihon shoki* jō, 302–303. For Aston's translation of this passage, see *Nihongi*, vol. 1, 203.

22. On the middle-kingdom ideology, see Q. Edward Wang, "History, Space, and Ethnicity: The Chinese Worldview," *Journal of World History*, 10: 2 (1999), 285–305; and Batten, *To the Ends of Japan*, 28–29.

23. From the "debate on fiction." *Genji monogatari* 3, NKBZ, vol. 14, 203–204.

24. *Kojiki norito*, NKBT, vol. 1, 213.

25. Yamaguchi Masao, "Kingship, Theatricality, and Marginal Reality in Japan," in *Text and Context: The Social Anthropology of Tradition,* ed. Ravindra K. Jain (Philadelphia: Institute for the Study of Human Issues, 1977), 151–179; Yamaguchi's major study of this subject is *Tennōsei no bunka jinruigaku,* esp. the chapter "Tennōsei no shinsō kōzō," 159–191. For a discussion and application of Yamaguchi's theory, see Akasaka Norio's chapter "Ōken, kuyō, keibatsu," in *Ijinron josetsu* (Sunagoya shobō, 1985), 134–163, esp. 140–144.

26. Yamaguchi, "Kingship," 157.

27. Ibid., 157–159. The trickster is described by Lévi-Strauss as follows: "Since his mediating function occupies a position halfway between two polar terms, he must retain something of that duality—namely an ambiguous and equivocal character . . . Not only can we account for the ambiguous character of the trickster, but we can also understand another property of mythical figures the world over, namely, that the same god is endowed with contradictory attributes—for instance, to be *good* and *bad* at the same time." Claude Lévi-Strauss, *Structural Anthropology* (New York: Doubleday Anchor, 1967), 224–227. Cited in Yamaguchi, "Kingship," 177 (endnote 8).

28. Ibid., 165.

29. Kōnoshi Takamitsu, *Kojiki no tassei: sono ronri to hōhō* (Tōkyō daigaku shuppankai, 1983), 134–176.

30. Still the definition of the word in the 1992 revised edition of the standard *Iwanami kogo jiten*.

31. Kōnoshi, *Kojiki no tassei*, 173.

32. Nishizawa Kazumitsu, "Ōken to bōryoku: *Kojiki* no mondai toshite," *KK*, 71: 11 (November 1994), 33–45.

33. *Kojiki norito*, NKBT, vol. 1, 149–165; Philippi, *Kojiki*, 163–177.

34. *Kojiki norito*, NKBT, vol. 1, 156–157.

35. *Nihon shoki* jō, 210–211 and 289–291; Aston, *Nihongi*, vol. 1, 129–130 and 194–195. On the tsuchigumo, see Saeki Shin'ichi, *Senjō no seishinshi: bushidō to iu gen'ei*, Enueichikei bukkusu 998 (Nihon hōsō shuppan kyōkai, 2004), 32–37; and on the graphs for tsuchigumo as an index of otherness, see Yamada Naomi, *Igyō no kodai bungaku: kiki fudoki hyōgen ron*, Shintensha kenkyū sōsho (Shintensha, 1993), 22–25. *Kojiki*, on the other hand, represents the sounds "tsuchigumo" by two graphs meaning "earth" and "cloud."

36. *Kojiki norito*, NKBT, vol. 1, 157–159.

37. Saigō Nobutsuna, *Kojiki chūshaku* 3 (Heibonsha, 1988), 65.

38. See Ueda Masaaki, "Kodai geinō no keisei," in *Genshi/kodai*, *Nihon geinōshi* 1 (Hōsei daigaku shuppankyoku, 1981), 15, and on the ancient banquet (*utage*), 204–209; and Hayashiya, *Chūsei geinōshi no kenkyū*, 62–70 and 79–90.

39. René Girard, *Things Hidden Since the Foundation of the World* (London: Athalone Press, 1987), 20.

40. Ibid., 24.

41. In addition to essentializing the moment of violence, Girard asserts that it was Christian myth alone that unmasked the arbitrary nature of the scapegoat system by granting the victim (Christ) self-awareness and thereby allowing him to reveal his own innocence.

42. Translation of Philippi, *Kojiki*, 42; *Kojiki norito*, NKBT, vol. 1, 47.

43. The *fudoki* are generally dated to the eighth century, sometime between the years 715 and 718, but survive only in relatively late manuscripts. The *Hitachi fudoki* is extant in an Edo period manuscript (1677) that transmits a previously abridged version of the text. According to the most widely held theory, the abridged text dates from the late Kamakura period. Another theory, proposed by Shida Jun'ichi, pushes the date for the abridgement back to the Enryaku era (782–806). For the first theory, see Akimoto, *Fudoki,SNKBT*, vol. 16, *NKBT*, vol. 2, 23; and Akimoto, "Fudoki denrai kō," in *Fudoki no kenkyū* (Osaka: Ōsaka Keizai Daigaku, 1963), 313–336. The second theory is discussed in Shida Jun'ichi, "Hitachi fudoki no seiritsu," *Hitachi fudoki to sono shakai* (Yūzankaku, 1974), 103–126. Both theories are reviewed in Akimoto Yoshinori, in *Hitachi fudoki*, vol. 1 of *Hitachi no kuni fudoki zen yakuchū*, 183–185. In English, see Aoki, *Records of Wind and Earth*, 1–4 and 25–33.

44. Akimoto Kichirō, *Fudoki*, NKBT, vol. 2, 35. I have also consulted the text and notes of Akimoto in *Fudoki*, *Hitachi no kuni fudoki zen yakuchū*, vol. 1, 13–14; and Aoki, in *Records of Wind and Earth*, 37.

45. Isomae Jun'ichi, "Myth in Metamorphosis: Ancient and Medieval Versions of the Yamatotakeru Legend," *MN*, 54: 3 (Autumn 1999), 366. I would like to thank Kate Wildman Nakai for bringing this article to my attention.

46. Mitani Kuniaki, "Kodai chimei kigen densetsu no hōhō," *Nihon bungaku*, 30: 10 (October 1981), 41–49.

47. Kamio Tokiko, "Yamato takeru tennō kō: Hitachi no kuni fudoki no chimei kigen denshō," in *Denshō no kosō: rekishi, gunki, shinwa*, ed. Mizuhara Hajime (Ōfūsha, 1991), 182–217, esp. 191–196 and 212. In *Kojiki*, the naming of the land in the lament spoken by the dying Yamato Takeru also suggests the form of a primitive "michiyuki." On this point, see Jacqueline Pigeot's observations on the michiyuki and the *kishu ryūri-tan* motif, in *Michiyuki-Bun: poétique de l'itinéraire dans la litérature du Japan ancien* (Paris: G.-P. Maisonneuve et Larose, 1982), 176–177 and 281–312.

48. On the magical properties of naming the land in the *fudoki* and other ancient texts, see Herbert E. Plutschow, *Chaos and Cosmos: Ritual in Early and Medieval Japanese Literature* (Leiden and New York: E. J. Brill, 1990), 75–77.

49. *Hōgen monogatari Heiji monogatari*, NKBT, vol. 31, 86.

50. Saigō, *Kojiki chūshaku* 3, 299–300.

51. *Hōgen monogatari Heiji monogatari*, NKBT, vol. 31, 175.

52. Tachibana no Hayanari died in Izu province where he had been exiled for rebellion: "Deprived of his original status, he received the status of non-person." Shōwa 9/7/28, *Shoku nihon kōki*. Discussed in Kuroda Toshio, *Nihon chūsei no kokka to shūkyō* (Iwanami shoten, 1975), 377.

53. *Nihon shoki* jō, 134; Aston, *Nihongi*, vol. 1, 64.

54. A representative example is the volume *Hyōhaku to teichaku: teijū shakai e no michi*, vol. 6 of *Nihon minzoku bunka taikei*, ed. Amino Yoshihiko (Shōgakukan, 1984).

55. Orikuchi Shinobu, "Gorotsuki no hanashi," in *Orikuchi Shinobu zenshū*, vol. 3, *Kodai kenkyū minzokugaku hen* 2, ed. Orikuchi hakushi kinenkai (Chūō kōronsha, 1955), 22–46.

56. Ibid., 23–24.

57. Marilyn Ivy, *Discourses of the Vanishing: Modernity, Phantasm, Japan* (Chicago: University of Chicago Press, 1995), 20–23.

58. Carlo Ginzburg, *The Night Battles: Witchcraft and Agrarian Cults in the Sixteenth and Seventeenth Centuries*, trans. John and Anne Tedeschi (New York: Penguin Books, 1985), 1–13; and *Deciphering the Witches' Sabbath*, trans. Raymond Rosenthal (New York: Pantheon Books, 1989). Covering a vast range of material from Europe to China, this latter work discloses interesting parallels between the rituals of the Italian *benandanti* and the Chinese Da Nuo festival (Jp. *tsuina*). See *Ecstasies*, 102–106.

59. Deleuze, *A Thousand Plateaus*, 237.

60. Gilles Deleuze, *Difference and Repetition*, trans. Paul Patton (London: Athlone Press, 1994), 36–37.

61. Deleuze, *A Thousand Plateaus*, 239–252 and 351–423. Deleuze's terminology sets up a series of paranomastic echoings that assonate with the term

"nomos": "anomalous" (*anomal*), "abnormal" (*anormal*), "animal" (*animal*). *A Thousand Plateaus*, 243–244.

62. Yōrō 1/5/2. *Shoku nihongi* 2, SNKBT, vol. 13, 28–29.

63. Wayne Farris, *Heavenly Warriors: The Evolution of Japan's Military, 500–1300* (Cambridge, MA, and London: Harvard University Press, 1992), 123.

64. On the term "hyakusho," see Amino Yoshihiko, "Emperor, Rice, and Commoners," *Multicultural Japan: Paleolithic to Postmodern*, ed. Donald Denoon et al., with an introduction by Gavan McCormack (Cambridge, England: Cambridge University Press, 1996), 235–244, esp. 236–237; and on Gyōki's followers, Gorai Shigeru, *Yūgyō to junrei* (Kadokawa shoten, 1989), 22.

65. Yōrō 1/4/3. *Shoku nihongi* 2, 26–27.

66. Janet Goodwin, *Alms and Vagabonds: Buddhist Temples and Popular Patronage in Japan* (Honolulu: University of Hawaii Press, 1994), 23–24. On the government's persecution of Gyōki, see also Nakai Shinkō, *Gyōki to kodai bukkyō* (Nagata bunshōdō, 1991), 10–15.

67. Tenpyō 2/9/29. *Shoku nihongi* 2, SNKBT, vol. 13, 238–239. Discussed in Masuo, *Man'yō kajin*, 110.

68. On the market as a site of vagabondage and government surveillance, see Saigō Nobutsuna, "Ichi to utagaki," in *Kodai no koe: uta odori ichi kotoba shinwa* (Asahi shinbunsha, 1985), 6–26.

69. Deleuze, *A Thousand Plateaus*, 246.

70. Yanagita divided shamans (*miko*) into sedentary shrine miko and itinerant mediumistic agents called *kuchiyose*. Ishimoda Shō viewed sedentary shamanism connected to agricultural communities as primary in Japan, whereas Ueda Masaaki regards both sedentary and ambulatory forms as coexisting, with the latter appearing only after the collapse of the ritsuryō state. Yanagita Kunio, "Miko kō," in *Teihon Yanagita Kunio shū*, vol. 9 (Chikuma shobō, 1962), 221–301, esp. 223–224 and 296–301. First published in 1913–1914.; Ishimoda Shō, "Kokka to Gyōki to jinmin," in *Nihon kodai kokka ron*, dai 1-bu: *Kanryōsei to hō no mondai* (Iwanami shoten, 1973), 90–101 and 109; and Ueda Masaaki, "Nihon kodai no ōken to fugeki," in *Higashi ajia ni okeru shakai to shūzoku*, *Higashi ajia sekai ni okeru nihon kodaishi kōza*, vol. 10, ed. Inoue Mitsusada et al. (Gakuseisha, 1984), 248–275, esp. 253–255; and by the same author, "Kodai geinō no keisei," 193–204. In English, see the opening chapter in Carmen Blacker, *The Catalpa Bow: A Study of Shamanistic Practices in Japan* (London: Unwin Hyman Limited, 1975, 1986), 19–33.

71. Nishimiya Hideki, "Nihon kodai 'fugeki' ron: sono jittai wo chūshin ni," in *Kodaishi ronshū* ge, ed. Naoki Kōjirō sensei koki kinenkai (Hanawa shobō, 1989), 203–233, esp. 211–212.

72. *Ryō no shūge: kōhen*, KST, vol. 24, 966–967. Cited and discussed in Gorai, *Yugyō to junrei*, 22–23.

73. Nishimiya, "Fugeki ron," 205.

74. Tenpyō-Shōhō 4/8/17. *Shoku nihongi* 3, SNKBT, vol. 14, 125; Nishimiya, "Fugeki ron," 206.

75. Nishimiya, "Fugeki ron," 215.

76. Ibid., 213.

77. Ninju 2/2/25. *Nihon montoku tennō jitsuroku*, KST, vol. 3, 38. Cited and discussed by Higuchi Kunio, *Chūsei no shijitsu to denshō* (Tōkyōdō shuppan, 1991), 20–21.

78. Nishimiya, "Fugeki ron," 207.

79. Sakamoto Tarō, *Rikkokushi*, Nihon rekishi sōsho 27 (Yoshikawa kōbunkan, 1970), 267.

80. Jōgan 5/5/20. *Sandai jitsuroku*, KST, vol. 4, 112–113; and *Kundoku nihon sandai jitsuroku*, ed. Takeda Yūkichi and Satō Kenzō (Kyoto: Rinsen shoten, 1986), 201.

81. The posthumous title Sudō Tennō that was conferred upon Prince Sawara in 799 carried the Daoist meaning of one who "reverenced the way."

82. On the excisions, see Sakamoto, *Rikkokushi*, 206–209; and on the Sawara incident, McCullough, CHJ, vol. 2, Heian Japan, 21–24. Each of the spirits to be placated was also a victim of political infighting and factional disputes. On the political background, see McCullough, CHJ, vol. 2, Heian Japan, 33–34 and 36–37; and Neil McMullin, "On Placating the Gods and Pacifying the Populace: The Case of the Gion *Goryō* Cult," HR, 27: 3 (February 1986), 270–293, esp. 288–289.

83. McMullin, "The Case of the Gion *Goryō* Cult," 289–290.

84. On the disasters rumored to be the result of Sudō's spirit, see McCullough, CHJ, vol. 2, Heian Japan, 24.

85. In an edict issued in response to natural calamities in 721, for example, Empress Genshō expressed misgivings about the virtuousness of her governance. See Yōrō 5/2/17. *Shoku nihongi* 2, SNKBT, vol. 13, 88–91. Discussed in Yamashita, *Heian jidai no shūkyō bunka to on'yōdō*, 34.

86. In the seventh year of Jōgan (865), the Yin-Yang Bureau issued instructions advising Seiwa Tennō to transfer first to the Daijōkan before proceeding from the tōgū to the dairi to avoid a prohibited direction. This is the earliest evidence for the observance of directional taboos (*kata-tagae*), although the term itself doesn't actually appear until the mid-Heian period. Murayama, *Sōsetsu*, 91; and Frank, *Kata-imi et kata-tagae: Étude sur les interdits de direction à l'époque Heian*, 59–120, esp. 88–89.

87. On the background and origins of goryō shinkō, see Kikuchi Kyōko, "Goryō shinkō no seiritsu to tenkai: shinkō no shijisō wo chūshin toshite," in *Goryō shinkō*, Minshū shūkyōshi sōsho 5, ed. Shibata Minoru (Yūzankaku, 1984), 37–61.

88. Kuroda Toshio, "Chinkon no keifu: kokka to shūkyō wo meguru tenbyō," in *Kenmitsu bukkyō to shaji seiryoku*, vol. 3 of *Kuroda Toshio chosakushū* (Hōzōkan, 1995), 131–140.

89. For an excellent discussion of the historical background to these events, including an analysis of *Dōken shōnin meidoki*, see Robert Borgen, *Sugawara no Michizane and the Early Heian Court* (Cambridge, MA: Harvard University Press, 1986), 310–320. *Dōken shōnin meidoki* is also important as one of the earliest texts to depict a tennō (in this case, Daigo) suffering the torments of hell,

further evidence that the ritual apparatus for managing violence was no longer under the control of the tennō's authority.

90. "Dōken shōnin meidoki," in *Kokusho itsubun*, ed. Wada Hidematsu (Mori katsumi, 1940), 31–37, with reference to Kawane Yoshiyasu's *kundoku*, in "Ōdo shisō to jinbutsu shūgō," *Kodai* 4, *Iwanami kōza nihon rekishi* 4, ed. Asao Naohiro (Iwanami shoten, 1976), 284–285. For historical background and an analysis of *Dōken shōnin meidoki*, see Borgen, *Sugawara no Michizane and the Early Heian Court*, 310–320.

91. For background and discussion, see Toda Yoshimi, *Nihon chūsei no min-shū to ryōshu* (Azekura shobō, 1994), 56–61.

92. Tengyō 8/7/27. *Honchō seiki, KST*, vol. 9, 109.

93. Tengyō 8/8/2. *Rihō ōki*, cited in Kawane, "Ōdo shisō," 283–284; and Sakurai Yoshirō, "Chūsei ni okeru hyōhaku to yūgei," in *Chūsei* 1, *Iwanami kōza nihon rekishi* 5 (Iwanami shoten, 1975), 311–312. The *Rihō ōki* was the journal of Emperor Daigo's fourth son, Prince Shigeaki.

94. Sakurai, "Chūsei ni okeru hyōhaku to yūgei," 312. Also discussed by Kawane, "Ōdō shisō," 286–290; and Toda, *Nihon chūsei no minshū to ryōshu*, 59–61.

95. Kōgyoku 2/10/12. *Nihon shoki* ge, 248–249; Aston, *Nihongi*, vol. 2, 181. From the reigns of Kōgyoku to Tenchi, the principal mediators of such songs were shamans, a role later taken over by priest-type figures. See Masuo, *Man'yō kajin*, 49–53. On the Chinese background to prophetic songs, including their connection to yin-yang five agents theory and omen-lore, see Oyanagi Shigeta, "Dōyō, toshin, kyōhi," in *Tōyō shisō no kenkyū* (Morikita shoten, 1943), 412–429; and on *Nihon shoki*'s "wazauta," Masuda Katsumi, "Shiyō no shisō: wazauta gogen kō," in *Kodai kayō*, Nihon bungaku kenkyū shiryō sōsho (Yūseidō, 1985), 221–230.

96. Translation of Judith Rabinovich, *Shōmonki: The Story of Masakado's Rebellion* (Tokyo: Monumenta Nipponica at Sophia University, 1986), 111–112.

97. Borgen, *Sugawara no Michizane and the Early Heian Court*, 314–315.

98. The *Gyokuyō* entries are Jishō 4/9/3 and Jishō 4/12/4. Cited in Higuchi, *Chūsei no shijitsu to denshō*, 3–4.

Chapter 5

1. *Gukanshō, NKBT*, vol. 8, 129 and 319–323; and Delmar Brown, Ichirō Ishida, *The Future and the Past: A Translation and Study of the Gukanshō, an Interpretive History of Japan Written in 1219* (Berkeley, Los Angeles, and London: University of California Press, 1979), 20 and 199–203.

2. M. M. Bakhtin, *The Dialogic Imagination: Four Essays by M. M. Bakhtin*, ed. Michael Holquist, trans. Caryl Emerson and Michael Holquist (Austin: University of Texas Press, 1981), 61.

3. For an example, see H. Mack Horton's discussion of language registers in medieval *renga* in *Song in an Age of Discord: "The Journal of Sōchō" and Poetic Life in Late Medieval Japan* (Stanford, CA: Stanford University Press, 2002).

4. Murai Osamu, *Moji no yokuatsu: kokugaku ideorogī no seiritsu*, 17–22. On print culture and orality, see Walter J. Ong's chapter "Print, Space, and Closure," in *Orality and Literacy: The Technologizing of the Word* (London and New York: Routledge, 1982), 117–138.

5. From the Preface by Naoki Sakai, in Motoori Norinaga, *Kojiki-den, Book 1*, Cornell East Asia Series 87, trans. Ann Wehmeyer (Ithaca, NY: East Asia Program), xii–xvi and xiv. See also Pollack's chapter, "Script and Scripture: The *Kojiki* and the Problem of Writing," where he traces the phonocentric bias back to the moment when Japan first adopted the Chinese writing system. *The Fracture of Meaning*, 14–54, esp. 53.

6. Shinada Yoshikazu, "*Man'yōshū*: The Invention of a National Poetry Anthology," in *Inventing the Classics*, 31–50; and Bialock, "Nation and Epic: *The Tale of the Heike* as Modern Classic," 170–176.

7. For a critique of "kotodama" as something unique to the Japanese language, see Roy Andrew Miller, "The 'Spirit' of the Japanese Language," *The Journal of Japanese Studies*, 3: 2 (Summer 1977), 251–298. According Plutschow, *Chaos and Cosmos*, 75, kotodama has "an ontic quality, being not only a sound that mediates between the mind and the object, but one that participates in the power or life of that object." It is also possible to understand kotodama as having what the linguist John Austin has characterized as illocutionary force, where the factive power of the magic formula derives from the ceremonial or ritual occasion that sets such utterance apart from ordinary speech. See Oswald Ducrot and Tsvetan Todorov, *Encyclopedic Dictionary of the Sciences of Language*, trans. Catherine Porter (Baltimore, MD: Johns Hopkins University Press, 1979), 342–345.

8. On this point, see Eguchi, *Onmyōryō*, 33.

9. Jesse M. Gellrich, *Discourse and Dominion in the Fourteenth Century: Oral Contexts of Writing in Philosophy, Politics, and Poetry* (Princeton, NJ: Princeton University Press, 1995), 123–191, esp. 148–149, and 39–78, which examines the role of voice (*vox*) in the theologian Ockham.

10. *Kojiki*, Shinchō nihon koten shūsei, ed. Nishimiya Kazutami (Shinchōsha, 1979), 288–289.

11. *Kojiki to norito*, NKBT, vol. 1, 47; and Philippi, *Kojiki*, 43.

12. As Watanabe Minoru suggests, Yasumaro's problem was not merely one of adapting Japanese sounds to Chinese graphs but related to the process of rendering any oral speech in writing, not specifically Chinese writing. The "verbosity" (*jōman*) of oral discourse overflows the container of written form. See Watanabe, *Heianchō bunshōshi* (Tōkyō daigaku shuppankai, 1981), 3–5. I would like to thank David Lurie for calling my attention to this article. For additional remarks on *Kojiki*'s Preface, see also Pollack, *The Fracture of Meaning*, 40–46.

13. *Kogo shūi: tsuketari chūshaku*, vol. 5 of *ST*, koten-hen, 3. In making the translation, I have also consulted *Kogo shūi Takahashi ujibumi*, Shinsen nihon koten bunko 4, ed. Yasuda Naomichi and Akimoto Yoshinori (Gendai Shinchōsha, 1976), 22–23. For a complete translation in English, see Bentley, *Historiographical Trends in Early Japanese Literature*, 67–92; and *Kogoshūi:*

Gleanings from Ancient Stories, trans. Genchi Katō and Hikoshirō Hoshino (London: Curzon Press, 1926).

14. Iida Isamu has argued that Hironari viewed the authority of his uji's ancient traditions (*furukotobumi*) as deriving precisely from their oral as opposed to their written character. In asserting the orthodoxy of his uji's oral traditions, he was consciously opposing the official discourse of *Nihon shoki*. Iida Isamu, "*Kogoshūi* no ronri to hōhō: 'kogo' to wa nan de atta ka," *Kodai bungaku*, 37 (March 1998), 14–23.

15. Fujii Sadakazu, *Monogatari bungaku seiritsushi: furukoto, katari, monogatari* (Tōkyō daigaku shuppankai, 1987), 116–133, esp. 119–120 and 133. As the vernacular gloss for a large number of Chinese compounds signifying old records, matters, oral traditions, and the like, the term "furukoto" remains conjectural. The term was extensively deployed by Motoori Norinaga in *Kojiki-den*, who was largely responsible for establishing it as a familiar usage, and is attested at least as early as *Nihon shoki shiki*, which appears to date from the latter half of the Heian period. For a discussion and review of the scholarship on furukoto, see Fujii, *Monogatari bungaku seiritsushi*, 111–115.

16. Ibid., 631–632.

17. *Kogo shūi*, vol. 5 of *ST*, koten-hen, 52.

18. Sheldon Lu, *From Historicity to Fictionality: The Chinese Poetics of Narrative* (Stanford, CA: Stanford University Press, 1994), 42–46 and 172 (note 6). In Japan, the term *xiao shuo* is recorded as early as the Nara period. On its occurrences and implications, see Fujii Sadakazu, *Nihon shōsetsu genshi* (Taishūkan shoten, 1995), 226–239.

19. Fujii, *Monogatari bungaku seiritsushi*, 685.

20. Mitani Eiichi, *Monogatari bungakushi ron* (Yūseidō, 1952), 10–23.

21. Saitō Hideki, "Sekkanki no nihongi kyōju," *Kokubungaku kaishaku to kanshō*, 64: 3 (March 1999), 35.

22. *Genji monogatari* 3, NKBZ, vol. 14, 203–204.

23. On the ironic and parodic potential of this passage, see Norma Field, *The Splendor of Longing in the Tale of Genji* (Princeton, NJ: Princeton University Press, 1987), 132–133.

24. *Sanshi* (*Three Histories*) consisted of *Shi ji*, *Han shu*, and *Hou han shu*. *Wujing* (*Five Classics*) consisted of the *Shujing*, *Shijing*, *Yijing*, *Chunqiu* (*The Spring Autumn Annals*), and *Li ji*. Earlier, in "Hahakigi" ("The Broom Tree"), the adjective *michimichishi* is used to describe *Sanshi wujing*. See *Genji monogatari* 1, NKBZ, vol. 12, 165. The ironic overtones of the word are discussed by Takahashi Tōru, in "In'yō toshite no junkyo: *Genji monogatari* ni okeru bungaku to rekishi," in *Heian jidai no rekishi to bungaku*, bungaku-hen, ed. Yamanaka Yutaka (Yoshikawa kōbunkan, 1981), 86.

25. For an overview of the debate, see Takahashi, "In'yō toshite no junkyo," 85–89; and Takahashi, "*Genji monogatari*: monogatari bungaku wo koete," 392–406, esp. 403–406.

26. Takahashi, "In'yō toshite no junkyo," 87–89.

27. On *Genji*'s oral reception, see Tamagami Takuya's classic study "*Genji*

monogatari no dokusha: monogatari ondokuron," *Joshidai bungaku*, Kokubun-hen, no. 7 (January 1955), 1–15.

28. I use the term *heteroglossia* (literally "other language") in the sense of "other-voiced" and therefore somewhat differently from Bakhtin, who uses it contrastively with *polyglossia* (his term for the awareness of foreign languages) to designate the differentiation of linguistic registers inside a single language that characterizes novelistic discourse. See Bakhtin, *The Dialogic Imagination*, 67.

29. Even a work like *Genji*, to the extent that its writing was in the hands of second-echelon nobility excluded from the highest positions in the hierarchy, can be characterized as a narrative peripheral to the center. On the social status of those who wrote monogatari, see Haruo Shirane, *The Bridge of Dreams: A Poetics of "The Tale of Genji"* (Stanford, CA: Stanford University Press, 1987), 4–16.

30. In *Gunsho Ruijū*, teiō bu, vol. 3, 425. On the role of praise in official court history, see Sakamoto Tarō, *Shūshi to shigaku*, in *Sakamoto Tarō chosakushū* 5 (Yoshikawa kōbunkan, 1989), 25–28.

31. In his book *Listening for the Text: On the Uses of the Past* (Baltimore, MD: Johns Hopkins University Press, 1990), Brian Stock defines a textual community "as a group that arises somewhere in the interstices between the imposition of the written word and the articulation of a certain type of a social organization. It is an interpretative community, but also a social entity," 150. The importance of oral communication at court well into the Heian period is indicated by Yoshikawa Shinji, who shows that it was not until about the middle of the tenth century that the government switched from predominantly oral to written modes of communication in the daily conduct of business. Yoshikawa Shinji, "Mōshibumi sashibumi kō: daijōkan seimu taikei no saihensei ni tsuite," *Nihonshi kenkyū*, 382 (June 1994), 1–36.

32. The lectures are discussed in Sakamoto, *Shūshi to shigaku*, 32–34; Kigoshi Takashi, "Nihongi kōen to Nihongi kyōen waka," *Kokubungaku kaishaku to kanshō*, 64: 3 (March 1999), 26–32; and Hashimoto Fumio, "Nihongi kyōen waka," in *Ōchō wakashi no kenkyū* (Kasama shoin, 1972), 14–27. Kigoshi lists the dates of only five readings (812, 843, 878, 904, 936), excluding the first (721) on the grounds that it was the inaugural presentation of the newly completed *Nihon shoki* and the last (965) due to the lack of information about its circumstances. In the Heian period, the lectures gradually evolved into the body of textual interpretation known collectively as "chūsei nihongi," represented by such commentaries as *Nihongi shiki* and *Shaku nihongi*. For some recent studies, see Kōnoshi Takamitsu, "Kodai tennō shinwa no kansei," *KK*, 73: 11 (November 1996), 1–14; Tsuda Hiroyuki, "Gishozukuri no waza: *Sendai kuji hongi* no hōhō to Nihongi-kō," *Nihon bungaku*, 43: 11 (November 1994), 80–83; and Tsuda, "Nihongi-kō to *Sendai kuji hongi*," *Nihon bungaku*, 46: 10 (October 1997), 62–67.

33. Saitō Hideki, "*Sendai kuji hongi* no gensetsu to seisei: hensei suru kodai shinwa ron no tame ni," *Kodai bungaku*, 37 (March 1998), 2–13. The discussion that follows is largely a summary of Saitō's views.

34. There is considerable disagreement on the antiquity of *Sendai kuji hongi*, including one school of scholarship that views the text as a "fraud." Bentley

takes up many of these issues and makes a case, on linguistic grounds, for *Kuji*'s antiquity. The present argument, following Saitō and Watanabe, relies on ritual as opposed to linguistic factors for its dating. For Bentley's discussion, see *Historiographical Trends in Early Japan*, 31–35.

35. Watanabe, "Kodai no chinkonsai," in *Chinkonsai no kenkyū*, 121–158, esp. 149–150.

36. Passages on the origin of the chinkon rite, in both the third and seventh scrolls, emphasize rites aimed at relieving pain and bringing the dead back to life. *Sendai kuji hongi*, vol. 8 of *ST*, koten-hen, scroll three, 41, and scroll seven, 124. See also Ōno Shichizō, *Sendai kuji hongi: kunchū* (Hihyōsha, 2001), 61 and 171–172.

37. Saitō, "*Sendai kuji hongi* no gensetsu to seisei," 9–10.

38. Watanabe, *Chinkonsai no kenkyū*, 150.

39. For a discussion and critique of this line of *Genji* commentary, see Doris Bargen, *A Woman's Weapon: Spirit Possession in the Tale of Genji* (Honolulu: University of Hawaii Press, 1997), 48 and 70–74.

40. Translation based on text in *Ise monogatari zenshaku*, ed. Morimoto Shigeru (Daigakudō shoten, 1973), 347. I have also consulted the version in *Taketori monogatari, Ise monogatari, Yamato monogatari, Heichū monogatari*, *NKBZ*, vol. 8, 201–202.

41. Okada, *Figures of Resistance: Language, Poetry, and Narrating in The Tale of Genji and Other Mid-Heian Texts* (Durham, NC, and London: Duke University Press, 1991), 140–141. As Okada also notes: "the possibility arises that the *Ise* compilers, through the opening gesture [of the first two episodes], wanted the reader-listener to recall both the Heijō site and the reign of Heizei to suggest an underside (*ura*) to a Fujiwara power structure based on the Heian capital."

42. Two modern commentaries that provide a selection of glosses from the main lines of ancient commentary are Takeoka Masao, *Ise monogatari zenhyōshaku: kochūshaku jūisshu shūsei* (Yūbun shoin, 1987), 1157–1174; and Yura Takuo, *Ise monogatari kōsetsu ge* (Meiji shoin, 1986), 183–191.

43. Yura, *Ise monogatari kōsetsu ge*, 187.

44. Ibid., 188; Takeoka, *Ise monogatari zenhyōshaku*, 1162.

45. Takeoka, *Ise monogatari zenhyōshaku*, 1166–1167.

46. Tokuda Kazuo, *Egatari to monogatari* (Heibonsha, 1990), 162–163.

47. As discussed earlier, the ascription of placenames by sacred figures was a way of reinscribing and thereby controlling the powers believed to inhere in specific sites. See Kamio, "Yamato Takeru tennō-kō," 183–191; and in the same volume, Komaki Satoshi, "Henkan sōchi toshite no chimei," 97–123. For additional comments on *meisho*, see Okada, *Figures of Resistance*, 308 (note 59); and on their ritual uses, especially the dangerous powers associated with the *meisho* of peripheral regions like Michinoku, Edward Kamens, *Utamakura, Allusion, and Intertextuality in Traditional Japanese Poetry* (New Haven, CT, and London: Yale University Press, 1997), 179, 218.

48. *Ōkagami*, NKBT, vol. 21, 35. I have also consulted the text and commentary in *Ōkagami zenhyōshaku*, jōge, ed. Hosaka Hiroshi (Gakutōsha, 1979); and the complete English translation and study of Helen McCullough, *Ōkagami: The Great Mirror, Fujiwara Michinaga (966–1027) and His Times* (Princeton, NJ: Princeton University Press, 1980). For the present passage, see *Ōkagami zenhyōshaku* jō, 15; and McCullough, *The Great Mirror*, 65.

49. *Imakagami Masukagami, KST*, vol. 21 (ge), 5–6.

50. *Mizukagami Ōkagami, KST*, vol. 21 (jō), 4–9.

51. *Ōkagami*, 59; *Ōkagami zenhyōshaku* jō, 174; McCullough, *The Great Mirror*, 86.

52. *Konjaku*, 15: 22, in *Konjaku monogatari shū* 3, NKBT, vol. 24, 374–375. On the background to the bodaikō, see Komine Kazuaki, "Ōkagami no katari: Bodaikō no hikari to kage," *Bungaku*, 55: 10, 132; and Matsumura Hiroji, *Rekishi monogatari: Eiga monogatari to shikyō*, Hanawa sensho 16 (Hanawa shobō, 1961), 89–92.

53. Michinaga is compared to a "wheel-turning sacred monarch" (*tenrin jōō*) and later to a Buddha or Buddha's provisional form (*hotoke, gonja*); see *Ōkagami*, 215 and 240; McCullough, *The Great Mirror*, 191, 208. In *Ōkagami*'s parodic narrative, however, the implications of being reborn as a Buddha are problematic because Yotsugi also relates a story about a dog that achieves rebirth as a Buddha. *Ōkagami*, 271; McCullough, *The Great Mirror*, 231.

54. *Ōkagami*, 248; McCullough, *The Great Mirror*, 213.

55. Seishi died on the twenty-fourth day of the Third Month. Discussed in Komine, "Ōkagami no katari," 134.

56. *Ōkagami*, 156; McCullough, *The Great Mirror*, 156.

57. Anecdotes about *onryō* or "vengeful spirits" include the deaths attributed to Michizane's spirit following his death in exile, *Ōkagami*, 75–79; McCullough, *The Great Mirror*, 99–102; Asahira's quarrel with Fujiwara no Koremasa and the destruction wrought against the latter's family by Asahira's vengeful spirit, *Ōkagami*, 141–142; McCullough, *The Great Mirror*, 145–146; and the vengeful spirits of Fujiwara no Kanemichi's eldest son Akimitsu and the latter's daughter, *Ōkagami*, 155–156; McCullough, *The Great Mirror*, 155–156.

58. On the dialogical form of *Ōkagami*, see Kawabata Yoshiaki, "Meguri monogatari tsuya monogatari," in *Setsuwa no gensetsu kōshō shoshō baitai*," ed. Honda Giken et al. (Benseisha, 1991), 205–225; and Abe Yasurō, "Taiwa yōshiki sakuhin josetsu: *Monjiki* wo megurite," *Nihon bungaku* (June 1988), 54–70.

59. On this point, see Kawakita Noboru, "Ōkagami no hihansei ni tsuite no ichikōsatsu," in *Ōkagami Eiga monogatari*, Nihon bungaku kenkyū taisei, ed. Kawakita Noboru (Kokusho kankōkai, 1988), 49. A division of roles that is approximate, since Yotsugi's narrative includes humorous anecdote and rumor, some of it critical of the Fujiwara.

60. Fukuda Akira views the link between genealogical recitation and placation tales as a synchronic feature of Japanese historical discourse. He documents

this in several studies of Ōsō sawaki (*The Tea-talk Chronicle of the Ōshū Sōma*, 1667), which preserves in written form the house history of the Sōma clan. According to its Preface, the chronicle was based on the oral traditions transmitted by a performer of ritual prayers (*kitōshi*) who resided in a small hut at the residence of the Sōma house's principal retainers, the Komegomezawa, and had charge of the transmission and preservation of the Sōma's house history, including its genealogies (*keizu*). As descendants of those who helped to defeat Masakado, the Komegomezawa also had a prerogative right over rituals aimed at placating Masakado. Hence, the dual role of Yotsugi (and his interlocutors) as genealogical lore-master and storyteller of the dispossessed. Fukuda Akira, *Gunki monogatari to minkan denshō*, Minzoku mingei sōsho 66 (Iwasaki bijutsu sha, 1972), 207–224; and his chapter "Sōma no yotsugi," in *Chūsei katarimono bungei: sono keifu to tenkai* (Miyai shoten, 1981), 20–45. The full text of *Ōsō sawaki* can be found in *Fukushima ken shiryō shūsei*, vol. 5, ed. Tago Kenkichi (Fukushima ken shiryō shūsei kankōkai, 1953), 427–540. For the Preface, see 427–429.

61. *Ōkagami*, 102; McCullough, *The Great Mirror*, 119.

62. Discussed by Matsumoto Haruhisa, *Ōkagami no kōsei* (Ōfūsha, 1969), 119–120.

63. Several well-known medieval examples are the *otogi zōshi* "Sannin bōshi" and "Shichinin bikuni" ("The Seven Nuns"). For a translation of the latter, see Margaret Helen Childs, *Rethinking Sorrow: Revelatory Tales of Late Medieval Japan* (Ann Arbor: Center for Japanese Studies, University of Michigan, 1991), 91–106.

64. *Ōkagami*, 255; McCullough, *The Great Mirror*, 218.

65. A famous example is "Kitano tsuya monogatari no koto" ("The Matter of the All-night Story-telling Vigil"), found in the thirty-fifth scroll of *Taiheiki*, in which three interlocutors representing opposing Confucian and Buddhist viewpoints take turns debating the cause of the political disorder in Japan. See *Taiheiki* 3, NKBT, vol. 36, 316–335. It is discussed by Otsu Yūichi, "*Taiheiki* to iu han 'monogatari' han 'rekishi,'" in *Heike monogatari Taiheiki*, Nihon bungaku kenkyū ronbun shūsei 14, ed. Saeki Shin'ichi and Koakimoto Dan (Wakakusa shobō, 1999), 191–205.

66. *Ōkagami*, 171; McCullough, *The Great Mirror*, 164–165.

67. Komine, "Ōkagami no katari," 127.

68. McCullough, *A Tale of Flowering Fortunes*, vol. 1, 138; and *Eiga monogatari zenchūshaku*, vol. 1, ed. Matsumura Hiroji, Nihon koten hyōshaku zenchūshaku sōsho (Kadokawa shoten, 1969), 327.

69. *Ōkagami*, 175–177; McCullough, *The Great Mirror*, 167–169.

70. *Ōkagami*, 39; McCullough, *The Great Mirror*, 68.

71. See McCullough, *Ōkagami*, 41–48; another view, discussed by Kawakita Noboru, is that the author of *Ōkagami* was male and thus deliberately tried to distance himself from the tradition of women's literature exemplified in *Genji*. Kawakita Noboru, "Rekishi monogatari dono yōni kakawatte iru ka," in *Ka-*

tari, hyōgen, kotoba, vol. 6 of *Genji monogatari kōza*, ed. Imai Takuji (Bensei-sha, 1992), 148–149.

72. Parody and laughter are not unique, of course, to *Ōkagami*, as numerous examples in *The Tale of Genji*, *A Tale of Flowering Fortunes*, and Sei Shōnagon's *The Pillow Book* attest. But by the time of *Ōkagami* (twelfth century), the parodic is being invested with ritual connotations pertaining to the conduct of royal authority that exceeds this earlier usage. For an interesting look at the humorous anecdote in *The Pillow Book*, see Mitamura Masako's discussion of laughter, in *Makura no sōshi: hyōgen to kōzō* (Yūseidō, 1994), 95–117.

73. On the early use of the term *rekishi monogatari*, see Matsumura, *Rekishi monogatari: Eiga monogatari to shikyō*, 6–17. Prior to Meiji, literary compilations like *Gunsho ichiran* (1802) classified *Ōkagami*, *Eiga monogatari*, *Heike monogatari*, *Taiheiki*, and other works under the category of *zatsushi*, a classical Chinese term for a variety of unofficial histories.

74. The term *yotsugi* had established itself as a general term by the late Heian to early medieval period. See Sakamoto, *Shūshi to shigaku*, 49.

75. Matsumura, *Rekishi monogatari*, 19.

76. For a detailed narratological analysis of this narrative mode, see Abe, "Taiwa yōshiki sakuhin ron josetsu," 54–60.

77. McCullough, *The Great Mirror*, 14–17, for example, echoing a well-established body of criticism, viewed *Ōkagami* as an advance in literary technique over *Eiga monogatari*.

78. Discussed in Monica Otter, *Inventiones: Fiction and Referentiality in Twelfth-Century English Historical Writing* (Chapel Hill, NC: University of North Carolina Press, 1996), 1–19, esp. 16. See also the important essay of Franz Bäuml, "Varieties and Consequences of Medieval Literacy and Illiteracy," *Speculum*, 55 (1980), 237–265, esp. 252–258.

79. Peter Haidu, "Repetition: Modern Reflections on Medieval Aesthetics," *Modern Language Notes*, 92 (1977), 875–887. According to Haidu, the language of fiction constituted "a turning away . . . from its proper function as redeemed language: that of focusing on God's message as inscribed both in Scripture and in the created world."

80. *Sandai jitsuroku*, KST, vol. 4, 2; Takeda, *Kundoku nihon sandai jitsuroku*, 3; and Sakamoto, *Rikkokushi*, 313.

81. On *Ōkagami* narrators and those of other mirror works as immortals, see Nakamae Masashi, "Koten bungaku no naka no shinsen sekai to dōkyō," in *Ajia sho-chiiki to dōkyō*, vol. 6 of *Kōza dōkyō*, 296–297.

82. The use of felicitous or congratulatory language is discussed by Matsumura, *Rekishi monogatari*, 45–46.

83. *Ōkagami*, 58; *Ōkagami zenhyōshaku*, jō, 165; McCullough, *The Great Mirror*, 85.

84. Ibid.

85. *Ōkagami*, 59; *Ōkagami zenhyōshaku*, jō, 170; McCullough, *The Great Mirror*, 85.

86. Ōkagami, 59; Ōkagami zenhyōshaku, jō, 171; McCullough, The Great Mirror, 86.

87. Ōkagami, 59; Ōkagami zenhyōshaku, jō, 174; McCullough, The Great Mirror, 86.

88. The primary sense of "utate" is to the extreme intensity or degree of a particular state. From this basic meaning, it comes to mean "unusual" or "strange."

89. Hayashiya Tatsusaburō, Rekishi, Kyōto, geinō, Asahi sensho 114 (Asahi shinbunsha, 1978), 30–32.

90. Aston, Nihongi, vol. 1, 220; Nihon shoki jō, 324–326.

91. Hayashiya, Rekishi, Kyōto, 33–34; and Chūsei geinōshi no kenkyū, 321. Hayashiya explicitly distinguishes the congratulatory function of the mirror as symbol for ancient Japanese history from the Chinese figure of the mirror as history that illuminates through exemplary patterns.

92. On Ōkagami's relationship to Shi ji and Chinese historical narrative, see Matsumura, Rekishi monogatari, 94–98; and Matsumoto, Ōkagami no kōsei, 90–109. The most detailed study on the relationship of Ōkagami to its Chinese sources is Mekada Sakuo's Ōkagami ron: kanbungei sakkaken ni okeru seiji hihan no keifu (Kasama shoin, 1979).

93. Cited in McCullough, The Great Mirror, 3.

94. Hanada Taneshige, Jōgan seiyō jō, SKT, vol. 95, 119.

95. Fujimura Tsukuru, "Ōkagami ni kansuru kōsatsu," KK (May 1924), 47–68.

96. For a complete list and discussion of these critical anecdotes, see Matsumoto, Ōkagami no kōsei, 110–132. The theory of Ōkagami's "critical spirit" and the early essays of Fujimura, Fujisawa, and others are reviewed by Kawakita, in "Ōkagami hihansei ni tsuite no ichikōsatsu," 49. Fujisawa Kesao's critique of the theory was first published in Kokugakuin zasshi (December 1941). On the presence of a "popular voice" critical of the tennō in Ōkagami, see Sakamoto, Shūshi to shigaku, 53.

97. Ōkagami, 282; McCullough, The Great Mirror, 239.

98. Discussed by Kawakita, "Ōkagami hihansei ni tsuite no ichikōsatsu," 56–57.

99. Ōkagami, 241; Ōkagami zenhyōshaku, jō, 390; McCullough, The Great Mirror, 209.

100. See Hirata Toshiharu's chapter, "Ōkagami no seiritsu to sakusha," in his Heian jidai no kenkyū (San'itsu shobō, 1943), 428–475, esp. 432–453; and Sakamoto, Shūshi to shigaku, 52. For an overview of recent debates on Ōkagami's authorship, see Kanō Shigefumi, Rekishi monogatari no shisō, Kyōto joshi daigaku kenkyū sōkan 19 (Kyōto joshi daigaku, 1992), 9–12. As Kanō observes, the later dating of Ōkagami to the period of rule by retired sovereigns is now largely accepted, although there continues to be wide variance of opinion regarding its authorship, with some supporting a Minamoto author and others a Fujiwara opposed to Michinaga.

101. McCullough, The Great Mirror, 53–58.

102. Matsumoto, *Ōkagami no kōsei*, 75–77.

103. Hosaka, *Ōkagami zenhyōshaku*, jō, 173.

104. On "tamashii," see McCullough, *The Great Mirror*, 43–53. As Mc-Cullough points out, the locus classicus and earliest appearance of the related term *yamatodamashii* occurs in *The Tale of Genji*, where it is contrasted with Chinese learning (*zae*): "After all, learning [*zae*] is what provides a firm foundation for the exercise of Japanese wit [*yamatodamashii*]." Cited from *The Tale of Genji*, vol. 1, trans. Royall Tyler (New York: Viking Press, 2001), 381.

105. *Ōkagami*, 78–81; McCullough, *The Great Mirror*, 102–105.

106. McCullough, *The Great Mirror*, 34 and 45.

107. *Ōkagami*, 81.

108. For a detailed discussion of this subject, see Tsukahara Tetsuo, "Ōkagami kōsei to kai-i genshō," in *Ōkagami Eiga monogatari*, 97–112. As Tsukahara observes, in *Ōkagami* the tennō's authority extends not only to the human world but to supernatural prodigies as well, 102.

109. *Ōkagami*, 217; McCullough, *The Great Mirror*, 194.

110. On the ritual implications of the okina figure, see Dōmoto Masaki, *Nō, kyōgen no gei*, Nihon no gei shirīzu (Tokyo shoseki, 1983), 24–27 and 112–116; Hayashiya, *Chūsei geinōshi no kenkyū*, 351–354; and for his link with exorcism, see Nose Asaji, *Nōgaku genryū kō* (Iwanami shoten, 1938), 176–188. In English, see Jin'ichi Konishi's remarks in *A History of Japanese Literature*, vol. 3, ed. Earl Miner and trans. Aileen Gatten and Mark Harbison (Princeton, NJ: Princeton University Press, 1991), 521.

111. Orikuchi Shinobu, "Okina no hassei," in *Orikuchi Shinobu zenshū*, vol. 2, *Kodai kenkyū minzokugaku hen* 1, ed. Orikuchi hakushi kinen kodai kenkyūjo (Chūō kōronsha, 1965), 371–415; and "Nōgaku ni okeru waki no igi: 'okina no hassei' no shūhen," in *Orikuchi Shinobu zenshū*, vol. 3, *Kodai kenkyū minzokugaku hen* 2, ed. Orikuchi hakushi kinen kodai kenkyūjo (Chūō kōronsha, 1966), 241–249.

112. On *dengaku*, see Benito Ortolani, *The Japanese Theatre: From Shamanistic Ritual to Contemporary Pluralism* (Leiden and New York: E. J. Brill, 1990), 72–74, and on the comic tradition behind *sangaku*, 61–64.

113. See Moriya Takeshi, *Chūsei geinō no genzō* (Tankōsha, 1985), 63–65. The dengaku phenomenon will be taken up at length in chap. 7.

114. See Abe Yasurō, "'Oko no monogatari toshite no *Heike monogatari*: Tsuzumi hōgan Tomoyasu to 'warai' no geinō," in *Heike monogatari kenkyū to hihyō*, ed. Yamashita Hiroaki (Yūseidō, 1996), 121–143; and Gomi Fumihiko, "Heike monogatari no monogatariteki kūkan–kyūtei shakai," in Kajihara Masaaki, ed., *Heike monogatari: shudai kōsō hyōgen*, Gunki bungaku kenkyū sōsho 6 (Kyūko shoin, 1998), 219–237.

115. *Ōkagami*, 150; McCullough, *The Great Mirror*, 151.

116. Abe, "'Oko no monogatari,'" 140–141.

117. McCullough (slightly modified by author), *The Great Mirror*, 179; *Ōkagami*, 195.

Chapter 6

1. Michel de Certeau, *Heterologies: Discourse on the Other*, Theory and History of Literature, vol. 17, trans. Brian Massumi, with a Foreword by Wlad Godzich (Minneapolis and London: University of Minnesota Press, 1986), 67–79, esp. 68.

2. Ibid., 75.

3. On the literary and historiographical construction of barbarian others in classical Chinese, see Paul Rouzer, "The Textual Life of Savages," in *Articulated Ladies: Gender and the Male Community in Early Chinese Texts* (Cambridge, MA: Harvard University Asia Center, 2001), 157–200.

4. *Man'yōshū* 1, *NKBT*, vol. 4, 149. In my translations of this and several of the other *Man'yōshū* poems that follow, I have consulted Ian Hideo Levy's *The Ten Thousand Leaves* and adopted some of his phrasing. For the present poem, see Levy, *The Ten Thousand Leaves*, 156. Many of the poems cited in this section are discussed in Ōkubo Hiroyuki, "Hina ni aru koto: Tabito ni okeru jikū ishiki," *KK*, 72: 2 (February 1995), 1–16.

5. *Man'yōshū* 2, *NKBT*, vol. 5, 153.

6. Levy, *The Ten Thousand Leaves*, 158, with the last two lines (*ku*) modified by the author; *Man'yōshū* 1, *NKBT*, vol. 4, 150–151.

7. The rhetorical strategy of casting Yamato as refined middle-kingdom (or *zhonghua* 中華) and its hinterlands as populated by "barbarians" (Yi-Ti 夷狄) is nicely expressed in *Nihon shoki*, where Emperor Kenzō's governance is characterized in the phrase, "Court (*miyako*) and hinterland (*hina*) looked up to him," where court is represented by the graph hau 華 (glossed as miyako) and hinterland by the graph yi 夷 (glossed as hina). See Aston, vol. 1, 390; *Nihon shoki*, jō, 522. Discussed in Narusawa Akira's chapter "'Hendo shōkoku' no nihon–chūseiteki seikaizō no ichisokumen ni tsuite," in *Seiji no kotoba–imi no rekishi wo megutte*, Heibonsha sensho 84 (Heibonsha, 1984), 106.

8. *Man'yōshū* 2, *NKBT*, vol. 5, 93; Levy, *The Ten Thousand Leaves*, 382.

9. Ōkubo, "Hina ni aru koto," 4.

10. Discussed in Hirohata, "Nihon koten ni okeru shinsensetsu oyobi chūgoku tenmonsetsu no eikyō," 150–151.

11. *Man'yōshū* 2, *NKBT*, vol. 5, 151.

12. Ibid., 153.

13. Ōkubo, "Hina ni aru koto," 3, 5–6, and 8.

14. Batten, *To the Ends of Japan*, 19–34, esp. 29.

15. Ibid., 35.

16. Amino Yoshihiko, *Nihonron no shiza: rettō no shakai to kokka* (Shōgakukan, 1990), 27–44, and 33 for the incidents of Jōgan 866 and 870.

17. Farris, *Heavenly Warriors*, 157.

18. Mori Kimiyuki, *Kodai nihon no taigai ninshiki to kōtsū* (Yoshikawa kōbunkan, 1998), 161–163; and Batten, *The Ends of Japan*, 28–29.

19. Kajihara Masaaki, vol. 2 of *Shōmonki*, Tōyō bunko 280, 291 (Heibonsha, 1975–1976), 130; and Rabinovich, *Shōmonki*, 116.

20. Kajihara, *Shōmonki* 2, 149–155; Rabinovitch, 117–118.

21. Morita Tei, "Shōmonki kō," *Nihon kodai no seiji to shūkyō* (Yūzankaku shuppan, 1997), 135–157, esp. 154–155.

22. Lefebvre, *The Production of Space*, 399.

23. Some of these works are discussed in Amino, "Chūsei no tabibito-tachi," in *Hyōhaku to teichaku: teijūshakai e no michi*, 155–266 esp. 159–163. The same phenomenon also gave rise to a new visual iconography, including *Shigisan engi*, *Chōjū giga*, and *Bandainagon e kotoba*, collected in Shibusawa Keizō, *Shinpan emakimono ni yoru nihon jōmin seikatsu ebiki*, 6 vols. (Heibonsha, 1984). A somewhat earlier figure than Masafusa is Sugawara no Michizane, who, in works like his "Kansō jushu," was one of the first classical writers to show an interest in the life of itinerant craftspeople and performers. Discussed in Amino, "Chūsei no tabibitotachi," 159–161.

24. Yamagishi, *Kodai seiji shakai shisō*, 158.

25. For a helpful comparison, see Rouzer, *Articulated Ladies*, 164–167, where he translates and discusses *Shi ji*'s account of the Xiongnu.

26. Discussed in Arai Takashige, *Chūsei akutō no kenkyū* (Yoshikawa kōbunkan, 1990), 15–17.

27. Amino, *Nihon chūsei no hinōgyōmin to tennō*, 230–235; and "Hyōhaku to teichaku," 175–178. On exoticization and *Kugutsuki*, see Thomas Keirstead, "The Gendering and Regendering of Medieval Japan," *U.S.–Japan Women's Journal*, English Supplement 9 (1995), 77–92; and Bernard Faure, *The Power of Denial: Buddhism, Purity, and Gender* (Princeton, NJ, and Oxford: Princeton University Press, 2003), 257–258.

28. Henri Lefebvre, *The Production of Space*, 36–46.

29. On *Konjaku*'s geography, see Takagi Yutaka, *Kamakura bukkyō shi kenkyū* (Iwanami shoten, 1982), 182–187. In a study on Japan–China trade in the Heian period, the economic historian Mori Katsumi notes how the sea shifts from being a source of fear in earlier court tales such as *Taketori monogatari* and *Utsubo monogatari* (*The Tale of the Hollow Tree*) to a site of trade and commerce in *Konjaku* and other tale collections from the late Heian period on. See Mori Katsumi, *Nissō bunka kōryū no shomondai* (zōho), in *Mori Katsumi chosaku senshū* 4 (Kokusho kankōkai, 1975), 70.

30. On triadic structuring and meguri monogatari in *Sangoku denki*, see Ikegami Jun'ichi, *Sangoku denki*, jō (Miyai shoten, 1976), 5–8; and Kuroda Akira, *Chūsei setsuwa no bungakushiteki kyōkan*, zoku, Kenkyū sōsho 160 (Izumi shoin, 1995), 330–338.

31. On the shift from the middle-kingdom ideology to the shinkoku or "divine country" ideology with the latter's geographical view of Japan as a "small country of the margin," see Narusawa, " 'Hendo shōkoku' no nihon–chūseiteki seikaizō no ichisokumen ni tsuite," in *Seiji no kotoba–imi no rekishi wo megutte*, 129–176. As Narusawa notes, 131–133, although the Indian Buddhist world-

view with its mythical geography of Jambu-dvīpa is recorded in the *Nin'nōkyō* (*Virtuous King Sutra*), a sutra already utilized in the Nara period, the positioning of Japan as a "small country of the margin" (*hendo no shōkoku*) dates only from the mid-Heian period, with the earliest example from *Shōtoku Taishi denryaku*, where Prince Taishi is referred to as "zokusan ō" 栗散王, "a scattered millet-seed king." Narusawa dates *Shōtoku Taishi denryaku* to the year 917, but other scholars to the late Heian period.

32. On how a once-dominant view of space may persist as a representation of space long after it has ceased to provide the basis for organizing a society's spatial practices, see Lefebvre's remarks on the Renaissance town, *Production of Space*, 40–41.

33. Jishō 4/9. *Meigetsuki*, vol. 1, 6; and Ivo Smits, "The Poet and the Politician: Teika and the Compilation of the *Shinkokinshū*," *MN*, 53:4 (Winter 1998), 427–428. Also discussed in Saeki Shin'ichi, "Iteki kannnen no juyō: *Heike monogatari* wo chūshin ni," in *Gunki to kanbungaku*, Wakan hikaku bungaku sōsho 15, ed. Wakan hikaku bungakukai (Kyūko shoin, 1993), 127.

34. Saeki Shin'ichi, "Shōgun to chōteki: *Heike monogatari* wo chūshin ni," *GK*, 27 (March 1991), 12–22.

35. *Heike monogatari sōsakuin* lists twenty-seven occurrences of the word *chōteki* for the standard Kakuichi text (Iwanami taikei edition). An example of the anachronistic use of the chōteki–shōgun dyad occurs in "Fujigawa": "In the past when a general set forth for the outer regions to subjugate a court enemy (*chōteki*), he first visited the Imperial Palace in order to receive the Sword of Commission." *Heike monogatari* jō, 368; McCullough, *Heike*, 186. A curious misuse of the graph "teki" (enemy) in the Kakuichi variant of "Su Wu" ("Sobu") discloses what "chōteki" conceals. In a letter to the Chinese emperor describing his exile among the Xiongnu, Su Wu describes himself as "a one-legged man among the *barbarians* (*koteki*)." Rather than "teki" meaning "barbarian," the scribe of this text has written "teki" (enemy), the same graph in the compound "chōteki." *Heike monogatari* jō, 206; McCullough, *Heike*, 94.

36. In *Taiheiki*, the son of the deceased Kusunoki no Masashige plays war games in which he refers to his father's enemy Takauji as chōteki and shōgun in the same breath, highlighting the interchangeability of the terms. In another *Taiheiki* episode, when the head of the slain warrior Yoshisada is paraded through the streets of the capital, the narrator comments, "the death of a court enemy is the valor of the warrior enemy" (*chōteki no sai buteki no yū nari*). *Taiheiki* 2, *NKBT*, vol. 35, 171 and 323. Discussed in Saeki, in "Shōgun to chōteki," 20.

37. McCullough, *Heike*, 246; *Heike monogatari* ge, 101.

38. On the sources for this passage, see Tomikura Tokujirō, *Heike monogatari zenchūshaku*, chū, Nihon koten hyōshaku zenchūshaku sōsho (Kadokawa shoten, 1966), 400–401. The rhetorical heightening found here and elsewhere in *Heike* has been characterized as "embellished style" (*bibunchō*), a term favored by Tomikura, or as a variety of "mixed Japanese-Chinese prose" (*wakan konkō bun*).

39. Translated by McCullough as "center of civilization."

40. *Heike monogatari* jō, 94; McCullough, *Heike*, 30.

41. Tomikura, *Zenchūshaku* jō, 86.

42. On structural inversion in the Kakuichi *Heike*, see Hyōdō Hiromi, *Katarimono josetsu: Heike katari no hassei to hyōgen*, Shin'ei kenkyū sōsho 8 (Yūseidō, 1985), 93–97; and Hyōdō, *Ōken to monogatari*, 82–96.

43. *Heike monogatari* jō, 85.

44. On first learning that Tadamori has been granted the privilege of entry into the Courtiers' Hall, the courtiers are referred to as "kumo no ue bito." *Heike monogatari* jō, 84. On the pair jige–tenjōbito, see Tomikura, *Zenchūshaku* jō, 53.

45. On the suppressed violence that pervades "The Night Attack in the Courtiers' Hall," see David T. Bialock, "Peripheries of Power: Voice, History, and the Construction of Imperial and Sacred Space in *The Tale of the Heike* and Other Medieval and Heian Historical Texts" (PhD diss., Columbia University, 1997), 353–381.

46. Murai Shōsuke, *Ajia no naka no chūsei nihon*, 37–40. The discussion that follows draws on Murai's observations.

47. On the Korean report, see Murai, *Ajia no naka no chūsei nihon*, 37.

48. *Taiheiki* 3, *NKBT*, vol. 36, 62–63.

49. Ibid., 61.

50. Kitano Tayuru, *Myōgoki* (Benseisha, 1983), 979–980.

51. Discussed in Saeki, "Iteki kannnen no juyō: *Heike monogatari* wo chūshin ni," 129.

52. I would like to thank Saeki Shin'ichi for elucidating the hansetsu method employed in *Myōgoki*.

53. The word *ezo* emerged as a new word in the medieval period to designate the Ainu peoples of Michinoku and Chishima in contradistinction to *ebisu*, which was frequently used of warriors from Tōgoku and northern parts of Japan. See Maeda Tomoyoshi, "Ezo," in *Goshi* 1, vol. 9 of *Kōza nihongo no goi*, ed. Satō Kiyoji (Meiji shoin, 1983), 128. On the overlap between ezo and defiled groups in the medieval period, see Ōishi Naomasa, "Soto-ga-hama ezo-ga-shimakō," *Nihon kodaishi kenkyū: Seki Akira sensei kanreki kinen*, ed. Seki Akira Kyōju Kanreki Kinenkai (Yoshikawa kōbunkan, 1980), 591.

54. Keiko Ikegami, *The Taming of the Samurai: Honorific Individualism and the Making of Modern Japan* (Cambridge, MA, and London: Harvard University Press, 1995), 113–117, and for the quote, 113.

55. Helen Craig McCullough, trans., *The Taiheiki: A Chronicle of Medieval Japan* (Tokyo: Charles E. Tuttle, 1959), 14–18.

56. Cited and discussed in Narusawa, *Seiji no kotoba–imi no rekishi wo megutte*, 169.

57. Ji, translated here as a placename, is poetic license. Its precise sense in the present passage is unknown. In Chinese, the graph can refer to the name of a mountain or family name. See Saeki, "Iteki no kannen," 142 (note 12).

58. *Engyōbon Heike monogatari honbun-hen* jō, ed. Kitahara Yasuo and Ogawa Eiichi (Benseisha, 1990), 195. The Kakuichi variant of this episode rounds out the first scroll.

59. According to *Chiribukuro*, "Those called *sendara* in India are butchers. They are wicked people, in appearance like *eta*, who kill and then sell living things." *Chiribukuro*, vol. 1, ed. Ōnishi Harutaka and Kimura Noriko, Tōyō bunko 723 (Heibonsha, 1998), 289.

60. Discussed in Kuroda Akira, "Sobu oboegaki: chūsei shiki no sekai kara," in *Heike monogatari: katari to gentai*, 7, 212–226.

61. Saeki, "Iteki kannen juyō," 139.

62. *Engyōbon* ge, 241–243.

63. Discussed by Ōishi Naomasa, in "Kita no shūen, rettō tōhokubu no kōki," in *Shūen kara mita chūsei nihon*, Nihon no rekishi 14, ed. Ōishi Naomasa, Takura Kurayoshi, and Takahashi Kimiaki (Kōdansha, 2001), 21–26.

64. Ibid., 26. For an extended discussion of Kiyohira's Hiraizumi and his creation of a counter-realm that appropriated the ideology of the center, see Mimi Hall Yiengpruksawan, *Hiraizumi: Buddhist Art and Regional Politics in Twelfth-Century Japan* (Cambridge, MA: Harvard University Press, 1998), 51–88.

65. On Soto-ga-hama and Ezo-ga-shima as a destination and source of defilements, see Ōishi, "Soto-ga-hama ezo-ga-shimakō," 574–582.

66. *Sankashū kinkai wakashū*, NKBT, vol. 29, 176. This and the following poem are cited and discussed in Ōishi, *Shūen kara mita chūsei nihon*, 21–23.

67. Tradition attributed the stone to the famous warrior Sakanoue Tamuramaro, who was said to have died there. *Shūchūshō*, in *Nihon kagaku taikei*, bekkan 2, ed. Kyūsōjin Hitaku (Kasama shoin, 1958), 315–316.

68. Fujiwara no Chikataka was the author of *Kyūan hyakushu* (*One-Hundred Poem Sequence of the Kyūan Era*, also known as *Kyūan rokunen on-hyakushu*), published in Nimpei 3 (1153). The present waka was included in the late Kamakura private poetry collection *Fuboku waka shō*, compiled by Fujiwara Nagakiyo, and can be found in *Fuboku waka shō*, 16, 9740, in *Shinpen kokka taikan*, vol. 2, Shinsenshū-hen kashū, ed. Shinpen kokka taikan (Kadokawa shoten, 1984), 679.

69. *Nihon kagaku taikei*, bekkan 2, 296.

70. Dan 15 from *Ise monogatari*, NKBT, vol. 9, 120–121. The Shinobu Mountains were located in the far northern provinces of Japan, known anciently as Michinoku. In the phrase "to see into the depths of your heart," the word translated as "depths" (*oku*) pivots on the name of the province Michinoku.

71. For Sei Shōnagon, Michinoku, which she lists as a "distant thing," lay culturally and geographically at the outer limit of what constituted civilization for the court. See *Makura no sōshi sōsakuin*, ed. Sakakibara Kunihiko (Yūbun shoin, 1967), 124, sect. 103.

72. Takahashi Kimiaki, "Chūsei nishi nihonkai chiiki to taigai kōryū," in *Nihonkai to Izumo sekai*, vol. 2 of *Umi to rettō bunka*, ed. Mori Kōichi (Shōgakukan, 1991), 344–346.

73. Discussed in Gomi Fumihiko, *Heike monogatari: shi to setsuwa* (Heibonsha, 1987), 217–221. On the Taira's contacts with Chinese merchants in Hakata and Ōwada, see also Charlotte von Verschuer, *Le commerce extérieur du Japon des origines au XVIe siècle* (Paris: Éditions Maisonneuve & Larose,

1988), 47–48; and on the competitive trade relations between the Taira and the rulers of Hiraizumi at this time, see Yiengpruksawan, *Hiraizumi: Buddhist Art and Regional Politics in Twelfth-Century Japan*, 99–100.

74. Watanabe Tamotsu, *Heike Ichimon* (Jinbutsu ōraisha, 1964), 124–125; and Mori Katsumi, *Nissō bunka kōryū no shomondai* (zōho), 58–59, and 149–158, which contains observations on the Song trade in Japanese timber, fragrant woods, fans, and other finished products.

75. Mori, *Nissō bunka kōryū no shomondai* (zōho), 223–227; Watanabe, *Heike ichimon*, 128; and von Verschuer, *Le Commerce exterieur du Japon*, 61.

76. Kaō 2/9/20. *Gyokuyō*, vol. 1 (Kokusho kankōkai, 1906), 106.

77. Shōan 2/9/17 and 2/9/22. *Gyokuyō*, vol. 1, 224 and 225–226.

78. Hashiguchi Kusaku, in "*Heike monogatari* no naka no nihon to gaikoku," *Kagoshima kenristsu tanki daigaku kiyō*, 44 (1993), 1–10, esp. 4–5. The same essay can also be found in *Kokubungaku nenji betsu ronbunshū, Chūsei 2*, ed. Gakujutsu bunken kankōkai (Hōbun shuppan, 1993), 37–42.

79. Mizuhara, *Shintei Genpei seisuiki*, vol. 3, 260; and Tsukamoto, *Genpei seisuiki* ge, 23. In my translation of this passage, I have ignored the break in Mizuhara's rescension of the text.

80. *Engyōbon* jō, 631–632.

81. An earlier school of *Heike* scholarship viewed this passage as evidence of the relatively late date of the Engyōbon, now widely regarded as transmitting the oldest extant version of *Heike*.

82. Discussed by Murai, *Ajia no naka no chūsei nihon*, 117–121; and by the same author, "The Boundaries of Medieval Japan," *Acta Asiatica*, 81 (2001), 72–91.

83. *Engyōbon* jō, 443. Variants of this dream are recorded in *Genpei jōsuiki, Genpei tōjōroku*, and the Myōhonjibon variant of *Soga monogatari*. Discussed in Hashiguchi, "*Heike monogatari* no naka nihon to gaikoku," 1 (37); and for a useful comparison of the variants, see *Genpei tōjōroku* jō, ed. Fukuda Toyohiko and Hattori Kōzō (Kōdansha, 1999), 171–191.

84. On Yoritomo and maps as a strategy of power, see Mary E. Berry's remarks in "Tōitsu kenryoku to chizu sakusei: aratana seiji bunka no tanjo," in *Chizu to ezu no seiji bunkashi*, ed. Kuroda Hideo, Mary E. Berry, and Sugimoto Fumiko (Tōkyō daigaku shuppankai, 2001), 146 and 181 (note 17).

85. *Heike monogatari* jō, 185.

86. Although Naritsune belonged to the provincial governor class, the viewpoint here is that of a cultured member of the capital elite.

87. Christopher Tilley, *A Phenomenology of Landscape, Places, Paths and Monuments* (Oxford: Berg, 1994), 11.

88. *Genpei seisuiki*, vol. 2, Chūsei no bungaku, 22; Mizuhara, *Shintei Genpei seisuiki*, vol. 1, 319.

89. Tilley, *A Phenomenology of Landscape*, 11.

90. 家中家柱中柱　空中七日有否　海中七日有否. The meaning of this phrase is not entirely clear. A tentative translation might read: "A house within a house, a pillar within a pillar; is it not seven days through the air; is it not seven days

by sea?" In a personal communication, Saeki Shin'ichi has suggested that it may involve a wordplay.

91. *Engyōbon* jō, 315–316.

92. Hirano Satsuki, "Engyōbon *Heike monogatari* no taichūgoku ishiki ni tsuite," in *Gunki to kanbungaku*, Wakan hikaku bungaku sōsho 15, 107–125. Hirano provides a complete chart of these expressions, 9. Mori Kimiyuki, cited earlier, lists scattered examples of such Japan-centrism from as early as the ninth century, but most of his examples date from the eleventh or twelfth century. See Mori, *Kodai nihon no taigai ninshiki to kōtsū*, 187–195.

93. Hirano, "Taichūgoku ishiki ni tsuite," 114–115.

94. On Edo attitudes toward Shigemori and "Kane watashi," see Sakakibara Chizuru, "Antoku tennō ibun: kinsei kōki ni miru *Heike monogatari*, kyōju no ittan," *KK*, 74: 1 (January 1997), 29–42. Haga Yaichi touches on the moral dimension of Shigemori's character in "Kokuminsei jūron," *Ochiai Naobumi, Ueda Kazutoshi, Haga Yaichi, Fujioka Sakutarō shū*, vol. 44 of *Meiji bungaku zenshū*, ed. Hisamatsu Sen'ichi (Chikuma shobō, 1968), 237–239. For Yamada Yoshio's views on the Confucian morality of Shigemori, see the essay in vol. 1 of his *Heike monogatari*, Iwanami bunko (Iwanami shoten, 1929), 13–39.

95. Studies on Shigemori's character and background include an early 1929 study by Mori Katsumi, "Shigemori to sono jidai," collected in *Nissō bunka kōryū no shomondai* (zōho), 127–148; Kobayashi Chishō, "Shigemori-zō zōkei no ronri," *Chūsei bungaku no shisō* (Shibundō, 1964), 52–102; Murai Yasuhiko, *Heike monogatari no sekai* (Tokuma shoten, 1973), 199–209; and Uwayokote Masataka, *Heike monogatari no kyokō to shinjitsu* jō (Hanawa shobō, 1985), 71–115. Some of these are discussed in Takehisa Tsuyoshi, *Heike monogatari no zentaizō*, Izumi sensho 103 (Osaka: Izumi shoin, 1996), 98–99.

96. *Heike monogatari* jō, 249.

97. A tentative yomikudashi and paraphrase of the letter (left untranslated here) is available in Saeki Shin'ichi, "'Kane watashi' senyūjō no honbun to sono shūhen," in *Enkyōbon heike monogatari kōshō* 2, ed. Mizuhara Hajime (Shintensha, 1993), 130–141. In his discussion, Saeki focuses mainly on debates connected to the letter in the medieval through the Meiji periods, including Ban Nobutomo's theory. Its historicity remains a matter of debate. Several phrases show Shigemori preoccupied with the survival of his fame in his afterlife.

98. *Engyōbon* jō, 293–294.

99. The term *taiten* has three distinct meanings: (1) to fall from a higher state (achieved as a result of ascetic practices or *shugyō*) to a lower state; (2) to be remiss or lapse in austerities; and (3) to degenerate or decline, particularly of a house or family. *Iwanami bukkyō jiten*, ed. Nakamura Hajime, Fukunaga Mitsuji, Tamura Yoshirō, and Konno Tōru (Iwanami shoten, 1989), 541.

100. Hirano, "Taichūgoku ishiki ni tsuite," 117.

101. An entry from Kujō Kanezane's journal *Gyokuyō*, for the year 1220 (Shōkyū 2/4/20), mentions a "Heike ki" or "chronicle," while the poet Fujiwara no Teika's copy of *Hyōhanki* contains an entry (dated 1240) on the manuscript's

back side (corresponding to Nin'an 3/10 or 1168) that mentions the copying of a "six scroll *Jishō monogatari* [*A Tale of the Jishō Era*] called *Heike*," an early version of *Heike* that probably drew on original documents. For the original citations, see *Heike monogatari*, vol. 9 of *Kokugo kokubungaku kenkyūshi taisei*, ed. Takagi Ichinosuke (Sanseidō, 1960), 51. Also discussed in Yamashita Hiroaki, *Heike monogatari no seisei* (Meiji shoin, 1984), 118–119.

102. Discussed by Tomikura, *Zenchūshaku* jō, 477–479; and Mori, *Nissō bunka kōryū no shomondai* (zōho), 167–184. Mori discusses the *Heike* variants of this episode as evidence of medieval commerce between Japan and Mount Yuwang in China.

103. This can be compared to the narrative centered on the mustering of Yoritomo's forces, another of the Engyōbon's alternative histories with a distinctive geopolitical space. See Engyōbon jō, 493–523. For a discussion and partial translation, see Bialock, "Peripheries of Power," 732–754.

104. In his discussion of the shift from the middle-kingdom worldview to the notion of Japan as a small country of the margin, Narusawa regards the emergence of the divine country or shinkoku ideology as an attempt to obviate or deny Japan's marginality. He attributes a similar logic to the contemporaneous doctrines of original enlightenment, achieving Buddhahood in this present body (*sokushin jōbutsu*), and this world is the Pureland (*kono do soku jōdo*). As I will argue in Chapter 8, however, the two can also be regarded as mutually reinforcing. On these points and the shinkoku worldview, see Narusawa, *Seiji no kotoba—imi no rekishi wo megutte*, 140–143 and 166–170; and on Japan's geographical marginality and shinkoku ideology, Murai, *Ajia no naka no chūsei nihon*, 34–37.

105. *Heike monogatari* jō, 172.

106. Ibid., 175.

107. *Genpei seisuiki*, vol. 2, Chūsei no bungaku, 93; Mizuhara, *Shintei Genpei seisuiki*, vol. 2, 38–39.

108. "Although the three Korean kingdoms have submitted to China, Japan has never yet belonged to a foreign country." *Hachiman gudō kun* (kō-text), in *Jisha engi*, ed. Sakurai Tokutarō, Hagiwara Tatsuo, and Miyata Noboru (Iwanami shoten, 1975), 170. Discussed by Murai, in *Ajia no naka no chūsei nihon*, 36–37. In a similar vein, Narusawa notes that in the ideology propagated in *Hachiman gudō kun*, Japan is shinkoku because it maintains distinctions between divinities and animals. Hence, the Mongols are the offspring of dogs and the Japanese are the descendants of divinities (*kami*). The medieval view departed sharply from Nara period texts like *Nihon shoki*, where the animal traits attributed to the Eastern Barbarians in the description of the Emishi (discussed in Chapter 4), for example, are reserved almost exclusively for populations on the archipelago. Apart from one exception, notes Narusawa, none of the four principal Chinese designations for barbarian—Yi 夷, Mang 蛮, Jung 戎, and Ti 狄—is used of the Korean kingdoms. Instead, these were typically designated by the Chinese graph "fan" 蕃, regularly glossed as "neighboring country" (*tonari no*

kuni). One of the rare exceptions occurs in Kōgyoku's chronicle (1/5/22, *Nihon shoki* ge, 240; Aston, vol. 2, 173), where a lack of mourning rites imputed to the Korean kingdoms is likened to the behavior of "birds and beasts" (*kedamono*). See Narusawa, *Seiji no kotoba-imi no rekishi wo megutte*, 105 and 169.

For Takagi Yutaka, the negative view of Korea in medieval Japan is also reflected in the "three country view," which delegitimized Korean Buddhism while elevating Japan's own status vis-à-vis the origin point of Buddhism, India. See Takagi, *Kamakura bukkyōshi kenkyū*, 187. On *Hachiman gudō kun* and its reworking of Empress Jingō's subjugation narrative in *Nihon shoki*, see the analysis of Kimura Saeko, "Chūsei hachiman shinkō ni okeru ikusa no kioku: Jingō kōgō denshō no hen'yō wo megutte," *Gengotai*, no. 5 (October 2004), 123–133.

109. Discussed in Hashiguchi, "*Heike monogatari* no naka nihon to gaikoku," 6–7 (40). On the introduction of Song medical arts, see Hattori Toshirō, *Kamakura jidai igakushi no kenkyū* (Yoshikawa kōbunkan, 1964), 46–48; and on Kanezane's secret consultation, 55–56.

110. *Engyōbon* jō, 287–290.

111. *Heike monogatari* jō, 242–243.

112. Ibid., 243.

113. On *Shōmonki*'s representation of fate, see Mizuhara Hajime, *Heike monogatari no keisei* (Katō chūdōkan, 1971), 285–286; and on the Chinese background to unmei in warrior chronicles more generally, see Komatsu Shigeto, "Gunkimono ni okeru unmeikan I: *Hōgen monogatari, Heiji monogatari, Heike monogatari*," in *Chūsei gunkimono no kenkyū* (Ōfūsha, 1962), 19–21.

114. Sudō Takashi, "Kotohirabon *Hōgen monogatari* no shishō kōsei: unmeikan to 'kudoki' to kanseki inyō," in *Gunki to kanbungaku*, Wakan hikaku bungaku sōsho 15, 24–41; and p. 37, where he comments specifically on "Ishi mondō." See also Nagafuji Yasushi on the shift from "shukusekan" to "unmeikan" in *Chūsei nihon bungaku to jikan ishiki* (Miraisha, 1984), 13–25.

115. *Heike monogatari* jō, 243–244.

116. Both the Yashirobon and Engyōbon employ "eshin" (dependent body). See Tomikura, *Zenchūshaku* jō, 464; and on the term *eshin*, *Iwanami bukkyō jiten*, 73.

117. On the background to "Ishi mondō" and some of its possible sources, see Mizuhara Hajime, *Engyōbon heike monogatari ronkō* (Katō chūdōkan, 1979), 253–257.

118. It has been argued that the differences between the Engyōbon and other texts of the so-called "read lineage" and the Kakuichi variant reflect an evolution from an earlier chronicle form (*ki*), focused equally on the Genji and Heike warrior clans, to a "lyrical" and "storylike" (*monogatari-teki*) narrative focused more narrowly on the destruction of the Heike. See Kitagawa Tadahiko, *Gunkimono ronkō* (Miyai shoten, 1989), 10–18.

119. *Jikkinshō*, 1: 21, *Shinpen Nihon koten bungaku zenshū*, vol. 1, annotated by Asami Kazuhiko (Shōgakukan, 1997), 61–62.

120. Minamoto no Tsunenobu (1016–1096), a late Heian poet skilled in Chinese and instrumental music. His title "Sochi no Minbu kyō" indicates that

he combined the offices of vice-governor of Dazai and head of the Home Affairs Bureau.

121. *Engyōbon* jō, 289–290.

122. The *Jikkinshō* variant may hint at an anti-Korean sentiment. Instead of the Engyōbon's "Crane Forest," it has 鶏林 (*keirin*), an old name for the country of Silla.

123. Discussed by Hirano, "Taichūgoku ishiki ni tsuite," 121.

124. *Engyōbon* jō, 290. A variant of the same anecdote is also collected in *Jikkinshō*.

125. Ingyō 3/8. Aston, *Nihongi*, vol. 1, 315–316; *Nihon shoki* ge, 436–437. For the *Kojiki* version, see Philippi, *Kojiki*, 332.

Chapter 7

1. Amino Yoshihiko, "Igyō no ōken: Go-Daigo, Monkan, Kanemitsu," in *Igyō no ōken*, Imēji rīdingu sōsho (Heibonsha, 1986), 159–212.

2. Tsuchiya Megumi, "Bugaku no chūsei: dōbu no kūkan, in *Chūsei no kūkan wo yomu*, ed. Gomi Fumihiko (Yoshikawa kōbunkan, 1995), 66–67.

3. *Hōgen monogatari, heiji monogatari, jōkyūki, SNKBT*, vol. 43, 305. I have also consulted the translation of William H. McCullough, in "*Shōkyūki: An Account of the Shōkyū War 1221*," *MN*, 19: 1 and 2 (1964), 163–215.

4. Akiyama Kiyoko, "Chūsei no omote to oku," in *Chūsei no kūkan wo yomu*, 106–137.

5. Ken'ei 1/9/1, *Meigetsuki*, vol. 1, 469; and Kenpo 1/2/5, *Meigetsuki*, vol. 2, 247. Akiyama, "Chūsei no omote to oku," 125. Likewise, at banquets held in Go-Toba's Seinan Palace in the year 1217, there were the same familiar accusations of wastefulness and extravagant use of gold, silver, and brocade cloths. On the occasion of a poetry contest held at Seinanji Temple in 1201, Go-Toba is observed willfully violating the customary seating arrangement by rank. On other occasions, recorded in *Gyokuyō* for the year 1221, shirabyōshi dances were held in the prayer hall (*jōdō*) and sangaku dancers performed "wild dances" (*ranbu*) in the courtyard of the palace. See Kenpō 5/2/9 and 5/2/13, *Meigetsuki*, vol. 2, 386; Kennin 2/5/26, *Meigetsuki*, vol. 1, 262–263; and Jōkyū 3/1/27 and 3/1/29, *Gyokuyō*. Discussed in Fujita Katsunari, "Tenkanki no Toba-den: chūsei jū-kūkan no senku," in *Inseiki bunka ronshū 3: Jikan to kūkan*, ed. Inseiki bunka kenkyūkai (Shinwasha, 2003), 211–235, esp. 220–223.

6. Okada, "Onmyōdō saishi no seiritsu to tenkai," *OMS*, vol. 1, *Kodai*, 165–171; Tamura, "Onmyōryō seiritsu izen," *OMS*, vol. 1, *Kodai*, 36.

7. Ōyama Kyōhei, *Nihon chūsei nōsonshi no kenkyū*, 390–399; Murai, *Ajia no naka no chūsei nihon*, 108–112; and Ōji Toshiaki, "Ninshiki kūkan toshite no 'nihon,'" in *Kosumoroji to shintai*, vol. 8 of *Iwanami kōza: Tennō to ōken wo kangaeru*, 71–95, esp. 71–77.

8. Translation of Bock (slightly modified by author), in *Classical Learning and Taoist Practices in Early Japan*, 45. See also *Engi shiki, KST*, vol. 26, 443; and *Kojiki norito, NKBT*, vol. 1, 458–459. Discussed in Murai, *Ajia no naka no chūsei nihon*, 109.

9. On the nanase no harae, see Okada, *Heian jidai no kokka to saishi*, 644–647; Endō, *Kinsei onmyōdōshi no kenkyū*, 34; and Wakamori Tarō, *Shugendōshi kenkyū, Wakamori Tarō chosakushū* 2 (Kōbundō, 1980), 70–74.

10. On the scope and character of the ritual topography, see Itō, *Nihon chūsei no ōken to ken'i*, 22–30.

11. Among the most important rituals for expelling defilements were the Miyashiro Four Corners Plague Deity Ritual (*Miyashiro shigū ekigami no matsuri*), the Miyashiro Four Corners Four Borders Ritual (*Miyashiro shikaku shikyō no matsuri*), and the Kinai Ten Site Plague Deity Ritual (*Kinai tosho ekigami no matsuri*). Itō, *Nihon chūsei no ōken to ken'i*, 25–26.

12. *Engi shiki* jō, vol. 11 of *ST*, koten-hen, 100–101; and Felicia G. Bock, *Engi-shiki: Procedures of the Engi Era* (Tokyo: Sophia University, 1970), 117. On the kō-otsu heitei system, see Ōyama, *Nihon chūsei nōsonshi no kenkyū*, 400–403; and Yamamoto, *Kegare to ōharae*, 42–46.

13. Yamamoto, *Kegare to ōharae*, 48–58.

14. Shōryaku 5/6/6. *Honchō seiki*, *KST*, vol. 9, 192. Ninpei 3/4/28. *Hyōhanki* 1, *ZST*, vol. 18, 189. Discussed in Okada, *Heian jidai no kokka to saishi*, 639–640.

15. Kobayashi Shigefumi, "Kodai no tojō ni okeru kyōkai: kyōkai girei to toshi no fūkei," in *Hōhō toshite no kyōkai*, Sōsho shisō wo horu 1, ed. Akasaka Norio (Shin'yōsha, 1991), 244; Nishigaki Seiji, "Minshū no seijin seikatsu: kegare to michi," *Rekishi kōron*, 101: 4 (April 1984), 101–107; and Yamamoto Kōji, "Kizoku shakai ni okeru kegare to chitsujo," *Nihonshi kenkyū*, 287 (July 1986), 35–36.

16. Okada, *Heian jidai no kokka to saishi*, 640.

17. Yamamoto, *Kegare to ōharae*, 54–56.

18. Itō, *Nihon chūsei no ōken*, 27. The Harima–Settsu border was the last and most distant from the capital of the ten sites listed in *Engi shiki*'s article on the Festival to the Deities of Epidemic at 10 Places on Boundaries of the Inner Provinces. See *Engi shiki* jō, vol. 11 of *ST*, koten-hen, 85; and Bock, *Engi-shiki: Procedures of the Engi Era*, 106.

19. Jishō 3/6/17. *Hyakurenshō*, in *Nihon kiryaku* kōhen/*Hyakurenshō*, *KST*, vol. 11, 98. Discussed by Mori Katsumi, *Nissō bōeki no kenkyū*, in *Mori Katsumi chosaku senshū* 1 (Kokusho kankōkai, 1975), 232–233.

20. On these points, see Watanabe, *Heike ichimon*, 118–119; Amino *Igyō no ōken*, 189; and von Verschuer, 81–83. For a detailed analysis of coins and currency-based trade, see also Matsunobu Yasutaka, "Zeni to kahei no kannen: Kamakura ki ni okeru kahei kinō no henka ni tsuite," in *Rettō no bunkashi* 6 (Nihon edeitā sukūru, 1989), 177–210. On the shiki system, see Cornelius J. Kiley, "Provincial Administration and Land Tenure in Early Heian," *CHJ*, vol. 2, *Heian Japan*, 244–252.

21. Amino, *Igyō no ōken*, 197–198. The major influence here is the writings of Max Weber.

22. Derek Gregory, *Geographical Imaginations* (Cambridge and Oxford: Blackwell, 1994), 373.

23. Lefebvre, *The Production of Space*, 263. Elsewhere, Lefebvre writes how "The urban landscape of the Middle Ages turned the space which preceded it, the space of the 'world,' upon its head," 256–257. This is exemplified in the cathedral that "decrypted" the dark, threatening subterranean spaces of preceding religious structures and represented an assertion of new secular rationality, a move toward "illumination and elevation." The heterotopic spaces were those that were not decrypted, connected to the darker sorts of magical knowledge that "took refuge in the subterranean parts of society, in places hidden away from face-to-face communication." Also discussed in Gregory, *Geographical Imaginations*, 387–388.

24. Lefebvre, *Production of Space*, 36.

25. On the overlap between the space of the market and burial grounds in medieval Japan, both linked to the imagery of birds and dogs and hence death defilement, see Kuroda Hideo, *Sugata to shigusa no chūseishi*, Imēji rīdingu sōsho (Heibonsha, 1986), 161–162. Markets were also one of the traditional sites for executions.

26. Yokoi Kiyoshi, *Chūsei minshū no seikatsu bunka*, 267–293, esp. 272–276.

27. Ibid., 275–276.

28. On the marketing of defilement by medieval temples, see Michele Marra, "The Aesthetics of Impurity," in *Representations of Power: The Literary Politics of Medieval Japan* (Honolulu: University of Hawaii Press, 1993), 55–114, esp. 61–76.

29. Satō Hiroo, *Nihon chūsei no kokka to bukkyō*, Chūseishi kenkyū sensho (Yoshikawa kōbunkan, 1987), 35–38.

30. Ibid., 42–44.

31. Discussed by Satō Hiroo, *Kami, hotoke, ōken no chūsei* (Hōzōkan, 1998), 227–230.

32. Akasaka, *Ijinron josetsu*, 119–120.

33. As Yamanaka Yutaka notes, throughout the Nara and early Heian periods, the taina, as it was then called, was closely modeled after the Chinese rite. By the early twelfth century, texts like *Ōe shidai* are referring to courtiers who no longer fire their arrows as a ritual gesture of expulsion in tandem with the exorcist but now aim them at the exorcist himself. Aristocrats, who once participated in the rite, also begin to regard the exorcist with feelings of taboo-like loathing, while the emperor views the spectacle in secret. See Yamanaka, *Heianchō no nenchū gyōji*, 266–267; and on the link with defilement, Itō *Nihon chūsei no ōken*, 140–141. For a translation of the Engi era protocol on the *tsuina*, see Bock, *Classical Learning and Taoist Practices in Early Japan*, 44–46; and on the Chinese Da nuo, Marcel Granet, *Danses et légendes de la Chine ancienne*, tome premier (Paris: Librairie Felix Alcan, 1926), 300–305.

34. On the Eichō Era and Rakuyō dengaku events, see Kuroda Hideo, *Nihon chūsei kaihatsushi no kenkyū* (Azekura shobō, 1984), 458–482; Inoue Mitsuo, "*Rakuyō dengakuki* wo megutte," in *Akamatsu Toshihide kyōju taikan kinen kokushiron*, 413–425; and Jacob Raz, "Popular Entertainment and

Politics: The Great *Dengaku* of 1096," *MN*, 40: 3 (Autumn 1985), 283–298. On the basara phenomenon, see Pierre François Souyri, *The World Turned Upside Down: Medieval Japanese Society*, trans. Käthe Roth (New York: Columbia University Press, 2001), 108–109.

35. On these points, see Moriya, *Chūsei geinō no genzō*, 5–40 and 183–218; Matsuoka Shinpei, *Utage no shintai: basara kara Zeami e* (Iwanami shoten, 1991), 7–46; and Hashimoto Hiroyuki, "Nekkyō no rutsubo kara: dengaku to irui igyō," in *Porifuōn*, vol. 9 (1991), 43–54.

36. On the popular character of the Yasurai and similar events, see Itō, *Nihon chūsei no ōken*, 70–73; Kuroda, *Nihon chūsei kaihatsushi no kenkyū*, 447–448; and Raz, 288–289.

37. *Ryōjin hishō*, Iwanami bunko 935, ed. Sasaki Nobutsuna (Iwanami shoten, 1933), 170–171. The sense of this passage, especially the relationship between the different participants, is not entirely clear, and my translation, drawing on the analysis of Kawane Yoshiyasu, remains tentative. For Kawane's detailed analysis, see his two-part study, "Yasurai matsuri no seiritsu (jō): hōgen shinsei no rekishiteki ichi wo meikaku ni suru tame ni," *Nihonshi kenkyū*, no. 137 (November 1973), 1–22, esp. 13–14; and Kawane, "Yasurai matsuri no seiritsu (ge): hōgen shinsei no rekishiteki ichi wo meikaku ni suru tame ni," *Nihonshi kenkyū*, no. 138 (January 1974), 44–72. See also Itō, *Nihon chūsei no ōken*, 74–80; and Matsuoka, *Utage no shintai*, 50.

38. Itō, *Nihon chūsei no ōken*, 75.

39. Kawane, "Yasurai matsuri no seiritsu" (jō), 12–15; and Kawane, "Yasurai matsuri no seiritsu" (ge), 50–56.

40. Kawane, "Yasurai matsuri no seiritsu" (jō), 17.

41. Itō, *Nihon chūsei no ōken*, 73–74 and 77. Another odd combination of dress would be the "red tights" (*akaki hitatare*) that are worn around the head of the demon, which is one conjectured reading for the garbled phrase "kubi ni akaki akatare wo tsuke" in the *kudenshū* text. In this case, the phrase would read "affixing red tights to the demon's head."

42. A provision in the *Ryō no shūge*, for example, indicates that one duty of the chief officer of the Bureau of Music was to expel licentious and heterodox sounds, and a phrase from an edict issued by Emperor Shōmu states: "When the rites and music are both in harmony, the realm will be peaceful and long-enduring." Tenpyō 15/5/3. *Shoku nihongi* 2, SNKBT, vol. 13, 419. On these points, see Kuroda Toshio, "Chūsei shakai ni okeru geinō to ongaku," in *Kuroda Toshio chosakushū*, vol. 3, *Kenmitsu bukkyō to jisha seiryoku*, 74–75; Kuniyasu Yō, "Nihon no ongakuron: gakusho ni mirareru ongaku shisō," *Bungaku*, 56: 4 (April 1988), 44; and Masuo, *Man'yō kajin*, 39–41.

43. On the oddness of the music, see Nagaike Kenji, "Itsudatsu no shōsei: chūsei inja bunka ni okeru ongaku to kayō," in vol. 6 of *Hyōshō toshite no ongaku, Iwanami kōza Nihon no ongaku Ajia no ongaku*, (Iwanami shoten, 1988), 61. As Itō notes, the formal gagaku elements that were initially incorporated into the goryōe-type rituals only later began to acquire an aura of oddness (*iyō*) after fusing with elements of dengaku and other "popular" musical forms.

44. *Rakuyō dengakuki,* in *Chōya gunsai, KST,* vol. 29 (jō), 68–69. Discussed in Moriya, *Chūsei geinō no genzō,* 69.

45. Kanji 8/5/20. *Chūyūki* 1, *ZST,* vol. 9, 153. Discussed in Itō, *Nihon chūsei no ōken,* 73–74 and 77; and Inoue, "*Rakuyō dengakuki* wo megutte," 415–417. See also Raz, 288, for a description of similar behavior at the Eichō era dengaku of 1096.

46. On the eating habits of carpenters, see *The Pillow Book of Sei Shōnagon,* trans. Ivan Morris (New York: Columbia University Press, 1991), 255; and McCullough, *A Tale of Flowering Fortunes,* vol. 2, 592.

47. An entry in *Azumakagami* for the year 1247 records the report of local residents in Sagami province concerning the "eerie strangeness" of nightly performances of dengaku in the fields. In successive entries in his journal *Entairyaku* for the year 1311, Tōin Kinkata characterizes the dengaku craze as "tenma no shoi" and refers to popular rumors linking dengaku and pestilence. A lampoon cited for the second year of Kemmu (1335) in *Kemmu nenkan ki* notes the continuing popularity of dengaku despite predictions that dogs and dengaku will be the ruin of the Bakufu. Hōji 1/9/16. *Azumakagami* (kōhen), *KST,* vol. 33, 395. Ōchō 1/3/2, 1/3/8. *Entairyaku,* vol. 7, Shiryō sanshū 76, 92 and 94. Discussed in Matsuoka, *Utage no shintai,* 27; and Hashimoto, "Dengaku to irui igyō," 45 and 49.

48. Jacques Le Goff, "Vestimentary and Alimentary Codes in *Erec et Enide,*" in *The Medieval Imagination,* trans. Arthur Goldhammer (Chicago: University of Chicago Press, 1988), 132–150.

49. Amino, *Igyō no ōken,* 106–116; Amino, *Nihon no rekishi wo yominaosu* (Chikuma shobō, 1991), 59–70. On the association between "persimmon-color" clothes and *hinin,* see also Kuroda Hideo, *Kyōkai no chūsei shōchō no chūsei* (Tokyo daigaku shuppankai, 1986), 151–152.

50. Amino, *Igyō no ōken,* 110–113.

51. *Shasekishū, NKBT,* vol. 85, 270; and Robert E. Morrell, *Sand & Pebbles (Shasekishū): The Tales of Mujū Ichien, A Voice of Pluralism in Kamakura Buddhism* (Albany: SUNY Press, 1985), 189.

52. On the role of categories and classifications in defining notions of purity and impurity, see Mary Douglas's classic study, *Purity and Danger: An Analysis of Concepts of Pollution and Taboo* (London and New York: Routledge, 1966), 42–58.

53. *Heike monogatari* jō, 92; McCullough, *Heike,* 29.

54. In "Itsukushima gokō," *Heike monogatari* jō, 271; McCullough, *Heike,* 131.

55. Moriya, *Chūsei geinō no genzō,* 53–59.

56. On the yin-yang background and the Jōgan incident, see Murayama, *Sōsetsu,* 106–107.

57. On this point, see Itō, *Nihon chūsei no ōken,* 141.

58. Niunoya Tetsuichi, *Kebiishi: chūsei no kegare to kenryoku* (Heibonsha, 1986), 21–65.

59. On the origins of the hōmen, see Kida Teikichi, "Hōmen kō," in *Kida Teikichi chosakushū* 10 (Heibonsha, 1982), 262–279.

60. For the iconography, see *Hōnen shōnin eden* chū, in *Zoku Nihon emaki taisei*, ed. Komatsu Shigemi (Chūō kōronsha, 1981), 134–137.

61. Amino, *Igyō no ōken*, 10–11.

62. Translation based on text in Kōda Toshio, *Kōhon gōdanshō to sono kenkyū* jō (Zoku gunsho ruijū kanseikai, 1987), 16. Discussed in Niunoya, *Kebiishi*, 10; Amino, *Igyō no ōken*, 10–11; and Amino, *Nihonron no shiza*, 234.

63. The qualifications for head of the imperial police are set forth in the *Hyakuryōkun yōshō*, a digest of rules pertaining to appointments to court offices: "The bettō is an officer to be selected from *major counselors (dainagon)* of especial talent and breeding. To be appointed he must conform to the five virtues mentioned by the Retired Sovereign Shirakawa: proper demeanor (*yōgi*), learning (*saigaku*), wealth (*fuki*), lineage (*fudai*), and close service to the tennō (*kinju*)." The requirement of wealth was directly related to another activity that devolved upon the Kebiishi, the distribution of alms (*segyō*). Like the requirement of wealth, the almsgiving of the Kebiishi was probably both an extension of and countermeasure to their work with defilement. *Hyakuryōkun yōshō*, vol. 4 of Shinchū kōgaku sōsho, ed. Mozume Takami (Kōbunko kankōkai, 1927), 520. Cited and discussed in Niunoya, *Kebiishi*, 8–10.

64. Niunoya, *Kebiishi*, 11–12.

65. Itō, *Nihon chūsei no ōken*, 143–144.

66. Moriya, *Chūsei geinō no genzō*, 196.

67. Eikyū 2/2/14. *Chūyūki* 4, ZST, vol. 12, 264.

68. Ninpei 2/5/17. *Chūyūki* 4, ZST, vol. 12, 307.

69. Moriya, *Chūsei geinō no genzō*, 196–197, who cites an edict for the year 1191 (Kenkyū 2/3/28) recorded in *Sandai seifu*.

70. Enryaku 2/11/23. *Meigetsuki*, vol. 2, 213. Cited in Moriya, *Chūsei geinō no genzō*, 50.

71. Hayashiya, *Chūsei geinōshi no kenkyū*, 345.

72. The earliest recorded example of shōzoku tabawari dates from 1148. See Moriya, *Chūsei geinō no genzō*, 47–48.

73. Kenryaku 2/3/22. Cited from the manuscript of *Gyokuzui* in Moriya, *Chūsei geinō no genzō*, 65.

74. On the overlap between the Kebiishi-chō and the underworld office of King Emma (*Emma-chō*), see Kuroda, "Jigoku no fūkei," in *Sugata to shigusa no chūseishi*, 172–177.

75. On this shift, see Moriya, *Chūsei geinō no genzō*, 186 ff.

76. "Semimaru," in *Yōkyokushū* 2, vol. 59 of *Shinpen nihon koten bungaku zenshū*, ed. Koyama Hiroshi and Satō Ken'ichirō (Shōgakukan, 1998), 97–98; and Royall Tyler, *Japanese Nō Dramas* (London and New York: Penguin Books, 1992), 244.

77. "Semimaru," *Yōkyokushū* 2, 98–99; Tyler, 245.

78. *Kyōkunshō*, in Hayashiya Tatsusaburō, ed., *Kodai chūsei geijutsu ron*, vol. 23 of *Nihon shisō taikei* (Iwanami shoten, 1973), 75. Discussed in Itō, *Nihon chūsei no ōken*, 83.

79. On these points, see Hattori Yukio's four-part study (jō, chū, ge ichi,

ge ni) on the Sakagami legend: "Sakagami no miya: hōrō geinō min no geinōshin shinkō ni tsuite," *Bungaku*, 46 (April 1978), 44–59; *Bungaku*, 46 (May 1978), 84–103; *Bungaku*, 46 (December 1978), 80–90; and *Bungaku*, 47 (August 1979), 32–53. On the negative connotations of Sakagami's hair in the Edo period, see part one (jō), 44–45; on the shamanistic and border deity aspect of Sakagami, part two (chū), 86–87; and on the ritual link between pools, shamaness figures, and blind musicians, part four (ge ni), 35–36. On zanbaragami as a sign of leprosy, see Itō, *Nihon chūsei no ōken*, 87–88.

80. Matsuoka, *Utage no shintai*, 36–37, where he likens the acrobatic style of dengaku performers to the guerrilla tactics described in *Taiheiki*'s battle narrative.

81. *Taiheiki* 1, NKBT, vol. 34, 161–163; McCullough, *The Taiheiki: A Chronicle of Medieval Japan*, 131–132.

82. Matsuoka, *Utage no shintai*, 31.

83. Matsuoka Shinpei, "Rikisha dengaku kō: gohō dōji no bassei-tachi," *Kanze*, 49: 6 (June 1982), 24.

84. Hashimoto, "Dengaku to irui igyō," 51–52.

85. *Taiheiki* 3, NKBT, vol. 36, 61–62.

86. On these points, see Arai, *Akutō no kenkyū*, 64–80.

87. Ibid., 104.

88. Tennin 1/3/23 and 1/3/30. *Chūyūki* 3, ZST, vol. 11, 339 and 341.

89. Discussed in Watanabe Morimichi, *Sōhei seisuiki*, Sanseidō sensho 108 (Sanseidō, 1984), 45.

90. *Genpei seisuiki*, vol. 1, Chūsei no bungaku, 135–136.

91. On the vocal style of the akusō, see Komine, *Setsuwa no gensetsu: chūsei no hyōgen to rekishi jojutsu* (Shinwasha, 2002), 305–308; and Amino Yoshihiko, "Kōshō to biin," in *Kotoba no bunkashi, Chūsei* 1, ed. Amino Yoshihiko (Heibonsha, 1988), 35–36, note 7.

92. On the culture, dress, and behavior of the akutō in *Taiheiki*, see Hyōdō Hiromi, *Taiheiki "yomi" no kanōsei: rekishi to iu monogatari* (Kōdansha, 1995), 56–64. See also *Taiheiki* 1, NKBT, vol. 34, 263; and McCullough, *Taiheiki*, 224.

93. Deleuze, "Becoming-Intense, Becoming-Animal, Becoming-Imperceptible," in *A Thousand Plateaus*, 232–309.

94. On the strange mixing of genres that characterized entertainments of the akusō and warrior monks, see Hayashiya, *Chūsei geinōshi no kenkyū*, 359 and 368–371; and Arai, *Akutō no kenkyū*, 105–106.

95. Discussed in Arai, *Kenkyū no akutō*, 148–152; Gorai Shigeru, in *Yoshino kumano shinkō no kenkyū*, Sangaku shūkyōshi kenkyū sōsho 4 (Meicho shuppan, 1975), 49–75; and Tsukudo Reikan, "Suwa honji: Agui saku *Shintōshū* ni tsuite," in *Chūsei shūkyō geibun no kenkyū* 1, *Tsukudo Reikan chosakushū*, vol. 3 (Serika shobō, 1976), 91–130, esp. 118–123.

96. The other "Lesser Secret Transmission" was the "Preface" ("Jo"), also called "Gion shōja." Discussed in Tomikura, *Chūshaku* ge ni, 228 and 256–257; and *Heike monogatari kenkyū jiten*, ed. Ichiko Teiji (Meiji shoin, 1978), 474.

97. Translation based on text in Tomikura, *Zenchūshaku* ge ni, 251–253.

98. Tomikura, *Zenchūshaku* ge ni, 254–256.

99. Discussed in Tomikura Tokujirō, *Heike monogatari kenkyū* (Kadokawa shoten, 1964), 299.

100. Written down with the help of sighted assistants, *Tōdōyōshū* records important guild-related traditions handed down among the blind reciters of *Heike*. According to *Enpekiken ki* and *Tōdōyōshū*, sekitōkai was performed on the sixteenth day of the Second Month and on the nineteenth day of the Sixth Month to commemorate the guild's patron founder Prince Hitoyasu, his brother Emperor Kōkō, and their empress mother. On sekitōkai's place in the guild rituals, see Watanabe Sadamaro, *Heike monogatari no shisō* (Hōzōkan, 1989), 36–39 and 70–71; Ubukata Takashige, *Heike monogatari no kisō to kōzō: mizu no kami to monogatari* (Kindai bungeisha, 1984), 275; and for the account in *Tōdōyōshū*, *Tōdōyōshū*, vol. 27 of *Kaitei shiseki shūran*, ed. Kondō Heijō (Kyoto: Rinsen shoten, 1984), 734–735.

101. *Heike monogatari* jō, 334; McCullough, *Heike*, 163–169, esp. 167.

102. *Heike monogatari* jō, 337–338.

103. Ibid., 335.

104. The malefic powers associated with the Demon Gate are alluded to in *Genpei seisuiki*, vol. 2, Chūsei no bungaku, 85; *Shintei Genpei seisuiki*, vol. 2, 29; and *Engyōbon* jō, 89. Discussed in Mizuhara Hajime, *Heike monogatari* chū, Shinchō nihon koten shūsei (Shinchōsha, 1980), 33 (headnote); and on the geomantic balancing, Fukunaga, *Dōkyō to nihon bunka*, 233–234.

105. *Genpei seisuiki*, vol. 3, Chūsei no bungaku, 137–138; *Shintei Genpei seisuiki*, vol. 2, 308–309.

106. See Frank, *Kata-imi et kata-tagae*, 50–51.

107. As Frank notes, kata-tagae is not verified until the early ninth century, casting doubt on the historical veracity of the anecdote, 87–88.

108. Narrated in "Mokke no sata" ("Strange Portents").

109. *Heike monogatari* jō, 347.

110. *Heike monogatari* ge, 153–154.

111. In the Engyōbon ge, 160, the expression used is "mikata no taishōgun nite" (in the capacity of general of the emperor's forces), the correct term for the battlefield. The expression used in the Kakuichi variant would normally have been reserved for public or ceremonial occasions. Discussed by Takagi Makoto, "Yoshinaka monogatari no kōzō: ijin hōmontan kara no itsudatsu," *Kodai bungaku kenkyū*, 1 (October 1992), 68–69.

112. On the ritual background to Tomoyasu's dance, including its link to the tsuina and other expulsion rituals, see Sasaki Kōichi. "Tsuzumi hōgan: *Heike monogatari* no warai," *Kokugakuin zasshi*, 67 (December 1966), 20–35. For Tomoyasu's links with the Kebiishi and other aspects of his career, see Sasaki, 25–28; and Abe, "Oko no monogatari toshite no Heike monogatari: Tsuzumi hōgan Tomoyasu to 'warai' no geinō," 131–135.

113. *Heike monogatari* ge, 152.

114. Translation of McCullough, *Heike*, 96; *Heike monogatari* jō, 209.

115. Sakakibara Chizuru, "Kakuichibon *Heike monogatari* ni okeru antoku tei no myakuraku," *Nihon bungaku*, 37: 12 (December 1988), 20.

116. Translation of McCullough, *Heike*, 103; *Heike monogatari* jō, 221.

117. On Antoku and the defilement of the imperial line, see Ubukata, *Heike monogatari no kisō to kōzō*, 61–78; and Sakakibara, "*Heike monogatari* ni okeru antoku tei no myakuraku," 23–24.

118. *Engyōbon* ge, 408–409.

119. *Shintei Genpei seisuiki*, vol. 6, 65. Tsukamoto, *Genpei seisuiki* ge, 642.

120. *Engyōbon* ge, 408.

121. On defilement and dogs, birds, and other animals, see Morino Muneaki, "Heian jidai ni okeru shokuekan to inu," *Bungei gengo kenkyū*, bungei-hen, 12 (1987), 1–14; and Kuroda, *Sugata to shigusa no chūseishi*, 147–168.

122. Kuroda, *Nihon chūsei no kokka to shūkyō*, 443–446; and Hosokawa Ryōichi, *Shi to kyōkai no chūseishi* (Yōsensha, 1997), 31–34. For more extended discussions, see Tamura Yoshirō, "Tendai hongaku shisō gaisetsu," in *Tendai hongaku ron*, vol. 9 of *Nihon shisō taikei*, ed. Tada Kōryū, Ōkubo Ryōjun, Tamura Yoshirō, and Asai Endō (Iwanami shoten, 1973), 477–548; and Jacqueline I. Stone, *Original Enlightenment and the Transformation of Medieval Japanese Buddhism* (Honolulu: University of Hawaii Press, 1999), esp. 77–85, where she reviews the literature critiquing *hongaku* doctrine, including Hazama Jikō's 1942 essay. On the oppositional potential of *hongaku*, see Ruben L. F. Habito, "The Logic of Nonduality and Absolute Affirmation: Deconstructing Tendai *Hongaku* Writings," *JJRS*, 22: 102 (Spring 1995), 83–102.

123. From *Sōmoku hosshin shugyō jōbutsu ki*, cited and discussed in Sueki Fumihiko, *Nihon bukkyō shi: Shisōshi toshite no apurōchi* (Shinchōsha, 1992), 168; and Sueki, "Two Seemingly Contradictory Aspects of the Teaching of Innate Enlightenment (*hongaku*) in Medieval Japan," *JJRS*, 22: 102 (Spring 1995), 3–15. For Sueki's most detailed discussion of these points, see *Heian shōki bukkyō shisō no kenkyū: Annen no shisō keisei wo chūshin toshite* (Shunjūsha, 1995), 363–421, esp. the sections on Annen, 369–373, and hongaku, 416–421. See also William R. Lafleur on Buddhahood in the plant world, in "Saigyō and the Buddhist Value of Nature," *Nature in Asian Traditions of Thought: Essays in Environmental Philosophy*, ed. J. Baird Callicott and Roger T. Ames (Albany: SUNY Press, 1989), 183–195.

124. Sueki, *Nihon bukkyōshi*, 168–171. See also Tamura, *Tendai hongaku ron*, 487, who characterizes the Chinese thinker Cheng Guan (738–839), a contemporary of Zhanran, as already moving away from the latter's doctrine of the void and "eshō funi" to the more monistic position that "buddha nature" (*busshō*) is a state of awakened knowledge immanent in the heart–mind of all living beings.

125. Stone, *Original Enlightenment*, 81.

126. Satō, *Kami, hotoke, ōken no chūsei*, 395–397.

127. The sequence includes the opening of "The Death of the Major Counselor" ("Dainagon no shikyo") and the episodes "Yasuyori's Prayer" ("Yasuyori notto"), "Stupas Cast Afloat" ("Sotoba nagashi"), "The Foot-Drumming" ("Ashizuri"), Ariō ("Ariō"), and "The Bishop's Death" ("Sōzu shikyo").

128. On background to the sequence, see Mizuhara, *Enkyōbon heike monogatari ronkō*, 296–334; and Tomikura, *Zenchūshaku* jō, 333–334, 361–362, and 454–456. On wandering hijiri and placation in the Ariō sequence, see Yanatida Kunio's classic study, "Ariō to Shunkan Sōzu," in *Yanagita Kunio zenshū*, vol. 9, Chikuma bunko (Chikuma shobō, 1990), 93–111; and Gorai Shigeru, *Kōyahijiri*, Kadokawa sensho (Kadokawa shoten, 1965), 123–134. For a reading of the sequence from a local as opposed to a capital perspective, see Taniguchi Hiroshi, "Kikai-gai-shima runin tan no seiritsu: Shunkan Ariō setsuwa wo megutte," *Dōshisha Kokubungaku*, 15 (January 1980), 15–27; and Taniguchi, "Setsuwa denshō to *Heike monogatori* no kōsō: kikai-ga-shima runin tan wo megutte," *Dōshisha Kokubungaku*, 17 (March 1981), 79–89.

129. *Heike monogatari* jō, 186–187.

130. Takahashi Kimiaki, "Higashi Ajia to chūsei bungaku," in *Jūsan jūshi seiki no bungaku, Iwanami kōza nihon bungakushi*, vol. 5 (Iwanami shoten, 1995), 311–327; and Ōji, "Ninshiki kūkan toshite no 'nihon,'" 77–80.

131. Hōji 1/5/29. *Azumakagami: kōhen, KST*, vol. 33, 378. On the portents, see Ōishi, *Shūen kara mita chūsei nihon*, 23–24.

132. *Heike monogatari* jō, 234.

133. In describing the island inhabitants, the Nagatobon narrator uses the same phrase that is here used of Shunkan's hair, stating that "their hair shoots up skyward" (*kami wa sorasama e oiagari*), and likens the inhabitants to "oni" (demons). *Nagatobon Heike monogatari no sōgō kenkyū*, vol. 1, ed. Asahara Yoshiko and Nanami Hiroaki (Benseisha, 1998–1999), 291; and *Heike monogatari Nagatobon*, ed. Kokusho kankōkai (Meicho kankōkai, 1974), 134–135.

134. *Heike monogatari* jō, 235

135. Some of these include 貴賀之嶋 / 貴海島 / and 貴賀井嶋. Discussed in Takahashi, *Shūen kara mita chūsei nihon*, 307–308.

136. *Heike monogatari* jō, 199.

137. On the two sequences, see Tomikura, *zenchūshaku* jō, 361–362 and 364.

138. From *Rakuyō dengakuki*, cited earlier.

139. On the dragon motif, see Bialock, "Outcasts, Emperorship, and Dragon Cults in *The Tale of the Heike*," 270–309.

140. *Heike monogatari* ge, 277.

141. Gorai Shigeru, "Kumano sanzan no rekishi to shinkō," in *Yoshino kumano shinkō no kenkyū*, 158–162; Gorai, "Kumano shinwa to kumano shintō," *Shugendō no bijutsu geinō bungaku*, vol. 2, Sangaku shūkyōshi kenkyū sōsho 15, ed. Gorai Shigeru (Meicho shuppan, 1981), 53–78. See also David Moerman, "The Ideology of Landscape and the Theater of State: Insei Pilgrimage to Kumano (1090–1220)," *JJRS*, 24: 3–4 (Fall 1997), 347–374.

142. "Shozan engi," in *Jisha engi*, vol. 20 of *Nihon shisō taikei*, 103.

143. Discussed in Nanami Hiroaki, "Inseiki no kumano mōde: metsuzai, chinkon, gohō-zuke wo meguru girei to shinkō, *Bungei gengo kenkyū*, 13 (February 1988), 30–32.

144. See Yamamoto Hiroko, "Chūsei kumano mōde no shūkyō sekai: jōdo toshite no kumano e," in *Henjōfu: chūsei shinbutsu shūgō no sekai* (Shunjūsha, 1993), 67; and Nanami, "Inseiki no kumano mōde," 32–33.

145. Nanami, "Inseiki no kumano mōde," 33–37.

146. Ibid., 50–52.

147. "Shozan engi," vol. 20 of *Nihon shisō taikei*, 104–108. Discussed in Nanami "Inseiki no kumano mōde," 53–56.

148. On the evolution of *shinbutsu shūgō* (amalgamating divinities and Buddhas) and the late Heian doctrine of honji/suijaku, see Tsuji Zennosuke, *Nihon bukkyōshi ronshū*, vol. 5 of *Nihon bukkyōshi kenkyū*, (Iwanami shoten, 1984), 1–62; and Satō, *Kami, hotoke, ōken no chūsei*, 348–375, on its medieval elaboration in the "wrathful" and "saving" deity paradigm.

149. The yokukai (*kāma-dhātu*) and shikikai (*rūpa-dhātu*) are two of the three worlds, the third being the mushokukai (*arūpya-dhātu*). In the yokukai world dwell those conditioned by desire and in the shikikai those who have transcended desire but continue to be caught in the world as conditioned by material things.

150. *Engyōbon* jō, 180–184.

151. See Philip B. Yampolsky, *The Platform Sutra of the Sixth Patriarch* (New York: Columbia University Press, 1967), 132.

152. On the historical background to the daruma shū, see Bernard Faure, "The Daruma-shū, Dōgen, and Sōtō Zen," *MN*, 42: 1 (1987), 25–55.

153. Akamatsu Toshihide, *Heike monogatari no kenkyū* (Hōzōkan, 1980), 372–373.

154. *Myōan Eisai: kōzen gokokuron, Ikkyū Sōjun: kyōun shū, hoka nihen*, in *Genten nihon bukkyō no shisō*, vol. 10, ed. Ichikawa Hakugen, Iriya Yoshitaka, and Yanagida Seizan (Iwanami shoten, 1991), 41. Cited and discussed in Akamatsu, *Heike monogatari no kenkyū*, 372.

155. From "Sanzen-in bunsho," cited and discussed by Amino, *Nihonron no shiza*, 115.

156. Makino Kazuo, "Engyōbon *Heike monogatari* no ichisokumen," *Geibun kenkyū*, 36 (March 1977), 1–22, esp. 8–15.

157. Yamamoto Hiroko, "Kikai-ga-shima setsuwa to chūsei shingi shinkō: Engyōbon *Heike monogatari* to *Genpei jōsuiki* wo megutte," in *Heike monogatari taiheiki*, 151–152. We can add that the Kegon doctrine of "sangai yuishin" (three worlds, one mind) also undermined hongaku in its substantialist form. "From the viewpoint of sangai yuishin, because the external world is formed by the mind of human beings, when human beings achieve Buddhahood the grass and trees that are the object of thought also achieve Buddhahood." Sueki, *Nihon bukkyōshi*, 170. On yuishin in relation to hongaku thought, see also Tamura, *Tendai hongaku ron*, 491.

158. Naritsune articulates the central doctrine of Kakuban's Shingon Pure Land, which emphasized "kaji no sokushin jōbutsu" and "tariki no ōjō" as teachings especially suited to the foolish and ignorant. Discussed in Makino, "Engyōbon *Heike monogatari* no ichisokumen," 9.

159. Commenting on the nondual epistemology that informed the practice of Buddhist pilgrimage on the Kunisaki Peninsula, Grapard writes: "The result of this system of symbolic correspondences was that walking in the mountains while listening to their natural sounds was equivalent to reading the scripture— assimilating it, letting it become one's body, one's mind." Allan G. Grapard, "Geosophia, Geognosis, and Geopiety: Orders of Significance in Japanese Representations of Space," in *NowHere: Space, Time, and Modernity*, 386.

160. *Genpei seisuiki*, vol. 2, Chūsei no bungaku, 91; *Shintei Genpei seisuiki*, vol. 2, 37.

161. Yamamoto, "Kikai-ga-shima setsuwa to chūsei shingi shinkō, 158–159.

162. *Genpei seisuiki*, vol. 2, Chūsei no bungaku, 92; *Shintei Genpei seisuiki*, vol. 2, 37–38.

163. *Genpei seisuiki*, vol. 2, Chūsei no bungaku, 93; *Shintei Genpei seisuiki*, vol. 2, 38–39.

164. Wittgenstein's *Tractatus* (6.54), cited in A. C. Grayling, *Wittgenstein* (Oxford and New York: Oxford University Press, 1988), 45.

165. The influx of new populations into temples from the late Heian period on made accommodations between the secular and profane spheres even more necessary, which was reflected in the ideological construction of "ninbō" (human law). See Satō, *Nihon chūsei no kokka to bukkyō*, 27–34.

166. As Paul Hamilton notes, Foucault "claims that he has defined a 'discursive formation,' and thus historically located an 'episteme,' when he 'can show that it may give birth simultaneously or successively to mutually exclusive objects, without having to modify itself.'" Hence, "The mapping of historical strata exposes the discursive formation whose tolerance of these contradictions keeps itself in power." Paul Hamilton, *Historicism* (London and New York: Routledge, 1996), 137–138; and Michel Foucault, *The Archaeology of Knowledge*, trans. A. M. Sheridan Smith (London: Tavistock, 1972), 44.

167. It underlies Jien's use of paradoxical logic (*dōri*) in *Gukanshō* to explain the complicity of Buddhism in the slaying of emperors during the ancient period.

168. On the ambiguous status of the demonic, see Abe Yasurō, "Tengu: ma no seishinshi," *Kokubungaku*, 44: 8 (August 1999), 61–67.

Chapter 8

1. The only other mention is the slaying of two kaburo in "The Execution of Tosabō" ("Tosabō kirare"), *Heike monogatari* ge, 387; McCullough, *Heike*, 406.

2. *Heike monogatari* jō, 91; McCullough, *Heike*, 28.

3. Mizuhara Hajime, *Heike monogatari* jō, Shinchō nihon koten shūsei, 38; and Takahashi Masaaki, *Kiyomori izen: Ise Heishi no kōryū*, Heibonsha sensho

85 (Heibonsha, 1984), 121. The *Ban dainagon ekotoba*, mentioned by Taka-hashi, shows what appears to be a low-ranking Kebiishi officer (*kado no osa*, responsible for arresting and jailing criminals) in red attire.

4. Moriya, *Chūsei geinō no genzō*, 197–198. On the wide latitude given to the notion of a childlike appearance and its associations with demonic behavior, see also Yanagita Kunio, "Oni no shison," in *Teihon Yanagita Kunio shū*, vol. 9 (Chikuma shobō, 1962), 427–433.

5. Moriya Takeshi, "Kyōwarawa no fubō," in *Nihon chūsei e no shiza: furyū basara kabuki*, Eneichikei bukkusu, 459 (Nihon hōsō shuppan kyōkai, 1984), 12–22; and Moriya, *Chūsei geinō no genzō*, 200–201.

6. *Shōtoku taishi denki*, in *Taishi den* jō, vol. 3 of *Shōtoku taishi zenshū*, ed. Fujiwara Yūsetsu (Ryūginsha sōritsu jimusho, 1944), 305. Cited and dis-cussed in Sakai Kimi, *Chūsei no uwasa johō dentatsu no shikumi* (Yoshikawa kōbunkan, 1997), 13. Sakai's chapter, "Uwasa no chikara," 5–18, contains insightful observations on the social, political, and supernatural role of rumor in medieval society. For the *Heike* occurrence of this same expression, see "The Burning of Kiyomizudera" ("Kiyomizudera enshō"), *Heike monogatari* jō, 114; and McCullough, *Heike*, 41.

7. *Genpei seisuiki*, vol. 2, Chūsei no bungaku, 31; *Shintei Genpei seisuiki*, vol. 1, 111.

8. *Genpei seisuiki*, vol. 1, Chūsei no bungaku, 31; *Shintei Genpei seisuiki*, vol. 1, 111; and *Nagatobon Heike monogatari no sōgō kenkyū*, vol. 1, 42. In the Nagatobon, it is not entirely clear if the meaning intended is that the kaburo are carrying the birds—implied by the verb "motasete"—or that the kaburo themselves are birds.

9. *Engyōbon* jō, 614.

10. On the link between the Kebiishi and entertainments, including dengaku, see Abe, "Oko no monogatari toshite no *Heike monogatari*: Tsuzumi hōgan Tomoyasu to 'warai' no geinō," 121–143; and Sunagawa Hiroshi, "Biwa hōshi ni tsuite no futatsu, mitsu no mondai," *GK*, 31 (March 1995), 75–83.

11. *Taiheiki* 1, *NKBT*, vol. 34, 323 and 178–179. Discussed in Sakai, *Chūsei no uwasa*, 16–17.

12. Apart from the circumstantial evidence linking the kaburo to the kebiishi and outcast populations, there are no "documents" corroborating their histori-cal existence.

13. Tomikura, *Zenchūshaku* jō, 72–73.

14. *Heike monogatari* jō, 83.

15. *Genpei jōsuiki*, for example, makes Kiyomori's identification with Xu-anzong explicit, although it does so by making the Bo Juyi allusion refer not directly to the kaburo but to the general tenor of Kiyomori's ambitions, thereby forecasting his eventual destruction. *Genpei seisuiki*, vol. 1, Chūsei no bungaku, 34; and *Shintei Genpei seisuiki*, vol. 1, 114.

16. Kuroda Akira, "Gion shōja oboegaki: chūshaku, shōdō, setsuwa shū," in *Heike monogatari Taiheiki*, 43.

17. Translation of McCullough, *Heike*, 27; *Heike monogatari* jō, 89.

18. Tomikura, *Zenchūshaku* jō, 64. The requirement to govern in harmony with the yin and the yang was a legacy of the earlier yin-yang Daoist assemblage discussed in Part One.

19. McCullough, *Heike*, 28; *Heike monogatari* jō, 91.

20. Lau, *Analects*, 11; Yoshida, *Rongo, SKT*, vol. 1, 166; Tomikura *Zenchūshaku* jō, 71.

21. Rebel figures that are held up as admonitory examples in the Preface later appear in a more favorable light. As Hyōdō has noted, in "Xiangyang Palace," the implicit sympathy for the rebel undermines the Buddhist logic of the Preface. Likewise, Saeki Shin'ichi has contrasted the Engyōbon variant, which expresses reverence toward the court, with the Kakuichi *Heike*'s more positive view of the rebel. See Hyōdō, *Ōken to monogatari*, 65–99, esp. 84 and 86–96; Saeki Shin'ichi, "*Heike monogatari* entan setsuwa no seiritsu," *GK*, 15 (March 1979), 1–13; and Kuroda, "Gion shōja oboegaki: chūshaku, shōdō, setsuwa shū," 43.

22. *Engyōbon* jō, 29–33.

23. On the felicitous mode in the Engyōbon, see Kobayashi, *Heike monogatari seiseiron*, 81–110.

24. *Heike monogatari* jō, 90; McCullough, *Heike*, 27.

25. Tomikura, *Zenchūshaku* jō, 66.

26. *Engyōbon* jō, 31.

27. Ibid.

28. That Kiyomori did consume the fish is made clear in a variant of the Kakuichi *Heike*, the Kyūrinsen bunkozō koshahon, which states that Kiyomori "had it cooked, ate it himself, and had all his attendants eat it with him." This text also places less emphasis on the mediation of the Kumano avatar by substituting the phrase "kore wa medetaki on koto nari" for the standard Kakuichi's "Kore wa gongen no go-rishō." See Tomikura, *Zenchūshaku* jō, 65.

29. See the discussion of Bishop Ikkai that follows.

30. A medieval audience would have typically associated impermanence with death, as in the expression *seisha hisshi* ("all living beings must die") in Hōnen's famous nirvana chant (*nehan wasan*). Hyōdō, *Ōken to monogatari*, 70–71, reads *Heike*'s swerve to *jōsha hissui* as indicative of an ideological intent. Tomikura, on the other hand, *Zenchūshaku* jō, 37–38, attributed the choice of *jōsha hissui*, with its emphasis on rise and fall, to the historical nature of the tale. For the wasan, see *Shōwa shinshū hōnen shōnin zenshū*, ed. Ishii Kyōdō (Kyoto: Heirakuji shoten, 1965), 1205; and on the Preface's multiple meanings and sources, Kuroda, "Gion shōja oboegaki: chūshaku, shōdō, setsuwa shū," 27–34.

31. *Engyōbon* jō, 17. A similar expression is also found in the Nagatobon. In both cases, the meaning is not entirely clear, and the translation remains tentative. See *Nagatobon Heike monogatari no sōgō kenkyū*, vol. 1, 5.

32. On the transcendent character of "ten" in the medieval period, see Satō, *Kami, hotoke, ōken no chūsei*, 231.

33. *Engyōbon* jō, 32–33. For the alternative reading, my thanks to Rieko Kamei.

34. For the other variants, see *Genpei seisuiki*, vol. 1, Chūsei no bungaku, 33; *Shintei Genpei seisuiki*, vol. 1, 113–114; *Nagatobon Heike monogatari no sōgō kenkyū*, vol. 1, 42–45; *Nagatobon* (1974), 18–19; and Fukuda, *Genpei tōjōroku* jō, 73–81. The Fukuda text also contains an excellent summary comparing the variants.

35. On possible sources, see Kuroda, "Gion shōja oboegaki: chūshaku, shōdō, setsuwa shū," 43–47; and Yanase Kiyoshi, "Kaburo ibun kō: 'dōyō' to Taira no Kiyomori zō shōkei no kankei," in *Nitchū koten bungaku ronkō* (Kyūko shoin, 1999), 471–486, originally published in *Nihon bungaku*, 46: 5 (May 1997), 25–34. For Yanase's remarks on the Dunhuang text, "Zenkan ryūke taishi den," see 482. *Nihon shoki* records the capture of a tortoise with the character for monkey written on its shell, an omen of disorder. See Tenchi 8/10/15, Aston, *Nihongi*, vol. 2, 291.

36. Yanase, *Nitchū koten bungaku ronkō*, 480.

37. *Genpei seisuki*, vol. 4, Chūsei no bungaku, 266. *Shintei Genpei seisuiki*, vol. 6, 152–153.

38. The *Han shu* portrays Wang Mang as one who establishes a false empire by cleverly making use of prophetic signs. Discussed in Yanase, *Nitchū koten bungaku ronkō*, 478.

39. The *Jin shu*, a Tang period history, states: "Thus, the five stars wax and wane. When someone loses rank, the star essence (*jing*) descends to earth and becomes a human being. Suixing descends in the form of a noble minister, and Yinghou in the form of a child." On the Chinese background to Keiwakusei and childlike singers of prophetic songs, see Oyanagi, "Dōyō, toshin, kyōhi," in *Tōyō shisō no kenkyō*, 412–414; and Yanase, *Nitchū koten bungaku ronkō*, 479 and 486, including a passage from the *Lunheng* (section on demons) on children's songs as messages of the red star Yinghou.

40. From *Shōtoku taishi denryaku*, in *Shiden-bu* 10, *Dainihon bukkyō zensho*, vol. 71, ed. Zaidan Hōjin Suzuki Gakujutsu Zaidan (Zaidan Hōjin Suzuki Gakujutsu Zaidan, 1972), 126–127. Cited and discussed in Sakai Kimi, *Chūsei no uwasa*, 11–12.

41. *Shōtoku taishi denki*, in *Taishi den* jō, 305. Cited in Sakai, *Chūsei no uwasa*, 13. For a slightly different version of the same passage, see also the recension in *Shōtoku taishi denki*, Denshō bungaku shiryō shūsei 1, ed. Makino Kazuo (Miyai shoten, 1999), 35–36.

42. As an example, *Taiheiki* tells of a meteorite that falls to Earth with signs portending the death and destruction of Shi huangdi. See *Taiheiki* 3, NKBT, vol. 36, 46. Discussed in Yanase, *Nitchū koten bungaku ronkō*, 486. For Keiwaku's destructive aspect, see also the "Governors of Heaven" in Yoshida, *Shiki* 4 (hassho), SKT, vol. 41, 164.

43. The conquest of Qin, the White Emperor, by Han Gaozu, identified with the red essence, was based on prophetic signs in the omen-lore. See Nakamura, "Onmyōdō ni juyō sareta 'isho' ni tsuite," OMS, vol. 4, *Tokuron*, 263.

44. For one series of weft-texts predicting Bochang's rise, see Yasui and Naka-mura, *Sho chūkō*, vol. 2 of *Jūshū isho*, 83. Also discussed in Yahagi, "Temmu-ki to sono shūhen," 134–135; and Hirohata, *Bansei ikkei ōchō shisō: Jimmu tennō no densetsu*, 300–331.

45. See *Engyōbon* jō, 31 and headnote 6.

46. On the magical properties of red, see Shinkawa, *Dōkyō wo meguru kōbō*, 56–58.

47. The characterization of Wang Mang as a minister of "outstanding talent and wisdom" is a trait that goes unmentioned in *Genpei jōsuiki*, which con-cludes its account of Kiyomori's kaburo strategy with the whispered remark that it was "the act of a demon" ("tengu no shoi"), clearly intended as a negative judgment.

48. *Genpei seisuiki*, vol. 1, Chūsei no bungaku, 32; *Shintei Genpei jōsuiki*, vol. 1, 112–113.

49. The biwa hōshi's historical ties to the area east of the Kamo River are well attested in documents. According to *Tōdōyōshū*, the founder of the Yasaka-kata school of Heike recitation, Jōgen, "lived near the Yasaka Pagoda." Located in the eastern part of the capital, the region about the Yasaka Pagoda included the East-ern Market and the ancient burial ground Toribeno, the latter stretching from Rokuhara Mitō—the site of the main residential quarter of the Taira until their defeat in the Genpei War—to the Kiyomizu slope near Kiyomizu Temple. On the topography of the biwa hōshi, see Ueki Yukinobu, "Tōdōza no keisei to hei-kyoku," in *Heike monogatari katari to gentai*, 7–29, esp. 14–16; Hyōdō Hi-romi, "Kakuichi-bon *Heike monogatari* no denshō wo megutte: Muromachi ōken to geinō," in *Heike biwa: katari to ongaku*, ed. Kamisangō Yūkō (Hitsuji shobō, 1993), 55–82, esp. 65–74; and Sunagawa Hiroshi, *Heike monogatari shinkō* (Tokyo Bijutsukan, 1982), 50–53. On the association between "ichi" in the names of Heike reciters and "market" (*ichi*), see Sunagawa, "Biwa hōshi ni tsuite no futatsu, mitsu no mondai," *GK*, 31 (March 1995), 75–83, esp. 78–79. For the *Tōdōyōshū* passage, see *Kaitei shiseki shūran*, vol. 27, 730.

50. On Shinzei's program, including his architectural, musical, and historio-graphical projects, see Gomi, "Shinzei seiken no kōzō," in *Heike monogatari: shi to setsuwa*, 176–210.

51. On these points, see Kobayashi Yoshikazu, "Engyōbon Heike monogatari no seiritsu," in *Heike monogatari no seiritsu, Anata ga yomu Heike monogatari* 1, ed. Tochigi Yoshitada et al. (Yūseidō, 1993) 91–111; and in the same volume, Asahara Yoshiko, "Heike monogatari no keisei to shingon ken," 167–194.

52. Shimizu Masumi, "Shi no Heike ju no Heike: *Heike monogatari* no seisei to kanjūjike no chikara," *GK*, 34 (March 1998), 41–52; and Shimizu, "Biwa hōshi no shūbun: jōsha hissui, kosha, shōgai," *Kokugakuin zasshi* 96: 1 (Janu-ary 1995), 65–83.

53. Kōwa 5/2/30. *Honchō seiki*, *KST*, vol. 9, 323–324. Discussed in Shi-mizu, "Shi no Heike," 42. On the market, see the previous note.

54. Shimizu, "Shi no Heike," 43–44.

55. Ibid., 47–51.

56. For the first citation from the *Guoyu*, see Shimizu, "Shi no Heike," 50; and "Biwa hōshi no shūbun," 70. The source for the second citation, *Guwen xiaojing*, was one of the standard texts used in educating an emperor. Cited in Shimizu, "Biwa hōshi no shūbun," 70.

57. There is a large literature on placation and *Heike*, a theory first proposed by Tsukudo Reikan. See Tsukudo Reikan, "*Heike monogatari* ni tsuite oboegaki," in *Shūkyō bungaku fukko to jojishi, Tsukudo Reikan chosakushū* 1 (Serika shobō, 1976), 270–299; and Tsukudo, "Rekishi to bungaku to no kyūsai," in *Heike monogatari: katari to gentai*, 1–6. The theory and its many variants are reviewed and critiqued in Saeki Shin'ichi, "Katarimono to rekishi: *Heike monogatari* wo chūshin ni," in *Sanbun bungaku "monogatari" no sekai, Kōza nihon no denshō bungaku*, vol. 3, ed. Minobe Shigekatsu and Hattori Kōzō (Miyai shoten, 1995), 272–287. See also Plutschow, *Chaos and Cosmos*, 217–228; and Bialock, "The Tale of the Heike," in *Medieval Japanese Writers, Dictionary of Literary Biography*, vol. 203, ed. Steven D. Carter (Detroit: Gale Group, 1999), 79–80. For Shimizu's remarks on placation and biwa hōshi, see "Biwa hōshi no shūbun," 67.

58. A reading followed by Yanase, *Nitchū koten bungaku ronkō*, 480–481.

59. Kuroda, "Gion shōja oboegaki: chūshaku, shōdō, setsuwa shū," 43.

60. Cited in Kuroda, 45–46, from the Hiroshima daigaku-bon, one of several texts belonging to the Shoryōbu lineage of rōei commentaries.

61. Ibid., 46.

62. In principle, Kuroda's theory does not rule out the possibility of orality influencing the textual tradition, but his remarks suggest that the kaburo are a pure product of textuality.

63. On the negative traits of the warrior in Indo-European myth, analyzed by George Dumézil and reinterpreted in relation to the nomadic, see Deleuze, *A Thousand Plateaus*, 351–355. The reference to Tadamori's squint-eyedness (*sugame*) occurs in "The Night Attack," *Heike monogatari* jō, 85–86. On the incest motif in *Heike*, see my remarks in Chapter 7.

64. On the marine model and the sea as "smooth space," see Deleuze, *A Thousand Plateaus*, 478–482.

65. *Nagatobon Heike monogatari no sōgō kenkyū*, vol. 1, 43. On metallurgy as an "ambulant science," see *A Thousand Plateaus*, 372–373 and 404–414.

66. That the kaburo tale overlaps at some level with craft groups in alliance with Kiyomori is suggested by the Engyōbon account of the construction of Tokujōjuin, where blacksmiths, carpenters, and woodsmen seemingly allied with Tadamori (Kiyomori's father) are placed under the authority of Enryakuji Temple. The narrative thereby performs a translation of the anomic–nomadic into an analogical sign of the sacred, a binary opposition expressive of defilement and purity that serves to display Enryakuji's sacred authority. On the Tokujōjuin narrative, see Bialock, "Outcasts, Emperorship, and Dragon Cults in *The Tale of the Heike*," 236–259.

67. *Nagatobon Heike monogatari no sōgō kenkyū*, vol. 1, 42.

68. *Genpei seisuiki*, vol. 1, Chūsei no bungaku, 31; and *Shintei Genpei sei-suiki*, vol. 1, 111. In a nomadic cultural assemblage, space is "held" or "occupied" rather than structured through oppositions, levels, and notions of inside–outside as it is in a sedentary culture. The former is the "smooth" space of the nomos; the latter is the striated space of centers or states. See *A Thousand Plateaus*, "The Smooth and the Striated," 474–500, esp. 474–475; and in "Treatise on Nomadology," 380–387.

69. On number, see *A Thousand Plateaus*, 387–394.

70. Translation of McCullough, *Heike*, 215; *Heike monogatari* jō, 417.

71. I have altered McCullough's language here.

72. McCullough, *Heike*, 217; *Heike monogatari* jō, 419.

73. An example of the demon-subjugating motif in *Heike* is "Nue" (The Thrush Monster), *Heike monogatari* jō, 324–328; McCullough, *Heike*, 160–163. On the "rich man motif" in *Heike*, see Higuchi, *Chūsei no shijitsu to denshō*, 54–93.

74. Studies of the Gion Lady episode and its different versions in the *Heike* variants include Sasaki Hachirō, in Part Two (ni-bu) of *Zōho Heike monogatari no kenkyū* (Waseda daigaku shuppanbu, 1967), 52–60; Tomikura, *Zenchūshaku* chū, 247–249; Akamatsu Toshihide's chapter "Kyōko to shijitsu 'Gion Nyōgo, Aosaburai no yume, Jishō monogatari': *Heike monogatari* no gentai ni tsuite dokuron," in *Heike monogatari no kenkyū*, 147–167, also published under the same title in *Heike monogatari* I, Nihon bungaku kenkyū taisei, ed. Takehisa Tsuyoshi (Kokusho kankōkai, 1990), 135–162; Higuchi, *Chūsei no shijitsu to denshō*, 71–93; and Tanaka Takako's chapter, "Dakiniten-hō 'ōken,' (1): Gion Nyōgo wo megutte," in *Gehō to aihō no chūsei*, Divinitasu sōsho 4 (Sunagoya shobō, 1993), 203–230.

75. *Nagatobon* (1974), 416–418, esp. 416; and *Engyōbon* jō, 632–636, esp. 632. Discussed in Akamatsu, *Heike monogatari no kenkyū*, 148; and Sasaki, *Heike monogatari no kenkyū*, ni-bu, 52–53. Sasaki, however, reads the rather vague Nagatobon version as implying that the nyōbō and Gion Nyōgo are one and the same figure, setting it apart from the Engyōbon that sharply differentiates the two. This view is not shared by Akamatsu.

76. For the second version, see *Shintei Genpei seisuiki*, vol. 3, 269; and Tsukamoto, *Genpei seisuiki*, ge, 31–32. Discussed in Sasaki, *Heike monogatari no kenkyū*, ni-bu, 56.

77. Discussed in Tomikura, *Zenchūshaku* chū, 247–248; and Ichiko Teiji, *Heike monogatari kenkyū jiten*, 133.

78. *Shintei Genpei seisuiki*, vol. 3, 262; Tsukamoto, *Genpei seisuiki* ge, 25–26.

79. Higuchi, *Chūsei no shijitsu to denshō*, 80–82.

80. Mizuhara, *Heike monogatari* chū, Shinchō nihon koten bungaku shūsei, 142–143.

81. Toda Yoshimi, "Ōchō toshi to shōen taisei," in *Kodai* 4, Iwanami kōza nihon rekishi 4 (Iwanami shoten, 1976), 187–189; and Higuchi, *Chūsei no shijitsu to denshō*, 61.

82. *Kojidan*, 1:81, in *Kojidan* jō, Koten bunko 60, ed. Kobayashi Yasuharu (Gendai shinchōsha, 1981), 97–99.

83. Gomi, "Ronsetsu: Insei to tennō," 93.

84. Higuchi, *Chūsei no shijitsu to denshō*, 84–85. As Higuchi notes, the verb "tsuihō" indicates a much more lenient punishment than either exile or imprisonment, let alone beheading.

85. Michele Marra has explained the Buddhist concept "hōben" in the domain of language as follows: "The Buddhist justification of language occurred at the metaphorical level, where a privileged kind of language—poetic—came to be accepted as a "skillful device" (*hōben*) to supplement the contingent, illusory logic of ordinary language." See Michele Marra, "Japanese Aesthetics: The Construction of Meaning," *Philosophy East & West*, 45: 3 (July 1995), 372. For Genji's classic use of "expedient means" as a defense of fiction, see Tyler, *The Tale of Genji*, vol. 1, 461.

86. On the codicil, see Yokoi Kiyoshi, " 'Kyōgen kigo no ayamari, sanbutsujō no in' no tenkyo," *Enkyōbon Heike monogatari kōshō* 1, ed. Mizuhara Hajime (Shintensha, 1992), 95–98; and on the Engyōbon's use of such language, Kubo Isamu, "Engyōbon *Heike monogatari* no kyōgen kigo kan: 'monogatari' no shikō shita mono," *Bungaku*, 10: 2 (April 1999), 55–69. For the codicil, see *Engyōbon* ge, 291.

87. Watanabe Yasuaki, "Korai futeishō to kyōgen kigo-kan," *KK*, 67: 11 (November 1990), 60–70; and William R. Lafleur, "Symbol and Yūgen: Shunzei's Use of Tendai Buddhism," in *The Karma of Words: Buddhism and the Literary Arts in Medieval Japan* (Berkeley: University of California Press, 1983), 80–106.

88. Discussed in Tanaka Takako, "Tendai kuden hōmon to setsuwa: *Keiranjūyōshū* no 'monogatari ni iwaku' wo megutte," in *Setsuwa no ba: shōdō, chūshaku, Setsuwa no kōza*, vol. 3, ed. Honda Giken et al. (Benseisha, 1993), 294–315.

89. Tanaka, *Gehō to aihō*, 295–296.

90. *Keiranjūyōshū*, vol. 76 of *Taishō shinshū daizōkyō*, ed. Takakusu Junjirō (Taishō issaikyō kankōkai, 1931), 633; and Tanaka, *Gehō to aihō*, 203–204. The name Ikkai suggests that he leapt over all the intervening ranks.

91. On "katari" as speech that is radically other to official discourse, see Hyōdō, *Katarimono josetsu: Heike katari no hassei to hyōgen*, esp. 3–36; and on categories of medieval discourse, Fukuda Hideichi, Shimazu Tadao, Komine Kazuaki, and Matsuoka Shinpei, " 'Shinpojiumu' hōkoku: Chūsei bungaku no han'i," *Chūsei bungaku*, 35 (June 1990), 1–23.

92. Tanaka, "Tendai kuden hōmon to setsuwa," 302.

93. On the heterodox force of the "zōdan" category, see Komine's remarks in " 'Shinpojiumu' hōkoku: Chūsei bungaku no han'i," 9–13; Komine Kazuaki, "Jitsugo to mōgo no 'setsuwa' shi," in *Kodai kōki, Nihon bungakushi wo yomu*, vol. 2 (Yūseidō, 1991), 240–262; and Tanaka, "Tendai kuden hōmon to setsuwa," 303.

94. A Tendai doctrine which held that the three forms of reality were fused into one.

95. Tanaka, "Tendai kuden hōmon to setsuwa," 302–303.

96. In "Shishi no tani," *Heike monogatari* jō, 122; McCullough, *Heike*, 45–46.

97. *Kojidan*, 3:70, *Kojidan* jō, 278–279.

98. Tanaka, *Gehō to aihō*, 221–222.

99. Tomikura, *Zenchūshaku* chū, 248; and Akamatsu, *Heike monogatari no kenkyū*, 154–167. The historian Mori Katsumi, *Nissō bunka kōryū no shomondai* (zōho), 185–202, devoted an entire chapter to these relics as evidence of trade between Japan and Mount Yuwang.

100. On the medieval use of relics in Japan, see Brian D. Ruppert, *Jewel in the Ashes: Buddha Relics and Power in Early Medieval Japan* (Cambridge, MA, and London: Harvard University Press, 2000).

101. Tanaka, *Gehō to aihō*, 148–175.

102. Based on the *Keishi Hōonji butsuge shari engi*, cited in Tanaka, *Gehō to aihō*, 156.

103. Ibid., 152.

104. Ibid., 159–160.

105. The episode is discussed in Kusaka Tsutomu, "*Heiji monogatari* Akugenda raika-banashi no tenkai: futatsu no taki to ryūjin shinkō," *GK*, 16 (March 1980), 12–26.

106. Generally thought to belong to a fluid stage in *Heiji monogatari*'s development when it came under the custodianship of biwa hōshi.

107. *Hōgen monogatari Heiji monogatari*, NKBT, vol. 31, 288–289.

108. Kusaka, "*Heiji monogatari* Akugenda raika-banashi no tenkai," 14–15 and 20; and on the biwa hōshi's ties to serpent/dragon cults, see Bialock, "Outcasts, Emperorship, and Dragon Cults in *The Tale of the Heike*," 283–287 and 306–308.

109. See Tanaka, *Gehō to aihō*, 139; and Bernard Faure, "Now You See It, Now You Don't: Relics and Regalia in Japanese Buddhism," Paper presented at the annual meeting of the American Academy of Religion, New Orleans, LA, November 17–18, 1996.

110. Recorded in *Yōwa gannen ki*. Cited in Tomikura, *Zenchūshaku* chū, 212–214 and 215–216.

111. *Heike monogatari* jō, 407–408; McCullough, *Heike*, 209–211.

112. A similar story about the death of the warrior Minamoto no Yoshiie relates how one of his female attendants dreams of demons that look like "demons painted on hell-scrolls." See *Kojidan* (326), vol. 2, 53.

113. The assumption is that, on occasion, they were performed in sequence, although, to my knowledge, no record exists of such a performance.

114. *Heike monogatari* jō, 412.

115. *Heike monogatari* jō, 412–416; McCullough, *Heike*, 213–215.

116. *Heike monogatari* jō, 412.

117. Ibid., 416.

118. On kanjin activity and *Heike*, see Saeki Shin'ichi, "Kanjin hijiri to setsuwa: aruiwa 'setsuwa' to 'katari,'" in *Heike monogatari: setsuwa to katari*, An-

ata ga yomu Heike monogatari, vol. 2, ed. Mizuhara Hajime (Yūseidō, 1994), 201–219.

119. Gotō's two early studies can be found in Gotō Tanji, "*Heike monogatari* shutten kō, dai-ni setsu meido sosei ki," in *Senki monogatari no kenkyū* (Tsukuba shoten, 1936), 56–71; and Gotō, "Heike monogatari no sho-mondai," in *Chūsei bungaku: kenkyū to shiryō, Kokubungaku ronsō* 2, ed. Keio Gijuku Daigaku Kokubungaku Kenkyūkai (Shibundō, 1958), 3–33. See also Mizuhara, *Ronkō*, 196–204.

120. Atsumi Kaoru, "Engyōbon *Heike monogatari* no jishinbō setsuwa ni tsuite: sono jūyosei to tokushūsei wo chūshin toshite," in *Gunki monogatari to setsuwa*, kasama sōsho 122 (Kasama shoin, 1979), 157–173; and Watanabe, "Jishinbō setsuwa no haikei," in *Heike monogatari no shisō*, 357–376. The latter, 360–362, provides a parallel citation of the *Meido sosei ki* original and the equivalent passage in the Engyōbon variant.

121. *Engyōbon* jō, 617.

122. Ibid., 619.

123. Atsumi Kaoru, *Gunki monogatari to setsuwa*, 163–164.

124. On Ryōgen's life, see Murayama Shūichi, *Hieizanshi: tatakai to inori no seiiki* (Tōkyō bijutsu, 1994), 117–143; and Wakabayashi Haruko, "From Conqueror of Evil to Devil King: Ryōgen and Notions of *Ma* in Medieval Japanese Buddhism," *MN*, 54: 4 (Winter 1999), 481–507. Wakabayashi's essay is a detailed examination of Ryōgen's contradictory roles in medieval Buddhism.

125. *Heian ibun*, 2: 303, cited in Arai, *Akutō no kenkyū*, 66.

126. On the akusō, see Mikael S. Adolphson, *The Gates of Power: Monks, Courtiers, and Warriors in Premodern Japan* (Honolulu: University of Hawaii Press, 2000), 62–63.

127. On practices associated with Jie's cult, see Murayama, *Hiezanshi*, 137–142; and Wakabayashi, "From Conqueror of Evil to Devil King," 487–488 and 502.

128. Makino, "*Meido sosei ki* sono sokkumen no ichimen," in *Heike monogatari: katari to gentai*, 119. The full name for Jie's demonic character would be Take jizai-ten no maō, with Take jizai-ten referring to the yokukai, or the world as conditioned by desire in the shingon concept of "three worlds." The Sixth Heaven, or Dairokuten, was located in this world.

129. *Engyōbon* jō, 85–86.

130. Ibid., 225.

131. Narrated in the twelfth section of scroll two in the Kakuichi *Heike*, *Heike monogatari* jō, 194. For an analysis, see Bialock, "Outcasts, Emperorship, and Dragon Cults," 244–251.

132. *Engyōbon* jō, 224.

133. A passage in *Keiranjūyōshū* describes sixth consciousness as follows: "Inside our water wheel are lungs, and in them a golden water. In the golden water is a three inch snake. This is our sixth consciousness. The lungs are the place of subtle insight and discernment of the western direction. Subtle insight and discernment are the sixth consciousness, the consciousness that dis-

cerns evil and good: namely, our intellectual faculty for discerning right and wrong. Its seed letter is the Sanskrit letter *un*. This seed letter is namely the seed letter for Benzaiten. Thus, our unformed originally enlightened inborn body has the form of a serpent." *Keiranjūyōshū*, vol. 76 of *Taishō shinshū daizō-kyō*, 623.

134. Makino, "*Meido sosei ki* sono sokkumen no ichimen," 121.

135. Tomikura, *Zenchūshaku* chū, 237.

136. Capping verses (*kanmuri*) refer to a type of acrostic in which the first graph in a series of Chinese verses spells out a phrase. The two capping verses "kyōrai Jie daisōjō" and "jigen saishō shōgunjin" first appear in *Jie Taishi kōshiki*, a Kamakura period text. For Makino's argument dating them back to the late Heian period, see 118. For a lengthier discussion of such verses, see Wakabayashi, "From Conqueror of Evil to Devil King," 495–499.

137. Akamatsu Toshihide, "Taira no Kiyomori no shinkō ni tsuite," in *Akamatsu Toshihide kyōju taikan kinen kokushiron*, 1–40, esp. 9–17 and 39–40.

138. *Engyōbon* jō, 55.

139. Akamatsu Toshihide, "Akusō no shinjō to Kamakura bukkyō," in *Bukkyō shisō ronshū: Okuda Jiō sensei kiju kinen* (Heirakuji, 1976), 455–470, esp. 460–465; and Makino, "*Meido sosei ki* sono sokkumen no ichimen," 121–122. See also Akamatsu's remarks in *Heike monogatari no kenkyū*, 355.

140. Tada, *Tendai hongaku ron*, 131.

141. Cited and discussed by Tamura, *Tendai hongaku ron*, 541–542; and by Makino, "*Meido sosei ki* sono sokkumen no ichimen," 123.

142. The analogies of the boar and kura-insect (*kurachū*) are also found in Kamo no Chōmei's *Hōbutsu shū* and the Buddhist meditative text *Maka shikan*. Although the insect referred to remains unknown, the kura (also written *kara-kura* 加羅求羅) was said to be extremely tiny but quickly increased in size upon contact with the wind and consumed everything. See *Hōbutsushū*, ed. Yamada Shōzen, Ōba Akira, and Mori Haruhiko (Ōfū, 1995), 94 (headnote 13).

143. *Engyōbon* jō, 620–622.

144. On this portion of the Engyōbon narrative, see Saeki Shin'ichi, "Engyōbon *Heike monogatari* no Kiyomori tsuitō wagun: 'shōdōsei' no ichidanmen," in *Heike monogatari* 1, Nihon bungaku kenkyū taisei, 329–341; Takehisa Tsuyoshi, "Kiyomori-katari no seitai: jikyōsha no keifu," in *Heike monogatari: setsuwa to katari*, Anata ga yomu Heike monogatari, vol. 2, 152–178; and on narratological issues in the sequence, Shidachi Masatomo, *Heike monogatari kataribon no hōhō to isō* (Kyūko shoin, 2004), 191–196.

145. This straightforward didactic application of the Devadatta analogy is most evident in the Shibubon variant of the episode: "It is said that Kiyomori was the manifestation of Jie Daishi. This is the meaning: 'Just as Devadatta committed sins against Buddhism in order to convert the multitudes, so too has Kiyomori committed great sins for the conversion of the multitudes in the latter age and fallen into the Hell Without Intermission.' So people say." Takayama Toshihiro, *Kundoku shibu kassenjō-bon Heike monogatari* (Yūseidō, 1995), 227.

146. Saeki, "Engyōbon *Heike monogatari* no Kiyomori tsuitō wagun: 'shōdōsei' no Ichidanmen," 330.

147. Murakami Mitoshi, "*Meido soseiki* to in'yō gogyō: Engyōbon *Heike monogatari* 'Jishinbō setsuwa' oboegaki," in *Chūsei bungaku no shosō to sono jidai*, Kenkyū sōsho 195 (Osaka: Izumi shoin, 1996), 615–630.

148. From "Mokke no sata" in scroll five, *Heike monogatari* jō, 341.

Epilogue

1. *Tōdai wajō tōseiden*, in vol. 3, denbu, of *Shinkō gunsho ruijū*, ed. Ueda Kazutoshi et al. (Naigai shoseki, 1930), 815. Discussed in Shimode, *Nihon kodai no jingi to dōkyō*, 221–222; and Shinkawa, *Dōkyō wo meguru kōbō*, 236–243.

2. Jorge Luis Borges, "Pierre Menard, Author of the *Quixote*," in *Labyrinths: Selected Stories and Other Writings* (London: Penguin Books, 2000), 69.

3. Bialock, "Nation and Epic: *The Tale of the Heike* as Modern Classic," 176–178.

BIBLIOGRAPHY

Primary Sources

Azumakagami kōhen. Vol. 33 of *KST*. Yoshikawa kōbunkan, 1933.

Chiribukuro. Ed. Ōnishi Harutaka and Kimura Noriko. Tōyō bunko 723 and 725. Heibonsha, 2004. 2 vols.

Chūyūki. Ed. Zōho shiryō taisei kankōkai. Vols. 9–15 of Zōho shiryō taisei. Kyoto: Rinsen shoten, 1965.

Dōken shōnin meidoki. In *Kokusho itsubun.* Ed. Wada Hidematsu, 31–37. Mori katsumi, 1940.

Engi shiki jō-ge. Ed. with notes by Torao Toshiya. Vols. 11–12 of *ST*, koten-hen. Shintō Taikei Hensankai, 1991–1993.

Engyōbon Heike monogatari honbun-hen jō-ge. Ed. Kitahara Yasuo and Ogawa Eiichi. Benseisha, 1990. 2 vols.

Entairyaku, vol. 7. Shiryō sanshū 76. Zoku gunsho ruijū kanseikai, 1985.

Fudoki. Ed. Akimoto Kichirō. Vol. 2 of *NKBT.* Iwanami shoten, 1958.

Genji monogatari. Ed. Abe Akio, Akiyama Ken, and Imai Gen'e. Vols. 12–17 of Nihon koten bungaku zenshū. Shōgakukan, 1970–1976.

Genpei seisuiki. Ed. Ichiko Teiji et al. Vols. 1–4, 6. Chūsei no bungaku. Miyai shoten, 1991–. 5 vols. to date.

Genpei seisuiki jō-ge. Ed. Tsukamoto Tetsuzō. Vols. 16–17 of Yūhōdō bunko. Yūhōdō shoten, 1929.

Godai teiō monogatari. In vol. 3 of *Gunsho ruijū,* teiō bu. Ed. Zoku Gunsho Ruijū Kanseikai, 425–459. Zoku gunsho ruijū, 1933.

Gukanshō. Ed. Okami Masao and Akamatsu Toshihide. Vol. 8 of *NKBT.* Iwanami shoten, 1967.

Gyokuyō. Kokusho kankōkai, 1906–1907. 3 vols.

Heike monogatari (jō-chū-ge). Ed. Mizuhara Hajime. Shinchō nihon koten shūsei. Shinchōsha, 1979–1981. 3 vols.

Heike monogatari Nagatobon. Ed. Kokusho kankōkai. Meicho kankōkai, 1974.

Heike monogatari (jō-ge). Ed. Ichiko Teiji. Vols. 29–30 of *NKBZ*. Shōgakukan, 1973–1975.

Heike monogatari. Ed. Takagi Ichinosuke, Ozawa Masao, Atsumi Kaoru, and Kindaichi Haruhiko. Vols. 32–33 of *NKBT*. Iwanami shoten, 1959–1960.

Heike monogatari. Vols. 44–45 of *SNKBT*. Ed. Kajihara Masaaki and Yamashita Hiroaki. Iwanami shoten, 1991–1993.

Hōbutsuhū. Ed. Yamada Shōzen, Ōba Akira, and Mori Haruhiko. Ōfū, 1995.

Hōgen monogatari Heiji monogatari. Ed. Nagazumi Yasuaki and Shimada Isao. Vol. 31 of *NKBT*. Iwanami shoten, 1961.

Hōgen monogatari, heiji monogatari, jōkyūki. Vol. 43 of *SNKBT*. Ed. Tochigi Yoshitada, Kusaka Tsutomu, Masuda Takashi, and Kubota Jun. Iwanami shoten, 1992.

Hōjōki hosshinshū. Ed. Miki Sumito. Shinchō nihon koten shūsei. Shinchōsha, 1976.

Honchō monzui. Ed. Ōsone Shōsuke, Kinbara Tadashi, and Gotō Akio. Vol. 27 of Shin Nihon koten bungaku taikei. Iwanami shoten, 1992.

Honchō seiki. Vol. 9 of *KST*. Yoshikawa kōbunkan, 1933.

Hyakuryōkun yōshō. Ed. Mozume Takami. Vol. 4 of Shinchū kōgaku sōsho. Kōbunko kankōkai, 1927.

Hyōhanki 1. Vol. 18 of Zōho shiryō taisei. Kyoto: Rinsen shoten, 1965.

Imakagami Masukagami. Vol. 21 (ge) of *KST*. Yoshikawa kōbunkan, 1940.

Ise monogatari zenshaku. Ed. Morimoto Shigeru. Daigakudō shoten, 1973.

Jikkinshō. Ed. Asami Kazuhiko. Vol. 51 of *Shinpen Nihon koten bungaku zenshū*. Shōgakukan, 1997.

Jisha engi. Ed. Sakurai Tokutarō, Hagiwara Tatsuo, and Miyata Noboru. Vol. 20 of *Nihon shisō taikei*. Iwanami shoten, 1975.

Kaifūsō, Bunka shūreishū, Honchō monzui. Ed. Kojima Noriyuki. Vol. 69 of *NKBT*. Iwanami shoten, 1964.

Keichū zenshū, vol. 1. Ed. Hisamatsu Sen'ichi. Iwanami shoten, 1973.

Keiranjūyōshū. Ed. Takakusu Junjirō and Watanabe Kaigyoku. Vol. 76 of *Taishō shinshū daizōkyō*. Taishō issaikyō kankōkai, 1931.

Kogo shūi. Vol. 25 of *Gunsho ruijū*, zatsu bu, 1–12. Zoku gunsho ruijū kanseikai, 1933.

Kogo shūi Takahashi ujibumi. Ed. Yasuda Naomichi and Akimoto Yoshinori. Shinsen nihon koten bunko 4. Gendai Shinchōsha, 1976.

Kogo shūi: tsuketari chūshaku. Ed. with notes by Iida Mizuho. Vol. 5 of Shintō taikei, koten-hen. Shintō Taikei Hensankai, 1986.

Kojidan (jō-ge). Ed. Kobayashi Yasuharu. Vols. 60–61 of Koten bunko. Gendai shichōsha, 1981.

Kojiki. Ed. Nishimiya Kazutami. Shinchō nihon koten shūsei. Shinchōsha, 1979.

Kojiki norito. Ed. Kurano Kenji and Takeda Yūkichi. Vol. 1 of *NKBT*. Iwanami shoten, 1958.

Konjaku monogatari shū. Ed. Yamada Yoshio, Yamada Tadao, Yamada Hideo, and Yamada Toshio. Vols. 22–26 of *NKBT*. Iwanami shoten, 1959–1963.

Kōtai shiki / Engi shiki / Kōnin shiki. Vol. 26 of *KST*. Yoshikawa kōbunkan, 1937.

Man'yōshū. Ed. Takagi Ichinosuke, Gomi Tomohide, and Ōno Susumu. Vols. 4–7 of *NKBT*. Iwanami shoten, 1957–1962.

Meigetsuki. Kokusho kankōkai, 1911–1912. 3 vols.

Mizukagami Ōkagami. Vol. 21 (jō) of *KST*. Yoshikawa kōbunkan, 1939.

Mutsuwaki. Ed. Kajihara Masaaki. Vol. 70 of Koten bunko. Gendai shichōsha, 1982.

Myōan Eisai: kōzen gokokuron, Ikkyū Sōjun: kyōun shū, hoka nihen. Ed. Ichikawa Hakugen, Iriya Yoshitaka, and Yanagida Seizan. Vol. 10 of *Genten nihon bukkyō no shisō.* Iwanami shoten, 1991.

Nagatobon Heike monogatari no sōgō kenkyū 1–2 (Kōchū-hen jō-ge). Ed. Asahara Yoshiko and Nanami Hiroaki. Benseisha, 1998–1999.

Nihon kiryaku kōhen / Hyakurenshō. Vol. 11 of *KST*. Yoshikawa kōbunkan, 1929.

Nihon kōki, Shoku nihon kōki, Montoku tennō jitsuroku. Vol. 3 of *KST*. Yoshikawa kōbunkan, 1934.

Nihon Sandai jitsuroku. Vol. 4 of *KST*. Yoshikawa kōbunkan, 1934.

Nihon shoki (jō-ge). Ed. Sakamoto Tarō. Vols. 67–68 of *NKBT*. Iwanami shoten, 1965–1967.

Ōkagami. Ed. Matsumura Hiroji. Vol. 21 of *NKBT*. Iwanami shoten, 1960.

Ōkagami zenhyōshaku (jō-ge). Ed. Hosaka Hiroshi. Gakutōsha, 1979. 2 vols.

Osō sawaki. Ed. Tago Kenkichi. In vol. 5 of *Fukushima ken shiryō shūsei*, 427–540. Fukushima ken shiryō shūsei kankūai, 1953.

Rakuyō dengakuki. In *Chōya gunsai*, 68–69. Vol. 29 (jō) of *KST*. Yoshikawa kōbunkan, 1938.

Ritsu / Ryō no gige. Vol. 22 of *KST*. Yoshikawa kōbunkan, 1939.

Ritsuryō. Ed. with notes by Inoue Mitsusada, Seki Akira, Tsuchida Naoshige, and Aoki Kazuo. *Nihon shisō taikei.* Iwanami shoten, 1976; reprinted 1994.

Ryō no shūge: zenpen. Vol. 23 of *KST*. Yoshikawa kōbunkan, 1966.

Ryō no shūge: kōhen. Vol. 24 of *KST*. Yoshikawa kōbunkan, 1966.

Ryōjin hishō. Ed. Sasaki Nobutsuna. Iwanami bunko 935. Iwanami shoten, 1933.

Ryōjin hishō, kanginshū, kyōgen kayō. Ed. Kobayashi Yoshinori et al. Vol. 56 of *SNKBT*. Iwanami shoten, 1993.

Sankashū kinkai wakashū. Ed. Kazamaki Keijirō and Kojima Yoshio. Vol. 29 of *NKBT*. Iwanami shoten, 1961.

Seiji yōryaku. Vol. 28 of *KST*. Yoshikawa kōbunkan, 1935.

Sendai kuji hongi. Ed. Kamatari Jun'ichi. Vol. 8 of Shintō taikei, koten-hen. Shintō Taikei Hensankai, 1980.

Shaku nihongi. Ed. with notes by Onoda Mitsuo. Vol. 5 of Shintō taikei, koten chūshaku-hen. Shintō Taikei Hensankai, 1986.

Shasekishū. Ed. Watanabe Tsunaya. Vol. 85 of *NKBT*. Iwanami shoten, 1966.

Shinkō gunsho ruijū. Ed. Ueda Kazutoshi et al. Naigai shoseki, 1928–1938. 24 vols.

Shinpen kokka taikan. Ed. Shinpen Kokka Taikan Iinkai. Kadokawa shoten, 1983–1992. 20 vols.

Shintei Genpei seisuiki. Ed. Mizuhara Hajime. Jinbutsu ōraisha, 1988–1991. 6 vols.

Shoku nihongi. Ed. Aoki Kazuo, Inaoka Kōji, Sasayama Haruo, and Shirafuji Noriyuki. Vols. 12–16 of *SNKBT*. Iwanami shoten, 1989–1998.

Shōmonki. Ed. Kajihara Masaaki. Vols. 280 and 291 of Tōyō bunko. Heibonsha, 1975–1976.

Shōmonki, Mutsuwaki, Hōgen monogatari, Heiji monogatari. Ed. Yanase Kiyoshi, Yashiro Kazuo, Matsubayashi Kiyoaki, and Inui Yoshihisa. Vol. 41 of Shinpen nihon koten bungaku zenshū. Shōgakukan, 2002.

Shōtoku taishi denki. Ed. Makino Kazuo. Denshō bungaku shiryō shūsei 1. Miyai shoten, 1999.

Shōtoku taishi denki. In *Taishi den* jō, 279–454. Vol. 3 of *Shōtoku taishi zenshū*. Ed. Fujiwara Yūsetsu. Ryūginsha sōritsu jimusho, 1944.

Shōtoku taishi denryaku. In *Shiden-bu* 10, 126–140. Vol. 71 of *Dainihon bukkyō zensho*. Ed. Suzuki Gakujutsu Zaidan. Suzuki Gakujutsu Zaidan, 1972.

Shōyūki 8. Vol. 8 of *Dai nihon kokiroku*. Ed. Shiryō hensanjo. Iwanami shoten, 1976.

Shūchūshō. In *Nihon kagaku taikei*, bekkan 2. Ed. Kyūsōjin Hitaku, 5–340. Kasama shoin, 1958.

Sumitomo tsuitōki. In *Gunsho ruijū*, vol. 20, kassenbu. Ed. Zoku Gunsho Ruijū Kanseikai, 21–22. Zoku gunsho ruijū kanseikai, 1933.

Taiheiki. Ed. Gotō Tanji, Kamada Kisaburō, and Okami Masao. Vols. 34–36 of *NKBT*. Iwanami shoten, 1960–1962.

Taketori monogatari, Ise monogatari, Yamato monogatari, Heichū monogatari. Ed. Katagiri Yōichi et al. Vol. 8 of *NKBZ*. Shōgakukan, 1972.

Taketori monogatari, Ise monogatari, Yamato monogatari. Ed. Sakakura Atsuyoshi et al. Vol. 9 of *NKBT*. Iwanami shoten, 1957.

Tōdōyōshū. In Vol. 27 of *Kaitei shiseki shūran*. Ed. Kondō Heijō, 705–736. Kyoto: Rinsen shoten, 1984.

Yashirobon kōyabon taishō: Heike monogatari. Ed. Asahara Yoshiko, Haruta Akira, and Matsuo Ashie. Shintensha, 1990–1993. 3 vols.

Yōkyokushū. Ed. Koyama Hiroshi and Satō Ken'ichirō. Vols. 58–59 of *Shinpen nihon koten bungaku zenshū*. Shōgakukan, 1997–1998.

Yunji qiqian. Beijing: Zhonghua shu ju, 2003. 5 vols.

Secondary Studies

Abe Yasurō. "Taiwa yōshiki sakuhin josetsu: Monjiki wo megurite." *Nihon bungaku* (June 1988), 54–70.

———. "Oko no monogatari toshite no *Heike monogatari*: Tsuzumi hōgan Tomoyasu to 'warai' no geinō." In *Heike monogatari kenkyū to hihyō*. Ed. Yamashita Hiroaki, 121–143. Yūseidō, 1996.

————. *Yuya no kōgō: chūsei no sei to seinaru mono.* Nagoya daigaku shuppankai, 1998.

————. "Tengu: ma no seishin shi." *Kokubungaku* (July 1999), 61–67.

Adolphson, Mikael S. *The Gates of Power: Monks, Courtiers, and Warriors in Premodern Japan.* Honolulu: University of Hawaii Press, 2000.

Akamatsu Toshihide. "Taira no Kiyomori no shinkō ni tsuite." In *Akamatsu Toshihide kyōju taikan kinen kokushi ronshū.* Ed. Akamatsu Toshihide Kyōju Taikan Kinen Jikyōkai, 1–40. Kyoto: Akamatsu Toshihide Kyōju Taikan Kinen Jikyōkai, 1972.

————. "Akusō no shinjō to kamakura bukkyō." In *Bukkyō shisō ronshū: Okuda Jiō sensei kiju kinen,* 455–470. Heirakuji, 1976.

————. *Heike monogatari no kenkyū.* Hōzōkan, 1980.

Akasaka Norio. *Ijinron josetsu.* Sunagoya shobō, 1985.

————, ed. *Hōhō toshite no kyōkai.* Sōsho shisō wo horu 1. Shin'yōsha, 1991.

Akatsuka Kiyoshi. *Sōshi* jō-ge. Vols. 16–17 of *ZKT.* Shūeisha, 1974–1977.

Akimoto Kichirō. *Fudoki no kenkyū.* Osaka: Ōsaka Keizai Daigaku, 1963.

Akimoto Yoshinori, ed. *Hitachi no kuni fudoki.* Vol. 1 of *Fudoki zen yakuchū.* Kōdansha gakujutsu bunko 385. Kōdansha, 1979.

Akiyama Kiyoko. "Chūsei no omote to oku." In *Chūsei no kūkan wo yomu.* Ed. Gomi Fumihiko, 106–137. Yoshikawa kōbunkan, 1995.

Amino Yoshihiko. *Nihon chūsei no hinōgyōmin to tennō.* Iwanami shoten, 1984.

————. "Chūsei no tabibito-tachi." In *Hyōhaku to teichaku: teijū shakai e no michi.* Vol. 6 of *Nihon minzoku bunka taikei.* Ed. idem, 155–266. Shōgakukan, 1984.

————. *Igyō no ōken.* Imēji rīdingu sōsho. Heibonsha, 1986.

————, ed. *Kotoba no bunkashi, Chūsei* 1. Heibonsha, 1988.

————. *Nihon ronno shiza: rettō no shakai to kokka.* Shōgakukan, 1990.

————. *Nihon no rekishi wo yominaosu.* Chikuma shobō, 1991.

————. "Emperor, Rice, and Commoners." In *Multicultural Japan: Paleolithic to Postmodern.* Ed. Donald Denoon, Mark Hudson, Gavan McCormack, and Tessa Morris-Suzuki, with an Introduction by Gavan McCormack, 235–244. Cambridge, England: Cambridge University Press, 1996.

Aoki, Michiko Y. *Records of Wind and Earth: A Translation of Fudoki with Introduction and Commentaries.* Monograph and Occasional Paper Series, Number 53. Ann Arbor, MI: Association for Asian Studies, 1997.

Arai Takashige. *Chūsei akutō no kenkyū.* Yoshikawa kōbunkan, 1990.

Araki Michio. "Onmyōdō." In *Nihon shisō* 2, 315–344. *Iwanami kōza tōyō shisō,* vol. 16. Iwanami shoten, 1989.

Asahara Yoshiko. "Heike monogatari no keisei to shingon ken." In *Heike monogatari no seiritsu.* Ed. Tochigi Yoshitada et al., 167–194. *Anata ga yomu Heike monogatari* 1. Yūseidō, 1993.

Asahara Yoshiko and Inui Yoshihisa, ed. *Nagatobon Heike monogatari no sōgō kenkyū* 3. Ronkyū-hen. Benseisha, 1999.

Aston, W. G. *Nihongi: Chronicles of Japan from the Earliest Times to* A.D. *697.* Rutland, Tokyo: Charles E. Tuttle, 1972.

Atsumi Kaoru. *Gunki monogatari to setsuwa.* Kasama sōsho 122. Kasama shoin, 1979.

Bakhtin, M. M. *The Dialogic Imagination: Four Essays by M. M. Bakhtin.* Ed. Michael Holquist and trans. Caryl Emerson and Michael Holquist. Austin: University of Texas Press, 1981.

————. *Rabelais and His World.* Bloomington: Indiana University Press, 1984.

Ban Nobutomo. *Ban Nobutomo zenshū,* vol. 2. Kokusho kankōkai, 1907.

Bargen, Doris. *A Woman's Weapon: Spirit Possession in the Tale of Genji.* Honolulu: University of Hawaii Press, 1997.

Barnes, Gina L. *China, Korea and Japan: The Rise of Civilization in East Asia.* London and New York: Thames & Hudson, 1993.

Batten, Bruce. *To the Ends of Japan: Premodern Frontiers, Boundaries, and Interactions.* Honolulu: University of Hawaii Press, 2003.

Baudrillard, Jean. *Système des objets.* Paris: Gallimard, 1968.

Bäuml, Franz. "Varieties and Consequences of Medieval Literacy and Illiteracy." *Speculum,* 55 (1980), 237–265.

Bentley, John R. *Historiographical Trends in Early Japan.* Japanese Studies, Vol. 15. Lewiston, NY: Edwin Mellen Press, 2002.

Benveniste, Emile. *Problèmes de linguistique générale,* 2 vols. Paris: Gallimard, 1974.

Berry, Mary E. "Tōitsu kenryoku to chizu sakusei: aratana seiji bunka no tanjo." In *Chizu to ezu no seiji bunkashi.* Ed. Kuroda Hideo, Mary E. Berry, and Sugimoto Fumiko, 137–184. Tōkyō daigaku shuppankai, 2001.

Bialock, David T. "Peripheries of Power: Voice, History, and the Construction of Imperial and Sacred Space in *The Tale of the Heike* and Other Medieval and Heian Historical Texts." PhD diss., Columbia University, 1997.

————. "The Tale of the Heike." In *Medieval Japanese Writers.* Ed. Steven D. Carter, 73–84. *Dictionary of Literary Biography,* vol. 203. Detroit: Gale Group, 1999.

————. "Nation and Epic: *The Tale of the Heike* as Modern Classic." In *Inventing the Classics: Modernity, National Identity, and Japanese Literature.* Ed. Haruo Shirane and Tomi Suzuki, 151–178. Stanford, CA: Stanford University Press, 2000.

————. "*The Tale of the Heike*: Its Modern Critics and the Medieval Past." In *Issues of Canonicity and Canon Formation in Japanese Literary Studies, PAJLS (Proceedings for the Association of Japanese Literary Studies),* 1 (Summer 2000), 141–152.

————. "Outcasts, Emperorship, and Dragon Cults in *The Tale of the Heike.*" In *Buddhist Priests, Kings and Marginals: Studies on Medieval Japanese Buddhism.* Ed. Bernard Faure. *Cahiers d'Extrême-Asie,* 13 (2002–2003), 227–310.

Blacker, Carmen. *The Catalpa Bow: A Study of Shamanistic Practices in Japan.* London: Unwin Hyman Limited, 1975, 1986.

Bock, Felicia G., trans. *Engi-shiki: Procedures of the Engi Era*. Tokyo: Sophia University, 1970.

———. *Classical Learning and Taoist Practices in Early Japan*, with a translation of Books XVI and XX of the Engi-Shiki. Occasional Paper No. 17. Tempe: Center for Asian Studies, Arizona State University, 1985.

Bokenkamp, Stephen R. *Early Daoist Scriptures*. Berkeley, Los Angeles, and London: University of California Press, 1997.

Borgen, Robert. *Sugawara no Michizane and the Early Heian Court*. Cambridge, MA: Harvard University Press, 1986.

Borges, Jorge Luis. *Labyrinths: Selected Stories and Other Writings*. London: Penguin Books, 2000.

Brown, Delmer M., ed. *The Cambridge History of Japan*, vol. 1, *Ancient Japan*. Cambridge: Cambridge University Press, 1993.

Brown, Delmar M., and Ichirō Ishida. *The Future and the Past: A Translation and Study of the Gukanshō, an Interpretive History of Japan Written in 1219*. Berkeley, Los Angeles, and London: University of California Press, 1979.

Butler, Kenneth Dean. "The Textual Evolution of the *Heike monogatari*." *Harvard Journal of Asiatic Studies*, 26: 5 (1966), 5–51.

Butler, Lee A. "The Way of Yin and Yang: A Tradition Revived, Sold, Adopted." *Monumenta Nipponica*, 51: 2 (Summer 1996), 189–217.

Ch'a Chu-huan. *Chōsen no Dōkyō*. Trans. Miura Kunio and Nozaki Mitsuhiko. Kyoto: Jinbun shoin, 1990.

Chamberlain, Basil Hall, trans. *The Kojiki: Records of Ancient Matters*. Tokyo: Charles E. Tuttle, 1981.

Chavannes, Édouard. *Les Mémoires Historiques de Se-Ma Ts'ien*, Tome Troisième. Paris: A. Maisonneuve, 1967.

Childs, Margaret Helen. *Rethinking Sorrow: Revelatory Tales of Late Medieval Japan*. Ann Arbor: Center for Japanese Studies, University of Michigan, 1991.

Colebrook, Claire. *New Literary Histories: New Historicism and Contemporary Criticism*. Manchester and New York: Manchester University Press, 1997.

de Bary, William Theodore et al., ed. *Sources of Chinese Tradition*, vol. 1. New York: Columbia University Press, 1960.

de Certeau, Michel. *Heterologies: Discourse on the Other*. Trans. Brian Massumi, with a Foreword by Wlad Godzich. Theory and History of Literature, vol. 17. Minneapolis and London: University of Minnesota Press, 1986.

———. *The Writing of History*. Trans. Tom Conley. New York: Columbia University Press, 1988.

Deleuze, Gilles. *Difference and Repetition*. Trans. Paul Patton. London: Athlone Press, 1994.

Deleuze, Gilles, and Felix Guattari. *A Thousand Plateaus: Capitalism and Schizophrenia*. Trans. Brian Massumi. Minneapolis and London: University of Minnesota Press, 1987.

Dōmoto Masaki. *Nō, kyōgen no gei.* Nihon no gei shirīzu. Tokyo shoseki, 1983.

Douglas, Mary. *Purity and Danger: An Analysis of Concepts of Pollution and Taboo.* London and New York: Routledge, 1966.

Ducrot, Oswald, and Tsvetan Todorov. *Encyclopedic Dictionary of the Sciences of Language.* Trans. Catherine Porer. Baltimore: Johns Hopkins University Press, 1979.

Dull, Jack L. "A Historical Introduction to the Apocryphal (Ch'an-wei) Texts of the Han Dynasty." PhD diss., University of Washington, 1966.

Ebersole, Gary L. *Ritual Poetry and the Politics of Death in Early Japan.* Princeton, NJ: Princeton University Press, 1989.

Eguchi Kiyoshi. *Kodai tennō to onmyōryō no shisō: Jitō tennōka no kaidoku yori.* Kawade shobō shinsha, 1999.

Endō Katsumi. *Kinsei onmyōdōshi no kenkyū.* Mirai kōbō, 1985.

Farris, Wayne. *Heavenly Warriors: The Evolution of Japan's Military, 500–1300.* Cambridge and London: Harvard University Press, 1992.

———. *Sacred Texts and Buried Treasures.* Honolulu: University of Hawaii Press, 1998.

Faure, Bernard. "The Daruma-shū, Dōgen, and Sōtō Zen." *Monumenta Nipponica,* 42: 1 (1987), 25–55.

———. "Now You See It, Now You Don't: Relics and Regalia in Japanese Buddhism." Paper presented at the annual meeting of the American Academy of Religion. New Orleans, LA, November 1996.

———. *The Power of Denial: Buddhism, Purity, and Gender.* Princeton, NJ, and Oxford: Princeton University Press, 2003.

Field, Norma. *The Splendor of Longing in the Tale of Genji.* Princeton, NJ: Princeton University Press, 1987.

Foucault, Michel. *The Archaeology of Knowledge.* Trans. A. M. Sheridan Smith. London: Tavistock Publications, 1972.

Frank, Bernard. *Kata-imi et kata-tagae: Étude sur les interdits de direction à l'époque Heian.* Paris: Collège de France, Institut des Hautes Études Japonaises, 1998.

Fujii Sadakazu. *Monogatari bungaku seiritsushi: furukoto, katari, monogatari.* Tōkyō daigaku shuppankai, 1987.

———. *Nihon shōsetsu genshi.* Taishūkan shoten, 1995.

Fujimura Tsukuru. "*Ōkagami* ni kansuru kōsatsu." *Kokugo to kokubungaku* (May 1924), 47–68.

Fujita Katsunari. "Tenkanki no Toba-den: chūsei jūkūkan no senku." In *Inseiki bunka ronshū 3: Jikan to kūkan.* Ed. Inseiki bunka kenkyūkai, 212–235. Shin'washa, 2003.

Fukuda Akira. *Gunki monogatari to minkan denshō.* Minzoku mingei sōsho 66. Iwasaki bijutsusha, 1972.

———. *Chūsei katarimono bungei: sono keifu to tenkai.* Miyai shoten, 1981.

Fukuda Hideichi, Shimazu Tadao, Komine Kazuaki, and Matsuoka Shinpei. "'Shinpojiumu' hōkoku: Chūsei bungaku no han'i." *Chūsei bungaku,* 35 (June 1990), 1–23.

Fukuda Toyohiko and Hattori Kōzō, ed. *Genpei tōjōroku: bandō de uma-reta Heike monogatari* (jō-ge). Kōdansha gakujutsu bunko. Kōdansha, 1999–2000.

Fukui Fumimasa. "Fukunaga Mitsuji cho: *Dōkyō to nihon bunka.*" *Tōhō shūkyō*, no. 60 (October 1982), 87–90.

———. "Kenkyū no nōto: Fukunaga kyōju no hanron ni tsuite." *Tōhō shūkyō*, no. 62 (October 1983), 60–73.

Fukunaga Mitsuji. "Tennō to shikyū to mahito–chūgoku kodai no shintō." *Shisō*, no. 637 (July 1977), 1–19.

———. *Dōkyō to nihon bunka.* Jinbun shoin, 1982.

———. "Kenkyū nōto: Tsuda Sōkichi hakushi to dōkyō: Fukui Fumimasa-shi no shohyō *Dōkyō to Nihon bunka* ni kotaete." *Tōhō shūkyō*, no. 61 (May 1983), 65–79.

———. *Dōkyō shisōshi kenkyū.* Iwanami shoten, 1987.

———. *Dōkyō to kodai nihon.* Jinbun shoin, 1987.

Fukunaga Mitsuji, Ueda Masaaki, and Ueyama Shunpei. *Dōkyō to kodai no tennōsei: Nihon kodaishi shinkō.* Tokuma shoten, 1978, 1986.

Fukushima Akiho. *Kiki shinwa densetsu no kenkyū.* Rokkō shuppan, 1988.

Furui Gen. *Tennō no keifu to shinwa.* Hanawa shobō, 1967.

Gellrich, Jesse M. *Discourse and Dominion in the Fourteenth Century: Oral Contexts of Writing in Philosophy, Politics, and Poetry.* Princeton, NJ: Princeton University Press, 1995.

Ginzburg, Carlo. *The Night Battles: Witchcraft and Agrarian Cults in the Sixteenth and Seventeenth Centuries.* Trans. John and Anne Tedeschi. New York: Penguin Books, 1985.

———. *Ecstasies: Deciphering the Witches' Sabbath.* Trans. Raymond Rosen-thal. New York: Pantheon Books, 1989.

Girard, René. *Things Hidden Since the Foundation of the World.* Trans. Ste-phen Bann and Michael Meteer. London: Athalone Press, 1987.

Goble, Andrew Edmund. *Kenmu: Go-Daigo's Revolution.* Cambridge, MA, and London: Harvard University Press, 1996.

Gomi Fumihiko. *Heike monogatari: shi to setsuwa.* Heibonsha, 1987.

———. "Ronsetsu: Insei to tennō." In *Iwanami kōza Nihon tsūshi*, vol. 7, *Chūsei I*, 75–103. Iwanami shoten, 1993.

———. "Heike monogatari no monogatariteki kūkan–kyūtei shakai." In *Heike monogatari: shudai kōsō hyōgen.* Ed. Kajihara Masaaki, 219–237. Gunki bungaku kenkyū sōsho 6. Kyūko shoin, 1998.

Goodwin, Janet. *Alms and Vagabonds: Buddhist Temples and Popular Patron-age in Medieval Japan.* Honolulu: University of Hawaii Press, 1994.

Gorai Shigeru. *Kōyahijiri.* Kadokawa sensho. Kadokawa shoten, 1965.

———. "Kumano sanzan no rekishi to shinkō." In *Yoshino kumano shinkō no kenkyū.* Ed. idem, 155–178. Sangaku shūkyōshi kenkyū sōsho 4. Meicho shuppan, 1975.

———. "Kumano shinwa to kumano shintō." In *Shugendō no bijutsu geinō bungaku*, vol. 2. Ed. idem, 58–78. Sangaku shūkyōshi kenkyū sōsho 15. Meicho shuppan, 1981.

———. "Kanjō no maki to nagarekanjō." In *Heike monogatari: katari to gentai*. Ed. Hyōdō Hiromi, 95–97. Nihon bungaku kenkyū shiryō shinshū 7. Yūseidō, 1987.

———. *Yūgyō to junrei*. Kadokawa shoten, 1989.

Gotō Tanji. *Senki monogatari no kenkyū*. Tsukuba shoten, 1936.

———. "Heike monogatari no sho-mondai." In *Chūsei bungaku: kenkyū to shiryō*. Ed. Keio Gijuku Daigaku Kokubungaku Kenkyūkai, 3–33. *Kokubungaku ronsō* 2. Shibundō, 1958.

Graham, A.C. *Disputers of the Tao: Philosophical Argument in Ancient China*. La Salle, IL: Open Court Publishing, 1989.

Granet, Marcel. *Danses et légendes de la Chine ancienne*, tome premier. Paris: Librairie Felix Alcan, 1926.

Grapard, Allan G. "Japan's Ignored Cultural Revolution: The Separation of Shinto and Buddhist Divinities in Meiji (*shimbutsu bunri*) and a Case Study: Tōnomine." *History of Religions*, 23: 3 (February 1984), 240–265.

———. *The Protocol of the Gods: A Study of the Kasuga Cult in Japanese History*. Berkeley: University of California Press, 1992.

———. "Geosophia, Geognosis, and Geopiety: Orders of Significance in Japanese Representations of Space." In *NowHere: Space, Time, and Modernity*. Ed. Roger Friedland and Deidre Boden, 372–401. Berkeley: University of California Press, 1994.

———. "Geotyping Sacred Space: The Case of Mount Hiko in Japan." In *Sacred Space: Shrine, City, Land*. Ed. Benjamin Z. Kedar and R. J. Zwi Werblowsky, 215–249. New York: New York University Press, 1998.

———. "Religious Practices." In *The Cambridge History of Japan*, vol. 2, *Heian Japan*. Ed. Donald H. Shively and William H. McCullough, 517–575. Cambridge: Cambridge University Press, 1999.

Grayling, A. C. *Wittgenstein*. Oxford and New York: Oxford University Press, 1988.

Gregory, Derek. *Geographical Imaginations*. Cambridge and Oxford: Blackwell, 1994.

Habito, Ruben L. "The Logic of Nonduality and Absolute Affirmation: Deconstructing Tendai Hongaku Writings." *Japanese Journal of Religious Studies*, 22: 102 (Spring 1995), 83–102.

Haga Yaichi. "Kokuminsei jūron." In *Ochiai Naobumi, Ueda Kazutoshi, Haga Yaichi, Fujioka Sakutarō shū*. Ed. Hisamatsu Sen'ichi, 237–239. Vol. 44 of *Meiji bungaku zenshū*. Chikuma shobō, 1968.

Haidu, Peter. "Repetition: Modern Reflections on Medieval Aesthetics." *Modern Language Notes*, 92 (1977), 875–887.

Hamilton, Paul. *Historicism*. London and New York: Routledge, 1996.

Harada Taneshige. *Jōgan seiyō*. Vols. 95–96 of *SKT*. Meiji shoin, 1978–1979.

Hashiguchi Kusaku. "*Heike monogatari* no naka no nihon to gaikoku." *Kagoshima kenritsu tanki daigaku kiyō*, 44 (1993), 1–10. Also collected in

Kokubungaku nenji betsu ronbunshū, Chusei 2. Ed. Gakujutsu bunken kankōkai, 37–42 (1–10). Hōbun shuppan, 1993.

Hashimoto Fumio. *Ōchō wakashi no kenkyū.* Kasama shoin, 1972.

Hashimoto Hiroyuki. "Nekkyō no rutsubo kara: dengaku to irui igyō." *Porifuōn,* 9 (1991), 43–54.

———. *Ō no mai no kenkyū.* Hitsuji shobō, 1997.

Hashimoto Masayoshi. "Chokumei genzoku to hōgi kanryō no keisei. In *Onmyōdō sōsho* 1, *Kodai.* Ed. Murayama Shūichi, 83–119. Meicho shuppan, 1991.

Hattori Toshirō. *Kamakura jidai igakushi no kenkyū.* Yoshikawa kōbunkan, 1964.

Hattori Yukio. "Sakagami no miya: hōrō geinō min no geinōshin shinkō ni tsuite." *Bungaku,* 46 (April 1978), 44–59; *Bungaku,* 46 (May 1978), 84–103; *Bungaku,* 46 (December 1978), 80–90; and *Bungaku,* 47 (August 1979), 32–53.

Hayashiya Tatsusaburō. *Chūsei geinōshi no kenkyū: kodai kara no keishō to sōzō.* Iwanami shoten, 1960.

———, ed. *Kodai chūsei geijutsu ron.* Vol. 23 of *Nihon shisō taikei.* Iwanami shoten, 1973.

———. *Rekishi, Kyōto, geinō.* Asahi sensho 114. Asahi shinbunsha, 1978.

Heinrich, Amy Vladeck. *Fragments of Rainbows: The Life and Poetry of Saito Mokichi, 1882–1953.* New York: Columbia University Press, 1983.

Higuchi Kunio. *Chūsei no shijitsu to denshō.* Tōkyōdō shuppan, 1991.

Hirano Satsuki. "Engyōbon *Heike monogatari* no taichūgoku ishiki ni tsuite." In *Gunki to kanbungaku.* Ed. Wakan Hikaku Bungakukai, 107–125. Wakan hikaku bungaku sōsho 15. Kyūko shoin, 1993.

Hirata Toshiharu. *Heian jidai no kenkyū.* San'itsu shobō, 1943.

Hirohata Sukeo. "Kōsojin takamimusubi no seiritsu ni kansuru ichikōsatsu." *Nihon chūgoku gakkai hō,* 25 (October 1973), 189–203.

———. "Nihon koten ni okeru shinsensetsu oyobi chūgoku tenmonsetsu no eikyō." In *Dōkyō kenkyū ronshū: Dōkyō no shisō to bunka Yoshioka hakushi kanreki kinen.* Ed. Yoshioka Yoshitoyo Hakushi Kanreki Kinen Ronshū Kankōkai, 645–664. Kokusho kankōkai, 1977.

———. *Bansei ikkei ōchō shisō: Jimmu tennō no densetsu.* Kasama shoin, 1993.

Hirokawa Katsumi and Komaki Satoshi. *Girei gengo no yōshiki.* Ōfūsha, 1989.

Holcombe, Charles. *The Genesis of East Asia, 221 B.C.–A.D. 907.* Honolulu: Association for Asian Studies and University of Hawaii Press, 2001.

Honda Wataru, Sawada Mizuho, and Kōma Miyoshi. *Hōbokushi, Ressenden, Sengaikyō.* Vol. 8 of *Chūgoku koten bungaku taikei.* Heibonsha, 1969.

Horton, H. Mack. *Song in an Age of Discord: "The Journal of Sōchō" and Poetic Life in Late Medieval Japan.* Stanford, CA: Stanford University Press, 2002.

Hosokawa Ryōichi. *Itsudatsu no nihon chūsei: kyōki tōsaku ma no sekai.* JICC Shuppankyoku, 1993.

———. *Shi to kyōkai no chūseishi.* Yōsensha, 1997.

Hyōdō Hiromi. *Katarimono josetsu: Heike katari no hassei to hyōgen.* Shin'ei kenkyū sōsho 8. Yūseidō, 1985.

———. *Ōken to monogatari.* Seikyūsha, 1989.

———. "Kakuichibon Heike monogatari no denrai wo megutte: Muromachi ōken to geinō." In *Heike biwa: katari to ongaku.* Ed. Kamisangō Yūkō, 55–82. Hitsuji shobō, 1993.

———. *Taiheiki "yomi" no kanōsei: rekishi to iu monogatari.* Kōdansha sensho mechie 61. Kōdansha, 1995.

Ichihara Kōkichi, Imai Kiyoshi, and Suzuki Ryūichi. *Raiki* jō-chū-ge. Vols. 12–14 of *ZKT.* Shūeisha, 1976–1979.

Ichikawa Yasuji and Endō Tetsuo. *Sōshi* ge. Vol. 8 of *SKT.* Meiji shoin, 1967.

Ichiko Teiji, ed. *Heike monogatari kenkyū jiten.* Meiji shoin, 1978.

Ienaga Saburō et al., ed. *Chūsei,* vol. 1. *Iwanami kōza nihon rekishi* 5. Iwanami shoten, 1962.

Ihara Akira. "Temmu tennō no aru ichimen." In *Man'yōshū kenkyū,* vol. 9. Ed. Gomi Tomohide and Kojima Noriyuki, 177–203. Hanawa shobō, 1980.

Iida Isamu. "*Kogo shūi* no ronri to hōhō: 'kogo' to wa nan de atta ka." *Kodai bungaku,* 37 (March 1998), 14–23.

Ikegami Jun'ichi. *Sangoku denki,* jō-ge. Miyai shoten, 1976. 2 vols.

Inaoka Kōji. *Hitomaro no hyōgen sekai: kotaika kara shintaika e.* Iwanami shoten, 1991.

Inoue Mitsuo. "*Rakuyō dengakuki* wo megutte." In *Akamatsu Toshihide kyōju taikan kinen kokushi ronshū.* Ed. Akamatsu Toshihide Kyōju Taikan Kinen Jikyōkai, 413–425. Kyoto: Akamatsu Toshihide Kyōju Taikan Kinen Jikyōkai, 1972.

Ishii Kyōdō, ed. *Shōwa shinshū hōnen shōnin zenshū.* Kyoto: Heirakuji shoten, 1965.

Ishii Masako. *Shinkō.* Chūgoku koten shinsho zoku hen. Meitoku shuppansha, 1991.

Ishimoda Shō. *Nihon kodai kokka ron,* dai 1-bu: *Kanryōsei to hō no mondai.* Iwanami shoten, 1973.

Isomae Jun'ichi. "Myth in Metamorphosis: Ancient and Medieval Versions of the Yamatotakeru Legend." *Monumenta Nipponica,* 54: 3 (Autumn 1999), 361–385.

Itano Chōhachi. *Jukyō seiritsushi no kenkyū.* Iwanami shoten, 1995.

Itō Kiyoshi. *Nihon chūsei no ōken to ken'i.* Kyoto: Shibunkaku shuppan, 1993.

Ivy, Marilyn. *Discourses of the Vanishing: Modernity, Phantasm, Japan.* Chicago: University of Chicago Press, 1995.

Kamens, Edward. *Utamakura, Allusion, and Intertextuality in Traditional Japanese Poetry*. New Haven, CT, and London: Yale University Press, 1997.

Kamio Tokiko. "Yamato takeru tennō kō: Hitachi no kuni fudoki no chimei kigen denshō." In *Denshō no kosō: rekishi, gunki, shinwa*. Ed. Mizuhara Hajime, 182–217. Ōfūsha, 1991.

Kanaya Osamu. *Rongo*. Iwanami kurashikku 13. Iwanami shoten, 1987.

Kanō Shigefumi. *Rekishi monogatari no shisō*. Kyōto joshi daigaku kenkyū sōkan 19. Kyōto joshi daigaku, 1992.

Katō, Genchi, and Hikoshirō Hoshino. *Kogoshūi: Gleanings from Ancient Stories*. London: Curzon Press, 1926.

Katō Jōken. *Shokyō* jō. Vol. 25 of *SKT*. Meiji shoin, 1983.

Kawabata Yoshiaki. "Meguri monogatari tsuya monogatari." In *Setsuwa no gensetsu kōshō shoshō baitai*. Ed. Honda Giken et al., 205–225. Benseisha, 1991.

Kawakita Noboru. "*Ōkagami* no hihansei ni tsuite no ichikōsatsu." In *Ōkagami Eiga monogatari*. Ed. idem, 48–57. Nihon bungaku kenkyū taisei. Kokusho kankōkai, 1988.

———. "Rekishi monogatari to dono yōni kakawatte iru ka." In *Katari, hyōgen, kotoba*. Ed. Imai Takuji, 139–153. Vol. 6 of *Genji monogatari kōza*. Benseisha, 1992.

Kawamura Hidene. *Shoki shikkai*. Kyoto: Rinsen shoten, 1969. 4 vols.

Kawane Yoshiyasu. "Yasurai matsuri no seiritsu (jō): hōgen shinsei no rekishiteki ichi wo meikaku ni suru tame ni." *Nihonshi kenkyū*, no. 137 (November 1973), 1–22.

———. "Yasurai matsuri no seiritsu (ge): hōgen shinsei no rekishiteki ichi wo meikaku ni suru tame ni." *Nihonshi kenkyū*, no. 138 (January 1974), 44–72.

———. "Ōdo shisō to jinbutsu shūgō." In *Kodai* 4. Ed. Asao Naohiro, 272–312. *Iwanami kōza nihon rekishi* 4. Iwanami shoten, 1976.

Keene, Donald. *Seeds in the Heart: Japanese Literature from Earliest Times to the Late Sixteenth Century*. History of Japanese Literature, Vol. 1. New York: Henry Holt, 1993.

Keirstead, Thomas. "The Gendering and Regendering of Medieval Japan." *U.S.–Japan Women's Journal*, English Supplement 9 (1995), 77–92.

Kida Teikichi. "Hōmen kō." In *Kida Teikichi chosakushū* 10, 262–279. Heibonsha, 1982.

Kidder, J. Edward. "The Newly Discovered Takamatsuzuka Tomb." *Monumenta Nipponica*, 27: 3 (Autumn 1972), 245–251.

Kigoshi Takashi. "Nihongi kōen to Nihongi kyōen waka." *Kokubungaku kaishaku to kanshō*, 64: 3 (March 1999), 26–32.

Kikuchi Kyōko. "Goryō shinkō no seiritsu to tenkai: shinkō no shijisō wo chūshin to shite." In *Goryō shinkō*. Ed. Shibata Minoru, 37–61. Minshū shūkyōshi sōsho 5. Yūzankaku, 1984.

Kiley, Cornelius J. "Provincial Administration and Land Tenure in Early Heian." In *The Cambridge History of Japan*, vol. 2, *Heian Japan*. Ed. Donald H. Shively and William H. McCullough, 244–252. Cambridge: Cambridge University Press, 1999.

Kimura Saeko. "Chūsei hachiman shinkō ni okeru ikusa no kioku: Jingō kōgō denshō no hen'yō wo megutte." *Gengotai*, no. 5 (October 2004), 123–133.

Kitagawa, Hiroshi, and Bruce T. Tsuchida, trans. *The Tale of the Heike*. With a Foreword by Edward Seidensticker. Tokyo: University of Tokyo Press, 1977. 2 vols.

Kitagawa, Joseph M. *On Understanding Japanese Religion*. Princeton, NJ: Princeton University Press, 1987.

Kitagawa Tadahiko. *Gunkimono ronkō*. Miyai shoten, 1989.

Kitano Tayuru. *Myōgoki*. Benseisha, 1983.

Klein, Susan B. "Allegories of Desire, Poetry and Eroticism in Ise Monogatari Zuino." *Monumenta Nipponica*, 52: 4 (Winter 1997), 441–465.

Knechtges, David R., trans. *Wen xuan, or, Selections of Refined Literature /Xiao Tong*, Vol. 1. *Rhapsodies on Metropolises and Capitals*. Princeton, NJ: Princeton University Press, 1982.

Knoblock, John, and Jeffrey Riegel. *The Annals of Lü Buwei: A Complete Translation and Study*. Stanford, CA: Stanford University Press, 2000.

Kobayashi Chishō. *Chūsei bungaku no shisō*. Shibundō, 1964.

Kobayashi Shigefumi. "Kodai no tojō ni okeru kyōkai: kyōkai girei to toshi no fūkei." In *Hōhō toshite no kyōkai*. Ed. Akasaka Norio, 218–262. Sōsho shisō wo horu 1. Shin'yōsha, 1991.

Kobayashi Toshio. *Kodai tennōsei no kisoteki kenkyū*. Azekura shoten, 1994.

Kobayashi Yoshikazu. *Heike monogatari seiseiron*. Miyai shoten, 1986.

———. "Engyōbon Heike monogatari no seiritsu." In *Heike monogatari no seiritsu*. Ed. Tochigi Yoshitada et al., 91–111. *Anata ga yomu Heike monogatari* 1. Yūseidō, 1993.

Kōda Toshio. *Kōhon gōdanshō to sono kenkyū* (jō-chū-ge). Zoku gunsho ruijū kanseikai, 1987–1989. 3 vols.

Kojima Noriyuki. *Jōdai nihon bungaku to chūgoku bungaku jō: shuttenron wo chūshin to suru hikaku bungakuteki kōsatsu*. Hirakawa shobō, 1962.

Komatsu Shigemi, ed. *Hōnen shōnin eden* (chū). *Zoku Nihon emaki taisei* 2. Chūō kōronsha, 1981.

Komatsu Shigeto. *Chūsei gunkimono no kenkyū*. Ōfūsha, 1962–1991. 3 vols.

Kominami Ichirō. *Seiōbo to tanabata denshō*. Heibonsha, 1991.

Komine Kazuaki. "Ōkagami no katari: Bodaikō no hikari to kage." *Bungaku*, 55: 10 (October 1980), 125–139.

———. "Jitsugo to mōgo no 'setsuwa' shi." In *Kodai kōki*, 240–262. *Nihon bungakushi wo yomu*, vol. 2. Yūseidō, 1991.

———. *Setsuwa no gensetsu: chūsei no hyōgen to rekishi jojutsu*. Shin'washa, 2002.

———. *Yaba taishi no nazo: rekishi jojutsu toshite no miraiki*. Iwanami shoten, 2003.

Konishi Jin'ichi. *A History of Japanese Literature, Vol. 1: The Archaic and Ancient Ages.* Trans. Aileen Gatten and Nicholos Teele and ed. Earl Miner. Princeton, NJ: Princeton University Press, 1984.

———. *A History of Japanese Literature, Vol. 3: The High Middle Ages.* Trans. Aileen Gatten and Mark Harbison and ed. Earl Miner. Princeton, NJ: Princeton University Press, 1991.

Kōnoshi Takamitsu. *Kojiki no tassei: sono ronri to hōhō.* Tōkyō daigaku shuppankai, 1983.

———. ed. *Ronshū: Nihon shoki jindai.* Izumi sensho 82. Izumi shoin, 1993.

———. "Kodai tennō shinwa no kansei." *Kokugo to kokubungaku*, 73: 11 (November 1996), 1–14.

———. "Constructing Imperial Mythology: *Kojiki* and *Nihon shoki*." Trans. Iori Joko. In *Inventing the Classics: Modernity, National Identity, and Japanese Literature.* Ed. Haruo Shirane and Tomi Suzuki, 51–67. Stanford, CA: Stanford University Press, 2000.

Koyama Satoko. "Chūsei zenki ni okeru dōji shinkō no ryūsei to mappō shisō." *Bukkyō shigaku kenkyū*, 43: 1 (January 2001), 45–69.

———. "Chūsei zenki ni okeru mappō shisō: sono rekishiteki igi no saikentō." *Shikyō*, no. 43 (September 2001), 21–39.

Kubo Isamu. "Engyōbon *Heike monogatari* no kyōgen kigo kan: 'monogatari' no shikō shita mono." *Bungaku*, 10: 2 (April 1999), 55–69.

Kubo Noritada. *Nitchū shūkyō bunka kōshōshi: kōshin shinkō no kenkyō, jō.* Hara shobō, 1980.

Kuniyasu Yō. "Nihon no ongakuron: gakusho ni mirareru ongaku shisō." *Bungaku*, 56: 4 (April 1988), 40–51.

Kuno Shōichi. "Zenkan makkan katoku setsu tonaerareta riyū ni tsuite" jō-ge. *Tōyō gakuhō*, 25: 3–4 (1938), 418–455 and 567–599.

Kuroda Akira. "Sobu oboegaki: chūsei shiki no sekai kara." In *Heike monogatari: katari to gentai.* Ed. Hyōdō Hiromi, 212–226. Nihon bungaku kenkyū shiryō shinshū 7. Yūseidō, 1987.

———. *Chūsei setsuwa no bungakushiteki kankyō* (zoku). Kenkyū sōsho 160. Izumi shoin, 1995.

———. "Gion shōja oboegaki: chūshaku, shōdō, setsuwa shū." In *Heike monogatari Taiheiki.* Ed. Saeki Shin'ichi and Koakimoto Dan, 27–55. Nihon bungaku kenkyū ronbun shūsei 14. Wakakusa shobō, 1999.

Kuroda Hideo. *Nihon chūsei kaihatsushi no kenkyū.* Azekura shobō, 1984.

———. *Kyōkai no chūsei shōchō no chūsei.* Tokyo daigaku shuppankai, 1986.

———. *Sugata to shigusa no chūseishi.* Imēji rīdingu sōsho. Heibonsha, 1986.

Kuroda Toshio. *Nihon chūsei no kokka to shūkyō.* Iwanami shoten, 1975.

———. "Shinto in the History of Japanese Religion." Trans. James C. Dobbins and Suzanne Gay. *Monumenta Nipponica*, 7: 1 (Winter 1981), 1–21.

———. "Chūsei shakai ni okeru geinō to ongaku." In *Kenmitsu bukkyō to jisha seiryoku*, 72–94. *Kuroda Toshio chosakushū*, vol. 3. Hōzōkan, 1995.

————. "Chinkon no keifu: kokka to shūkyō wo meguru tenbyō." In *Kenmitsu bukkyō to jisha seiryoku*, 131–163. *Kuroda Toshio chosakushū*, vol. 3. Hōzōkan, 1995.

Kuroita Katsumi. "Waga jōdai ni okeru dōka shisō oyobi dōkyō ni tsuite." *Shirin*, 8: 1 (January 1923), 40–54.

Kuroita Masao. "Nara jidai no dōjutsu ni tsuite no shiron." In *Nara bukkyō to higashi ajia*. Ed. Nakai Shinkō, 185–199. Vol. 5 of *Ronshū nara bukkyō*. Yūzankaku, 1995.

Kusaka Tsutomu. "*Heiji monogatari* Akugenda raika-banashi no tenkai: futatsu no taki to ryūjin shinkō." *Gunki to katarimono*, 16 (March 1980), 12–26.

Kusuyama Haruki. *Enanji* jō-chū-ge. Vols. 54–56 of *SKT*. Meiji shoin, 1979–1988.

Lafleur, William R. *The Karma of Words: Buddhism and the Literary Arts in Medieval Japan*. Berkeley: University of California Press, 1983.

————. "Saigyō and the Buddhist Value of Nature." In *Nature in Asian Traditions of Thought: Essays in Environmental Philosophy*. Ed. J. Baird Callicott and Roger T. Ames, 183–209. Albany: SUNY Press, 1989.

Lamarre, Thomas. *Uncovering Heian Japan: An Archaeology of Sensation and Inscription*. Durham, NC: Duke University Press, 2000.

Lau, D. C. *Confucius: The Analects (Lun yü)*. London: Penguin Books, 1979.

Le Blanc, Charles. *Huai-Nan Tzu: Philosophical Synthesis in Early Han Thought, The Idea of Resonance (Kan-Ying)*. With a translation and analysis of Chapter 6. Hong Kong: Hong Kong University Press, 1985.

Le Goff, Jacques. *The Medieval Imagination*. Trans. Arthur Goldhammer. Chicago: University of Chicago Press, 1988.

Lefebvre, Henri. *The Production of Space*. Trans. Donald Nicholson-Smith. Oxford and Cambridge, MA: Blackwell, 1991.

Legge, James, trans. *Li Chi: Book of Rites, An Encyclopedia of Ancient Usages, Religious Creeds, and Social Institutions*, vol. 1. Ed. with Introduction and Study Guide by Ch'u Chai and Winberg Chai. New York: University Books, 1967.

Levy, Ian Hideo. *The Ten Thousand Leaves: A Translation of the Man'yōshū, Japan's Premier Anthology of Classical Poetry*, vol. 1. Princeton, NJ: Princeton University Press, 1981.

Livia Kohn, ed. *Daoism Handbook*. Leiden and Boston: E. J. Brill, 2000.

Loewe, Michael. *Divination, Mythology and Monarchy in Han China*. Cambridge: Cambridge University Press, 1994.

Lu, Sheldon. *From Historicity to Fictionality: The Chinese Poetics of Narrative*. Stanford, CA: Stanford University Press, 1994.

Maeda Masayuki. "Setsuwa to rekishi jojutsu: Heianchō setsuwa shū no rekishi jojutsu wo megutte." In *Setsuwa to wa nanika*. Ed. Honda Giken, Ikegami Jun'ichi, Komine Kazuaki, and Mori Masahito, 202–223. *Setsuwa no kōza*, vol. 1. Benseisha, 1991.

Maeda Tomiyoshi. "Ezo." In *Goshi* 1. Ed. Satō Kiyoji, 126–129. Vol. 9 of *Kōza nihongo no goi*. Meiji shoin, 1983.

Makino Atsushi. "Engyōbon *Heike monogatari* hōō go-kanjō no koto ronri: Dōsen risshi to idaten no monogatari to sono shaku wo tegakari ni." *Gunki to katarimono*, 34 (March 1998), 55–65.

Makino Kazuo. "Engyōbon Heike monogatari no ichisokumen." *Geibun kenkyū*, 36 (March 1977), 1–22.

———. "*Meido sosei ki* sono sokkumen no ichimen." In *Heike monogatari: katari to gentai*. Ed. Hyōdō Hiromi, 117–128. Nihon bungaku kenkyū shiryō shinshū 7. Yūseidō, 1987.

Marra, Michele. *The Aesthetics of Discontent: Politics and Reclusion in Medieval Japanese Literature*. Honolulu: University of Hawaii Press, 1991.

———. *Representations of Power: The Literary Politics of Medieval Japan*. Honolulu: University of Hawaii Press, 1993.

———. "Japanese Aesthetics: The Construction of Meaning." *Philosophy East & West*, 45: 3 (July 1995), 367–386.

Maruyama Yumiko. *Nihon kodai no iryō seido*. Rekshigaku sōsho. Meicho kankōkai, 1998.

———. "Kodai no tennō to byōsha." In *Kosumoroji to shintai*. Ed. Amino Yoshihiko et al., 203–226. Vol. 8 of *Iwanami kōza: Tennō to ōken wo kangaeru*. Iwanami shoten, 2002.

Masuda Katsumi. "Shiyō no shisō: wazauta gogen kō." In *Kodai kayō*. Ed. Nihon bungaku kenkyū shiryō kankōkai, 221–230. Nihon bungaku kenkyū shiryō sōsho. Yūseidō, 1985.

Masuo Shin'ichirō. *Man'yō kajin to chūgoku shisō*. Yoshikawa kōbunkan, 1997.

———. "Nihon kodai no dōkyō juyō to gigi kyōten." In *Dōkyō no rekishi to bunka*. Ed. Yamada Toshiaki and Tanaka Fumio, 297–320. Yūzankaku shuppan, 1998.

———. "Nihon kodai no shūkyō bunka to dōkyō." In *Ajia sho-chiiki to dōkyō*. Ed. Noguchi Testurō, Yusa Noboru, Nozaki Mitsuhiko, and Masuo Shin'ichirō, 256–284. *Kōza dōkyō* 6. Yūzankaku, 2001.

———. "Nihon shoki no hensan to tennō-gō no seiritsu." *Higashi Ajia no kodai bunka*, no. 106 (February 2001), 47–60.

———. "Tojō no chinsai to 'ekigami' saigi no tenkai." In *Kankyō to shinsei no kattō*. Ed. Masuo Shin'ichirō, Kudō Ken'ichi, and Hōjō Katsutaka, 316–341. *Kankyō to shinsei no bunkashi* 3 (ge). Bensei shuppan, 2003.

Matsuda Tomohiro. *Kodai nihon no dōkyō juyō to sennin*. Iwata shoin, 1999.

Matsumoto Haruhisa. *Ōkagami no kōsei*. Ōfūsha, 1969.

Matsumura Hiroji. *Rekishi monogatari: Eiga monogatari to shikyō*. Hanawa sensho 16. Hanawa shobō, 1961.

———. *Eiga monogatari zenchūshaku*. Nihon koten hyōshaku zenchūshaku sōsho. Kadokawa shoten, 1969–1982. 9 vols.

Matsunobu Yasutaka. "Zeni to kahei no kannen: Kamakura ki ni okeru kahei kinō no henka ni tsuite." In *Rettō no bunkashi* 6, 177–210. Nihon edeitā sukūru, 1989.

Matsuoka Shinpei. "Rikisha dengaku kō: gohō dōji no bassei-tachi." *Kanze*, 49: 6 (June 1982), 18–26.

Matsuoka Shinpei. *Utage no shintai: basara kara Zeami e*. Iwanami shoten, 1991.

McCullough, Helen Craig, trans. *The Taiheiki: A Chronicle of Medieval Japan.* Tokyo: Charles E. Tuttle, 1959.

———. *Ōkagami: The Great Mirror, Fujiwara Michinaga (966–1027) and His Times*. Princeton, NJ: Princeton University Press, 1980.

———. *Brocade By Night: "Kokin wakashū" and the Court Style in Japanese Classical Poetry*. Stanford, CA: Stanford University Press, 1985.

———, trans. *The Tale of the Heike*. Stanford, CA: Stanford University Press, 1988.

McCullough, William H. "*Shōkyūki: An Account of the Shōkyū War 1221*." *Monumenta Nipponica*, 19: 1–2 (1964), 163–215.

McCullough, William H., and Helen Craig McCullough. *A Tale of Flowering Fortunes*. Stanford, CA: Stanford University Press, 1980. 2 vols.

McMullin, Neil. "On Placating the Gods and Pacifying the Populace: The Case of the Gion *Goryō* Cult." *History of Religions*, 27: 3 (February 1986), 270–293.

Mekada Sakuo. *Ōkagami ron: kanbungei sakkaken ni okeru seiji hihan no keifu*. Kasama sōsho 107. Kasama shoin, 1979.

Miller, Roy Andrew. "The 'Spirit' of the Japanese Language." *The Journal of Japanese Studies*, 3: 2 (Summer 1977), 251–298.

Mitamura Masako. *Makura no sōshi: hyōgen to kōzō*. Yūseidō, 1994.

Mitani Eiichi. *Monogatari bungakushi ron*. Yūseidō, 1952.

Mitani Kuniaki. "Kodai chimei kigen densetsu no hōhō." *Nihon bungaku*, 30: 10 (October 1981), 41–49.

Miura Kunio. "Dōten fukuchi shōron." *Tōhō shūkyō*, no. 61 (May 1983), 1–23.

Miyazaki Kenji. "Nara-matsu Heian shoki ni okeru ekigami saishi." In *Nihon kodai no shakai to shūkyō*. Ed. Hino Akira, 151–169. Ryūkoku daigaku bukkyō bunka kenkyū sōsho 6. Kyoto: Ryūkoku daigaku bukkyō bunka kenkyūjo, 1996.

Mizuhara Hajime. *Heike monogatari no keisei*. Katō chūdōkan, 1971.

———. *Enkyōbon heike monogatari ronkō*. Katō chūdōkan, 1979.

Moerman, David. "The Ideology of Landscape and the Theater of State: Insei Pilgrimage to Kumano (1090–1220)." *Japanese Journal of Religious Studies*, 24: 3–4 (Fall 1997), 347–374.

Mori Katsumi. *Nissō bunka kōryū no shomondai*. Tōkō shoin, 1950.

———. *Nissō bunka kōryū no shomondai* (zōho). *Mori Katsumi chosaku senshū* 4. Kokusho kankōkai, 1975.

————. *Nissō bōeki no kenkyū. Mori Katsumi chosaku senshū* 1. Kokusho kankōkai, 1975.

Mori Kimiyuki. *Kodai nihon no taigai ninshiki to kōtsū.* Yoshikawa kōbunkan, 1998.

Morino Muneaki. "Heian jidai ni okeru shokuekan to inu." *Bungei gengo kenkyū,* bungei-hen, vol. 12 (1987), 1–14.

Morita Tei. *Nihon kodai no seiji to shūkyō.* Yūzankaku shuppan, 1997.

Moriya Takeshi. *Nihon chūsei e no shiza: furyū basara kabuki.* Enueichikei bukkusu 459. Nihon hōsō shuppan kyōkai, 1984.

————. *Chūsei geinō no genzō.* Kyoto: Tankōsha, 1985.

Morrell, Robert E. *Sand & Pebbles (Shasekishū): The Tales of Mujū Ichien, A Voice of Pluralism in Kamakura Buddhism.* Albany: SUNY Press, 1985.

Morris, Ivan, trans. *The Pillow Book of Sei Shōnagon.* New York: Columbia University Press, 1991.

Morris, Mark. "Waka and Form, Waka and History." *Harvard Journal of Asiatic Studies,* 46: 2 (December 1986), 551–610.

Mostow, Joshua S. *Pictures of the Heart: The Hyakunin Isshu in Word and Image.* Honolulu: University of Hawaii Press, 1996.

Motoori Norinaga. *Kojikiden* 1–4. In *Motoori Norinaga zenshū,* vols. 9–12. Chikuma shobō, 1968–1974.

————. *Kojiki-den, Book 1.* Trans. Ann Wehmeyer with a Preface by Naoki Sakai. Cornell East Asia Series 87. Ithaca, NY: East Asia Program, 1997.

Murai Osamu. *Moji no yokuatsu: kokugaku ideorogī no seiritsu.* Seikyūsha, 1989.

Murai Shōsuke. *Ajia no naka no chūsei nihon.* Azekura shobō, 1988.

————. "The Boundaries of Medieval Japan." *Acta Asiatica,* 81 (2001), 72–91.

Murai Yasuhiko. *Heike monogatari no sekai.* Tokuma shoten, 1973.

Murakami Mitoshi. *Chūsei bungaku no shosō to sono jidai.* Kenkyū sōsho 195. Osaka: Izumi shoin, 1996.

Murayama Shūichi. *Nihon onmyōdōshi sōsetsu.* Hanawa shobō, 1981.

————. "Kodai nihon no onmyōdō." In *Onmyōdō sōsho* 1, *Kodai.* Ed. Murayama Shūichi, 17–31. Meicho shuppan, 1991.

————. *Hieizanshi: tatakai to inori no seiiki.* Tōkyō bijutsu, 1994.

————. *Shugen onmyōdō to shaji shiryō.* Hōzōkan, 1997.

Naba Toshisada. "Dōkyō no nihonkoku e no ruden ni tsukite (1)." *Tōhō shūkyō,* 1: 2 (September 1952), 1–22.

————. "Dōkyō no nihonkoku e no ruden ni tsukite (2)." *Tōhō shūkyō,* 1: 4–5 (January 1954), 58–122.

Nagafuji Yasushi. *Chūsei nihon bungaku to jikan ishiki.* Miraisha, 1984.

Nagaike Kenji. "Itsudatsu no shōsei: chūsei inja bunka ni okeru ongaku to kayō." In *Hyōshō toshite no ongaku,* 57–81. Vol. 6 of *Iwanami kōza Nihon no ongaku Ajia no ongaku.* Iwanami shoten, 1988.

Nakada Norio. *Nihon ryōiki*. Vol. 6 of *NKBZ*. Shōgakukan, 1975.

Nakai Shinkō. *Gyōki to kodai bukkyō*. Nagata bunshōdō, 1991.

Nakamae Masashi. "Koten bungaku no naka no shinsen sekai to dōkyō." In *Ajia sho-chiiki to dōkyō*. Ed. Noguchi Testurō, Yusa Noboru, Nozaki Mitsuhiko, and Masuo Shin'ichirō, 285–312. Vol. 6 of *Kōza dōkyō*. Yūzankaku, 2001.

Nakamura Hajime, Fukunaga Mitsuji, Tamura Yoshirō, and Konno Tōru, ed. *Iwanami bukkyō jiten*. Iwanami shoten, 1989.

Nakamura, Kyoko Motomochi, trans. *Miraculous Stories from the Japanese Buddhist Tradition: The Nihon ryōiki of the Monk Kyōkai*. Cambridge, MA: Harvard University Press, 1973.

Nakamura Shōhachi. *Hōbokushi*. Chūgoku koten shinsho. Meitoku shuppansha, 1967.

———. *Gogyō taigi*. Chūgoku koten shinsho. Meitoku shuppansha, 1973.

———. "Onmyōdō ni juyō sareta 'isho' ni tsuite." In *Onmyōdō sōsho 4 Tokuron*. Ed. Murayama Shūichi, Shimode Sekiyo, and Nakamura Shōhachi, 259–277. Meicho shuppan, 1993.

Nakamura Shōhachi, Kotō Tomoko, and Shimizu Hiroko. *Gogyō taigi* jō-ge. Shinpen kanbunsen shisō rekishi shirīzu 7, 8. Meiji shoin, 1998.

Nanami Hiroaki. "Inseiki no kumano mōde: mestuzai, chinkon, gohō-zuke wo meguru girei to shinkō." *Bungei gengo kenkyū*, no. 13 (February 1988), 25–101.

Narusawa Akira. *Seiji no kotoba: imi no rekishi wo megutte*. Heibonsha sensho 84. Heibonsha, 1984.

Needham, Joseph. *Science and Civilization in China*, vol. 5, *Chemistry and Chemical Technology*, Part 2, *Spagyrical Discovery and Invention: Magisteries of Gold and Immortality*. Cambridge: Cambridge University Press, 1974.

Nishigaki Seiji. "Minshū no seijin seikatsu: kegare to michi." *Rekishi kōron*, 101: 4 (April 1984), 101–107.

Nishimiya Hideki. "Nihon kodai 'fugeki' ron: sono jittai wo chūshin ni." In *Kodaishi ronshū* ge. Ed. Naoki Kōjirō Sensei Koki Kinenkai, 203–233. Hanawa shobō, 1989.

Nishizawa Kazumitsu. "Ōken to bōryoku: *Kojiki* no mondai toshite." *Kokugo to kokubungaku*, 71: 11 (November 1994), 33–45.

Niunoya Tetsuichi. *Kebiishi: chūsei no kegare to kenryoku*. Heibonsha, 1986.

Nōda Chūryō. *Koyomi: Gijutsu no ue kara jidai no rekishi wo miru* zōhoban. Nihon rekishi shinsho. Shibundō, 1966, 1980.

Noda Kosaburō. "Onmyōdō no ichisokumen: Heian chūki wo chūshin to shite." In *Onmyōdō sōsho* 1, *Kodai*. Ed. Murayama Shūichi et al., 121–152. Meicho shuppan, 1991.

———. "Onmyōdō no seiritsu." In *Onmyōdō sōsho* 1, *Kodai*. Ed. Murayama Shūichi et al., 61–82. Meicho shuppan, 1991.

Noguchi Tetsurō, ed. *Dōkyō jiten*. Hirakawa shuppansha, 1994.

Nosco, Peter. *Remembering Paradise: Nativism and Nostalgia in Eighteenth-*

Century Japan. Cambridge, MA, and London: Council on East Asian Studies, Harvard University Press, 1990.

Nose Asaji. *Nōgaku genryū kō*. Iwanami shoten, 1938.

Nylan, Michael. "The *Chin wen/Ku wen* Controversy in Han." *T'oung pao*, 80 (1994), 83–145.

———. "A Problematic Model: The Han 'Orthodox Synthesis,' Then and Now." In *Imagining Boundaries: Changing Confucian Doctrines, Texts, and Hermeneutics*. Ed. Kai-wing Chow, On-cho Ng, and John B. Henderson, 17–56. Albany: SUNY Press, 1999.

Ōhama Itsuhiko. *Man'yō genshikō*. Shūeisha, 1978.

Ōishi Naomasa. "Soto-ga-hama ezo-ga-shima kō." In *Nihon kodaishi kenkyū: Seki Akira sensei kanreki kinen*. Ed. Seki Akira Kyōju Kanreki Kinenkai, 567–598. Yoshikawa kōbunkan, 1980.

———. "Kita no shūen, rettō tōhokubu no kōki." In *Shūen kara mita chūsei nihon*. Ed. idem, Takura Kurayoshi, and Takahashi Kimiaki, 13–64. Nihon no rekishi 14. Kōdansha, 2001.

Ōji Toshiaki. "Ninshiki kūkan toshite no 'nihon.'" In *Kosumoroji to shintai*. Ed. Amino Yoshihiko et al., 71–95. Vol. 8 of *Iwanami kōza: Tennō to ōken wo kangaeru*. Iwanami shoten, 2002.

Okada Masayuki. "Kenpō jū shichi jō ni tsuite." In *Ōmi nara chō no kanbungaku*, 37–51. Nara-ken Tanbaichi-chō: Yōtokusha, 1946.

Okada, Richard H. *Figures of Resistance: Language, Poetry, and Narrating in The Tale of Genji and Other Mid-Heian Texts*. Durham, NC, and London: Duke University Press, 1991.

Okada Shōji. "Onmyōdō saishi no seiritsu to tenkai." In *Onmyōdō sōsho* 1, *Kodai*. Ed. Murayama Shūichi et al., 153–195. Meicho shuppan, 1991.

———. *Heian jidai no kokka to saishi*. Zoku gunsho ruijū kanseikai, 1994.

Ōkubo Hiroyuki. "Hina ni aru koto: Tabito ni okeru jikū ishiki." *Kokugo to kokubungaku*, 72: 2 (February 1995), 1–16.

Ong, Walter J. *Orality and Literacy: The Technologizing of the Word*. London and New York: Routledge, 1982.

Ōno Shichizō. *Sendai kuji hongi: kunchū*. Hihyōsha, 2001.

Orikuchi Shinobu. "Yamato jidai no bungaku." In *Orikuchi Shinobu zenshū*, vol. 8. Ed. Orikuchi hakase kinenkai, 93–158. Chūō kōronsha, 1955.

———. "Gorotsuki no hanashi." In *Kodai kenkyū minzokugaku hen* 2. Ed. Orikuchi hakushi kinenkai, 22–46. *Orikuchi Shinobu zenshū*, vol. 3. Chūō kōronsha, 1955.

———. "Okina no hassei." In *Kodai kenkyū minzokugaku hen* 1. Ed. Orikuchi hakushi kinen kodai kenkyūjo, 371–415. *Orikuchi Shinobu zenshū*, vol. 2. Chūō kōronsha, 1965.

———. "Nōgaku ni okeru waki no igi: 'okina no hassei' no shūhen." In *Kodai kenkyū minzokugaku hen* 2. Ed. Orikuchi hakushi kinen kodai kenkyūjo, 241–249. *Orikuchi Shinobu zenshū*, vol. 3. Chūō kōronsha, 1966.

Ortolani, Benito. *The Japanese Theatre: From Shamanistic Ritual to Contemporary Pluralism*. Leiden and New York: E. J. Brill, 1990.

Otsu Yūichi. "Taiheiki to iu han 'monogatari' han 'rekishi.'" In *Heike mono-gatari Taiheiki*. Ed. Saeki Shin'ichi and Koakimoto Dan, 191–205. Nihon bungaku kenkyū ronbun shūsei 14. Wakakusa shobō, 1999.

Otter, Monica. *Inventiones: Fiction and Referentiality in Twelfth-Century English Historical Writing*. Chapel Hill, NC: University of North Carolina Press, 1996.

Ōyama Kyōhei. *Nihon chūsei nōsonshi no kenkyū*. Iwanami shoten, 1978.

Ōyama Seiichi. *Nagaya ōke mokkan to kinsekibun*. Yoshikawa kōbunkan, 1998.

Oyanagi Shigeta. "Dōkyō to shingon mikkyō to no kankei wo ronjite shu-gendō ni oyobu." *Tetsugaku zasshi*, 39: 450 (August 1924), 617–645, and 451 (September 1924), 733–746.

———. *Tōyō shisō no kenkyū*. Morikita shoten, 1943.

Philippi, Donald. L. *Kojiki*. University of Tokyo Press, 1968.

———. *Norito: A Translation of the Ancient Japanese Ritual Prayers*. With a new Preface by Joseph M. Kitagawa. Princeton, NJ: Princeton University Press, 1990.

Pigeot, Jacqueline. *Michiyuki-Bun: poétique de l'itinéraire dans la littérature du Japan ancien*. Paris: G.-P. Maisonneuve et Larose, 1982.

Piggott, Joan R. *The Emergence of Japanese Kingship*. Stanford, CA: Stanford University Press, 1997.

Plutschow, Herbert E. *Chaos and Cosmos: Ritual in Early and Medieval Japa-nese Literature*. Leiden and New York: E. J. Brill, 1990.

Pollack, David. *The Fracture of Meaning: Japan's Synthesis of China from the Eighth Through the Eighteenth Centuries*. Princeton, NJ: Princeton Univer-sity Press, 1986.

Queen, Sarah A. *From Chronicle to Canon: The Hermeneutics of the Spring and Autumn, According to Tung Chung-shu*. Cambridge and New York: Cambridge University Press, 1996.

Rabinovitch, Judith. *Shōmonki: The Story of Masakado's Rebellion*. Monu-menta Nipponica at Sophia University, 1986.

Rambelli, Fabio. "True Words, Silence, and the Adamantine Dance: On Japa-nese Mikkyō and the Formation of the Shingon Discourse." *Japanese Jour-nal of Religious Studies*, 21: 4 (December 1994), 373–405.

Raz, Jacob. "Popular Entertainment and Politics: The Great *Dengaku* of 1096." *Monumenta Nipponica*, 40: 3 (Autumn 1985), 283–298.

Ricoeur, Paul. *Time and Narrative*, Vol. 3. Chicago: University of Chicago Press, 1985.

Robinet, Isabelle. *Taoism: Growth of a Religion*. Trans. Phyllis Brooks. Stanford, CA: Stanford University Press, 1997.

Rouzer, Paul. *Articulated Ladies: Gender and the Male Community in Early Chinese Texts*. Cambridge, MA: Harvard University Asia Center, 2001.

Saeki Shin'ichi. "*Heike monogatari* entan setsuwa no seiritsu." *Gunki to ka-tarimono*, 15 (March 1979), 1–13.

———. "Engyōbon Heike monogatari no Kiyomori tsuitō wagun: 'shōdōsei' no ichidanmen." In *Heike monogatari* 1. Ed. Takehisa Tsuyoshi, 329–341. Nihon bungaku kenkyū taisei. Kokusho kankōkai, 1990.

———. "Shōgun to chōteki: *Heike monogatari* wo chūshin ni." *Gunki to katarimono*, 27 (March 1991), 12–22.

———. "'Kane watashi' senyūjō no honbun to sono shūhen." In *Engyōbon heike monogatari kōshō* 2. Ed. Mizuhara Hajime, 130–141. Shintensha, 1993.

———. "Iteki kannnen no juyō: *Heike monogatari* wo chūshin ni." In *Gunki to kanbungaku*. Ed. Wakan hikaku bungakukai, 127–143. Wakan hikaku bungaku sōsho 15. Kyūko shoin, 1993.

———. "Kanjin hijiri to setsuwa: aruiwa 'setsuwa' to 'katari.'" In *Heike monogatari: setsuwa to katari*. Ed. Mizuhara Hajime, 201–219. *Anata ga yomu Heike monogatari*, vol. 2. Yūseidō, 1994.

———. "Katarimono to rekishi: *Heike monogatari* wo chūshin ni." In *Sanbun bungaku "monogatari" no sekai*. Ed. Minobe Shigekatsu and Hattori Kōzō, 272–287. Vol. 3 of *Kōza nihon no denshō bungaku*. Miyai shoten, 1995.

———. *Senjō no seishinshi: bushidō to iu gen'ei*. Enueichikei bukkusu 998. Nihon hōsō shuppan kyōkai, 2004.

Saigō Nobutsuna. *Shinwa to kokka: kodai ronshū*. Heibonsha sensho 53. Heibonsha, 1977.

———. *Kodai no koe: uta odori ichi kotoba shinwa*. Asahi shinbunsha, 1985.

———. *Kojiki chūshaku*, vol. 3. Heibonsha, 1988.

Saitō Hideki, ed. *Nihon shinwa: sono kōzō to seisei*. Nihon bungaku wo yomikaeru 1. Yūseidō, 1995.

———. "Sendai kuji hongi no gensetsu to seisei: hensei suru kodai shinwa ron no tame ni." *Kodai bungaku*, 37 (March 1998), 2–13.

———. "Sekkanki no nihongi kyōju." *Kokubungaku kaishaku to kanshō*, 64: 3 (March 1999), 34–42.

Saitō Mokichi. *Man'yōshū kenkyū* (jō-ge). Iwanami shoten, 1940. 2 vols.

Sakai Kimi. *Chūsei no uwasa jōhō dentatsu no shikumi*. Yoshikawa kōbunkan, 1997.

Sakai Tadao and Fukui Fumimasa. "Dōkyō to wa nanika: dōkyō, dōka, dōjutsu, dōshi." In *Dōkyō no sōgōteki kenkyū*. Ed. Sakai Tadao, 429–449. Kokusho kankōkai, 1977.

———. "Nihon ni okeru dōkyō kenkyū." In *Dōkyō no sōgōteki kenkyū*. Ed. idem, 419–428. Kokusho kankōkai, 1977, 1981.

———. "Shohyō: *Dōkyō jiten* tsuketari *Dōkyō no daijiten*." *Shikyū*, no. 29 (September 1994), 153–162.

Sakai, Naoki. *Voices of the Past: The Status of Language in Eighteenth-Century Japanese Discourse*. Ithaca, NY: Cornell University Press, 1991.

Sakakibara Chizuru. "Kakucihibon *Heike monogatari* ni okeru antoku tei no myakuraku." *Nihon bungaku*, 37: 12 (December 1988), 19–29.

———. "Antoku tennō ibun: kinsei kōki ni miru *Heike monogatari*, kyōju no ittan." *Kokugo to Kokubungaku*, 74: 1 (January 1997), 29–42.

Sakakibara Kunihiko, ed. *Makura no sōshi sōsakuin*. Yūbun shoin, 1967.

Sakamoto Tarō. *Rikkokushi*. Nihon rekishi sōsho 27. Yoshikawa kōbunkan, 1970.

————. *Shūshi to shigaku. Sakamoto Tarō chosakushū* 5. Yoshikawa kōbunkan, 1989.

————. *The Six National Histories of Japan.* Trans. John S. Brownlee. Vancouver: University of British Columbia Press, 1991.

Sakurai Yoshirō. "Chūsei ni okeru hyōhaku to yūgei." In *Chūsei* 1, 300–339. *Iwanami kōza nihon rekishi* 5. Iwanami shoten, 1975.

Sansom, George. *A History of Japan to 1334.* Stanford, CA: Stanford University Press, 1958.

Sasaki Hachirō. *Zōho Heike monogatari no kenkyū.* Waseda daigaku shuppanbu, 1967.

Sasaki Kōichi. "Tsuzumi hōgan: *Heike monogatari* no warai." *Kokugakuin zasshi,* 67 (December 1966), 20–35.

Satō Akira. "Fukunaga Mitsuji-shi no 'dōkyō' to 'nihon bunka' ni kansuru ichiren no kenkyū wo megutte." *Chugoku tetsugaku ronshū,* no. 14 (October 1988), 19–34.

Satō Hiroo. *Nihon chūsei no kokka to bukkyō.* Chūseishi kenkyū sensho. Yoshikawa kōbunkan, 1987.

————. *Kami, hotoke, ōken no chūsei.* Hōzōkan, 1998.

Schafer, Edward H. *Pacing the Void: T'ang Approaches to the Stars.* Berkeley: University of California Press, 1977.

————. "Blue Green Clouds." *Journal of the American Oriental Society* 102: 1 (January–March 1982), 91–92.

Schipper, Kristopher. "The Taoist Body." *History of Religions,* 17: 3–4 (February–May 1978), 355–385.

Schwartz, Benjamin. *The World of Thought in Ancient China.* Cambridge, MA: Belknap Press of Harvard University Press, 1985.

Seidel, Anna K. "Imperial Treasures and Taoist Sacraments: Taoist Roots in the Apocrypha." In *Tantric and Taoist Studies in Honour of R. A. Stein,* vol. 2. Ed. Michel Strickmann, 291–371. Melanges chinois et bouddhiques, no. 21. Brussels: Institut Belge des Hautes Études Chinoises, 1983.

Shida Jun'ichi. *Hitachi fudoki to sono shakai.* Yūzankaku, 1974.

Shidachi Masatomo. *Heike monogatari kataribon no hōhō to isō.* Kyūko shoin, 2004.

Shigeta Shin'ichi. *Onmyōji to kizoku shakai.* Yoshikawa kōbunkan, 2004.

Shimizu Masumi. "Biwa hōshi no shūbun: jōsha hissui, kosha, shōgai." *Kokugakuin zasshi,* 96: 1 (January 1995), 65–83.

————. "Shi no Heike ju no Heike: *Heike monogatari* no seisei to kanjūjike no chikara." *Gunki to katarimono,* 34 (March 1998), 41–52.

Shimode Sekiyo. *Shinsen shisō.* Nihon rekishi sōsho 22. Yoshikawa kōbunkan, 1968.

————. *Dōkyō: sono kōdō to shisō.* Nihonjin no kōdō to shisō 10. Hyōronsha, 1971.

————. "Saimei ki no Futa-tsuki no miya ni tsuite: shoki no dōkyō kiji kō." In *Zoku nihon kodaishi ronshū,* jō. Ed. Sakamoto Tarō Hakushi Koki Kinenkai, 171–196. Yoshikawa kōbunkan, 1972.

————. *Nihon kodai no jingi to dōkyō.* Yoshikawa kōbunkan, 1972.

————. *Kodai shinsen shisō no kenkyū.* Yoshikawa kōbunkan, 1986.

————. "Nihon ni okeru onmyōdō no shiteki isō." In *Onmyōdō sōsho 4, Tokuron.* Ed. Murayama Shūichi, Shimode Sekiyo, and Nakamura Shōhachi, 1–18. Meicho shuppan, 1993.

————. *Nihon kodai no dōkyō onmyōdō to jingi.* Yoshikawa kōbunkan, 1997.

Shinada Yoshikazu. "*Man'yōshū*: The Invention of a National Poetry Anthology." In *Inventing the Classics: Modernity, National Identity, and Japanese Literature.* Ed. Haruo Shirane and Tomi Suzuki, 31–50. Stanford, CA: Stanford University Press, 2000.

Shinkawa Tokio. "Nihon kodai ni okeru bukkyō to dōkyō." In *Kodai bunka no tenkai to dōkyō.* Ed. Noguchi Tetsurō and Nakamura Shōhachi, 51–83. *Senshū dōkyō to nihon* 2. Yūzankaku, 1997.

————. *Dōkyō wo meguru kōbō: Nihon no kun'nō, dōshi no hō wo agamezu.* Ajia bukkusu 13. Taishūkan shoten, 1999.

————. *Nihon kodai no girei to hyōgen: Ajia no naka no seiji bunka.* Yoshikawa kōbunkan, 1999.

Shirane, Haruo. *The Bridge of Dreams: A Poetics of "The Tale of Genji."* Stanford, CA: Stanford University Press, 1987.

Smits, Ivo. *The Pursuit of Loneliness: Chinese and Japanese Nature Poetry in Medieval Japan, ca. 1050–1150.* Stuttgart: Franz Steiner Verlag, 1995.

————. "The Poet and the Politician: Teika and the Compilation of the *Shinkokinshū*." *Monumenta Nipponica*, 53: 4 (Winter 1998), 427–472.

Souyri, Pierre François. *The World Turned Upside Down: Medieval Japanese Society.* Trans. Käthe Roth. New York: Columbia University Press, 2001.

Stock, Brian. *Listening for the Text: On the Uses of the Past.* Baltimore: Johns Hopkins University Press, 1990.

Stone, Jacqueline I. *Original Enlightenment and the Transformation of Medieval Japanese Buddhism.* Honolulu: University of Hawaii Press, 1999.

Strickmann, Michel. *Chinese Magical Medicine.* Ed. Bernard Faure. Asian Religions & Cultures. Stanford, CA: Stanford University Press, 2002.

Sudō Takashi. "Kotohirabon *Hōgen monogatari* no shishō kōsei: unmeikan to 'kudoki' to kanseki inyō." *Gunki to kanbungaku.* Ed. Wakan Hikaku Bungakukai, 24–41. Wakan hikaku bungaku sōsho 15. Kyūko shoin, 1993.

Sueki Fumihiko. *Nihon bukkyōshi: Shisōshi toshite no apurōchi.* Shinchōsha, 1992.

————. "Two Seemingly Contradictory Aspects of the Teaching of Innate Enlightenment (hongaku) in Medieval Japan." *Japanese Journal of Religious Studies*, 22: 102 (Spring 1995), 3–15.

————. *Heian shōki bukkyō shisō no kenkyū: Annen no shisō keisei wo chūshin toshite.* Shunjūsha, 1995.

Sunagawa Hiroshi. *Heike monogatari shinkō.* Tokyo bijutsu, 1982.

————. "Biwa hōshi ni tsuite no ni, san no mondai." *Gunki to katarimono*, 31 (March 1995), 75–83.

Sunayama Minoru. *Zui Tō dōkyō shisōshi kenkyū.* Hirakawa shuppansha, 1990.

Suzuki Yoshijirō. *Ekikyō* jō-ge. Vols. 9–10 of *ZKT.* Shūeisha, 1974.

Tada Kōryū, Ōkubo Ryōjun, Tamura Yoshirō, and Asai Endō, ed. *Tendai hongaku ron.* Vol. 9 of *Nihon shisō taikei.* Iwanami shoten, 1973.

Takagi Ichinosuke, ed. *Heike monogatari.* Vol. 9 of *Kokugo kokubungaku kenkyūshi taisei.* Sanseidō, 1960.

Takagi Makoto. "Hangyaku no gengo / seido no gengo: Manabon *Soga monogatari* no hyōgen to kōzō." *Nagoya daigaku kokugo kokubungaku,* 64 (July 1989), 1–17.

———. "Yoshinaka monogatari no kōzō: ijin hōmontan kara no itsudatsu." *Kodai bungaku kenkyū,* 1 (October 1992), 59–75.

———. "Seisei hen'yō suru 'sekai' aruiwa manabon *Soga monogatari*: 'kami' no tanjō to 'tsumi' no hassei." In *Gikeiki, soga monogatari.* Ed. Murakami Manabu, 357–371. Nihon bungaku kenkyū taisei. Kokusho kankōkai, 1993.

Takagi Yutaka. *Kamakura bukkyōshi kenkyū.* Iwanami shoten, 1982.

Takahashi Kimiaki. "Chūsei nishi nihonkai chiiki to taigai kōryū." In *Nihonkai to Izumo sekai.* Ed. Mori Kōichi, *Umi to rettō bunka,* vol. 2, 341–363. Shōgakukan, 1991.

———. "Higashi Ajia to chūsei bungaku." In *Jūsan jūshi seiki no bungaku,* 311–327. Vol. 5 of *Iwanami kōza nihon bungakushi.* Iwanami shoten, 1995.

Takahashi Masaaki. *Kiyomori izen: Ise Heishi no kōryū.* Heibonsha sensho 85. Heibonsha, 1984.

Takahashi Sadaichi. *Kundoku gyokuyō.* Takashina shoten, 1988–1990. 8 vols.

Takahashi Tōru. "In'yō toshite no junkyo: *Genji monogatari* ni okeru bungaku to rekishi." In *Heian jidai no rekishi to bungaku,* bungaku-hen. Ed. Yamanaka Yutaka, 83–111. Yoshikawa kōbunkan, 1981.

Takahashi Yōichirō. "*Kaifūsō* to chūgoku bungaku." In *Jōdai bungaku to kanbungaku.* Ed. Wakan hikaku bungakukai, 191–207. Wakan hikaku bungaku sōsho 2. Kyūko shoin, 1986.

Takashima Masato. "Shichi hasseki ni okeru nihon no dōkyō." In *Rekishi ni okeru minshū to bunka: Sakai Tadao Sensei koki shukuga kinen ronshū.* Ed. Sakai Tadao Sensei Koki Shukuga Kinen no Kai, 923–938. Kokusho kankōkai, 1982.

Takayama Toshihiro. *Kundoku shibu kassenjō-bon Heike monogatari.* Yūseidō, 1995.

Takeda Sachiko. *Kodai kokka no keisei to ifukusei: hakama to kantōi.* Yoshikawa kōbunkan, 1984.

Takeda Yūkichi and Satō Kenzō. *Kundoku nihon sandai jitsuroku.* Kyoto: Rinsen shoten, 1986.

Takehisa Tsuyoshi. *Heike monogatari seiritsu katei kō.* Ōfūsha, 1986.

————. "Kiyomori-katari no seitai: jikyōsha no keifu." In *Heike monogatari: setsuwa to katari*. Ed. Mizuhara Hajime, 152–178. *Anata ga yomu Heike monogatari*, vol. 2. Yūseidō, 1994.

————. *Heike monogatari no zentaizō*. Izumi sensho 103. Osaka: Izumi shoin, 1996.

Takeoka Masao. *Ise monogatari zenhyōshaku: kochūshaku jūisshu shūsei*. Yūbun shoin, 1987.

Takeuchi Teruo. *Raiki* jō-chū-ge. Vols. 27–29 of *SKT*. Meiji shoin, 1971–1979.

Takigawa Masajirō. "Kokka seihō no hajime, Jōgū taishi kenpō jū shichi kajō." In *Ritsuryō kyakushiki no kenkyū*, 15–78. Kadokawa shoten, 1967.

————. "Ritsuryō to onmyōdō." *Tōhō shūkyō*, no. 35 (July 1970), 1–19.

Tamagami Takuya. "*Genji monogatari* no dokusha: monogatari ondokuron." *Joshidai bungaku*, Kokubun-hen, no. 7 (January 1955), 1–15.

Tamba Akira. *La théorie et l'esthétique musicale japonaises*. Paris: Publications Orientalistes de France, 1988.

Tamura Enchō. "Onmyōryō seiritsu izen." In *Onmyōdō sōsho 1, kodai*. Ed. Murayama Shūichi et al., 35–60. Meicho shuppan, 1991.

Tamura Yoshinaga. *Asukakyō Fujiwarakyō kōshō*. Kyoto: Sōgeisha, 1965.

Tanaka, Stefan. *Japan's Orient: Rendering Pasts into History*. Berkeley: University of California Press, 1993.

Tanaka Takako. *Gehō to aihō no chūsei*. Divinitasu sōsho 4. Sunagoya shobō, 1993.

————. "Tendai kuden hōmon to setsuwa: *Keiranjūyōshū* no 'monogatari ni iwaku' wo megutte." *Setsuwa no ba: shōdō, chūshaku*. Ed. Honda Giken et al., 294–315. *Setsuwa no kōza*, vol. 3. Benseisha, 1993.

Tanaka Taku. "Futatabi yasoshima matsuri ni tsuite: Okada Seiji-shi setsu no hihan." *Shintōshi kenkyū*, 25: 3 (May 1977), 2–23.

Taniguchi Hiroyuki. "Kikai-gai-shima runin tan no seiritsu: Shunkan Ariō setsuwa wo megutte." *Dōshisha Kokubungaku*, 15 (January 1980), 15–27.

————. "Setsuwa denshō to *Heike monogatari* no kōsō: kikai-ga-shima runin tan wo megutte." *Dōshisha kokubungaku*, 17 (March 1981), 79–89.

Thornhill, Arthur H. *Six Circles, One Dewdrop: The Religio-Aesthetic World of Komparu Zenchiku*. Princeton, NJ: Princeton University Press, 1993.

Tilley, Christopher. *A Phenomenology of Landscape, Places, Paths and Monuments*. Oxford: Berg, 1994.

Toda Yoshimi. "Ōchō toshi to shōen taisei." *Kodai 4*, 160–191. *Iwanami kōza nihon rekishi 4*. Iwanami shoten, 1976.

————. *Nihon chūsei no minshū to ryōshu*. Azekura shobō, 1994.

Tokuda Kazuo. *Egatari to monogatari*. Imēji rīdingu sōsho. Heibonsha, 1990.

Tomikura Tokujirō. *Heike monogatari kenkyū*. Kadokawa shoten, 1964.

————. *Heike monogatari zenchūshaku*. Nihon koten hyōshaku zenchūshaku sōsho. Kadokawa shoten, 1966–1968. 4 vols.

Tōno Haruyuki. *Shōsōin bunsho to mokkan no kenkyū.* Hanawa shobō, 1977.

Tsuchiya Megumi. "Bugaku no chūsei: dōbu no kūkan. In *Chūsei no kūkan wo yomu.* Ed. Gomi Fumihiko, 59–99. Yoshikawa kōbunkan, 1995.

Tsuda Hiroyuki. "Gishozukuri no waza: *Sendai kuji hongi* no hōhō to Nihongi-kō." *Nihon bungaku,* 43: 11 (November 1994), 80–83.

———. "Nihongi-kō to *Sendai kuji hongi.*" *Nihon bungaku,* 46: 10 (October 1997), 62–67.

Tsuda Sōkichi. *Tsuda Sōkichi zenshū.* Iwanami shoten, 1963–1966. 33 vols.

Tsugita Masaki. *Nihon shinwa no kōsei.* Meiji shoin, 1973.

———. *Kojiki* (chū). Kōdansha gakujutsu bunko 208. Kōdansha, 1980.

Tsuji Zennosuke. *Nihon bukkyōshi ronshū.* Vol. 5 of *Nihon bukkyōshi kenkyū.* Iwanami shoten, 1984.

Tsukahara Tetsuo. "*Ōkagami* kōsei to kai-i genshō." In *Ōkagami Eiga monogatari.* Ed. Kawakita Noboru, 97–112. Nihon bungaku kenkyū taisei. Kokusho kankōkai, 1988.

Tsukudo Reikan. "Suwa honji: Agui saku shintōshū ni tsuite." In *Chūsei shūkyō geibun no kenkyū* 1, 91–130. *Tsukudo Reikan chosakushū,* vol. 3. Serika shobō, 1975.

———. "*Heike monogatari* ni tsuite oboegaki." In *Shūkyō bungaku fukko to jojishi,* 270–299. *Tsukudo Reikan chosakushū,* vol. 1. Serika shobō, 1976.

———. "Rekishi to bungaku to no kyūsai." In *Heike monogatari: katari to gentai.* Ed. Hyōdō Hiromi, 1–6. Nihon bungaku kenkyū shiryō shinshū 7. Yūseidō, 1987.

Tsumaki Chokuryō. "Nihon ni okeru dōkyō shisō." *Ryūkoku gakuhō,* 306, 308.

Twitchett, Denis. *The Writing of Official History Under the T'ang.* Cambridge: Cambridge University Press, 1992.

Tyler, Royall. *Japanese Nō Dramas.* London and New York: Penguin Books, 1992.

———.*The Tale of Genji.* New York: Viking, 2001. 2 vols.

Ubukata Takashige. *Heike monogatari no kisō to kōzō: mizu no kami to monogatari.* Kindai bungeisha, 1984.

Ueda Masaaki. "Wafū shigō to jindaishi." In *Akamatsu Toshihide kyōju taikan kinen kokushi ronshū.* Ed. Akamatsu Toshihide Kyōju Taikan Kinen Jikyōkai, 123–138. Kyoto: Akamatsu Toshihide Kyōju Taikan Kinen Jigyōkai, 1972.

———. *Daiō no seiki.* Nihon no rekishi 2. Shōgakukan, 1973.

———. "Kodai geinō no keisei." In *Genshi / kodai.* Ed. Geinōshi kenkyūkai, 171–228. *Nihon geinōshi* 1. Hōsei daigaku shuppankyoku, 1981.

———. "Nihon kodai no ōken to fugeki." In *Higashi ajia ni okeru shakai to shūzoku.* Ed. Inoue Mitsusada et al., 248–275. *Higashi ajia sekai ni okeru nihon kodaishi kōza,* vol. 10. Gakuseisha, 1984.

Ueki Yukinobu. "Tōdōza no keisei to heikyoku." *Heike monogatari katari to gentai.* Ed. Hyōdō Hiromi, 7–29. Nihon bungaku kenkyū shiryō shinshū 7. Yūseidō, 1987.

Umemura Takashi. "Tennō no koshō." In *Tōchiteki sho kinō to tennōkan*. Ed. Nagahara Keiji, 9–42. *Kōza zenkindai no tennō*, vol. 4. Aoki shoten, 1995.

Uwayokote Masataka. *Heike monogatgari no kyokō to shinjitsu* (jō-ge). Hanawa shobō, 1985.

Van Ess, Hans. "The Old Text/New Text Controversy: Has the 20th Century Got It Wrong?" *T'oung pao*, 80 (1994), 146–170.

Verschuer, Charlotte von. *Le commerce extérieur du Japon des origines au XVIe siècle*. Paris: Éditions Maisonneuve & Larose, 1988.

Wada Atsumu. "Kusurigari to *Honzōshūchū*: Nihon kodai no minkan dōkyō no jittai." *Shirin*, 61: 3 (March 1978), 333–378.

———. "Jitō jotei no Yoshino miya gyōkō." In *Matsurigoto no tenkai*. Ed. Kishi Toshio, 71–98. Nihon no kodai 7. Chūō kōronsha, 1996.

Wakabayashi Haruko. "From Conqueror of Evil to Devil King: Ryōgen and Notions of *Ma* in Medieval Japanese Buddhism." *Monumenta Nipponica*, 54: 4 (Winter 1999), 481–507.

Wakamori Tarō. *Shugendōshi no kenkyū*. Wakamori Tarō chosakushū 2. Kōbundō, 1980.

Wang, Q. Edward. "History, Space, and Ethnicity: The Chinese Worldview." *Journal of World History*, 10: 2 (1999), 285–305.

Watanabe Katsuyoshi. *Chinkonsai no kenkyū*. Meichō shuppan, 1994.

Watanabe Minoru. *Heianchō bunshōshi*. Tōkyō daigaku shuppankai, 1981.

Watanabe Morimichi. *Sōhei seisuiki*. Sanseidō sensho 108. Sanseidō, 1984.

Watanabe Sadamaro. *Heike monogatari no shisō*. Hōzōkan, 1989.

Watanabe Tamotsu. *Heike Ichimon*. Jinbutsu ōraisha, 1964.

Watanabe Yasuaki. "Korai futeishō to kyōgen kigo-kan." *Kokugo to kokubungaku*, 67: 11 (November 1990), 60–70.

Watase Masatada. "Hitomaro kashū tanabata kagun no kōzō: sono dai-sanjū-ichi shu made." *Man'yō*, no. 169 (1999), 30–43.

———. *Hitomaro kashū hi ryakutaika ron* ge: *Tanabata kagun ron*. Vol. 4 of *Watase Masatada chosakushū*. Ōfū, 2002.

———. *Shima no miya no bungaku*. Vol. 6 of *Watase Masatada chosakushū*. Ōfū, 2003.

Watson, Burton. *The Complete Works of Chuang Tzu*. New York: Columbia University Press, 1968.

Watson, Michael Geoffrey. "A Narrative Study of the Kakuichi-bon *Heike monogatari*." PhD diss., University of Oxford, 2003.

Wilhelm, Richard. *The I Ching or Book of Changes*. Trans. Cary F. Baynes with a Foreword by C. C. Jung. London and Melbourne: Routledge & Kegan Paul, 1951, 1965.

Yahagi Takeshi. "Temmu-ki to sono shūhen: dōkyō isho ni kanren shite." In *Jōdai bungaku to kanbungaku*. Ed. Wakan Hikaku Bungakukai, 123–142. Wakan hikaku bungaku sōsho 2. Kyūko shoin, 1986.

Yajima Genryō. *Nihonkoku genzaisho mokuroku: shūshō to kenkyū*. Kyūko shoin, 1984.

Yamada Naomi. *Igyō no kodai bungaku: kiki fudoki hyōgen ron*. Shintensha kenkyū sōsho 57. Shintensha, 1993.

Yamada Yoshio. *Heike monogatari*. Iwanami bunko. Iwanami shoten, 1929.
2 vols.

Yamagishi Tokuhei, Takeuchi Rizō, Ienaga Saburō, and Osone Shōsuke, ed. *Kodai seiji shakai shisō*. Vol. 8 of *Nihon shisō taikei*. Iwanami shoten, 1979.

Yamaguchi Masao. "Kingship, Theatricality, and Marginal Reality in Japan." In *Text and Context: The Social Anthropology of Tradition*. Ed. Ravindra K. Jain, 151–179. Philadelphia: Institute for the Study of Human Issues, 1977.

———. *Tennōsei no bunka jinruigaku*. Rippū shobō, 1989.

Yamamoto Hiroko. *Henjōfu: chūsei shinbutsu shūgō no sekai*. Shunjūsha, 1993.

———. "Kikai ga shima setsuwa to chūsei shingi shinkō: Engyōbon *Heike monogatari* to *Genpei seisuiki* wo megutte." In *Heike monogatari taiheiki*. Ed. Saeki Shin'ichi and Koakimoto Dan, 145–172. Nihon bungaku kenkyū ronbun shūsei 14. Wakakusa shobō, 1999.

Yamamoto Kōji. "Kizoku shakai ni okeru kegare to chitsujo." *Nihonshi kenkyū*, 287 (July 1986), 28–54.

———. *Kegare to ōharae*. Heibonsha sensho 144. Heibonsha, 1992.

Yamanaka Yutaka. *Heianchō no nenchū gyōji*. Hanawa sensho 75. Hirakawa shobō, 1972.

Yamashita Hiroaki. *Heike monogatari no seisei*. Meiji shoin, 1984.

———. "Ikusa monogatari hyōgenshi I: *Kojiki* to *Nihon shoki*." *Nagoya daigaku bungakubu kenkyū ronshū*, 35 (March 1989), 195–207.

Yamashita Katsuaki. *Heian jidai no shūkyō bunka to on'yōdō*. Iwata shoin, 1996.

Yampolsky, Philip B. *The Platform Sutra of the Sixth Patriarch*. New York: Columbia University Press, 1967.

Yanagita Kunio. "Miko kō." In *Teihon Yanagita Kunio shū*, vol. 9, 221–301. Chikuma shobō, 1962.

———. "Oni no shison." In *Teihon Yanagita Kunio shū*, vol. 9, 427–433. Chikuma shobō, 1962.

———. "Ariō to Shunkan Sōzu." *Yanagita Kunio zenshū*, vol. 9, 93–111. Chikuma shobō, 1990.

Yanase Kiyoshi. "Kaburo ibun kō: 'dōyō' to Taira no Kiyomori zō shōkei no kankei." *Nihon bungaku*, 46: 5 (May 1997), 25–34.

———. *Nitchū koten bungaku ronkō*. Kyūko shoin, 1999.

Yasui Kōzan. "Hirata Atsutane no ishogaku: Shunjū meireki jokō wo chūshin to shite." In *Dōkyō kenkyū ronshū: Dōkyō no shisō to bunka Yoshioka hakushi kanreki kinen*. Ed. Yoshioka Yoshitoyo Hakushi Kanreki Kinen Ronshū Kankōkai, 735–751. Kokusho kankōkai, 1977.

———. *Isho no seiritsu to sono tenkai*. Kokusho kankōkai, 1979.

———. *Chūgoku shinpi shisō no nihon e no tenkai*. Taishō daigaku sensho 5. Taishō daigaku shuppanbu, 1983.

———. *Isho to chūgoku no shinpi shisō*. Hirakawa shuppansha, 1988.

Yasui Kōzan and Nakamura Shōhachi. *Isho no kisoteki kenkyū*. Kangibunka kenkyūkai, 1966.

————. *Sho chūkō*. Vol. 2 of *Jūshū isho shūsei*. Meitoku shuppansha, 1975.

Yiengpruksawan, Mimi Hall. *Hiraizumi: Buddhist Art and Regional Politics in Twelfth-Century Japan*. Cambridge, MA: Harvard University Press, 1998.

Yoda, Tomiko. "Literary History Against the National Frame, or Gender and the Emergence of Heian Kana Writing." *Positions: East Asia Cultures Critique*, 8: 2 (2000 Fall), 465–497.

Yokoi Kiyoshi. "Heike monogatari seiritsu katei no ichikōsatsu: hachi-jō-bon no sonzai wo shimesu ichi shiryō." *Bungaku*, 42: 12 (December 1974), 52–64.

————. *Chūsei minshū no seikatsu bunka*. Tokyo daigaku shuppankai, 1975.

————. " 'Kyōgen kigo no ayamari, sanbutsujō no in' no tenkyo." In *Enkyōbon Heike monogatari kōshō* 1. Ed. Mizuhara Hajime, 95–98. Shintensha, 1992.

Yoshida Kenkō. *Rongo*. Vol. 1 of *SKT*. Meiji shoin, 1960.

————. *Shiki* 4 (Hassho). Vol. 41 of *SKT*. Meiji shoin, 1995.

Yoshikawa Shinji. "Mōshibumi sashibumi kō: daijōkan seimu taikei no saihensei ni tsuite." *Nihonshi kenkyū*, 382 (June 1994), 1–36.

Yoshino Hiroko. *In'yō gogyō shisō kara mita nihon no matsuri: Ise jingū saishi daijōsai wo chūshin to shite*. Kōbundō, 1978.

————. *Eki to nihon no saishi: shintō e no ichi shiten*. Kyoto: Jinbun shoin, 1984.

Yukawa Hisamitsu. "Kikajin no fukuzoku girei / sono keisei to igi: Yamato Kawachi Fumi Imiki-be no norito wo megutte." *Jōdai bungaku*, no. 52 (April 1984), 76–88.

Yura Takuo. *Ise monogatari kōsetsu ge*. Meiji shoin, 1986.

GLOSSARY OF CHINESE CHARACTERS

Ai 哀

bai hu 白虎

baiguan 稗官

Baihu tongyi 白虎通[義]

Ban Gu 班固

Ban Zu 斑足

Baopu zi 抱朴子

benji 本紀

Bianque 扁鵲

Bo Juyi 白居易

Bowu zhi 博物志

cang long 蒼竜

chen 讖

Cheng Guan 澄観

Chengdi 成帝 (Jp. Seitei)

chenwei 讖緯

Chijing zi 赤精子

Chuxue ji 初学記

Daigong 大公

Da nuo 大儺

Daode jing 道徳經

daoguan 道観

Daozang 道蔵

Di 帝

Dixi pu 帝系譜

Dong wang fu 東王父

Dong Zhongshu 董仲舒

fan tu 犯土

fangshi 方士 (Jp. hōshi)

fangxiang shi 方相氏

fangzhang 方丈

fangzhong 房中

fu 符

fu ming 符命

furui 符瑞

fuyao 服薬

gaitian 蓋天

gongdian 宮殿

guaiyi 怪異

guan 観

Guangwu di 光武帝

Guoyu 国語

guwen 古文

Han Gaozu 漢高祖

Han shu 漢書

Han Wu di 漢武帝

Haotian shangdi 昊天上帝

Hong fan 洪範

Hou han shu 後漢書

Huainan zi 淮南子

huangdi 皇帝

Huangdi 黃帝

Huangting neijing yujing 黃庭內景
玉經

Huineng 慧能

hun 魂

huntian 渾天

jiaosi 郊祠

jing 精

jing 經

jingshu 經書

Jin shu 晉書

jinji 禁忌

jinwen 今文

Jīvaka 耆婆

keyi 科儀

Kunlun 崑崙

Laozi 老子

Li ji 礼記

Liexian zhuan 列仙傳

lingwan 靈丸

Liu Bang 劉邦

Liu Xiang 劉歆

Liu Xin 劉向

lu 籙

Lü Buwei 呂不韋

Lunheng 論衡

Lunyu 論語

Lushan 祿山

Lüshi chunqiu 呂氏春秋

Ma Rong 馬融

Mengzi 孟子

Miao Dian 妙典

Mingyi bielu 名医別錄

Mozi 墨子

po 魄

Pozhen yue 破陣樂

Qi 齐

qi 氣

Qianjin yaofang 千金要方

Qin 秦

Qing Bu 黥布

ruixing 瑞星

ruiyun 瑞雲

San wu li ji 三五曆記

shangdi 上帝

shen 震

Shennong benjing 神農本經

Shennong bencao jing jizhu 神農
本草經集注

shenqi 神器

shenxian 神仙

Shenxian zhuan 神仙傳

Shi huangdi 始皇帝

shi 史

Shi ji 史記

Shijing 詩經

Shujing 書經

sitian dai 司天台

Sui shu 隋書

Suixing 歲星

Sun Simiao 孫思邈

Taiji 太極

Taiping jing 太平經

Taiping yulan 太平御覽

taiyi 太一

taizi 太子

Taizong 太宗

Tang Gaozu 唐高祖

tanyao 丹藥

Tao Hongjing 陶弘景

te 德

tian 天

tian di ren 天地人

Tiandi 天帝

tianguan 天官

tianhuang 天皇

tianzun 天尊

tongyao 童謠

tu 圖

Wang Chong 王充

Wang Mang 王莽

Wangxian [Palace] 望仙宮

wei 緯

weishu 緯書

wuwei 無為

Wuxing dayi (Jp. Gogyō taigi)
五行大儀

Wuxing zhi 五行志

Xi Bochang 西伯昌

Xia 夏

xian 仙

xian chi 咸池

Xiang'er 想爾

xiangrui 祥瑞

Xianliang duice 賢良対策

xianren 仙人

Xiaojing 考經

xiao shuo 小説

Xiaoyao you 逍遙遊

xie 契

xie 邪

xingqi 行気

Xinxiu benjing 新修本經

Xiongnu 匈奴

Xi wang mu 西王母

xuan wu 玄武

xuanye 宣夜

Xuanzong 玄宗

Yang Guifei 楊貴妃

yang qi 陽気

yi 異

Yijing 易經

Yin 殷

Yinghou 熒惑

Yingzhou 瀛州

Yuandi 元帝 (Jp. Gentei)

Yuanjun 元君

Yunji qiqian 雲笈七籤

Yuwang 育王

zai 災

zaihai 災害

zaiyi 災異

zhaijiao 斎醮

Zhang Lao 長老

Zhanran 湛然

Zhao Gao 趙高

zheng 政

Zhengao 真誥

Zhenguan zhengyao (Jōgan seiyō)
貞観政要

zhenren 真人

Zhenzhong ji 枕中記

Zhonghua (Jp. Chōka) 重花

Zhou 周

Zhou Wang 紂王

zhu 朮

zhu niao 朱鳥

Zhu Yi 朱异

Zhuangxiang (Jp. Sōjō) 莊襄

Zhuangzi 莊子

Zhuoan Deguang 拙庵徳光

ziwei yuan 紫薇垣

ziwei gong 紫薇宮

Ziyang zhenren neizhuan 紫陽眞人
内傳

Zou Yan 騶衍

Zuo zhuan 左傳